LEGAL RIGHTS, DUTIES, AND LIABILITIES OF CRIMINAL JUSTICE PERSONNEL

LEGAL RIGHTS, DUTIES, AND LIABILITIES

OF CRIMINAL JUSTICE PERSONNEL

HISTORY AND ANALYSIS

SECOND EDITION

By

CYRIL D. ROBINSON, LL.B.

Professor Emeritus
Southern Illinois University at Carbondale
Carbondale, Illinois

CHARLES C THOMAS • PUBLISHER
Springfield • Illinois • U.S.A.

Published and Distributed Throughout the World by

CHARLES C THOMAS • PUBLISHER
2600 South First Street
Springfield, Illinois 62794-9265

© *1992 by* CHARLES C THOMAS • PUBLISHER
ISBN 0-398-05779-6
Library of Congress Catalog Card Number: 91-40243

With **THOMAS BOOKS** *careful attention is given to all details of manufacturing and design. It is the Publisher's desire to present books that are satisfactory as to their physical qualities and artistic possibilities and appropriate for their particular use.* **THOMAS BOOKS** *will be true to those laws of quality that assure a good name and good will.*

Printed in the United States of America
SC-R-3

Library of Congress Cataloging-in-Publication Data

Robinson, Cyril D.
    Legal rights, duties, and liabilities of criminal justice
personnel : history and analysis / by Cyril D. Robinson. — 2nd ed.
        p.   cm.
    Includes bibliographical references and index.
    ISBN 0-398-05779-6 (cloth)
    1. Criminal justice personnel — Legal status, laws, etc. — United
States.   I. Title.
KF5399.R6   1992
344.73'0136322 — dc20
[304176136322]
                                                          91-40243
                                                          CIP

This Second Edition is dedicated to my daughters, Anne and Nathalie

FOREWORD

As a legal historian who is also interested in contemporary problems of criminal justice, I am especially pleased to have a small part in the publication of the second edition of Cyril Robinson's treatise. Unlike other books on this subject, *Legal Rights, Duties, and Liabilities of Criminal Justice Personnel* places its subject in a multidimensional framework that takes into account the social, historical, and economic aspects of how the law affects law enforcement officials.

By placing the law in this larger context, Professor Robinson does more than help satisfy the curiosity of those of us who ask "why" as well as "what"; he also helps people less interested in the "why" question to nevertheless understand the "what" more fully. To put this issue less abstractly: we cannot understand where we are until we can get some sense of where we have been. Nor can we understand fully what the law does to us without having at least some knowledge of how and why the law grew as it did. In this enormously impressive treatise, Professor Robinson places his analysis of the current law in a context that allows us to understand how the law got to where it is.

This book is enormously useful as a resource for scholars, teachers, practitioners, and law enforcement personnel. Professor Robinson provides us with a wealth of information that can be quickly applied to research, teaching, law practice, and labor relations. Despite the wonderful electronic tools and data bases available to modern researchers, there is still nothing quite like a treatise that puts it all together in one place for the scholar, practitioner, or layman. This book will not always be the place to end research on issues involving the law and criminal justice personnel. A database search will yield new cases, and new statutes will change the law in the future. But, it is quite likely that this volume will remain the standard place to begin research on these subjects, at least until Professor Robinson offers us a third edition in another decade or so.

Like the best treatise writers, Professor Robinson has not simply given us a nuts and bolts summary of the law as it is today. Rather, he has also presented an invaluable historical dimension to this subject. Thus, we can learn not only what the law is, but how it got to be that way. Such a perspective allows us to avoid reinventing the wheel in each generation and at the same time to avoid repeating the mistakes of previous generations. More importantly, perhaps, this volume allows scholars, students, and new members of the criminal justice community to better understand present-day personnel practices. To use but one simple example, remedies against the use of excessive force by police officers may seem almost unnecessary to a new officer, certain that she/he will be fair, reasonable, and never unnecessarily violent. But, knowledge of the horrors of police brutality in such cases as *Screws v. United States* (1945) may help law students and enforcement officers to better understand the need to protect all citizens from the arbitrary abuses of those who we entrust to keep the peace and guard the persons and property of the nation. Thus, happily Professor Robinson had provided us with a historical dimension to the issues he so ably details in this volume. Similarly, by understanding the development of fair procedures for all government personnel, all people interested in this subject can better understand why we must be scrupulously fair to the law enforcement officer when judging her/his rights to due process in personnel decisions.

When he published the first edition of this book, in 1984, Cyril Robinson joined a long and distinguished line of legal scholars: the treatise writers. The first important American legal treatise was St. George Tucker's edition of *Blackstone's Commentaries,* published in 1803. *Tucker's Blackstone,* as the treatise has always been called, combined Blackstone's analysis of English law with constitutional and legal developments in the new United States. Tucker's purpose in publishing the volume was patriotic as well as utilitarian. He wanted to show Americans that as new legal system—a truly American law—had emerged in the new nation.

Tucker was the first of a long line of American treatise writers who produced vast numbers of volumes in the first half of the nineteenth century. The best known, of course, are James Kent's *Commentaries on American Law* (4 vols., 1826–1830) and Joseph Story's *Commentaries on the Constitution* (1833). Story also wrote treatises on Agency, Bailments, Conflicts of Laws, Equity, and Promissory Notes. His son, William Wetmore

Story, published his *Treatise on the Law of Contracts* in 1844. Other scholars and attorneys of the Golden Age of American law wrote treatises on such topics as bills of exchange, equity jurisprudence, common carriers, criminal law, evidence, railroads, slavery, torts, and watercourses. Illustrative of the wide range of treatises are: Joseph Angell and Samuel Ames, *Treatise of the Law of Private Corporations Aggregate* (1832); Simon Greenlead, *Evidence* (1842); Theodore Sedgwick, *Treatise on International Law* (1847); and Thomas R.R. Cobb, *An Inquiry into the Law of Negro Slavery* (1858).

Professor Robinson's impressive and very valuable treatise fits nicely into this long heritage of legal scholarship. The topic and materials illustrate the unique mix of Constitutional principles, federal statutes, and common law precedents that go into the development of most American law. Moreover, as Professor Robinson demonstrates, much of the subject of this book is deeply rooted in events that took place more than a hundred years ago—the amendments and federal civil rights statutes growing out of the civil war.

The subject matter of this treatise illustrates the importance of law in our democratic society. In some nations the citizen has few, if any, recourses against the actions of the police. This is true, to some extent, even in other democracies. In the United States, as Cyril Robinson's book teaches us, you can "sue city hall" and even win. Moreover, in some circumstances the federal courts will apply the Constitution and federal statutes to help the citizen win such a suit.

At the same time, the due process procedures that protect citizens also apply to law enforcement officers. No executive can arbitrarily fire a law enforcement officer. Civil rights legislation, which one day might be used in a suit against a police officer, might just as easily be applied to protect that officer from arbitrary actions by a superintendent. Labor laws and constitutional rights protect strikers from the kind of police brutality that was all too prevalent from the late nineteenth century to the eve of World War II; those same laws and constitutional provisions also allow law enforcement officers to organize unions. Prohibitions on sexual harassment protect the citizen from police officers and simultaneously protect police officers from their supervisors.

Unfortunately, the rights of law enforcement officers are not always the same as the average citizen. We have come a long distance from Oliver Wendell Holmes's misguided notion that "The petitioner may have a constitutional right to talk politics, but he has no constitutional right to be a policeman."[1] The First Amendment which protects those who would protest actions of the police similarly protects the rights of law enforcement officials to express their private views. As the U.S. Supreme Court noted: "policemen, like teachers and lawyers, are not regulated to a watered-down version of constitutional rights."[2] However, courts have also accepted the concept with that "The public employee may speak freely so long as he does not impair the administration of the public service in which he is employed."[3] Professor Robinson's book explains these contradictions and helps us to better understand the complex thicket of the rights and responsibilities of public employees.

The publication of this edition comes in the middle of the war on drugs, the latest in our country's various crusades against crime. This war places law enforcement officers in greater physical danger than earlier crackdowns on crime. Such physical danger may lead to tougher responses by the police, which could lead to more suits against law enforcement officers and agencies. Moreover, the war on drugs also places the constitutional rights of law enforcement personnel in greater danger, as drug testing of public employees has become routine in many places. This new edition of *Legal Rights, Duties, and Liabilities of Criminal Justice Personnel* is thus especially timely in incorporating this changing and growing area of law. No doubt the law and doctrine will continue to expand and evolve. But, even as court decisions, statutes, and technology modify the law, because of its historical, sociological, and economic analysis and data, Professor Robinson's book will remain timely and indispensable to students, scholars, practitioners, and law enforcement personnel.

PAUL FINKELMAN, PH.D.
Brooklyn Law School

---

[1]*McAuliffe v. Mayor of New Bedford,* 155 Mass 216, 29 N.E. 517 (1892). At the time Holmes sat on the Massachusetts Supreme Judicial Court.

[2]*Garrity v. New Jersey,* 385 U.S. 493 (1967).

[3]*In re Gioglio,* 248 A2d 570, 575 (N.J., 1968). Here the Court found no such impairment.

PREFACE TO THE FIRST EDITION

The field of legal rights, duties and liabilities of criminal justice personnel is so new that at least at the time this book is written there is no text available to teach this material. Texts tend to follow rather than to lead. Therefore it is only natural that there are adequate texts on the rights of suspects and defendants and more recently on prisoners' rights but none as to rights of criminal justice employees. The publishing of a textbook in an area of legal rights itself signifies that those rights have "arrived."

Like many books issuing in a new field of law, this one originally consisted of teaching materials used in a course entitled Legal Rights, Duties and Liabilities of Criminal Justice Personnel. During the first terms the course was taught, I used an enormous and varied mass of materials, cases, articles, and excerpts from books, most of which could only be made available by daily visits to the Library Reserve Room. This placed a heavy burden on students both in terms of the amount of material to be read and the inconvenience of having to read it in the library.

In an effort to overcome that kind of problem and to provide a cohesiveness to the materials, cases were summarized, and numerous articles and books were synthesized in order to provide the student with the conceptual tools to cope with constitutional law problems likely to be met by criminal justice personnel. Nevertheless, in its present form the book represents more than the mere summarization of the views of others. A particular critical view of the origin and purposes of law is presented. It is essential that students understand that law is neither neutral nor political; that it is a powerful force in molding the social forces around us and in turn is subject to these same forces in its development. Moreover, law is not a free-floating mass, but works within an economic, political and social structure. This point is particularly true for constitutional law and is self-evident for the subject-matter of this book, criminal justice personnel, a group at the center of social problems and efforts to deal with them. Therefore, some understanding of this structure and its relation to law is prerequisite to an understanding of the dynamics of rights and how they are acquired by criminal justice personnel.

Because this is the first time such material is available in text form, there are bound to be mistakes, in the kinds of material selected, their interpretation, and from a more mundane point of view, in such things as citations, accuracy of the table of contents, table of cases, and so forth. I would be most grateful for any suggestions or corrections from students or from instructors using the text that may help in improving the materials. Just as this text attacks certain assumptions on which much writing on law is based, the thesis here presented also rests on assumptions. The student should try to discover these and question their accuracy and logic.

I want to thank earlier classes for their tolerance and generosity in helping me along as I learned the material myself, particularly my Winter 1977 class which took the initiative in organizing the material in a form more convenient for them and for me. More particularly, I wish to thank my former secretary, Patti Stein, for her endurance and patience for the many times I said, "It's fine, but could you make just this one little change," to Linda Cline who did all the original cutting, sorting and rearranging; kept everything in order, and made a book out of a muddle, and most recently to Linda Patrick who brought into my life that miracle of modern technology, the word processor; and to her gang Rita Sobkowiak, Julie Donton and Rebecca Leidigh. I would also like to thank my legal assistants, Charles Stowe, Ray Taseff and Steve Glancy, for their intelligent aid, and my graduate assistants, Robert Russo, Donald Schoen and Stephen L. Ewell for their indefatigable efforts. The Southern Illinois University Law Library staff, Ann Puckett, Laurel Wendt and Larry Spears were also of incomparable help. I also wish to acknowledge financial aid from the College of Human Resources, Southern Illinois University Faculty Development Fund, to fund a legal assistant.

CYRIL D. ROBINSON
Carbondale, Illinois

PREFACE TO THE SECOND EDITION

Because of the enormous amount of new material that had to be included in this second edition, I thought of ways to reduce the volume of material. I decided to drop the first two chapters. Chapter 1, which deals with a theory of the origin and assertion of legal rights, and chapter 2, which concerns the history of legal rights applicable to criminal justice personnel, if included in this edition, would have been substantially the same as in the first edition. Readers interested in the material should refer to the first edition of this book. In addition, I have eliminated what I considered unnecessary footnotes with the result that every reference within a case that is not to an actual quotation may not have a citation. I have also removed some dated documentation, and have rejected the temptation to cover all points with law review or other scholarship. Nevertheless, I have tried to suggest texts where the reader could find additional explanatory material. Many of these treatises are kept up to date by pocket parts or insertions when an important development in the law occurs so that the reader, once having found a pertinent point of law, can search for the latest statutory or case developments.

The period from 1984 to the present has witnessed substantial changes in the law: a new Chief Justice of the United States Supreme Court, the appointment of justices with a more conservative philosophy who now dominate the Court, the change of the US Justice Department from a partisan in favor of to one against affirmative action, and therefore somewhat of a shift in civil rights litigation from federal to state courts. Several altogether new areas of law have arisen or evolved in new directions: AIDS, testing government employees for drug use, sexual preference and disabilities, physical or mental; inaction on the part of the State as state action, and many others. Sexual harassment, age discrimination, and clashes between seniority and affirmative action have also undergone important developments since the early eighties.

Apart from the elimination of the first two chapters, the organization of the book largely follows that of the first edition. Research has been made easier and more current by the Lexis system, made available to me by the library staff of Southern Illinois University Law School. I wish to acknowledge the expert and generous help and counsel of the Law School's excellent lawyer-librarians, James E. Duggan, Kathy Garner and Laurel Wendt.

I would like also to thank the College of Education Operations Support Center, under the able direction of Linda Patrick, who was everready to help out with the many drafts that were necessary to complete the task. Most of these drafts were processed by Margaret Highland, whose skill and tolerance for my excessive demands I will always marvel at and be thankful for. Finally, I would like to thank the Southern Illinois University Crime Study Center for its support of graduate assistants, and for the efficient and useful work of graduate assistants, Amy Clark, Rebecca Cruse and Gary Nelson.

CYRIL D. ROBINSON
Carbondale, Illinois

INTRODUCTION

This book concentrates on constitutional doctrines involved in claims by and against criminal justice personnel from the particular standpoint of the person employed within the criminal justice system. It starts from the assumption that there are certain common constitutional principles applicable to all criminal justice personnel, be they law enforcement, correctional, probation or parole officers, or court employees.

This is not a book on criminal procedure. Therefore, the reader will find little material on the powers of arrest, search and seizure law, trial procedures and post-conviction rights, except as those matters are relevant to the main theme of the book, legal rights, duties and liabilities of criminal justice personnel. There are many books that deal with such procedural matters, especially as concerns the police. Moreover, an arrangement of material that adequately examines those matters would not have lent itself to the present organization which emphasizes an understanding, not of individual rules of law, but of the social, political, historical, as well as the constitutional underpinnings to law applicable to criminal justice personnel.

A major theme of this book is that the assertion of rights by minorities and women sensitized and raised the consciousness of all criminal justice personnel to these same rights. "If 'criminals' have a right to *Miranda* warnings when they are interrogated about a crime, why aren't we entitled to the same right when we are interrogated," say criminal justice employees. As cases in this new edition reflect, one result is the discovery by and the assertion by criminal justice personnel of their own rights, particularly procedural and substantive rights as employees within their own organizations.

The text assumes a certain basic knowledge of federal and state government, the Constitution, and the court system. On the other hand, there has been an attempt to explain in detail all concepts necessary to understand the case analysis presented. Part I, chapters 1 through 4, explores various remedies and defenses used by and against criminal justice personnel in asserting or defending claims; Part II, the Specific Part of the book, utilizes the rights and remedies found in Part I to explain the kinds of legal problems confronting criminal justice personnel.

Chapter 1 describes procedural remedies fashioned by legislatures and courts to implement constitutional rights, including civil rights statutes. Chapter 2 continues this discussion with special emphasis on affirmative action suits of particular interest to criminal justice personnel. Chapter 3 details certain defenses to the actions outlined in the prior two chapters, especially the defense of sovereign immunity. Chapter 4 covers the special remedy of injunctive relief and the problems in its employ.

Chapter 5, the first chapter of Part II of the book, concerns the rights of criminal justice personnel within their own organization. It describes the legal and political environment of the criminal justice system, the rise of police and correctional unions, and the police and prison guards as a political force. The most expanded chapter in this edition, chapter 6, discusses the procedural rights of criminal justice employees to disciplinary and dismissal hearings. Chapter 7, the final chapter, covers first amendment rights of criminal justice personnel inside and outside their organization.

In sum, the goals of the book are to provide criminal justice personnel with an understanding of the social, political and especially the legal events that affect their lives; to allow readers to come away from the text with an appreciation of their rights, how they came into being, how they can be expanded, and how rights of criminal justice personnel are related to and dependent on the rights of others.

Research for the book stopped about October 1, 1991. At that time, the Civil Rights Bill, intended to return the law to the state it was after the US Supreme Court's decision in Griggs v Duke Power Co (1971), was still before Congress. I had held up the book several months hoping I could include the civil rights law as part of chapter 2. I finally decided to go ahead even before Congress tried again to pass the bill because it became obvious that no bill would be likely to satisfy President Bush's characterization of the bill's provisions as requiring a quota. Moreover, even were a bill to pass, its effect on the law would be uncertain until lower courts, and finally the Supreme Court itself, passed on it, many months, if not years in the future.

Cyril D. Robinson
Carbondale, Illinois

CONTENTS

**PART II—SPECIFIC RIGHTS, DUTIES, AND LIABILITIES
OF CRIMINAL JUSTICE PERSONNEL**

LEGAL RIGHTS, DUTIES, AND LIABILITIES OF CRIMINAL JUSTICE PERSONNEL

PART I:
REMEDIES AND DEFENSES

Chapter 1

PROCEDURAL REMEDIES FOR ASSERTION OF RIGHTS BY AND AGAINST CRIMINAL JUSTICE PERSONNEL

Introductory remarks

An important legal principle prescribes that where there is a right, there is a remedy. By *remedy* is meant the legal procedure by which a right is asserted in court. Remedies may be provided, either by legislation or by court decision. Without a means to assert a right in court, the right would be legally unenforceable and of little use.

Remedies may be thought of as being divided into three categories depending on the relief desired by the litigant. Relief may be sought (1) for past misconduct on the part of a defendant (money damages or criminal sanctions); (2) to question the legality or constitutionality of a present incarceration (habeas corpus) or to request a declaration of rights (declaratory judgment); or (3) to ask that government officials be ordered to do something or not to do something in the future (injunctive relief). None of these categories are independent of each other. Both a civil action for damages and a criminal prosecution will hopefully deter like action in the future both on the part of the official sued or prosecuted and others in a like position who learn of this action.

Because of the nature of our federal system, claimants often have a choice between a federal and a state forum. The decision of which one to choose can be crucial to the determination of the cause. Such a choice may be limited by constitutional or legislative restrictions on a court's jurisdiction. Courts themselves may devise obstacles to access for reasons of federalism or because of fear of overloading their capacity to decide cases.

Jurisdiction of state and federal courts will be first briefly described; then the different remedies available in each forum will be listed; thereafter these remedies will be elaborated, and finally the obstacles to be met in bringing the various types of claims will be suggested. The balance of the chapter will be a discussion of the means of asserting the various civil rights acts.

Jurisdiction of state and federal courts

State courts are courts of *general* jurisdiction while federal courts are courts of *limited* jurisdiction.[1] There should be nothing surprising about this distinction for a state has plenary, that is, full power as a semi-sovereign government to pass any law within its broad police power. Police power is the power of a state to legislate all measures necessary to maintain the health, safety, morals and welfare of the people within the state's jurisdiction. Because laws are passed by representatives elected by the people — laws that these representatives believe will sustain the health, safety, morals or welfare of the people of the state — these laws are given great weight (are presumed to be constitutional) by courts against any constitutional challenge.

The federal government, on the other hand, has only the power the states delegated to it in the United States Constitution. The United States Supreme Court can adjudicate only "cases or controversies" arising under the Constitution or laws of the United States, while inferior (lower) federal courts are limited to the jurisdiction set forth in congressional legislation establishing those courts.[2]

It follows that one claiming jurisdiction in a federal court must specifically allege (1) a denial of some right derived from the Constitution or laws of the United States, and (2) a statutory ground for the district court's jurisdiction. Failure to allege and prove this ground will result in dismissal of the case for lack of jurisdiction. Once a basis for federal jurisdiction is established, however, state claims may be asserted in the same action. For instance, a claim of assault derived from state law may be added to a federal civil rights action. In a state court, an opposite presumption is true. Unless the contrary is shown, there is a presumption that the court has jurisdiction over the subject matter.

Summary of remedies available in state and federal courts

Following the above scheme of broad state and narrow federal power, state remedies derive from both common and statutory law while federal remedies are derived from the federal constitution and are generally statutory. State remedies fall into the following categories: Torts (civil wrongs); violations of criminal statutes; habeas corpus; and declaratory judgments (a demand for a declaration by the court that plaintiff's rights are being violated by defendant). Because plaintiffs normally wish more than just a declaration of rights, a prayer for injunctive relief usually accompanies a petition for declaratory judgment. Contempt of court is also available where the court decides that a person under jurisdiction of the court has disobeyed a previous order of the court.

Federal remedies generally parallel state remedies. Federal statutes allow tort, habeas corpus, declaratory judgment and injunctive relief. The principal difference between state and federal remedies lies in the availability of the federal Civil Rights Acts, which include both civil and criminal remedies. These acts have become the main vehicle for the assertion of claims against criminal justice personnel. They have also been used by criminal justice personnel to assert rights against their own organizations.

STATE REMEDIES

Tort

A tort is a civil action in which plaintiffs seek to recover money damages from persons they claim wrongfully injured them. Torts may be either intentional (an assault) or unintentional (negligence). In order to recover, the plaintiff must allege and prove that there was a duty owed from the defendant to the plaintiff; that the defendant breached that duty, that as a result of the breach of the duty the plaintiff was in some way damaged, and (in some states) that the plaintiff did not contribute to the injury. The duty is usually expressed in terms of "reasonable care."

Prison officials, for example, have the duty to provide inmates with basic necessities of life such as food, lodging, and medical care and to use reasonable care to prevent injuries to inmates. Because of the doctrine of sovereign immunity, discussed in chapter 3, a state may not be sued in tort without its consent. The federal government and some states, however, by statute, have given their consent to be sued. But even where such a statute is present, the consent may be so drawn as to exclude the suit in question, or the statute may limit the nature and amount of the claim that may be made.

Habeas corpus

Habeas corpus literally means—to have the body. It is used when petitioners wish to challenge by what right the state (or other custodian) holds someone in custody. Petitioners may complain that they are illegally confined because of some procedural defect in their conviction, or that conditions under which they are confined are illegal or unconstitutional. Thus, convicted offenders may employ this remedy to seek relief from an alleged illegal conviction or sentence, particularly where the result of granting the prisoner's request would result in release.

Prisoners (or their attorneys) file the application or petition for habeas corpus and become the applicants or petitioners in the action. The respondent, usually the director of the state department or division of corrections, or the warden of a state institution, is the person having legal custody of the applicant. The writ has the effect of (1) empowering the court to direct the custodian to produce the person in custody before the court; (2) requiring the custodian to show the legal basis for the detention and (3) permitting the court to determine whether this basis is legally valid.[3] State habeas generally reaches *any* arbitrary or capricious action whether it is of constitutional dimension or breaches a specified law, and in this way the state habeas differs from the federal writ. But since each state has its own habeas law, to be sure of its application, students must address the law in their own state.

Obstacles to bringing state habeas corpus

According to the rule in many states, habeas cannot be brought by a person no longer in custody because the purpose of the writ is to liberate one in custody. Thus, a person on probation or parole may not be able to use the remedy to test the conditions of release or the validity of the underlying conviction. This is not an obstacle to federal habeas. A federal or state parolee is considered to be "in custody" for the purposes of federal habeas.[4] State prisoners are entitled to one full evidentiary hearing on habeas claims in state courts plus an appeal from an order denying relief, but are not entitled to repeatedly raise the same issue nor present claims a bit at a time.

Contempt of court

Prison officials are regarded as officers of the court because they are responsible for executing sentences. They are therefore subject to conviction for contempt of court if they wilfully fail to carry out an order of court, for example, to correct prison conditions that the court has found in violation of the Constitution.

Declaratory judgment

This remedy is used where parties assert uncertainty as to their legal rights with reference to another and ask for a judicial determination of respective rights and responsibilities so that they may legally act without incurring legal liability.

Action for equitable relief

Equitable relief historically grew out of the inability of law courts to do more than give money damages. A separate remedy and even a separate court structure (the court in equity) evolved to give equitable (injunctive) relief, that is, to order people to do something or to forbid them from doing something. Today, the courts of law and equity are merged into one court system providing both legal and equitable relief. Because equity historically has always been an exceptional remedy and because equitable relief involves control by the court over future behavior, certain restrictions have become attached to its use. Injunctive relief will be considered in chapter 4.

State criminal penalties

In the absence of a privilege to act differently, criminal justice personnel are covered by the same statutes as anyone else so that what would be a breach of a criminal statute for any other person would also be a violation for criminal justice personnel (criminal assault, for instance).

FEDERAL REMEDIES

Federal Tort Claims Act[5]

The Federal Tort Claims Act, passed in 1946, is a waiver of the government's defense of sovereign immunity, thus permitting the federal government to be sued for torts committed by its agents. The waiver of immunity is not, however, complete. Suit is permitted subject to the procedures and terms set out in the statute.

In the Act's statement of purpose, immunity is said to be waived because of "a desire on the part of the federal government in the interests of justice and fair play to permit a private litigant to satisfy his legal claims for injury or damage suffered at the hands of a United States employee in the scope of his employment."[6]

The essence of the statute is stated in 28 USC § 1346(b):

[T]he district courts . . . shall have exclusive jurisdiction of civil actions on claims against the United States, for money damages, . . . for injury or loss of property, or personal injury or death caused by the negligent or wrongful act or omission of any employee of the Government while acting within the scope of his office or employment, under circumstances where the United States, if a private person, would be liable to the claimant in accordance with the law of the place where the act or omission occurred.

For the purposes of this Act, an " 'employee of the government' includes officers or employees of any federal agency, members of the military or naval forces of the United States, members of the National Guard while engaged in training or duty . . . and persons acting on behalf of a federal agency in an official capacity, temporarily or permanently in the service of the United States, whether with or without compensation."[7]

Federal Employees Liability Reform and Tort Compensation Act of 1988

New amendments to the FTCA were made necessary in the aftermath of the 1988 case of Westfall v Erwin,[8] in which the Court was asked to decide whether certain federal officials were "absolutely immune from liability under state tort law for conduct within the scope of their employment without regard to whether the challenged conduct was discretionary in nature."[9] Erwin was employed by the federal government as a warehouseman and while so employed he complained that through the negligence of federal employees he came into contact with bags of toxic soda ash resulting in burns to his eyes and throat. Defendant federal officials defended that they had absolute immunity for ordinary torts committed within the scope of their jobs.

After reviewing the rationale for giving absolute immunity to decision-makers—to protect their freedom to make decisions without fear of law suits for incorrect decisions—the Court noted that acting "within the outer scope of their duties" will not alone entitle federal officials to absolute immunity. "A material issue of fact thus exists as to whether [federal officials] exercised sufficient discretion in connection with the alleged tort to warrant the shield of absolute immunity. . . . [A]bsolute immunity does not shield official functions from state-law tort liability unless the challenged conduct is within the outer perimeter of an official's duties *and* is discretionary in nature."[10]

The effect of the *Westfall* decision was to place the entire federal workforce at risk. In the words of one writer, "Federal employees, especially lower ranking functionaries performing ministerial duties, were left after *Westfall* not knowing whether the most routine of their official duties would expose them to state law lawsuits jeopardizing their personal assets."[11] Recognizing this problem, in its decision, the Court suggested that "Congress is in the best position to provide guidance for the complex and often highly empirical inquiry into whether absolute immunity of federal employees involved in state-law tort actions would be useful."[12] The bill finally made law in November 1988, therefore, had for its purpose the restoration of the status quo before *Westfall.*[13]

The Federal Employees Liability Reform and Tort Compensation Act of 1988 provides the sole and exclusive remedy for persons bringing common law actions for torts committed by federal employees within the scope of their employment.[14] By its terms, the Act does not extend to constitutional torts, that is, those based on violations of rights arising out of the Constitution of the United States.[15]

No action under the act can be instituted until the claimant has presented the claim to the appropriate federal agency, and either the agency has made a determination or six months have passed without a decision by the agency.[16] "Upon certification by the Attorney General that the defendant employee was acting within the scope of his office or employment at the time of the incident out of which the claim arose," the claim shall be deemed to be against the United States.[17] If the claim is begun in a state court the Attorney General may move it to a federal district court.[18]

> With respect to any claim under this chapter, the United States shall be entitled to assert any defense upon judicial or legislative immunity, which otherwise would have been available to the employee of the United States whose act or omission gave rise to the claim, as well as any other defenses to which the United States is entitled.[19]

Two issues concerning federal employee tort liability under the FTCA are of importance to criminal justice personnel. The first involves injuries growing out of "a discretionary function or duty" and the second concerns a 1974 amendment extending liability to federal employees who commit intentional torts.

Discretionary function or duty under the FTCA

A claim is *excluded* from coverage which is:

> based upon the exercise or performance or the failure to exercise or perform a discretionary function or duty on the part of a federal agency or any employee of the Government, whether or not the discretion involved be abused.[20]

The question becomes whether the act causing the injury was in the exercise of a discretionary or a ministerial function. A ministerial act may be defined as the carrying out of an act, the policy for which is set by another—the discretionary act. In general, in a bureaucratic structure, the persons at the top (by definition) are engaged in discretionary acts while the persons at the bottom are engaged in ministerial acts.

The interpretation of this section has been the subject of a number of Supreme Court opinions.[21] What function is "discretionary" and what "ministerial," or which acts, even though discretionary, are still not immune is unclear. The Supreme Court case of Berkovitz v United States[22] attempted to define a discretionary act under the section. To a complaint that a government agency wrongfully distributed a polio vaccine that gave plaintiff's baby the polio virus, the government responded that the release of the vaccine was a discretionary act, which gave the government immunity under the FTCA. In rejecting that view, Justice Marshall defined the discretionary function:

> In examining the nature of the challenged conduct, a court must first consider whether the action is a matter of choice for the acting employee. . . . Thus, the discretionary function exception will not apply when a federal statute, regulation, or policy specifically prescribes a course of conduct for an employer to follow. In this event, the employee has no rightful option but to adhere to the directive. And if the employee's conduct cannot appropriately be the product of judgment or choice, then there is no discretion in the conduct for the discretionary exception to protect. . . . Moreover, assuming the challenged conduct involves an element of judgment, a court must determine whether that judgment is of the kind that the discretionary exception was designed to shield. The basis for the discretionary function exception was Congress' desire to "prevent judicial 'second-guessing' of legislative and administrative decisions grounded in social, economic, and political policy through the medium of an action in tort." The exception, properly construed, therefore protects only governmental actions and decisions based on considerations of public policy. In sum, the discretionary function exception insulates the Government from liability if the action challenged in the case involves the permissible exercise of policy judgment.[23]

In effect, the Court seems to be limiting the discretionary function exemption to those acts involving "actual public policy considerations."[24]

Liability based on intentional conduct

Prior to March 1974, the FTCA excluded from coverage most intentional torts, thus limiting the Act almost entirely to negligent acts by federal employees. But a series of transgressions taken under federal authority sensitized Congress to the necessity of providing protection for injuries due to omissions or intentional acts of law enforcement officers.[25]

As one commentator reflected, "From a background of the Jackson State and Kent State tragedies in May 1970, the Supreme Court's decision in Bivens v Six Unknown Named Agents of Federal Bureau of Narcotics in June 1971,[26] the May Day mass arrests in Washington in 1971, and the Attica debacle in September 1971, the focus upon responsibilities for abuses of governmental authority is not surprising."[27]

As amended, the section, which originally excluded claims against the federal government for the enumerated intentional torts, now permits such suits for "acts or omissions of investigative or law enforcement officers of the United States Government," defined in the amendment to mean "any officer of the United States who is empowered by law to execute searches, to seize evidence, or to make arrests for violations of Federal law."[28]

Federal habeas corpus

Federal habeas is used to test both the conditions as well as the legality of confinement on the theory that if the conditions of confinement are made more burdensome than allowed by law, the imprisonment is illegal.[29] Where the result of the claim for relief will be reduction of the term of or the release of the prisoner, habeas is the proper, and in the case of state prisoners, the only remedy.[30]

A short history of federal habeas

The present use of federal habeas corpus by *state* prisoners grows out of the Judiciary Act of February 5, 1867, that was intended to give freed slaves the right to challenge in federal courts their incarceration by state authorities.[31] Before the Civil War, habeas had never been available as a remedy to the large portion of the population represented by slaves and Indians who had no substantive rights to enforce. Although today the principal use of habeas is by state prisoners trying to obtain relief in federal courts for alleged violation of federal constitutional rights, such a use was expressly forbidden in the original act of 1789.[32] That law authorized federal courts to issue the writ "agreeable to the principles and usages of law . . . for the purpose of an inquiry into the cause of commitment." But "writs of *habeas corpus* shall in no case extend to state prisoners in jail. . . . "[33] Availability of the habeas remedy thus depended on the custodian. Federal habeas was available solely in federal court for free persons held under federal restraint. Persons in state custody had to rely on state habeas. Otherwise stated, such prisoners were forced to rely for recognition of their rights on the same authorities that had repeatedly denied them.

This early use of habeas carefully followed the lines of division of power between federal and state courts, a policy that continued until the exigencies of the Civil War period demanded an expansion of the remedy. As federal agents moved into southern states with advancing northern troops, enlisting former slaves in the army or arresting offenders against federal statutes, they were in turn sued in state courts by recalcitrant southern citizens "for such offenses as trespassing, illegal arrest, false imprisonment, and assault."[34] Congress responded by passing the habeas corpus indemnity removal law of March 1863 that allowed the sued federal officer to petition the local federal court to remove the case from state to federal court for trial. Counsel was to be provided and the officers were to be indemnified for their monetary losses while engaged in carrying out their official duties.

As southern resolve solidified to deny the freedmen the civil rights granted them, Congress, by Act of February 1867, strengthened the removal power by authorizing the removal of a case from state to federal court in any instance in which a person "is denied or cannot enforce in the courts of such state a right under any law providing for the equal civil rights of citizens of the United States."[35] The mere filing of the removal petition in federal court had the effect of depriving the state court of jurisdiction over the cause until the petitioner's assertions were determined by that federal court.

In a further effort to counter the Black Codes that threatened to return blacks to penal slavery, Congress also empowered federal courts "to grant writs of habeas corpus in all cases where any person may be restrained of his or her liberty in violation of the constitution, or of any treaty or law of the United States . . . , and to inquire into the facts surrounding the detention."[36]

For the first time, legislation extended the federal writ to all persons held by state authority in violation of federal law. The importance of the writ can be understood only when it is considered in combination with its powerful counterparts, the fourteenth amendment's due process and equal protection clauses. For it is the writ that acts as a procedural device whereby substantive rights guaranteed by the due process and equal protection clauses may be brought before the courts. Habeas and the fourteenth amendment are thereby permanently entwined. As court decisions enlarge the scope of the rights drawn from the fourteenth amendment, the breadth of coverage of the writ is likewise broadened. The combined effect of this merger of right and remedy can be summed up as follows: (1) federal habeas has been extended to persons held in state custody in violation of federal law; (2) the scope of a federal court's inquiry into the legality of confinement after a final judgment of conviction has been constantly enlarged; (3) the meaning of due process of law and equal protection in criminal proceedings has been expanded by numerous Supreme Court decisions.

Obstacles to use of habeas in federal courts

As time went on, the determination of claims against the state in federal courts became a source of irritation between the two systems. In 1948, to cope with this problem, the federal statute on habeas corpus was modified to provide that state prisoners, before they come to federal courts seeking habeas, must exhaust the remedies available in state courts; or the federal court must find that there is either no available state means of relief, or that the relief provided is ineffective in protecting the rights of the prisoner.[37]

Therefore, before state prisoners can gain access to federal court by way of habeas, they must show that they have exhausted state remedies. Normally, this would mean a decision by the highest court of the state denying the claim, or that it would be useless to pursue that course because, for example, the state supreme court has already decided the precise issue the petitioner wishes to raise.

Federal prisoners using federal habeas meet the doctrine of exhaustion of *administrative* remedies.[38] Before they use habeas they must exhaust any remedies provided within the prison structure, and must also have applied for relief to the court that originally sentenced them.[39] Even where the prisoner has been successful in the claim, the result has rarely been release. Of 3,702 federal habeas petitions filed in one four year period, only five resulted in the discharge of the prisoner. In most others, a new trial was granted in which there was usually a new conviction.[40]

Obstacles to actions by state prisoners in federal courts

In addition to the requirement that state administrative and legal remedies must be exhausted before a state prisoner can bring a habeas action in federal court, two additional doctrines influence both federal and state courts to refrain from accepting complaints: the *hands-off* doctrine that can apply to any case involving court intervention in the workings of state administration, including the criminal justice system, and the *abstention* doctrine, that is concerned only with problems created by federal intervention in state court systems.

Hands-off doctrine

This doctrine ultimately derives from concern for separation of powers: that it is the function of the executive power to enforce the law and to run a prison system or a police department, and not the function of the courts to dictate such policy. Prison and law enforcement authorities are often accepted by courts as "experts" in their field who can better evaluate the nature of the problems to be solved and the best way to solve them than can courts. It follows from this view that courts should intervene in agency policymaking only when agencies have clearly stepped beyond the bounds of their expertise or have acted in such an obviously illegal or unconstitutional way that their actions result in denial of rights to large numbers of persons. Finally, courts have voiced a concern that their intervention in the affairs of police departments or prisons will weaken discipline in a system where discipline is a key to order.

Any court, state or federal, may use the hands-off doctrine to refuse to intervene in a case involving agency decision making. While this doctrine had been in decline under the Warren Court, it has resumed importance in recent years as the Burger and the Rehnquist Courts have relied on such reasoning to support their less "activist" role of judicial intervention. Justice Powell summed up this rationale with reference to prison affairs:

> The problems of prisons in America are complex and intractable, and, more to the point, they are not readily susceptible of resolution by decree. Most require expertise, comprehensive planning, and the commitment of resources, all of which are peculiarly within the province of the legislative and executive branches of government. For all of those reasons, courts are ill-equipped to deal with the increasingly urgent problems of prison administrators and reform. Judicial recognition of that fact reflects no more than a healthy sense of realism.[41]

One is entitled to ask, however, whether in instances in which the legislative and executive branches do not supply the "expertise, comprehensive planning, and commitment of resources" to maintain the "prisons of America" within constitutional limits, does it not then become the duty of the judicial branch to set that process in motion? The Court majority has moved, in recent years, to a return to the hands-off doctrine of the pre-Warren Court, a subject to be discussed in more detail in chapter 4.

Abstention

This doctrine relies on the principle that our government rests on a federal relationship in which there are two separate court systems, federal and state, in which the state court system has primary responsibility for the administration of criminal law. Therefore, before a federal court will take a case involving the construction of a state law or the evaluation of state administrative policies, a federal court may require that the matter first be heard in a state court.[42] In this way, statutes which may be overbroad or vague, as written, may be so construed by state courts so as to be constitutional. On the other hand, where the state statute or regulation is clearly unconstitutional on its face, or where the issue of state law to be decided is clear, or where the state and federal constitutional provisions to be construed are substantially similar, the doctrine does not apply.

Civil rights actions

Because of the procedural problems in bringing a habeas corpus proceeding, in particular the necessity of exhausting state remedies, civil rights actions have become the favored means of asserting a claim for deprivation of a constitutional right.

These sections can be divided into civil and criminal sanctions. All but §§ 241, 242 and 245 are civil.

Civil Rights Acts can be further divided into:

(1) Those laws enacted during the post-Civil War period:
   a) *Civil Statutes*

42 USC § 1981 (1866)	contract rights
42 USC § 1982 (1866)	property rights
42 USC § 1983 (1871)	constitutional rights
42 USC § 1985 (1871)	conspiracy

b) *Criminal Statutes*

18 USC § 241 (1870)	criminal sanctions
18 USC § 242 (1866)	criminal sanctions

(2) Civil rights statutes enacted following the 1960s civil rights movement:
   a) *Civil Statutes*

42 USC § 2000a (1964)	public accommodations
42 USC § 2000e (1964)	employment

   b) *Criminal Statutes*

18 USC § 245 (1968)	racially-motivated violence

Before proceeding with a discussion of the present use of these sections, the historical background will provide a perspective by which to understand both the revitalization of the Reconstruction legislation and the more recent civil rights legislation of the 1960s, a period sometimes known as the Second Reconstruction.

The Second Reconstruction

The Reconstruction Period provided a battery of civil rights, constitutional principles and laws that were quickly made moribund by the economic realities of the day and by hostile Supreme Court decisions. Conversely, during the 1930s, 40s and 50s, numerous decisions of the Supreme Court revitalized the fourteenth amendment's due process clause. Faced with repeated instances in which the South's repressive criminal justice system clearly silhouetted one system for whites and another for poor blacks, the Court, on a case by case basis, began to set forth rules that provided at least minimum standards of due process against which to measure southern state court procedures. Because many of these cases involved poor southern blacks, they laid a foundation for a later resurgence of black rights.

Among those cases were decisions that fleshed out and extended the right to the selection of an unprejudiced jury;[43] an absolute right to counsel in capital cases[44] and where defendants are mentally ill;[45] the exclusion of confessions extorted through torture,[46] or through systematic psychological pressure.[47] Once enunciated by the Supreme Court, these rights became the property of all Americans.

That one hundred years had passed had not modified the basic economic and social principles that had generated post-Civil War public policy. One of those principles continued to be that racial prejudice was private action, a matter of personal taste, not to be regulated by law.

Restaurant and hotel owners would have the right, under this perspective, to deny blacks entry into their "private" establishments. Such denial was merely a matter of personal and local concern.

But by the 1960s, though the idea of government regulation of such activity continued to trouble many whites, the economic base of the country had changed. The small-town innkeeper had been replaced by national chains of motels; nationally-affiliated supermarkets supplanted the mom and pop corner grocery. People traveled from state to state in a way that was unknown in the Reconstruction era. Consistent with these changes in our national commercial structure and image, Congress, in many instances, sought its source of legislative power in the Commerce Clause, Article I, Section 8 of the US Constitution. It was natural for Congress to rely on the Commerce Clause to pass the first significant civil rights measure since Reconstruction, Title II of the Civil Rights Act of 1964, to be known as the Public Accommodations Law.[48] That law guaranteed to all persons the right to equal services in places of public accommodations such as hotels, motels, restaurants and motion picture houses without regard to race, color, religion, or national origin.

A companion measure, Title VII, the Equal Employment Opportunities Law,[49] provided protection against discrimination by employers, employment agencies and labor unions, and will be discussed in chapter 2. The Voting Rights Act of 1965 protected the right to vote against state attempts to restrict that right to white voters. The last of the major civil rights statutes, the Fair Housing Law of 1968, dealt with discrimination in the sale and rental of private housing. Each of these measures carried out the Reconstruction Period conception that blacks would be able to help themselves if they were given the opportunity to individually assert their rights. For this purpose, they were to be provided with civil rather than criminal sanctions that would have necessitated governmental intervention.

As in the post-Reconstruction era, these legislative enactments were soon tested in the courts. A 1964 Supreme Court decision, Katzenbach v McClung,[50] held that a small restaurant's connection with interstate commerce was sufficient to authorize Congress to pass the Public Accommodations Law. Still more important was the Court's opinion in the 1968 case of Jones v Alfred H Mayer Co.,[51] because it gave new life to the thirteenth amendment. The dispute involved a claim by a black man, Jones, that Mayer had refused to sell him a house because of his color. No question of state action was involved. The Fair Housing Law of 1968 was not yet on the books. As mere private action, the denial seemed unreachable by the courts. But Jones' resourceful attorney found a long-forgotten Reconstruction civil rights statute, what is now 42 USC § 1982. This statute gave to all citizens the same right to inherit, purchase, lease, sell, hold and convey real and personal property as is enjoyed by white citizens. Relying on the enabling clause of the thirteenth amendment, the Court concluded that Congress had power *"to pass all laws necessary and proper for abolishing all badges and incidents of slavery in the United States."*[52]

This 1968 decision was of monumental importance on several counts: (1) It gave clear authority to Congress to act directly against both public and private discrimination without the need to utilize the rather indirect and awkward reasoning connected with the Commerce Clause (that racial discrimination is an "impediment" to the free flow of interstate commerce); (2) *Jones* gave a signal to lower courts that they should interpret civil rights measures to the limits of constitutional power; (3) *Jones* revitalized and brought to the attention of the legal profession the whole battery of Reconstruction civil rights measures, civil and criminal, that will be discussed in the balance of this chapter.

Section 1983—deprivation of constitutional rights

Section 1983 is intended to provide a remedy for persons denied federal rights under color of state law or authority. The section is the civil counterpart of § 2 of the Civil Rights Act of 1866, now 18 USC § 242, which, using substantially the same language, provided criminal sanctions. Section 1983 originates as section 1 of the Ku Klux Act of April 20, 1871, that was enacted by Congress pursuant to and as a means of enforcing the fourteenth amendment and creates "a remedy as broad as the protection that the Fourteenth Amendment affords the individual."[53] Section 1983 reads as follows:

> Every person who, under color of any statute, ordinance, regulation, custom, or usage, of any State or Territory, subjects, or causes to be subjected, any citizen of the United States or other person within the jurisdiction thereof to the deprivation of any rights, privileges, or immunities secured by the Constitution and laws, shall be liable to the party injured in an action at law, suit in equity, or other proper proceeding for redress.[54]

For claims by and against criminal justice personnel, § 1983 is the most important and most frequently used of all civil rights statutes. It is therefore worth reciting the story of the section's revitalization after a long period of dormancy.

The hibernation and revival of § 1983

One researcher found that between 1871 and 1920, only twenty-one cases were decided under § 1983, and "an appraisal of the statute's application in 1920 would have revealed little promise that it might develop into an effective bulwark against all invasions of civil liberties."[55] Other researchers discovered only 53 reported cases from 1951–1967."[56] Factors said to be responsible for the section's long period of hibernation include: "restrictive application of the state action doctrine,[57] a narrow reading of the fourteenth amendment's privileges and immunities clause,[58] a similarly narrow reading of § 1983's jurisdictional counterpart,[59] and the Court's refusal to completely incorporate the provisions of the Bill of Rights. . . . "[60]

The revival of § 1983 can be divided into four stages: (1) from Reconstruction to 1939 when neither litigants nor courts recognized § 1983 as a cause of action; (2) from 1939 to 1961 when courts interpreted the section to mean that it applied only to situations in which state law authorized a state official to violate someone's federal rights; (3) when claims for deprivations of federal rights were allowable against state but not against federal officials, a point passed in 1971 when the United States Supreme Court created a 1983-like remedy to apply to federal agents;[61] and (4) a period ending in 1978, when municipalities, which had heretofore been immune, were made subject to § 1983 actions.[62]

A 1939 case, Hague v CIO,[63] involving an injunction against the mayor and the local police from interfering with peaceful labor picketing, announced the re-entry of § 1983 into the field of civil rights litigation. But the case that opened the way for its current usage is the 1961 decision of Monroe v Pape.[64] The complaint alleged that, without a warrant, "13 Chicago police officers broke into petitioner's home in the early morning, routed them from bed, made them stand naked in the living room, emptying drawers and ripping mattress covers," thereafter arresting, interrogating and releasing the husband without taking him before a magistrate or having any charges preferred against him. In deciding the case, the Court examined the Reconstruction backdrop against which § 1983 was passed. During the debates on the bill, Congress had before it a 600 page report on Ku Klux Klan activities "and the inability of the state governments to cope with it."

The Court cited contemporary comments by congressmen, one of whom stated:

> While murder is stalking abroad in disguise, while whippings and lynchings and banishment have been visited upon unoffending American citizens, the local administrations have been found inadequate or unwilling to apply the proper corrective. Combinations, darker than the night that hides them, conspiracies, wicked as the worst of felons could devise, have gone unwhipped of justice. Immunity is given to crime, and the records of the public tribunals are searched in vain for any evidence of effective redress.[65]

The section was thus aimed not at the laws on the books but at their unequal enforcement. Its purpose was "to create a federal remedy independent of state law for the protection of constitutional rights from official lawlessness or derogation of duty,"[66] and "to 'involve the federal judiciary' in the effort to exert federal control over state officials who refused to enforce the law."[67] Monroe v Pape decided a number of issues that thereafter made § 1983 an attractive vehicle for civil rights attorneys: (1) plaintiffs need allege only facts constituting a deprivation of a federal right under color of state authority; (2) the section could be used "against those who carry a badge of authority of a State and represent it in some capacity, whether they act in accordance with their authority or misuse it;"[68] (3) it is a remedy independent of and additional to any state remedy and the claimant need not exhaust state remedies before seeking § 1983 relief; (4) plaintiffs need allege no specific intent by the defendant to deprive them of federal rights; and (5) the section "should be read against the background of tort liability that makes a man responsible for the natural consequences of his actions."[69]

Justice Powell has summed up the increase in civil rights actions following Monroe v Pape:

> Between 1961 and 1977, the number of cases filed in federal court under civil rights statutes increased from 296 to 13,113. . . . New filings have remained relatively constant from 1977 to date. . . . These filings do not include the many prisoner petitions filed annually under 42 U.S.C. § 1983. . . . If prisoner petitions are included, the number of civil rights cases filed in 1979 rises to 24,951.[70]

Problems in using § 1983.

During the course of its use, a number of problems have appeared. These include the meaning of the words "under color of" law; the mental state required before it can be said that a person "caused" a constitutional violation; the extent to which a private person's action may be brought within the section; rights protected by the section; coverage of acts committed by federal officers, the applicable statute of limitation,[71] and defenses to the action (discussed in Chapter 3).

Deprivation of federal rights

Plaintiffs may recover under the section if they can show that (1) as a result of the action of the defendant the plaintiff was deprived of some right, privilege or immunity guaranteed by the Constitution or laws of the United States, and (2) the defendant acted under color of state or local law.

Plaintiffs must prove that they were deprived of "rights, privileges, or immunities secured by the Constitution and laws of the United States." In terms of precedence of proof, the Supreme Court has clearly stated that "The first inquiry in any § 1983 suit, therefore, is whether the plaintiff has been deprived of a right 'secured by the Constitution and laws.' "[72] Deprivations "secured by the Constitution and [federal] laws" may include (1) violations as determined by Supreme Court decisions interpreting the fourteenth amendment's due process and equal protection clauses; (2) violations of those provisions of the bill of rights incorporated by the due process clause of the fourteenth amendment and made applicable to the states; (3) violations of constitutional rights found by the Supreme Court to be fundamental such as the right to privacy and access to courts although not explicitly present in the Constitution; (4) violations of rights of national citizenship originating in the fourteenth amendment's privileges and immunities clause such as the right to interstate travel; (5) violations of rights judicially protected under any part of the Constitution; (6) violations of rights that have been judicially declared or recognized by federal courts as originating in the Constitution or federal laws; and (7) violations of rights secured by federal statutes or treaties.

During the past fifty years, the Supreme Court has selectively incorporated most provisions of the bill of rights into the fourteenth amendment's due process clause, thus applying to the states the same constitutional standards as apply to the federal government. The following provisions have been incorporated:

1. First amendment's freedom of speech, press, assembly and petition; free exercise and establishment of religion;
2. Fourth amendment's protection under unreasonable search and seizure.

3. Fifth amendment's protection against double jeopardy, self-incrimination and the right to just compensation;
4. Sixth amendment's right to a speedy, public and impartial jury trial and right to notice, confrontation, compulsory process and counsel;
5. Eighth amendment's freedom from cruel and unusual punishment and excessive bail.[73]

The deprivation must be based on a federal source, either the Constitution or laws of the United States. Section 1983 cannot be used to redress a violation of a statute if the "statute provides an exclusive remedy for violations of its terms."[74] It cannot have its origin in state law. Thus, in Monroe v Pape, the action of the police officers in unlawfully invading a family's home was a constitutional violation of the fourth amendment's search and seizure provision. It also involved state common law violations such as assault and battery, and home invasion. But it was only by virtue of the violation of federal rights, that is, the fourth amendment violation, that the plaintiffs could charge a 1983 violation. The state infraction provided no such basis. Thus § 1983 "is not itself a source of substantive rights," merely providing "a method for indicating federal rights elsewhere conferred."[75]

In the 1989 case of Graham v Connor,[76] the Court refined the proof needed, at least with reference to § 1983 claims that were based on the use by government agents of "excessive force" in carrying out their duties. Such claims may not be founded on substantive due process analysis. Rather, proof of such a claim

> begins by identifying the specific constitutional right allegedly infringed by the challenged application of force. . . . In most instances, that will be either the Fourth Amendment's prohibition against unreasonable seizures of the person, or the Eighth Amendment's ban on cruel and inhuman punishments, which are the two primary sources of constitutional protection against physically abusive government conduct.[77]

The constitutional tort—mental state required

A related question concerns the legal basis by which the deprivation of a federal right is to be shown. When Monroe v Pape stated that § 1983 "should be read against the background of tort liability that makes a man responsible for the natural consequences of his actions,"[78] it sowed a field of confusion. Which of the mental states normally applied to tort liability cases—intent, knowledge, ordinary negligence—or gross negligence was to be employed in 1983 cases? Is "mere" negligence sufficient to show that plaintiff was deprived of a constitutional right?

To many courts and commentators, the 1981 case of Parratt v Taylor,[79] appeared to answer that question affirmatively. There, a prisoner charged that in violation of his due process rights prison officials negligently lost hobby material that he had received in the mail. While the court decided that prison officials did not deprive the prisoner of due process on the facts of this case, in the course of their opinion, they opined that "§ 1983 affords a 'civil remedy' for deprivations of federally protected rights caused by persons acting under color of state law without any express requirement of a particular state of mind."[80] This vague statement sparked two lines of cases, some of which insisted that mere negligence was a sufficient base for § 1983 liability, while others argued that such liability could be founded only on gross negligence, recklessness, or deliberate indifference to the plaintiff's constitutional rights. Such a determination has crucial importance because it is much easier to show "mere" negligence than it is "deliberate" indifference. Such proof becomes particularly difficult when plaintiffs wish to show that their deprivation of constitutional rights emanates, not from the individual officer committing the violation, but from higher up.

In the case of Smith v Wade,[81] that conflict was resolved against mere negligence as a basis for 1983 liability—at least where the defendant has a qualified immunity defense. Wade, a state prisoner, had been placed in a cell with known violent offenders and had subsequently been beaten and sexually assaulted. The trial court had instructed the jury that because of the guard's qualified immunity defense (see chapter 3) Wade could recover only if defendants were guilty of " 'gross negligence' (defined as 'a callous indifference or a thoughtless disregard for the consequences of one's act or failure to act'). . . . "[82] The Court agreed: "Smith is protected from liability for mere negligence because of the need to protect his use of discretion in his day-to-day decisions in the running of a correctional facility."[83]

Whitley v Albers[84] relied on deprivation of rights under the eighth (cruel and unusual punishment) and fourteenth amendments (due process). There, a prison guard shot a prisoner who was attempting to protect elderly prisoners following a disturbance in which another guard was held hostage. The question was whether such use of deadly force was justified even though the original disturbance had already quieted down at the time the guard fired. Although the opinion written by Justice O'Connor was a five-four decision, all judges agreed that "the correct standard" for an eighth amendment violation is "unnecessary and wanton" conduct. As stated by Justice O'Connor:

> Unless it appears that the evidence, viewed in the light most favorable to the plaintiff, will support a reliable inference of wantonness in the infliction of pain under the standard we have described, the case should not go to the jury.... Under these circumstances, the actual shooting was part and parcel of a good faith effort to restore prison security. As such, it did not violate [the prisoner's] Eighth Amendment right to be free from cruel and unusual punishments.[85]

In Daniels v Williams,[86] the Court returned to *Parratt* to "reconsider our statement . . . that 'the alleged loss, even though negligently caused amounted to a deprivation'" under the due process clause of the fourteenth amendment.[87] In a § 1983 action, the plaintiff, a prisoner, sought to recover damages for injuries suffered when he slipped on a pillow negligently left on the stairs by a jail employee, the argument being that that negligence "deprived" plaintiff of his "liberty" interest in freedom from bodily injury.

Reasoning that the purposes of the due process clause to promote fairness and to guard against arbitrary state decisions "are quite remote" from "leaving a pillow on the prison stairs," six justices concluded, in an opinion written by Chief Justice Rehnquist that *Parratt* should be overruled "to the extent that it states that mere lack of due care by a state official may 'deprive' an individual of life, liberty or property under the Fourteenth Amendment."[88] Therefore, the Court decided, for mere negligence on the part of state officials, the fourteenth amendment "does not afford him a remedy."[89]

Even though decisions have now excluded both negligence and gross negligence as a remedy for deprivation of due process and eighth amendment violations, the Court left open the possibility that "there are other constitutional provisions that would be violated by mere lack of care."[90] As one writer has concluded: "in a marked clarification of its ruling in *Monroe,* the Supreme Court has recently held that § 1983 has no state-of-mind requirement of its own, that it adopts the state-of-mind requirement of the constitutional right that the plaintiff seeks to enforce."[91]

Acting "under color of" law

In addition to showing that they have been deprived of a federal right, plaintiffs must show that defendants acted "under color of" state or local authority. Although Congress has power to eliminate this requirement by making deprivation of a federal right the sole test for liability, it has not chosen to do so.[92] The terms, "under color of" law, and "state action," have been found by the courts to be equivalent so that the huge fund of fourteenth amendment due process cases is available for interpreting the words.[93]

To be acting under color of law, state or local government agents must be either fulfilling or purporting to fulfill some assigned task, or obligation or be engaged in some act made possible by the power conferred on them by government. Action taken under state law has been held to include misuse of such power, actions taken in excess of authority or without authorization, even where contrary to state law; or failure to carry out a duty where there is a legal duty to act. A 1945 Supreme Court case, Screws v United States, sets forth a concise interpretation of the term:

> It is clear that under "color" means under "pretense" of law. Thus acts of officers in the ambit of their personal pursuits are plainly excluded. Acts of officers who undertake to perform their official duties are included whether they hew to the line of their authority or overstep it.[94]

A more recent statement on the definition of action "under color of law" is found in West v Adkins:

> To constitute state action, "the deprivation must be caused by the exercise by some right or privilege created by the State . . . or by a person for whom the State is responsible," and "the party charged with the deprivation must be a person who may fairly be said to be a state actor. [S]tate employment is generally sufficient to render the defendant a state actor." It is firmly established that a defendant in a § 1983 suit acts under color of state law when he abuses the position given him by the state. Thus, generally a public employee acts under color of state law while acting in his official capacity or while exercising his responsibilities pursuant to state law.[95]

One writer has separated problems arising out of the section's state action requirement into those in which (1) the state employee deprives the plaintiff of a right while acting pursuant to state authority; (2) employees act in such a way as to misuse or abuse their authority; (3) a private person or entity acts in such an interdependent or symbiotic relationship with the state, or exercises a traditionally state function, that it amounts to state action; or (4) officials go so far beyond the scope of their authority that the action amounts to private pursuit rather than state action.[96]

The first category would include any situation in which local law is in conflict with federal rights, for example, racial conflict of the 1950s and 1960s when southern police arrested violators of state segregation laws.[97] The second category is illustrated by a case in which a young woman who was making a complaint for assault was photographed in the nude by city police officers who thereafter distributed the photos to fellow officers.[98] The last two categories, whether action by officials may sometimes be private pursuit, or its opposite, whether action by private persons may sometimes be state action, are complex issues and will be considered below.

State versus private action

Because § 1983 relies for its authority on the fourteenth amendment which exclusively restrains state action, it can apply only to state and not to private action. Action by state or local officials that can be characterized as mere private pursuit therefore cannot be actionable under 1983. Because there is no facile way to tell a public from a private function, courts have had considerable difficulty in coming up with a usable test to distinguish between the two species of act. One author, taking her cue from Monroe v Pape, groups the cases into two categories: (1) those in which the excesses or abuses in authority are committed while the officer is acting or purporting to act in the line of duty, and (2) although not purporting to act in the line of duty, the wrongful act is facilitated or made possible only because of the agent's government status.[99] Unless the behavior falls in one of these two categories, it will be deemed by the courts to be private and not state action.

Into the first category falls Stengel v Belcher[100] in which an out of uniform, off-duty police officer intervened in a tavern brawl in an effort to restore order. In the struggle which followed, the officer, using mace and his service revolver, killed two men and wounded a third. Departmental regulations required off-duty police officers to carry pistols and take action at any time there was criminal activity in their presence. In addition, the court considered that the officer had used departmentally-issued mace; that a departmental board of inquiry had found his actions to be in "line of duty" and that he had received workmen's compensation. Thus, the officer acted as he did because he was under an obligation to do so. Even though his action was excessive, it was in the line of duty and as such was taken under color of law.

Belcher can be compared to Gibson v City of Chicago,[101] in which a police officer who had been declared mentally unfit for duty, for unknown reasons, shot and killed an individual, whose estate later sued the city. The court held the officer had not acted under color of law because he "was not authorized to use any police authority; he could not misuse power he could not exercise in the first place."

Several cases are suggested as candidates for the second category. Catlette v United States involved a situation in which several Jehovah's Witnesses sought protection from Deputy Sheriff Catlette against a threatening gang.[102] Catlette, instead of protecting them, joined with the others in forcing his victims to drink castor oil and submit to other indignities. In Crews v United States, a town marshall bull-whipped a black man and then forced him to leap to his death from a bridge.[103] In Henry v Cagle, an off-duty constable beat a prisoner in the custody of another to settle a private grievance.[104] In each case, the officials were found to be acting under color of law. While *Belcher* was a case in which the officer acted under authority of a departmental regulation but abused that authority, in *Catlette, Crews* and *Henry,* there was no such authority to act as they did. Rather, it was their office as local officials that made it possible for them to engage in such conduct.

Although this rationale makes some sense in terms of the above cited cases, other decisions make it unclear what test courts are applying. A sheriff and deputy in uniform moonlighting at a race track ejected a patron on the instruction of the race track owners;[105] a sheriff and his deputy illegally arrested a citizen as a means of pressure to force him to pay a debt to a creditor;[106] police officers in uniform and on duty called a citizen names and offered to fight with him;[107] and a corrections officer beat and threw feces at a prisoner who rejected his sexual advances.[108] In each case, defendants were found to be engaged in private pursuits. One writer criticized such decisions, suggesting that problems of this sort are better handled in terms of defendant's immunities or defenses than in denying that the official was acting under color of law.[109]

In the 1988 case of National Collegiate Athletic Association v Tarkanian,[110] a five to four decision, the Court did little to clarify the concept. The Court decided that the University of Nevada (UNLV), which fired a basketball coach on the recommendation of the National Collegiate Athletic Association (NCAA), was not engaged in state action. The plaintiff coach had argued that "the NCAA was a state actor because it misused power that it possessed by virtue of state law."[111]

The NCCA consists of voluntary members, one of which is UNLV, a state-funded university. NCAA's bylaws provide for a Committee on

Infractions to oversee its enforcement program. That Committee initiated an investigation of alleged violations by UNLV, which resulted in
findings that UNLV had violated NCAA's rules and recommended,
among other things, that Tarkanian be removed as basketball coach.
Other sanctions against UNLV's basketball program would follow if
Tarkanian were not removed. UNLV did remove him from the program
and Tarkanian filed this § 1983 suit, claiming his due process rights
under the fourteenth amendment had been violated.

In response, the majority answered that "in the usual case we ask
whether the State provided a mantle of authority that enhanced the
power of the harm-causing individual actor,"[112] but under the facts of
this case, "It would be more appropriate to conclude that UNLV has
conducted its athletic program under color of the policies adopted by the
NCAA, rather than that those policies were developed and enforced
under color of Nevada law."[113]

This case is unlikely to have much impact on the doctrine because of
its "unusual" facts, the lack of any theory to sustain its reasoning, and the
thinness of the majority.

Inaction as state action

Under the due process clause of the fourteenth amendment, does the
state's knowledge of the individual's predicament or its expressions of
intent to help him, create an affirmative duty to protect which satisfies
the amendment's state action requirement? Or is that requirement activated only by the "state's affirmative act of restraining the individual's
freedom to act on his own behalf—through incarceration, institutionalization, or other restraint of personal liberty—which is the 'deprivation
of liberty' triggering the protections of the Due Process Clause"?[114]

Adopting the second proposition as its guiding rule, Chief Justice
Rehnquist in DeShaney v Winnebago County DSS,[115] writing for a
majority of six, decided that the failure of a county department of social
services to heed several warnings that a child would be harmed by the
child's father unless the child was removed from his custody did not
engage the responsibility of the state because it did not amount to state
action. The Court concluded that brain damage resulting to the child
from the father's beatings was caused by private and not state action.

> Because . . . the State had no constitutional duty to protect [the child] against
> his father's violence, its failure to do so—though calamitous in hindsight—
> simply does not constitute a violation of the Due Process Clause.[116]

In the course of its opinion, the Court rejected a doctrine relied on by plaintiffs and followed until then by a number of courts of appeals, the "special relationship" doctrine:

> Once the State learns that a third party poses a special danger to an identified victim, and indicates its willingness to protect the victim against that danger, a "special relationship" arises between State and victim, giving rise to an affirmative duty, enforceable through the Due Process Clause, to render adequate protection.[117]

The Court proposed a more restricted view of state action.

> The affirmative duty to protect arises not from the State's knowledge of the individual's predicament or from its expressions of intent to help him, but from the limitation which it has imposed on his freedom to act on his own behalf. In the substantive due process analysis, it is the State's affirmative act of restraining the individual's freedom to act on his own behalf—through incarcerations, institutionalization, or other similar restraint of personal liberty— which is the "deprivation of liberty" triggering the protections of the Due Process Clause, not its failure to act to prevent his liberty interests against harms inflicted by other means. . . . While the State may have been aware of the dangers that [the child] faced in the free world, it played no part in their creation, nor did it do anything to render him any more vulnerable to them.[118]

Court of Appeals cases following *DeShaney* have taken a rather tortuous path in maneuvering between state action and inaction. Like *DeShaney*, Brown v Grabowski,[119] involved "calamitous" circumstances. Two women were sexually assaulted by a former boyfriend of one of the women, incidents that finally resulted in the death of one of them. While these assaults were proceeding, the women themselves and their families complained to the police but the assailant was never arrested. A subsequent investigation of the department showed that it was completely "unsupervised" by the chief of police (one of the defendants in a § 1983 suit), and that there was a failure to follow up on domestic violence cases. Nevertheless, on the basis of *DeShaney* the court found itself compelled to conclude that

> plaintiff has adduced insufficient evidence to create a genuine issue of material fact as to her claim that [the detective to whom she reported the assault], much less [the police officer] acted so as to create a special relationship with [the victim], triggering a constitutional duty to assist her in obtaining protection from [the assailant] in the civil courts. Plaintiff has provided no evidence, as *DeShaney* would appear to require, that either defendant affirmatively barred the door to the civil courts to [the victim], that he otherwise limited her

freedom to act on her own behalf, or that he created or exacerbated the danger that [the assailant] posed to her.[120]

On the other hand, in Gregory v City of Rogers, Ark,[121] police had arrested a "designated driver," so designated after the two passengers had been at a party where they had become intoxicated. On the arrest of the driver for a traffic violation, the police found that the driver was wanted for a warrant for another traffic offense. Even though they were told of the circumstances, the officers nevertheless placed the intoxicated persons in possession of the car, which was shortly thereafter involved in a fatal accident.

> In this case, unlike in *DeShaney*, the state *did* do something to create a danger for Gregory and Fields and render them more vulnerable, i.e., a police officer took their designated driver from them. Gregory and Fields had taken the precaution of appointing a designated driver; by removing that driver, the state exposed the two passengers to grave danger, as the result of which one was killed and the other was seriously injured.[122]

Acts of private persons as state action

The notion that there be a significant distinction between the public and private sectors, underlies much of the Reconstruction legislation, including the fourteenth amendment's state action requirement, and dominates judicial thinking on the subject today. Nevertheless, regardless of the belief that these two sectors are separate and distinct, there are many places where they intersect and are interdependent. The fuzziness of these boundaries creates problems in determining whether in any particular case "private action" is really state action so as to become actionable under § 1983. Courts have used several tests in making this determination. The general rule is that acts by private persons or entities are not subject to § 1983 suits. But there are exceptions to this rule when (1) there exists between the private person and state or local government an interdependent and symbiotic relationship; (2) the government requires, encourages, conspires with or acts in concert with the private party; or (3) there is a delegation of a state function to private persons or entities.[123]

A symbiotic relationship exists between the state and the private person when the acts of the two are so interwoven that "the acts of the individuals can reasonably be said to be the acts of the political state."[124] For example, police benevolent organizations, such as the Fraternal Order of Police, have been found to be in such a close relationship with the police department that the act of such associations in excluding black officers could be considered state action.[125]

Where the government and the private party conspire together or act jointly or in concert in connection with the deprivation of plaintiff's rights, the private party may be acting under color of law. In Adickes v S H Kress & Co,[126] the Supreme Court held that if the plaintiff can prove that the defendant restaurant refused her service because she was in the company of blacks and that her arrest for vagrancy immediately after was the result of joint activity with the state or its agents, these actions could be found to be under color of [state] law. All that is necessary to satisfy the state action "joint participation" requirement is "invoking the aid of state officials to take advantage of state created . . . procedures."[127] Likewise, where the state has created a system for the seizure of private property at the instance of a private party instituting the procedure, the private party is engaged in "joint participation" with state officials,[128] but where persons violating a court injunction are arrested by other citizens, their later detention by the police, does not satisfy the joint activity test.[129]

The state action test most applicable to criminal justice personnel is that known as the public function theory. As one author expresses this idea, "Policing the community and enforcing the laws is an essential and traditional governmental function, and those private persons who assume this function will generally be acting" under color of law.[130] Cases using this rationale include a special patrolman who acted "pursuant to a statutory grant of police power," even though he was paid by a private employer;[131] a towing service that acted at the direction of the sheriff;[132] and a business employing security guards, who were extensively regulated by the state and had the same power to arrest as sheriffs.[133] Most recently the Supreme Court found that a private physician under contract to provide orthopedic services at a state prison on a part-time basis who treated plaintiff, a prisoner, for leg injuries was "engaged in state action fairly attributable to the State, and that [the physician] therefore acted under color of state law for purposes of § 1983."[134] Shopkeepers, who detain persons on authority of a shoplifter statute, have generally not been found to be acting under color of law on the theory that these persons are acting in their own self-interest rather than performing a public function.[135]

A problem, as yet legally unresolved, has been posed by the appearance in a number of cities of "Guardian Angels," groups of community volunteers that attempt to control crime in city streets and subways. After some friction between city police and the Angels, in most cities, the two factions have come to an accommodation. In New York City, a "memorandum of understanding" was entered into between the City, the police department, and the Angels to establish the legal relationship between them, and to protect the city as much as possible against suit by citizens allegedly injured by Angel activity. In the memorandum, the City recognized the Angels as "an independent, autonomous, volunteer citizens group," not as "employees of the City of New York," and providing that the city would not be liable to indemnify the Angels for any judgment arising out of actions taken by them. This agreement cannot of course bind third parties. Claims by injured parties brought against cities on the basis of cooperation of city police with the Angels raise interesting and important public function questions.[136]

1983-like claims against federal officers

Section 1983 applies to deprivation "under color of . . . State" law and thus does not cover wrongful acts committed by the federal government or its agents. Such a limitation follows from § 1983's source of authority in the fourteenth amendment that applies only to state action. But in Bivens v Six Unknown Named Agents,[137] the Court carved out a 1983-like federal common law remedy to cover situations in which federal agents deprived persons of federal constitutional rights. The Court recognized the injustice and irony in a situation in which persons had a remedy for deprivation of federal constitutional rights by state officers but not by federal officers. In order to fill this gap the Court created a remedy based in the bill of rights and the fundamental constitutional rights derived therefrom by the Court's decisions.

Since *Bivens*, which was grounded in the fourth amendment's search and seizure provisions, the Court has taken a number of steps to limit the doctrine. In Carlson v Green the Court affirmed the use of the *Bivens* action but set forth "two situations" where it might be defeated:

> The first is when defendants demonstrate "special factors counseling hesitation in the absence of affirmative action by Congress." The second is when defendants show that Congress has provided an alternative remedy which it explicitly disclosed to be a *substitute* for recovery directly under the Constitution, and viewed as equally effective.[138]

This reasoning, which naturally came to be known as the "special factors" doctrine, was reaffirmed and expanded in Schweiker v Chilicky:

In sum, the concept of "special factors counseling hesitation in the absence of affirmative action by Congress" has proved to include an appropriate judicial deference to indications that congressional inaction has not been inadvertent. When the design of a government program suggests that Congress has provided what it considers adequate remedial mechanisms for constitutional violations that may occur in the course of its administration, we have not created additional *Bivens* remedies.[139]

Use of § 1983 by whites

The original purpose of the civil rights sections was to protect both blacks and their white supporters. Several instances have surfaced of cases in which whites have relied on 1983 for relief against discriminatory practices. In one, Bentley v Beck, a white prisoner in a Georgia jail complained that he was denied kitchen duty because the kitchen orderly did not like whites working in the kitchen. As long as he was deputy, the deputy said, only blacks would work there. The court found such a policy unconstitutional in that "inmates have the constitutional right to be free from racial discrimination."[140] Others will be cited in future chapters.

Federal jurisdiction

As has been suggested earlier, in order for a federal court to entertain a cause of action, it must have a specific grant of jurisdiction from Congress; the litigant in turn must assert this ground of jurisdiction in filing suit. For example, many suits in federal court are based on a diversity of jurisdiction (that is, the plaintiff and defendant must come from different states or territories), in which case, there is a requirement that the plaintiff assert a claim in excess of $50,000.

But for civil rights actions, a special jurisdictional provision, 28 USC 1343(3) authorizes the civil claimant to file a case in federal court without naming any amount in controversy. Such actions cover deprivations, under color of state authority, "of any right, privilege or immunity secured by the Constitution of the United States or by any Act of Congress providing equal rights of citizens or of all persons within the jurisdiction of the United States."[141]

Although, as a federal statute, 1983 actions are normally brought in federal court, state courts can and perhaps must accept such actions.[142]

Who may be a Section 1983 plaintiff?

The language of the section describes a plaintiff as "any citizen of the United States or other person" who has suffered the deprivation of a federal right. These words are interpreted the same as similar language in the fourteenth amendment's due process clause. Although a corporation is not a citizen, it is a "person" and may therefore sue. Likewise, the language has been held to include aliens, convicted felons, unions and other associations, but probably does not include a fetus, cities, states or state divisions such as counties.[143] A plea of guilty does not preclude a § 1983 suit to recover damages by or against state officers who violate plaintiff's constitutional fourth amendment rights.[144] Enlisted military personnel, however, may not maintain suit to recover damages from superior officers for injuries incurred in military service from violation of their constitutional rights.[145]

Who may be a Section 1983 defendant?

Like the plaintiff, the language, "every person," defines the defendant through the perspective of the fourteenth amendment's due process clause. Therefore, all natural persons, corporations and associations may be sued. Cities are suable, but "neither a state nor its officials acting in their official capacities," nor state subdivisions are "persons" under § 1983.[146] Federal officials, acting in their official capacity, under color of federal law, cannot be sued under § 1983 because § 1983 applies to actions taken under color of *state* law. These matters will be further developed in chapter 3.

Availability of punitive damages in 1983 actions

In law, there are two kinds of damages that may be requested as relief—compensatory and punitive. Compensatory damages have the object of making the injured person "whole," that is, to return persons to the same economic status they had before the injury took place. Such damages may include compensation for pain and suffering, medical expenses, loss of pay, and the like. Punitive damages, on the other hand, "are not intended to compensate the injured party, but rather to punish the tortfeasor whose wrongful conduct was intentional or malicious, and to deter him and others from similar extreme conduct."[147] Thus, punitive damages are possible only where the defendant's conduct rises above ordinary negligence and can be shown to be at least grossly negligent or reckless. Moreover, punitive damages are allowable only if there has been a finding of compensatory damages, although the amount awarded may be nominal. In City of Newport v Fact Concerts,[148] the Court decided that in § 1983 actions punitive damages may be found against city officials but not against cities. City officials had unconstitutionally denied the right of one of several musical groups to play at a concert. As a result of the ensuing publicity severe losses were suffered by plaintiff. The trial resulted in both compensatory and punitive damages against city officials and the city. In denying the right of punitive damages against cities, the Court concluded that neither purpose of punitive damages—punishment nor deterrence—would be served by allowing such a judgment. First, the primary requirement before a jury can find punitive damages, malice, cannot be attributed to cities, but only to those acting for them, city officials. Secondly, the punishment objective is not furthered by the use of punitive damages against the city (the Court does not say why). Finally, deterrence (to prevent future misconduct of city officials), is unlikely to result from punitive awards against the city that employed them. Rather, "by allowing juries and courts to assess punitive damages in appropriate circumstances against the offending official, based on his personal financial resources, the statute directly advances the public's interest in preventing repeated constitutional deprivations."[149] Thus, the Court concluded, cities are immune from punitive damages under § 1983.

Which remedy to use—federal habeas corpus or § 1983?

Where the question involves the "conditions of confinement," the proper action is under § 1983; where challenge is made to "the very fact or duration of his physical imprisonment and the relief he seeks is a determination that he is entitled to immediate release or a speedier release from that imprisonment," federal habeas must be used.[150] If it were otherwise, a state prisoner could avoid resort to state administrative and judicial remedies simply by filing a 1983 action. Therefore, where the prisoner's release is in prospect, habeas is the exclusive remedy and before using it, administrative remedies must be exhausted. In a proper case for the use of § 1983, a person need not exhaust state remedies. This should include any case in which the relief sought is damages or injunctive relief rather than speedier release from prison.

Other Civil Rights Acts—Civil Sanctions

Although 1983 is presently the most frequently used of Reconstruction legislation, civil rights acts still on the books include 42 USC §§ 1981, 1982, and 1985. Sections 1981 and 1982 have a common origin in the Civil Rights Act of 1866 while § 1985 is derived from an Act of 1871.

Section 1981 protects the right to contract and relies for its authority on the implementing clauses of both the thirteenth and fourteenth amendments. Section 1982 protects the right to inherit, purchase, lease, sell, hold and convey real and personal property and is authorized by the thirteenth amendment. Section 1985 gives a right of action in conspiracies to interfere with civil rights, and like the other two sections, takes its authority from the thirteenth amendment. Since all three are based on the thirteenth amendment, they reach private as well as state action. There is thus no color of law requirement under these sections.[151]

42 USC § 1981—the right to contract[152]

Section 1981 was re-enacted after the adoption of the fourteenth amendment as an Act of May 31, 1870, and thereafter was codified as 42 USC § 1981. As amended, it reads:

> All persons . . . shall have the same right, in every State and Territory to make and enforce contracts, to sue, be parties, and give evidence, and to full and equal benefit of all laws and proceedings for the security of person and property, as is enjoyed by white persons, and shall be subject to like punishment, pains, penalties, taxes, licenses, and exactions of every kind, and to no other.[153]

In Saint Francis College v Majid Ghaidan Al-Khazraji, a 1987 case,[154] a unanimous Court found that a person of Arab ancestry had an action under § 1981. The plaintiff was a US citizen, born in Iraq, claiming he was denied tenure by a university because he was of the "Arabian race." After looking into the meaning of "race" in the nineteenth century at the time § 1981 was passed, the Court concluded:

> Congress intended to protect from discrimination identifiable classes of persons who are subjected to intentional discrimination solely because of their ancestry or ethnic characteristics. . . . whether or not it would be classified as racial in terms of modern scientific theory. . . . If respondent on remand can prove that he was subjected to intentional discrimination based on the fact that he was born an Arab, rather than solely on the place or nation of his origin, or his religion, he will have made out a case under § 1981.[155]

This section was intended to strike at one of the primary impediments of slavery, the inability of a slave to make and enforce contracts. Action lies under the section for any racially discriminatory refusal to enter into a contract. Because, by its words, the section includes "all persons," all races are equally covered.[156] The purpose of § 1981 is "to provide for equality of rights as between persons of different races"[157] by prohibiting "all racial discrimination, whether or not under 'color of law,' with respect to the rights enumerated therein."[158] There is no *Bivens* equivalent for § 1981 and therefore federal employees having an employment complaint cannot file under this section but are limited to Title VII for employment discrimination.[159]

The principal case interpreting the section is Runyon v McCrary,[160] a 1976 case which held that Section 1981 prohibits racial discrimination caused by private as well as state action. That interpretation was based on a reading of thirteenth amendment legislative history. Congress could pass laws for the purpose of eradicating badges and incidents of slavery, including the inability to hold property or to make contracts. Pursuant to Section 2 of that amendment, Section 1 of the Civil Rights Act of 1866 was passed, and Section 1981 derives its power from this section. Therefore, Section 1981, under the authority of the thirteenth amendment, covers the actions of private persons. The Court in *McCrary* found that refusal to admit black children to a private school solely because of their race violated the section.

The future of the section has been clouded by a recent opinion by a bare majority of the Court that first reconsidered their decision in *McCrary*, that is, whether Section 1981 should be interpreted as reaching private action, and then declined to overrule it. In Patterson v McLean Credit Union,[161] Patterson, a black woman, relying on § 1981, charged that her employer had racially harassed her, intentionally failed to promote her and discharged her because she was black. The Court, in a 5 to 4 decision, first held that § 1981 does indeed reach private action but went on to hold that "racial harassment relating to conditions of employment is not actionable under § 1981 because that provision does not apply to conduct that occurs after the formation of a contract and that does not interfere with the right to enforce established contract obligations."[162] The Court also decided plaintiff's burden of proof requirement to prove a claim of discrimination in employment; and how a § 1981 claim interacts with a Title VII employment discrimination claim. This portion of the case will be discussed in chapter 2.

In explaining its rather narrow interpretation of § 1981, the majority reasoned that "by its plain terms, the relevant provision in § 1981 protects two rights: 'the same right . . . to . . . make . . . contracts' and 'the same right . . . to . . . enforce contracts' " as is enjoyed by white people.[163] From this statutory language, the court concluded that "the first of these protections extends only to the formation of a contract, but not to problems that may arise later from the conditions of continuing employment. . . . The second of these guarantees . . . embraces protection of a legal process . . . [I]t prohibits discrimination that infects the legal process in ways that prevent one from enforcing contract rights, by reason of his or her race, and this is so whether this discrimination is attributed to a statute or simply to existing practices," and would include "wholly *private* efforts."[164]

Applying these principles to plaintiff's case, the Court concluded that racial harassment that does not amount to "a refusal to make a contract with her or the impairment of her ability to enforce her established contract rights," does not establish a § 1981 claim.[165] A person with such a claim must look to Title VII of the Civil Rights Act of 1964 for her remedy.

As to plaintiff's claim that she was denied promotion for racial reasons, "whether a promotion claim is actionable under § 1981 depends upon whether the nature of the change in position was such that it involved the opportunity to enter into a new contract with the employer," that is, "only where the promotion rises to the level of an opportunity for a new and distinct relation between the employee and the employer is such a claim actionable under § 1981."[166] Justice Brennan's dissent for a four-man minority described the majority's interpretation of § 1981 as "needlessly cramped" in ruling out Patterson's racial harassment claim.[167]

In Jet v Dallas Independent School District,[168] decided in the Court's term after *Patterson,* Justice O'Connor, for a five to four majority, wrote that

> the express "action at law" provided by § 1983 for the "deprivation of any rights, privileges, or immunities secured by the Constitution and laws," provides the exclusive federal remedy for the violation of the rights guaranteed by § 1981 when the claim is pressed against a state actor.[169]

The import of this decision is that all of the immunity defenses, applicable to § 1983, and discussed in chapter 3, are equally applicable to § 1981. Justice Brennan, again dissented, questioning whether these two cases (*Patterson* and *Jet*) raise "the possibility that this landmark civil rights statute [now] affords no civil redress at all."[170]

Cases following *Patterson* have generally arisen in pending cases in which defendants on the basis of the Court's holding in *Patterson*, filed requests for summary judgments (that is, they asked the court to find in their favor on the basis of the law, without the necessity of taking any evidence). Defendants have often successfully argued that racial discrimination, discriminatory work assignment, denial of equal training opportunities, discriminatory promotion or wrongful discharge are not, under *Patterson*, violations of § 1981.[171]

42 USC § 1982—property rights

Section 1982 has the same origin and purpose as § 1981 and can be similarly employed, in appropriate cases, by blacks and non-blacks. The section reads:

> All citizens of the United States shall have the same right, in every State and Territory, as is enjoyed by white citizens thereof to inherit, purchase, lease, sell, hold, and convey real and personal property.[172]

Defendants may be private persons, and no proof of state action or color of law is necessary for the same reasons applicable to § 1981. The section cuts through defenses of sovereign immunity (see chapter 3), and thus the federal government, its agencies and personnel, state and local government, are all potential defendants.[173] The section has been used to seek redress against the firebomber of plaintiff's house;[174] against a housing authority which maintained racially-segregated housing;[175] against a fishing and hunting club that denied membership and the opportunity on the part of a black man to share in club property ownership;[176] and to obtain damages from a landlord who refused to lease to a white that would have black visitors.[177] Both money and equitable relief are available for injuries alleged and proven under the section.

In a companion case to the Saint Francis case (see section on § 1981), Shaare Tefila Congregation v Cobb,[178] under § 1982 a Jewish congregation sued persons who allegedly defiled their synagogue and thereby deprived the congregation of the right to hold property. Defendants defended that because "Jews today are not thought to be members of a separate race, they cannot make out a claim of racial discrimination within the meaning of § 1982."[179] Relying on the same construction of § 1982 as the Court used in *Saint Francis*, the Court held that "the question before us is not whether Jews are considered to be a separate race by today's standards, but whether, at the time § 1982 was adopted, Jews constituted a group of people that Congress intended to protect. . . . Jews are not foreclosed from stating a cause of action against other members of what today is considered to be part of the Caucasian race."[180]

42 USC § 1985—conspiracy[181]

Section 1985 is aimed at conspiracies that deprive black citizens of "basic rights that the law secures to all free men."[182] Its modern interpretation is not limited to blacks, but brings other classes within its protection.[183] The section is divided into three subsections. Subsection (1) allows an action by "any person" against persons who "conspire to prevent, by force, intimidation, or threat" the holding of or discharging the duties of any United States office; subsection (2)[a][184] authorizes an action by a party or witness against any persons who "conspire to deter" them "by force, intimidation, or threat," from gaining access to *federal* courts or [b] who conspire with the intention of impeding, hindering or obstructing "the due course of justice" in any *state* court with intent to deny to any citizen the equal protection of the law; subsection (3)[a] allows an action by "any person or class of persons" against individuals who "conspire or go in disguise on the highway or on the premises of another, for the purpose of depriving" these persons of the "equal protection of the laws, or of equal privileges and immunities under the laws," or (3)[b] any person who conspires to prevent anyone from voting in a *federal* election.[185] Section 3 provides a remedy applicable to all sections: "The party so injured or deprived may have an action for the recovery of damages occasioned by such injury or deprivation, against one or more of the conspirators."

In order to prove a claim under 1985(3), the plaintiff must establish (1) a conspiracy, (2) motivated by some racial or other invidiously discriminatory animus, (3) an act in furtherance of the conspiracy, and (4) an injury to person or property or a deprivation of any right or privilege of a citizen of the United States.[186] As long as there is a denial of a federal right, the section authorizes action against private conspirators without any color of law requirement.[187] Subsection (3) has been the subsection most frequently used. Rights protected relevant to criminal justice personnel include the right to be free from conspiracies to unlawfully arrest and imprison;[188] a right of reasonable access to the courts;[189] a remedy for an accused's confession by illegal means;[190] a right of police protection from racial violence.[191]

In determining whether it was necessary for a plaintiff to prove an intention to deprive the victims of the equal protection of the laws, sometimes referred to as "racial or class-based invidiously discriminatory animus," the Kush v Rutledge Court distinguished between the statute's reference to interference with state or federal functions. Where the statute refers to protection of federal functions [sections 1, 2(a) and 3(a)], there is no necessity of showing such a mental state, but where the statute refers to protection of state functions [sections 2(b) and 3(b)], such proof is necessary. The Court bases its conclusions on the statute's "legislative history," namely, that given the "disorder and anarchy in the Southern States," at the time it became law (1871), "neither proponents nor opponents . . . had any doubt that the Constitution gave Congress the power to prohibit intimidation of parties, witnesses, and jurors in federal courts" while there was a great deal of objection to such extension of power to state courts.[192]

Use of Civil Rights Acts by criminal justice personnel

One of the fundamental propositions of this text is that criminal justice personnel are direct beneficiaries of legislation, doctrines and decisions originally won by other groups. The use by criminal justice employees of the Civil Rights Acts has been rising in recent years, a point more fully discussed in chapters 2, 6 and 7. Moreover, it is likely that as criminal justice employees become more accustomed to asserting their rights, a matter to be discussed in chapter 5, their use of civil rights legislation will increase. For example, criminal justice personnel have used § 1983 to challenge the dismissal of a black police officer for permitting two white women to board in his home;[193] the refusal of a police fraternal association to admit to membership black police officers;[194] a dismissal by a sheriff of his deputy for membership in a police union;[195] a transfer from the officer's home city for punitive reasons;[196] to declare certain sick leave regulations unconstitutional.[197]

18 USC §§ 241, 242 and 245—criminal sanctions

In addition to the civil remedies that have been described, Reconstruction legislation also provided criminal sanctions, now designated as §§ 241 and 242 of the Federal Criminal Code.

Section 241 is the criminal counterpart of § 1985 and applies to conspiracies of two or more persons who (1) threaten to intimidate or (2) go in disguise on the highway or on premises of another, with intent to interfere with a citizen's enjoyment of rights secured by the Constitution or federal laws.

Section 242 is the criminal counterpart of § 1983 and applies to any person who under color of law willfully subjects any inhabitant to the deprivation of rights secured by the Constitution or federal laws.

Section 245 was passed in 1968, following the massive violent reaction by private individuals and state authorities to attempts to desegregate southern schools, restaurants and other public facilities, and the disorders in northern cities in the late 1960s. The section makes it a federal crime to forcibly interfere with the rights of any person to attend public schools, use state facilities, or obtain employment or public accommodations on account of race, color, religion or national origin; or to engage in looting or vandalism during a riot.

Before proceeding to a discussion of the legal interpretations of these sections, it will be useful to discuss certain elements common to §§ 241 and 242. Over the course of time, the courts have been no kinder to the criminal provisions of the Reconstruction Period than they have been to the civil sections. Part of the problem has been the lack of precision in the language used to draft the statutes, a fault particularly deadly when dealing with criminal statutes, the constitutionality of which is judged in part by the clarity in defining the crime they are sanctioning.

As Justice Frankfurter so well stated:

> The dominant conditions of the Reconstruction Period were not conducive to the enactment of carefully considered and coherent legislation. Strong postwar feelings caused inadequate deliberation and led to loose and careless phrasing of laws related to the new political issues.[198]

Section 241, for example, covers two or more persons who conspire to injure any *citizen* in the exercise of rights secured by the Constitution or laws of the United States while § 242 protects any *inhabitant.* Section 245 protects the more expansive any *person.*

History and purpose of the sections

What is now § 241 is derived from § 6 of the Enforcement Act of 1870; § 242 has its origin in § 2 of the Civil Rights Act of 1866. The sections have maintained their present wording since 1874.[199] Section 242 is known as the *substantive* section, protecting unspecified "rights, privileges and immunities," while § 241 is known as the *conspiracy* section, applying to conspiracies to deprive citizens of their federal rights.

United States v Price,[200] the case that resurrected these sections from relative oblivion, sets forth their history. As the Court emphasizes, "the purpose and scope of the 1866 and 1870 enactments must be viewed against the events and passions of the time."[201] The Court briefly recounts the struggle between the ten "unreconstructed" states and the federal government. Following the formation of the Ku Klux Klan and the Knights of the White Camellia in 1866, there came by "1868 a wave of murders and assaults . . . including assassinations designed to keep Negroes from the polls. The States themselves were helpless, despite the resort of some of them to extreme measures such as making it legal to hunt down and shoot any disguised man."[202] The sections were to provide federal authorities with a means to curb these outrages. It was hoped that they would be broadly interpreted by the courts. But it was a long time before the federal authorities and the courts came to that conclusion.

The enforcement history of the sections

In 1939, the Civil Rights Section, as it was then known, was created in the US Department of Justice, the first time that any part of the United States government had been specifically assigned responsibility for civil rights enforcement since the post-Civil War Freedmen's Bureau.[203] The Department of Justice's policy in initiating civil rights prosecutions was that of self-imposed restraint because of fear on the part of federal authorities that a more forceful approach would alienate southern police forces. Justice Roberts, in his dissent in Screws v United States, quotes the Attorney General's policy statement with reference to civil rights prosecutions as one of "strict self-limitation. . . . When violations of such statutes are reported, the Department requires that efforts be made to encourage state officials to take appropriate action under state law."[204] The consequence of this policy is evident in the Attorney General's activity report that reveals that "less than one per cent of the complaints received by the Civil Rights Section are ever fully investigated and a still smaller percentage ever reached the prosecution stage."[205]

Some forty years later (1978), in testimony before the US Commission on Civil Rights, Drew S Days III, the Assistant Attorney General in charge of the Civil Rights Division, provided enforcement procedures and statistics. He testified that all civil rights investigations are conducted by the FBI. When the results are available, the findings are conveyed to the local office of the United States Attorney and to the Civil Rights Division. These offices jointly decide whether prosecution is warranted and what form it will take.[206] Approximately 10,000 complaints of police misconduct are received by the Civil Rights Division each year. Many of these are considered to be outside the jurisdiction of the federal government. After an FBI investigation of the remaining 3,000, about 50–100 matters are presented to grand juries and 25–50 actually result in indictments. The conviction rate in 1971 was about 70 percent, as compared with the rate of conviction for other federal crimes of above 95 percent.[207]

In his testimony, Days pointed out the weakness of relying on criminal sanctions for enforcement of civil rights statutes:

> The chief limitation on the effectiveness of prosecution as a deterrent is in the nature of the criminal charge itself. A prosecution for police misconduct does not address itself to the activities of a police department as such or of a city administration per se, but only to the actions of one or more officers in a given circumstance, framed by and limited to the wording of the criminal indictment. Moreover, criminal prosecutions are reactive litigations involving only the calling to account of individuals who have already engaged in acts of misconduct. Any conscious effort to anticipate instances of police misconduct and head them off before they occur must arise from some other source than the Federal criminal code.[208]

In reply to these comments by Days, it can be said that while the criminal sanction leaves much to be desired as a guarantor of civil rights, its effect is not limited to deterrence of the individual who committed the offense. Another purpose of the penalty is to serve as an example to others in order to deter them from committing the same or a similar offense. In organized bodies such as police departments or prisons where information about and interest in such a case is likely to be intense, such a penalty promises to have even more of a deterrent effect than with the general public.

Because § 242 deals with individual violations of substantive federal rights while § 241 is aimed at conspiracies of two or more persons to deprive citizens of these rights, it has been the substantive section, § 242 that has been used most frequently by the government and whose court interpretation has been most influential on the course of civil rights litigation.

18 USC § 242—substantive provision

Section 242 reads as follows:

> Whoever, under color of any law, statute, ordinance, regulation, or custom, willfully subjects any inhabitant of any State, Territory, or District to the deprivation of any rights, privileges, or immunities secured or protected by the Constitution or laws of the United States, or to different punishments, pains, or penalities, on account of such inhabitant being an alien, or by reason of his color, or race, than are prescribed for the punishment of citizens, shall be fined not more than $1,000 or imprisoned not more than one year, or both; and if bodily injury results shall be fined . . . or imprisoned not more than ten years, or both; and if death results shall be subject to imprisonment for any term of years or for life[209]

This section can be divided into two separate offenses: wilfully subjecting any inhabitant (1) to the deprivation of federal rights, or (2) to different penalties because of alienage, color or race. It is apparent that the second of these offenses was inspired by the discriminatory treatment of blacks by the southern criminal justice system following the Civil War. It has seen very little use. Our discussion, therefore, will be limited to the provision dealing with wilful deprivation of federal rights.

Before the establishment of the Civil Rights Section of the Department of Justice, § 242 had been employed in only two reported cases.[210] Thereafter, the numbers of cases filed somewhat increased. One in 1945, Screws v United States, and another in 1966, United States v Price, have determined the scope and interpretation of the section.

Court interpretation of § 242

Section 242 is a criminal statute and therefore is subject to the due process claim that a law that makes it a crime to wilfully deprive one of a right, privilege or immunity secured by the Constitution or laws of the United States is so vague and indefinite that it does not give "a person acting with reference to the statute fair warning that his conduct is within its prohibition."[211] That claim made in Screws v United States allowed the Supreme Court to construe the word "willfully" in such a way as to sustain the section's constitutionality.

Justice Douglas, speaking for himself and three concurring justices, began his reply to the claim of vagueness by admitting that prior decisions construing the due process clause have revealed conflicting views. In order to save the Act from this impasse Justice Douglas pointed to the well-known rule of statutory construction that states that the Court will not declare a federal law unconstitutional if a narrow interpretation of its language can preserve it. Turning to the word, "willfully," in the statute, Justice Douglas interpreted it to require "an intent to deprive a person of a right which has been made specific either by the express terms of the Constitution or laws of the United States or by decisions interpreting them."[212]

Although six members of the *Screws* Court agreed on the decision, Justice Douglas was able to carry only three other members to support his reasoning for sustaining the statute. The section stood on this weak reed until the 1966 Supreme Court case of United States v Price,[213] in which the Court made clear that § 242 is based on the enabling clause of the fourteenth amendment: "We have no doubt of 'the power of Congress to enforce by appropriate criminal sanction every right guaranteed by the Due Process Clause of the 14th amendment.' "[214]

The facts presented in *Price* dramatized the kind of situation that gave rise to the Reconstruction Period criminal sanction. Three young men, active in the 1964 desegregation demonstrations, were arrested and detained in a Mississippi jail. Thereafter, the defendants released the prisoners for the express purpose of waylaying and killing them.

As private persons participating with law enforcement officers in the murders, the defendants contended that they could not be acting under color of law. The Court replied:

> Private persons, jointly engaged with state officials in the prohibited action, are acting "under color" of law for purposes of the statute. To act "under color" of law does not require that the accused be an officer of the State. It is enough that he is a willful participant in joint activity with the State or its agents.[215]

Thus, *Price* decided that (1) under color of law means the same thing in § 242 that it does in § 1983 and that (2) the concert of action theory is equally applicable to §§ 1983 and 242. Two later court of appeals cases have solidified the *Screws* approach, both heavily relying on that case's reasoning. A 1975 5th circuit case, United States v Stokes,[216] involved a Georgia police officer, who after taking the victim into custody, physically abused him to the point that he suffered a fractured skull and was still in a coma at the time of trial, six months later. Stokes, relying on certain language in *Screws,* argued that the only constitutional right of which the prisoner could be deprived was his right to a courtroom trial. But the court concluded that the scope of § 242 is not so limited. It includes as well "a right not to be treated with unreasonable, unnecessary or unprovoked force by those charged by the state with the duty of keeping accused and convicted offenders in custody."[217]

In sum, to succeed in a § 242 prosecution, the government must show that (1) the person was an inhabitant of a state, territory, or district of the United States; (2) the accused person acted under color of law; (3) the person acted with an intent to deprive the inhabitant of a right that has been made specific either by the express terms of the Constitution, the laws of the United States, or by decisions interpreting them.

Questions have also been raised about sentencing provisions. United States v Hayes,[218] a 1979 case, dealt with the 1968 amendment to § 242 that increased the penalty, "if death results" from the defendant's act, to "any term of years or for life." The effect of this amendment was to raise the offense in case of death from misdemeanor to felony. Hayes had arrested and then physically mistreated the victim, a Mexican, by poking him with a shotgun, which had discharged, killing the prisoner. Hayes contended that the 1968 amendment obligated the government to show intent on his part to kill the victim. The court answered that the "Amendment alters the statute only insofar as requiring the additional element that death ensued as a proximate result of the accuseds' willful violation of a victim's defined rights."[219]

In another case interpreting the penalty clause, it was held that where the penalty for violation of § 241 is for "any term of years or for life," and where the defendant was sentenced to 10 years imprisonment, the district court exceeded its authority in suspending execution of the sentence by placing defendants on probation.[220]

Rights protected by § 242

In its original 1866 wording, § 242 had very limited coverage, restricted to deprivation under color of law of specific rights:

> to make and enforce contracts, to sue, be parties, give evidence, and to the full and equal benefit of all laws and proceedings for the security of person and property as is enjoyed by white citizens [and to] be subject to like punishment, pains, penalities, taxes, licenses, and exactions of every kind, and none other.[221]

In the general revision of the Civil Rights Acts in 1874, the specific enumeration of these rights was eliminated and the broader language substituted: "deprivation of any rights, privileges or immunities secured or protected by the Constitution or laws of the United States."[222] In

United States v Hayes,[223] taking *Screws* as its guiding light, the Court sets forth the means of applying § 242 to specific substantive rights:

> Thus, *Screws* makes it perfectly clear that once a due process right has been defined and made specific by court decisions, the right is encompassed by § 242. Further, in order to violate § 242, one must have a specific intent to willfully violate that defined right. Defendant concedes, as he must, that there are numerous cases which support the proposition that one's right to be tried by a court, and not by ordeal, and thus to be free from unlawful assault by state law enforcement officers when lawfully in their custody, has been made a definite and specific part of the body of due process rights protected by the fourteenth amendment of the Constitution, and therefore within the purview of § 242.[224]

Although in *Hayes* the court was interested only in a due process violation, this approach should be equally applicable to deprivation of equal protection of the laws or to other rights secured by federal law. The color of law language in § 1983 and § 242 is identical so that 1983 cases can be used in determining the rights covered by § 242.[225] Thus, the *Stokes* court, referring to a number of § 1983 cases, suggested that § 242 covers such actions as failure of state prison employees and correctional officers to prevent unprovoked knife assaults by one inmate on another; assault of pre-trial detainees by correctional officers; beatings of convicted federal prisoners by state jailers while in custody to answer state criminal charges; unreasonable and unnecessary force used by police to restrain arrested persons; beating of inmates in state correctional facilities and unreasonable and unnecessary force used by municipal police officers in making arrests.[226]

18 USC § 241—conspiracy

Section 241 reads as follows:

> If two or more persons conspire to injure, oppress, threaten, or intimidate any inhabitant of any state, territory, or district in the free exercise or enjoyment of any right or privilege secured to him by the Constitution or laws of the United States, or because of his having so exercised the same; or
>
> If two or more persons go in disguise on the highway, or on the premises of another, with intent to prevent or hinder his free exercise or enjoyment of any right or privilege so secured—
>
> They shall be fined not more than $10,000 or imprisoned not more than ten years, or both; and if death results, they shall be subject to imprisonment for any term of years or for life.[227]

History and purpose of § 241

As is apparent from the language quoted earlier from United States v Price, § 241 was aimed at private individuals such as members of the Ku Klux Klan who conspire together in groups to deprive citizens, that is, blacks just granted citizenship, of their newly-acquired federal rights. It was passed a few months after the fifteenth amendment and was particularly directed at attempts to prevent blacks from asserting their newly-won right to vote.[228] The colorful and situation-specific language of subsection two has not been used for many years although the resurgence of hate groups may revive its utility.

Court interpretation of § 241

In United States v Price, the Supreme Court made clear the breadth of interpretation to which the section is entitled:

> Within the Congress pressures mounted in the period between the end of the war and 1870 for drastic measures. . . . In this context, it is hardly conceivable that Congress intended § 241 to apply only to a narrow and relatively unimportant category of rights. We cannot doubt that the purpose and effect of § 241 was to reach assaults upon rights under the entire Constitution, including the 13th, 14th and 15th amendments, and not merely a part of it.[229]

The majority was replying to those on the Court and elsewhere who argued that the rights and privileges referred to were only those arising from the relation of the victim to the federal government. This view represented a resurgence of the dual citizenship concept of separate state and federally-derived rights.

To put that notion to rest, the Court forcefully concluded:

> The language of § 241 is plain and unlimited. . . . [I]ts language embraces *all* of the rights and privileges secured to citizens of *all* of the Constitution and *all* of the laws of the United States.[230]

The question arises as to what extent the basic premises of the criminal law, such as the necessity to show specific intent to violate a constitutional right as found in *Screws,* also applies to § 241. Even though the word "willfully", found in § 242, does not appear in § 241, the Supreme Court, relying on *Screws,* has said that "there is no basis for distinction between the two statutes in this respect," that is, the same requirement for intent is required in the two sections.[231]

In a similar vein, it has been asserted that the application of *Screws* to § 241 means that the government must show that the violation of the specific constitutional right was the *predominant* purpose of the conspiracy. In United States v Ellis, the court rejected that view, commenting that while *Screws* did "require such a specific intent, [it does] not require that the immediate intent to violate constitutional rights predominate over the ultimate purposes which that violation is designed to achieve,"[232] and it has been further held that an allegation that defendant intended to deprive plaintiff of the right to due process satisfies the statutory requirement that the indictment allege the deprivation of a constitutional right.[233]

Rights protected by § 241

The Supreme Court in the *Price* case explicitly stated that § 241 applied to all rights and privileges made specific by the Constitution and laws of the United States. It was further emphasized that both § 241 and § 242 covered the same rights. United States v Johnson,[234] showed the possible reach of the section. That case involved a conspiracy by "outside hoodlums to assault Negroes for exercising their right to equality in public accommodations" (in this case a restaurant), under the Civil Rights Act of 1964. It was contended that the 1964 Act provided an injunction as its exclusive remedy. Based on a reading of the Act's legislative history, the Court concluded that the injunction was exclusive only where the violator was the proprietor, not where as here, the persons prosecuted were "outside hoodlums." This case has broad implications, giving the government power to employ criminal sanctions to protect persons against any conspiracy that deprives them of rights granted by federal legislation.

18 USC § 245—racially-motivated violence

Section 245 grew out of the violent acts committed against blacks and white civil rights workers in the process of desegregating the South in the 1950s and 1960s. In many ways, these years were a replay of the Reconstruction Period with the result that Reconstruction legislation such as §§ 241 and 242 were reactivated and put to the test. But in attempting to use these sections as a means of deterring violence, it became evident that they had the defects already discussed, particularly problems of vagueness as to the particular rights protected. To deal with these problems of statutory construction and as a means of coping with the renewed violence, § 245 was enacted.[235]

In United States v Guest, a 1966 companion Supreme Court case to

United States v Price, Justice Brennan clearly invited Congress to take action:

> [S]ince the limitation on the statute's effectiveness derives from Congress' failure to define—with any measure of specificity—the rights encompassed, the remedy is for Congress to write a law without this defect.[236]

One aspect of the vagueness of §§ 241 and 242 stems from language such as "right or privilege" in § 241 and "rights, privileges, or immunities" in § 242, language that the Court had considerable difficulty in saving from unconstitutional infirmity in *Screws*. In the words of a Senate report, § 245

> meets this need by spelling out the kinds of activity to be protected, and [by providing] an effective means of deterring and punishing forcible interference with the exercise of Federal rights. The clear language of the bill would avoid unnecessary litigation concerning coverage and would provide unmistakable warning to lawless elements not to interfere with any of these activities.[237]

In carrying out the task of specifying federally-protected activities, Congress provided a statute with extremely detailed coverage to forbid three types of conduct: forceful interference with (1) federal activities involving elections, federally-administered programs, employment, jury duty and programs of financial assistance; (2) state activities involving public school, colleges, private or state employment, labor unions, public transport and accommodations, because of race, color, religion, or national origin; and (3) forceful interference during a riot or civil disorder with persons engaged in a business in commerce.

Coverage of the section

In addition to the problem of vagueness, it was unclear whether §§ 241 and 242 reached purely private actions denying federal rights; whether § 241 applied only to conspiracies, not individual action, and finally, the claim that the penalties for violation of the sections were inadequate to deter the violence at which they were aimed. By its terms, § 245 applied to anyone "whether or not acting under color of law," and since it is based on the implementing clauses of the fourteenth and fifteenth amendments, it extends to private as well as state interference with the enumerated rights and protects persons participating in both federal and state activities. In the case of state activities, the forceful interference must be "because of his race, color, religion or national origin."

Federal courts of appeals have concluded, consistent with *Screws*, that while there must be a purpose to interfere with one of the activities specified in the statute, there is no necessity to show that the defendant knew he was violating a federal right. In United States v Griffin,[238] the defendant, participating in an antibusing demonstration, attacked a black man who had no connection with school busing. To an argument that the act was not carried out with the thought that the beating would tend to prevent busing, the court stated:

> It was enough under 18 USC § 245 that he purposely sought to interfere with the right of black children to go to school; he need not know the exact extent, or the federal character of that right.[239]

Although the Supreme Court has not yet passed on the constitutionality of the section, the Court has ruled on a minor point of statutory construction, and lower federal courts have upheld the section's constitutionality. In United States v Kozminski,[240] a couple was charged under section 241 of forcing two laborers to work involuntarily on their farm. The Court decided that the section reaches such conduct—a violation of the thirteenth amendment prohibition against involuntary servitude. It overturned the decision, however, because the judge's instructions to the jury had permitted a finding of involuntary servitude on the basis of psychological coercion. The Court limited the meaning to forcible coercion.

A court of appeals decision, United States v Bledsoe,[241] found subsection 241(b)(2)(B) constitutional. That subsection acts against a wilful "force or threat of force" against "any person because of his race, color, religion, or national origin and because he is or has been engaging in any benefit . . . provided by any state." Defendant was convicted of killing a black man while the man was using a state park toilet. On appeal from a conviction, the defendant argued that the statute took its authority from the fourteenth amendment and therefore had no power to reach private action. The court responded that the deceased had a right to enjoy "state provided benefits free from private harassment motivated by racial animus," and that power to reach private parties derives from both the thirteenth and fourteenth amendments.

In a better-reasoned case, United States v Lane[242] the court found constitutional section 245(b)(2)(C) which prohibits any wilful interference with the enjoyment of "employment . . . by any private employer. . . . " Violation of section 245(b)(2)(C) arose out of the killing of a Jewish radio talk show host, Alan Berg, by members of a white supremacy group. As in *Bledsoe,* the defendants urged that this subsection was limited to regulation of state action and could not touch private action. But after a search of the section's statutory history, the court concluded that the subsection found its origin in the Commerce Clause of the United States Constitution and thus could reach acts by private persons.

Other cases have found, as is likewise true of other criminal civil rights statutes, that the sections do not give rise to private actions for damages;[243] that section 245 covers situations in which whites interfered with black's living in an all-white neighborhood;[244] or where correctional officers conspired to introduce false evidence into prison disciplinary proceedings;[245] but a conspiracy to bribe voters was found not to be within the section's coverage.[246]

Summary and Conclusions

Because ours is a federal system, both federal and state remedies are available for the assertion of rights and the redress of harms. The federal system also means that federal courts are more restricted in their jurisdiction than are state courts. State remedies derive from both common and statutory law while federal remedies are derived from the federal constitution and are generally statutory.

The federal government has waived its immunity to tort claims except for discretionary acts, that is, those injuries committed at the highest levels. At the same time, intentional injuries, which had been excluded from protection, were brought within the Act as a result of the reaction to a number of particularly outrageous incidents by law enforcement officers.

Habeas corpus became important in state-federal relations after the Civil War. The writ was broadened to allow state prisoners to call on federal courts to protect federal constitutional rights. Both state and federal tribunals have erected obstacles to keep habeas from interfering with state-federal relations and from overloading the court system. As part of this more general concern the courts have developed the abstention and hands-off doctrines, the first of which inhibits federal courts from interfering with state court proceedings, and the second allows courts to withhold intervention in state or federal prisons and police departments on the ground that they are in the care of experts delegated by the legislature to handle these problems without court interference.

After a period of dormancy following Reconstruction, changes in the economic structure of the country, pressures from blacks for equal rights, and a series of favorable Supreme Court decisions, revitalized and brought the Civil Rights Acts to the attention of the Bar. After the 1961 Monroe v Pape decision, use of § 1983 skyrocketed. Proof requirements are two: (1) the plaintiff must be shown to have been deprived of some right, privilege, or immunity guaranteed by the US Constitution or laws; (2) and the defendant must have acted under color of state or local law. With reference to the first proof requirement, the defendant must be shown to have been recklessly or deliberately indifferent to the violation of plaintiff's federal rights. Allegations of mere negligence are not enough. Deprivation of rights may be claimed for violation of the US Constitution as interpreted by the federal courts, and for violations of rights secured by federal statutes or treaties.

To be acting under color of law, state or local government agents must either be carrying out or purporting to carry out some assigned task or obligation, or be engaged in some act made possible by the power conferred on them by government. Mere inaction on the part of the government, in the absence of some affirmative act to restrain the individual's freedom to act, does not constitute state action. A further issue involves the determination whether a particular action is state or private. If it is shown to be private, § 1983 does not apply. Exceptions include instances in which the state and private persons are involved in some interdependent act; the government acts in concert with the individual, or the state delegates to the private person some public function. Although § 1983 does not apply to federal officers, the Supreme Court, in the *Bivens* case, has fashioned a common law remedy that allows persons injured by federal action to use a 1983-like remedy.

In addition to § 1983, other civil rights acts have been revived: § 1981 protects the right to contract; recent Supreme Court cases, however, have somewhat crippled this section by limiting its application to a person's entry into an employment contract denying its application to conditions arising thereafter; § 1982 protects equal rights to purchase and use property, and § 1985 protects against conspiracies to deprive persons of federal rights. Because all three draw all or part of their authority from the thirteenth amendment, they reach private as well as state action.

Sections 241, 242, and 245 of the Federal Criminal Code provide criminal sanctions to deter violation of constitutional rights. These sections, however, have seen only modest use because of lack of resources, because of concern by federal enforcement authorities that such prosecutions would destroy working relationships with police, and because of a continued belief that the solution to these violations lies more in civil action by the injured parties than in criminal action by the federal government. Nevertheless, the legislation has been favorably interpreted by Supreme Court decisions providing power to the government should it decide to use these Acts, and may be employed more often as hate groups become more active.

As court decisions recognize and declare additional rights and as federal statutes have expanded the role of the federal government in attempts at alleviating various societal inequities, the claims possible under § 1983 have increased. The Supreme Court has held that § 1983 claims are not limited to civil rights but may be based on any federal statute establishing a benefit. Therefore, the current attempt to substantially reduce the federal role in aiding those groups in society that no longer fit within the market structure (unskilled and "unneeded" workers) means that the ability of those groups to assert rights under federal laws are likely to materially decrease.

ENDNOTES

1. Both state legislatures and Congress may create special "legislative" courts to hear designated matters. The federal Court of Claims, which hears claims against the federal government, is one such court.
2. US Constitution, Art III § 2.
3. Meador, J: Habeas Corpus and Magna Carta, Charlottesville, University Press of Virginia, 1966, pp 9, 55.
4. Jones v Cunningham 371 US 236 (1963).
5. 28 USCA § 1346 (West Supp 1991). The Act does not cover injuries to federal civilian employees. Such injuries come under the Federal Employees Compensation Act (FECA), 5 USCA § 8102(a) (1980), an exclusive remedy to a federal employee injured in the course of employment.
6. 28 USCA § 1346 (West Supp 1991).
7. 28 USCA § 2671 (West Supp 1991).
8. 484 US 292.
9. Id at 293.
10. Id at 300 (emphasis added).
11. Cornell, Wm T, Note, An evaluation of the Federal Employees Liability Reform and Tort Compensation Act: Congress responds, 26 San Diego L Rev 137, 145 (Jan–Feb 1989).
12. 484 US at 300. Cornell, *supra* n 11 at 140.
13. Id at 141.
14. 28 USCA § 1346(b) (1976); 28 USCA 2679 (West Supp 1991). In US v Smith 111 SCt 1180 (1991), the Court decided that this section covered an injury by a military physician to plaintiff while overseas even though the FTCA pre-

cluded a claim for injuries incurred outside the US, so that such a plaintiff was without an effective remedy for his loss.

15. 28 USCA § 2679(b)(2). Constitutional torts are considered in ch 3.
16. Id at § 2675.
17. Id at § 2679(d)(1).
18. Id at § 2679(d)(2).
19. Id at § 2674.
20. 28 USCA § 2680(a) (1965).
21. See Meredith, Kathleen H and Pressman, Jennifer S, Suing the federal government: Can the king still do no wrong? 18 U of Balt L Rev 475, 515 (Sp 1989).
22. 486 US 531 (1988).
23. Id at 536–37 (citations omitted). Meredith and Pressman, *supra* n 21 at 526.
24. In Zumwalt v US 928 F2d 951, 955 (10th Cir 1991), using the *Berkowitz* definition, the court denied a FTCA claim by an injured hiker in a national park because "the exercise of discretion in determining what safety measures to implement . . . is shielded from judicial review by the discretionary function exception."
25. 28 USCA § 2680(h) (West Supp 1991). Only specified intentional torts—"assault, battery, false imprisonment, false arrest, malicious prosecution, abuse of process, libel, slander, misrepresentation, deceit, or interference with contract rights"—are excluded. Those such as trespass and invasion of privacy, for example, are still actionable. See Boger et al, "The Federal Tort Claims Act intentional torts amendment: An interpretive analysis," 54 North Carolina L Rev 497, 518 (1976).
26. 403 US 388 (1971). The *Bivens* action, which allows suit against federal officers for civil rights violations, will be discussed in this chapter under § 1983 actions.
27. Boger et al supra n 25 at 498–99.
28. 28 USCA § 2680(h) (West Supp 1991).
29. Coffin v Reichard 143 F2d 443, 445 (6th cir 1944).
30. Preiser v Rodriguez 411 US 475, 487 (1973).
31. 28 USCA § 2241 (West Supp 1991).
32. Fay v Noia 372 US 391, 400 (1963) sets forth a short history of the writ:

> Received into our own law in the colonial period, given explicit recognition in the Federal Constitution, Art. I, § 9, cl. 2,* incorporated in the first grant of federal jurisdiction, Act of September 24, 1789, c. 20 § 14, 1 Stat. 81–82, habeas corpus was early confirmed by Chief Justice Marshall to be a "great constitutional privilege."
>
> *"The Privilege of the Writ of Habeas Corpus shall not be suspended, unless when in Cases of Rebellion or Invasion the Public Safety may Require it."

See also McCleskey v Zant 111 SCt 1454, 1461–62 (1991).
33. 1 Stat 81–2 (1789).
34. Hyman, H: A more perfect union, New York, Knopf, 1973, p 249.

35. 28 USCA § 1443(1) (West Supp 1991).
36. 28 USCA § 2241 (West Supp 1991).
37. 28 USCA § 2254(b) (West Supp 1991).
38. Willis v Ciccone 506 F2d 1011 (8th Cir 1974).
39. 28 USCA § 2254 (West Supp 1991).
40. Kerper, H and Kerper, J: Legal rights of the convicted, St Paul, West, 1974, p 218. Although no disposition figures appear to be currently available, for the 12-month period ending June 30, 1989, of 1,651 habeas petitions filed, only 6 went to trial. Annual Report of the Director of the Administrative Office of US Courts, twelve month period ended June 30, 1989, Appendix I, Table C-5B, Washington, D.C., 1989.
41. Procunier v Martinez 416 US 396, 404–5 (1976). Justice O'Connor, citing *Martinez* in Turner v Safley 482 US 78 (1987), a case involving prison regulations governing inmate marriages and correspondence, affirmed that "separation of powers concerns counsel a policy of judicial restraint." Id at 85. This same "recognition that prison authorities are best equipped to make difficult decisions regarding prison administration" resulted in a reduced standard of review of alleged violations of prisoner's "fundamental" constitutional rights from strict scrutiny to one of reasonableness, Washington v Harper 110 SCt 1028, 1037–38 (1990). In McCleskey v Zant 111 SCt 1454 (1991), the Court substantially increased the difficulty of state prisoners filing a second habeas in that the second habeas can contain no matters that could have been raised in the first habeas.
42. See Doe v Hirsch 731 FSupp 627 (SD NY 1990) (where police officers who had been cut while transporting a bloody body challenged state law making blood test information about the HIV virus confidential, and state agrees officers have remedy under state law, federal court will abstain from adjudicating officers' constitutional claims until state case is determined).
43. In Morris v Alabama 294 US 587 (1935), nine blacks were indicted for rape. The Court reversed on the ground that exclusion of all blacks from the grand jury denied due process.
44. Powell v Alabama 287 US 45 (1932).
45. McNeal v Culver 365 US 109 (1960).
46. Brown v Mississippi 297 US 45 (1932).
47. Harris v South Carolina 338 US 68 (1948).
48. Civil Rights Act of 1964, Tit II, § 201, 78 Stat 243, July 2, 1969; 42 USCA § 2000(a) et seq (1981).
49. Civil Rights Act of 1964, Tit VII, § 703, 78 Stat 243, July 2, 1969; 42 USCA § 2000(e)-2 et seq (1981).
50. 379 US 294.
51. 392 US 409.
52. 392 US at 439 (emphasis in original).
53. Lugar v Edmondson Oil Co 457 US 922, 934 (1982).
54. Ch 22, § 1, 17 Stat 13. In 1874, Congress codified existing law so that the substantive portion of § 1 of the 1871 Act became a separate section

identical to the present § 1983. At that time, coverage was extended to include deprivations of rights secured by federal laws as well as by the Constitution. Maine v Thiboutot 448 US 1, 7, 14–22 (1980). In addition, however, the civil rights sections, that had originally formed a "distinctive, coherent" whole, were redistributed among unrelated chapters of the revised statutes. It was only in 1952 that all civil rights sections to be discussed in this chapter were codified in their present form. Gressman, E: "The unhappy history of civil rights legislation," 50 Mich L Rev 1323, 1343 (1952). The history of each of these statutes will be found in Wechsler, H: "The nationalization of civil liberties and civil rights," XII Texas Quar 10, App p 44 (1969).

55. Comment, "The Civil Rights Act: Emergence of an adequate federal civil remedy?" 26 Ind L J 361, 363, 366 (1951).

56. Ginger, A and Bell, L: "Police misconduct litigation—plaintiff's remedies," 15 Am Jur Trials 555, 580–90 (1968).

57. Civil Rights Cases 109 US 3 (1883).

58. Slaughterhouse Cases 83 US 36 (16 Wall) (1873).

59. Hague v CIO 370 US 496 (1939).

60. Adamson v California 332 US 46 (1947). For a more detailed statement of the legal "suppression of § 1983, see Collins, Michael G, "Economic rights," implied constitutional actions, and the scope of section 1983, 77 Georgetown L J 1493, 1497–1507 (Apr 1989).

61. Bivens v Six Unknown Named Agents 403 US 388 (1971).

62. Monell v Dept. of Social Services 436 US 658 (1978).

63. 307 US 496.

64. 365 US 167.

65. Id at 175.

66. Kates, D: "Police misconduct litigation in the federal courts," in Days III, Rosen, S and Strickler, Jr, G: Federal civil rights litigation, NYC, Practicing Law Institute, 1977, p 758.

67. Maine v Thiboutot 448 US 1, 20 (1980), Justice Powell dissenting.

68. 365 US at 172.

69. Id at 187.

70. Maine v Thiboutot 448 US 1, 27 fn 16, Justice Powell dissenting. Since 1979 the number of civil rights cases has continued to climb. In the twelve month period ending June 30, 1988, 19,367 civil rights cases were filed, plus 25,905 prisoner petitions, for a total of 45,262 cases. Annual Report of the Director of the Administrative Office of US Courts, Twelve month period ended June 30, 1989, Appendix J, Table C-2, Washington, D.C., 1989. An analysis concluding that § 1983 have "low success rates" will be found in Eisenberg, Theodore, Litigation models and trial outcomes in civil rights and prisoner cases, 77 Georgetown L J 1567, 1601 (Sp 1989).

71. In Owens v Okure, 488 US 235, 251 (1989), the Court decided, in a case based on intentional injuries by police officers, that the proper state statute of limitations to apply was the three year "general" statute rather than the one

year "intentional" tort statute. Congress provided no statute of limitations for § 1983 actions but merely authorized courts to borrow the appropriate limitation from state law. See 42 USC § 1988 (1988).

72. Baker v McCollan 443 US 137, 140 (1979); see also Graham v Connor 490 US 386, 394 (1989).

73. Nahmod, S: Civil rights and civil liberties litigation, the Law of Section 1983, Colorado Springs, Shepard's, 1986, 2d ed § 2.03 listing cases.

74. Uniformed Firefighters Assn v City of New York 676 F2d 20, 28 (2nd Cir 1982), cert den 459 US 838 (1982).

75. Baker v McCollan 443 US 137, 144 n 3 (1979).

76. 490 US 386.

77. Id at 393. Plaintiffs are now precluded from asserting both a fourth amendment and due process claim in excessive force cases but must restrict themselves to a fourth amendment theory. Walker v Norris 917 F2d 1449, 1455 (6th Cir 1990).

78. 365 US 167, 187 (1961). In Wilson v Garcia 471 US 261, 277 (1985) the Court held that section 1983 actions were "analogous to tort claims for personal injury."

79. 451 US 527.

80. Id at 535.

81. 461 US 30 (1983).

82. Id at 33.

83. Id at 55.

84. 475 US 312 (1986).

85. Id at 321, 327.

86. 474 US 327 (1986).

87. Id at 328. Later cases construed *Parratt* to mean that negligence by a state prison employee could not be the basis of a constitutional violation. Hudson v Palmer 468 US 517, 535 (1984) held that the same reasoning precluded recovery for intentional deprivation as long as the state provided the injured party other means of recovering his loss, for example, by an action in tort.

88. 474 US at 330, 331.

89. Id at 336.

90. Id at 334. See also the companion case of Davidson v Cannon 474 US 344, 345 (1986), a § 1983 action against state prison officials "for injuries he suffered when they negligently failed to protect him from another inmate". The Court concluded that "As we held in *Daniels*, the protections of the Due Process Clause, whether procedural or substantive, are just not triggered by lack of due care by prison officials" (at 348). For a discussion of the mental state problem, see Gregory v City of Rogers Park 921 F2d 750, 756–57 (8th Cir 1990). See also de Jesus Benavides v Santos 883 F2d 385, 388 (8th Cir 1989) involving injury to prison guards during an attempted escape where the court distinquishes between prisoners who may have an action of constitutional tort while guards "are employees 'who enlisted, on

terms they found satisfactory, and [who] were free to quit whenever they pleased.' "

91. Abernathey, Charles F, Section 1983 and constitutional torts, 77 Georgetown L J 1441, 1491 (Apr 1989).

92. Congress could rely on the implementing clause of the thirteenth amendment which has no state action requirement. See the discussion hereafter of §§ 1981, 1982, 1985 and § 245 which eliminate the color of law requirement.

93. United States v Price 383 US 787, 794 fn 7 (1966); Lugar v Edmondson Oil Co Inc 457 US 922, 928 (1982), but see 457 US at 935, 936 fn 18 where the Court makes some distinction between "state action" and "under color of law."

94. 325 US 91, 111 (1945).

95. 487 US 42, 49–50 (1988; citations omitted).

96. Antieau, C: Federal Civil Rights Acts, Rochester, Lawyers Co-op, 1980, 2d ed, Vol I, §§ 57–61, 1989 Cum Supp; Nahmod *supra* n 73 at §§ 2.04-2.08.

97. Pierson v Ray 386 US 547 (1967).

98. York v Story et al 324 F2d 450 (9th Cir 1963).

99. Kanovitz, J: "Civil rights and civil rights legislation," Klotter, J and Kanovitz, J: Constitutional law, Cincinnati, Anderson, 1991, 6th ed, pp 560–563. A substantial part of the analysis in this section relies on this material.

100. 522 F2d 438 (6th Cir 1975) cert granted 425 US 910 cert dismissed as improvidently granted 429 US 118 (1976).

101. 701 FSupp 666, 671 (ND Ill 1988); revd in part but affd as to no color of law claim 910 F2d 1510 (7th Cir 1990). See also Rivera v LaPorte 896 F2d 691, 696 (2nd Cir 1990) in which plaintiff and police officers were in a traffic dispute while officer was off duty. After striking plaintiff, defendant yelled, "I'm a police officer, you're under arrest, handcuffed and arrested plaintiff." "Though the dispute that precipitated the arrest was private, the response, including the arrest and the use of excessive force, was unquestionably action under color of law;" and Revene v Charles County Comrs 882 F2d 870, 873 (4th Cir 1989) (sheriff's deputy, "off-duty," who while driving private car, stopped, had an "altercation" with and killed a party, was acting under color of law, by local ordinance placing him on duty 24-hours a day—even though he may have overstepped his duty).

102. 132 F2d 902 (4th Cir 1943).

103. 160 F2d 746 (5th Cir 1947).

104. 482 F2d 137 (6th Cir 1973).

105. Watkins v Oaklawn Jockey Club 183 F2d 440 (8th Cir 1950).

106. Simmons v Whitaker 252 F2d 224 (5th Cir 1958).

107. Johnson v Hackett 284 FSupp 933 (ED Pa 1968).

108. Rembert v Holland 735 FSupp 733, 736 (WD Mich 1990).

109. Antieau p 109, *supra* n 96.

110. 488 US 179.

111. Id at 191.

112. Id at 192.

113. Id at 199.

114. DeShaney v Winnebago Cty Soc Serv Dept 489 US 189, 200 (1989).

115. Id.

116. Id at 202.

117. Id at 198 fn 4.

118. Id at 200–201 (citations omitted).

119. 922 F2d 1097 (3rd Cir 1990).

120. Id at 1116. See Bishop, Gary M, Note, Section 1983 and domestic violence: A solution to the problem of police officer's inaction, 30 Boston College L Rev 1357–1389 (Sept 1989) who criticizes *Deshaney* for its likely effect in discouraging aggressive police action in domestic violence cases.

121. 921 F2d 750 (8th Cir 1990).

122. Id at 754. See also Chrissy F v Miss DPW 925 F2d 844, 852 (5th Cir 1991) (where social workers, district attorney and judge repeatedly ignored reports of child abuse by father, allowing him visitation privileges and custody, state child protective statutes created a liberty interest); Sodal v County of Cook 923 F2d 1241, 1247 (7th Cir 1991) (state action where sheriff's deputies aided landowner to enforce illegal eviction); KH through Murphy v Morgan 912 F2d 846, 852 (7th cir 1990) (where state officers gave child custody to foster parents "whom the state knows or suspects to be a child abuser," such foster parents can be "fairly considered an instrument of the state"); and Walker v Norris 917 F2d 1449 (6th Cir 1990), where guards stood, taking no action while one prisoner stabbed another, issue of *DeShaney* not even discussed by court). For a detailed analysis of the three examples of state action, involuntary confinement, analogies to confinement, and special relationships, see Eaton, Thom A and Wells, Michael, Governmental inaction as a constitutional tort: *DeShaney* and its aftermath, 66 Washington L Rev 107, 124–127, 143–158 (Jan 91), and Davis, Robert G, Note, State has no affirmative duty to provide protective services absent custodial relationships, 24 Suffolk U L Rev 246–254 (Sp 1990).

123. See Cook, J.G., and Sobieski, Jr J: Civil Rights Actions, Sec 7.10, New York, Matthew Bender, 1990.

124. Antieau p 109, *supra* n 96.

125. Adams v Miami Police Benev Assn 454 F2d 1315 (5th Cir) cert den 409 US 843 (1972).

126. 392 US 144 (1970).

127. Lugar v Edmondson Oil Co 457 US 922, 942 (1982).

128. Id.

129. Collins v Womancare 878 F2d 1145 (9th Cir 1989), cert den 110 SCt 865 (1990).

130. Antieau p 177, *supra* n 96.

131. Temple v Albert 719 FSupp 265, 267 (SD NY 1989).

132. Bins v Artison 721 FSupp 1034 (ED Wis 1989), affd 1991 US App Lexis 1665.

133. Thompson v McCoy 425 FSupp 407 (D SC 1976).

134. West v Adkins 487 US 42, 57 (1988).

135. White v Scrivner Corp 594 F2d 140 (5th Cir 1979).

136. Office of the Mayor's Criminal Justice Coordinator, "Memorandum of understanding," New York City, March 25 1981, pp 6–7.

137. 403 US 388 (1971).

138. 446 US 14, 18–19 (1980) (citations omitted, emphasis in original).

139. 487 US 412, 423 (1988) (social security claimants who were unconstitutionally denied benefits did not have a *Bivens* remedy even though administrative remedies provided only reimbursement but no damages because Congress had "addressed the problems" and had not created a broader damage remedy). See also Saul v US 928 F2d 829, 835 (9th Cir 1991) (Social Security Administration employee claiming violation of his fourth amendment rights cannot rely on *Bivens* claim where the Civil Service Reform Act provides remedy). Woodley, John Paul, Constitutional tort actions against federal officials after Schweiker v Chilicky 1989 Army Lawyer 10–15 and Nichol, Jr, Gene R., *Bivens, Chilicky,* and constitutional damage claims 75 Virginia L Rev 1117–1154 (Sept 1989). Between 1975 and 1985, the government's Torts Branch successfully defended 99% of the 11,000 *Bivens* suits filed during this decade. Annual Report of the Attorney General of the US 1985, p 154.

140. 625 F2d 70, 70–71 (5th Cir 1980). See generally Manak, J P: "The police plaintiff: making the system work for law enforcement," 56 Police Chief 16–19 (Sept 1989). This article discusses both § 1983 and common law actions brought by police. Race of plaintiffs is not indicated but most officers are white.

141. 28 USC § 1343(3) began, like § 1983, as § 1 of the Ku Klux Act of 1871, enacted by Congress to enforce the fourteenth amendment. Thereafter, it followed the course of § 1983. See *supra* n 54.

142. Yellow Freight System, Inc v Donnelly 494 US 820 (1990) decided that state courts have jurisdiction in Title VII actions. Justice Stevens, for a unanimous Court, states that in "our system of dual sovereignty," for state courts to be divested of jurisdiction "Congress must, in an exercise of its powers under the Supremacy Clause, affirmatively divest state courts of their presumptively concurrent jurisdiction."

143. Cook and Sobieski, sec 7.07, *supra* n 123.

144. Haring v Prosise 462 US 306 (1983).

145. Chappell v Wallace 462 US 296 (1983).

146. Will v Michigan Dept of State Police 491 US 58, 71 (1989). In Ngiraingas v Sanchez 110 SCt 1737, 1743 (1990), the Court held "that neither the Territory of Guam nor its officers acting in their official capacities are 'persons' under § 1983."

147. City of Newport v Fact Concerts 453 US 247, 266–7 (1981).

148. 453 US at 247.

149. Id at 269.

150. Preiser v Rodriguez 411 US 475, 498, 500 (1973). Preiser claimed that he had been improperly disciplined in violation of his due process rights, the

result of which was to lose 120 days of good conduct time. Restoration of these credits would have resulted in his immediate release.

151. Jones v Alfred H Mayer Co 392 US 409, 438 (1968) and Memphis v Greene 451 US 100, 120 (1981).

152. Portions of this chapter covering §§ 1981 and 1982 rely on Antieau chaps 4 and 5, *supra* n 96.

153. Act May 31 1870, ch 114 § 16, 16 stat 144, re-enacted as 42 USC § 1981. See *supra* n 54.

154. 481 US 604.

155. Id at 612–613. In Walker v Secretary of Treasury, IRS 713 FSupp 403, 408 (ND GA 1989), the Court held that § 1981 permitted a light-skinned black person to sue a dark-skinned black person for discriminatory discharge on the basis of skin color but in the trial stage of the same case 742 FSupp 670 (ND GA 1990) held evidence insufficient to sustain plaintiff's claim she was fired because of racial discrimination.

156. Runyon v McCrary 427 US 160, 170–1 (1976).

157. Agnew v Compton 239 F2d 226, 230 (9th Cir 1956), cert den 353 US 959 (1957).

158. Jones v Alfred H Mayer Co 392 US 409 (1968).

159. Brown v GSA 425 US 820 (1976).

160. 427 US 160.

161. 491 US 164 (1989).

162. Id at 170.

163. Id at 176.

164. Id at 176–77 (emphasis in original).

165. Id at 183.

166. Id at 185.

167. Id at 189.

168. 491 US 701 (1989).

169. Id at 735.

170. Id at 739.

171. Lynch v Belden & Co 882 F2d 262, 217 (7th Cir 1989), cert den 110 SCt 1134 (1990) (racial discrimination, and discriminatory promotion and transfer do not involve a refusal to make a contract or interfere with employee's ability to enforce his contract rights); Courtney v Canyon TV & Appliance Rental 899 F2d 845, 849 (9th Cir 1990) ("Discharge is the type of post-formation 'breach of contract' conduct not protected by section 1981"); Artis v US Industry 1990 US Dist Lexis 12007 (ND Ill 1990), from *Artis* following McKnight v General Motors Corp 908 F2d 104 (7th Cir 1990), the Court held a racially motivated discharge is not actionable under § 1981, and neither is a failure to train claim to avoid discharge as a result of a layoff; and in Hicks v Brown Group 902 F2d 630 (8th Cir 1990), a finding that § 1981 prohibited racially-based discharge was vacated by the Supreme Court in Brown Group v Hicks 111 SCt 1299 (1991), and remanded to the 8th circuit for further consideration in light of that court opinion to be filed in Taggert v Jefferson County Child Support Enforcement Court 915

F2d 396 ("the Supreme Court's decision in *Patterson* precludes section 1981 suits for discriminary termination of employment"); and CPC Int'l, Inc v Aerojet-General Corp 731 FSupp 783, 798 (WD Mich 1989) ("An employer's decision to fire the employee is not the refusal to make a contract, but the termination of an existing contractual relationship").

172. Act Apr 9 1866 ch 31 § 1, 14 stat 27, codified as 42 USCA § 1982 (1981).

173. Jones v Alfred H Mayer 392 US 409, 413 (1968).

174. Stirgus v Benoit 720 FSupp 119, 122 (ND Ill 1989), and same case, motion for summary judgment, 1990 US Dist Lexis 17593, 4 (1990) ("The firebombing of Stirgus' home is precisely the type of discriminatory conduct that section 1982 is designed to remedy. When racially-motivated firebombing destroys a person's home, that person does not truly enjoy the same freedom to acquire and 'hold' property as a similarly situated white person").

175. Young v Pierce 628 FSupp 1037 (E D Tex 1985); for subsequent litigation on the appropriate injunction, see 822 F2d 1368 (5th Cir 1987).

176. Durham v Red Lake Fishing & Hunting Club 666 FSupp 954, 961 (W D Tex 1987).

177. Laudon v Loos 694 FSupp 253, 255 (E D Mich 1988).

178. 481 US 615 (1987).

179. Id at 617.

180. Id.

181. Act of July 31 1861, ch 33 12 Stat 284; apr 20 1871, 17 Stat 13, codified as 42 USCA § 1985 (1981).

182. Griffin v Breckenridge 403 US 88, 105 (1971).

183. Kush v Rutledge 460 US 719 (1983) discussed below.

184. Subsections indicate the divisions described by the Court in *Kush,* 460 US 719. The [a] and [b] designations are added for discussion purposes, and do not appear in the statute.

185. 42 USCA § 1985 (1981) (emphasis added.). For a constitutional history of the section, see Cook and Sobieski, sec 13.02, *supra* n. 123.

186. Griffin v Breckenridge 403 US at 102–103.

187. Id at 98.

188. Curtis v Peerless Ins Co 299 FSupp 429 (DC Minn 1969).

189. Yeadon v NYC Transit Authority 719 FSupp 204, 212 (SD NY 1989) (race-based false arrests of subway passengers).

190. Wakat v Harlib 253 F2d 59 (7th Cir 1958).

191. Hawk v Perillo 642 FSupp 380, 385 (ND Ill 1985) (police pursuit of violent offenders was both "belated and futile").

192. Kush v Rutledge 460 US 719, 726, 727 (1983).

193. Battle v Mulholland 439 F2d 321 (5th Cir 1971).

194. Johnson v Capitol City Lodge No 74, Fraternal Order of Police 477 F2d 601 (4th Cir 1973).

195. Lontine v VanCleave 483 F2d 966 (10th Cir 1973).

196. Ruhlman v Barger 435 FSupp 447 (WD Pa 1976).

197. Crain v Board of Police Comrs 920 F2d 1402 (8th Cir 1990); 1991 US App Lexis 2044 (1991) pet for rehr by panel denied; see Manak, *supra* n 140.
198. United States v Williams 341 US 70, 74 (1951).
199. United States v Price 383 US 787, 803 (1966), and articles cited at n 54.
200. 383 US 787 (1966).
201. Id at 803.
202. Id at 804.
203. Gressman pp 1323, 1343–4, *supra* n 54.
204. 325 US 91, 159 (1945).
205. Gressman p 1344 fn 58, *supra* n 54.
206. United States Commission on Civil Rights, Police practices and the preservation of civil rights, Dec 12–13, Govt Printing Office, 1978, p 140.
207. Id at 139–40. "During the Fiscal Year 1985, the Section reviewed over 9,000 complaints alleging criminal interference with civil rights; approximately 3,000 of these complaints were investigated by the Federal Bureau of Investigation. The results of 56 investigations were presented to federal grand juries; 35 indictments were returned and 13 informations were filed charging a total of 106 defendants, including 67 law enforcement officers. Thirty cases were tried, resulting in conviction of 41 defendants. In addition, the 31 defendants who pled guilty to violations of criminal civil rights statutes led to a success rate of almost 80 percent for the Section." Annual Report of the Attorney General of the US, 1985, p. 164.
208. United States Commission on Civil Rights, *Supra* n 206 at 141.
209. 18 USCA § 242 (West Supp 1991), as amended, Nov 18, 1988, Pub L 100-690, Title VII § 7019, 102 Stat 4396.
210. Gressman p 1350, *supra* n 54, citing United States v Buntin 10 F 730 (1882) and United States v Stone 188 F 836 (1911).
211. Screws v United States 325 US 91, 104 (1945).
212. Id at 101. The word "willfully" was added to the statute in 1909. Id at 103.
213. 383 US 787.
214. Id at 789, quoting from United States v Williams 341 US 70, 72 (1951).
215. 383 US at 794.
216. 506 F2d 771.
217. Id at 776.
218. 589 F2d 811 (5th Cir) cert den 444 US 847 (1979).
219. 589 F2d at 820.
220. United States v Denson 588 F2d 1112, 1125 (5th Cir 1979).
221. United States v Price 383 US 787, 902 (1966).
222. Id at 803.
223. 589 F2d 811 (5th Cir) cert den 444 US 847 (1979).
224. 589 F2d at 820.
225. United States v Price 383 US 787, 794 fn 7 (1966).
226. United States v Stokes 506 F2d 771, 776 (5th Cir 1975).
227. 18 USCA § 241 (West Supp 1991), as amended Nov 18, 1988, Pub L 100-690, Title VII, § 7018(a), (b) (1), 102 Stat 4396.

228. Gressman p 1345, *supra* n 54.
229. United States v Price 383 US 787, 804–5 (1966).
230. Id at 800 (emphasis in original).
231. Id at 806, fn 20.
232. 595 F2d 154, 162 (3rd Cir), cert den Ellis v United States 444 US 838 (1979).
233. United States v Purvis 580 F2d 853 (5th Cir 1978), cert den Purvis v United States 440 US 914 (1979).
234. 390 US 563 (1968).
235. Senate Rep No 721, Judiciary Com, Nov 2, 1967, 90th Cong 1st Session, 1968 US Code Cong and Adm News, pp 1837, 1840–41.
236. 383 US 745, 786 (1966). *Guest*, involving the murder of well-known black educator, Lemuel Penn, while driving through Georgia, decided the same point as *Price* but for the equal protection clause of the fourteenth amendment.
237. Sen Rep p 1841 n 235.
238. 525 F2d 710 (1st Cir 1975), cert den Griffin v United States 424 US 945 (1976).
239. 525 F2d at 712.
240. 487 US 931, 950 (1988).
241. 728 F2d 1094, 1097 (8th Cir 1984), cert den Bledsoe v United States 469 US 838 (1984).
242. 883 F2d 1484, 1493 (10th Cir 1989), cert den Pierce v United States 110 SCt 872 (1990).
243. Larsen v Larsen 671 FSupp 718 (D Utah 1987), cert den 110 SCt 135 (1989).
244. United States v Callahan 659 FSupp 80, 84 (ED Pa), affd without op 826 F2d 1057 (1987).
245. United States v Wallace 673 FSupp 205, 206 (S D Tex 1987).
246. United States v McLean 808 F2d 1044, 1049 (4th Cir 1987).

Chapter 2

AFFIRMATIVE ACTION REMEDIES
AGAINST EMPLOYMENT DISCRIMINATION

Introductory remarks

Title VII of the Civil Rights Act of 1964, also known as the Equal Employment Opportunity Act,[1] recognized the prevalence of discriminatory employment practices among employers and labor organizations and the need for federal legislation to eliminate such practices. Originally enacted pursuant to the Commerce Clause to regulate private employment practices, a 1972 amendment relied on the implementing clauses of the thirteenth and fourteenth amendments to make the Act applicable to state and local governments, including criminal justice agencies.[2]

A report of the US Commission on Civil Rights suggests the rationale for affirmative action:

> Individuals are discriminated against because they belong to groups, not because of their individual attributes. . . . [W]hen group wrongs pervade the social, political, economic, and ideological landscape they become self-sustaining processes that only a special set of antidiscrimination techniques—affirmative action—can effectively dismantle. Such group wrongs simply overwhelm remedies that do not take group designations into account.[3]

The Act has been called "a watershed in American history. All previous acts of regulation by the Federal Government had been regulations of things and standards—of railroads and wavelengths, of foods and drugs, weights and measures. The Civil Rights Act was a departure: it undertook to regulate behavior. Its purpose was to change the customs and manners of the American people."[4] It also departed from the Reconstruction tradition in that instead of relying on the individual litigant to institute change, a large part of the momentum for change was in the hands of and was to be the responsibility of the federal government.

In the intervening years, however, changes in the composition of the Supreme Court have brought with it a change in the Court's view of Title VII from that of a remedy for group wrongs to that of a remedy for individual wrongs. In Wygant v Jackson Board of Education,[5] the Court stated:

> No one doubts that there has been serious racial discrimination in this country. But as the basis for imposing discriminatory *legal* remedies that work against innocent people, *societal* discrimination is insufficient and overly expansive. In the absence of *particularized findings,* a court could uphold remedies that are ageless in their reach into the past, and timeless in their ability to affect the future.[6]

Scope of Title VII

Title VII permits job classifications based upon race, religion, sex, or national origin only when such classifications are the result of bona fide (good faith) occupational qualifications that are reasonably necessary to the normal operations of a particular business.[7] Section 703(h) of the Act provides that differences in terms of employment and compensation may be based upon different locations of employment, or upon bona fide seniority or quality of production, or upon professionally developed tests, so long as they are not the result of discrimination because of race, color, religion, sex, or national origin.[8]

The heart of Title VII is § 703(a):

> It shall be an unlawful employment practice for an employer [of 15 or more persons]
> (1) to fail or refuse to hire or to discharge any individual, or otherwise to discriminate against any individual with respect to his compensation, terms, conditions, or privileges of employment, because of such individual's race, color, religion, sex, or national origin; or (2) limit, segregate, or classify his employees or applicants for employment in any way which would deprive or tend to deprive any individual of employment opportunities or otherwise adversely affect his status as an employee, because of such individual's race, color, religion, sex, or national origin.[9]

The philosophy behind the original legislation was that conciliation between employers and complaining minorities and women could be expected to change the discriminatory patterns at which the Act was aimed. Therefore, in the original Act, the Equal Employment Opportunity Commission (EEOC), created to enforce the Act, was given no power to enforce its orders and could file suit only if it found a pattern of discrimination in a particular industry. But by 1972, the inability of the Commission to bring about the changes sought by the Commission by conciliation alone had become so apparent that in that year Congress amended the Act, giving the Commission the power to bring a civil suit in federal court to enforce its orders.[10]

Another amendment made "governments, governmental agencies [and] political subdivisions" subject to the provisions of Title VII.[11] Under this amendment, federal, state, and local government employees are protected by Title VII to the same extent as private employees. The prohibition against discrimination in employment includes hiring, promotions, assignments, compensation, testing to secure employment and promotions, conditions of employment, retirement and other fringe benefits, pensions, layoffs and rehirings, and any employment practice in which one group is treated more harshly than another by reason of race, color, religion, sex or national origin.

Recent Supreme Court decisions have threatened to upend this recent history, and start affirmative action on a new and uncertain path. As stated by one commentator:

> In the quarter century since its passage, the Civil Rights Act of 1964 left unmistakable evidence of the power of law to change deeply entrenched patterns of discrimination. In the early years the Supreme Court interpreted the Statute expansively. . . . Recently, though, the jurisprudential climate that fostered the growth of Title VII has changed. This change culminated in a spate of decisions . . . in which the Supreme Court turned on Title VII and the Civil Rights Act of 1866.[12]

Asserting a Title VII claim

Congress created the Equal Employment Opportunity Commission (EEOC) to interpret and enforce the Act. Its members are appointed by the President with the advice and consent of the Senate. The Commission issues regulations as guidelines for statutory interpretation and has subpoena power for the purpose of gathering evidence and holding hearings.[13]

Where there is a state or local ordinance covering the discriminatory practice complained of, the complainant must first file a claim with the state agency and follow that procedure before resorting to the EEOC. If the state agency has not resolved the matter within 60 days, the aggrieved person may file a complaint with the EEOC within 180 days after the alleged unlawful discrimination occurred. The Commission must render a decision within 120 days of the filing of the complaint after which an individual can bring suit in federal court.[14]

Where the respondent is a government agency, and the EEOC has been unable to obtain an acceptable conciliation agreement, it may refer the case to the US Attorney General who may sue in federal court. If the Attorney General does not bring a Title VII action within a specified period, aggrieved individuals may themselves file an action in federal district court.[15] If the grievants prevail, they are entitled to reasonable attorney fees.[16]

District courts are given full power to enforce their decrees by enjoining the discriminatory practice and ordering "such affirmative action as may be appropriate . . . or any other equitable relief as the court deems appropriate."[17] The EEOC has defined affirmative action as "actions appropriate to overcome the effects of past or present practices, policies, or other barriers to equal employment opportunity."[18] Much of this chapter will be concerned with disputes about what is the "appropriate" affirmative action relief for discriminatory practices.

Minority representation in criminal justice agencies

In order to understand the causes of the social and legal conflict that led to the enactment of Title VII, it will be necessary to reconstruct the social history that led up to it, including the historically small representation of minorities, blacks and hispanics, in criminal justice agencies, why this has been so, the growth of pressures to place blacks in these agencies, the partial success of these efforts, legal attempts to require such representation, white backlash to these efforts, and consequences on minority and female employment of recent economic problems.

Until the 1970s, minority representation in criminal justice agencies was miniscule. Because the police played such an important part in provoking the initiation of these programs, and because such a large percentage of initial funding and hence pressure for change in their minority representation focused on the police much of the following discussion will center on that agency. Nevertheless, the record of minority and female employment has been every bit as bad in correctional facilities.[19] In the 1970s, minority groups constituted about 20% of the US population, about 50% of the prison population, but only about 10% of correctional personnel.[20]

1967 was a time of full employment, when there was reputed to be a need nationally for 50,000 police officers, and urban police forces were under authorized strength. Yet, the US Commission on Civil Rights, after a national survey of cities with large black populations, concluded:

> Barriers to equal opportunity are greater in police and fire departments than in any other area of State and local government. . . . Although 27 percent of all central city jobs surveyed are in police and fire departments, only 7 percent of the black employees in central cities are policemen and firemen. . . . Negro policemen and firemen hold almost no positions in the officer ranks. . . . State police forces employ very few Negro policemen.[21]

A nation-wide survey of state police in 1974 showed that blacks constituted no more than 1.5% of all such forces.[22] As one report concluded, "The historical paucity of blacks in police forces is merely reflective of low black employment in government as a whole."[23]

Blacks' relation to the labor market

Following their release from slavery, blacks entered the labor market at the lowest levels. They were in constant competition for bottom-level jobs with newly arrived Irish, German, and Italian immigrants. When over time these latter groups were able to worm their way into government and industry, they tried to maintain protective ethnic enclaves against invasion by other groups. Much of this competitive antagonism was aimed at blacks who were at the bottom pushing up.

Until the mid-20th century, the vast number of blacks remained in the South where barriers against equal employment opportunity were firm and impenetrable. When in the 1940s and 1950s the first large migrations of blacks to the North took place since World War I, obstacles to their entrance into government employment were formidable. Irish and Italian groups, that had hitherto successfully struggled to carve out jobs within local government, were especially effective in fending off black entry.

Thus, the traditional means by which most ethnic groups rose through government employment was virtually closed to blacks. Not only did the government take no affirmative action to repair this situation, but government practices often actively encouraged job discrimination. For example, until 1942, the US Civil Service Commission required applicants to submit photographs with job applications, thus permitting race identification. After World War II pressures from civil rights advocates increased and some minor governmental remedial measures were undertaken to reduce discriminatory hiring in government. But it was really the post-World War II economic expansion that permitted blacks to emigrate to northern industrial cities where they were able to fill lower-level government jobs abandoned by whites who left to take better-paying jobs in private industry.[24]

The years 1950–1970 saw an enormous expansion of the service sector of government. By the end of this period nearly one in five jobs were with some governmental agency. Increases in government employment were related to mounting black demands in the late 1960s for jobs, public housing, welfare, health and other services that the private economy had been unable or unwilling to furnish on an equal basis. White middle-class demands rose in reaction to black action. Calls for maintenance of public order, particularly containment of ghetto street crime and drug offenses, pushed up criminal justice expenditures. Contemporaneous with the movement by poor blacks for increased rights was the growth and militancy of public sector unions (to be discussed in chapter 5), primarily controlled by various ethnic groups: Irish police, Jewish school teachers, and Italian construction workers. During the period 1965–1975, state and local governments as well as the criminal justice system, expanded at a rate of approximately 5% per year, rising from $101 to 318.5 billion. Costs of education, health, hospitals and public welfare increased most rapidly.[25]

Ironically, this surge into government employment resulted in instances where blacks and other minorities held government jobs in numbers greater than their proportion in the population. But these jobs "are characterized by few, if any, entry skills, relatively low pay, and limited opportunity to advance through the ranks. . . . Such jobs, principally those of common laborer and general service worker, traditionally have been considered 'Negro jobs.' "[26] Moreover, where blacks work in police departments they represented a much higher percentage of civilian than sworn personnel. In Philadelphia, for instance, blacks made up 63% of the civilian employees but only 20% of sworn personnel.[27]

Pressures for minority employment

Mid-1960s riots in northern American inner-city areas had shaken and threatened to tear asunder American society. Nearly every one of these disturbances had its origin in the police arrest of inner-city black residents. Although it was clear from the beginning that the police were merely scapegoats for the long-smouldering grievances of blacks against unemployment, deteriorating housing, inadequate educational opportunities and city services, the problem and the remedy focused on the police.[28] The post-Eisenhower, Kennedy, and Johnson years were akin to the Reconstruction period as far as the rise of black rights is concerned. Black discontent was clear as city after city with Democratic administrations erupted in riots. Federal action led by a Democratic President was needed to turn the tide for the Democrats. In 1967, President Johnson appointed an elite commission, the President's Commission on Law Enforcement and Administration of Justice, to examine the criminal justice system. That Commission concluded that the appointment of minority police was "a high priority objective of all departments in communities with a substantial minority population."[29]

> In neighborhoods filled with people suffering from a sense of social injustice and exclusion, many residents will reach the conclusion that the neighborhood is being policed not for the purpose of maintaining law and order but for the purpose of maintaining the status quo.[30]

Other reasons given for hiring minority police are "to gain the general confidence and acceptance of a community"; personnel within a police department should be representative of "a community as a whole"; it "can help to reduce stereotyping and prejudice of white officers"; the minority officers can provide a department with an understanding of minority groups with different subcultures; it can "lead to information not otherwise available, to earlier anticipation of trouble, and to increased solution of crime"; it can "lessen the odds of race rioting"; give jobs to minorities; lead to better understanding between ghetto communities and police; and help control any disorders that do break out.[31] On the political front, as important a reason was that the hiring of minority officers accommodated the demands of civil rights organizations. Thus, until a national elite, concerned about the stability of the economy, pressured northern city governments to contain large restive black populations by increasing minority recruitment in their police forces, little change took place.

Difficulties blacks have had in entering police forces are not limited to intentional discrimination, although there is plenty of that. The problem is more apt to derive from the application of the *same* standards (physical, mental and character investigation) to blacks and other minorities as to whites. Because candidates are likely to be ghetto youths (minority youths with more attractive backgrounds do not usually seek police or correctional jobs), they arrive with educational, physical and "moral" (arrest record) deficiencies that derive from the social problems endemic to their neighborhoods.

EEOC'S effectiveness in reducing job discrimination

Has the EEOC managed to eliminate or substantially decrease discriminatory hiring practices? A 1976 report to Congress assessing the EEOC's effectiveness in eliminating employment discrimination found that its "great promise . . . remains essentially unfulfilled."[32] More recent evidence, however, suggests that affirmative action, perhaps accompanied by other factors (changing attitudes toward minorities and women, their increasing educational attainments, and more of them in posts where they influence hiring decisions), has positively affected hiring of minorities and women.[33]

Nevertheless, demographic trends (more working-age minorities in the population), and movement of the economy from higher-paying industrial to lower-paying service sector jobs "meant that Title VII had not produced the employment opportunities its creators anticipated."[34] Moreover, recent Supreme Court decisions, the lesser activity of federal agencies in litigating discrimination cases, the appointment of federal judges unfriendly to Title VII suits, the increased complexity, and therefore, rising cost in bringing such cases, has made it difficult for plaintiffs, mostly poor blacks, hispanics or women, to obtain legal counsel to pursue Title VII cases.[35]

Regardless of whether Title VII has substantially decreased discriminatory employment practices, minority employees and women have unleashed a veritable tidal wave of affirmative action suits, both public and private, claiming that they have been discriminated against by their employers. At the end of 1986, about 40% of all police departments in cities over 250,000 population operated under court orders or consent decrees, 42% had adopted voluntary affirmative action plans, and 43% had no such policy at all.[36] From the standpoint of criminal justice personnel, the most important litigation has been those suits challenging the hiring and promotion policies of police departments and correctional agencies. White males and their unions have often countered with claims that orders issued to make up for past discrimination constitute "reverse discrimination," and are unconstitutional as a denial of equal protection of the laws. This action and counter-action has become a country-wide pattern.

Some idea of the effectiveness of Title VII to increase the percentages of minorities and women in police forces can be seen by examining Table I. This table, covering the period, 1967–1977, is a combination of a survey obtained from the Police Foundation for the book's first edition together with more recent data modified from the *Sourcebook of Criminal Justice Statistics*. Even from this incomplete data it is evident that as of 1967 none of these cities had as much as 10% blacks in their departments, notwithstanding that percentages of minorities in these cities' populations often was several times this percentage. By 1977, with a few exceptions, these cities had made substantial progress, some doubling or even quadrupling these percentages. Though less dramatic, this progress is continued for the period, 1983–1988. There were also gains in the employment of women police, but the percentages, to begin with, are so small that even with substantial improvement, women's share in 1977 remains tiny.

If we examine Table II the widespread presence of affirmative action plans is apparent. Every city for which information is available has one. Out of 47 cities where there is data, 31, or about two-thirds, increased black officer representation by at least 10%. Nine, however, or about 20%, had either none or negative progress in numbers of black officers during the 1983–1988 period. It is likely that these departments got caught in the lay-offs of city workers as a result of the 1983 recession. During this period, black officers (and women), who had recently been hired under affirmative action plans, were the first laid off under earlier white male-dominated union contracts containing seniority provisions, a matter dealt with at the end of this chapter.

If we look at the index of black representation (dividing the percent of black officers in a department by the percentage of blacks in the local population), for 1988, out of 48 departments where information is available, only 14 have indexes less than 50%. Likewise, looking at the period, 1983–1988, all but 18 departments increased their index of black representation by more than 5 points. Only 10 departments reduced their index, and two of these merely went from a perfect index (1.00) to a few points below.

The effect of affirmative action on women police is dealt with later in this chapter under the heading, "Women in criminal justice agencies."

Recent Legislative efforts to require minority representation

What has been the nature of recent legislative attempts to require criminal justice agencies to accept minorities and women? What success have they had and what has been the reaction of white male employees?

As of March 1974, the EEOC was substituted for the Justice Department as the governmental institution enforcing Title VII prohibitions

Table 1
Minority and Female Representation in Selected Police Departments,
1967–1977

NAME OF JURISDICTION	1967 MIN POP %	1977 MIN POP %	1967*	1977*	1967 MIN* %	1977 MIN* %	1967 FEMALE* %	1977 FEMALE* %
Chicago, (IL)	34.4	NA	11,300	13,300	NA	19.2	1.1	2.8
Philadelphia (PA)	26.7	36.2	6,979	8,345	NA	17.6	0.8	1.1
Memphis (TN)	39.7	45.2	(1972) 1,096	1,249	8.9	5.6	2.3	4.2
Washington, D.C.	67.3	76.1	2,758	4,237	NA	44.1	1.1	7.3
Cleveland (OH)	35.0	61.8	2,011	2,023	6.7	9.2	2.1	2.2
Boston (MA)	9.8	18.8	2,494	NA	NA	NA	0.1	NA
New Orleans (LA)	45.5	46.0	(1968) 1,364	1,583	5.1	11.2	0.8	2.5
Atlanta (GA)	44.8	60.4	NA	1,226	NA	32.4	NA	9.2
Miami (FL)	6.0	77.0	664	726	6.9	24.2	1.5	6.3
Newark (NJ)	34.1	54.2	1,388	1,558	NA	19.8	NA	0.4

*Refers to sworn personnel. 1967–1977 figures from J. Heaphy, ed: Police Practices, the general administration survey. Police Foundation 1978.

against discrimination in employment.[37] Pursuant to this authority the EEOC has issued a series of guidelines requiring public employers to report on the racial and ethnic composition of their work force,[38] and has limited testing and screening devices that may have discriminatory consequences.[39] Cases involving public employees which cannot be settled by conciliation or negotiation are referred to the Justice Department for litigation.[40] The Crime Control Act of 1976, as amended in 1979, triggers mandatory enforcement procedures upon a finding of discrimination in any agency of a public recipient unless the recipient comes into satisfactory compliance within a specified time period.[41]

Enforcement procedures were further tightened by the President's Reorganization Plan No. 1 of 1978. That Plan designated the EEOC as the government agency that would "provide leadership and coordination to the efforts of Federal departments and agencies to develop uniform standards and procedures for EEOC compliance under all federal programs,"[42] and was to be responsible for equal employment opportu-

Table 2
Black Representation in Selected Police Departments, 1983-1988

| | TOTAL NUMBER OF OFFICERS | | BLACK OFFICERS | | | | INDEX OF BLACK REPRE-SENTATION | | % CHANGE | AFFIRMA-TIVE ACTION PLAN |
| | | | 1983 | | 1988 | | | | | |
	1983	1988	#	%	#	%	1983	1988		
Chicago (IL)	12,472	12,362	2,508	20.1	2,805	22.0	0.51	0.55	7.8	YES
Philadelphia (PA)	7,265	6,519	1,201	16.5	1,300	19.9	0.44	0.53	20.4	YES
Memphis (TN)	1,216	1,264	268	22.0	371	29.3	0.46	0.62	34.7	YES
Washington, D.C.	3,851	3,855	1,931	50.1	1,596	41.4	0.71	0.59	−16.9	NA
Cleveland (OH	2,091	NA	238	11.3	NA	NA	NA	NA	NA	NA
Boston (MA)	1,871	1,943	248	13.2	336	17.2	0.59	0.77	30.5	YES
New Orleans (LA)	1,317	1,347	276	20.9	445	33.0	0.38	0.60	57.8	YES
Atlanta (GA)	1,313	1,365	602	45.8	771	56.4	0.69	0.85	23.1	NA
Miami (FL)	1,051	1,033	181	17.2	180	17.4	0.69	0.69	0.0	YES
Newark (NJ)	1,144	1,064	275	24.0	296	27.8	0.41	0.48	17.0	NA

Note: Cities listed are ranked in order of size based on the 1980 population Census. The index of black representation is calculated by dividing the percent of black police officers in a department by the percent of blacks in the local population. An index approaching 1.0 indicates that a city is closer to achieving a representation of black police officers equal to their proportion in the local population. The black population of a city is derived from the 1980 census of the population. A "yes" in the table indicates the presence of an affirmative action plan for blacks operating at some point during 1983–1988. Table adapted from *Sourcebook of Criminal Justice Statistics*, 1988, Table 1.55. These cities were selected from the table because data from 1967 was available for these cities.

nity for all federal employees. Administration of several key civil rights statutes was transferred to the EEOC. Responsibility for state equal opportunity compliance formerly administered by other federal agencies was consolidated in the Office of Federal Contract Compliance Programs (Department of Labor). Overseeing all of these agencies was the Office of Management and Budget.[43]

In 1984, the Justice System Improvement act was amended, abolishing LEAA.[44] The amendment establishes the Office of Justice Programs (OJP) within the Department of Justice. OJP is comprised of the Bureau of Justice Assistance, Bureau of Criminal Justice Assistance, the National Institute of Justice, the Bureau of Justice Statistics and the Office of Juvenile Justice and Delinquency Prevention. By placing OJP within the Department of Justice, Congress attempted to enhance the stature of the organization, provide for more accountability, and maximize limited resources. OJP is headed by an Assistant Attorney General, while the four individual bureaus are headed by directors appointed by the Attorney General.[45]

OJP is to review recipients of federal funding appearing to have "the most serious equal employment opportunity problem, or the greatest disparity in the delivery of services to minority and non-minority or male and female communities they serve." Selection for review shall be made on the basis of:

(1) The relative disparity between the percentage of minorities, or women, in the relevant labor market, and the percentage of minorities, or women, employed by the recipient;

(2) The percentage of women and minorities in the population receiving program benefits;

(3) The number and nature of discrimination complaints filed against a recipient with OJARS or other Federal agencies;

(4) The scope of the problems revealed by an investigation commenced on the basis of a complaint filed with the Office [OJARS] against a recipient . . . ; and

(5) The amount of assistance provided to the recipient."[46]

The Justice System Improvement Act requires the OJP to initiate cut-off proceedings when there is a determination that either (1) the recipient is in noncompliance with the prohibition against discrimination; (2) OJP is notified that there has been a finding that there has been a pattern or practice of prohibited discrimination; or (3) the US Attorney General files a civil action alleging a pattern or practice of prohibited discriminatory conduct in any program or activity of a state government or unit of local government, and no preliminary injunction has been issued by the court enjoining such cut-off.[47]

If after appropriate notice of the Title VII violation and hearings there is a determination of noncompliance, OJP is required to institute administrative proceedings resulting in recommendations for compliance. If these recommendations are not met, OJP shall notify the Attorney General so that the Attorney General can institute a civil action to terminate payment of funds.[48] Cases involving public employees are referred to the Justice Department for litigation. The Justice Department is authorized to initiate broad "pattern or practice" suits against public agencies under Title VII and other laws. The Attorney General may initiate a Title VII action without waiting for the EEOC to act where a "pattern or practice" of discrimination is found.[49]

In 1978 Congress amended Title VII to specify that the Act's prohibition of sex discrimination includes discrimination based on pregnancy, child-birth or related medical conditions.[50] This amendment had the effect of reinstating a provision of the EEOC Sex Discrimination Guidelines overruled by the Supreme Court in General Electric v Gilbert[51] which decided that the exclusion by a private employer of pregnancy-related benefits from a comprehensive disability plan did not constitute sex discrimination in violation of Title VII.

Taking into consideration the governmental enforcement mechanism, together with the strong professional organizations that grew up to represent minority groups (see ch 5), it is likely that minorities and women in law enforcement did better in affirmative action suits than did minorities as a whole.

Interpretation of Title VII

The Supreme Court has stated "that a primary objective of Title VII is prophylactic: to achieve equal employment opportunity and to remove the barriers that have operated to favor white male employees over other employees."[52] Following the different ways that employment discrimination is manifested, the Court has developed two theories to interpret Title VII. These theories reflect distinctions in whether the discriminatory practice is intentional or unintentional. Where the practice is intentional it is designated as disparate *treatment,* and where unintentional, it is called disparate *impact.*

Disparate treatment involves *intentionally* less favorable employer treatment of an individual or group because of race, color, religion, sex, or national origin. Proof that the employer's action was motivated by one of these Title VII criteria is essential. Such motivation may, however, be inferred from the surrounding facts.

Disparate Impact involves *facially neutral* (unintentional) treatment of different groups but where the employment practice impacts more harshly on one of the statutorily-protected groups and cannot be justified by business necessity. A nondiscriminatory purpose is no defense. The sole defense is job-relatedness of the offending requirement. Both theories may apply in the same case.

Disparate treatment

The proof requirements for establishing disparate treatment were originally set forth in the 1973 case of McDonnell Douglas Corporation v Green.[53] There a laid-off black employee was arrested, convicted, and fired for obstructing traffic into the employer's plant. Thereafter, he applied for an available job with the company. When the company refused to rehire him while at the same time rehiring whites who had engaged in the same illegal acts, he alleged a Title VII violation. After determining that he was entitled to a hearing, the Court set forth the proofs necessary to sustain a claim of disparate treatment. A plaintiff "must carry the initial burden under the statute of establishing a prima facie case of racial discrimination."[54] Once the plaintiff has satisfied the prima facie requirements, the burden of proof shifts to the employer "to articulate some legitimate, nondiscriminatory reason for the employee's rejection."[55] The plaintiff is then to be given a chance to demonstrate that the employer's stated reason for its action is a mere pretext for a discriminatory decision.

In a later case, Texas Dept of Community Affairs v Burdine,[56] the Court had a chance to expand on the defendant employer's burden of proof. *Burdine* involved the claim by a female that she was discriminated against when her former employer hired a male who was equally qualified but who the employer believed would better contribute to the efficiency of the agency. The defendant employer, in articulating "some legitimate, nondiscriminatory reason" for the employee's rejection "need only produce admissible evidence which would allow the trier of fact rationally to conclude that the employment decision had not been motivated by discriminatory animus."[57] There is no requirement that the employer "hire the minority or female applicant whenever the person's objective qualifications were equal to those of a white male applicant. . . . Rather, the employer has discretion to choose among equally qualified candidates, provided the decision is not based upon unlawful criteria."[58]

In another sex discrimination case, Price Waterhouse v Hopkins,[59] Justice Brennan, for a plurality of four, provided a more detailed blueprint of proof requirements for disparate treatment cases. Justices O'Connor and White, who filed concurring opinions, would require a different burden of proof for the employer than would the plurality.

Hopkins charged a violation of Title VII in that the accounting firm, for which she worked as a senior manager, had refused to accept her as a partner because of her sex. The issue concerned "the respective burdens of proof of a defendant and plaintiff in a suit under Title VII when it has been shown that an employment decision resulted from a mixture of legitimate and illegitimate motives."[60]

At the time, of 662 partners, 7 were women, and of the 88 proposed for partnership that year, the only woman was Hopkins. About half of those proposed were admitted to partnership; about half of those rejected, including Hopkins, were placed on "hold," to be reconsidered next year. Part of the acceptance process required partners to comment on the candidate. Such comments were considered by an Admissions Committee. The major criticism of Hopkins was that she was "sometimes overly aggressive, unduly harsh, difficult to work with and impatient with staff." Various comments by partners tended to indicate that their attitudes were affected by her sex: that she was "macho," that she "overcompensated for being a woman," that she ought to take a course at a "charm school"; and that she used too much foul language for a lady. What the Court regarded as the *coup de grace* was administered by the partner who explained to her the reasons for the negative decision: that she might in the future be more favorably considered if she would "walk more femininely, talk more femininely, dress more femininely, wear make-up, have her hair styled, and wear jewelry."[61]

The Court was called on to construe 42 USC §§ 2000e-2(a)(1), (2) that prohibits employment discrimination "which would deprive any individual of employment opportunities . . . *because* of such individual's . . . sex." In reviewing the facts here, there seemed to be both legitimate and illegitimate, that is, sexually discriminatory motives, for the employment decision:

> . . . Title VII meant to condemn even those decisions based on a mixture of legitimate and illegitimate considerations. When, therefore, an employer considers both gender and legitimate factors at the time of making a decision, that decision was "because of" sex and the other, legitimate considerations — even if we may say later, in the context of litigation, that the decision would have been the same if gender had not been taken into account.[62]

The Court distinguished this case from those like *McDonnell supra,* which it designates a *pretext* case (whether the employer's stated reason for its decision was *the* reason for its action) and this case, designated as one of "mixed motives." Even if the plaintiff proves that the defendant relied on sex-based considerations in coming to its employment decision, the employer may still avoid liability if it can prove that, even if it had not taken gender into account, it would have come to the same decision regarding the particular person.[63]

The Court's rationale for this arrangement of proof is that:

> while an employer may not take gender into account in making an employment decision (except in those very narrow circumstances in which gender is a BFOQ), it is free to decide against a woman for other reasons. We think these principles require that, once a plaintiff in a Title VII case shows that gender played a motivating part in an employment decision, the defendant may avoid a finding of liability only by proving that it would have made the same decision even it had not allowed gender to play such a role. This balance of burdens is the direct result of Title VII's balance of rights.[64]

Next, the Court considered the question of burden of proof. The burden was placed on the employer to show that the reason for its action toward the complaining employee was legitimate. Rejecting the proof requirement demanded by the court of appeals that the employer must prove by "clear and convincing" evidence that it would have made the same decision absent the sexual discrimination, the plurality concluded that the "better rule" is "that the employer must make this showing by a preponderance of the evidence."[65] Because the lower courts had required proof of the employer's defense by clear and convincing evidence rather than by a preponderance, the case was remanded to the district court for a rehearing.

Justice White, in his concurring opinion, would substantially lighten the burden of the employer in rebutting the employee's claim of discrimination. All he would require is that "employer credibly testifies that the action would have been taken for the legitimate reasons alone," a rather self-serving species of proof.[66]

Justice O'Connor differs from the plurality in that she believes that the word, "because," in Title VII means that the illegitimate action must have "caused" the injury complained of. In terms of proof, the plaintiff would have to show that the "illegitimate criterion was a *substantial* factor in an adverse employment decision . . . ,"[67] whereupon the "burden shifts to the employer to show that regardless of the discriminatory events, the plaintiff would not have received the partnership anyway because of independently adequate factors. The reason for shifting the proof to the employer (whereas in other Title VII cases the burden always stays with the plaintiff), is "that the employer is [not] entitled to the same presumption of good faith where there is direct evidence that it has placed substantial reliance on factors whose considerations is forbidden by Title VII."[68]

Summing up, in "mixed motive" cases—that is, where the objected to discriminatory action results from a mixture of legitimate and illegitimate motives—the plaintiff must show that one of these factors was illegitimate (O'Connor would require the illegitimate motive to be "substantial"). The proof then shifts to the defendant employer who must show by a preponderance of the evidence, that the same adverse decision with reference to the employee would have been made regardless of the improper motive.

Disparate impact—Proving a disparate impact Title VII violation

The theory of disparate impact applies to employment practices that are neutral on their face but which disadvantage one of the protected groups and cannot be justified by business necessity.

In the 1989 case of Wards Cove Packing Co v Atonio,[69] discussed below, the Court completely revamped the proof necessary to prove a disparate impact Title VII claim. Prior to *Wards Cove,* the leading case was Griggs v Duke Power Co,[70] in which the company argued that even though the effect of its testing and promotion policies resulted in preferential treatment of whites, there was no intent on its part to discriminate and it had therefore not violated Title VII. But the Court found irrelevant the intention of the company not to discriminate because "Congress directed the thrust of the Act to the *consequences* of employment practices, not simply the motivation. More than that, Congress has placed on the employer the burden of showing that any given requirement must have a manifest relationship to the employment in question."[71]

Thus, for plaintiffs to establish a disparate impact Title VII violation where the issue is selection procedure, "*Griggs* and its progeny have established a three-part analysis": (1) The plaintiff must make a prima facie case of discrimination by showing that the facially neutral employment practice had a significantly discriminatory impact; (2) to avoid a finding of discrimination, the employer then must demonstrate that the practice has a manifest relationship to the employment, and (3) plaintiffs may still prevail if they show that the employer is using the practice "as a mere pretext for discrimination."[72]

While *Griggs* dealt with disparate impact of a *testing* procedure, Watson v Fort Worth Bank & Trust Co[73] decided "what evidentiary standards should be applied under Title VII . . . in determining whether an employer's practice of committing promotion decisions to the *subjective discretion* of supervisory employees has led to illegal discrimination."[74] Watson, a black woman, working as a bank teller, applied over time for several supervisory positions. White employees were selected over her by supervisors, all of whom were white, who used their subjective judgment to determine the qualifications of the competing job candidates. Watson claimed unlawful discrimination in promotion and other bank procedures in violation of Title VII.

After reviewing both the *Griggs* line of disparate impact cases and the disparate treatment cases, a plurality (O'Connor, Rehnquist, White, and Scalia) of the Court noted that the *Griggs* line was limited to questions involving employment testing while disparate treatment cases dealt with hiring and promotion decisions. This finding led the Court to ask "whether the reasons that support the use of disparate impact analysis apply to subjective employment practices, and whether such analysis can be applied in this new context under workable evidentiary standards."[75] The Court reasoned that where "objective" criteria (usually tests) and "subjective" standards (interviews, for example) are mixed, the end result must be considered "subjective," and that subjective procedures should be analyzed under the disparate impact approach.

The Court then turned to reconsideration of and detailing how a plaintiff should prove a disparate impact claim. Because only a plurality could agree on this burden of proof question, the issue was again raised and more definitely determined in the more recent case of Wards Cove Packing Co v Atonio.[76] In that case, the Court's five to four majority, speaking through Justice White, completely revamped the proof necessary in Title VII cases, substantially shifting proof requirements from the employer to plaintiff employees. In so doing, it placed serious obstacles of proof before plaintiffs using disparate impact theory.

Plaintiffs were nonwhite workers allegedly assigned by the defendant salmon canning company to unskilled jobs while whites were assigned skilled higher-paying jobs. Because the work took place in a remote area of Alaska, the company provided living quarters. Such quarters, however, segregated living and eating places for whites and nonwhites.

Addressing itself to the means by which a plaintiff could establish disparate impact statistically, the majority rejected the idea that a racial unbalance was sufficient proof. "[S]tatistics showing a high percentage of nonwhite workers in the cannery jobs and a low percentage of such workers in the noncannery positions" cannot alone make out a prima facie case. The proper comparison should be "between the racial composition of the qualified persons in the labor market and the persons holding at-issue jobs," or if that comparison is not possible, then "the racial composition of 'otherwise-qualified applicants' for at-issue jobs" would pass muster.[77]

Because the Court remanded the case to the district court, and wished to instruct that court how to proceed, the Court decided questions of "causation" and the burden of proof the plaintiff must carry in showing disparate impact.

In order to demonstrate a prima facie case of disparate impact, employees "will . . . have to demonstrate that the disparity they complain of is the result of one or more of the employment practices that they are attacking here [nepotism, separate hiring channels and rehiring preferences], specifically showing that each challenged practice has a significantly disparate impact on employment opportunities for whites and nonwhites." Such a showing is necessary to prove a "causal link between challenged employment practices and racial imbalances in the work force."[78]

Once plaintiff employees make a prima facie case, "the case will shift to any business justification" the employer offers for its use of these practices. This second phase of proof consists of two successive but independent requirements: "a consideration of the justifications an employer offers for his use of these practices; and second, the availability of alternate practices to achieve the same business ends, with less racial impact."[79]

While noting that "the employer carries the burden of producing evidence of a business justification for his employment practice," the Court emphasized that "the burden of persuasion . . . remains with the disparate-impact plaintiff" because "the ultimate burden of proving that discrimination against a protected group has been caused by a specific employment practice remains with the plaintiff *at all times,*" citing *Watson.*[80]

Finally, if employees do not prevail in overcoming the business necessity defense, they may still proceed on the theory that selection devices that do not have an undesirable racial impact would just as well serve the employer's interest. Employees would thereby show that an employer, who nevertheless used the objectionable hiring procedure, would be using it solely as a pretext for discrimination. To be acceptable, such alternative procedure must be "equally effective" in achieving the employer's goals. The Court cautioned that "the judiciary should proceed with care before mandating that an employer must adopt a plaintiff's alternative selection or hiring practice in response to a Title VII suit."[81]

Justice Stevens, speaking as well for three other justices, accused the majority of "turning a blind eye to the meaning and purpose of Title VII"[82] and departing "from the body of law engendered by this disparate impact theory, reformulating the order of proof and the weight of the parties' burden."[83] In a separate dissent, Justice Blackmun, joined by Justices Brennan and Marshall, "sadly" queries "whether the majority still believes that race discrimination—or, more accurately, race discrimination against nonwhites—is a problem in our society, or even remembers that it ever was."[84]

One commentator charged that *Wards Cove* had reduced the goal of Title VII from a remedy for group discrimination (see page 1 of this chapter) to that for individual discrimination; that in effect the decision had "changed the disparate impact analysis scheme to approximate that of disparate treatment" in that the equivalent of intent was now required for both; and that cases decided during the Court's 1988 term spelled the end of the Second Reconstruction.[85]

Whether the results of *Wards Cove* were so dire can only be determined by seeing the effect the case has on subsequent decisions. Federal courts still see a difference in the proof necessary between disparate treatment and disparate impact cases. One court of appeals stated in dicta (because the case did not involve disparate impact): "No proof of intentional discrimination is necessary" in disparate impact claims.[86]

Perhaps the most significant effect of *Wards Cove* will be on the enhanced proof requirements for statistical evidence. In Green v USX Corp,[87] black applicants for unskilled labor positions presented data showing that more whites than blacks were being hired. The court found the interviewing process in which the employer determined employment based on the interviewer's "gut" reaction to have caused the discriminatory impact. The employer countered that it had found interviews to be the best way to select qualified employees. To this self-serving assertion, the court responded: "Although *Wards Cove* may have relaxed the employer's burden to rebut the plaintiff's *prima facie* case, we do not read the decision as requiring us to accept at face value an employer's explanation of the adverse impact of its hiring practices on blacks."[88]

The "burden of persuasion" was the issue in Allen v Seidman.[89] Plaintiffs, black bank examiners, had disproportionately failed in program evaluations by the employers, the Federal Deposit Insurance Corporation (FDIC), and were therefore not promoted. The case was remanded to the district court because on trial that court had placed the burden of persuasion on the employer to show that the evaluation program was a reliable selection device whereas *Wards Cove* places the burden on the plaintiff, "at all times."

In EEOC v Joint Apprenticeship Committee,[90] the EEOC, suing under Title VII on behalf of black men and women, attacked as discriminatory the diploma requirement of the joint labor-management board (JAC) to admit apprentice electricians to its training program. Because the district court's reasoning concluding that the plaintiff had proved disparate impact "appeared to disclaim the need for exploration of the causal nexus between criterion and disparity," the matter was returned to the district court for such a finding.[91]

Harris v Lyng[92] shows the difficulty plaintiffs may have in proving the causal connection. Black employees of the Foreign Agricultural Service, suing under Title VII, showed a disparity between blacks and whites promoted. The black employees argued that the disparity was due to the actions of the Personnel Assignments Committee, which passed on promotions, and which for 20 years never had a black employee. Pointing to the fact that PAC's decisions were merely recommendations, and that PAC had offered several nondiscriminatory reasons for the disparity, the court held that the plaintiffs had not proved a causal connection.

Statistical proof of discrimination

In Teamsters v United States,[93] a case considered at length in the section on seniority, the Court suggested how statistical evidence might be used to show disparate treatment. The case, a pattern or practice suit by the Attorney General, "had to establish by a preponderance of the evidence that racial discrimination was the company's standard operating procedure—the regular rather than the unusual practice."[94] The Government showed a clear statistical pattern of discriminatory hiring, bolstered by testimony of personal experiences of over 40 specific instances of discrimination. "The company's principal response to this evidence is that statistics can never in and of themselves prove the existence of a pattern or practice of discrimination, or even establish a prima facie case shifting to the employer the burden of rebutting the inference raised by the figures."[95] While statistical evidence, like other evidence, may be rebutted, said the Court, it serves " 'an important role' in cases in which the existence of discrimination is a disputed issue."[96] Statistical evidence has been extensively used to make a prima facie showing that tests employed for recruiting or promotions are in violation of Title VII. As discussed above in the *Wards Cove* case, the Court is now closely scrutinizing proof based principally on statistical disparaties.

In the City of Richmond v JA Croson,[97] the Court found an ordinance that purported to award a specified percentage of city construction contracts to minority contractors, unconstitutional in violation of the equal protection of the laws clause. The Court concluded that mere gross statistical disparities between blacks in the population and contractors receiving contracts was insufficient to establish a prima facie case of Title VII violation. The case arose when a white contractor, who had lost a bid to a minority competitor, challenged the ordinance.

The Court relied on the fact that there was no "direct evidence" of discrimination on the part of the city in letting contracts; that the figure of 30% of the money amount of each contract to be awarded was "chosen arbitrarily"; and that "a generalized assertion that there has been past discrimination in an entire industry provides no guidance for a legislative body to determine the precise scope of the injury it seeks to remedy."[98] The proper statistical standard, the Court continued, would be "the number of minorities qualified to undertake the particular task," a number the city does not even know.[99]

> While the States and their subdivisions may take remedial action when they possess evidence that their own spending practices are exacerbating a pattern of prior discrimination, they must identify that discrimination, public or private, with some specificity before they may use race-conscious relief. . . . In sum, none of the evidence presented by the city points to any identified discrimination in the Richmond construction industry. We, therefore, hold that the city has failed to demonstrate a compelling interest in apportioning public contracting opportunities on the basis of race.[100]

Hereafter, any law or ordinance that uses race as a basis for distribution of some benefit, with the object of correcting some prior wrong, must pass the Court's strict scrutiny test of showing a compelling state interest for its legislation. Such a heavy burden of proof, heretofore, was limited to those authorities who were discriminating *against* minorities.

Testing as a means of discrimination

Most often this issue arises when a testing procedure used by employers to determine qualification for hiring or promotion falls more harshly on minorities or women. Three issues are crucial in understanding the context of this discrimination: the growth of tests as a means of validating qualifications for employment, the cultural context of the tests, and the method for proving that the test discriminates against a protected group.

Testing has become an indicia of industrial society. Except for the lowest paying and least skilled jobs, almost every application to an educational institution or for a job requires a qualifying examination. In an economy with more applicants than jobs, tests have become a means to eliminate the vast majority of applicants. Although tests are widely billed as verifying the qualifications and aptitude of the applicant for the particular job, closer investigation has shown that a large percentage are culturally based, are not job-related, and depend on values and knowledge that can be acquired most easily through participation in the dominant male white middle-class culture.[101]

Thus, a woman, or more particularly, a minority male, is disadvantaged in taking a test that is culturally biased. Many minority applicants for criminal justice positions have been raised in areas where educational facilities have been minimally effective, and where their family background (parents with little formal education, a broken home or frequent moves) does not allow them to take full advantage of any education available. Therefore, an examination that may seem fair on its face, in practice, may test areas of conception and knowledge that are accessible to one group but not to another.

Written tests are only one kind of selection device. Personnel interviews, observation of the candidate's performance of job-related tasks, simulation exercises, or some combination thereof, are other possibilities. But the ease and low-unit cost of giving written tests to large numbers of applicants, and their apparent objectivity as compared to tests based on subjective observation, have made written tests the preferred selection device for most criminal justice agencies.[102]

Testing the tests

Challenging test results has been a major means by which minorities and women have sought to enter criminal justice agencies. Craig v County of Los Angeles,[103] a class action by Mexican-American applicants for deputy sheriff posts, questioned the use of a written examination that failed 33% Mexican-Americans but only 13% whites. Proof of the test's disparate impact shifted the burden to the defendant county to show that the challenged test was significantly job-related, a validation process involving three steps: the employer must (1) specify the particular trait or characteristic that the test is being used to measure; (2) determine that that particular trait or characteristic is an important element of work behavior; and (3) demonstrate by "professionally acceptable methods" that the test is "predictive of or significantly correlated" with the element of work behavior identified in the second step.

Plaintiffs took the position that the test must predict performance on the job while the county argued that it need show performance validity only at the training academy. The Court held that both of these validations were necessary: the test must correlate "significantly with important elements of academy performance *and* [show] that those elements of academy performance are important to actual job performance."[104] The Court accepted the county's argument that the law-related academy courses and training in telecommunications were essential to the "increasingly complex requirements of police work," and that the test correlated with success in academy performance in these areas. In effect, the county was able to demonstrate "that persons excluded from the academy . . . because they failed the . . . entrance exam would not have succeeded in the academic training program."[105] On remand to the district court, the county would have to prove the additional requirement "that the level of academic training given to new recruits manifestly relates to the knowledge that deputy sheriffs must possess to perform the job successfully."[106] Thus, this case does not require correlation of the selection device to actual job performance but only to knowledge necessary to perform the job.

Guardians Assn of New York City v Civil Service Commission[107] illustrates the complexity of validating a testing device. Claiming a Title VII violation, the Guardians Association and the Hispanic Society, respectively representing black and hispanic officers of the New York City Police Department, challenged the test used for hiring police officers. The district court found for the plaintiffs and ordered "a 50% minority hiring quota."[108] In a 35-page opinion, the court detailed how the test was prepared, the standards for judging validity, the application of these standards and the use of the test in ranking candidates. The disparate impact of the test was apparent from the results: "the passing rate for Whites was 45.9% compared to 17% for Blacks and 20.5% for Hispanics." From the final list of candidates, of those chosen "89.2% were White, 3.5% were Black, and 6.8% were Hispanic."[109]

The more difficult question was whether the test was job-related. For guidance the court turned to the EEOC Uniform Guidelines on Employee

Selection Procedures[110] which described three test validation methods: content, construct and criterion-related. Content validation is appropriate when (1) the test attempts to measure knowledge or ability, and not a general trait such as intelligence, and (2) it does not measure knowledge or ability that the applicant is expected to learn on the job. Construct validation attempts to measure general mental traits such as intelligence, aptitude, commonsense, judgment, or leadership ability. Criteria-related validation involves a job analysis showing production or error rate, tardiness, length of service or other behavior critical to the particular employment. Plaintiffs argue that construct validation is the proper means to evaluate the test because that method requires empirical data showing that the test successfully predicts job performance. The defendant, on the other hand, contends that content validation is the proper method. The court reasons that it can begin with the less demanding content validity for if the test fails to satisfy that requirement, it cannot successfully overcome the more difficult prima facie evidence of disparate impact.

The department's exam tests three basic abilities: to remember details, fill out forms, and apply general principles to specific facts. This third ability is assessed in three contexts: the application of general statements (1) of criminal offenses to the facts of specific events, (2) to the facts of specific policing activities, and (3) to the facts of specific situations involving human relations problems. These qualities are appropriate for content validation because they are based on observable behavior rather than on abstract qualities such as intelligence and leadership, more appropriate for construct validation.

Using content validity as a guide, the court then asked whether the exam had sufficient reliability to select applicants. Five requirements were distilled from the EEOC guidelines: (1) the test-makers must have conducted a suitable job analysis; (2) they must have used reasonable competence in constructing the test; (3) the test content must be related to job content; (4) test content must be representative of job content; and (5) it must use a scoring method that selects among the applicants those who can better do the job.

By interviewing police officers the police department identified 42 job-related tasks significant to entry-level officers. By questionnaire, a large number of officers were then asked to rank these tasks by importance; thereafter, the tasks were submitted to panels of officers who were requested to specify the knowledge skills and abilities necessary to effectively perform the tasks. The court found this procedure faulty because the department developed the questionnaire without any specialized help; officers framing the questions had little access to the job analysis material; the questions were never tested on a sample population, and the testing for human relations skill, when reduced to written questions, merely tested the applicant's ability to apply general written standards to specific fact situations. Nevertheless, the court concluded that the test satisfied "the central requirement of Title VII, . . . adequate assurance that the identified tasks are in fact the tasks that a police officer performs."[111] The test likewise met the requirement that it be a "representative sample of the content of the job. . . . [T]he job analysis identified as important . . . memory, the ability to fill out forms, and the ability to apply rules to factual situations . . . all significant aspects of entry-level police work."[112]

The court then turned to the way the test was used to distinguish among candidates. The city used the exam to rank candidates and then arbitrarily selected a passing "cut-off" score sufficient to provide the number of trainees it desired. The court noted that "where as here, the test scores reveal a disparate racial impact, and that disparity is greater at high passing scores than at low passing scores, the appropriateness of inferring that higher scores closely correlate with better job performance must be closely scrutinized."[113] In this instance, the test results precluded such correlation. Two-thirds of all who passed were bunched between a score of 94 and 97 because the exam constructed was "too easy," thus making "the use of rank-ordering an extremely unreliable basis for hiring decisions."[114] In addition, the cut-off score determining the rejection of the applicant was placed at the point calculated to supply the department with the number of candidates it needed without any relationship to ability levels. Thus the court concluded that the exam, as used, had a significant disparate racial impact; had not been shown to be job-related; and therefore, violated Title VII and was invalid. These cases dealing with testing remain the law except as modified by the *Wards Cove* "burden of persuasion" on the plaintiff to prove all aspects of the case.

Post *Wards Cove* Test cases

Since the 1980s, when *Craig* and *Guardians* were decided, cases involving testing have gone through a number of phases: (1) after findings of discrimination and/or consent decrees, testing procedures were established to end discrimination against minorities and women, and district courts issued decrees to monitor these procedures; (2) validating these tests increasingly employed sophisticated statistical techniques and hence, the use of experts on each side; (3) these procedures were often challenged by white males acting through their law enforcement organizations; (4) most recently, white males have claimed that the decrees, heretofore entered, have served their purpose, and should now be dissolved.

The case of Bridgeport Guardians, Inc v City of Bridgeport[115] illustrates these developments. Two organizations dedicated to the eradication of racial employment discrimination in the Department and 10 minority police officers who took the 1989 Sergeant examination brought the suit claiming a discriminatory selection process. Intervening white officers opposed it.[116]

Sixty-eight percent of whites against 38% of minorities passed the written test. The highest scoring minority candidate ranked 20th. As there were 19 sergeant posts available, no minorities would be promoted. Both plaintiffs and the psychologist hired by the City urged the City to promote based on a banding technique rather than strict rank order. Banding "takes a range of scores whose differences are not statistically significant, and within that band range, provides promotions of candidates on the basis of considerations such as race or ethnicity, gender, work experience, past job dependability, and other factors that the hiring authorities deem pertinent."[117] It was the psychologist's opinion that the tests were not constructed in so precise a fashion that rank order of test scores was justified.

On appeal from a finding of a violation of Title VII and relief to remedy it, the court of appeals concluded that

> While the court ruled . . . that the City proceeded to meet its task of showing that the examination was content valid and justified by the City's business needs, the court also properly ruled that plaintiffs had sufficiently rebutted that evidence by showing that the City could have chosen to use banding in order to alleviate the disparate racial effect of the examination without disserving its legitimate interests.[118]

Police Officers v City of Columbus[119] turned on the validity of the test rather than on whether rank order or banding is more appropriate to apply to the results of the test. In an earlier version of the case, Police Officers for Equal Rights (POER) obtained a finding of discrimination against blacks in promotions, assignments, transfers and other conditions of employment, and that the sergeant examination had a discriminatory impact on black officers and was not job related. Plaintiffs also charged that the lieutenant examination was not job related. The Fraternal Order of Police, the collective bargaining agent for all sworn officers, supported the validity of the examination.

Evidence showed that in order to constitute the examination the Civil Service Commission employed a nationally recognized expert in preparing promotion examinations for public safety organizations. He, in turn, consulted with an expert at a local university. The staff that prepared the test consisted of one Ph.D., three persons with masters degrees in psychology, and two with bachelor degrees.

POER charged that the test was defective because it was based solely on knowledge rather than on skills and abilities. Turning to the EEOC Uniform Guidelines, the court concluded that the Guidelines language does not preclude a test simply because it is a test of knowledge.

POER next argued that "the lieutenant examination does not represent the requirements of the position of lieutenant because the test does not measure attributes in proportion to their importance and frequency of use in the performance of the job."[120] In reply, the court cited evidence presented by the city to establish content validity, namely it

> identif[ied] the tasks involved in the job, that it rated them according to importance and frequency and in the process identified the most important task categories. It constructed a test which tested for all or nearly all of the task categories, and emphasized the most important task categories.[121]

In order to attain content validity, there is no requirement that the test measure all aspects of the job, no matter how insignificant. Precise proportionality is not required. POER further contended that the job relatedness was insufficient for rank ordering and that banding should have been the selection device. The City's expert suggested that three requirements were necessary to justify rank ordering of test scores:

> (1) there must be a sufficient spread among the scores of candidates; (2) there must be composite reliability (the whole test must be reliable) and component reliability (each component must be reliable); and (3) there must be a reasonable job analysis.[122]

The City experts, in a battle with the POER expert, were able to demonstrate to the court's satisfaction, that the exam was sufficiently reliable to justify rank ordering. POER also complained that the district court had failed to grant any relief with reference to lieutenant and captain promotions, to which the court responded that the pool of minority candidates from which to choose was so small that there would be no basis for selection. In effect, the court concluded that time and the procedure already ordered by the court would take care of the problem. As more blacks became sergeants, a pool for lieutenants and captains would thereby be created.

The "bottom line" defense—rejected

What about the situation in which a test favorably impacts on a protected group *as a whole* but still denies opportunities for advancement for individuals of that group? In Connecticut v Teal,[123] black employees who had been temporarily advanced to welfare supervisors of a state agency were required to take a test to retain that promotion. Of the blacks who took the examination, 22.9% were promoted, while of the whites who took the examination, 13.5% were promoted. Plaintiffs, not among those promoted, challenged this "bottom-line" result claiming that the test was not job-related. The issue was whether, given this prima facie lack of disparate racial impact on the protected group, was it still necessary for the employer to demonstrate job relatedness of the test?

Relying on the language of § 703(a)(2) which forbids an employer from depriving "any individual of employment opportunities," the Court decided that such a demonstration was still required. A "suggestion that disparate impact should be measured only at the bottom line ignores the fact that Title VII guarantees these individual respondents the *opportunity* to compete equally with white workers on the basis of job-related criteria."[124] The rights of the protected groups are violated under the section unless the employer "can demonstrate that the examination given was not an artificial, arbitrary, or unnecessary barrier, because it measured skills related to effective performance" on the job.[125] Finally, the "bottom-line" defense is rejected because "it is clear that Congress never intended to give an employer license to discriminate against some employees on the basis of race or sex merely because he favorably treats other members of the employee's group."[126] But where females were selected from a pool consisting solely of female applicants, there was no discrimination as to females although if the pool consisted of both male and female applicants, such a height requirement which disproportionately disqualified women, would be discriminatory.[127]

Measure of damages

Given that an employer has violated Title VII, what should be the measure of damages? In Albemarle Paper Co. v Moody,[128] black employees brought a Title VII class action charging both their employer and the plant employees' union with discrimination. The North Carolina employer

> had "strictly segregated" the plant's departmental "lines of progression" prior to January 1, 1964, reserving the higher paying and more skilled lines for whites.... Because of the plant's previous history of overt segregation, only whites had seniority in the higher job categories. Accordingly, the court ordered the petitioners to implement a system of "plantwide" seniority.[129]

But the district court denied a request for backpay to make up for the losses plaintiffs suffered as a result of the discrimination. Under the Act, backpay liability is limited to discriminatory practices occurring after its effective date, July 2, 1965, and may be asserted only for a period beginning two years prior to filing a charge with the EEOC.

In determining whether Title VII authorized district courts to award backpay as damages in proven cases of discrimination, the Court looked to the purpose of the Act. Citing *Griggs,* the Court noted that the purpose was "a prophylactic one ... to achieve equality of employment opportunities and remove barriers that have operated in the past to favor an identifiable group of white employees over the other employees."[130] Backpay has a clear connection to this object for it is the prospect of a backpay award that may spur employers and unions to eliminate discriminatory practices. But even more important, the Court went on to provide a means of measuring damages, well-known in tort litigation. Title VII has a "make whole" purpose "to make persons whole for injuries suffered on account of unlawful employment discrimination"[131] —that is, to place claimants in the same position they would have been in if the injury had not occurred.

Having discussed the history and interpretation of Title VII, we can now turn to specific areas of application such as women's rights, seniority and layoffs, affirmative action plans, voluntary agreements, reverse discrimination and equal protection of the law violations.

Women in criminal justice agencies

Jobs in criminal justice "have historically and traditionally been firmly embedded in the male domain. Judges, lawyers, sheriffs, wardens, police and corrections officers have almost exclusively been male occupations for most of the history of the country.... In fact, such positions are the very antithesis of what is usually perceived as 'women's work.' "[132] Although there were isolated cases of women police as early as the mid-nineteenth century, it was not until the opening of the twentieth century that women began to be regularly employed to care for female and juvenile prisoners in local jails. As part of the Progressive movement philosophy, police departments were pressured by elitist reform groups to adopt a preventive as well as a repressive function, for example, concerns for juvenile delinquency and the morals of young working women subjected to tavern and dance hall influences. Women were seen as the natural guardians of these groups. Drives against prostitution by reform organizations also produced female prisoners who could not easily be processed by males. On the theory that women police were really engaged in social work, women were paid less and required to attain higher educational standards than men.[133] Their role was thus strictly limited to duties that would not threaten men's jobs, that is, to jobs involving "women, children and typewriters."[134] They were forbidden to wear uniforms, patrol regular beats or arrest adults. By the mid-1920s, because of this narrow job definition, the movement had declined. The concept of police professionalism changed from emphasis on the preventive function to that of "managerial efficiency, technological sophistication, and an emphasis on crime fighting."[135] Until the late 1960s the women's police movement remained dormant.

Thereafter, particularly in corrections, women have registered important, though limited, gains:

> There are increasing numbers of women appearing in the corrections work force. Traditionally, women in corrections have staffed women's prisons, but now they are moving into all-male correctional institutions. The move has been gradual—from the strictly protected clerical area of work to the remote watch on the prison tower, the highly visible processing of visitors far away from the cellblocks, to structured classroom teaching situations under male officer surveillance, the nursing area of the prison hospital, the counselling room—and now into direct supervision of male inmates in the cellblocks. The smallest number of women occupies administrative managerial positions and there are almost no female wardens of male institutions. A negligible number of women have achieved the offices of deputy commissioners and commissioners.[136]

Quantifying the above summary, another writer states:

> A 1979 survey [the most recent available] reported that only 29.3 percent of correctional workers were female; moreover, these women were overrepresented in clerical and support functions, and only 41 percent of them had contact with prisoners. Many of these women worked in institutions for females and juveniles. . . . [O]nly 56 percent of the facilities for women are headed by women.[137]

Increase in female employment demands

By the first half of 1979 women constituted 41% of the labor force, representing nearly 51% of all women of working age. By 1988 the percentage of women in the work force had increased to 46.1%. Since 1972, over a million women have entered the work force each year. A number of reasons have been given for this influx: (1) changes in what is thought to constitute an adequate standard of living and rising prices necessary to attain and retain this standard; (2) inability of many families to maintain their living standards without a second income; (3) fewer children; (4) rapid growth of white collar and service jobs where women are primarily employed; (5) social acceptability of women with young children working outside the home; (6) advances in household technology allowing women to economize their time; (7) availability of post-secondary education so that employable skills may be acquired outside the normal educational cycle; (8) more part-time and flexi-time work allowing more women to combine work and household duties.[138]

Although there have been sensational advances by women into occupations which a few years ago were all but closed to them (US Supreme Court Justice O'Connor being a prime example), women still are principally found in "female" jobs, those in service and clerical categories. For example, as of 1988, women comprise 98.2% of all stenographers, typists and secretaries, and 60.5% of all those in service work. Because these jobs are at the bottom of the employment hierarchy, they are low-paying, women earning about 66% of wages paid to men. The discrepancy in earnings can be partially explained by the fact that women's education, even where equal or superior to that of men, often does not fit the technical needs of employers. Women also usually begin their working career later in life after their child-bearing years, so that they do not accumulate seniority or acquaintances who can ease their way into the "old-boy" networks that permit entry into higher-level jobs.[139]

Nevertheless, one recent 1986 survey of women police concluded that "affirmative action policies have had a major impact on both the current entry rate and overall representation of women in policing."[140] The survey found that the percentage of women officers was directly related to whether their agency was under court order to comply (10%); was subject to a voluntary plan (8.3%), or without a plan (6.1%). The same relationships were true for numbers of minority and for women in supervisory positions. Earlier surveys have shown that as of 1972, women represented no more than 2% of uniformed law enforcement personnel, and were generally excluded from patrol duties. By 1978, the percentage of women as sworn personnel in municipal departments had risen to 4.2% and at the end of 1986, to 8.8%, 40% of whom were minority women.

Not surprisingly, increase in supervisory positions showed the least progress. In 1978, 1% of municipal supervisors were women. In 1986, that figure had increased to 3.3%, most of whom were at the rank of sergeant. Only 1.4% had attained a rank above lieutenant. Some of that restricted advance may be explained by the short time women have been in the system. Women were actually being promoted at or above their proportion in the departments. An unknown number of women police while normally assigned to field operations, may actually be assigned to clerical or staff support positions. Moreover, they are less likely than men to be assigned to "elite" squads such as criminal investigations or vice. The author of the study suggests that if present trends continue, by the end of the century, women will still comprise no more than 20% of police personnel.[141]

Title VII claims by women

Discriminatory employment practices against women by criminal justice agencies have restricted women to processing and maintaining custody of female and juvenile prisoners, resulting in very limited employment opportunities at low-paying jobs. 1978 statistics show that women represent 23% of the correctional jobs; 3.2% of law enforcement officers; 9% of lawyers, 5.8% of judges, and about 1% of administrators in each of these fields.[142] In 1988, those figures, not exactly comparable, show that 17.8% of "correctional institution officers" and 20% of "guards"; 10.1% "supervisors, police and detectives"; "sheriffs, bailiffs, and other law enforcement officers" 17.4%; and a combined total of judges and lawyers, 19.3%, were women.[143] Until recently, this job segregation had been bolstered by imposing height, weight, and physical strength entry criteria which barred all but a small percentage of women. Women have used Title VII to challenge these barriers as not being job related.

In Dothard v Rawlinson,[144] a 22-year-old female college graduate majoring in correctional psychology sought and was denied a job as a prison guard in the Alabama prison system because she did not meet the 120-pound weight or 5'2" minimum height requirements. She attacked both those requirements as well as administrative Regulation 204 that established gender-based criteria for "contact positions" in maximum-security institutions. The Court summarized employment at the correctional facility at the time of the litigation as follows:

> [T]he Board of Corrections employed a total of 435 people in various correctional counselor positions, 56 of whom were women. Of those 56 women, 21 were employed at the Julia Tutwiler Prison for Women, 13 were employed in noncontact positions at the four male maximum-security institutions, and the remaining 22 were employed at the other institutions operated by the Alabama Board of Corrections. Because most of Alabama's prisoners are held at the four maximum-security male penitentiaries, 336 of the 435 correctional counselor jobs were in those institutions, a majority of them concededly in the "contact" classification. Thus, even though meeting the statutory height and weight requirements, women applicants could under Regulation 204 compete with men for only about 25% of the correctional counselor jobs available in the Alabama prison system.[145]

The Court further noted that

> When the height and weight restrictions are combined, Alabama's statutory standards would exclude 41.13% of the female population while excluding less than 1% of the male population.[146]

Because these requirements had a discriminatory impact on the women applicants the Court concluded that plaintiffs had established a prima facie Title VII violation. But because the Board of Corrections produced no evidence to show that the height and weight requirements were job related they may not be applied to Rawlinson or the class she represents. The Court then turned to Regulation 204 which explicitly made sex a basis for prison assignments and was therefore a clear case of disparate treatment of a protected group. The Corrections Board argued that the regulation was permitted by § 703(e) of Title VII as a "bona fide occupational qualification [bfoq] reasonably necessary to the normal operation of that particular business or enterprise."[147] While the court conceded "that the bfoq exception was in fact meant to be an extremely narrow exception to the general prohibition of discrimination on the basis of sex, in the particular factual circumstances of this case, however, we conclude that . . . Regulation 204 falls within the narrow ambit of the bfoq exception."[148]

The "particular factual circumstances" on which the decision rested included an "environment of violence and disorganization," where it was estimated that sex offenders represented 20% of the prisoners who might be again moved to assault women if given the chance, or that "other inmates, deprived of normal heterosexual environment, would assault women guards because they were women."[149] Such potential assaults

> would pose a real threat not only to the victim of the assault but also to the basic control of the penitentiary and protection of its inmates and the other security personnel. The employee's very womanhood would thus directly undermine her capacity to provide the security that is the essence of a correctional counselor's responsibility.[150]

To support its conclusions the Court rather weakly cited two prison assaults, one of a female clerical worker and another of a student taken hostage during a prison visit. No comparison was made with male guards assaulted nor was there any evidence that the assaults were sexually based. Justice Marshall, dissenting, argued that the Court's analysis "sounds distressingly like saying that two wrongs make a right."[151] Rather than condemning a "prison system operating in blatant violation of the Eighth Amendment, . . . it is women who are made to pay the price in lost job opportunities for the threat of depraved conduct by prison inmates."[152] Marshall noted that the Court's bfoq decision was limited to the special facts of that decision. To date, although *Dothard* has often been cited for that part of the decision invalidating the height, weight, and strength requirements, it has not spawned any bfoq progeny.[153]

Earlier cases are represented by Blake v City of Los Angeles[154] which sets forth conditions under which women have operated during the 1960s and 1970s in most criminal justice agencies. Past, present and future female applicants to the Los Angeles Police Department (LAPD) brought this Title VII class action against the city administration complaining of a number of sex-based discriminatory employment practices. Prior to July 1 1973 the department maintained separate, gender-based job classifications in entry-level police positions.

> Men in the "policeman" classification performed general police patrol assignments and could be promoted through all ranks of the department. Women in the "policewoman" classification generally performed "tasks relating to women and children, desk duty, and administration." Policewomen were barred from regular police patrol assignments and were ineligible for promotion above the level of sergeant. Between 1970 and 1973 no women were appointed to sworn positions in the LAPD, although the department hired more than 2,000 men. The percentage of women in sworn positions in the LAPD declined from 2.62 percent in 1970 to 2.15 percent in 1973.[155]

Even after the abolition of these classifications in July 1973 and the reduction of the height requirement from 5'7" to 5'6", as of 1976, women represented only 2.08% of all sworn personnel and 0.48% of all ranks of sergeant and above.

> The undisputed evidence revealed that the 5'6" height requirement excluded 87 percent of all women, but only 20 percent of all men between the ages of 18 and 79. The 5'7" requirement excluded 95 percent of all women, but only 32 percent of all men [citations omitted]. The physical abilities test excluded half of all women who took it, but only 2.6 percent of all men who took the test.[156]

Based on discriminatory impact, the plaintiffs had established a prima facie Title VII violation. The department responded that taller officers could more easily control suspects and observe field situations and were therefore a bfoq business necessity. But empirical evidence submitted by the defendant to support this assertion was found by the court to be insufficient to overcome plaintiff's prima facie case.[157]

In the 1991 case of Bouman v Block, Sheriff of Los Angeles County,[158] plaintiff filed for herself and a class of potential female applicants for sergeant in the county sheriff's department charging sex discrimination. Although Bouman placed highest on the list developed for promotion to sergeant, she was not promoted. In order to determine if there had been sex discrimination, the court applied the same test as for racial discrimination, asking if

> 1) she belongs to a protected group; 2) application was made for the job for which the employer was seeking applicants; 3) despite plaintiff's qualifications for that job, she was rejected; and 4) after plaintiff was rejected, the position remained open and the employer continued to seek applicants from persons of plaintiff's qualification. The employer must then show a legitimate, non-discriminatory reason for the challenged employment action. Plaintiff must then persuade that court that a discriminatory reason more likely motivated the employer, or that the employer's proffered explanation is unworthy of credence.[159]

Plaintiff's main claim was that the 1975 and 1977 sergeant examinations had a disparate impact on women. To determine this fact, the court applied what had become known as the 4/5th rule, originating in the EEOC's 1978 Uniform Guidelines on Employee Selection Procedures.[160] In the words of the court,

> The federal agency guidelines . . . require a showing that the protected group is selected at less than four-fifths or 80 percent of the rate achieved by the highest scoring group. . . . Of the 79 women who took the 1975 written test, ten, or roughly 13 percent, scored high enough on a combination of written and appraisal scores to be considered candidates for promotion. Four women, or roughly five percent of the women who took the examination, were ultimately

promoted. Of the 1312 men who took the 1975 written test, 250, or approximately 19 percent, received sufficiently high combined scores to be eligible for promotion. 127 men, or approximately ten percent, were ultimately promoted. . . . These figures clearly show a violation of the 80 percent rule. The women's pass rate—the number of persons placed on the eligibility list over the number who took the test—was only 66 percent of the men's pass rate, while the women's promotion rate—the number of people promoted over the number who took the test—was less than 53 percent of the men's promotion rate.[161]

For the 1977 examination, the results were similar: "The women's pass rate was only 67 percent of the men's pass rate, while the women's promotion rate was only 66 percent of the men's promotion rate."[162] Although the mere violation of this rule is not in itself sufficient to show disparate impact, the plaintiffs were able to show that these figures were "statistically significant." The County, in turn, failed to produce any evidence validating the exam, that is, showing that it was a realistic measure of job performance.

Bouman also claimed that the County had retaliated against her for filing a claim with the EEOC by denying her request for a transfer to another station. The County gave as reasons for the refusal to transfer "her attitude, immaturity and failure to understand her role as a Deputy Sheriff." The court, however, found such reason was "pretextual," and that in terms of reprimands and rewards, females were treated differently from males.[163]

For the relief, the court of appeals approved the district court's order that the County develop a "validated" sergeant exam, and hire female sergeants consistent with their percentage representation until the proper selection procedures are in place.[164]

In Johnson v Transportation Agency, Santa Clara County, CA,[165] the Court was faced with a male's challenge to the hiring of a female for a road dispatcher job pursuant to an affirmative action plan seeking to correct underrepresentation of women, where the qualifications for the job of the two were approximately equal. The Court held that employers could take into consideration the sex of the applicant where the hiring followed the guidelines of a proper affirmative action plan (this case is further discussed below in the section on Affirmative Action Agreements).

In the 1981 case of County of Washington v Gunther,[166] the Court was faced with the contention that the Equal Pay Act[167] had the effect of restricting Title VII sex-based claims to equal pay for equal work. Female jail guards, caring for women prisoners, alleged that they were paid lower wages than male guards and that part of that differential was attributable to intentional sex discrimination. It was conceded that female guards were not performing work equal to that of male guards, a standard for recovery under the Equal Pay Act. Nevertheless, the Court decided under Title VII, that the women guards were not limited to equal pay claims. Such a restriction would mean that Title VII claims could succeed only when there were males employed doing like work. Title VII allows a claim for sex discrimination where it can be shown that a woman is being intentionally paid less than a market analysis (available in this case) showed she was worth.

Another significant question arose in Arizona Governing Committee v Norris.[168] That case involved the question "whether Title VII... prohibits an employer from offering its employees the option of receiving retirement benefits from one of several companies selected by the employer, all of which pay a woman lower monthly retirement benefits than a man who has made the same contributions; and if there is such a Title VII violation, whether the relief to be awarded should be retroactive or prospective only. In a split decision, in which Justice O'Connor provided the swing vote, the Court decided that such an insurance arrangement, paying women lower retirement benefits than men, was a violation of Title VII, but because "[i]mposing such unanticipated financial burdens would come at a time when many States and local governments are struggling to meet substantial fiscal deficits,"[169] the liability will be prospective only.

In a rare opinion without a dissent, International Union, UAW v Johnson Controls,[170] decided that a company manufacturing batteries containing lead could not exclude women from such work on the supposition that such work might result in a health risk to them or to their unborn child. As formulated by the Court, the question was "whether an employer, seeking to protect potential fetuses, may discriminate against women just because of their ability to become pregnant."[171]

The Court rejected *Johnson Controls* argument that the company's concern for the unborn children constituted a BFOQ.

> Fertile women, as far as appears in the record, participate in the manufacture of batteries as efficiently as anyone else. Johnson Controls' professed moral and ethical concerns about the welfare of the next generation do not suffice to establish a BFOQ of female sterility.[172]

Seniority and Title VII

Seniority affects employee's promotions, transfers, benefits, vacations, pensions, and most important for our present consideration, layoffs and recalls. For different purposes, seniority may be calculated on the basis of job, departmental, bargaining unit, or plant seniority. Seniority has been a hard-won union benefit and has been thought of by both management and labor as an objective standard by which to allocate benefits among competing employees. In the case of layoffs and recalls, it has spawned the last hired, first fired result that falls most severely on those who have recently entered the employment picture—minorities and women.

In passing the Civil Rights Act of 1964 Congress specifically tried to protect the accrued rights of employees incorporated in seniority systems. Section 703(h) of that Act states:

> [I]t shall not be an unlawful employment practice for an employer to apply different standards of compensation, or different terms, conditions, or privileges of employment pursuant to a bona fide seniority or merit system . . . provided that such differences are not the result of an intention to discriminate because of race, color, religion, sex, or national origin. . . . [173]

Senators Joseph S. Clark and Clifford P. Case, floor managers of Title VII, submitted an interpretive memorandum stating that the section was intended to (1) affect no existing seniority rights; (2) operate only prospectively, and (3) permit different employee treatment because of seniority, particularly mentioning the last hired, first fired provisions of many contracts.[174] In effect, § 703(h) was to allow disparate employee treatment pursuant to a "bona fide seniority or merit system" so long as the "differences are not the result of an intention to discriminate because of race, color, religion, sex, or national origin." The term "bona fide" seniority system was left undefined and became an important issue in ensuing litigation.

Most seniority systems, because they were instituted at a time when women and minorities were customarily excluded from all but the least skilled and lowest paying jobs, have discrimination locked into their structures. Moreover, where layoffs and recalls are concerned, most labor contracts call for seniority to be calculated on a departmental rather than on a plant basis. For minorities and women who have just recently become eligible for jobs in higher paying departments, even where their plant seniority is high, their departmental seniority is likely to be low.

One commentator has suggested that

the pervasive institutionalization of seniority after 1935 should be understood as a policy decision arrived at by management, often in conjunction with unions, to meet the threat of unemployment by enhancing the security of some workers [white males] while heightening the insecurity of others. Although black unemployment levels have been high, and teenage black unemployment levels have been extremely high, white male workers over the age of thirty experienced very little unemployment in the postwar United States until the early 1980s.[175]

Courts have had to face questions as to whether in computing seniority for purposes of layoffs they can discount departmental seniority in favor of plant seniority. And for those who were discriminatorily denied employment in the past, whether courts can create "rightful place" seniority which would give protected groups constructive seniority from the time of the discriminatory hiring or transfer. Because seniority is inevitably a means of establishing priorities, in a time of scarce employment opportunities, any reordering of the seniority system must result in conflicts, not only between protected groups and their employers, but between these groups and labor unions, which in criminal justice agencies have principally represented white males.[176]

These issues first made their way to the Supreme Court in the 1976 case of Franks v Bowman Transportation Co.[177] Black applicants, who had been denied employment, sued Bowman and the employee union claiming various racial discriminatory practices. The district court found a pattern of discrimination in hiring, transfer and discharge of employees and that such practices were perpetuated in the company's union agreement. The issue, as seen by the Court, was whether nonemployee black applicants who applied for and were denied over-the-road (OTR) truck driver positions because of race and in violation of Title VII may be awarded seniority status retroactive to the dates of their employment application, that is, "rightful place" seniority.

The Court first concluded that § 703(h) did not bar an award of seniority. In arriving at the extent of the award, the Court recalled the "make whole" objective of Title VII.

That goal can be attained only by an award of the seniority credit [the employee] presumptively would have earned but for the wrongful treatment. . . . Without an award of seniority dating from the time when he was discriminatorily refused employment, an individual who applies for and obtains employment as an OTR driver pursuant to the District Court's order will never obtain his rightful place in the hierarchy of seniority according to which these various employment benefits are distributed. He will perpetually remain subordinate to persons who, but for the illegal discrimination, would have been in respect to entitlement to these benefits his inferiors.[178]

As the Court later said, the essence of *Franks* was "that 703(h) does not bar the award of retroactive seniority to job applicants who seek relief from an employer's post-Act hiring discrimination."[179]

But what about a seniority system otherwise bona fide that perpetuates *pre-Act* discrimination in lay-offs and recalls? That issue was decided in the *Teamsters* case.[180] The US Attorney General brought suit under § 707(a) of the Civil Rights Act of 1964[181] against the International Brotherhood of Teamsters, the employee union, and the employer, T.I.M.E.-D.C., Inc., charging a pattern and practice of discrimination in assigning minorities as lower-payed local city drivers rather than as higher-payed long distance drivers. The government sought "make whole" relief which would allow discriminatees to transfer to long-distance driver jobs without loss of company seniority. Under company-union rules, an employee transferring from department to department would lose all seniority and start at the bottom, locking minority workers "into inferior jobs and perpetuating prior discrimination by discouraging transfers to jobs as line drivers."[182]

The United States argued that "Because the company discriminated both before and after the enactment of Title VII, the seniority system is said to have operated to perpetuate the effects of both pre- and post-Act discrimination."[183] Under *Franks,* post-Act discriminatees may obtain relief without the necessity of attacking the seniority system. The Court recognized that the seniority system had a harsher effect on minorities because of pre-Act discriminatory practices. Were it not for § 703(h) such result would be unlawful under *Griggs,* but the Court concluded that the legislative history and the literal terms of the section indicated that Congress wished to extend a certain immunity to pre-Act seniority systems.

> Accordingly, we hold that an otherwise neutral, legitimate seniority system does not become unlawful under Title VII simply because it may perpetuate pre-Act discrimination.[184]

A seniority system that (1) applies equally to all, (2) is neither designed nor (3) maintained with a discriminatory purpose is "bona fide" under § 703(h) even though it does not extend retroactive seniority to pre-Act discriminatees. Thus, plaintiffs must show a discriminatory purpose before a seniority system will be found to fail the bona fide test. Otherwise said, Title VII permits retroactive seniority only to post-Act discriminatees. In the case of criminal justice agencies, post-Act would be after March 1972, the date when Title VII took effect for government bodies.

Teamsters dealt with seniority systems agreed to before Title VII was enacted. What of post-Civil Rights Act seniority plans that have a discriminatory impact on minorities and women? In American Tobacco Co v Patterson,[185] the Court, in a 5 to 4 opinion, decided that such post-Act plans were legal, regardless of their impact on minorities and women, as long as they were not adopted for a discriminatory purpose. Relying on the "plain language" of the section, the Court noted that "[o]n its face § 703(h) makes no distinction between pre- and post-Act seniority systems,"[186] and "[t]o be cognizable, a claim that a seniority system has a discriminatory impact must be accompanied by proof of a discriminatory purpose."[187] The majority of the Court concluded that in passing § 703(h)

> Congress was well aware in 1964 that the overall purpose of Title VII, to eliminate discrimination in employment, inevitably would, on occasion, conflict with the policy favoring minimal supervision by courts and other governmental agencies over the substantive terms of collective bargaining agreements. Section 703(h) represents the balance Congress struck between the two policies, and it is not this Court's function to upset that balance.[188]

Therefore, seniority systems, whether entered into before or after the 1964 Civil Rights Act, which result in "differentials among employees . . . are not unlawful employment practices unless the product of an intent to discriminate. . . . As § 703(h) was construed in *Teamsters,* there must be a finding of actual intent to discriminate on racial grounds on the part of those who negotiated or maintained the system."[189]

The Court was also presented with the question of "whether an employer charged with discrimination in hiring can toll the continuing accrual of backpay liability under Title VII simply by unconditionally offering the claimant the job previously denied, or whether the employer also must offer seniority retroactive to the date of the alleged discrimination."[190] Three women were wrongfully denied jobs at the Ford Motor Company because of their sex. Two years after they first made their application, Ford offered them jobs which did not include seniority retroactive to the date of their applications. When the women refused the jobs, the question became the legal effect of that job offer on their Title VII claim for back pay. Justice O'Connor, speaking for six members of the Court, relied on the language of § 706(g) which provided that where the trial court finds that an employer has intentionally engaged in unlawful discrimination the court *may* order affirmative action in "hiring of employees, with or without back pay."[191] Arguing that language in the section required employees to accept an unconditional job offer even without retroactive security,[192] the Court held that "absent [unspecified] special circumstances, the simple rule that the ongoing accrual of backpay liability is tolled when a Title VII claimant rejects the job he originally sought comports with Title VII's policy of making discrimination victims whole."[193]

In the more recent case of Lorance v AT & T Technologies,[194] the Court, in a six to three decision, continued to make it more difficult for minorities and women to challenge a seniority system established at a time when white males dominated the workplace. The case involved the question as to when the applicable statute of limitations begins to run so as to bar claims: at the time when the seniority agreement is changed, or at the time that change directly affects the plaintiff.

Plaintiffs were three women employees working for AT & T, an electronics manufacturer, as hourly-wage employees since the early 1970s.

> Until 1979 all hourly wage earners accrued competitive seniority exclusively on the basis of years spent in the plant, and a worker promoted to the more highly skilled and better paid "tester" position retained this plantwise seniority. A collective-bargaining agreement executed by [the union, also a defendant] on July 23, 1979, altered the manner of calculating tester seniority. Thenceforth a tester's seniority was to be determined not by length of plantwide service, but by time actually spent as a tester . . . The present action arises from that contractual modification.[195]

Although plaintiffs became testers between 1978 and 1980, when an "economic downturn" came in 1982, their low seniority under the 1979 collective-bargaining agreement resulted in their demotion. Had their seniority been calculated on the earlier plantwide seniority, they would not have been demoted. Plaintiffs claimed that the 1979 seniority agreement was an attempt to preserve a situation in which tester positions were almost exclusively held by men and therefore was sexually discriminatory under Title VII.

As the Court read the statute of limitations applicable to Title VII actions, their claim failed. Plaintiffs filed their action only after they were demoted in 1982, well within the 300 days from the alleged unfair employment practice. The Court decided, however, that the statute ran not from that 1982 date but from 1979, the time of the seniority agreement which changed their status.

Justice Marshall, writing for dissenters Justices Brennan and Blackmun, complained that the "harsh reality" of the decision applied

> even if the employee who subsequently challenges that [seniority] system could not reasonably have expected to be demoted or otherwise concretely harmed by the new system at the time of its adoption, and indeed, even if the employee was not working in the affected division of the company at the time of the system's adoption.[196]

Affirmative action agreements—the Weber case

Constant pressure from civil rights groups, minority and women's professional unions, and government agencies have brought some recalcitrant police departments and correctional agencies into affirmative action compliance. As discussed earlier in this chapter, Title VII law suits have had an important part to play in this movement.

Affirmative action plans have assumed two forms: those proposed by the government employer without court intervention, and consent decrees, where, following a successful Title VII action, the government agency and minority or women plaintiffs agree on an affirmative action plan. These cases usually arise when whites adversely affected by the proposed or agreed to affirmative action plan intervene complaining either that such an agreement is in violation of Title VII because the plan relies on racially-based hiring, or is in violation of their rights under the equal protection of the laws clause of the fourteenth amendment. Can a white male legally complain that he has been discriminated against in violation of Title VII because the plan provides for favored treatment of women or minority employees?

United Steelworkers of America v Weber[197] decided that such plans could legally reserve "for black employees 50% of the openings in an in-plant craft-training program until the percentage of black craftworkers in the plant is commensurate with the percentage of blacks in the local labor force."[198] As part of a 1974 collective bargaining agreement Kaiser Aluminum and Chemical Corporation and the United Steelworkers, the employee union, agreed to modify the "almost exclusively white craftwork force." This suit challenges that part of the plan reserving 50% of the on-the-job training openings for black employees.

Prior to the agreement the company hired as craftworkers only those with experience. Because blacks historically had been all but excluded from craft unions, they could rarely meet this requirement. Although 39% of the area labor force was black, only 1.83% of Kaiser's craftworkers was black. Based on other cases and available studies the Court took judicial notice that such racial exclusion from crafts was a national problem. Neither the company nor the union, however, admitted past discrimination, and the district court made no finding that they had engaged in discriminatory practices.

During the program's first year, 1974, on the basis of seniority, 13 employees were selected to participate. 7 were black and 6 white, but the most senior black had less seniority than several of the whites. One of these, Weber, brought suit urging that the plan was a violation of § 703(d) of Title VII which made it "an unlawful employment practice for any employer, [or] labor organization . . . controlling . . . on-the-job training programs to discriminate . . . because of his race. . . . "[199]

The Court first specified what it was deciding:

> The only question before us is the narrow statutory issue of whether Title VII *forbids* private employers and unions from voluntarily agreeing upon bona fide affirmative action plans that accord racial preferences in the manner and for the purposes provided in the Kaiser-USWA plan.[200]

Weber, in his arguments, said the Court, relied on a "literal interpretation" that Title VII forbade any racial preference. But in so arguing, the Court said, Weber overlooked the Act's legislative and historical context. "Congress' primary concern" was the economic plight of blacks, particularly the recognized fact that they were largely restricted to unskilled and semi-skilled jobs which were decreasing because of automation. Therefore, a principal purpose of the legislation was to open up occupations traditionally closed to blacks. Voluntary affirmative action was not precluded as one means of attaining that objective.

Replying to another Weber argument, the Court observed that § 703(j) states that Title VII shall not "be interpreted to *require* any employer . . . to grant preferential treatment . . . to any group because of race. . . . " The section does not say, however, that it shall not "be interpreted to *permit*" preferential treatment.[201] Congress might have so written the section had it wished to prohibit such agreements.

In finding the plan within the limits of employer-union action permitted by Title VII, the Court pointed out that

> [T]he plan does not unnecessarily trammel the interests of the white employees. The plan does not require the discharge of white workers and their replace-

ment with new black hirees.... Nor does the plan create an absolute bar
to the advancement of white employees; half of those trained in the program will be white. Moreover, the plan is a temporary measure.... Preferential selection of craft trainees ... will end as soon as the percentage of black
skilled craftworkers ... approximates the percentage of blacks in the local
labor force.[202]

In the case of Texas Department of Community Affairs v Burdine,[203]
the Court decided that "the employer has discretion to choose among
equally qualified candidates, provided the decision is not based upon
unlawful criteria."[204] In Johnson v Transportation Agency,[205] Justice
Brennan, speaking for the Court, applied that holding to a situation in
which the County government chose a woman over an equally qualified
man in carrying out the goals of an affirmative action plan to remedy the
underrepresentation of women in the workforce. Johnson, the male
employee who lost out to a woman for the job of road dispatcher, sued
claiming that in making the decision the employer "impermissibly took
into account the sex of the applicants in violation of Title VII.... "[206]
The issue posed by the facts was whether an employer could hire pursuant to an affirmative action plan that made the sex of the applicant one of
the factors in the hiring decision.

In entering into the Affirmative Action Plan the Agency provided the
following data as the reasons for the plan:

> women were represented in numbers far less than their proportion of the
> county labor force in both the Agency as a whole and in five of seven job
> categories. Specifically, while women constituted 36.4% of the area labor market,
> they composed only 22.4% of Agency employees. Furthermore, women work-
> ing at the Agency were concentrated largely in EEOC job categories traditionally
> held by women: women made up 76% of Office and Clerical Workers, but only
> 7.1% of Agency Officials and Administrators, 8.6% of Professionals, 9.7% of
> Technicians, and 22% of Service and Maintenance workers. As for the job
> classification relevant to this case, none of the 238 Skilled Craft Worker posi-
> tions was held by a woman ... , and [the employer] had never employed a
> woman as a road dispatcher.[207]

The Court viewed the issue as substantially the same as in *Weber:*
Weber found that taking race into account was consistent with Title VII's
objective of 'break[ing] down old patterns of racial segregation and
hierarchy.' "[208]

Following *Weber,* the Court asked "whether [the *Burdine*] decision was
made pursuant to a plan prompted by concerns similar to the employer
in *Weber.* Next, we must determine whether the effect of the plan on

males and non-minorities is comparable to the effect of the plan in that case."[209] Thus, the Court first asked "whether consideration of the sex of applicants for skilled craft jobs was justified by the existence of a 'manifest imbalance' that reflected underrepresentation of women in 'traditionally segregated job categories.' "[210] In determining whether sex as a factor in hiring may be taken into account the Court would normally make "a comparison of the percentage of minorities or women in the employer's work force with the percentage in the area labor market."[211] But where the job in question requires " 'special training,' . . . the comparison should be with those in the labor force who possess the relevant qualifications."[212]

Turning to the Agency Affirmative Action Plan, it was clear that the plan directed that "sex or race be taken into account for the purpose of remedying underrepresentation."[213] But in seeking this goal the Agency realized that its long-term goal of attaining the same percentage of women in the workplace as in the area labor market could not then be reached because of the lack of training that would qualify women for these jobs. Therefore, the "Plan . . . directed that annual short-term goals be formulated that would provide a more realistic indication of the degree to which sex should be taken into account in filling particular positions."[214] These "short-term" goals took into account "factors such as 'turnover, layoffs, lateral transfers, new job openings, retirements and availability of minorities, women and handicapped persons who possess the desired qualifications or potential for placement.' "[215]

The Court concluded that

> had the Plan simply calculated imbalances in all categories according to the proportion of women in the area labor pool, and then directed that hiring be governed solely by those figures, its validity fairly could be called into question. This is because analysis of a more specialized labor pool normally is necessary in determining underrepresentation in some positions. If a plan failed to take distinctions in qualifications into account in providing guidance for actual employment decisions, it would dictate mere blind hiring by the numbers. . . . [216]

It is important that the reasoning of Justice O'Connor be set forth because it was her concurrence that made possible a majority opinion. Her concurrence was based on the following factors:

1. "the sex [of the employee] was but one of numerous factors [the employer] took into account in arriving at his [hiring] decision;
2. "*No* persons are automatically excluded from consideration; *all* are able to have their qualifications weighed against those of other applicants";

3. "the Agency's Plan was intended to *attain* a balanced work force, not to maintain one"; and

4. Employment decisions "must rest on a multitude of practical, realistic factors."[217]

According to Justice O'Connor, the Court held as follows:

the Agency appropriately took into account as one factor the sex of [the employee] in determining that she should be promoted to the road dispatcher position. The decision to do so was made pursuant to an affirmative action plan that represents a moderate, flexible, case-by-case approach to effecting a gradual improvement in the representation of minorities and women in the Agency's work force.[218]

Justice Scalia, joined by the Chief Justice and Justice White, dissented, arguing that the effect of the majority view of Title VII, as interpreted by *Weber,* "effectively *requires* employers, public as well as private, to engage in intentional discrimination on the basis of race or sex,"[219] suggesting that because the majority has substituted "judicial improvisation for statutory text" of Title VII, *Weber* should be overruled.[220] This opinion, according to the dissent, is unlikely to "displease the world of corporate and governmental employers . . . for whom the cost of hiring less qualified workers is often substantially less—and infinitely more predictable than the cost of litigating Title VII cases. . . . In fact, the only losers in the process are the Johnsons of the country, for whom Title VII has been not merely repealed but actually inverted. The irony is that these individuals—predominantly unknown, unaffluent, unorganized—suffer this injustice at the hands of a Court fond of thinking itself the champion of the politically impotent."[221]

Applicability of *Weber* to criminal justice agencies

In assessing the significance of *Weber* for criminal justice agencies it should be noted that the case had the following characteristics: (1) Kaiser was a private concern; (2) there was no finding or admission by the company or union of discriminatory past conduct; (3) the plan aimed to correct a stated objective of the Act—to eliminate discrimination in jobs traditionally closed to minorities; (4) the plan displaced no white employees; and (5) it was temporary and terminated when blacks in the plant were proportionate to those in the local labor force.

One case, Baker v City of Detroit,[222] is of particular interest because it spells out the social and economic conflicts leading to the adoption of Detroit's affirmative action plan. The attitude of the department towards its black officers was reflected in its treatment of the black community and the resulting view that the community had of the department. As stated by the court:

> There is extensive evidence in the record which shows that the Police Department and the black community were at each other's throats at least until the early 1970's. A phrase which was constantly used at trial was that the Police Department was regarded as an "occupation army" in the black community and was treated as such. Precinct stations in the black community looked like armed fortresses; they were shot at by passing cars of black youths. Officers were afraid to venture into the community for fear of being harassed or worse.[223]

The department first aggressively started to recruit blacks in 1971 through an extensive advertising campaign in the black community, and by changes in written and oral examinations. But it was not until 1973 that discriminatory hiring practices were eliminated. Discrimination against women ended in December 1973 as a result of affirmative action litigation. The turning point for blacks came in July 1974 when Detroit adopted a new city charter that required the mayor to appoint a Board of Police Commissioners (BPC) to which he would submit promotions recommended by the chief of police. That same month the BPC adopted an affirmative action plan, the subject of this suit, selecting a 50/50 black-white hiring ratio because that was the relationship between the races in the city. This plan was bitterly opposed by the white-dominated Detroit Police Lieutenants and Sergeants Association and defended by the black Guardians of Michigan. These two groups ended up on opposite sides of the law suit.

The challenge to the affirmative action plan by the white sergeants was summarized by the district court:

> It is undisputed that the City's affirmative action plan promoted officers on the basis of race and that absent affirmative action, white officers would have been promoted where black officers were in fact promoted. By choosing equal numbers of white and black officers according to their rank on the promotional eligibility list, the Department effectively bypassed a group of white officers.
>
> Plaintiffs claim that this was blatant discrimination against them as whites which is illegal under the above mentioned statutes and the Constitution. . . . Reconciling the rights of white and black officers is not easy. Whether the City acted reasonably when it adopted its affirmative action plan is the principal question for this Court.[224]

"Reasonableness" of the plan was crucial because "Weber stands for the general proposition that voluntary affirmative action is proper if it is reasonable under all the circumstances."[225] The court noted that, unlike *Weber,* here the employer admitted past discrimination, thus giving more justification for such voluntary compliance. Plaintiffs complained that white sergeants were unfairly passed over. But, said the court, the same thing occurred in *Weber.* Moreover, even if as claimed the white sergeants were more qualified than the blacks, "affirmative action promotions would still be permissible given the broad deference *Weber* gives to employers."[226] Like *Weber,* Detroit's plan is a temporary measure, not meant to be an attempt to permanently eliminate racial imbalance. These principles should apply even more strongly to public than to private employees.

In considering the question of "reasonableness" the court looked to the "operational" needs of the department. It reviewed at some length the bad relations the department had with the black community and concluded that the presence of an all white department was instrumental in creating such a condition, and that "The presence of black officers was a critical factor in changing the black community's perception of the police and winning their cooperation in fighting crime."[227]

In Detroit Police Officers' Assn v Young[228] a companion case to *Baker,* plaintiff police officers' association and a number of white police officers complained that on the basis of the same affirmative action plan described in *Baker* they were passed over for promotion to sergeant in favor of black officers with lower eligibility ratings. The white officers argued that the plan was a violation of Title VII and the equal protection of the laws clause of the fourteenth amendment. After surveying the same history of discriminatory practices that has been set forth above for the *Baker* case, the court turned to *Weber* and concluded that "the question is not what Title VII requires or what a court might order to remedy a proven Title VII violation. Rather, the question is what voluntary actions may lawfully be taken."[229] The court then looked to the "reasonableness" of the 50/50 promotion ratio:

> The reasonableness test includes a determination whether the affirmative action plan is "substantially related" to the objectives of remediation of prior discrimination and improved law enforcement. A racial preference plan is reasonable when it provides an effective remedy for past discrimination without unnecessarily trammeling the interests of white candidates for promotion [citing *Weber*]. . . . On remand, the district court must consider . . . the urgency of effectuating the state's objectives, practical limitations in doing so, and the degree of hardship to be borne by whites. However, concern for the interest

of white employees cannot be allowed to thwart achievement of the state's goals. It is reasonable for some persons innocent of wrongdoing to bear some burden in order to correct the harsh effects of a grievous wrong of constitutional dimensions and enhance public safety by improved law enforcement.[230]

The court pointed out that white employees were not losing vested employment rights but "at most, . . . an expectation of promotion under certain conditions."[231] Finally, the plan satisfied *Weber's* requirement that it be a "temporary measure to eliminate a manifest racial imbalance, not a measure to maintain a given balance."[232]

Weber's application to consent decrees

In the 1986 case of Local Number 93 v City of Cleveland,[233] black and Hispanic firefighters, employed by the City of Cleveland, claimed that they had been intentionally discriminated against because of their race and national origin in the awarding of promotions. After extensive litigation in which the city resisted the suit, the city and plaintiffs' organization, the Vanguards, entered into negotiations terminating in a consent decree:

> [T]he decree required that the City immediately make 66 promotions to Lieutenant, 32 promotions to Captain, 16 promotions to Battalion Chief and 4 promotions to Assistant Chief. These promotions were to be based on a promotional examination that had been administered during the litigation. The 66 initial promotions to Lieutenant were to be evenly split between minority and nonminority firefighters. . . . Promotions from the lists produced by these examinations were to be made in accordance with specified promotional "goals" that were expressed in terms of percentages and were different for each rank.[234]

Both the union for all firefighters and the US, which filed an *amicus curiae* brief, argued that Section 706(g) of Title VII "precludes a court from awarding ["race-conscious"] relief under Title VII that may benefit individuals who were not the actual victims of the employer's discrimination."[235]

The pertinent sentence of Section 706(g) reads:

> "*[n]o order of the court shall require* the admission or reinstatement of an individual as a member of a union, or *the hiring, reinstatement, or promotion of an individual as an employee,* or the payment to him of any back pay, *if such individual* was refused admission, suspended, or expelled, or *was refused employment or advancement* or was suspended or discharged *for any reason other than discrimination on account of race,* color, religion, sex, or national origin or in violation of section 2000e-3(a) of this title." 42 USC § 2000e-5(g).[236]

After examining their prior decisions, including *Weber,* and the legislative history of § 706(g), the Court concluded:

whatever the limitations Congress placed in § 706(g) on the power of federal courts to impose obligations on employers or unions to remedy violations of Title VII, those simply do not apply when the obligations are created by a consent decree.[237]

Therefore, even though § 706(g) might preclude a court from entering such a decree after a trial, the voluntary aspect of the consent decree permits race-conscious relief such as ordered in this case.

In Martin v Wilks,[238] the Court, in another five to four opinion, decided that firefighters who claimed that they were being denied promotions in favor of less qualified firefighters because of a previously entered consent decree, could nevertheless now challenge employment decisions taken pursuant to that decree. Such a decision opens up all consent decrees to challenge by disgruntled "sideline-sitters," that is, those who declined to enter the litigation at an earlier stage.

This consent decree was the result of a 1974 Title VII suit by black plaintiffs claiming that Birmingham, Alabama authorities racially discriminated in their hiring and promotion practices. A consent decree provided for hiring and promotion of blacks in equal numbers with whites until blacks attained their percentage in the local labor market.

After the decree was entered, white firefighters brought this suit claiming they were denied promotions because of their race in favor of less-qualified blacks. Their claim was dismissed by the district court as an impermissible collateral (side) attack on the consent decree. The court of appeals reversed, and the Supreme Court affirmed the decision of the court of appeals, holding that "a voluntary settlement in the form of a consent degree between one group of employees and their employer cannot possibly 'settle,' voluntarily or otherwise, the conflicting claims of another group of employees who do not join in the agreement."[239] This principle applies even when the complaining parties knew of the law suit and did not attempt to intervene.

Two results may be expected from this case: (1) increased attacks on consent degrees by white males, and (2) reluctance on the part of employers to enter into consent decrees which thereafter may be subject to attack.

Reverse discrimination, equal protection, and § 1981

In an economy with scarce desirable jobs, affirmative action, which prefers some groups over others, is bound to create dissatisfaction among newly "disfavored" groups. Legally, this discontent is translated into claims of reverse discrimination. White claimants have principally relied on Title VII, equal protection of the laws, and 42 USC § 1981 (discussed in chapter 1).

Title VII purportedly had been enacted to protect the employment rights of blacks. Does it also apply to whites? One of the major principles proposed by this book is that rights once granted to one social group cannot be contained but will spread to other groups on the same economic level. McDonald v Sante Fe Trail Transportation Co[240] illustrates this point: whether Title VII prohibitions applied equally to majority white as well as to minority black employees, or specifically "whether a complaint alleging that white employees charged with misappropriating property from their employer were dismissed from employment, while a black employee similarly charged was not dismissed, states a claim under Title VII."[241]

The facts in the case are simple. Three employees, two white and one black, were charged with stealing items belonging to the company. The white employees were fired and the black retained. Both the employees' union and the EEOC rejected the complaint of the white employees who then brought this Title VII claim. Relying on the words of § 703(a)(1) that "prohibits the discharge of 'any individual' because of 'such individual's race,' " the Court held "that Title VII prohibits racial discrimination against the white petitioners in this case upon the same standards as would be applicable were they Negroes. . . . "[242] The Court rejected the company's claim that because the complaining employee was engaged in a serious crime Title VII does not apply. "While Sante Fe may decide that participation in a theft of cargo may render an employee unqualified for employment, this criterion must be "applied, alike to members of all races, and Title VII is violated if, as petitioners alleged, it was not."[243]

Equal protection claims

Perhaps because cases like *Weber* and the appellate cases earlier cited have approved Title VII affirmative action plans, white complainants have turned to constitutional remedies, particularly the equal protection clause of the fourteenth amendment. Further, while *Weber* applies most clearly to private employers, the equal protection clause applies to public employers. Moreover, such plans may be seen as purposeful discrimination, the very essence of equal protection violation. Although Washington v Davis[244] involved the due process clause of the fifth amendment it set forth the proof requirements as well for equal protection violations. Black officers from the District of Columbia Metropolitan Police Department complained that a test used in recruiting was in violation of their rights under the due process clause because it had a disproportionate impact on blacks. Plaintiffs sued under the due process clause rather than Title VII because at the time the suit was filed (1970), public employers were not covered by Title VII.

Following the reasoning in *Griggs,* the circuit court concluded that even though the employer was not shown to have had a discriminatory purpose in using the test, the result of a substantially higher percentage of whites passing than blacks could not be justified on the basis of its measurement of job performance. The Supreme Court reversed, holding that the circuit court had erroneously applied the *statutory* standards of *Griggs* to a *constitutional* issue.

The Court pointed out that the "central purpose of the Equal Protection Clause of the Fourteenth Amendment is the prevention of official conduct discriminating on the basis of race. . . . But our cases have not embraced the proposition that a law or other official act, without regard to whether it reflects a racially discriminatory purpose is unconstitutional *solely* because it has a racially disproportionate impact."[245] Therefore, in a claim depending on constitutional grounds rather than on the statutory base of Title VII, a plaintiff cannot rely solely on disproportionate impact but must establish a discriminatory purpose on the part of the employer.

A third opinion that has affected equal protection reverse discrimination claims is Regents of the University of California v Bakke.[246] Bakke, a white applicant to medical school, complained about an affirmative action plan that admitted minority students over Bakke even though Bakke had a higher score judged by admittance criteria. The plan reserved 16 of 100 places for qualified minorities. The *Bakke* opinion spanned more than 150 pages without producing a majority. Four judges lined up on each side, with Justice Powell providing the swing vote that held the medical school's plan in violation of the equal protection clause of the fourteenth amendment and Title VI of the Civil Rights Act of

1964, which prohibits exclusion of persons from programs receiving federal funds on the basis of race, color, or national origin.[247]

It is Justice Powell's analysis that has become the guiding light in subsequent reverse discrimination litigation involving criminal justice agencies. Because Justice Powell was engaged in interpreting the equal protection clause his first task was to determine if the matter under discussion required strict scrutiny or reasonable relationship analysis. Given that the issue dealt with a racial admissions policy, it was simple to decide that the university's rejection of Bakke called for strict scrutiny analysis.[248] Justice Powell next sought to determine if the state had a compelling interest to make such a classification. The university argued that it had a compelling interest in maintaining a diverse student body. Though Justice Powell granted that this was "clearly a constitutionally permissible goal for an institution of higher education[249] ... ethnic diversity, however, is only one element in a range of factors a university properly may consider in attaining a goal of a heterogeneous student body."[250] The question is "whether the program's racial classification is necessary to promote this interest."[251] Justice Powell suggested that race may constitutionally serve as one of several factors, a "plus, ... without the factor of race being decisive when compared" with other qualities.[252] Such a program would treat "each applicant as an individual in the admissions process."[253] It was this failure to afford Bakke "the chance to compete with applicants from the preferred groups for the special admissions seats,"[254] thereby disregarding his individual rights, that proved fatal. Nevertheless, the state may legitimately have "a properly devised admissions program involving the competitive consideration of race and ethnic origin."[255]

It has been difficult to maneuver the rocky waters between *Weber,* which approved race-based affirmative action plans in the private sector, and *Bakke,* which disapproved a race-based affirmative action plan in the public sector. In Johnson v Transportation Agency,[256] discussed above with the Weber case, the Court allowed the use of sex as one of the hiring criteria. But as stated earlier, the disagreements among the justices on the proper interpretation of Title VII makes the water in this area very murky indeed.

In United States v Paradise,[257] another 5 to 4 decision, the Court found the district court had power to order the promotion of blacks while the dissent believed the district court could not impose such a "quota" without first considering certain less stringent alternatives. The issue was: whether relief awarded in the case, in the form of a one-black-for-one-white promotion requirement to be applied as an interim measure to state trooper promotions in the Alabama Department of Public Safety, is permissible under the equal protection guarantee of the fourteenth amendment. Although the suit was originally filed by the National Association for the Advancement of Colored People (NAACP), the United States joined the suit as a party plaintiff. As the suit developed, the United States reversed itself and opposed the relief granted plaintiff blacks.

Facts developed at trial showed that at the time the suit was filed in 1972, "in the thirty-seven year history of the patrol there has never been a black trooper and the only Negroes ever employed by the department have been nonmerit system laborers."[258] As the district court proceded over the years from hearing to hearing the department was ordered but constantly stalled in supplying a promotion plan that was non-discriminatory. After twelve years of hearings, corporal was still the highest rank attained by blacks. There were only four of these, and no acceptable promotion procedures had been submitted. In 1984, the district court ordered "at least 50% of the promotions to corporal must be awarded to black troopers, if qualified black candidates were available."[259]

Although the United States conceded that the district court's order serves a compelling state "interest the Government insists that it was not narrowly tailored to accomplish its purposes—to remedy past discrimination and eliminate its lingering effects. . . . "[260] The Court considered the following factors to determine "whether race-conscious remedies are appropriate . . . the necessity for the relief and the efficacy of alternative remedies, the flexibility and duration of the relief, including the availability of waiver provisions; the relationship of the numerical goals to the relevant labor market; and the impact of the relief on the rights of third parties."[261]

After finding that the order was "flexible, waivable, and temporary in application,"[262] the Court asked whether the order imposed "an unacceptable burden on innocent third parties."[263] Because the one-for-one ratio required no layoffs or discharges, only postponed promotions of qualified whites, and required black candidates to be qualified so that white candidates may compete with them; any advantage that black candidates would have in that competition would be only temporary. Finally, the Court concluded that the decree was "narrowly tailored" to achieve its purpose of eliminating unconstitutional discrimination. With reference to the equal protection point, the Court concluded that in shaping this remedy, the district judge "properly balanced the individual and collective interests at stake, including the interests of the white troopers eligible for promotion. . . ."[264]

In Local 28 of Sheet Metal Workers v EEOC,[265] in which a union was found guilty of discriminating against nonwhite workers in recruitment, selection, training, and admission to the union, the Court held that "in appropriate circumstances" (there was "pervasive and egregious discrimination," the goals set by the district court were necessary to combat the effects of such discrimination, the goals are not set to maintain racial balance but "as a means by which [the court] can measure [the union's] compliance with its orders," the goals and the court's order are "temporary measures," and the order does not "unnecessarily trammel the interests of white employees"), the district court may "order preferential relief benefitting individuals who are not the actual victims of discrimination as a remedy for violations of Title VII. . . ."[266]

Recent Supreme Court cases have turned the emphasis from protecting groups to that of protecting individuals, thus making the challenges in reverse discrimination suits by "trammeled" white males more legitimate. In Krupa v New Castle County,[267] white patrolmen claimed their equal protection rights were violated by a sergeant's examination that used racial preferences to exclude them.

Because of a number of assertions in the past of discrimination against blacks and women, and reports by the EEOC and other regulatory agencies of disparity between numbers of blacks and women in the police force compared to those in the general population, the County passed an ordinance setting forth a County Affirmative Action Program under which future promotions were to be made. The Program required that "the Personnel Director shall certify the names of the three highest ranked *members of a protected class* [women and/or members of minority groups] on the list."[268]

Pursuant to this plan, In order to select a sergeant, the County placed qualified individuals passing a validated test in bands. Three positions for sergeants were filled; the two highest qualified whites were selected from band 1, and one black male, who had scored somewhere between 45th and 69th in band 3. Thus, according to the court, the chief of police who selected the black male, ignored "the validated testing process [which] demonstrated that those who scored in band 1 were more qualified than those who placed in lower bands."[269]

The district court concluded that recent Supreme Court decisions required it to apply strict scrutiny analysis to a "race based affirmative action plan." Thus, a compelling governmental interest is required to justify a racial classification together with "a showing that the means selected to effectuate that objective are narrowly tailored to meet that goal. . . . Put another way, an affirmative action plan adopted by a public employer may satisfy the burdens imposed by Title VII and yet not pass constitutional muster,"[270] a frightening, although as we will see, not unlikely prospect.

In order to satisfy the first prong, a compelling interest, there must be some "showing of prior discrimination by the public employer to justify the remedial use of race-preferential measures."[271] The County's effort to meet this prong by pointing to the disparity between percentages of blacks in the police force and those in the general population was rejected: "the Supreme Court itself has indicated that there are many reasons for a statistical disparity other than discrimination."[272] The County was therefore unable to show a compelling interest for the racial preference in promotions. For the second prong, whether the Plan was sufficiently narrowly tailored to achieve the goal, the court suggested an alternative constitutionally allowable plan, one that selected the top three candidates, and then allowed race to be considered as one of the factors in the final selection.[273] But in the selection procedure used, ignoring the objective test results constituted an "arbitrary and subjective racial preference."[274] The court therefore granted the plaintiff's motion for summary judgment invalidating the Plan.

Section 1981 as a remedy for reverse discrimination

Section 1981, by virtue of the fact that it provides that "citizens, of every race and color . . . shall have the same right . . . to make and enforce contracts"[275] can be used by whites who complain that affirmative action plans unconstitutionally deprive them of equal treatment with respect to employment contracts. On trial, the question becomes whether plaintiffs must show purposeful discrimination or merely the disparate impact demanded by Title VII. Based on the section's legislative history, the Court has decided that "like the Equal Protection Clause [§ 1981] can be violated only by purposeful discrimination."[276]

Competing rights: seniority and layoffs as a Title VII issue

As a result of the relative boom times in the 1960s and the continuing pressures by minorities to share in this larger economic pie, substantial economic gains were registered by minorities in the 1960s and by women in the 1970s. Among nonwhites, 20 years of age and over, unemployment rates dropped from 11% in 1961 to less than 5% in 1969. Likewise, women's participation in the labor market increased from 33.9% to 44.7% in the period 1950 to 1973.[277]

In a capitalist (or perhaps in all industrial societies) political rights are limited by the economic capacities of that system to satisfy those rights, and that when such a squeeze ensues, the role of the courts is to pare down political rights to conform to economic limits. Such a situation arises as a result of the boom and bust nature of the US economy.[278] Although minorities and women made impressive gains in employment opportunities, in part as a result of affirmative action programs, those gains were impressive only because of the near zero point at which they began. In examining the permanency of recently acquired employment opportunities, it is necessary to look at the economic results of the recessions of 1974–75 and 1980–83. In a recession period, recently hired employees are also the first laid off. In lean times conflicting claims of different parts of the working class collide. Hard fought rights to seniority gained in the 1940s and 50s, principally for white males, contend against rights to equal employment gained in the 1960s and 70s for minorities and women.

Impact of recessions on minority and female employment

In a 1977 report on the last hired first fired problem, the US Commission on Civil Rights observed:

> [J]ob loss is an integral part of the employment pattern for many nonwhite and female workers, regardless of the overall conditions of the economy. When the current recession struck, it hit these vulnerable workers disproportionately hard. . . . [J]ob loss unemployment – layoffs – rose most sharply during the current recession in those blue-collar occupations where minorities are employed in greater numbers. . . . [B]lack male workers [are overrepresented] among the recent job losers. In early 1975 blacks accounted for about 18 percent (725,000) of the job loss employment, though they were only 11 percent of the total labor force.[279]

Because women are disproportionally employed in low-paying trade and service industries, they have been less affected by lay-offs. Where, however, they work in "male" jobs such as that of police officer, they are subject to the same rate of layoffs as recently-hired minority workers. Layoffs take on legal content when they are made on the basis of the time the employee has been employed. Employees with the least seniority, usually minority workers or women, are laid off first. In a 1975 survey of major collective bargaining agreements, it was found that 90 percent contained layoff provisions, of which 85% took seniority into consideration.[280]

Almost every employer contemplating layoffs uses the last hired first fired principle. For the 1974–75 recession this has meant that where minorities represented 10 to 12% of the workforce, they accounted for 60–70% of layoffs. Out of 25,930 NYC police officers, 680 were female. 371 of these, all of whom had been hired since January 1973, were laid off in mid-1975.[281]

Detroit, during 1979, laid off approximately 1100 police officers, about 75% of whom were black, largely because these officers had the least seniority. As explained earlier in this chapter, the Detroit police department did not begin hiring numbers of black police officers until 1974.[282] Looked at over the period of black freedom, blacks, other minorities and women, have been used by employers as a reserve army of unemployed which would be called in as needed in emergencies and good times, and layed off during bad.[283]

Application of seniority-layoff cases to criminal justice agencies

In Acha v Beame,[284] women police officers of the NYC police department sought to enjoin a layoff that would have reduced the number of female officers by 73.5% while the reduction for males would have been 23.9%. The case had been appealed on a procedural matter but in the course of its opinion, the court set forth the proof requirements necessary for seniority relief. Plaintiffs must first establish a post-Act (after March 1972) Title VII violation: that after that date the department maintained a policy which limited female hiring, assignment, transfer, promotion, or discharge. The district court may then consider the award of retroactive seniority to the effective date of the Act, the criterion being as for all equitable relief, to seek to "recreate the conditions and relationships" that would have existed if there had been no unlawful discrimination.[285]

Whether plaintiffs, who had been discriminated against by a post-Act hiring procedure, could obtain retroactive seniority (a question earlier decided in *Franks* as to a private company) was presented as to a police department in the *Guardian* cases.[286] Initiated as a result of the same last hired, first fired layoff in June 1975 as in *Acha*, minority New York City police officers charged that but for a discriminatory examination they would have been hired earlier and thus would have had enough seniority to resist layoffs. In addition to claims under Title VII, the plaintiffs also asked for relief under § 1981 (discussed above), and Title VI (treated hereafter).

Relying on *Acha*, the court of appeals concluded that the challenged examinations did indeed result in a Title VII violation in that they had a disproportionate impact on minorities. No evidence, however, was found of intentional discrimination on the part of the municipal employer. Defendants tried to bring their hiring system under the immunity cloak of *Teamsters* by arguing that since the hiring system was not designed to be discriminatory it must be a bona fide merit system within the meaning of § 703(h). The court rejected this approach stating that "[i]t is one thing to utilize the system that locks in the effects of past discriminatory hiring decisions; it is a very different thing to lock in a discriminatory method of making hiring decisions."[287] The circuit court therefore affirmed the district court position that "the only effect *Teamsters* has on a post-Act discriminatory refusal to hire claim is to limit awards of compensatory seniority to the effective date of Title VII."[288] The court determined that for both Title VI and § 1981, relief could be obtained only where plaintiffs could show that they had been subjected to purposeful employment discrimination. But since no intentional discrimination had been shown, plaintiffs were limited to their Title VII relief.

Title VI claims

Title VI became important to the *Guardian* plaintiffs because *Teamsters* had limited Title VII relief to discrimination occurring after March 24, 1972, the date when the act became applicable to local governments. In their complaint, therefore, plaintiffs relied as well on Title VI, which applied to such discrimination since its enactment in 1964. Title VI reads as follows:

> No person in the United States shall, on the ground of race, color, or national origin, be excluded from participation in, be denied the benefits of, or be subjected to discrimination under any program or activity receiving Federal financial assistance.[289]

Because almost every major municipality had received some form of federal assistance, municipal employers were generally subject to claims under Title VI.

In Guardians Assn v Civ Serv Comn of City of NY,[290] black and hispanic members of the NYC police department alleged they were discriminated against in entrance exams. Although they had passing scores and were hired, because of the discrimination, they argued they were hired later than they otherwise would have been; if they had been hired when they should have been, they would have had enough seniority to avoid the layoff.

In deciding the case, the Court considered the following questions: Could private plaintiffs bring suit to enforce the provisions of Title VI? If so, what proof is to be required—purposeful discrimination or discriminatory impact? Once discrimination was proved, to what relief is the plaintiff entitled? In a multi-opinion decision in which Justice White, speaking for the majority, became the swing vote, it was decided that private plaintiffs did have an action under Title VI; that such a claim could be maintained for both intentional and disparate discriminatory action, but that prospective injunctive relief only was to be permitted. As the majority read the statute, compensatory relief was not allowed, at least where no intentional discrimination had been shown. Thus, the possibility of compensation was held out to a victim of purposeful discrimination.

The rationale underlying the decision poses dangers for civil rights advocates. Justice White reasoned that while Title VI legislative history did not itself show a legislative intention to make discriminatory impact a basis for relief, rules issued by regulatory agencies did so, and those regulations were consistent with the purposes of Title VI. Such an interpretation permits regulatory agencies, by merely changing their regulations, to reduce the scope of Title VI coverage to cases in which intentional discrimination can be proved, a near impossible task.

Seniority and layoffs as competing rights

The current economic crunch has brought many cities to their fiscal knees. They have often sought to alleviate their distress through extensive layoffs of city workers. This act, in turn, has brought into conflict several of the legal doctrines heretofore discussed—seniority, consent decrees, minority rights and counter claims of reverse discrimination. This witch's brew was served up to the courts in Boston Chapter NAACP v Beecher,[291] a case which had as bizarre a history as the events that produced it. Layoffs resulting from budgetary restrictions on city finances set the stage for conflicting claims between minority workers' rights under earlier consent decrees and majority workers' rights under statutorily mandated seniority. As a result of a suit brought by black and hispanic police officers, the Boston police department (BPD) had entered into consent decrees providing for minority hiring. During the years the decree was in force, minority representation had substantially increased. When, because of financial constraints, the city decided to reduce the size of its police force, it was required by a Massachusetts statute to do so on the basis of seniority—last hired, first fired—a means that would have decimated the ranks of the newly-hired minorities. Blacks and hispanics, who had filed the original Title VII suit, returned to ask that the decree, which was silent on the layoff question, be modified to maintain the gains that minorities had won. The district court thereupon modified its decree prohibiting the BPD from reducing the percentage of blacks and hispanics below the level which obtained before the Spring 1981 reduction in forces was put into effect. The police union, representing the white majority police, then appealed to the 1st circuit court of appeals.

That court found that the case involved "three fundamental. issues: did the district court have the power to modify the consent decrees and, if so, did its orders impermissibly supersede a valid Massachusetts civil service statute or unconstitutionally impose reverse discrimination."[292]

As the court stated, "[t]he statistics are undisputed" as to the facts of departmental discrimination:

> At the time of the original filing of these actions, racial discrimination had led to the virtual exclusion of blacks and hispanics from Boston's Police and Fire Departments. In 1970, only 65 of 2,805 police officers were blacks or hispanic, representing but 2.3 percent of the total.... In contrast the minority population of Boston was more than 16 percent in 1970 ... and approximately 23 percent by 1974.[293]

As a result of the district court's remedial orders,

> between 1974 and 1980, the Boston Police Department hired 492 officers, of whom 213 (43 percent) were black or hispanic. As of July 6, 1981, 224 out of a total of 1,912 officers were black or hispanic [11.7%].[294]

The layoff program would have a "devastating" effect on this newly achieved integration.

> The police department planned to lay off 252 officers, of whom 122 were black or hispanic. Of the officers to be laid off, 48 percent were minority, which

comprised 54.5 percent of the department's entire complement of minority officers. . . . By mid-August 1981 only 103 of 1,660 police officers would have been black or hispanic, and minority representation would have fallen from 11.7 percent to 6.2 percent.[295]

It was also possible that future layoffs might worsen this record. The threshold question was whether the district court was empowered to modify the prior consent decrees as a result of changed conditions brought on by layoffs. By looking at the overall purpose of these decrees, the court concluded that the goal was to shape "ongoing relief so as to eliminate the *condition* precipitating the original decrees: gross discriminatory underrepresentation of persons in the fire and police departments who are not members of the 'prevailing white culture' . . . [A] court of equity, upon a sufficient showing," has the power " 'to modify an injunction in adaptation to changed conditions though it was entered by consent.' "[296]

Ironically, events after the decision in the Boston layoff case illustrate the continued political dominance of the "prevailing white culture." The result of the district court's order was that "several hundred senior white officers were laid off while blacks with less seniority remained on the job." In the meantime, a petition for certiorari was granted by the Supreme Court. That case was never heard by the Court because the legislation reinstating the laid off police officers and firefighters had the effect of mooting the issues. The Court therefore dismissed the petition.

Among other things, the case exposed the Reagan administration's weak commitment to civil rights when it filed a brief supporting the position of the "predominantly white police and firefighters' unions."[297] Of more significance was the reaction of the Massachusetts legislature to the plight of the white officers. To protect that group, it first legitimatized the seniority procedures in case of layoffs and when that strategy failed, it provided funds to permanently protect this group from unemployment. Query, if minorities had been the ones laid off, whether the legislature would have as diligently come to their aid.

The issue was not laid to rest because essentially the same question was presented in Memphis Firefighters Local Union No 1784 v Stots.[298] As in the Boston layoff case, all white firefighters had been returned to work and therefore, in the Supreme Court, the losing white firefighters met the objection that the reinstatement of the laid-off firefighters made the case moot—that is, that there was no longer anything for the Court to decide. Therefore, the minorities argued, the case should be dismissed.

The original plaintiffs took this stance because they were unsure what reception the Burger Court would give to their claim. As it turned out, their apprehension was justified. First, the Court held that the case was not moot because "the judgment below will have a continuing effect on the City's management of the Department. . . ."[299] It then faced the main issue: "whether the District Court exceeded its powers in entering an injunction requiring white employees to be laid off, when the otherwise applicable seniority system would have called for the layoff of black employees with less seniority."[300]

The Court made explicit in its decision that it was operating from values different from those of the district court:

> As our cases have made clear Title VII protects bona fide seniority systems, and it is inappropriate to deny an innocent employee the benefits of his seniority in order to provide a remedy in a pattern or practice suit such as this.[301]

In overriding the seniority system, said the Supreme Court, the district court had surpassed its authority. Earlier cases had made it

> clear that mere membership in the disadvantaged class is insufficient to warrant a seniority award; each individual must prove that the discriminatory practice had an impact on him. Even when an individual shows that the discriminatory practice has an impact on him, he is not automatically entitled to have a non-minority employee laid off to make room for him. He may have to wait until a vacancy occurs, and if there are non-minority employees on layoff, the Court must balance the equities in determining who is entitled to the job. Here, there was no finding that any of the blacks protected from layoff had been a victim of discrimination and no award of competitive seniority to any of them. Nor had the parties in formulating the consent decree purported to identify any specific employee entitled to particular relief other than those listed in the exhibits attached to the decree. It therefore seems that in light of *Teamsters*, the Court of Appeals imposed on the parties as an adjunct of settlement something that could not have been ordered had the case gone to trial and the plaintiffs proved that a pattern or practice of discrimination existed.[302]

Thus, the Court reduces an important social conflict between major parts of the working class over the lack of sufficient work for all of them to a conflict between individuals of each group for the same job.

In another decision, the Court, by a 5 to 4 decision, held that an attempt by a Board of Education to use layoffs as a means to accomplish the valid purpose of retaining minority teachers was nevertheless a violation of the Equal Protection Clause.[303] The Board, in retaining tenured teachers over probationary/minority teachers, breached a union contract which provided for the retention of minority teachers in case of layoffs. Because "layoffs impose the entire burden of achieving racial equality on particular individuals, often resulting in serious disruption of their lives,"[304] such a remedy must be more narrowly tailored than it was in this case where the court based its remedy merely on the desire to maintain the number of minority members so as to serve as a "role model" for minority students.

Layoffs represent the means by which employers attempt to shift the burden of the boom and bust cycle, endemic to the capitalist system, to the worker. It is one instance of the employment at will rule discussed in chapter 6. Unions try to protect workers by collective bargaining agreements which require that in the event of layoffs, workers be laid off according to their seniority. As we have seen, such a system usually shifts the burden to minorities with short tenure on the job. In the case of Grace v Local Union 759,[305] the Court was faced with the complicated legal maneuvering of one employer caught between its obligations to women and blacks and claims by male workers based on seniority rights. The company had discriminated against blacks and women. When challenged by the EEOC, the company entered into a conciliation agreement, which among other things, covered possible layoffs of minorities and women. Because of economic conditions, the company laid off some of its workers according to the terms of the conciliation agreement. Such a layoff, however, conflicted with the last-hired, first-fired, seniority provisions of the collective bargaining agreement with the white majority union. Male workers disfavored by these layoffs then sued for back pay. The specific issue decided by the Court arose when an arbitrator acting pursuant to the collective bargaining agreement decided against the company in determining that the company was bound by the seniority agreement and thus must pay back pay to the laid off male workers.

Although technically the issue decided by the Court revolved around the policy of enforcing an arbitrator's award, the real question, according to the Court, was which group was to bear the burden for the company's conduct:

> Because of the Company's alleged prior discrimination against women, some readjustments and consequent losses were bound to occur. The issue is whether the Company or the Union members should bear the burden of those losses.... [T]he collective bargaining agreement placed this unavoidable burden on the Company. By entering into the conflicting conciliation agreement,

by seeking a court order to excuse it from performing the collective bargaining agreement, and by subsequently acting on its mistaken interpretation of its contractual obligations, the Company attempted to shift the loss to its male employees, who shared no responsibility for the sex discrimination. The Company voluntarily assumed its obligations under the collective bargaining agreement and the arbitrators' interpretations of it. No public policy is violated by holding the Company to those obligations, which bar the Company's attempted reallocation of the burden.[306]

Summary and conclusions

Title VII, the Equal Employment Opportunity Act, set about righting group wrongs by providing affirmative action remedies for individuals or groups discriminated against because of race, color, religion, sex, or national origin. A 1972 amendment to the original 1964 act brought state and local government employees, including criminal justice personnel, within the same protections as the earlier act had provided to private employees.

A tidal wave of suits resulted in which minorities and women challenged the hiring and promotional policies of police departments and correctional agencies. Often on one side of such suits are minorities or women, and their unions, claiming discrimination, while on the other side are found white males and their unions claiming reverse discrimination.

Blacks have historically had a very small representation in police and correctional agencies. Also shut out of the private sector, blacks have sought to penetrate the public sector. Government employment has been a customary way for new groups to enter and mount in the labor market. But when blacks entered that market after the Civil War, it was already filled by immigrant groups. Blacks could only make gains after the Second World War when they filled lower-level government jobs abandoned by whites seeking better jobs in private industry. The expansion of service jobs during the next twenty years enabled blacks to make further gains. Most of the jobs, however, continued to be at the lowest level.

Riots in northern city ghettoes during the 1960s triggered a series of presidential reports, which in turn recommended higher minority representation in criminal justice agencies. The LEAA was the legislative effort most successful in placing pressure on criminal justice agencies to comply with Equal Employment Opportunity provisions. By the late 1970s, after a series of hesitant years, compliance procedures were tightened and the Attorney General began to file a number of "pattern or practice suits." But as the country began to hit on less prosperous times, whites became less generous. The LEAA and revenue sharing was terminated toward the end of the 1970s. Nevertheless, the procedures set up to enforce the Civil Rights Act of 1964, particularly Title VII apparently have had important effects in increasing blacks and women in state, county, and city criminal justice agencies.

Two theories have been developed by the Supreme Court to interpret Title VII: disparate treatment and disparate impact. Disparate treatment involves intentionally less favorable employer treatment of an individual or group because of race, color, religion, sex, or national origin. Law had developed in which disparate impact consisted of facially neutral (unintentional) treatment of different groups but where the employment practice impacted more harshly on one of the statutorily protected groups and could not be justified by business necessity. Proof of such disparate impact usually comprised statistical evidence. Recent Supreme Court decisions, however, both increased the difficulty of using statistical evidence to prove disparate impact, and required the plaintiff to carry the burden of proof at all stages of the proof process.

A large number of cases revolve around the question of determining whether a test is job-related. Three validation methods have been devised: content validation in instances in which the test attempts to measure knowledge or ability, and not a general trait such as intelligence; construct validity, in which the attempt is to measure general mental traits such as intelligence, aptitude, judgment, or leadership ability; and criteria-related validation, in which a job analysis shows production or error rate, tardiness, length of service or other behavior critical to the particular employment.

A key to affirmative action enforcement is the amount and kind of damages that may be obtained in a Title VII suit. The Court has said that the legislation has a "make whole" purpose, to fully compensate the persons for the losses suffered as a result of unlawful employment discrimination. On that basis the Court allowed a backpay award but concluded that the section limited recovery of back pay to two years prior to filing the claim with the EEOC.

Criminal justice agencies have always been controlled by males, with women permitted to engage in strictly limited duties such as caring for female and juvenile prisoners. But the increasing number of women in the work force, and the pressing of Title VII suits on behalf of women claimants has placed great pressure on criminal justice agencies to hire women. Obstacles to female hiring have often taken the form of out-moded height, weight and physical endurance test rules. These rules have not been upheld except in the few instances in which an agency can show that the job requires a male officer. In recent years, women have made substantial gains in criminal justice employment, although their representation in the higher ranks is still miniscule.

Seniority has been the backbone of most labor union contracts. In passing Title VII, Congress sought to protect minorities, but not at the expense of the accrued seniority rights of workers. Yet those seniority rights were acquired, for the most part, within a system that has discriminated against minority and female workers. When Title VII claims are measured against the rights of workers with seniority, who is to win? In most cases, the Court has decided, on the basis of § 703(h) of Title VII, that as long as the special privileges (different compensation, conditions of work, promotions) are gained pursuant to a "bona fide seniority system" and that the system is not the result of an intention to discriminate because of race or sex, seniority will win out. One way to get around this result has been the award by the courts of "rightful place" (constructive) seniority to those who have been discriminated against. But this result applies only to post-Act discrimination. A seniority system which (1) applies equally to all, (2) is neither designed nor (3) maintained with a discriminatory purpose, is "bona fide" under § 703(h) even though it does not extend retroactive seniority to pre-Act discriminatees. Thus, plaintiffs must show that a seniority system has a discriminatory purpose before the system will be found to fail the bona fide test. A later case applied this same criterion to a post-Civil Rights Act seniority plan.

The constant pressure on criminal justice agencies has resulted in numerous compliance agreements. These have taken two forms: those proposed by the government employer without court intervention, and consent decrees, where, following a successful Title VII action, the government agency and minority or women plaintiffs agree on an affirmative action plan. Once such a decree is entered, a further phase of litigation develops in which white males and their unions claim that the plan is racially based and therefore in violation of their equal protection rights. A voluntary plan entered into between a union and a steel company in which equal numbers of blacks and whites were to be eligible for a craft-training program brought this issue before the Supreme Court. One excluded worker argued that the plan was in violation of his equal protection rights. The Court decided that voluntary agreements to carry out the purposes of Title VII were permitted by the section. Such plans are permissible as long as they do not unnecessarily trammel the interests of white workers, require their replacement with blacks, absolutely bar their advancement, and are temporary measures with a precise end. Moreover, even though a court could not have entered a decree providing for race-conscious relief to relieve violations of Title VII after a trial, where there is a consent decree, the court has such power, despite the provisions of § 706(g).

Cases have also held that Title VII applies to whites as well as to blacks who have suffered job discrimination. Whites have relied on the equal protection of the laws clause to press their reverse discrimination claims. Such a claim must show purposeful discrimination. The question becomes whether and to what degree race may be considered in hiring and promotions. The *Bakke* case decided that (1) race may be considered as a "plus" factor if that applicant is not insulated from comparison with other candidates, and (2) candidates not credited with the plus will not be excluded from receiving a fair consideration as to all places available. For a criminal justice agency, to use race as a "plus" factor, it must have some compelling reason. One court found sufficiently compelling the reason that hiring minorities and women would tend to enhance the safety and efficiency of prisons.

The boom and bust nature of the US economy has a particularly disastrous effect on minorities and women who have recently made gains in criminal justice employment. In such times, employees with the least seniority tend to be laid off first under the last hired first fired rule of most collective bargaining agreements. At the point of lay-off the Title VII issue has been raised whether minorities and women can claim retroactive seniority to give them constructive seniority back to the time when discriminatory hiring occurred. They argued that but for the discriminatory hiring they would have been hired earlier and thus would have had enough seniority to resist the layoffs. Some circuit courts have allowed such claims but have given constructive seniority only to the point when Title VII was applied to state agencies, March 1972. Efforts to use Title VI to extend constructive seniority back to the effective date of that Act, 1964, have been unsuccessful. The Supreme Court, in an opinion construing Title VI, decided that an action could be had for both intentional and unintentional discrimination, but that at least where discrimination was shown by disparate impact, the relief accorded could be only prospective, that is, injunctive relief.

The Court also found that § 1981, a Reconstruction statute attacking racially discriminatory contracts, required proof of purposeful discrimination. The result is that compensation for discriminatory hiring or promotions can be obtained only under Title VII, thus limiting monetary and seniority relief to discriminatory actions after March 1972.

In conflicts between the seniority provisions of collective bargaining contracts and recently-hired minorities and women under an affirmative action decree, the Court decided that when layoffs occur, employers must adhere to the seniority agreement. If minorities and women have less seniority, as they normally would have, they must be laid off regardless of the affirmative action decree.

ENDNOTES

1. 42 USCA 2000e et seq (1981).
2. Id at 2000e(a).
3. Affirmative action in the 1980's: Dismantling the process of discrimination, Government Printing Office, Nov 1981, pp 39–40.
4. White, T: "Summing Up" The New York Times Magazine, Apr 25 1982, Sec 6, pp 32–3.
5. 476 US 267 (1986).
6. Id at 276. An article evaluating Clarence Thomas, a Reagan appointee, as head of the EEOC, 1982–1990, concluded that during his tenure, the EEOC had "eliminated use of minority hiring goals and timetables by employers to correct racial and ethnic barriers; and "largely abandoned the use of class-action lawsuits [in favor of] those who could show they personally had been hurt by discrimination." McAllister, Bill, What happened to the EEOC when Thomas was there? The Washington Post National Weekly Edition, Sept 16–22, 1991, p. 31.
7. 42 USCA § 2000e-2 (1981).
8. Id at § 2000e-2(h).
9. Id at § 2000e-2(a).
10. Id at § 2000e-5(f)(1).
11. Id at § 2000e(a). Title VII does not apply to United States citizens employed abroad. EEOC v Arabian American Oil Co 111 SCt 1227 (1991).
12. Norton, Eleanor Holmes, The end of the *Griggs* economy: doctrinal adjustment for the new American workplace, 8 Yale Law & Policy Rev 197 (Fall 1990).
13. Id at § 2000e-4(a).
14. Id at § 2000e-5(e).
15. Id at § 2000e-5(f)(1).
16. Id at § 2000e-5(k).
17. Id at § 2000e-5(g).

18. 29 CFR § 1608.1(c) (1990).
19. Skoler, D and Loewenstein, R: "Minorities in correction, non-discrimination, equal opportunity, and legal issues," Crime & Delinquency, Oct 1974, pp 339–346; Joint Commission on Correctional Manpower and Training, A Time to Act, Washington, JCCMT, 1969, stated in part: "While Negroes make up 12 percent of the total population, only 8 percent of correctional employees are black . . . [T]hey form only 3 percent of all top-and-middle-level administrators." More important, of course, is that over 50% of many prison populations are composed of minority groups. See also Montilla, M: Prison employee unionism: Management guide for correctional administrators, LEAA, Washington, Government Printing Office, Jan 1978, pp 382–91.
20. The inequality of justice: A report on crime and the administration of justice in the minority community, National Minority Advisory Council on Criminal Justice, Washington DC, Government Printing Office, Jan 1982, p 299.
21. US Commission on Civil Rights, "For all the people . . . By all the people," Washington, Government Printing Office, 1969, pp 72, 119–20. See also United States v Alexandria 614 F2d 1358, 1363, fn 12 (5th Cir 1980). Kuykendall, J and Burns, D: "The Black Police Officer: A Historical Perspective," Journal of Contemporary Criminal Justice, Nov 1980, found that the percentage of black police in the period 1890–1960 varied from less than 1% to 3.55% in 1960.
22. The New York Times, Dec 10 1974, p 22.
23. Locke, H: The impact of affirmative action and civil service on American police personnel systems, LEAA, Washington, Government Printing Office, 1979, p 3. Although, until recently, there has been much less research on hispanic representation, the same can be said of them.
24. Id. For a somewhat opposing view that reviews the federal government's efforts to reduce discrimination, see Jones, J., The Genesis and Present Status of Affirmative Action in Employment: Economic, Legal and Political Realities, 70 Iowa L Rev 900 (1985).
25. Mollenkopf, J: The crisis of the public sector in America's cities, Essays on the political economy of urban America with special reference to New York, Alcaly, R, and Mermelstein, D, eds, New York, Vintage, 1977.
26. US Commission on Civil Rights, pp 4–5, *supra* n 21.
27. Id at 16.
28. Robinson, C: "The mayor and the police—the political role of the police in society," Police forces in history, Mosse, G, ed, Beverly Hills, Sage, 1975, pp 277–315.
29. President's Commission on Law Enforcement and Administration of Justice, The challenge of crime in a free society, Washington, Government Printing Office, 1967, p 102.
30. President's Commission on Law Enforcement and Administration of Justice, Task force report on the police, Washington, Government Printing Office, 1967, p 167.

31. Id; Alex, N: Black in blue, A study of the Negro policeman, New York, Appleton-Century Crofts, 1969, pp 27–8.

32. Comptroller General of the United States, Report to the Congress: The Equal Employment Opportunity Commission has made limited progress in eliminating employment discrimination, 62HRD-76-147, Washington, General Accounting Office, Sept 28 1976. But see Blumrosen, A and Blumrosen, R: "Layoff or work sharing: The Civil Rights Act of 1964 in the recession of 1975," Equal Employment Opportunity Reader, 1976, pp 39, 46–48.

33. Martin, S E: White Male, Black Male, Female: The Impact of Affirmative Action on Women in Policing, p. 1, Washington, D.C., Police Foundation, unpublished paper, 1989; Zimmer, L E: Women guarding men, Chicago, University of Chicago Press, 1986; Fuchs, Lawrence H, The American kaleidoscope, Wesleyan University Press, 1991, pp 443–44.

34. Blumrosen, Alfred W, Society in transition I: broader congressional agenda for equal employment—the peace dividend, leapfrogging, and other matters, 8 Yale Law & Policy Rev 257, 264 (Fall 1990). One economic study concluded "that federal employment discrimination law played a significant role in accelerating the rate of improvement in black relative wages and occupational status during the period 1965 to 1975, particularly in the South [but] it appears to have had little aggregate effect since then." Heckman, James J and Verkerke, Hault J, Racial disparity and employment discrimination law; an economic perspective, Id at 297. For doubts if the legislation resulted in any minority gains at all, see Epstein, Richard A, The Paradox of Civil Rights, Id at 299.

35. The New York Times, July 24, 1991, p A17. A May 1991 survey by the National Employment Lawyers Association, an organization of plaintiff's lawyers, found 44% of its members rejected more than 90% of such cases. Id at p 1. The EEOC, itself filed only 524 court cases in 1990 while having a backlog of 45,000 cases. Id at A17.

36. Martin at 36, n 33.

37. 42 USCA § 2000e-6(c) (1981).

38. 29 CFR 1602.12–1602.14 (1990).

39. Id at § 1607 et seq.

40. 42 USCA § 2000e-6(a) (1981); Affirmative Action IV-3, July 1979, 29 CFR 1608 et seq (1990).

41. 42 USC § 3789(d)(c)(1) (West Supp 1991).

42. Executive Order 12067, June 30, 1978; 3 CFR 206(1979).

43. Id.

44. 42 USCA § 3711 et seq (West Supp 1991).

45. PL 98-473, 98 Stat 2078 (1984); 28 CFR 42.2 (1990); Legislative history 4 USCCAN 3455 (1984).

46. 28 CFR 42.206(c) (1990).

47. 42 USCA § 3789d(c) (West Supp 1991).

48. Id at 3789d(g)(2)(c); 28 CFR § 42.106 (1989).

49. Id at 3789 (c)(2)(h).

50. 42 USC 2000e(k) (1988).
51. 429 US 125 (1976).
52. Teamsters v United States 431 US 324, 354 (1977).
53. 411 US 792.
54. Id at 802.
55. Id.
56. 450 US 248 (1981).
57. Id at 257.
58. Id at 259. Thus where a female police applicant minimally qualified but was not among the top five interviewed, the court concluded there was "no requirement to adopt hiring procedure to maximize hiring of minority employees," Mallory v Lee City, Fla 694 FSupp 851, 854 (MD Fla 1988).
59. 490 US 228 (1989).
60. Id at 232.
61. Id at 235.
62. Id at 241.
63. Id at 242.
64. Id at 244.
65. Id at 253.
66. Id at 261.
67. Id at 265.
68. Id at 271.
69. 490 US 642.
70. 401 US 424 (1971).
71. Id at 432.
72. Connecticut v Teal 457 US 440, 446–447 (1982). In Davis v City of Dallas 777 F2d 205 (5th Cir 1985), requirements for applicants for patrolman's position to have college education, to be free from recent or excessive marihuana use and hazardous driving convictions, were valid even though result was disparate impact on blacks because job-related.
73. 487 US 977 (1988).
74. Id at 982 (emphasis added).
75. Id at 989.
76. 490 US 642 (1989).
77. Id at 650.
78. Id at 658.
79. Id.
80. Id at 659 (emphasis in original).
81. Id at 661.
82. Id at 663.
83. Id at 678.
84. Id at 662.
85. Belton, R: "The dismantling of the Griggs' disparate impact theory and the future of Title VII: the need for a third reconstruction 8 Yale Law & Policy Review 223–224, 243 (1990); Kelman, Mark: Concepts of discrimination in

"general ability" job testing 104 Harv L Rev 1158, 1167 fn 23 (April 1991) concludes that "*Wards Cove* requires the plaintiff to convince the factfinder by a preponderance of the evidence that the practice serves no valid business purpose," a burden representing "a substantial departure from previous understandings of Title VII in many federal courts."

86. EEOC v Metal Service Co 892 F2d 341, 346–7 (3rd Cir 1990); see also Baltzer v City of Sun Prairie Police Dept 725 FSupp 1008, 1023 (WD Wis 1989), as modified Baltzer v City of Sun Prairie 1989 US Dist Lexis 13938.

87. 896 F2d 801 (3rd Cir 1990), cert den US Corp v Green 111 SCt 53 (1990).

88. Id at 805; and see Nash v City of Jacksonville 905 F2d 355, 358 (11th Cir 1990) ("a comparison between the racial composition of Jacksonville firefighters who passed the promotion exam, the specific employment practice, and those who did not pass" does not suffer from same defects as in *Wards Cove*).

89. 881 F2d 375, 381 (7th Cir 1989). In a Title VII suit by female police officers, Davis v City of Dallas 748 FSupp 1165, 1171 (ND Tex 1990), under *Wards Cove*, the city still "bears the burden of producing a clear, reasonably specific, legitimate, nondiscriminatory reason for each of its challenged hiring decisions."

90. 895 F2d 86 (2nd Cir 1990).

91. Id at 91.

92. 717 FSupp 870, 875 (DDC 1989). See also Walls v City of Petersburg 895 F2d 188, 191 (4th Cir 1990) (plaintiff civilian employee of police department was not able to show any connection between her refusal to answer questions and their disparate impact on black employees).

93. 431 US 324 (1977).

94. Id at 336.

95. Id at 339.

96. Id.

97. 488 US 469 (1989).

98. Id at 498.

99. Id at 501.

100. Id at 504.

101. Kelman, *supra* n 85 at 1217–20; and Com of Pa v Flaherty 760 FSupp 472, 479 (WD Pa 1991).

102. Commission on Civil Rights, For all the people, pp 39–46, *supra* n 21.

103. 626 F2d 659 (9th Cir 1980), cert den, 450 US 919 (1981).

104. Id at 663 (emphasis in original).

105. Id at 665.

106. Id at 666.

107. 630 F2d 79 (2nd Cir 1980), cert den, 452 US 940 (1981).

108. Id at 83.

109. Id at 86, 88.

110. 28 CFR § 50.14 (1990).

111. 630 F2d at 98.

112. Id at 98–9.

113. Id at 100.
114. Id at 103.
115. 933 F2d 1140 (2nd Cir 1991). For a different result with private employees, see Bernard v Gulf Oil Co 890 F2d 735 (5th Cir 1989), cert den 110 SCt 3237 (1990).
116. 933 F2d at 1142.
117. Id at 1144.
118. Id at 1148. For a detailed discussion of job relatedness, see Canton, Doreen, Adverse impact analysis of public sector employment tests: Can a city devise a valid test?, 56 Cinn L Rev 691–695 (1987).
119. 916 F2d 1092 (6th Cir 1990).
120. Id at 1099.
121. Id at 1099–1100.
122. Id at 1102. See Canton, *supra* n 118 at 695.
123. 457 US 440 (1982).
124. Id at 451 (emphasis in original).
125. Id.
126. Id at 455.
127. Costa v Markey 694 F2d 876, 880 (1st Cir 1982) cert den 461 US 920; reaffd 706 F2d 1 (1983); cert den 464 US 1017 (1983).
128. 422 US 405 (1975).
129. Id at 409.
130. 422 US at 417.
131. Id at 419, 418.
132. Flynn, E: "Women in the criminal justice professions," Rafter, N, and Stanko, E, eds, Judge, lawyer, victim, thief: Women, gender roles, and criminal justice, Boston, Northeastern U Press, 1982, pp 305–340, and Price, B, and Sokoloff, N: The criminal justice system and women, New York, Clark Boardman, 1982, part 3.
133. Walker, S: A critical history of police reform, Lexington, Lexington Books, 1977, pp 84–94; Walker, S: Popular justice, A history of American criminal justice, Oxford, Oxford U Press, 1980, pp 138–40.
134. Milton, C.: Women in Policing, Washington, D.C., Police Foundation, 1972.
135. Walker, A critical history, p 93 fn 124, *supra* n 133.
136. Graham, C: "Women are succeeding in male institutions," Hadley, O et al, eds, Women in Corrections, College Pk, Md, American Correctional Assoc, Feb 1981, pp 27, 32; and Zimmer, *supra* n 33, discussing legal problems of privacy raised by women guards in men's prisons. See also Crouch, B M: "Pandora's box: women guards in men's prisons," 13 J of Criminal Justice 535–548 (1985), and Horne, P: "Female correction officer: A status report" 49 Fed Prob 46 (Sept 1985) ("women in the corrections field have probably made the slightest progress" compared to progress in the rest of the criminal justice system).
137. Pollock-Byrne, J.M.: Women, Prison, and Crime p. 114, Pacific Grove, CA, Brooks/Cole Publishing Co., 1990.

138. Leshin, G: 1980 report, equal employment opportunity and affirmative action, the roots grow deeper, Los Angeles, University of California, Institute of Industrial Relations, Sept 1980, pp. 64–73; The Statistical Abstract of the United States, 1990 (Washington, DC 1990) at Table 634.

139. Leshin *supra* n 138 at 272–3, 275–6 and Statistical Abstract *supra* n 138, Tables 645, 673.

140. Susan, S. E.: "Women on the move?: a report on the status of women in policing," Women and Criminal Justice 21, 35 (1989).

141. Id at 32. See also, Steel, B. and Lovrich, Jr, N: "Equality and efficiency tradeoffs in affirmative action—real or imagined? The case of women in policing," 24 The Social Science Journal 53, 57 (1987) who predict on the basis of 1980 data that "by the turn of the century, women will only constitute 10–15% of total police employment and will hold 5% of all law enforcement administrative posts."

142. Flynn p 311, *supra* n 132; Statistical Abstract, *supra* n 138.

143. Statistical Abstract, *supra* n 138 at Table 645.

144. 433 US 321 (1977).

145. Id at 328–9.

146. Id at 330–31.

147. Id at 333, 42 USC § 2000e-2(e) (1976). The same bfoq argument has been successfully made that female prisoners need an environment free of the male world to bar male guards from a women's prison. See Torres v Wise Dept of Health & Social Services 859 F2d 1523, 1532 (7th Cir 1988), cert den 489 US 1017 (1989) and Rider v Com of Pa 850 F2d 982 (3rd Cir); cert den 488 US 993 (1988); but see *contra* Sims v Montgomery County Com 766 FSupp 1052, 1065 (MD Ala 1990).

148. 433 US at 334.

149. Id at 335.

150. 433 US at 336. This idea of the incapacity of womanhood is turned on its head in US v Gregory 871 F2 1239, 1246 (4th Cir 1989), 110 SCt 720 (1990) cert den, where the court found a disparate treatment violation because the sheriff accepted "the proposition that women were incapable of performing the duties of deputies."

151. Id at 342.

152. Id at 341, 345.

153. As of 1986, one study reports that less than 4% of municipal police departments had minimum height and weight requirements. Martin, *supra* n 33 at 6 and Zimmer, *supra* n 33 discuss post-*Dothard* cases.

154. 595 F2d 1367 (9th Cir 1979), cert den 446 US 928 (1980).

155. Id.

156. Id at 1374.

157. Id at 1379, 1381, 1383; Byrne v City of Naperville 1991 US Dist Lexis 7464 (ND Ill) where evidence that 50% of females could not handle the type of firearm required to qualify as police officer was enough to establish prima facie case of disparate treatment; and Scott v City of Topeka Police and Fire

Civil Serv Com 1990 US Dist Lexis 4037, p5 (D Kan), 739 FSupp 1434 (D Kan 1990) mo for judgment nwv denied (where plaintiff female police applicant was rejected because of "poor credit record," but males were not, that reason was pretexual and sheriff was guilty of intentional sex discrimination); Scimeca v Village of Lincolnwood 1989 US Dist Lexis 424 (ND Ill) (physical agility test having disparate impact on women found not to be job related), but see Evans v City of Evanston 695 FSupp 922, 928 (ND Ill 1988) (women fire fighters complained that a physical agility test discriminated against them. The court found, however, that "the acts performed . . . are exactly the sort of activities a firefighter performs while on duty," and is therefore valid even though it disparately impacts on women); and US v City of Wichita Falls 704 FSupp 709, 715 (ND Tex 1988) (even though physical agility test has disparate impact on women, "successful completion of these test is necessary to be an effective police officer in Wichita Falls Texas"). See Canton, Doreen, *supra* n 118 at 703.

158. 1991 US App Lexis 15783 (9th Cir).

159. Id at 23.

160. 28 CFR 50.14.4(d). See Canton, *supra* n 118 at 687.

161. 1991 US App Lexis 15783 at 29–30. In Black Law Enforcement Officers Assoc v City of Akron 1990 US App Lexis 21742 (6th), the 4/5 rule was used to deny black officers relief as to a sergeant exam.

162. 1991 US App Lexis 15783 at 30.

163. See also Gallegos v Thornburgh 1989 US Dist Lexis 13964 (DC) (Drug Enforcement agent who had represented hispanic agents in their EEOC claims against agency and who was severely disciplined for supposed violation "out of line with penalties imposed on others" had been subject to retaliatory action.

164. Where the city had consistently refused to obey a decree that required it to develop a promotion plan that did not discriminate against women, the court ordered promotions of particular women to sergeant, lieutenant and captain, with back pay awards where appropriate, US v City of Montgomery Ala 1991 US Dist Lexis 11862, p 20 (ND Ala).

165. 480 US 616 (1987).

166. 452 US 161.

167. 29 USC § 206(d) (1988). The Equal Pay Act of 1963 was originally enacted as an amendment to the Fair Labor Standards Act of 1938. 29 USC §§ 201–19. The Fair Labor Standards Amendments of 1974 added municipal workers to those affected. See Cook and Sobieski: Civil Rights Actions Vol 4, sec 20.01, New York, Matthew Bender 1990.

168. 463 US 1073 (1983).

169. Id at 1106, 1107, Justice Powell concurring.

170. 111 SCt 1196 (1991).

171. Id at 1202.

172. Id at 1207. Women are also often disadvantaged by the use by many law enforcement agencies of veterans preference points that are added to

applicant's test scores, a usage much more likely to benefit males than females. Upheld in Com of Pa v Flaherty 760 FSupp 472, 479 (WD Pa 1991).

173. 42 USCA § 2000e-2(h) (1981).
174. Franks v Bowman Transportation Co 424 US 747, 759 (1976).
175. Keyssar, A.: "History and the Problem of Unemployment," 89 Socialist Review 15–34 (1989).
176. US Commission on Civil Rights, Nonreferral Unions and Equal Employment Opportunity, Washington, Government Printing Office, March 1982.
177. 424 US 747.
178. Id at 767–8.
179. Teamsters v United States 431 US 324, 346 (1977).
180. Id at 324.
181. 42 USCA § 2000e-6 (1981).
182. 431 US at 344.
183. Id at 347.
184. Id at 353, 354.
185. 456 U.S. 63 (1982).
186. Id at 69.
187. Id.
188. Id at 76, 77 (citations omitted).
189. Pullman-Standard v Swint 456 US 273, 289 (1982).
190. Ford Motor Co v EEOC 458 US 219, 220 (1982).
191. 42 USC § 2000e-5(g) (1988).
192. "Interim earnings or amounts earnable with reasonable diligence by the persons or persons discriminated against shall operate to reduce the back pay otherwise allowable." Id.
193. 458 US at 238, 239.
194. 490 US 900 (1989).
195. Id at 902.
196. Id at 913.
197. 443 US 193 (1979).
198. Id at 197.
199. 42 USCA § 2000e-2(d) (1981).
200. 443 US at 200 (emphasis in original).
201. Id at 205–6 (emphasis in original).
202. Id at 208–9.
203. 450 US 248 (1981).
204. Id at 259.
205. 480 US 616 (1987).
206. Id at 619.
207. Id at 620–621.
208. Id at 628.
209. Id at 631.
210. Id.
211. Id.

212. Id at 632.
213. Id at 634.
214. Id at 635.
215. Id.
216. Id at 636.
217. Id at 639–41.
218. Id at 641.
219. Id at 676.
220. Id at 672.
221. Id at 676.
222. 483 FSupp 930 (ED Mich 1979); see also Detroit Police Officers' Assn v Young 608 F2d 671 (6th Cir 1979); for a similar history for Pittsburgh, see Com of Pa v Flaherty 760 FSupp 472 (WD Pa 1991).
223. Baker v City of Detroit 483 FSupp 930, 996 (ED Mich 1979).
224. Id at 930, 979–80.
225. Id at 983.
226. Id at 986.
227. Id at 998.
228. 608 F2d 671 (6th Cir 1979), cert den 452 US 938 (1981).
229. Id at 690.
230. Id at 696 (citations omitted).
231. Id at 696 fn 12.
232. Id at 698. In NAACP v Detroit Police Officers Assoc (DPOA) 591 FSupp 1194 (ED Mich SD 1984) the court enjoined city layoffs of police officers because the number of black officers laid off decimated the affirmative action agreement, reversed NAACP, Detroit Branch v DPOA 900 F2d 903 (6th Cir 1990) *infra* n 302; NAACP v Detroit Police Officers Association 685 FSupp 1004, 1007 (ED Mich 1988) case dismissed based on court's finding that "everything the court sought to accomplish in its original judgment . . . has been accomplished. . . . Presently, blacks constitute 51.3 percent of the Department and 70 percent of new hires," and the majority of the police union now is black.
233. 478 US 501.
234. Id at 510.
235. Id at 514.
236. Id (emphasis added by Court).
237. Id at 522–23. See also Donaghy v City of Omaha 933 F2d 1448, 1461 (8th Cir 1991) (deciding that the consent decree was "incontrovertibly valid," the court turned back an attempt by a white officer to overturn promotions made pursuant to it. Decisions made pursuant to a valid consent decree do not violate officer's constitutional rights).
238. 490 US 755 (1989).
239. Id at 768.
240. 427 US 273 (1976).
241. 427 US at 275–6.

242. Id at 280.
243. Id at 283.
244. 426 US 229 (1976).
245. Id at 239 (emphasis in original).
246. 438 US 265 (1978).
247. 42 USC § 2000d (1988).
248. 438 US at 305.
249. Id at 311–12.
250. Id at 314.
251. Id at 314–15.
252. Id at 316–17.
253. Id at 318.
254. Id at 319.
255. Id.
256. 480 US 616 (1987).
257. 480 US 149 (1987).
258. Id at 155.
259. Id at 164.
260. Id at 172.
261. Id.
262. Id at 179.
263. Id at 186.
264. Id at 185.
265. 478 US 421 (1986).
266. Id at 479.
267. 732 FSupp 497 (D Del 1990).
268. Id at 504 (emphasis in original).
269. Id at 500.
270. Id at 507.
271. Id. For similar reasoning and result, see Com of Pa v Flaherty 760 FSupp 472, 487 (WD Pa 1991).
272. Id at 513.
273. citing Higgins v City of Vallejo 823 F2d 351, 359–60 (9th Cir 1987), at 516. See also Officers for Justice et al v Civil Service Com for the City and Cty of San Francisco 1991 US Dist Lexis 8259 (ND Cal), revd in part on other grounds, 934 F2d 1092 (9th Cir 1991) (use of race as the sole criterion within each band to select minorities for sergeant is in violation of the equal protection clause).
274. 732 FSupp at 517. See Tinio, Ferdinand S, Annotation, Affirmative action benefiting particular employees or prospective employees as violating other employee's rights under federal constitution or under federal civil rights legislation—Supreme Court cases, 92 LEd2d 849 (1986).
275. 42 USCA § 1981 (1981).
276. General Bldg Contractors Assn v Pennsylvania 458 US 375, 391 (1982).

277. US Commission on Civil Rights, Last hired, first fired: Layoff and civil rights, Washington, Government Printing Office, Feb 1977, p 7.

278. Counting the 1980–81 and 1981–83 bust, since 1834 there have been 35 recorded such cycles. Moore, G: "Business cycles, panics, and depressions," Encyclopedia of American economic history, Porter, G, ed, New York, Scribner, 1980, pp 151–56.

279. US Commission on Civil Rights, Last hired, first fired: layoff and civil rights, Washington, Government Printing Office, Feb 1977, p 12 n 296. Recent Labor Department studies show during the 1980s, "black workers bore a relatively heavier burden of widespread job displacement . . . because of the industries and occupations in which they were concentrated; they were less likely to be reemployed and were out of work longer." Rich, Spencer, Black, White and pink slips, The Washington Post National Weekly Edition, Sept 2–8, 1991.

280. US Commission on Civil Rights, *Supra*, n 279 at 23.

281. Id at 25–6.

282. NAACP v Detroit Police Officers Association (DPOA) 591 FSupp 1194 (ED Mich 1984).

283. Blumrosen, A and Blumrosen, R: "Layoff or work sharing: The Civil Rights Act of 1964 in the recession of 1975," in Equal employment opportunity law reader, New York, Executive Enterprises Publications, 1976, p 36.

284. 570 F2d 57 (2nd Cir 1978).

285. Id at 65, citing *Franks* 424 US at 769.

286. Guardians Association v Civil Service Commission 490 F2d 400 (2nd Cir 1973); 431 FSupp 526 (SD NY 1977); 466 FSupp 1273 (SD NY 1979), and 633 F2d 232 (2nd Cir 1980), all representing various stages of the same case.

287. 633 F2d at 253.

288. Id at 251.

289. 42 USC § 2000d (1988).

290. 463 US 582 (1983). In Neighborhood Action Coalition v Canton, Ohio 882 F2d 1012, 1017 (6th Cir 1989), a neighborhood organization complained that the city refused to invest federally-received funds in minority-occupied areas or to provide police protection to the same extent provided in white areas. The court allowed the action, but in reliance on *Guardians Association* allowed only a claim for injunctive relief.

291. 679 F2d 965 (1st Cir 1982).

292. 679 F2d at 966.

293. Id at 970.

294. Id.

295. Id.

296. Id at 972 (Emphasis in original).

297. Id.

298. 467 US 561 (1984).

299. Id at 571.

300. Id at 572, 573.

301. Id at 575.
302. Id at 579. NAACP v DPOA 900 F2d 903 (6th Cir 1990) reversed a district court decision that enjoined city layoffs on the ground that the Detroit affirmative action plan was subordinated to the seniority provision, § 703(h) of Title VII.
303. Wygant v Jackson Bd. of Education 476 U.S. 267 (1986).
304. Id at 283.
305. 461 US 757 (1983).
306. Id at 770.

Chapter 3

SOVEREIGN IMMUNITY AND GOOD FAITH AS DEFENSES TO CIVIL ACTIONS AGAINST CRIMINAL JUSTICE PERSONNEL

Introductory remarks

The two previous chapters dealt with remedies that allowed plaintiffs to pursue various legal and constitutional theories in federal and state forums. This chapter looks at the other side—certain defenses that individuals (criminal justice personnel) and their employers (the federal, state, county or city governments) can raise in defense of common law and § 1983 actions seeking money damages for their illegal or unconstitutional acts. Suits seeking prospective relief (declaratory judgments and injunctions) are not subject to the immunity defense. Injunctive relief for constitutional violations will be discussed in chapter 4.

Immunity defenses have important historical roots in the growth of state power. During formation of the nation-state and the accompanying evolution of the court system, the king (and later the state) said in effect: You can use the courts to sue each other but you cannot use them to sue me. Thus, the concept of sovereign immunity from suit developed as one element of state power: the judiciary (one part of the state) could not be used to sue the state, or any of the state's components, without the state's consent.

This doctrine has been extended to cover government components (governmental immunity) and various employees of the state. Governmental units—cities and counties—may be sued under § 1983 and have no immunity defense,[1] while states and state agencies, boards, and other subdivisions, have retained their complete immunity from suit.[2] State, county, and municipal employees each have their own variety of immunity: legislators (legislative immunity), judges and prosecutors (judicial immunity) and executive officials (executive immunity). Government employees may have either absolute or qualified immunity depending on their function. Employees having a legislative or judicial function have absolute immunity. Those with nonjudicial functions have a lesser qualified immunity that they must assert. Police, correctional, probation and parole officers, while acting as executive officers, have qualified immunity, permitting them a defense where their actions, though illegal or unconstitutional so as to cause injury, were reasonable and taken in good faith.

A number of events indicate the ongoing erosion of the doctrine: the 1946 passage of the Federal Tort Claims Act (discussed in Chapter 1), that substantially reduced the federal government's immunity for nondiscretionary acts; the replacement of absolute immunity with a good faith defense against liability for governmental torts, the increasing numbers of § 1983 suits that forced the Supreme Court to rethink the doctrine, and the enactment in a majority of states of tort claims acts or the abolition of the doctrine by some state courts. This area of the law is still rather unrefined and is developing on a case by case basis. Founded on a federal doctrine and on admitted inequities resulting from the denial of recovery to persons injured by illegal or unconstitutional governmental acts, recent decisions indicate that the Court is in the process of completely revamping the doctrine.[3]

Sovereign immunity—its significance

The legal effect of the common law doctrine of sovereign immunity is to deny a person the right to sue the state, or one of its subdivisions, for an injury done to that person by the state, unless the state consents to that suit. Such a defense may intervene in any action against a state, or subsidiary unit of a state such as a township, school, parole board, or prison. No action against a state government unit can be successful in the absence of consent by the state to such action. Consent, when given, usually takes the form of a statute that defines the kind of claims that may be made against the state. Different rules, to be considered hereafter, now apply to § 1983 actions against cities and counties.

Analogous to the defense of sovereign immunity are the defenses of legislative, executive, and judicial immunity that clothe government officials who represent these governmental units in a legislative, executive or judicial capacity. There are two separate but related doctrines: (1) sovereign immunity that affects the right of claimants to recover against the state or its subdivisions for its wrongful acts; and (2) the derivative doctrines of legislative, executive or judicial immunity, applicable to individual employees who injure third parties while in the exercise of their governmental functions.

The exact application of these doctrines may depend upon the injury claimed, and the remedy employed. Claimants injured by a governmental act may base their claims either on common law torts or what has come to be known as constitutional torts, in which case they will probably file a § 1983 claim.[4]

Claims fall into the following categories:

    I. Claims against *state* government, grounded in
        (1) state tort claims acts for ordinary torts;
        (2) § 1983 for constitutional torts.
    II. Claims against the *federal* government, grounded in
        (1) the Federal Tort Claims Act for ordinary torts;
        (2) *Bivens* type actions for constitutional torts.

For the most part, this chapter will be concerned with § 1983 claims against state, county, or municipal officers.

Sovereign immunity—its historical base

Sovereign immunity can be best explained as a device developed during the feudal period to strengthen the growth of a fledgling state, in which the king was, for certain purposes, the real, and for other purposes, the symbolic head of an evolving state. Sovereign immunity, part of the doctrine of the divine right of kings, was one means by which kings sought to resist claims against themselves that might weaken their power. To this end, the concept of the "ideal king" was developed, from which flows the notion that kings can do no wrong.

> The ideal king is the foundation of justice, and therefore no court can have jurisdiction over him. From this principle, it is deduced as a consequence, that no suit or action can be brought against the real king, and that his person must be sacred, because there can be no tribunal that has a power to try him.[5]

In effect then, the king's courts are said to have no jurisdiction over the king. This notion developed from the dominant characteristics of the feudal period. Each lord in the pyramidal structure lorded over his own domain, but at the same time was a vassal to the person above him.[6] The only exception to this hierarchical vassalage was the king who was beholden to no one on earth—only to God on high. This same scheme applied to courts. Each lord had his own court where no one could sue the lord without his consent. This did not mean that the lord or the king could do no wrong. Lords, though not answerable to their underlings in their own courts, were subject to the jurisdiction of the lord above them in the hierarchy. By virtue of Magna Carta, the king was also bound by the law. The medieval concept that the king could do no wrong merely signified that there was no legal structure above the king that was capable of coercing the king to answer for his wrong.

Legislative immunity developed in an attempt by Parliament to protect itself and declare its independence from regal power. Judicial immunity evolved in tandem with the king's immunity. Because judges were seen as the king's agents, an attack on the king's judges was viewed as an indirect attack on the king himself. Thus, sovereign immunity and all of its progeny was a means to maintain power of the governing class as against claims by its subjects, most of whom were serfs, who might be injured as a result of acts of government, that is, their lord.

By the eighteenth century the notion that the king could do no wrong had been reinvented in different form: "[S]ince the king could do no wrong, any wrong that was done in his name, was, in the eyes of the law, not done by the king at all,"[7] but by his agents, thereby providing the legal fiction for personal liability of government agents acting for the government. In the United States, the notion of sovereign immunity is largely court created. Its acceptance by United States courts was motivated by fears of the effects of suits by citizens for the recovery of Revolutionary War debts resulting from the decision in Chisholm v Georgia.[8] That case held that Article III of the United States Constitution gave federal courts jurisdiction to hear suits by citizens of another state, even if the state had not consented to the suit. Article III, § 2 provides in part:

> The judicial power of the United States shall extend to all cases . . . between a state and citizen of another state.

In an effort to avoid such suits, Congress passed the eleventh amendment to the United States Constitution. The amendment, ratified in 1795, provides:

> The judicial power of the United States shall not be construed to extend to any suit in law or equity, commenced or prosecuted against one of the United States by citizens of another state, or by citizens or subjects of any foreign state.

The effect of the amendment was to foreclose the use of federal courts as a forum for individual claims against states. Likewise, the Supremacy Clause of the US Constitution precludes states from interposing their state-created immunity defense to protect the state from § 1983 claimants.[9]

Between the early eighteenth century and the Civil War the immunity doctrine was strongly criticized for violating the democratic principle that a government is responsible to its citizens for its wrongs. After the Civil War, however, state governments found themselves heavily in debt, much as they had been after the Revolutionary War, so that many states that had given their consent to be sued, withdrew that consent. Within fifty years most state courts and the United States Supreme Court had decided that sovereign immunity applied across the board. In United States v McLemore, the Court held that "the [United States] government is not liable to be sued, except within its own consent, given by law."[10] The Supreme Court has recently confirmed this interpretation of the eleventh amendment:

> [W]e have understood the Eleventh Amendment to stand not so much for what it says, but for the presupposition of our constitutional structure which it confirms: that the States entered the federal system with their sovereignty intact; that the judicial authority in Article III is limited by this sovereignty, and that a State will therefore not be subject to suit in federal court unless it has consented to suit, either expressly or in the "plan of the [constitutional] convention."[11]

Thereafter, the only legal recourse open to parties injured by wrongful state action was to sue the government agent responsible.

Sovereign immunity—its scope and rationale

Because a government can act only through its officials and employees and because one of the purposes of the doctrine is to protect government operations, it was natural that courts also found that employees of the executive branch had some protection from suits as long as they were acting within the scope of their functions. The questions then became: what agents of government are covered by the immunity doctrine and what is the extent of that coverage?

Courts have fashioned three approaches to the immunity question: (1) *absolute immunity,* that gives the defendant official a complete defense that can be raised at an early stage of the proceeding; (2) *qualified immunity,* that permits officials to interpose a defense showing that the contested action was reasonable and taken in good faith; and (3) *no immunity,* in which case the claimant, to recover, need show only the unlawfulness of the official's action causing the loss.

Federal and state legislators, engaged in the legislative function, and all members of the judiciary, including prosecutors, while they are engaged in a judicial or quasi-judicial function, have absolute and unqualified immunity, while employees with executive functions have only qualified immunity. Where immunity is absolute, even acts done with malice or in bad faith find no remedy in law as long as they are taken within the actor's scope of employment. Where however there is qualified immunity, the harmful act must be taken in "good faith" and be reasonable to constitute a defense.[12]

American courts have suggested three rationales to support some form of immunity for legislative, judicial, and executive functions: (1) Because public officials have a duty to make difficult decisions, mistakes are inevitable and it would be unfair to hold them liable; (2) the threat of liability would have two practical consequences—it would discourage courageous decision making and would encourage the avoidance of public service by able individuals; and (3) it would result in a waste of energy by public officials in defending claims rather than in attending to public business.[13] Thus, for American courts, the reasoning behind immunity relies on the practical difficulties in governmental decision making rather than on its historical antecedents.

Criticism of the doctrine has been constant and vehement. Even apparent beneficiaries such as the National Association of Attorneys General have noted that it seems strange that the doctrine

> came to be accepted legal principle in a democracy like the United States. . . . One can scarcely imagine any idea more antithetical to the basic tenets of democratic government than that which holds that the people, at whose pleasure and for whose benefit the government exists, cannot sue their representatives when they have been wronged by them.[14]

Historical development of executive immunity

Executive officials are not generally liable for common law torts that result from the exercise of discretion in the conduct of affairs within the scope of their authority. Problems of defining what is within the "scope of their authority," and what is a "discretionary act," and to what extent these concepts apply to § 1983 actions, will be discussed below.

Because it is clear that a state cannot be directly sued for the torts of its employees without its consent, officials committing the act are customarily named in their suit, usually in their individual *and* in their official capacity. The question then becomes, is the suit against the official (which is permissible), or is the official named merely as a subterfuge to sue the state (which is impermissible)? The landmark opinion on this question is the 1908 case of Ex Parte Young.[15] There the Court found that although it was improper to sue a state's attorney general for money damages, it was proper to enjoin his act because he was acting unconstitutionally. The Court reasoned that because of the illegality of the act, that act could not be the act of the state. Rather, it was the act of the attorney general acting in his individual capacity. As such, the illegal act could be enjoined, and the official held personally responsible for the consequences of his illegal individual conduct.[16]

Whether a *federal* court can examine the constitutionality of *state* executive action was raised in Sterling v Constantin.[17] There, a state attorney general used the state militia to enforce an order of a state commission against a railroad. The Court rejected the state's argument that the governor's call out of troops was unreviewable. Instead, it found that at the time the troops were summoned the governor was acting in his civilian rather than in his military capacity. Civilian decisions are reviewable by courts; further, state officials who invade rights secured by the federal constitution are subject to review of such actions so that persons injured may have appropriate relief.

The scope of authority question

If employees act *outside* the scope of governmental authority given them, they are acting not for the government but on their own, and therefore cannot claim immunity. This is the lesson of Ex Parte Young. An official is said to be acting within his authority if the action taken had "more or less connection with the general matters committed by law to his control or supervision."[18] In Barr v Matteo, Justice Harlan suggested that an action taken "within the outer perimeter of petitioner's line of duty is enough to render the privilege applicable. . . ."[19] To Justice Black, concurring in the same opinion, immunity was applicable if the act was not "plainly beyond the scope" of defendant's official business.[20] The "outer perimeter" of the executive's duty continues to be the test for judging whether an executive has absolute immunity.[21]

The discretionary-ministerial distinction

One method by which courts have attempted to deal with the problem of executive immunity is to distinguish between what the courts call a discretionary and ministerial act. The idea behind the distinction is similar to that earlier expressed for sovereign immunity—that discretionary functions are said to require risk taking and the exercise of judgment—often on short notice and without adequate information. If officials were to be held liable for mistakes in judgment under such circumstances, courts fear that they would hesitate in making necessary decisions. Ministerial functions are those in which discretion is said to be an insignificant factor, where the task is ordinarily repetitive and automatic, and where the employee has relatively little option on which way to act.[22] It follows from this reasoning that officials with greater responsibility for decision making, that is, those who have more discretion, need immunity while those who have lesser responsibility and minimum discretion need or should have little or no immunity for their wrongful actions.

On the whole, the higher one stands in the government hierarchy, the greater the discretion in policy making, and therefore the greater the scope of immunity accorded.[23] Such a result indicates continued deference by the courts to the feudal model of authority and its continued utility to the state as a means of limiting liability of its upper echelons. The Court, however, has questioned this belief, noting that "the greater power of [high] officials . . . affords a greater potential for a regime of lawless conduct."[24] The balance of the chapter will consider the immunity defense in relation to § 1983 claims.

Immunity in § 1983 cases

Prior to 1951, § 1983 cases had been treated as an exception to the absolute immunity of executive officials to suit because the section's imperative language making liable "every person" who violated federal rights, seemed to have bypassed the doctrine. But in Tenney v Brandhove,[25] a case involving legislative immunity, the Court observed that in 1871, when § 1983 was enacted, immunity was an accepted legal principle that Congress could not have intended to nullify. Legislators, who benefited from absolute immunity to suit at the time § 1983 became law, were therefore also immune from a 1983 claim.

Immunity for judges and prosecutors was addressed in the 1967 case of Pierson v Ray.[26] This case, growing out of activities to desegregate southern public facilities, rejected attempts to hold a judge and a police officer liable under § 1983 for an alleged false arrest and conviction of peaceful demonstrators. Judges, the Court held, have absolute immunity from a suit for damages even where the action of the judge is corrupt and malicious. The object of the doctrine is not to protect corrupt judges but to allow all judges "to exercise their functions with independence and without fear of consequences."[27] Police officers, however, do not have absolute immunity. Instead, they have a defense if they can show that their act, though wrongful, was committed in good faith and with probable cause (that is, that the officer acted reasonably).[28]

Scheuer v Rhodes[29] raised the issue of immunity of a state governor, and therefore of other high executive officials. The case arose out of the Kent State University disturbances in which the governor ordered the national guard onto the campus. The guard shot several students, who in turn sued the governor and other high state executives for their injuries. The governor defended that he had absolute immunity from suit. Chief Justice Burger noted that contrary to Ex Parte Young and Sterling v Constantin, cases that involved injunctive relief, the plaintiffs here demanded money damages. In an earlier case, where persons tried to recover money damages from federal officials under the theory of Ex Parte Young, the Supreme Court held that the suit "is in essence one for the recovery of money from the state, the state is the real, substantial party in interest and is entitled to invoke its sovereign immunity from suit even though individual officers are nominal defendants."[30] But in *Scheuer* the Court concluded that "damages against individual defendants are a permissible remedy—notwithstanding the fact that they hold public office."[31]

Addressing the argument that the governor, as a member of the executive branch making discretionary decisions, had absolute immunity, the Court repeated the "root considerations" on which the doctrine of immunity rests. The Court then reasoned that for these values to be protected, absolute immunity was unnecessary. It would be sufficient for state executive officers to have a qualified immunity. Its extent would vary according to the scope of discretion exercised, the responsibility of the office, and the circumstances as they reasonably appeared at the time of the action in question.

Asserting the qualified immunity defense

While the *Scheuer* Court determined that state executive officials had a qualified immunity defense, the Court did not delineate how that defense was to be asserted. In the 1975 case of Wood v Strickland[32] the Court reviewed its earlier decisions and set its course for the future. Although *Wood* involved the liability of school board officials, this case enunciated the principles that would later be applied to criminal justice personnel. The *Wood* case grew out of an incident in which a school board expelled three 10th grade girls for "spiking" some punch with a "beer-like beverage" in violation of a school regulation. Two of the students filed a § 1983 complaint demanding damages and injunctive relief. The Court was presented with the question as to what, if any, immunity the school board officials were entitled.

In attempting to respond to this question, the Court examined the competing values for and against granting absolute immunity, arguments that are relevant for all executive officers, not merely school board officials.

> The most capable candidates for school board positions might be deterred from seeking office if heavy burdens upon their private resources from monetary liability were a likely prospect during their tenure.... But at the same time, the judgment implicit in this common-law development is that absolute immunity would not be justified since it would not sufficiently increase the ability of school officials to exercise their discretion in a forthright manner to warrant the absence of a remedy for students subjected to intentional or otherwise inexcusable deprivations.[33]

On the basis of this reasoning, the Court held that a school board

> member is not immune from liability for damages under § 1983 if he knew or reasonably should have known that the action he took within his sphere of official responsibility would violate the constitutional rights of the student affected, or if he took the action with the malicious intention to cause a deprivation of constitutional rights or other injury to the student.... A compensatory award will be appropriate only if the school board member has acted with such an impermissible motivation or with such disregard of the student's clearly established constitutional rights that his action cannot reasonably be characterized as being in good faith.[34]

Three years later, in Procunier v Navarette,[35] the Court applied these standards to state prison officials who had allegedly interfered with a prisoner's mailing privileges in violation of his first amendment rights. The Court recalled its two-pronged test in *Wood*—the first "objective" and the second "subjective." The defense of qualified immunity would be rejected (1) "if the constitutional right allegedly infringed by them was clearly established at the time of their challenged conduct, if they knew or should have known of that right, and if they knew or should have known that their conduct violated the constitutional norm"; or (2) if the official had maliciously intended to deprive the claimant of a constitutional right.[36]

But in Harlow v Fitzgerald,[37] the Supreme Court, concerned with the difficulties of proving the subjective prong of the *Wood* test, clipped that prong leaving only the objective criterion, that "government officials performing discretionary functions generally are shielded from liability for civil damages insofar as their conduct does not violate clearly established statutory or constitutional rights of which a reasonable person would have known."[38]

In the 1991 case of Siegert v Gilley,[39] the Court decided that an employee of a federal hospital had not sufficiently alleged grounds to overcome the government's claim of qualified immunity. Justice Rehnquist set forth what a plaintiff must show in his pleadings:

> A necessary concomitant to the determination of whether the constitutional right asserted by the plaintiff is "clearly established" at the time the defendant acted is the determination of whether the plaintiff has asserted a violation of a constitutional right at all. Decision of this purely legal question permits courts to expeditiously weed out suits which fail the test without requiring a defendant who rightly claims qualified immunity to engage in expensive and time consuming preparation to defend the suit on its merits.[40]

One court of appeals reasoned that the Court now required a "two level progressive inquiry:"

(1) Was the law clearly established at the time? If the answer to this threshold question is no, the official is immune.

(2) If the answer is yes, the immunity defense ordinarily should fail unless the official claims extraordinary circumstances and can prove that he neither knew nor should have known that his acts invaded settled legal rights.[41]

Application of immunity to federal executive officials

Pierson, Scheuer, Wood and *Procunier* were all § 1983 cases involving claims of immunity by state officials. In Butz v Economou,[42] plaintiffs asserted a *Bivens*-type claim against federal officials arising directly from alleged violations of their constitutional rights under the United States Constitution. Plaintiffs cannot sue the federal government directly because the federal government is protected by its sovereign immunity. Therefore *Bivens* suits are available only against federal officials in their personal capacities.[43]

In *Butz,* the Court decided that there was no absolute immunity cover for all federal executives. Liability of federal executives charged with constitutional violations would follow the same immunity rules as do state officials. The Court adopted a "functional" approach—that immunity attached to the official's *function* and not to the office. Those who exercised functions, such as judges and prosecutors, who historically had been clothed with absolute immunity, should have absolute immunity even though they were employed by the executive branch. Thus, the administrative law judge, performing acts analogous to the common law judge, and executive officials who make decisions to initiate administrative proceedings or conduct trials, functions analogous to the prosecutor, therefore should have the same absolute immunity as their common-law counterparts. Only the President, among executives performing an executive function, has absolute "immunity from damages liability for acts within the 'outer perimeter' of his official responsibility." This is because of the "special nature of the President's constitutional office and functions."[44] Presidential aids, however, are entitled only to qualified immunity.

This position was affirmed by the Court in Mitchell v Forsyth,[45] a 1985 case in which Attorney General John Mitchell authorized the tapping of anti-war activist Forsyth's phone allegedly for security reasons. Forsyth sued under section 1983 for damages and Mitchell defended that he had absolute, or in the alternative, qualified immunity, for his action. The Court rejected Mitchell's attempt to piggyback on the President's absolute immunity concluding "that the Attorney General is not absolutely immune from suit for damages arising out of his allegedly unconstitutional conduct in performing his national security functions."[46] Looking at the function Mitchell was performing in this case, the Court concluded that he was not acting in a prosecutorial capacity and therefore was not entitled to absolute immunity. Furthermore, "the danger that high federal officials will disregard constitutional rights in their zeal to protect the national security is sufficiently real to counsel against affording such officials an absolute immunity."[47]

After *Butz* and *Harlow,* the immunity available to federal officials can be said to fall into one of three categories: (1) no immunity if officials act outside the scope of their duties; (2) qualified immunity if they commit a constitutional tort *and* were not performing a special function; (3) absolute immunity if they commit a common law tort or were performing a special function.[48]

Judicial and prosecutorial absolute immunity

Regardless of whether a suit is based on common law or § 1983, judges have absolute immunity from damage claims for their wrongful acts as long as they act within the "outer perimeter" of their judicial functions.[49] State supreme court judges have been found to have absolute immunity in both their judicial and rulemaking capacities, but while immune for *damage* actions, they are subject to § 1983 *injunctive* relief for deprivations of plaintiff's federal rights.[50] In Imbler v Pachtman,[51] the judge's immunity was extended to prosecutors on the theory that prosecutors are engaged in a quasi-judicial function requiring the same protection as judges.

In *Imbler*, a prosecutor was alleged to have knowingly used false testimony and to have suppressed material evidence at the plaintiff's trial causing the plaintiff's wrongful conviction and imprisonment. After a complicated series of court maneuvers, the prosecution was finally dismissed and this suit against the prosecutor for damages followed. The prosecutor defended by claiming absolute immunity to suit. The Court began its analysis by pointing out that earlier cases had decided that § 1983 "is to be read in harmony with general principles of tort immunities and defenses. . . . "[52] It then reasoned that common law immunities for judges carried over to the prosecutor who enjoys "absolute immunity from § 1983 suits for damages when he acts within the scope of his prosecutorial duties,"[53] that is, when prosecutors act in their quasi-judicial capacity. The distinction between the prosecutor's function as an "advocate," the initiation and pursuit of prosecutions, where absolute immunity would apply, and the function of "administrator or investigative officer," where the prosecutor would have the same qualified immunity as a police officer has been worked out in later cases and is considered below. A police officer who commits perjury during testimony at plaintiff's criminal trial has absolute immunity from a later § 1983 claim for damages because the officer is exercising a judicial function.[54]

Judicial and prosecutorial qualified immunity

Court of appeals decisions have somewhat clarified the distinction between absolute and qualified immunity for judges and prosecutors, principally based on whether, at the time of the act in question, they were engaged in a "judicial" or a "non-judicial" function. Where judges and prosecutors are engaged in "non-judicial" functions, they are entitled only to qualified immunity. The narrowness of this exception can be illustrated by the leading Supreme Court case of Stump v Sparkman,[55] in which a judge was sued for damages in a § 1983 action. The defendant judge had been presented with an *ex parte* petition by plaintiff's mother to have her "somewhat retarded" daughter sterilized. At the time, the plaintiff daughter was told she was undergoing an appendectomy. Later, when she was unable to conceive, she consulted a doctor who told her what had occurred. The Court found the judge absolutely immune from suit because, regardless of the irreparable harm he had caused plaintiff, his determination was a "judicial act," and did not clearly fall outside his subject matter jurisdiction. Using this same reasoning, two courts of appeals have found that judges' "nonjudicial" conduct have caused them to lose their absolute immunity. In Rankin v Howard,[56] a judge granted a petition to appoint a guardian to deprogram an adult child belonging to a religious cult, knowing that the purpose was to kidnap and hold that plaintiff captive until he agreed to leave the cult. The court considered three factors: "the nature of the act itself, i.e., whether it is a function normally performed by a judge, . . . the expectation of the parties, i.e., whether they dealt with the judge in his judicial capacity," and whether the acts were taken in the "clear absence of all jurisdiction."[57] If, as here alleged, the judge's jurisdiction is based on allegations that he knew were fraudulent, then the judge, acting as part of a conspiracy, has no personal jurisdiction of the case and loses his absolute immunity.

In Harper v Merckle,[58] plaintiff came to the courthouse, where his ex-wife worked, to make a support payment. The defendant judge, in street clothes, seated in an adjacent office, intervened on behalf of the ex-wife, a friend. He began to question plaintiff about his address, tried to place him under oath, and when plaintiff attempted to leave, first chased him, and failing to catch him, sent deputies after him. When the plaintiff was returned to court, the judge held him in contempt and then committed him to jail for the weekend. Although the requirement to be sworn in and the contempt proceedings were normal judicial functions, and took place in a judicial setting, they did not center around any matter then pending before the court, and "were brought to the Judge's attention in a social, not judicial, forum." In effect, the judge was acting as a police officer rather than a judge, and therefore should have only qualified immunity. The court, however, cautioned that its holding was "exceedingly narrow and is tailored to this, the rarest of factual settings."[59] To illustrate the unusual circumstances in which such cases might arise, the court pointed to Zarcone v Perry.[60] There, a judge sent a deputy sheriff to purchase coffee from a vendor, coffee that the judge concluded was "putrid." On the judge's orders, the vendor was brought before him in handcuffs, and subjected to 20 minutes of vilification. The judge's conduct was so clearly outside the judicial function that the defendant judge did not even raise the immunity defense.[61]

In the 1988 case of Forrester v White,[62] a state court judge hired a juvenile and adult probation officer and discharged her thereafter, allegedly because of her sex. When Forrester sued the judge under equal protection of the laws, the judge claimed his actions were protected by absolute immunity from civil suit for damages. But the Court, relying on its distinction between judicial and nonjudicial functions decided that the judge "was acting in an administrative capacity when he demoted and discharged" the plaintiff, and therefore the judge was not entitled to claim absolute, though he might be able to claim, qualified immunity.[63]

Stepanian v Addis[64] applied this same notion to prosecutors. In connection with his function of presenting evidence to a grand jury, a prosecutor held a press conference during which he allegedly made a statement defaming the plaintiff. The prosecutor claimed absolute immunity from suit. A federal prosecutor, the court suggested, has "two paths" to absolute immunity: (1) quasi-judicial activity, and (2) executive activity which if done by an executive, would have absolute immunity. Statements made at a press conference, the court concluded, do not constitute quasi-judicial activity. Turning to the second claim for immunity, that the prosecutor was acting within his executive function, this argument too, the court rejected. Prosecutors' absolute immunity is limited to action in which the prosecution merely repeats the information in the indictment or where their statements stay within the authority given by the guidelines set forth by the federal regulation covering release of such information. Like judges, if prosecutors exceed their authority, they are merely entitled to qualified immunity.

Hampton v Hanrahan[65] involved the participation of the Illinois state's attorney in the planning, execution and post-raid coverup of allegedly unconstitutional violations of plaintiff's rights. The court was called on to give content to the *Imbler* distinction between a prosecutor's advocacy and investigative or administrative functions. In an earlier version of the same case, the court rejected absolute immunity for the state's attorneys' planning and execution of the raid.[66] State's attorneys were absolutely immune for the decision to prosecute the survivors of the raid, presentation of evidence to the grand jury, a compromise worked out with the federal attorney general's office to drop state charges, and the alleged deliberate use of perjured testimony, all of which compose the judicial function. But the state's attorney's "generation of post-raid publicity," that "allegedly violated specific statutory and constitutional guarantees" was entitled only to qualified immunity.[67]

These precedents were relied on by the recent case of Burns v Reed.[68] There the Court decided that a state prosecutor had absolute immunity for claims against him arising out of a probable cause hearing in which he examined a witness and successfully supported police application for a search warrant. But where he gave legal advice to the police which led to the plaintiff's improper arrest and charge of attempted murder, he had only qualified immunity.

Public defenders, who engage in intentional misconduct are not protected by absolute immunity. In Tower v Glover,[69] it was alleged that public defenders engaged in a conspiracy with state officials to convict plaintiff. The Court concluded that "state public defenders are not immune from liability under § 1983 for intentional misconduct, 'under color of' state law, by virtue of alleged conspiratorial action with state officials that deprives their clients of federal rights."[70]

Application of the immunity defense to criminal justice personnel

Davis v Scherer,[71] posed the question: whether state officials lose their qualified immunity if they violate a "clear command" of a state administrative regulation. All justices agreed that violation of such a regulation would not be sufficient, in itself, to show that an official had deprived the plaintiff of a *federal* constitutional right. The minority, however, disagreed with the majority's finding that the plaintiff had failed to show the additional necessary requirement—that at the time of the alleged constitutional deprivation, the right was clearly established.

Scherer, a radio-teletype operator for the Florida Highway Patrol, sought additional outside employment as a reserve deputy for the county sheriff's office. A departmental rule required that such outside employment have prior approval. Such approval was sought by Scherer, initially given, and then revoked because his superiors had determined that such a job might conflict with his duties with the highway patrol. Nevertheless, Scherer continued his outside employment, at the same time carrying on conversations and written communications with his superiors denying there was any conflict of interest. Without notice or hearing, a higher officer in the highway command terminated his employment. Scherer filed a § 1983 suit claiming that in violation of his fourteenth amendment due process rights, the discharge had taken place without a formal pretermination or post-termination hearing.

The district court found and the Supreme Court agreed that it was undisputed that the state had violated Scherer's fourteenth amendment due process rights. The question then was whether the plaintiff was barred from any damages because of the government employee's qualified immunity.

Even defendants who violate constitutional rights enjoy a qualified immunity that protects them from liability for damages unless it is further demonstrated that their conduct was unreasonable under the applicable standard.... Whether an official may prevail in his qualified immunity defense depends upon the "objective reasonableness of [his] conduct as measured by reference to clearly established law."[72]

As this plaintiff had not shown to the Court's satisfaction that these rights were clearly established at the time of their violation, the Court remanded the case to the district court for the plaintiff to make such a showing.

Malley v Briggs[73] held that a police officer who caused § 1983 plaintiffs to be unconstitutionally arrested by presenting a judge with a complaint and supporting affidavit failing to establish probable cause could be held liable under the objective standard. On the basis of some information learned on tapping the phone of an acquaintance of the plaintiffs' daughter, the Rhode Island state police presented affidavits to a judge and obtained arrest warrants for the plaintiffs and others. When the grand jury failed to indict, the charges against plaintiffs were dropped. After plaintiffs filed their 1983 suit, it was successfully argued by the police defendants in the district court that "an officer who believes that the facts stated in the affidavit are true and who submits them to a neutral magistrate may thereby be entitled to immunity under the 'objective' reasonableness' standard of Harlow...."[74] Before the Supreme Court, defendants argued that police officers presenting affidavits and complaints before magistrates should have absolute immunity (comparing the function of the police officer to the prosecutor), thereby relieving officers of any responsibility for their own negligence. The Court rejected that argument principally for policy reasons: that the effect of making officers liable for their own misconduct would require officers to reflect before applying for a warrant and that a damages remedy would better serve the criminal justice system and the parties than if the matter were to be raised in a suppression hearing. The Court held that

Defendants will not be immune if, on an objective basis, it is obvious that no reasonably competent officer would have concluded that a warrant should issue; but if officers of reasonable competence would disagree on this issue, immunity should be recognized.... The ... question in this case is whether a reasonably well-trained officer in petitioner's position would have known that his affidavit failed to establish probable cause and that he should not have applied for the warrant.[75]

The Court remanded the case for the lower court to determine if the police officer's conduct was "objectively reasonable."

The "settled law" approach has been criticized in that it reduces executive liability to the near vanishing point by "giving public officials one 'free' constitutional violation."[76] While the effect of revealing such a violation may be to help others in the future to obtain a "settled" constitutional violation, a "first violation" suit will be unlikely to obtain relief for the particular client bringing the action. Thus, instead of encouraging litigation to reveal constitutional violations, such a policy tends to discourage attorneys from breaking new legal ground. This problem is apparent in the consideration of pre- and post-*Harlow* cases.

Whereas in *Malley,* the Court held an officer legally liable for negligence in applying for an arrest warrant, in Anderson v Creighton,[77] a 1987 *Bivens*-type case, the Court found a federal officer not liable because "the officer could have believed that the search comported with the Fourth Amendment."[78] Federal officers had searched plaintiffs' home without a warrant in the mistaken belief that a bank robbery suspect would be found there. There was no probable cause for such search. The question under *Harlow,* said the Court, is not that the officer "violated—the right to be free from warrantless searches of one's home unless the searchers have probable cause and there are exigent circumstances,"[79] but rather "the objective . . . question whether a reasonable officer could have believed Anderson's warrantless search to be lawful, in light of clearly established law and the information the searching officers possessed."[80]

> We have recognized that it is inevitable that law enforcement officials will in some cases reasonably but unmistakenly conclude that probable cause is present . . . [L]ike other officials who act in ways they reasonably believe to be lawful—[they] should not be held personally liable.[81]

With this decision "officials can know that they will not be held personally liable as long as their actions are reasonable in light of current American law."[82]

But to Justice Stevens, the majority in *Anderson* is establishing a "double standard of reasonableness," one "that affords a law enforcement official two layers of insulation from liability. . . ."[83] The first of these is the requirement for a right "clearly established" at the time of the violation; and the second that a reasonable person in his position could reasonably have believed that his particular conduct would not violate rights that he concedes are clearly established.[84] In effect, Stevens argues, the Court has taken the *Harlow* doctrine, crafted to fit the needs of the federal executive to make discretionary decisions and applied it to low-level law enforcement officers who have no need for this policy making protection.[85]

Two cases decided by the Court in 1989 give some insight into the Court's criteria for judging what conduct will be considered as "objectively reasonable." In Brower v County of Inyo,[86] the police, in order to stop a speeding stolen car, placed a roadblock across the highway, at a spot around a curve, and shined headlights in the direction the car was coming from, in such a way that the car's driver could not see the roadblock, hit it and was killed. In a § 1983 action, his heirs claimed a violation of his fourth amendment rights to be free from unreasonable search and seizure. The Court decided that the situation should be analyzed using fourth amendment rather than the substantive due process analysis that had been applied by the court of appeals. Setting up a roadblock in order to stop the driver, the Court concluded, constitutes a seizure under fourth amendment law. The question of reasonableness of the seizure was to be determined by proof of the allegation that the road block was set up in such a way as would be likely to kill the driver. Although no claim of immunity was made in this case, conceivably outrageous facts such as these are most likely to be the kind necessary to overcome the *Anderson* objective reasonableness doctrine.

The second case, Graham v Connor,[87] likewise failed to raise the immunity defense. There police officers arrested Graham, a diabetic, as he was having a "sugar reaction" on a city street, ignoring pleas from friends informing them that his true condition was diabetic and not drunkenness as the officers presumed. As a result, Graham was roughly handled, physically injuring him during the arrest. The Court notes that the " 'reasonableness' of a particular use of force must be judged from the perspective of a reasonable officer on the scene, rather than with the 20/20 vision of hindsight. . . . The Fourth Amendment inquiry is one of 'objective reasonableness' under the circumstances, and subjective concepts like 'malice' and 'sadism' have no proper place in that inquiry."[88]

A law review article, reviewing cases since *Anderson,* concluded that

The history of the qualified immunity defense indicates the Court's interest in protecting officials from frivolous civil rights suits. The Court first articulated a standard that denied immunity if officials had acted maliciously or if they had violated clearly established constitutional or statutory rights. It later eliminated subjective good faith as a factor in its attempt to articulate a qualified immunity standard that would be "wholly objective," one that would allow courts to dispose of insubstantial suits prior to discovery. The Court recognized that the issue of qualified immunity could be resolved as a matter of law in three situations: (1) if the law pertaining to the plaintiff's claims was not clearly established, then the officer had immunity; (2) if the facts as alleged by the plaintiff indicated that a reasonable officer could have believed the conduct to be lawful, then the officer had qualified immunity; and (3) if the facts as alleged by the defendant indicated that a reasonable officer could not have believed the conduct to be lawful, then the officer did not have immunity.

Recently, however, the Court has expanded the scope of immunity by recognizing that the standard for qualified immunity was also fact-specific. According to the Court, officials have qualified immunity even if the general principle of law relied on by the plaintiff was clearly established. Officials have qualified immunity, the Court reasoned, if the "contours" of the asserted right were not sufficiently clear to give officials notice that their conduct was unlawful.[89]

These cases raise considerable difficulty for plaintiffs. *Harlow* has eliminated the "subjective" alternative and *Davis* requires the plaintiff to bear the burden of showing that a defendant raising a good faith immunity defense has violated "settled" constitutional law. On the other hand, *Malley* places a reasonable burden on police officers to examine their own warrants before presenting them to magistrates. The case also seems to indicate that as the Court on the one hand makes it more difficult to suppress evidence in criminal proceedings, on the other hand, the Court makes it easier for plaintiffs to obtain damages from officers who unreasonably obtain warrants. *Davis* gives signals to lower courts that they should decide every doubt in terms of "objective reasonableness" and "clearly established law" in favor of the defendant government employee. *Anderson* also weakens the ability of innocent victims to recover in cases in which the illegal act was reasonable from the officer's point of view.

Constitutional and common law torts

As numbers of § 1983 cases were decided, the Supreme Court developed a different immunity approach to *constitutional* torts (see chapter 1) and to *common law* torts. This distinction was recognized in *Butz*.[91] Federal and state officials have absolute immunity from common law tort liability (where not covered by federal or state claims acts) whereas they have only qualified immunity for constitutional torts. One writer suggested that the rationale for the distinction is

Because unchecked government can lead to abuses, there must be curbs to government action built into the system. When the public official violates the Constitution, he is violating the very instrument which gives, and in the case of state officials, limits his power; that instrument is written to check the actions of federal and, through the fourteenth amendment, the state government. . . . Moreover, plaintiffs suing to challenge constitutional deprivations are vindicating not only private, but also public interests. . . . This factor, when weighed in the balance, can justify tipping the scales toward only qualified immunity where constitutional values are at stake, while leaving the public official protected when the conduct is much less affected with a public interest.[92]

We have seen that § 1983 defenses present formidable obstacles to 1983 plaintiffs seeking money damages for violations of their federal rights. Nevertheless, these cases represent a complete rethinking of the doctrine of sovereign immunity by the Court. A further aspect of this evolution is to be found in the Court's treatment of the liability of local governments that employ criminal justice personnel.

Local government liability for § 1983 actions

Monroe v Pape[93] decided that municipalities were absolutely immune from § 1983 suits because, as the Court then concluded, the statutory history of the section showed that cities were not "persons" within the meaning of the statute. That history was reconsidered in the 1978 case of Monell v Dept of Social Services of the City of New York[94] with the result that *Monroe* was overruled as to the city immunity issue. Local governmental units (cities and counties) were henceforth to be considered "persons" under § 1983 and could be sued. But whether such local government entities might have the type of qualified immunity good faith defense allowed police officers in *Pierson,* the Court specifically reserved for another day.

That day arrived with the 1980 case of Owen v City of Independence Mo,[95] in which Owen, a police chief, was dismissed by the city manager, who gave no reasons for his action. Relying on § 1983, Owen sued his employer, the city, claiming denial of procedural due process because he was fired without a hearing or a specific statement of charges. In its decision, the Court not only rejected absolute immunity for cities but also found that municipalities may not even "assert the good faith of its officers or agents as a defense to liability under § 1983."[96] The Court reasoned that "[b]y its terms, § 1983 'creates a species of tort liability that on its face admits of no immunities,' "[97] and "[b]y including municipalities within the class of 'persons' subject to liability for violations of the Federal Constitution and laws, Congress—the supreme sovereign on matters of federal law—abolished whatever vestige of the State's sovereign immunity the municipality possessed."[98]

Focusing on the "central aim of the Civil Rights Act...to provide protection to those persons wronged by" misuse of power by state authorities, the Court indicated concern that the result of applying the same immunity to cities as was applied to their employees would mean that "many victims of municipal misfeasance would be left remediless."[99]

The decision was an attempt by the Court to equitably allocate costs of municipal liability

> among the three principals in the scenario of the § 1983 cause of action: the victim of the constitutional deprivation; the officer whose conduct caused the injury; and the public, as represented by the municipal entity. The innocent individual who is harmed by an abuse of governmental authority is assured that he will be compensated for his injury. The offending official, so long as he conducts himself in good faith, may go about his business secure in the knowledge that a qualified immunity will protect him from personal liability for damages that are more appropriately chargeable to the populace as a whole. And the public will be forced to bear only the costs of injury inflicted by the "execution of a government's policy or custom, whether made by its lawmakers or by those whose edicts or acts may fairly be said to represent official policy."[100]

Thus, a local government is a "person" under § 1983 but is without an immunity defense. Its liability is limited to injuries "inflicted by the 'execution of a government's policy or custom, whether made by its lawmakers or by those whose edicts or acts, may fairly be said to represent official policy,'" a point to be considered in more detail in the next section dealing with the liability of local governments and supervisory personnel.

While the law on municipal liability is in a state of continual development, the law on § 1983 liability of states has now been settled by the case of Will v Michigan Department of State Police.[101] In a five to four opinion, the Court held "that neither a State nor its officials acting in their official capacities are 'persons' under § 1983,"[102] explaining that the reason for differentiating between municipalities, which remain liable, and states is that "States are protected by the Eleventh Amendment while municipalities are not...."[103]

The liability of sheriffs, who are state officers for some purposes and county officers for other purposes, is complex. Although counties are "creatures" of states, they are not so considered for the purposes of the eleventh amendment, and thus may be sued.[104] This immunity likewise has been breached for cities in § 1983 actions by the *Owen* case, discussed earlier in this chapter. Although the Supreme Court has not yet specifically dealt with county liability under § 1983, lower courts have.

Parker v Williams[105] involved a woman prisoner, who during her incarceration, was released on bond, then kidnapped and raped by the county jailor. The county and the sheriff, in his official and individual capacity, were sued both in state tort law and § 1983. In earlier cases, the state supreme court had decided that the sheriff was a state officer. Relying on that finding, the court of appeals held that both the county and the sheriff are immune to suit on the basis of state tort law. As to the 1983 action, the sheriff is immune to damage claims in his official capacity inasmuch as such a claim is really a suit against a state official for damages the state would have to pay. But the sheriff may be liable in his individual capacity and thereby incurr the liability of the county because the sheriff is the official policymaker for the county.

That the state supreme court had decided that the sheriff is a state official is not definitive in terms of immunity because the sheriff may be a state official for some purposes and a county official for others—as county jailor, for example. "One official may exercise county authority over some matters and state authority over other matters,"[106] to say the least, a foggy concept on which to base either policies or legal advice.

Vicarious liability of municipalities and their supervisory employees for acts of subordinates in § 1983 actions

All criminal justice agencies consist of hierarchical (bureaucratic) structures in which policy is supposedly formulated at the top by highranking officials, to be executed by lower echelon line officers. The Supreme Court has never formulated an adequate legal theory to deal with the intricate practical aspects intervening between policymaking and the implementation of these decisions. The Court has rejected theories of vicarious liability applicable to private industry without putting anything in its place. By vicarious liability is meant liability resulting from actions of someone other than oneself. Under the common law, employers were legally responsible for the tortious acts of their employees as long as the employees' acts were within the scope of their employment. Thus, the employer of a truck driver who negligently injured a third party in the course of making a delivery, would have to legally respond to the victim.

That doctrine, called *respondeat superior,* means that superiors are legally responsible for their subordinate's wrongdoing. The rationale behind such a doctrine is not that the superiors have themselves negligently caused the injury to the plaintiff by their own actions and are therefore at fault. Rather it is that because subordinates are really acting for the benefit of their superiors, those superiors should be legally responsible for the tortious acts of the subordinates acting in their stead. The doctrine further recognizes that suing the negligent employee would be useless, for a lower-level employee would not ordinarily be financially able to respond in damages. Employers are better able to absorb the loss as a cost of doing business by spreading it among the public to whom they sell their products than if injured individuals had to bear the entire loss themselves. To a limited extent, the Supreme Court has now recognized this cost-spreading principle, evidenced by the quotations from *Owen* set forth above.

There are good reasons why plaintiffs would want to apply this doctrine to 1983 actions. The state cannot be sued because of the defense of sovereign immunity. Individuals who have committed the injury can, of course, be made subject to suit under the conditions set forth above. Local governments can also be sued for their constitutional violations. Yet, the interests of plaintiffs in suing criminal justice personnel often includes objectives other than money damages, in particular the desire to force a change in agency policies. Such policies, especially those that may result in constitutional torts, are likely to be manifested in the actions of lower-level personnel such as police or correctional officers, while being directed by upper-level personnel. Where such an interest is involved, the right to seek damages from cities or high-level officers would be an effective tool. Litigants, therefore, have naturally turned to local governments and superior officers as defendants both because they are more likely to be able to pay damages and because it is the local government that often determines the policy complained of. In such suits, plaintiffs can and must place in issue not only the alleged wrong of the individual officer but of the departmental "policies and customs" under which the officer acted.

Attempts, however, to apply this species of liability to § 1983 actions or other claims against local governments or criminal justice superiors for the acts of their subordinates have been generally unsuccessful in the absence of some proven fault on the part of the superior officer. This trend was confirmed in *Monell,* which while dealing with cities rather than with supervisory personnel, had implications for both classes of defendants. There, the Court found "that a municipality cannot be held *solely* because it employs a tortfeasor—or in other words, a municipality cannot be held liable under § 1983 on a *respondeat superior* theory."[107] The Court drew its conclusion from the statutory language, as originally passed, which made liable "*Any person who . . . shall subject, or cause to be subjected,* any person," to a deprivation of federal rights.[108] Such language, the Court reasoned, showed an intention on the part of Congress to place liability on a government only when that government "causes" its employees to commit a constitutional tort. The mere fact of the employer-employee relationship is insufficient. Summing up its holding on this issue, the Court stated:

> We conclude, therefore, that a local government may not be sued under § 1983 for an injury inflicted solely by its employees or agents. Instead, it is when execution of a government's policy or custom, whether made by its lawmakers or by those whose edicts or acts may fairly be said to represent official policy, inflicts the injury that the government as an entity is responsible under § 1983.[109]

Where the cause of action is based on custom, long-standing unconstitutional acts of low-level employees will be insufficient in themselves to sustain liability because such officials cannot, on their own, create a departmental "custom." Before finding liability, courts require knowledge or approval of the custom by high-ranking officials. Referring to Justice Harlan's opinion in an earlier civil rights case, the Court quoted the following passage, indicating its understanding of the use of custom in § 1983 cases:

> Congress included customs and usages [in § 1983] because of the persistent and widespread discriminatory practices of state officials. . . . Although not authorized by written law, such practices of state officials could well be so permanent and well settled as to constitute a 'custom or usage' with the force of law.[110]

Monell applied to supervisory personnel—proof requirements

Although the facts of *Monell* dealt uniquely with a municipality, the Court went out of its way to apply the same logic to supervisory personnel. In a footnote, the Court suggests that "the mere right to control without any control or direction having been exercised and without any failure to supervise is not enough to support § 1983 liability,"[111] implying that where control or direction is exercised or where the constitutional tort results from a failure to supervise, liability of supervisory personnel is possible. Thus, standards to be applied for liability seem to be the same for both municipalities and for supervisory personnel employed by these cities: unless these "persons" are shown to have "caused" the injury complained of, the 1983 plaintiff cannot recover. Further, it must be shown that the acts of subordinates resulting in injury can be said to fairly represent official policy formulated by superiors. Only then can the city and the superiors be required to financially respond for the subordinates' conduct. As in the case of other torts, the plaintiff must show both a duty (based on official government policy or custom) from the defendant to the plaintiff and a breach of that duty causing plaintiff's constitutional injury.

Superiors may be sued in either their individual or official capacities. Sued in their individual capacities they have the good faith immunity defense that has been described above. Sued in their official capacity (this is done by merely making such an allegation in plaintiff's complaint), they have no immunity defense because such suit is the legal equivalent of suing the local government body. A finding of liability against superiors in their official capacity is a judgment against their local government employer. As in the suit against their local government entity, the official must be shown to have acted pursuant to some established government policy or custom that resulted in plaintiff's deprivation of federal rights.[112]

The distinction between individual and official liability has caused so much confusion, that the Court felt called upon to explain the point:

> Personal-capacity suits seek to impose personal liability upon a government official for actions he takes under color of state law. Official-capacity suits, in contrast, "generally represent only another way of pleading an action against an entity of which an officer is an agent." As long as the government entity receives notice and an opportunity to respond, an official-capacity suit is, in all respects other than name, to be treated as a suit against the entity. It is *not* a suit against the official personally, for the real party in interest is the entity. Thus, while an award of damages against an official in his personal capacity can be executed only against the official's personal assets, a plaintiff seeking to recover on a damages judgment in an official-capacity suit must look to the government entity itself.
>
> On the merits, to establish *personal* liability in a § 1983 action, it is enough to show that the official, acting under color of state law, caused the deprivation of a federal right. More is required in an official-capacity action, however, for a

governmental entity is liable under § 1983 only when the entity itself is a "'moving force'" behind the deprivation; thus, in an official-capacity suit the entity's "policy or custom" must have played a part in the violation of federal law.[113]

Further clarification of this difficult distinction was attempted in Pembaur v City of Cincinnati.[114] Deputy Sheriffs armed with a court order but without a search warrant, after first trying to persuade plaintiff to allow them to enter his medical clinic so as to search for two witnesses sought by the order, broke down the door with an axe, arresting two persons who later turned out not to be the wanted persons. Before making the decision to break down the door the deputies called the assistant county prosecutor, who in turn conferred with the County Prosecutor. The deputies were instructed to "go in and get" the witnesses.[115] The question presented to the Court was "whether, and in what circumstances, a decision by municipal policymakers on a single occasion may satisfy this requirement."[116]

The Court first concluded that absent exigent circumstances, entry into Pembaur's clinic without a search warrant was in violation of his fourth amendment rights. A re-examination of *Monell* showed clearly that "the basis for municipal liability under § 1983, must be pursuant to a municipality's 'official policy'. . . ."[117] The Court then went on to clarify the meaning of "official policy."

> Municipal liability attaches only where the decisionmaker possesses final authority to establish municipal policy with respect to the action ordered. . . . Authority to make municipal policy may be granted directly by a legislative enactment or may be delegated by an official who possesses such authority, and of course, whether an official had final policymaking authority is a question of state law. . . . We hold that municipal liability under § 1983 attaches where—and only where—a deliberate choice to follow a course of action is made from among various alternatives by the official or officials responsible for establishing final policy with respect to the subject matter in question. . . . Applying this standard to the case before us, we have little difficulty concluding that the Court of Appeals erred in dismissing petitioner's claim against the county. . . . The Prosecutor made a considered decision based on his understanding of the law and commanded the officers forcibly to enter petitioner's clinic. That decision directly caused the violation of petitioner's Fourth Amendment rights.[118]

In the 1988 case of City of St Louis v Praprotnik,[119] the Court attempted to clarify "the proper legal standard for determining when isolated decisions by municipal officials or employees may expose the municipality itself to liability under 42 USC § 1983."[120] The plurality decision of four, written by Justice O'Connor, sought to set forth the "guiding principles" a majority had agreed to in *Pembaur:*

> municipalities may be held liable under § 1983 only for acts for which the municipality itself is actually responsible, "that is, acts which the municipality has officially sanctioned." Second, only those municipal officials who have "final policymaking authority" may by their actions subject the government to § 1983 liability. Third, whether a particular official has "final policymaking authority" is a question of *state law . . .* Fourth, the challenged action must have been taken pursuant to a policy adopted by the official or officials responsible under state law for making policy in *that area* of the city's business.[121]

The application of the rules to the fact situation in *Praprotnik* illustrates the difficulty of determining the last of these criteria. Proprotnik was a city architect who fell out of favor with his supervisors for filing a grievance against them. He alleged that in retaliation, a first amendment violation, his supervisors initially transferred him to a dead-end job and then laid him off. The Court reiterated that "an unconstitutional government policy could be inferred from a single decision taken by the highest officials responsible for setting policy in that area of the government's business."[122]

In applying the above standards to the facts, the Court determined that Praprotnik had not shown that those able to make a final decision in such matters—according to state law, the mayor and alderman—had set a city policy with reference to the personnel matter that governed his case. Rather, the city had empowered a Civil Service Commission to review such matters. Therefore, the supervisors who decided the action that injured Praprotnik could not be said to be carrying out city policy, and the city was not therefore liable.

This decision seems far from a satisfactory resolution of this complex issue. As Justice Brennan said in his concurrence:

> the plurality suggests that whenever the decisions of an official are subject to some sort of review—however limited—that official's decisions are nonfinal. . . . Therefore, even where an official wields policymaking authority with respect to a challenged decision, the city would not be liable for that official's policy decision unless *reviewing* officials affirmatively approved both the "decision and the basis for it" . . . Even the hollowest promise of review is sufficient to divest all city officials save the mayor and governing legislative body of final policymaking authority.[123]

Thus, only where the act done by line personnel carries out a policy attributable to an official who has the authority to establish the "final policy" on the matter, is the liability of the municipal corporation engaged.

The 1989 case of Jett v Dallas Independent School District,[124] another five to four opinion, allowed the Court to further direct trial courts on how to determine what official has final policymaking authority. Jett, the white male plaintiff, was a teacher and head football coach at a high school that went through a racial change from predominantly white to predominantly black. After a black principal, Todd, was appointed, continual clashes developed between the two. Todd, among other things, objected to statements made by Jett to local newspapers about the lack of academic qualification of most of the players. Following a letter from Todd informing Jett that Todd intended to relieve Jett of his coaching duties, Jett met with the district superintendent who decided to follow the recommendation of Todd and reassign Jett to another school. Jett resigned and then brought suit against the school district and Todd, in his personal and official capacities, under §§ 1981 and 1983 claiming due process, first amendment and equal protection of the law violations.

The question decided by the Court was "whether 42 USC § 1981 provides an independent federal cause of action for damages against local governmental entities, and whether that cause of action is broader than the damage remedy available under 42 USC § 1983, such that a municipality may be held liable for its employees' violations of § 1981 under a theory of *respondeat superior.*"[125]

After an extensive historical analysis of the statutory history of the above sections the Court held

> that the express "action at law" provided by § 1983 for the "deprivation of any rights, privileges, or immunities secured by the Constitution and laws," provides the exclusive federal damages remedy for the violation of the rights guaranteed by § 1981 when the claim is pressed against a state actor. Thus to prevail on his claim for damages against the school district, petitioner must show that the violation of his "right to make contracts" protected by § 1981 was caused by a custom or policy within the meaning of *Monell* and subsequent cases.[126]

If respondeat superior cannot be used as a basis of liability, then the Court must determine if the principal or superintendent "can be considered policymakers for the school district such that their decisions may rightly be said to represent the official policy of the [district] subjecting it to liability under § 1983."[127] Referring to *Praprotnik* (holding that policymaking authority was to be determined by state law), the Court

declared that identification of which officials make official local governmental policy is a question to be determined by the trial judge *before* the
case goes to the jury.

> [T]he trial judge must identify those officials of governmental bodies who
> speak with final policymaking authority for the local governmental actor
> concerning the action alleged to have caused the particular constitutional or
> statutory violation at issue. Once those officials who have the power to make
> official policy on a particular issue have been identified, it is for the jury to
> determine whether *their* decisions have caused the deprivation of rights at
> issue by policies which affirmatively command that it occur [citing *Monell*], or
> by acquiescence in a longstanding practice or custom which constitutes the
> "standard operating procedure" of the local governmental entity."[128]

The Court remanded the case to the court of appeals to determine,
based on Texas law, whether the superintendent had final policymaking
authority and whether a new trial is required to determine the school
district's liability for the principal's actions.

Alternatives to respondeat superior to find superior officers liable

Although it is now clear that criminal justice superiors are not responsible for the torts of their subordinates on the basis of respondeat superior,
the following "exceptions" to that rule, based in most instances on actual
fault of the superiors themselves, have developed over time from statutory or case law:

(1) the common law or statutes of the state in which the tort takes place
provides for liability of superiors;
(2) the superior was or should have been aware of the misconduct, but nevertheless took no remedial action to prevent it;
(3) the superior was deliberately indifferent in the selection, training or retaining
of the subordinate who caused the injury;
(4) the superior intentionally acted through subordinates to deprive persons of
their constitutional rights.

Monroe holds that § 1983 liability is to be considered against a background of tort law to be found in the state in which the tort takes place.[130]
The same principle should apply in deciding whether superiors are
responsible for torts of subordinates.

(1) Common law and statutory liability of superiors

In the case of sheriffs and their deputies, an ancient common law
doctrine relies on the legal fiction that sheriffs and their deputies are
legally one. An act of the deputy can therefore be said to be the act of the

sheriff. No question of respondeat superior is therefore involved. A further basis of liability for sheriffs arises from their freedom to appoint as deputy whomever they wish. Like private employers, sheriffs are responsible for the actions of the individuals they have employed. Where this common law or statutory principle is in operation § 1983 cases have generally followed this doctrine.[131]

In Scott v Vandiver,[132] the fourth circuit federal court of appeals, in part, based its finding of liability of a sheriff for the actions of his deputies on a state statute empowering the sheriff to call upon a posse "to assist in enforcing the laws and in arresting violators."[133] The action arose out of an assault on the plaintiff by sheriff's deputies recruited under the above statute to assist the sheriff in the investigation of a shooting. As a result of a long-standing agreement that county employees would assist the sheriff upon request, such recruitment was found to constitute a "custom" within the meaning of § 1983. In addition, the common law of the state authorized sheriffs to summon bystanders to assist them in apprehending felons. All three grounds, custom, common law, and statute, were cited by the court as § 1983 bases of liability of the sheriff for the actions of his deputies. A Missouri statute placing responsibility on the sheriff for the county jail, the custody of prisoners, and for the appointment of jailers "makes the Sheriff liable for jail conditions even though he may not have had actual knowledge of them."[134]

State laws have been found to place an affirmative responsibility on criminal justice personnel to oversee their area of responsibility. Thus, in Messimer v Lockhart,[135] the director of corrections "has statutory responsibility over precisely the conditions giving rise to the [alleged constitutional] violations," even though he may have no knowledge of the particular incident involving the plaintiff.

(2) Knowledge of subordinate's wrongdoing

Just at what point knowledge of the unconstitutional actions of their subordinates places an affirmative duty on the local government unit or on the supervisor to act to end those violations has not yet been clearly established. If the Court takes the position that he who sees no evil knows no evil (as it appears to be doing), it will give a signal to supervisory personnel that the less they know about the doings of their subordinates the better; and that a department that has no policy or has a vague policy in a constitutionally sensitive area is better off legally than one that sets forth clear guidelines for its officers.[136]

In Jett v Dallas Independent School District,[137] the Court in dicta, through Justice O'Connor, hinted that either action or nonaction could trigger supervisor liability. Deprivations may occur either "by policies which affirmatively command that it occur [citing *Monell*], or by acquiescence in a longstanding practice or custom which constitutes the 'standard operating procedure' of the local governmental entity."[138]

Elaborating further on this point, Justice O'Connor, in concurring and dissenting, in part, in City of Canton, Ohio v Harris,[139] stated:

> Where, as here, a claim of municipal liability is predicated upon a failure to act, the requisite degree of fault must be shown by proof of a background of events and circumstances which establish that the "policy of inaction" is the functional equivalent of a decision by the city itself to violate the Constitution. ... Where a § 1983 plaintiff can establish that the facts available to city policymakers put them on actual or constructive notice that the particular omission is substantially certain to result in the violation of the constitutional rights of their citizens, the dictates of *Monell* are satisfied.[140]

Thus, a superior's liability based on knowledge of prior misdoings by subordinates is usually based on a finding that the supervisor knew or should have known that the constitutional violation would be likely to occur—a common law tort foreseeability concept. In effect, plaintiffs must show that the supervisor defendant had notice, either actual or constructive (the supervisor should have known), of the unconstitutional practice. But Justice Rehnquist, and a majority, including Justice O'Connor herself, appear to have taken a position at odds with Justice O'Connor's earlier dicta.

DeShaney v Winnebago Cty Soc Serv Dept,[141] considered under the state action section in ch 1, also has important implications for supervisor liability. There, social workers were sued under § 1983 for failing to act to remove a child from his father's custody even though they had received reports that the father was abusing him. In the course of the Court's opinion, it seemed to eliminate knowledge of wrongdoing as a basis for a cause of action under the due process clause of the fourteenth amendment:

> The affirmative duty to protect arises not from the State's knowledge of the individual's predicament or from its expressions of intent to help him, but from the limitation which it has imposed on his freedom to act on his behalf.[142]

Cases following this view of a superior's liability, where the state's knowledge of the plaintiff's vulnerability was the sole basis of the claim, have refused to find liability on the part of the superior. In Brown v

Grabowski,[143] two women were sexually assaulted and despite repeated reports to them, the police took no action to arrest their tormentor. On the authority of *DeShaney,* the court could not find the chief of police responsible.

> Plaintiff has presented considerable evidence that Chief Trolan presided over a detective bureau that was carelessly apathetic at best and greviously incompetent at worst. The prosecutor's office found the . . . Detective Bureau completely lacked supervision . . . and did nothing to follow up on crimes involving domestic violence. Plaintiff has supplied no evidence, however, that Chief Trolan directed or affirmatively participated in any of the actions claimed to have deprived Evans of her constitutional rights and ultimately her life.[144]

There seems to be agreement, therefore, that some minimal "personal" involvement in the deprivation of rights is necessary before a supervisor may be legally held. In Williams v Smith,[145] a state prisoner charged the prison superintendent had prevented him from calling witnesses in a disciplinary hearing. The court stated that there were several ways that such a defendant could be personally involved in the deprivation: (1) by personal involvement; (2) by failing to remedy the wrong, after learning of it; (3) by creating a policy or custom under which the deprivations occurred, or allowing such policies or customs to continue; or (4) by being grossly negligent in managing subordinates who cause the unlawful condition or event.[146] Even though the superintendent claimed he did not "personally know, acquiesce or participate" in the deprivation of plaintiff's constitutional rights,

> [W]e cannot say . . . that as Superintendent of Attica he was not directly responsible for the conduct of prison disciplinary hearings, or that, given the frequency with which Attica has violated inmate rights to call witnesses during Smith's tenure, Smith did not accept a custom or policy at Attica allowing that unconstitutional practice to occur.[147]

Applying tort principles, as the Court admonished in *Monroe,*[148] the proper question to ask is "whether the supervisor has done something, or failed to do something that he ought to have done, which was the direct cause of the violation of the plaintiff's constitutional rights."

In Guterrez-Rodriguez v Cartagena,[149] plaintiff, in a § 1983 action, sued the police department superintendent for injuries resulting from a stop by drug enforcement officers. In that incident, the officers approached plaintiff's car with guns drawn, neglected to identify themselves as officers, and when plaintiff drove off, shot and seriously wounded him. The superintendent's liability could not be based on respondeat superior; rather it had to be based on his acts or omissions shown to amount to callous indifference, and that an "affirmative link" must be shown between the conduct of the line officers and the action or inaction of the supervisory officials. Thus in this instance

> It could be found that Cartagena's conduct reflected a reckless or callous indifference to the rights of the citizens of Puerto Rico. Both his failure to identify and take remedial action concerning Sato [the offending employee] and his employment of a disciplinary system that was grossly deficient . . . made it highly likely that the police officers under his command would engage in conduct that would deprive the citizens of Puerto Rico of their constitutional rights. Had the disciplinary system been in place, Soto would have been identified as an officer prone to misconduct.[150]

In Doe v Angelina County, Texas,[151] Doe was arrested for an offense carrying only a fine, but nevertheless, pursuant to a policy of the county, Doe was imprisoned because he was unable to pay the fine. Under earlier Supreme Court decisions this procedure was clearly unconstitutional. The question was the sheriff's liability, if any, for the deprivation of plaintiff's rights. Even though here, the sheriff adopted this procedure at the request of the county judge, it was the sheriff who

> promulgated the procedure that jail officials followed when they incarcerated plaintiffs. Where subordinates act pursuant to a policy or procedure adopted by their supervisor and their compliance with the policy or procedure results in a constitutional violation, promulgation of the policy or procedure is sufficient personal participation in the constitutional violation to give rise to individual liability on the part of the supervisory official.[152]

In Murray v Koehler,[153] a prisoner on Rikers island alleged he was assaulted by several correctional officers because they believed he had punched an assistant deputy warden during a prison altercation. Plaintiff also named a supervisor who plaintiff alleged was notified of the altercation but did nothing to protect prisoners even though he knew from previous incidents that prisoners would be in danger. Knowledge of a past history of such incidents

> would permit a reasonable person to conclude that [the supervisors] had "actual or constructive notice" of foreseeable unconstitutional practices and "demonstrate[d] 'gross negligence' or 'deliberate indifference by failing to act.[154]

A classic case of imputed knowledge of wrongdoing is Brandon v Holt,[155] in which the defendant officer's reputation for brutality was well-known. Twenty complaints had been filed against him; he was known to his fellow officers as a "mental case"; he rode in his squad car alone because other officers would not ride with him; he boasted of killing a man on duty; and he wore what he called "killing gloves." As to these matters in the department, there was a "code of silence"; the department's procedure for dealing with civilian complaints was to send a form letter under the Director's signature assuring the person that appropriate action had been taken even if, in fact, nothing had been done, so that the effect was both a cover up of such misconduct as far as the public was concerned and keeping the officer's superiors in ignorance of his conduct. Under such facts the liability of the officer and the Director were not even in issue.

On the other hand, a prison warden is not legally responsible for the deliberate indifference of physicians with whom he merely contracted to provide inmate care. A warden has no duty to monitor treatment of individual prisoners to make sure they receive proper medical treatment.[156]

(3) Deliberate indifference in selection, training or retention of subordinates

Because every police officer has received *some* training and because there has been so much criticism of the adequacy of training procedures, failure to properly train has been a favored basis of § 1983 liability. Negligence in the selection or retention of officers which in turn resulted in the constitutional violation complained of has not been found to be a sufficient allegation. Instead, deliberate indifference must be alleged. Connecting the particular violation to inadequate training, sometimes years in the past, has also been difficult to establish.

In the landmark case in this area, Justice White, in a rare unanimous opinion (on the main issue in the case), spoke for the Court in City of Canton, Ohio v Harris,[157] succinctly setting forth the issue, and the Court's disposition:

> [W]e are asked to determine if a municipality can ever be liable under 42 U.S.C. § 1983 for constitutional violations resulting from its failure to train municipal employees. We hold that, under certain circumstances, such liability is permitted by the statute.[158]

Harris was arrested by the City of Canton police for reasons not disclosed in the case. She was carried to the police station in a patrol wagon, and upon her arrival police noticed she was sitting on the wagon floor; that when asked if she needed medical attention she answered incoherently; in the station, she slumped to the floor on two occasions; police finally left her lying there to prevent her from falling again. No medical attention was ever provided by the police. After an hour, she was released in custody to her family who took her by ambulance to a hospital where she was diagnosed to be suffering from "emotional ailments."

She sued the City and its officials claiming a violation of her due process right to receive proper medical attention while in custody. At a jury trial, evidence was presented that showed that there was a municipal ordinance authorizing shift commanders to determine, solely at their discretion, whether a detainee required medical care. No special training was provided commanders on how to determine who was entitled to medical care.

The Court rejected the city's argument that only unconstitutional policies can be a basis for an action under § 1983. Next, it set forth the "degree of fault [that] must be evidenced by the municipality's inaction before liability will be permitted":

> We hold today that the inadequacy of police training may serve as the basis for § 1983 liability only where the failure to train amounts to deliberate indifference to the rights of persons with whom the police come into contact.[159]

In elaborating its reasoning, the Court added:

> Thus, in the case at hand, respondent must still prove that the deficiency in training actually caused the police officers' indifference to her medical needs. Would the injury have been avoided had the employee been trained under a program that was not deficient in the identified respect?[160]

Justice O'Connor, concurring (and dissenting only as to the necessity for remand), suggests one instance when a city would be clearly liable: where a city fails to train an officer in the use of deadly force, an area in which the Court had clearly established constitutional limitations, and where the failure to train effectively will create an "extremely high risk that constitutional violations will ensue."[161]

Lower courts have constructed a three pronged approach to determining if supervisors are liable for inadequate training:

> (1) whether, in failing adequately to train and supervise subordinates, he was deliberately indifferent to the [plaintiff's constitutional rights]; (2) whether a reasonable person in the supervisor's position would know that his failure to train and supervise reflected deliberate indifference; and (3) whether his conduct was causally related to this constitutional infringement by his subordinate.[162]

One of the foreseeable situations *Canton* referred to was the use of deadly force by officers.

> [C]ity policymakers know to a moral certainty that their police officers will be required to arrest fleeing felons. The city has armed its officers with firearms, in part to allow them to accomplish this task. Thus, the need to train officers in the constitutional limitations on the use of deadly force can be said to be "so obvious," that failure to do so could properly be characterized as "deliberate indifference" to constitutional rights.[163]

In Cooper v Merrill,[164] police pursued Cooper, a robbery suspect believed to be armed and dangerous. After a car chase, Cooper ran from his car and hid in some bushes. Officers fired a number of shots at him, three of which hit him. Cooper sued the borough of Trainer for, among other claims, a lack of any policy on the use of deadly force. In order to maintain such a claim the court suggested he would have to show "1) inadequate training, 2) the inadequate training represents a policy which reflects a deliberate indifference to plaintiff's constitutional rights, and 3) the policy caused the alleged violation of constitutional rights."[165] Other than the use of the state force statute, the county here had no oral or written policy with reference to use of deadly force. "There was no evidence that the Borough provided any practice training either in the field or in the form of a manual or procedure to guide its officers,"[166] and therefore the requested summary judgment for the Borough was denied.

Another foreseeable problem, on which police departments today must have a policy is the arrest and disposition of persons with AIDS. In Doe v Borough of Barrington[167] defendant police officers stopped plaintiffs, a husband and wife riding in a truck. The husband informed police, as they were about to search him, that he had tested HIV-positive and that he had "weeping lesions." In a later incident that same day occurring opposite the plaintiffs' house, the police officers informed plaintiffs' neighbors that the husband had tested positive for AIDS. The neighbors immediately notified others, many of whom withdrew their children from the school the plaintiffs' children attended; newspaper and TV stories appeared, as a result of which plaintiffs suffered much embarrassment, humiliation and discrimination.

Plaintiffs argued that the town was legally responsible because of the lack of training in the way to handle confidentiality problems involving AIDS arrestees. The court agreed:

> In light of the duties assigned to police officers, the need for police training about AIDS is obvious. . . . The failure to instruct officers to keep information

about AIDS carriers confidential was likely to result in disclosures and fan the flames of hysteria. [The town's] failure to train officers, therefore, was likely to result in a violation of constitutional rights. . . . Knowing that other communities had taken precautions to protect officers from AIDS, [the town] did not establish its own policy or instruct officers about precautions. As such, [the town] made a conscious decision not to train its officers about the disease. . . . Clearly [the officer's] ignorance about the disease caused the improper disclosure.[168]

(4) Intentionally wrongful acts of superiors

All of the above cases involve some degree of culpability on the part of defendant superior officers. The highest degree of culpability has always been reserved for intentional acts. Therefore, superiors who intentionally act through subordinates to deprive persons of constitutional rights are liable to § 1983 actions. Examples include high level officials who conspired to discharge a police officer,[169] and a police chief who improperly discharged a police officer.[170]

Summary and conclusions

Over time, courts and state legislatures have wavered in their support for sovereign immunity, a doctrine that is hard to reconcile with the democratic principles that neither the state nor its officials are above the law and that every wrong should have its appropriate remedy. Even though courts and legislatures are beginning to reduce the doctrine to rational limits, sovereign immunity remains an important defense against both common law and constitutional torts. Because of the special history of § 1983 and the increased number of 1983 cases that have come before it in recent years, the Supreme Court has begun to refine its views, basing its approach on the function performed by the particular defendant rather than on whether the defendant is formally part of the legislative, executive, or judicial branch. The concepts employed by the Court have been that of absolute and qualified immunity; the legislative, executive or judicial functions, scope of authority, and a distinction between common law and constitutional torts.

Where a defendant (the state, or a state or federal employee) has absolute immunity, plaintiffs have no legal remedy for their injuries, even if the tort is committed with malice and in bad faith. The reason given by the Court for the different degree of protection is that absolute immunity is needed in situations where the decisionmakers (judges, prosecutors, and legislators) are likely to make numerous discretionary decisions as a part of their work that would constantly expose them to suit for alleged wrongs. If such actions were allowed, litigation would interfere both with their liberty to make independent decisions and with the likelihood that capable persons would accept decisionmaking posts. In contrast, where qualified immunity is assigned, the Court believes that the decisionmaker is sufficiently protected by a rule that requires the law to be so settled at the time of the violation that the act breaking the rule could not have been taken in good faith.

Following this logic, past and current court decisions, for both common law and constitutional torts, have found that persons performing legislative and judicial functions have absolute immunity. This defense is applicable even to executive officials, such as prosecutors, police, and administrative trial examiners, who perform judicial functions. Officials who perform executive functions in which some degree of discretion is exercised are given qualified immunity for decisions that result in injury to others.

With reference to § 1983 claims, the Court has constructed an order of proof and defense first requiring plaintiffs to show that the defendant, while acting under color of law, deprived them of a federal right. If the defendant is a line officer, the question is whether a reasonable officer could have believed his illegal act to be lawful, in light of clearly established law and the information he possessed at the time.

Higher-level defendant officials wishing to assert a qualified immunity defense must assert that defense by showing that their function was discretionary (decisionmaking) rather than ministerial and that they acted within the "outer perimeter" of their authority. The plaintiff must then show that the constitutional right violated was clearly established at the time of the alleged violation; if the defendant officials knew or reasonably should have known of the right, but nevertheless, the official's conduct violated the constitutional norm, then the immunity defense will be rejected. These requirements are applicable equally to state and federal officials. Liability of federal officials, however, is grounded in provisions of the Constitution, (a *Bivens*-type claim) rather than in § 1983. In a *Bivens* type claim, plaintiffs can neither sue the federal government directly, nor the federal official in her official capacity. Suit must be against the official in her personal capacity.

Until the *Monell* decision, states, counties and cities, had absolute immunity from suit. *Monell* removed cities from this privileged position, finding they were "persons" within the meaning of § 1983. But since cities can act only vicariously through their employees, city liability is tied to the actions of its officials, particularly those who execute a government's policy or custom in such a way that it represents "official" policy. Both superiors and the municipalities they represent are tied to the same standard of liability. To be liable under § 1983, the city must "cause" the constitutional violation, a fact that can occur only when the violation is the result of "official policy," that is, a consequence of actions taken by superior officers who have final policymaking authority. Whether the defense allowed is absolute or qualified immunity, the defense applies only where officials act within the scope of their authority. Where they act beyond that scope, they are personally liable to the injured party for their acts.

While there has been little success in founding liability of cities or of superiors on vicarious liability, there has been more success in asserting liability on the basis of actual fault of superiors where that fault has been based on common law or statute; on the failure to take action to prevent unlawful conduct of which they were aware; where their negligence in the selection, training, or retaining of subordinates has caused injury, or where the wrongful action of superiors was intentional.

The Supreme Court has not yet clearly decided that a failure to act when there is a duty to act will result in supervisor or municipal liability. Court opinions appear in conflict on this issue. Mere negligence as a mental state is insufficient to trigger liability. Deliberate indifference on the part of the official is necessary, a standard much closer to a reckless or intentional than a negligent mental state. The Court has applied this doctrine recently in finding that where failure to train amounts to deliberate indifference to the rights of persons with whom criminal justice personnel come in contact, municipal liability may result.

In addition to the legal side of sovereign immunity, there is also a social perspective. From feudal times, the doctrine has represented a means by which the class controlling the feudal domains or the state could protect itself against those who wished to use the judiciary as a battering ram to assault its privileges. Sovereign immunity has been the legal shield used by a privileged governing class to avoid providing a remedy against themselves for the wrongs committed in the course of governing. Putting aside the various rationalizations advanced by its proponents, the practical result of the doctrine has been to permit the state (and therefore those who controlled the state apparatus) (1) to make policy decisions with little control by or concern for the persons who might be wronged by those decisions; (2) to maintain a front of absolutism that prevented an inquiry into the nature of the decisions taken; (3) to place the costs of injuries caused as a result of these decisions on the victims themselves; and (4) to allow the state, in the few instances where it consented to recompense the injury, to appear as a beneficent and charitable monarch.

Although there has been a substantial democratization of the political structure as compared to feudal times, nonetheless, even now, the government follows a feudal, bureaucratic, hierarchical model in which the highest to lowest posts generally represent a descending ladder of policymaking (discretionary) responsibility. Thus, it is the highest-placed groups in our society, from both a social and economic perspective, that are most frequently the policymakers. But it is the middle-level policymakers (police chiefs and prison wardens) who are most highly represented as § 1983 defendants. On the other hand, most 1983 plaintiffs (to be considered in the next chapter), consist largely of minorities and the poorest part of the population, groups which are likely to be under the surveillance of police or correctional personnel. While other groups, such as students (*Davis* and *Wood*), women (*Monell*) and criminal justice personnel (*Owen*), have asserted rights under § 1983, most 1983 plaintiffs will be found in prisons and center-city ghettos.

Thus, the effect of the doctrine, to the extent it restricts law suits against the state and its policymaking employees, does not strike the population in an even-handed manner. Rather, it protects the more powerful from claims by the least favored and powerful groups, those who are more often subject to constitutional injury. On the other hand, restrictions on the doctrine have the effect of reducing the absolute power of administrators, requiring more accountability for their decisions and opening these decisions to public examination.

With these thoughts in mind it is possible to re-examine the latest decisions of the Supreme Court in order to better understand their import. These cases have resulted in significant breaches in the immunity defense. The rise in the number of § 1983 suits, itself related to the civil rights activities of the 1950s and 1960s, forced the federal courts, especially the US Supreme Court, to reconsider the history of § 1983 in light of the Reconstruction Period. Sovereign immunity has roots in feudal landlord-serf relations. Immunity reinforced a relationship in which the landlord was all-powerful and the serf powerless, remarkably close to the South's pre-Civil War master-slave relations. Reconstruction legislation, including § 1983, was directed at eradicating that condition with all its incidents. The Court called on that history in *Monell* where it found that cities were persons and therefore subject to suit. But in addition to the history of 1983 and the feudal roots of the doctrine, the Court decided the case subject to the fundamental values of today's liberal democratic state with a capitalist economic organization, that is, a state limited by law that proclaims that every person deprived of a right is entitled to a remedy and that fault is individual rather than collective. Nevertheless, the overriding purpose of the doctrine and the Court's interpretation of it remains—to limit liability within the constraints of a hierarchically-oriented elite structure. More recent cases of the Rehnquist Court, making it more difficult for § 1983 plaintiffs to sue, are consistent with that purpose.

ENDNOTES

1. Monell v Dept of Social Services 436 US 658, 690 (1978) (local government bodies), and Owen v City of Independence Mo 445 US 622, 638 (1980) (cities). See generally, Civil actions against state government: its divisions, agencies and officers, Griffin, Jr, L, and Sheiring, D, eds, Colorado Springs, Shepard's/McGraw-Hill, 1982, Nov. 1989 Cumulative Supplement.
2. Moor v County of Alameda 411 US 693 (1973). Neither states nor their subdivisions, nor their employees acting in their official capacities, are "persons" under § 1983. Will v Michigan Dept. of State Police 491 US 58, 71 (1989) and Griffin and Sheiring, n 1 *supra* § 10.4.
3. See, for example, Port Authority Trans-Hudson Corp v Feeney 110 SCt 1868, 1875 (1990) where Justice Brennan, concurring, argued that the eleventh amendment "did not constitutionalize some general notion of state sovereign immunity" but rather was a "jurisdictional provision," and Jackson, Vicki C, the Supreme Court, the eleventh amendment, and state sovereign immunity 98 Yale L J 1, 3–4 (Nov 1988) stating that "this principle of immunity is in tension with two other fundamental constitutional principles that the law will generally provide a remedy for rights violated by the government (government accountability) and that the judicial power of the United States over claims answering under federal law is as broad within its sphere, as is the legislative power of the United States ('full judicial power')." As of 1982, only two states, South Dakota and Virginia, retained sovereign immunity without some modifications. Gray, Beecher

R, Local government sovereign immunity: the need for reform 18 Wake Forest L Rev 43, 46 (Feb 1982). See McQuillin, E, The Law of Municipal Corporations § 53.02, 3rd ed (1984) which describes the doctrine in each state.

4. See ch 1 for a description of both varieties of claim.
5. Allen, J: Inquiry into the rise and growth of the royal prerogative in England, London, Longman, Brown, Green, and Longmans, 1849, pp 31–3.
6. Engdahl, D: Immunity and accountability for positive government wrongs, 44 Colorado L Rev 1, 2–3 (1972). The following historical account relies heavily on this article and on National Association of Attorneys General, Sovereign immunity: The tort liability of government and its officials, Sept 1979.
7. Engdahl p 4, *supra* n 6.
8. 2 US (2 DALL) 419 (1793).
9. Howlett by and through Howlett v Rose 110 SCt 2430, 2446–47 (1990).
10. 45 US (4 How) 286, 287–8 (1846).
11. Blatchford v Native Village of Noatak 111 SCt 2578, 2581 (1991) (Indian tribe not a sovereign nation so as to escape the effects of the amendment).
12. Pierson v Ray 386 US 116 (1967).
13. Freed, M: Executive official immunity for constitutional violations: An analysis and a critique, 72 NW U L Rev 527 fn 8 (1977); Harlow v Fitzgerald 457 US 800, 814–816 (1982).
14. National Assoc of Attorneys General: The liability of government and its officials, Jan 1975, p 1. This statement has been dropped from later editions of this report.
15. 209 US 123.
16. The Court has sought to distinguish between official and personal capacity suits. See Kentucky v Graham 473 US 159, 166–167 (1985) (where the state was dismissed as defendant because the eleventh amendment bars damage claims against states).
17. 287 US 378 (1932).
18. Spalding v Vilas 161 US 483, 498 (1896).
19. 360 US 564, 575 (1959).
20. Id at 577–8.
21. Nixon v Fitzgerald 457 US 731, 756 (1982).
22. Government employees exercising a "ministerial" duty have no immunity for the consequences of their act. See Davis v Scherer 468 US 183, 196 fn 14 (1984).
23. Harlow v Fitzgerald 457 US 800, 809 (1982).
24. Id.
25. 341 US 367 (1951).
26. 386 US 547.
27. Id at 554. For a history of the doctrine, see Pulliam v Allen 466 US 522, 530–36 (1984). Even though absolutely immune for their illegal acts, judges are still subject to injunctive relief for such acts in section 1983 actions.

28. 386 US at 556–7.

29. 416 US 232 (1974).

30. Ford Motor Co v Dept of Treasury 323 US 459, 464 (1945).

31. 416 US at 238.

32. 420 US 308.

33. Id at 320.

34. Id at 322.

35. 434 US 555 (1978).

36. Id at 562, 566.

37. 457 US 800, 818–19 (1982).

38. Id at 818.

39. 111 SCt 1789 (1991).

40. Id at 1793.

41. Trejo v Perez 693 F2d 482, 484 (5th Cir 1982).

42. 438 US 478 (1978). For a short history of the case law of federal immunity, see Cornell, Wm T, Note, An evaluation of the Federal Employees Liability Reform and Tort Compensation Act: Congress' response, 26 San Diego Rev 137, 142–147 (Jan–Feb 1989). The rationale that federal officials "should not be under an apprehension that the motives that control his official conduct may, at any time, become the subject of inquiry in a civil suit for damages," first enunciated in Spalding v Vilas 161 US 483, 498–99 (1896), is the same as that noted for state officials earlier in this chapter.

43. Cook, JG and Sobieski, JL: Civil Rights Actions § 14-18[A], New York, Matthew Bender 1990.

44. Nixon v Fitzgerald 457 US 731, 756 (1982).

45. 472 US 511.

46. Id at 520.

47. Id at 523. On the facts of this case, the Court found that the unconstitutionality of a warrantless tapping of phones for national security purposes was not "clearly established" at the time the phones were tapped. 472 US at 535.

48. Comment, Qualified immunity for federal officials: A proposed standard for defamation cases, 58 Tex L Rev 789, 793–4 (1980).

49. Stump v Sparkman 435 US 349, 362 (1978).

50. Supreme Court of Va v Consumers Union 446 US 719, 734, 736–7 (1980); Pulliam v Allen 80 466 US 522, 541 (1984).

51. 424 US 409 (1976). For a reaffirmation of a judge's immunity in the face of a claim that the judge had issued an injunction as a result of a bribe, see Dennis v Sparks 449 US 24 (1980).

52. 424 US at 418.

53. Id at 420.

54. Briscoe v LaHue 460 US 325, 328 (1983). See Chrissy F v Mississippi DPW 925 F2d 844, 850 (5th Cir 1991) (failure of district attorney to comply with statute to report child sexual abuse to youth court outside his prosecutorial function), and Snell v Tunnell 920 F2d 673, 696 (10th Cir 1990) (district attorney who applied to court for seizure of children after others in his

office had refused to do so "was without color of authority . . . and absolute immunity is unwarranted").

55. 435 US 349 (1978).

56. 633 F2d 844 (9th Cir 1980), cert den Zeller v Rankin 451 US 939 (1981).

57. Id at 847–848.

58. 638 F2d 848 (5th Cir 1981), cert den Merkle v Harper 454 US 816 (1981).

59. Id at 859. See also Maestri v Jutkofsky 860 F2d 50, 51 (2nd Cir 1988), cert den 489 US 1016 (1989) (judge who issues an arrest warrant for an offense committed in a town where judge has no jurisdiction is not entitled to absolute immunity).

60. 572 F2d 52 (2nd Cir 1978).

61. 638 F2d at 859 fn 17. See also Lucarell v McNair 453 F2d 836, 838 (6th Cir 1972) (no immunity where judge assaults individual in courtroom).

62. 484 US 219.

63. Id at 229.

64. 699 F2d 1046 (11th Cir 1983), revd in part on other grounds, 782 F2d 902 (1986).

65. 600 F2d 600 (7th Cir 1979), revd in part on other grounds, 446 US 754 (1980).

66. Hampton v City of Chicago 484 F2d 602 (7th Cir 1973), cited at 600 F2d at 631.

67. 600 F2d at 632–3.

68. 111 SCt 1934 (1991).

69. 467 US 914 (1984).

70. Id at 923.

71. 468 US 183, 185 (1984).

72. Id at 192.

73. 475 US 334 (1986).

74. Id at 340.

75. Id at 342, 346.

76. Freed p 558, *supra* n 13.

77. 483 US 635.

78. Id at 637.

79. Id at 640.

80. Id at 641.

81. Id.

82. Id at 646. *Anderson* has been criticized as investing "The trial judge with the responsibility of making a judgment [of reasonableness] based on personal predictions," Garcia, A: "The scope of police immunity from civil suit under Title 42 section 1983 and *Bivens:* A realistic appraisal," 11 Whittier L Rev 511, 531 (1989).

83. 483 US at 659.

84. Id. at 648. One comment argues that police officers should not have the same qualified immunity as do high executive officials because, among other reasons, police already have a defense of probable cause good faith defined under *Pierson*. Stoelting, David P, Qualified immunity for law enforcement officials in section 1983 excessive force cases, 58 U of Cinn L Rev 243, 259 (1989). See Petit v City of Chicago 1991 US Dist Lexis 3615, p. 20 (ND

Ill) in which the city was held to have a qualified immunity defense to a reverse discrimination claim because "under the then prevailing law, defendants were not on notice that adhering to the affirmative action program . . . would be unlawful. Moreover, given the state of the law, defendants could have reasonably believed that failing to act in the face of the list's disparate impact would be unlawful."

85. Id at 649.
86. 489 US 593.
87. 490 US 386 (1989).
88. Id at 396, 398.
89. Urbonya, Kathryn R, Problematic standards of reasonableness: qualified immunity in Section 1983 actions for a police officer's use of excessive force, 62 Temple L Rev 61, 115 (Feb 1989), adding that "in applying the current standard for qualified immunity to excessive force claims alleging a violation of the fourth amendment, courts should recognize that qualified immunity is an unnecessary defense because the standard for qualified immunity is identical to the fourth amendment standard for liability." Id. See also Stoelting, *supra* n 84 at 255, 261 suggesting that "the court comes close to . . . transform[ing] qualified immunity for officers into the absolute immunity enjoyed by judges and legislatures."
91. 438 US 478, 495 (1978).
92. Freed p 550, *supra* n 13.
93. 365 US 167 (1961).
94. 436 US 658.
95. 445 US 622.
96. Id at 638.
97. Id at 635.
98. Id at 647–8.
99. Id at 650, 651.
100. Id.
101. 491 US 58 (1989).
102. Id at 71.
103. Id at 70. One writer suggests that the decision does not preclude actions against officials in their personal capacities. If a state then decides to reimburse this official for any judgment against him, that act is done with the consent of the state and therefore does not implicate the eleventh amendment. Bartels, Robert, Why *Will* won't destroy Section 1983 damages actions, 27 Criminal Law Bulletin 59, 65 (Jan–Feb 1991); see Ruark v Solano 928 F2d 947, 950 (10th Cir 1991) (complaint of prisoner suing state department of corrections director in his official capacity properly dismissed); McCord v Maggio 927 F2d 844, 847 (5th Cir 1991) (prisoner alleging eighth amendment violation could not sue warden in his official capacity but could in his individual capacity); and Walker v Norris 917 F2d 1449, 1457 (6th Cir 1990), suit by prisoner's estate against warden and commissioner of

department of corrections could only proceed in individual capacity and lack of proof of their supervisory liability may indicate problems of proof in the light of *Will*.

104. See Civil actions against state government, divisions, agencies, and officers, sec 10.5, Colorado Springs, Colo, Shephard's/McGraw-Hill 1982; Nov 1990 Supp). The same issue may arise with district attorneys. See, for example, Chrissy F v Mississippi DPW 925 F2d 844, 849 (5th Cir 1991).

105. 862 F2d 1471 (11th Cir 1989).

106. Id at 1479. But see Gulledge v Smart 691 FSupp 947, 954–55 (DSC 1988), affd without op 878 F2d 379 (4th Cir 1989) (sheriff's deputy is agent of state and § 1983 claim is therefore barred by eleventh amendment).

107. Monell v Dept of Social Services 436 US 658, 691 (1978) (emphasis in original).

108. 436 US at 691 (emphasis in original).

109. Id at 694.

110. Adickes v S H Kress and Co 398 US 144, 167–8 (1970).

111. Monell v Dept of Social Services 436 US 658, 694 fn 58.

112. Owen v City of Independence Mo 455 US 622, 657 (1980).

113. Kentucky v Graham 473 US 159, 165–66 (1985) (emphasis in original, citations omitted).

114. 475 US 469 (1986).

115. Id at 473.

116. Id at 471.

117. Id at 479.

118. Id at 481–82. In Crowder v Sinard 884 F2d 804, 828 (5th Cir 1989), cert den 110 SCt 2617 (1990), the court found that sheriffs were statutorily made the chief law enforcement policymaker in the county. But generally, for police, the mayor or city manager would be the policymaker, unless, as here, such policymaking power was delegated to the police chief).

119. 485 US 112.

120. Id at 114.

121. Id at 121 (emphasis in original, citations omitted).

122. Id at 123.

123. Id at 144–45 (emphasis in original).

124. 491 US 701.

125. Id at 705 (emphasis in original).

126. Id at 735–36.

127. Id at 736.

128. Id at 737 (emphasis in original). See Auriemma et al v City of Chicago 747 FSupp 465, 472 (N D Ill 1990) (police supt who demoted white officers and promoted black officers cannot through his action make city liable because only the City Council can make employment policy).

130. Monroe v Pape 365 US 167, 187 (1961).

131. 70 Am Jur2d, Sheriffs, Police, and Constables § 6 (1987).

132. 476 F2d 238 (4th Cir 1983); see also Whited v Fields 581 FSupp 1444, 1455 (WD Va 1984); for a discussion of the issue, see Avery, M and Rubovsky, D:

Police misconduct, law and litigation 2d ed § 3.4(a) fn 9, New York: Clark Boardman Co 1989.

133. 476 F2d at 241 fn 5.

134. Tatum v Houser 642 F2d 253, 254 (8th Cir 1981).

135. 702 F2d 729 (8th Cir 1983). See also Hendrickson v Griggs 672 FSupp 1126, 1142 (ND Iowa 1987), app on other issues, Hendrickson v Branstad 934 F2d 158 (1991) (where state did not comply with federal regulations refusing removal of juveniles from adult jails, court could order compliance); and Leach v Shelby County Sheriff 891 42d 1241, 1247 (6th Cir 1989) reh den en banc Leach v Barksdale 1990 US App Lexis 4833 and cert den Shelby County Sheriff v Leach 110 SCt 2173 (1990) (state laws place on sheriff the responsibility to provide prisons with adequate health care that cannot be delegated to private agency).

136. See Eaton, Thom A, and Wells, Michael, Government inaction as a constitutional tort: *DeShaney* and its aftermath, 66 Washington L Rev 107, 131 (Jan 91) criticizes the *DeShaney* case, discussed below in the text, for this very reason.

137. 491 US 701 (1989).

138. Id at 737.

139. 489 US 378 (1989).

140. Id at 394–96.

141. 489 US 189 (1989).

142. Id at 200.

143. 922 F2d 1097 (3rd 1990).

144. Id at 1116.

145. 781 F2d 319 (2nd Cir 1986).

146. Id at 323–24.

147. Id at 324 (citations omitted).

148. 365 US 167, 187 (1961).

149. 882 F2d 553 (1st Cir 1989).

150. Id at 566.

151. 733 FSupp 245 (ED Tex 1990).

152. Id at 258.

153. 734 FSupp 605 (SD NY 1990).

154. Id at 607. See also Leach v Shelby County Sheriff 891 F2d 1241, 1247 (6th Cir 1989), cert den Shelby Cty Sheriff v Leach 110 SCt 2173 (1990) (sheriff who failed to supervise his employees with reference to the health care of paraplegic prisoners has an affirmative duty to know and act); and Wzorek v City of Chicago 906 F2d 1180, 1183 (7th Cir 1990) where the city, in an action to hold it in civil contempt for failure to obey a court order, could not argue it was not responsible for middle managers who violated the decree. "[I]t was under an obligation to police its own employees. . . . Blind faith in middle managers will not do."

155. 469 US 464 (1985).

156. Miltier v Beorn 896 F2d 848, 854 (4th Cir 1990), appealed on other issue 935

F2d 660 (1991) (in death of prisoner from heart attack, warden entitled to rely on health care provider's expertise).

157. 489 US 378 (1989).

158. Id at 380.

159. Id at 388.

160. Id at 391.

161. Id at 396.

162. Greason v Kemp 891 F2d 829, 836–37 (11th Cir 1990).

163. City of Canton v Harris 489 US 378, 390 fn 10 (1989), Justice O'Connor concurring at 1209. See Davis v Mason County 927 2d 1473, 1483 (9th Cir 1991) (involving several incidents of sheriff's deputies' use of excessive force, sheriff liable because "while they have had some training in the use of force, they received no training in the constitutional limits of the use of force").

164. 736 FSupp 552 (D Del 1990).

165. Id at 567.

166. Id at 568.

167. 729 FSupp 376 (D NJ 1990).

168. Id at 389.

169. Williams v Codd 459 FSupp 804 (SD NY 1978).

170. Cale v City of Covington 586 F2d 311 (4th Cir 1978); Britt v Little Rock Police Dept 721 FSupp 189, 192 (ED Ark 1989) ("clear that an intentional deprivation of life, liberty and property interests by a state actor does state a cause of action under § 1983 . . . "), and see Hudson v Palmer 468 US 517, 533 (1984) where the Court in a § 1983 action decided there was "no logical distinction between negligent and intentional deprivations of property").

Chapter 4

INJUNCTIVE RELIEF—COURT CONTROLS OVER CRIMINAL JUSTICE AGENCIES

Introductory remarks

This chapter discusses court injunctions and other controls over criminal justice agencies or personnel. Persons claiming that they have been injured by criminal justice personnel have often sought to avoid *future* injuries of the same sort to themselves or others by seeking a court injunction—a court order that orders persons or agencies to do or refrain from doing something in the future. Whether judicial controls over criminal justice personnel and the agencies for which they are employed are necessary will depend on whether there are other societal institutions or modes through which recourse is possible, and the adequacy of that relief. Criminal justice institutions are different from every other institution in society. It is they which have the monopoly of force that is the very essence of state organization and it is only they which hold legitimate power of life and death over individual citizens.

Government power has been distrusted from the earliest days of the Republic. It has been surrounded with constitutional restrictions and has been placed in conflict with itself by a series of checks and balances that would hopefully keep any unchallengeable center of power from developing. Both separation and division of powers are further limitations on the exercise of a central and unrestricted source of state action. The court system itself, particularly the recognized power of the United States Supreme Court to overturn federal and state legislation in conflict with the United States Constitution, is an additional check on the exercise of unbridled and arbitrary power. The fourteenth amendment's due process clause is the most specific source of attack on such power. These formal restraints on governmental arbitrary action have perhaps helped to obscure a plentitude of such practices by government authorities,[1] including the actions of police toward persons suspected of crimes, and the actions of correction officials towards prisoners. Probation and parole

203

officers may also engage in arbitrary conduct in instances when they arrest or improperly control their probationers or parolees.

But for the reasons set forth below the remedies fashioned by legislatures and courts to control abuses of power have been found to be insufficient. Even where the remedy was adequate to recompense a particular injury, the result, though helpful to that litigant, had little if any effect on police or correctional policies. In most cases, these individual officers were carrying out long-term departmental or prison practices or customs. A remedy, therefore, has been sought that would have the effect, not merely of punishing individuals, but of changing institutional procedures. That remedy is injunctive relief. Injunctive relief has the additional advantage of avoiding the immunity defenses discussed in chapter 3. Government officials may have qualified immunity to actions for damages. This defense, however, is inapplicable to petitions for injunctive relief because such suits seek to stop future illegal or unconstitutional acts by government officials rather than seeking money damages for past injuries. Moreover, a suit for injunctive relief is unique in that it allows a person to coerce a defendant to do or not do something under the threat of civil or criminal contempt. Such a possibility is of particular significance in the area of civil rights where the government is often the culprit and therefore unlikely to be the initiator of deterrent or preventive action.[2]

A brief history of recent use of injunctive relief[3]

Because injunctive relief first came into use during the feudal period when land was the source of wealth, its utilization came to be associated with the protection of property rights, not personal rights. An infamous example of the application of this ancient doctrine to protect powerful groups is its use against Eugene Debs, a socialist leader of the 1894 Pullman strike which managed to paralyze the nation's railroads. The Supreme Court upheld a lower court injunction against the strike on the ground that the workers by striking were physically obstructing interstate commerce.[4] Federal courts continued to use the injunction to protect employer property in labor disputes until the coming of the New Deal turned the political tide. Congress then passed the 1932 Norris-LaGuardia Act which denied to federal courts power to issue injunctions in labor disputes.

Thereafter, the injunction remedy lay dormant until the 1954 decision, Brown v Board of Education,[5] when it took on new life as a remedial measure, being thereafter employed in such diverse areas as legislative reapportionment, mental hospitals, jails, prisons, and environmental concerns. The *Brown* case and the growing civil rights movement gave birth to the "structural" or institutional injunction "which seeks to effectuate the reorganization of an ongoing institution."[6] Civil rights suits are frequently characterized by group rather than individual plaintiffs and institutional rather than individual defendants.

Because local governments were often the source of the civil rights violations, they could not be depended upon to protect minority rights. Likewise, these same minority groups were themselves unlikely to have the means to enforce civil rights laws. That was one of the lessons of the Reconstruction Period when it was thought that to protect newly-won rights it would be enough to provide ex-slaves with the possibility of asserting those rights in court. Blacks neither had the means nor could have asserted rights in the face of the social and political structure that pressed upon them. In order to cope with this problem Congress attached provisions to most civil rights legislation of the 1960s and the 1970s authorizing the attorney general of the United States to initiate suit for injunction when the Civil Rights Acts were violated.

Such authority did not have its origin in civil rights legislation. The 1890 Sherman Antitrust Act contained a like authorization. Within recent years, Congress has authorized the attorney general to enforce laws dealing with voting rights, access to public and state facilities, public schools, employment, housing and the environment, among others. The superior resources available to the attorney general make such authority a valuable increment to the individual right to sue for injunction. An additional quality of modern legislation, missing from most earlier laws, is that injunctions now draw their authority from the legislative rather than the judicial branch. Congressional authorization for the issuance of the injunction tends to rob the modern injunction of its appearance as a bare assertion of judicial power and arrogance, thereby clothing it with legislative legitimacy. Thus, the growth of the structural injunction has been a near revolutionary force in efforts to transform criminal justice and other institutions. The injunction has gradually evolved from an instrument to change individual behavior to a means to modify the social or power relationship between the social group (blacks, Indians, students, women, prisoners, etc.) and the institution with power over them.

Injunctive relief has allowed such social groups to accomplish this goal in two ways: (1) It permits the individual citizen or social group to seize the initiative, using the power of courts to reform the institution within constitutional limits; and (2) it has allowed a challenge to the traditional hierarchy of responsibility in which the higher up the decision is made the less accountable the institution or individual official is for its consequences. The rise and the wane of the structural injunction, as told in this chapter, must be seen within the context of the role that the injunction continues to play in power struggles between more and less powerful groups in our society.

Other types of relief available[7]

There are a number of state common law remedies, including suits for false arrest and false imprisonment against police, and suits for assault against both police and correctional officers, all of which seek money damages. In addition, there is the relief provided by § 1983 suits, and its related sections, treated in chapter 1. The exclusionary rule has also been used to exclude evidence obtained in violation of constitutional rights; civilian review boards have been advocated to review police action directed at minorities. Many police departments and some prisons have internal review procedures for complaints by citizens against police officers or by prisoners against correctional officers.

Problems in seeking relief

Most observers agree that false arrest and false imprisonment suits complaining of illegal arrests are ineffective either in obtaining money damages for the complainant or in deterring future like conduct. To a large extent this result flows from the nature of the claimant, who is more often than not poor and uneducated. Such plaintiffs do not usually make particularly articulate or presentable witnesses; frequently they may have a criminal record or may be under arrest or in prison at the time of the incident. Because a substantial part of the expected damages may be based on loss of reputation, a jury may think such plaintiffs have no reputation to lose.

Moreover, the fate of the case will frequently depend on the word of the plaintiff against that of the defendant, a police or correctional officer. Many arrests and assaults take place in situations in which there are several police present to testify that no more than normal force was used whereas plaintiffs will often have to rely on their own testimony. Juries and judges usually take the word of criminal justice personnel over that of accuseds or prisoners. Legally, all that police officers need show is that they acted reasonably and in good faith.[8] Damages are hard to estimate and many kinds of damage cannot be compensated for by money. Juries may be critical of one who sues the police. To the extent that it is difficult to win such suits, lawyers are discouraged from taking them. Many criminal justice personnel will also be judgment-proof; that is, they will not have the money to pay any judgment rendered against them, although bonds that some police are statutorily required to carry, or state indemnification, might, in certain instances, eliminate this problem.

The fact that judges and prosecutors are usually elected and are therefore the target of political and community pressures if they are dubbed "anti-police," is also a significant factor. Plaintiffs may, in addition, be subject to substantial harassment for pressing a claim. Police may bring criminal charges against plaintiffs or may file a countersuit and may agree to dismiss it only in exchange for plaintiffs dropping their suit; or as has been the practice in some courts, the judge may require defendants in a minor criminal matter to waive all charges against the police before charges against them are dismissed. Criminal charges, such as assault and battery, are also a possibility. But prosecutors who must bring them have a relationship with the police that they normally do not want to sacrifice by prosecuting a police officer. Political aspects, mentioned above, would apply even more strongly to criminal action.

The exclusionary rule became a possible deterrent to police conduct when the Court decided in *Mapp v. Ohio*[9] that it was a violation of due process for a state court to use evidence in a criminal prosecution that was obtained by police through an unreasonable search and seizure. Underlying the rule was the assumption that the police object in search was to secure evidence to convict the defendant. It was therefore initially presumed by the courts that the threat of a court excluding evidence on the ground that the search was unreasonable would deter police from making unlawful searches. But police have many other reasons for searching besides the desire to convict the person searched.[10] Such reasons may include search for evidence solely for the purpose of harassment as in the case of some vice raids, or in order to confiscate weapons, or where there is enough other evidence to convict the accused so that the fact of unlawful search becomes merely one factor in the plea bargaining process; and of course if the unlawful search finds no incriminating evidence, the rule does not apply at all.[11]

Moreover, under the Burger and later Courts, the exclusionary rule has been weakened and is under attack. In recent years the Court has carved out several exceptions to the rule among which are: illegally seized evidence may be used in grand jury proceedings;[12] federal habeas corpus relief is not available for a constitutional claim that illegally seized evidence was introduced at the state trial;[13] and illegally seized evidence may be used to impeach the testimony of defendants testifying in their defense.[14]

Perhaps the most important reason that administrative and judicial controls on police and correctional officers do not work is that the working environment of criminal justice personnel places them in situations of danger, in which, for reasons of self-preservation, they must act as they do. Whether it is minorities who complain of brutality by the police or police who complain of their own injuries while on duty, both most frequently occur in high-density areas where police see residents as dangerous enemies and residents view police as a colonial army of occupation. Police working in such areas tend to believe that the most dangerous and crime-prone persons are young males and these persons, in turn, are the ones most likely to react violently to interpellation. Because to the officer, any young male carrying a knife or gun represents a personal threat, the officer is likely to stop young males to search for a knife or gun in order to reduce that threat. Prisons, whose population is made up of a high percentage of young male minority members, also have a heavily charged violence-prone atmosphere.

Civilian review boards

Most large police departments have an internal investigation division purportedly for the purpose of investigating complaints against their own officers accused of some offense against a citizen. In most cases, however, these divisions have been instituted as a buffer against complaints by civil liberties and civil rights organizations charging that police departments practice brutality against minority groups.

These organizations call for civilian control of the police through a civilian review board while police departments reply that their internal review procedure is adequate to handle such complaints, and that only police officers (of which the internal review boards are generally entirely composed) can understand the decisions police have to make. One outspoken Chicago police officer got himself into trouble with his department by describing its internal inspection division as "a great big washing machine. Everything they put in it comes out clean."[15] In a few cities, civil liberties groups were temporarily successful in pressuring mayors to appoint groups of elite civilian-dominated review boards to oversee these complaints but the opposition of police has been so solid that the boards were short-lived. A good deal of the muscle for their elimination has come from police unions:

> In New York City a civilian review board lasted just four months. It was discontinued as a result of a campaign by the Patrolmen's Benevolent Association, representing the largest police force in the nation, that urged the public to vote out the board. In Boston, the Patrolmen's Association showed its influence in city politics by defeating a proposed Model Cities program in November, 1968. The program included a proposal to allow citizens to hear, but not to judge, complaints against the police.[16]

Even where the Boards have survived they have had little effect on police-community relations problems. Because the boards have been so concerned about their image with the police, their actions have been feeble and hesitant. In addition, they were authorized to hear only individual cases, whereas poor police-community relations stem from causes beyond the control of the individual officer, and his superior as well. Hence, civilian review boards have been ineffective and are unlikely to be decisive in controlling police misconduct. Because their other remedies have so seldom met with success, complainants have more and more turned to the courts, particularly the federal courts, for relief.

Injunctions as a means to control criminal justice personnel

Most suits for injunctive relief involving criminal justice agencies or personnel are brought under the provisions of Title 42 USC § 1983, considered in chapter 1. By its terms this statute allows a person deprived of a federal right by state action to proceed by a "suit in equity," that is, to ask for injunctive or other equitable relief.[17] The leading case of Lankford v Gelston[18] illustrates the kind of case in which a court is likely to issue an injunction. Following a shootout in which one police officer was killed and another wounded, police, on the basis of anonymous tips, conducted over 300 searches, mostly of black persons' dwellings. No warrants were obtained and none could have been on the sparse information available. Officers often entered houses, heavily armed, with little warning, sometimes in the middle of the night, terrifying the occupants and causing them substantial discomfort and embarrassment. While the lower court denied relief, the court of appeals issued the injunction believing that there was sufficient probability of future misconduct to justify equitable relief. Even where no statute provides for such relief, federal courts have been held to have power to enjoin state action that violates federal constitutional rights.[19]

Problems in obtaining injunctive relief

Because injunctive relief is extraordinary (that is, outside the normal procedure of courts which are usually limited to providing money damages for past injury) courts place obstacles in the path of persons asking for injunctive relief. These obstacles are customarily verbalized by courts as follows: (1) equitable remedies are discretionary; (2) the applicant must come into equity with "clean hands"; (3) the legal remedy must be shown to be inadequate; (4) equity will not interfere with law enforcement.[20]

(1) Equitable remedies are discretionary

Before a court may issue an injunction, it must make two findings. First, it must decide if there has been a violation of one of plaintiff's rights. Once such a violation is found, the court must determine whether in the case at hand injunctive relief is proper. Thus, one court has observed that injunctive relief should be used with caution and that where proof was lacking of an officially tolerated pattern of racism by the police, it should be denied.

> Vigorous and forceful police action was absolutely necessary to control the violence and restore calm.... As sometimes happens in cases of riotous magnitude, there were some excesses; but they were not descriptive of police behavior generally when this entire panorama of events is considered.[21]

Lower courts, which have an opportunity to weigh all the factors involving the need for such relief, are given considerable discretion to grant or reject an injunction. Appellate courts will not disturb this decision unless it is clearly an abuse of discretion.

(2) The clean hands doctrine

Those asking for injunctive relief must come to the court with "clean hands," that is, without themselves having violated the law. This state of purity is often difficult to attain where the complainants, by the very nature of the matter, may have "dirty hands" in the form of criminal records, or at the moment are engaged in illegal activity. Courts often articulate this idea by stating that equity should not aid law-breakers. Some cases have overridden this doctrine on the theory either that the danger to society by police misconduct is more important than the policy reasons for the dirty hands doctrine or that the plaintiff's misconduct does not relate to a matter before the court and therefore the court is not bound to consider it.[22]

(3) The adequacy of the legal remedy

Historically, equity developed after common law remedies. It therefore became a special means to seek relief for other than money damages, available only where the petitioner had no remedy at law. Requiring plaintiffs to show that there is no adequate remedy at law before they can obtain equitable relief has been incorporated into American law and continues to retain some vitality today even though there is no longer a separation of law and equity. Courts usually consider three factors in arriving at a decision as to whether there is an adequate remedy at law: (a) whether there will be irreparable injury to property if the injunction is not granted; (b) whether there are adequate *legal* remedies available, and (c) whether there will be serious procedural problems associated with providing injunctive relief.

(a) Irreparable injury to property

Early cases restricted injunctive relief to the protection of property rights.[23] Because most claimants for injunctive relief about whom we are concerned wish to enjoin violation of personal as opposed to property rights, such a limitation would substantially reduce the usefulness of the injunction in these cases. Recent decisions, however, have generally refused to require an injury to a property interest before giving relief. The case usually cited for this point is a 1946 decision, Kenyon v City of Chicopee,[24] in which Jehovah's witnesses, seeking to enjoin local officials from interfering with their right to distribute handbills, were met with the argument that no property interest was involved. The court retorted that "If equity would safeguard their right to sell bananas it ought to be at least equally solicitous of their personal liberties guaranteed by the Constitution."[25]

Nevertheless, "most courts still require irreparable injury to some interest of the plaintiff before an injunction will issue."[26] An irreparable injury is said to be "that which cannot be repaired, restored, or adequately compensated for in money, or where the compensation cannot be safely measured."[27] A deprivation of constitutional rights would seem to fit that definition.

(b) The availability of legal remedies

Injunctive relief is different in its very nature from common law remedies, for its purpose is to prevent future harm rather than to repair harm already done. Nonetheless, because equity historically grew out of the inadequacy of common law remedies to right certain wrongs, the courts still look closely to see if other legal remedies are adequate before turning to injunctive relief.

In cases involving criminal justice agencies (as has been noted earlier in this chapter), civil suits do not offer an adequate remedy. Most pertinent to the need for injunctive relief is the fact that damage judgments provide only uncertain protection against future injuries. There are, therefore, substantial arguments to be made urging a court to issue an injunction on the ground that there are no available legal remedies.

(c) Problems in issuing injunctions

Even though a court is satisfied that the above conditions for the issuance of an injunction are fulfilled it might not issue an injunction because of the very special procedural difficulties inherent in issuing a proper injunction. These include procedural hardships to the defendant, problems of framing and enforcing the decree, and mootness. The first problem is of special importance to criminal justice personnel. Defendants in injunction proceedings have no right to jury trials. Equity proceedings, coming from an entirely separate historical source than common law actions, have never provided for juries. Where criminal justice personnel violate an injunction, they may be subject to contempt of court for violation of a court order with the result that judges may be hesitant to issue injunctions. When this potential loss of rights with jury protection is coupled with difficulties in wording the decree in such a way as to warn police or correctional officers what they may or may not legally do, this judicial caution is understandable. The answer is not, however, to deny injunctive relief because of these dangers, but rather to provide jury trials in contempt proceedings. This solution has already been constitutionally mandated in cases in which the contempt could result in imprisonment of six months or more.[28]

A further safeguard would be to make sure that the injunction, when issued, is understandable to the public official who must obey it, and that compliance is within the officer's capability. Decrees may be framed either to prohibit certain conduct, the *prohibitory* injunction, or to require that something be done, the *mandatory* injunction. Courts may be reluctant to issue mandatory injunctions because they may be harder to supervise and are more burdensome to defendants. Whether mandatory or prohibitory, the injunctions must state clearly and precisely what the government officer must or must not do so as to be an understandable guide to conduct. When dealing in constitutional matters involving such terms as "unreasonable search" or "probable cause," precision is difficult. An injunction which merely charges police officers to refrain from engaging in "unreasonable searches and seizures" might be challengeable as unconstitutionally vague in violation of the due process provision of the fourteenth amendment.

(4) Equity will not interfere with law enforcement

A rule that discourages courts from interfering with law enforcement is obviously significant for criminal justice personnel. In recent years this rule seems to be emerging as the most important of the self-imposed obstacles to courts issuing injunctions. The problem at which this rule is aimed arises most acutely when a federal court is asked to enjoin a state criminal proceeding on the ground that the continuation of the state case will result in violation of a federal right.

Issuing an injunction in such circumstances places the federal court in the awkward position of regulating state judicial proceedings and it is for this reason that the cautionary rule exists. Near equally difficult situations arise when federal courts are asked to enjoin a state prosecutor from proceeding with a prosecution as in Younger v Harris,[29] or when federal courts are asked to enjoin state court judges from engaging in violations of plaintiffs' civil rights as in O'Shea v Littleton.[30] These cases raise fundamental questions about the limitations that our federal system places on the power of federal courts to restrain the actions of state law enforcement agencies. This topic will be discussed later in the chapter.

Recent developments in the law of injunctions[31]

Cases brought under § 1983, or Title VII, by civil rights, civil liberties, legal services or professional law enforcement organizations have increasingly looked to the injunction as a means to regulate police or correctional activity. Progressively these cases have demanded that the court enjoin (1) unconstitutional or illegal acts aimed at a single individual; (2) future actions based on a proven past pattern of unconstitutional or illegal conduct; (3) substantial change in the structure and policy of police or correctional procedures or prison conditions. Using similar categories, another authority would call the successive categories, reparative, preventive and structural injunctions.[32]

A typical case of the first category is Rafoule v Ellis.[33] Police suspected that the plaintiff had murdered his wife, but they did not have sufficient evidence to arrest him. Instead, on four occasions, they took him into custody and questioned him for prolonged periods, ignoring his requests to see counsel and friends. His suit for an injunction under § 1983 alleged a denial of due process of law and requested that the conduct complained of be enjoined and that a confession obtained from him relating to another crime be suppressed. The first request was granted, but the second was disallowed on the ground that he had an adequate remedy at law. The rationale, the extent of the relief given, and the circumspection of the court in giving it are illustrated in this statement by the court:

> This [injunction] does not violate the general principle that equity does not ordinarily interfere with the administration of criminal laws. Plaintiff seeks to enjoin not the administration of criminal laws by the state of Georgia, but the illegal manner of administration of defendants as agencies of the State.
>
> Defendants do not deny the detentions and questionings above described and *have failed to express any intention to cease the commission of such acts* in the future, but on the other hand, have strongly insisted that they were within their rights in doing what they have done and in continuing to do so in the future if they find it desirable to do so.
>
> In view of this attitude, it seems that a preliminary injunction is demanded to protect plaintiff from infringements of his rights under the Constitution and Civil Rights Statute.
>
> A preliminary injunction will issue enjoining the exercise of personal restraint over plaintiff by defendants without a warrant or confinement without lawful arrest, and from further questioning plaintiff without his consent after being afforded an opportunity of consulting with his counsel.[34]

The next step in the progression dealt with a practice antedating the particular incident complained of and resulted in a decree with a more general sweep. *Lankford v Gelston*[35] described earlier, involved police searches of more than three hundred buildings in nineteen days, most of which were private homes in a black section of Baltimore. Relief was sought in a class action against the police commissioner under the authority of § 1983 and the fourteenth amendment.

The district court denied the petition on grounds that the injunction would be "difficult to frame, difficult to enforce and its enforcement would place severe burdens on the police and on this Court."[36] Moreover, said the court, the action complained of had ceased, and the police would make a bona fide effort to observe the rules of the law formulated by the court. According to trial testimony, the use of anonymous, unverified tips to authorize searches was standard procedure for the department. During the trial the police commissioner promulgated a general order directing police officers to arrest a person upon a warrant only if there is probable cause to believe the suspected person is on the premises. The Court of Appeals rejected this attempt to moot the issue, stating:

> The grave character of the department's conduct *places a strong obligation on the court to make sure that similar conduct will not occur.* Police protestations of repentence and reform timed to anticipate or to blunt the force of a lawsuit offer insufficient assurance that similar raids will not ensue when another aggravated crime occurs. . . . In fact, it is perhaps more reasonable to view the cessation of the raids and the promulgation of General Order 10388 not as belated acts of repentence but as the recognition of the futility of continuing the searches when it had become manifest that the Veneys had made their escape.[37]

The Lankford court demonstrated none of the caution and need for self-supporting rationalizations expressed by the decision in *Rafoule:*

> After so vast a demonstration of disregard of private rights, the complainants are entitled to a clear response. While the immediate pressure of wholesale raids had been withdrawn, the practice of indiscriminate searches of homes has been renounced only obliquely, if at all, and the danger of repetition has not been removed. The sense of impending crisis in police-community relations persists, and nothing would so directly ameliorate it as a judicial decree forbidding the practices complained of. [The decree granted should enjoin] the Police Department from conducting a search of any private house to effect the arrest of any persons not known to reside therein, whether with or without an arrest warrant, where the belief that the person is on the premises is based only on an anonymous tip and hence without probable cause.[38]

The opinion is unique in that the court legislates a specific rule of *future* conduct for the police for *all like* situations, permitting, in the event of infractions, later access to the court through its power to defend its own injunctive decrees—the contempt power.

The structural or institutional reform injunction began its modern history with Brown v Board of Education[39] and subsequent litigation that forced the Court to regulate school desegregation decrees. During the 1960s and 1970s, as the Supreme Court lifted its "hands off" policy and began to intervene in prisons and other state institutions, institutional reform lawsuits seized on the structural injunction as its favorite weapon.[40] The revitalization of § 1983 and other civil rights sections, together with the enactment of Title VII of the Civil Rights Act of 1964 greatly magnified the power of federal courts to provide remedial relief. The particular characteristic of this type of injunction is that after the relief is granted, the district court will often retain jurisdiction in order to monitor compliance, a process that might take years.

Once plaintiffs prove racial discrimination, for example, the duty of the district court becomes clear:

> The framing of a remedial decree is within the discretionary authority of the trial judge. Where racial discrimination is concerned, a "district court has not merely the power but the duty to render a decree which will so far as possible eliminate the discrimination effects of the past as well as bar like discrimination in the future."[41]

Out of this situation, a new procedure has arisen, that of "dissolution," a claim that the original circumstances that gave rise to the original decree, for example, racial discrimination, is no longer a departmental policy, and therefore the court's order should be "dissolved."[42] Such cases will be treated in more detail at the end of this chapter.

The earlier "hands off" policy by the legislative and executive branches, together with the increasingly more conservative bent of the middle and upper classes against upward pressures of lower-class groups, a subject discussed in chapter 2, resulted in counter-pressures on courts to tone down their remedial efforts. These pressures had developed by the end of the 1960s and were symbolized in the retirement of Earl Warren and the appointment of Warren Burger and later William Rehnquist as Chief Justices of the Supreme Court. While the result of the confluence of these events—restrictions on power of federal courts to control unconstitutional acts of state criminal justice agencies—would not have been "inevitable" under the Warren Court, it did naturally follow from the way the Burger and future Courts conceived of their role. Their more conservative approach to state-individual relations and prison administration was expressed in terms of federal-state relations (federalism). Federal courts were to be restricted from "interfering" in the internal operations of criminal justice agencies. This issue was raised in the *Younger* and *O'Shea* cases, and finally came into sharp focus in the *Rizzo* and *City of Los Angeles* cases to be discussed below.

"Our Federalism" resurrected

Because ours is a federal system in which the national and state governments are separate sovereignties, there must be some means of establishing a legal relationship between them. The United States Constitution carefully delineates the powers of Congress and those of the states. Article VI (the Supremacy Clause) provides that where there is a conflict between national and state laws, in an area where the national government may properly legislate, it is the national law that will prevail. The first great crisis in this arrangement culminated in the Civil War. Out of the Reconstruction Period came the fourteenth amendment and civil rights legislation that substantially changed the relationship between the national and state governments. The fourteenth amendment legitimized a means by which federal courts could intervene in state governmental operations. Because the criminal justice system was frequently used to oppress freed blacks and whites aiding them, many of the early cases were aimed at enjoining state criminal proceedings. Yet even before *Younger v Harris*,[43] "Although the precise reasons for this longstanding public policy against federal court interference with state court proceedings have never been specifically identified . . . the primary sources of the policy are plain."[44] These sources, the Court said, were that:

> [C]ourts of equity should not act, and particularly should not act to restrain a criminal prosecution, when the moving party has an adequate remedy at law and will not suffer irreparable injury if denied equitable relief. . . . This underlying reason for restraining courts of equity from interfering with criminal prosecutions is reinforced by an even more vital consideration, the notion of "comity," that is, a proper respect for state functions, a recognition of the fact that the entire country is made up of a Union of separate state governments, and a continuance of the belief that the National Government will fare best if the States and their institutions are left free to perform their separate functions in their separate ways. This, perhaps for lack of a better and clearer way to describe it, is referred to by many as "Our Federalism," and one familiar with the profound debates that ushered our Federal Constitution into existence is bound to respect those who remain loyal to the ideals and dreams of "Our Federalism."[45]

Concerned that this rather romantic view of federalism could be seen by some as adoption by the Court of the idea of "States' Rights," used by southern conservatives in the 1960s to counter the civil rights movement, the Court went on to explain:

> The concept does not mean blind deference to "States' Rights". . . . What the concept does represent is a system in which there is sensitivity to the legitimate

interests of both State and National Governments, and in which the National Government, anxious though it may be to vindicate and protect federal rights and federal interests, always endeavors to do so in ways that will not unduly interfere with the legitimate activities of the States.[46]

This homily on federalism was induced by the facts of *Younger.* Harris, the plaintiff, having been indicted for violation of California's Criminal Syndicalism Act, asked a federal court to enjoin the district attorney, Younger, from prosecuting him. Harris was joined by other plaintiffs who complained that the prosecution of Harris would inhibit them, as members of the Progressive Labor Party, from peacefully advocating their program which was to replace the capitalist with a socialist system of government; another plaintiff, a college history instructor, said he was uncertain whether the law made him criminally liable for teaching marxist doctrines.

The Court quickly disposed of the latter two parties, stating:

> A federal lawsuit to stop a prosecution in a state court is a serious matter. And persons having no fears of state prosecution except those that are imaginary or speculative, are not to be accepted as appropriate plaintiffs.[47]

Then turning to Harris, the Court first agreed that being under indictment he had a clear interest in seeking relief. The question then became whether an injunction by a federal court of the state proceedings was the proper relief. In setting forth the criteria by which to judge this matter, the Court said that it was not enough for a plaintiff to prove that failure of a federal court to interfere would result in irreparable injury. In addition, plaintiffs must show that injury would "be one that cannot be eliminated by his defense against a single criminal prosecution."[48] The Court noted that there was already a case pending against Harris in which he could assert his constitutional claims, concluding that

> the possible unconstitutionality of a statute "on its face" does not justify an injunction against good-faith attempts to enforce it, and that appellee Harris has failed to make any showing of bad faith, harassment, or any other unusual circumstance that would call for equitable relief.[49]

Justice Stewart, concurring, further explained the Court's restricted view of injunctive relief.

> [W]e hold that a federal court must not, save in exceptional and extremely limited circumstances, intervene by way of either injunction or declaration in an existing state criminal prosecution. Such circumstances exist only when there is a threat of irreparable injury "both great and immediate."[50]

Justice Stewart suggests two such circumstances: if "the criminal statute in question were patently and flagrantly unconstitutional on its face," "or if there has been bad faith and harassment—official lawlessness—in a statute's enforcement."[51] Justice Douglas' views in dissent are worthy of attention because his rejected argument clarifies the disputes between the two Court factions on the injunction issue. He took the position that "Whatever the balance of the pressures of localism and nationalism prior to the Civil War, they were fundamentally altered by the war."[52] The fourteenth amendment and § 1983 in particular interposed "the federal government between the states and their inhabitants"[53] so as to give the federal courts an affirmative duty to act when those rights are endangered by state action. Justice Burger and his colleagues dispute this view, at least where injunctive relief is called for.

A further step in the Burger Court's limitation on the use of the federal injunction to restrict state law enforcement was taken in the 1974 case of O'Shea v Littleton.[54] *O'Shea* is important because it represents a prototype of the Reconstruction Period oppression of blacks that civil rights laws were aimed at eliminating. The complaint arose out of long-standing antagonisms between wealthier and more powerful white residents of Cairo, Illinois against poorer blacks who were seeking equal political and economic rights.[55] One means by which black citizens sought to assert these rights was by engaging in an economic boycott of white merchants practicing racial discrimination. The complaint, relying on 42 USC § § 1981, 1982, 1983 and 1985 (see chapter 1), charged that in response to plaintiffs' lawful and peaceful attempt to seek "equality of opportunity and treatment in employment, housing, education, [and] participation in governmental decisionmaking,"[56] the state's attorney, the police commissioner, and the county magistrate deliberately applied the law more harshly to blacks than to whites, specifically alleging discriminatory bond setting procedures, sentencing, and the required payment of certain legal fees. Without finding it necessary to get to the merits of the matter, the Court determined that "The complaint failed to satisfy the threshold requirement imposed by Art. III of the Constitution that those who seek to invoke the power of federal courts must allege an actual case or controversy."[57] The problem with this complaint was that "None of the named plaintiffs is identified as himself having suffered any injury in the manner" complained of.[58] The Court noted that the complaint did not question the constitutionality of a single law nor attempt to enjoin any particular prosecution. Rather, the Court observed, plaintiffs seek to control future criminal trials, contemplating "interruption of state proceedings to adjudicate assertions of noncompliance" by the defendants.[59] "This seems to us nothing less than an ongoing federal audit of state criminal proceedings that Younger v Harris . . . sought to prevent." Such an injunctive order would be "intrusive and unworkable" and should be denied.[60]

Compared to the case next to be discussed, Rizzo v Goode,[61] *Younger* and *O'Shea* were merely preliminary skirmishes that resurrected federalism as the conceptual big gun to counter the developing structural injunction. This type of injunction threatened to use the federal courts to reform state criminal justice institutions. Rizzo v Goode presented the supreme challenge—an attempt by minority groups to restructure the police-community relations program of a big-city police department.

Rizzo v Goode

Two civil rights groups filed separate § 1983 suits, eventually consolidated, seeking equitable relief in federal district court charging the mayor, the city managing director, the police commissioner and two other police supervisors with failure to act in the face of numerous instances of police misconduct, and having provided no adequate procedure for handling complaints about such behavior. These suits proceeded as class actions in which two complainant classes were delineated: all residents of Philadelphia and an included class of all black residents of that city. The district court, after hearing extensive evidence of alleged police abuses, ordered the police department to submit for the approval of the court "a comprehensive program for improving the handling of citizen complaints alleging police misconduct. . . ."[62] After months of negotiation between plaintiffs and defendants, such a plan was incorporated into a final judgment, from which the mayor and other defendants appealed.

The Supreme Court reversed the decree of the district court on the basis of a refinement of the case or controversy doctrine developed in *Younger* and *O'Shea.* But in this case, the Court phrased the plaintiffs' problems in terms of a failure to prove a violation of their constitutional rights as required by § 1983, namely:

(1) "there was no affirmative link [causal relationship] between the occurrence of the various incidents of police misconduct and the adoption of any plan or policy by [the defendants] . . . showing their authorization or approval of such misconduct."[63] Thus, the plaintiffs did not make out the "requisite

Article III case or controversy between the individually named" defendants and plaintiffs.[64]

(2) Defendants "played no affirmative part in depriving any members of the" plaintiff classes of their constitutional rights.[65] "[F]*ailure* to act in the face of a statistical pattern" of violations is insufficient to incurr § 1983 liability.[66]

(3) Principles of federalism preclude the injection of the injunctive decree into the internal disciplinary affairs of a state agency "except in the most extraordinary circumstances."[67]

Part of plaintiffs' difficulty arose from the nature of their complaint. In the words of the Court:

> The central thrust of respondent's efforts . . . was to lay a foundation for equitable intervention . . . because of an assertedly pervasive pattern of illegal and unconstitutional mistreatment by police officers. This mistreatment was said to have been directed against minority citizens in particular and against all Philadelphia residents in general.[68]

Plaintiffs alleged injuries against both the minority population and all Philadelphians, apparently to make the point that police misconduct affected everyone in Philadelphia, and not merely a small portion of the population. But in drafting their complaint with this idea in mind, they left themselves vulnerable to a charge that

> this lawsuit — a heated dispute between individual citizens and certain policemen — has evolved into an attempt by the federal judiciary to resolve a "controversy" between the entire citizenry of Philadelphia and the petitioning elected and appointed officials over what steps might, in the Court of Appeals' words, "[appear] to have the potential for prevention of future police misconduct."[69]

Plaintiffs were able to substantiate no more than 20 instances of misconduct, causing the Court to imply that the 20 incidents "in a city of three million inhabitants, with 7,500 policemen," was not in their view, the "unacceptable high" rate found by the district court. A number of lower federal courts have been called on to determine the importance of *Rizzo*.

Lower court interpretations of *Rizzo*

In Lewis v Hyland,[70] the third circuit court of appeals was called on to decide the application of *Rizzo* to a claim by a class of motorists who traveled New Jersey highways, and a subclass of "long-haired highway-travelers," that they were subjected to a "pattern and practice of unreasonable searches of vehicles and travelers" without probable cause. A § 1983 action sought injunctive relief against New Jersey's attorney general, superintendent of state police, and 14 individual state troopers alleged to have engaged in these practices.

The circuit court affirmed the decision of the district court denying the request for injunctive relief entirely on the authority of *Rizzo.*

> The district court's extensive findings of fact reveal what can only be described as callous indifference by the New Jersey State Police for the rights of citizens using New Jersey roads. Were it not for the Supreme Court's opinion in *Rizzo v Goode* ... our original mandate in this case ... would have required that we reverse the district court's denial of injunctive relief in light of plaintiff's demonstration of numerous violations of their constitutional rights.[71]

Like *Rizzo,* the court concluded that the relatively small number of proved incidents of police abuse (66) "paled in comparison with the overwhelming number of routine contacts between Troopers and travelers" "revealing no 'deliberate pattern and practice' of abuse by responsible officials; rather the fault lay in the 'willful and random acts ... of a minority of the Troopers.'"[72]

Also like *Rizzo,* plaintiffs here failed "to prove the existence of an unconstitutional policy or plan adopted and enforced by the official defendants. Throughout, the Court emphasized the complete absence of any causal link between the individual officers' conduct and the responsible authorities."[73] Mere "failure" to act on the part of the responsible officials was insufficient.[74] The court concluded that "the now-required additional element of a 'causal relation to responsible authorities' is fatal to the relief sought where proof of such a relationship is wanting."[75]

In his dissent to a denial of a petition for certiorari in *Lewis,*[76] Justice Marshall suggested the following to be the distinguishing characteristics of *Rizzo:*

(1) In *Rizzo* the policemen who were found to have violated constitutional rights were not named as defendants ... The only named defendants were supervisory officials."[77]

(2) "the extent of the defendant officials' knowledge of their subordinate's unconstitutional actions was uncertain [in that] plaintiffs apparently proceeded on the theory that the officials had a duty to act to correct a statistical pattern of abuse, regardless of their knowledge of the pattern."[78]

(3) There must be "a closer nexus here between the inaction of responsible officials and the violation of rights by subordinates than there was in *Rizzo.*"[79]

(4) One of the "plaintiff classes in *Rizzo* were co-extensive with the city's electorate and thus had recourse to the political process to remedy official

tolerance of abuse of civil rights, a factor that may have made the need for federal-court intervention appear less compelling."[80]

(5) "The injunction in *Rizzo* "significantly revised the internal procedures of the Philadelphia police department."[81]

Regardless of the restrictions of *Rizzo,* a number of federal courts have nevertheless been able to argue that their facts could be sufficiently distinguished from *Rizzo* to issue injunctive relief against criminal justice agencies. These post-*Rizzo* cases fall into the same categories established earlier in this chapter, namely, injunctions issued to enjoin (1) illegal acts of a single individual or organization; (2) future actions based on a proven past pattern of unconstitutional or illegal conduct; or (3) to order a substantial change in the structure of police or correctional institutions. It is the last of these at which *Rizzo* was most pointedly aimed.

All of the cases to be discussed were § 1983 suits seeking injunctive relief but no damages. Commonwealth of Pennsylvania v Porter[82] involved a suit by the state of Pennsylvania and certain aggrieved individuals against the mayor, chief of police, named members of the borough of Millvale council, and one police officer, Baranyai, whose actions were the object of the suit. Baranyai was alleged to have repeatedly subjected the named plaintiffs and others to illegal arrest and search, assault, harassment, retaliation and intimidation. On the basis of *Rizzo,* defendants sought to dismiss the action. In denying the motion, the court pointed out that in *Rizzo* there had been no proof of any plan or policy on the part of the defendant's police superiors showing their authorization or approval of the officer's conduct while in the instant case there was ample evidence of such authorization or approval. In *Rizzo,* defendant police officers were not named as parties. Here the officer was named as defendant and most of the evidence at the trial involved his conduct. Further, here there was no request that the court assume supervision of a large metropolitan police department. Moreover, rather than asserting that an injunction would interfere with state law enforcement, the state here asked for the injunction in the name of the citizens.

The court concluded that "*Rizzo* does allow limited federal intervention into state police practices in those instances where it could be found that a pervasive pattern or policy of unconstitutional behavior was causally related to the named official defendants. . . . [T]his case goes far beyond the mere failure to act as in *Rizzo.* "[83] In consequence, the court issued a permanent injunction enjoining the defendants from future conduct of the kind complained of.

In Ruiz v Estelle,[84] an inmate and the United States, which intervened on the side of the inmate, charged that numerous prison conditions — overcrowding, inadequacy of recreational, sanitation, health care facilities, and access to courts — were in violation of the constitution and asked that they be enjoined. Defendant prison officials argued that *Rizzo* precluded such a comprehensive federal injunction. In contrast to *Rizzo,* the court here was able to catalogue in over 300 pages of analysis a pattern of unconstitutional practices that victimized the entire prison population. The state statutory structure placed management and control duties on the department of corrections so that "the defendants are clearly charge-able with notice of the type of constitutional violations which have been proven."[85]

Finally, in Campbell v McGruder,[86] plaintiffs, consisting of pretrial detainees in the District of Columbia jail sought injunctive relief "to cease housing pretrial detainees in any space smaller than 48 square feet per inmate. . . . " The district court, in response, "set limits on the total number of inmates that could be housed at the jail and established a procedure for reducing the inmate population should those limits be exceeded."[87] On appeal, the court was met with the objection that the decree exceeded the bounds set by *Rizzo* for federal court intervention. Although it was not clear that the doctrine obliging federal courts to abstain from interfering in state criminal justice agencies except in exceptional circumstances was applicable to the District of Columbia, the court assumed for the sake of argument that it was. Nevertheless, it found *Rizzo* inapplicable to the facts of this case:

> [*Rizzo*] actually holds that a federal court should refrain from assuming a comprehensive supervisory role via its injunctive powers over broad areas of local government for the purpose of preventing speculative and probably only sporadic future misconduct by local officials toward an imprecise class of potential victims, especially when that misconduct is not part of a pattern of persistent and deliberate official policy. The case at bar stands in clear contrast to the situation in *Rizzo.* Here, the constitutional violations are alleged to have actually affected the entire, clearly defined plaintiff class and to have stemmed from continuing policies of the Department of Corrections, so that only injunctive relief classwide in scope can effectively end the multiple and con-tinuing wrongs.[88]

City of Los Angeles v Lyons

In Lyons v City of Los Angeles,[89] the plaintiff sought to curb a particular practice of the police department rather than the acts of a single officer. Plaintiff alleged that four city police officers, with the active encouragement of the police department, were applying strangleholds to the necks of motorists stopped for minor traffic offenses. The plaintiff asked the court "to restrain the City from authorizing the use of the stranglehold controls except where the victim reasonably appears to be threatening the immediate use of deadly force."

On appeal from the issuance of an injunction, the Court tightened the rope around the injunction, leaving little slack for plaintiffs seeking injunctive relief against illegal police action. As in *Rizzo, City of Los Angeles* was to turn on the question of whether the plaintiff had a "case or controversy" sufficient to permit a federal court, in the Supreme Court's view, to issue an injunction. The answer was an emphatic no.

> Lyons' standing to seek the injunction requested depended on whether he was likely to suffer future injury from the use of the chokeholds by police officers. Count V of the complaint alleged the traffic stop and choking incident five months before. That Lyons may have been legally choked by the police ... while presumably affording Lyons standing to claim damages against the individual officers and perhaps against the City, does nothing to establish a real and immediate threat that he would again be stopped for a traffic violation, or for any other offense, by an officer or officers who would illegally choke him into unconsciousness without any provocation or resistance on his part. The additional allegation in the complaint that the police in Los Angeles routinely apply chokeholds in situations where they are not threatened by the use of deadly force falls far short of the allegations that would be necessary to establish a case or controversy between these parties.[90]

Therefore, because Lyons cannot show "that he is realistically threatened by a repetition of his experience of October, 1976, then he has not met the requirements for seeking an injunction in a federal court...."[91] The majority cautioned that "In exercising their equitable powers federal courts must recognize '[t]he special delicacy of the adjustment to be preserved between federal equitable power and State administration of its own law.'"[92] Endeavoring to answer the criticism that the withdrawal of the federal injunction from the service of civil rights and liberties would tend to encourage constitutional violations, the Court responded that there are other remedies available to deter such violations: a § 1983 damage action, federal criminal laws, and the option for state courts to fill the gap. As indicated earlier in this chapter, none of these alternatives have appeared particularly viable in the past.

Justice Marshall, dissenting and speaking for three other justices, warns that

The Court's decision removes an entire class of constitutional violations from the equitable powers of a federal court. It immunizes from prospective equitable relief any policy that authorizes persistent deprivations of constitutional rights as long as no individual can establish with substantial certainty that he will be injured, or injured again, in the future.... The federal judicial power is now limited to levying a toll for such a systematic constitutional violation.[93]

Post-Warren use of the structural injunction

Even though the post-Warren Supreme Court has tightened the reigns on the structural injunction, it still represents a formidable remedy. In US v Paradise,[94] after the department had stalled for twelve years in forming its own plan to end racially discriminatory promotions, the Court approved a district court's order requiring the police department to promote to corporal one black for every white promoted.

Within the criminal justice community, suits for injunctive relief, at least in terms of claims of racial or gender discrimination, may be divided into suits asking for injunctive relief to cure these practices; and thereafter, suits claiming that the relief granted had resulted in reverse discrimination, that is, the violation of the constitutional rights of white male officers. Such litigation, often lengthy and bitter, tends to pit law enforcement organizations representing black members against organizations representing white members. One court, frustrated with the length and vituperation of the litigation, compared such suits to Dickens' famous novel, Bleak House, in which a suit in equity went on for generations.[95]

A good illustration of the process is Gralak v City of Chicago,[96] a 1991 case which began in 1970. At this stage Chicago Police Department white male sergeants alleged that certain officials racially altered scores in order to promote black sergeants to lieutenants in the 1988 lieutenant's exam. The district court's frustration with the unending nature of the case is evident from its description of the case's history:

For brevity and sanity's sake, we have not included a section titled "Background".... Those who seek a detailed summary of background facts, including the entire procedural history of the cases involving discrimination by or within the Chicago Police Department, might be interested in [reading five district court and four court of appeals decisions]. Then again, they might not.[97]

The main case, United States v City of Chicago,[98] challenged hiring and promotion practices of the Chicago Police Department for allegedly discriminating against blacks, hispanics and women. After finding that such discrimination did exist, the district court imposed numerical hiring and promotion quotas and enjoined the payment of federal revenue sharing funds pending compliance. The suit commenced in 1970 by an action brought by the Afro-American Patrolmen's League. A second suit in 1973 challenged "the full range of departmental practices with respect to recruiting, screening and hiring." A third suit by the United States in 1973 alleged a pattern and practice of discrimination against the same groups in their assignment, promotions, and discipline of personnel.

In 1979 the Fraternal Order of Police intervened to demand a modification of the 1976 decree (joined by the City and the United States), to reduce the percentage of minorities promoted from 40 to 25. After a review of the results of examinations taken under the prevailing decree, the court concluded that "the essential purpose of that quota (parity of minority representation . . . between patrol officers and sergeants) has been achieved . . . ,"[99] and the decree was thereby modified.

In another 1989 court of appeals decision, US v City of Chicago,[100] the court allowed the intervention of a group of female sergeants who were affected by the promotion order. Finally in 1990,[101] the Fraternal Order of Police was denied a stay of the current list of promotions because they were unable to show that they would suffer irreparable damage if the process proceeded. The court of appeals summed up the court's supervisory injunctive relief:

> For approximately the last twenty years the Chicago Police Department promotion process has been a fountain of substantial protracted litigation. Since 1976, when the district court determined that the 1971 sergeant's promotion exams had a discriminatory impact upon blacks, Hispanics and females, the process of promoting patrol officers has been conducted pursuant to the district court's equitable decree and in accordance with court-imposed quotas. The City's attempts to develop and administer subsequent, nondiscriminatory exams have not met with complete success. These efforts have confronted the district court with the difficult question of how to proceed with the necessary task of fairly promoting police officers within the Department. The equitable orders of the district court have spawned numerous appeals to this court.[102]

In a new phase of civil rights litigation, groups, usually representing white males, claim that decrees heretofore entered have achieved their results and therefore should be dissolved. In Com of Pa v Flaherty,[103] an injunction, which had governed police officer hiring for 15 years, was challenged by white male candidates for employment. The court agreed, setting forth the basis of such dissolution:

[W]e find that the ultimate burden of proving unconstitutional discrimination justifying judicial intervention must remain with the plaintiffs. To justify dissolution of the preliminary injunction, intervenors . . . must merely show that the injunction is no longer valid under existing law. This can be accomplished by showing that the plaintiffs cannot meet their burden of proving intentional discrimination and that the City is unlikely to discriminate intentionally against women and blacks.[104]

Thus, to continue an injunction in the face of a constitutional challenge, those defending the decree must show the government is guilty of intentional discrimination, not merely the discriminatory impact of policies that may have led to the injunction in the first place.

The structural injunction is important in other areas as well in which unconstitutional institutional conditions may be shown.[105]

Summary and conclusions

After an early history in which powerful groups used injunctions to thwart challenges to that power from labor organizations, in recent years minorities have sought to use the injunction to challenge some of the major instruments of power—police departments, prisons, mental institutions, educational systems and other majoritarian social institutions. Injunctions, however, have always been viewed by courts as extraordinary remedies. They are provided only when litigants can show that they have no remedy at law and that if they are not helped by a court of equity they will be irreparably damaged. A more serious objection arises from the nature of our federal arrangement of sovereign national and state governments. This necessitates caution on the part of the federal courts in regulating state government proceedings.

Such a problem becomes even more delicate when a federal court is called on to intervene in state trial proceedings or in police and prison administration. The issue is especially sharp when the form of decree sought is the structural injunction, that is, one that not only seeks to enjoin behavior of individual state government agents but attempts to restructure the internal operations of a government agency. In a series of cases, *Younger, O'Shea* and finally *Rizzo,* the Court sought to re-establish "Our Federalism" as a rationale for restraining the use of the injunction by federal courts as a means of social change. Using such concepts as case and controversy and causation, the Court seemed to be trying to push the genie back into the bottle by reducing the social content of the litigation to the simple one-on-one adversary model. Whether in its latest attempt in *City of Los Angeles* the Court has succeeded in capping the bottle, only future cases will tell. In the meantime, plaintiffs will have to skillfully draft their complaints so as to come within the Court's demands for a case and controversy.

In the final analysis, it becomes a question of power. The injunction has provided a potent weapon whereby minorities and civil rights advocates have used the federal courts as a counterweight to the power majoritarian institutions have over them. Because, as has been indicated earlier, such groups have only weak remedies to rely on for relief, the Court's limitation on the use of the structural injunction must be seen as a power shift away from such groups. Foreclosing this means of complaint is important to criminal justice personnel. To the extent that legitimate means of protest are closed, protesting groups will be forced to assert their rights by the methods used in the 1960s—public marches, occupation of buildings and even open violence. In such demonstrations criminal justice personnel become the object of the protest and the anger which could be worked out through political and judicial means is turned against them.

ENDNOTES

1. For essays on American attitudes toward government authority, see Veysey, L, ed: Law and resistance, American attitudes toward authority, New York, Harper Torchback, 1970. For arbitrary government actions, see O'Reilly, Kenneth, Racial matters: the FBI's secret file on black America, 1960–1972, New York, Free Press, 1989; Mitgang, Herbert, Dangerous dossiers: exposing the secret war against America's greatest authors, New York, Donald I Fine, 1988; Churchill, Ward, Agents of Repression: the FBI's secret war against the Black Panther Party and the American Indian movement; and Garrow, David J, the FBI and Martin Luther King, Jr, New York, NY, Penguin, 1983.
2. Fiss, O: The civil rights injunction, Bloomington, Indiana U Press, 1978, pp 18–20, 88.
3. This section relies heavily on Fiss, ch I, *supra* n 2.
4. In re Debs 158 US 564 (1895). For a brief account of the strike and the devastating effect of the injunction on union organizing, see Hofstadter, R et al: The United States, The history of a republic, 2d ed, Englewood Cliffs, Prentice-Hall, 1967, pp 537–8.
5. 347 US 483 (1954).
6. Fiss p 7, *supra* n 2.

7. Bent, A: The politics of law enforcement, Lexington, Heath, 1974, has been relied upon in this section.

8. Pierson v Ray 386 US 547 (1967). See ch 3 for a more detailed discussion of this point.

9. 367 US 643 (1961).

10. This theme is carefully developed in Skolnick, J: Justice without trial, New York, Wiley, 1975, 2d ed, pp 143ff and 219ff. Skolnick vividly describes the reasons why narcotic addicts are unlikely to file a claim against police even though their constitutional rights have been repeatedly violated.

11. The foregoing material relies on Tiffany, L: "Judicial attempts to control police," 61 Current History 13–19 (1971).

12. United States v Calandra 414 US 338 (1974).

13. Stone v Powell 428 US 465 (1976).

14. United States v Havens 446 US 620 (1980).

15. Muller v Conlisk 429 F2d 901, 902 (7th Cir 1970).

16. Bent p 73, *supra* n 7.

17. 42 USC § 1983 (1988).

18. 364 F2d 197 (4th Cir 1966).

19. Hague v CIO 307 US 496 (1939).

20. For a more detailed explanation of these problems see Dobbyn, John F, Injunctions in a nutshell, St Paul, Mn, West Publ Co, 1974; and for the requirements for a court to issue a preliminary injunction, see Heiny, Ann E, Formulating a theory for preliminary injunctions, 72 Iowa L Rev 1157, 1158 (May 1987).

21. Barton v Eichelberger 311 FSupp 1132 (MD Pa 1970), affd 451 F2d 263 (1971).

22. Johnson v Yellow Cab 321 US 383 (1943).

23. Spelling, T: A Treatise on the law governing injunctions, St Louis, Thomas Law Book Co, 1926, pp 8–9.

24. 320 Mass 528, 70 NE2d 241 (1946).

25. 320 Mass at 533–4, 70 NE2d at 244.

26. Seidel, G: "Injunctive relief for police misconduct in the United States," 50 J Urban Law 681, 690 (1973). A recent treatment of the subject concluded that "specific relief is problematic only occasionally. . . . [T]he irreparable injury rule is dead. It does not describe what the cases do, and it cannot account for the results." Laycock, Douglas, The death of the irreparable injury rule, New York, Oxford University Press, 1991, p 5. See, for example, Anderson v Grand Rapids Police Dept 1990 US Dist Lexis 14170, p 9 (WD Mich) (police officers who sought injunction against further proceeding with sergeant promotions "have not shown that it is likely or imminent that they will not be promoted to the position of sergeant").

27. Comment, "Injunctive relief for violations of constitutional rights by the police," 45 U of Colorado L Rev 90, 106 (1973).

28. Bloom v Illinois 391 US 194 (1968).

29. 401 US 37 (1971).

30. 414 US 488 (1974).

31. This section relies on Robinson, C: "A goal-oriented model code of pre-arraignment procedure for Wisconsin," 2 Prospectus 1, 110 (Dec 1968).

32. Fiss p 7, *supra* n 2; Easton, R E: "The dual role of the structural injunction" 99 Yale LJ 1983 (1990).

33. 74 FSupp 336 (ND Ga 1947).

34. Id at 343 (emphasis in original). A court may enjoin a judge from unconstitutionally jailing a person convicted of a misdemeanor who could not pay a fine; or from discharging police officer on basis of illegally disclosed information about her drug use, Jeanette A v Condon 728 FSupp 204, 207 (SD NY 1989). Under Title VII, a court may enjoin an employer from retaliating against an employee while the claim is in process, Wagner v Taylor 836 F2d 566, 578 (DC Cir 1987); and a police department that violates an order to promote female may be ordered to promote plaintiff within 21 days, US v City of Montgomery 744 FSupp 1089, 1094 (MD Ala 1990). Survey, Employment discrimination, Title VII retaliation claims 57 George Washington L Rev 1168–1186 (May 1989); and court orders to enjoin batterer from further violence on their spouses. Finn, Peter, Statutory authority in the use and enforcement of civil protection orders against domestic abuse, 23 Family LQ 43–73 (Sp 1989).

35. 364 F2d 197 (4th Cir 1966).

36. Lankford v Schmidt 240 FSupp 550, 561 (D Md 1965), revd Langford v Gelston 364 F2d 197 (1966).

37. Langford v Gelston 364 F2d 193, 203 (4th Cir 1966) (emphasis added).

38. Id at 204, 206. In a case where there are repeated instances of past sexual discrimination a court may continue its injunctive relief against sheriff's department when "there are not sufficient assurances that the employer is unlikely to repeat its discriminatory actions," Bouman v Sheriff of Los Angeles Cty 1991 US App Lexis 15783, p 56 (9th Cir).

39. 349 US 483 (1954).

40. Cohen, F: "The discovery of prison reform," 21 Buffalo L Rev 855–887 (1972).

41. Davis v City of Texas 748 FSupp 1165, 1177 (ND Tex 1990).

42. Welling, Sarah N and Jones, Barbara W, Prison reform issues for the eighties: modification and dissolution of injunctions in the federal courts, 20 Conn L Rev 865–894 (Sum 1988).

43. 401 US 37 (1971). See Mason, David, Note, Slogan or substance? Understanding "our federalism" and *Younger* abstention 73 Cornell L Rev 852–882 (May 1988).

44. 401 US at 43.

45. Id at 44.

46. Id.

47. Id at 42.

48. Id at 46.

49. Id at 54.

50. Id at 56.

51. Id.

52. Id at 61.
53. Id at 63.
54. 414 US 488.
55. See Cairo, Illinois: A symbol of racial polarization, Report of United States Commission on Civil Rights, US Govt Printing Office, Feb 1973.
56. 414 US at 491.
57. Id at 493.
58. Id at 495.
59. Id at 500.
60. Id.
61. 423 US 362 (1976).
62. Id at 365.
63. Id at 371.
64. Id at 371–2.
65. Id at 377.
66. Id at 376 (emphasis in original).
67. Id at 379.
68. Id at 366–7.
69. Id at 371 (citation omitted).
70. 554 F2d 93 (3d Cir 1977), cert den 434 US 931, Justice Marshall dissenting.
71. Id at 94–5.
72. Id at 97, 101.
73. Id at 98.
74. Id.
75. Id at 101.
76. Cert den, Lewis v Hyland 434 US 931 (1977).
77. Id at 934 fn 3.
78. Id at 933.
79. Id.
80. Id at 933 fn 2.
81. Id at 934 fn 4.
82. 480 FSupp 686 (WD Pa 1979); affd in part and revd in part 659 F2d 306, 323 (3d Cir 1981), cert den Porter v Pennsylvania 458 US 1121 (1982).
83. 480 FSupp at 703.
84. 503 FSupp 1265 (SD Tex 1980).
85. Id at 1385.
86. 580 F2d 521 (DC Cir 1978), disapproved in Bell v Wolfish 441 US 520, 533, 543 (1979) on other grounds.
87. Id at 524.
88. Id at 526. In Orantes-Hernandez v Thornburgh 919 F2d 549, 566 (9th Cir 1990) (where Immigration and Naturalization Service coerced illegal immigrants to sign "voluntary" departure agreements and did not inform them of their right to counsel, permanent injunction had been properly issued); Lopez v Garriga 917 F2d 63, 68 (1st Cir 1990) (where jury found that plaintiff did not have a fourth amendment claim to unreasonable detention, injunction

based on this fact must fail); and Perales v Casillas 903 F2d 1043, 1051 (5th Cir 1990) (where states gives INS "discretionary grant of mercy," court may not issue injunction to require agency to act in particular way).

89. 461 US 95 (1983).

90. Id at 105.

91. Id at 109.

92. Id at 112.

93. Id at 137.

94. 480 US 149 (1987).

95. US v City of Chicago 870 F2d 1256, 1259 (1989).

96. 1991 US Dist Lexis 9683.

97. Id at 2.

98. 549 F2d 415 (7th Cir 1977).

99. 663 F2d 1354, 1360 (7th Cir 1981).

100. 870 F2d 1256, 1259 (7th Cir 1989).

101. 894 F2d 943, 947 (7th Cir 1990).

102. Id at 944. See also Bouman v Sheriff of Los Angeles Cty 1991 US App Lexis 15783 (court ordered county to develop "validated" sergeant exam and to hire female sergeants consistent with their percentage representation as deputies until county instituted validated selection procedures); Black Law Enforcement Officer's Association v City of Akron 1990 US App 21742 (6th Cir) (injunction to prevent police department from promoting sergeants based on challenged test); and Perez v FBI 714 FSupp 1414 (WD Tex 1989) (appointment of a panel of three special masters to supervise extensive informal reform of FBI hiring and promotion processes to eliminate discrimination against hispanic agents).

103. 760 FSupp 472 (WD Pa 1991).

104. Id at 477.

105. See Thompson v Enomoto 915 F2d 1383, 1385 (9th Cir 1990) (death row inmates complaining of living conditions frustrated by failure of authorities to adhere to terms of earlier decree could have special master appointed to supervise conformity); Langston v Johnston 928 F2d 1206, 1208 (1st Cir 1991) (request for appointment of receiver to release or reassign "sexually dangerous persons" to other institutions, alleging failure to adequately provide for them); Northeast Women's Center, Inc v McMonagle 1991 US App Lexis 15251 (3rd Cir) (injunction ordering anti-abortion activists not to interfere with women entering women's center); Roe v Operation Rescue 919 F2d 857, 868 (3rd Cir 1990), to same effect.

Part II:
SPECIFIC RIGHTS, DUTIES,
AND LIABILITIES
OF CRIMINAL JUSTICE PERSONNEL

Chapter 5

RIGHTS OF CRIMINAL JUSTICE PERSONNEL WITHIN THEIR ORGANIZATIONS OR WHILE AT WORK.

Introductory remarks

This chapter will discuss the rights criminal justice personnel have within their own organizations (the police department or the prison), and the process by which these rights have been acquired. Among these rights are freedom of association, the right to privacy, the right to form a union, and to bargain collectively for improved pay and better working conditions. Two characteristics seem crucial in determining the rights of criminal justice personnel: (1) their relationship as employees of a police department, bureau of corrections, or board of parole, making them economically and socially members of the working class (those working for others); and (2) their relationship to the state as public employees. Public employment is defined by political decisions, and not, as is true in private employment, by the economics of the marketplace.[1] Every assertion of rights by public employees, therefore, becomes a political act. The most important vehicle in mobilizing these characteristics for the acquisition of additional rights has been the public employee union, a potent political force in protecting members against arbitrary and capricious state action.

Though both characteristics, as workers and as public employees, are more obviously true for the police and correctional officers than for parole and probation officers, the principles to be developed apply to all. Police and correctional workers will first be placed in their current legal and political environment; the growth of police and correctional unions will be related to the development of the union movement in general and of public employee unions in particular; these movements will be linked to the legal claims by criminal justice personnel for union representation and collective bargaining, and to the gains obtained by criminal justice personnel as a result of collective bargaining.

Political environment surrounding police personnel[2]

Police administration in the United States is largely a matter of local responsibility, principally concerned with the enforcement of state laws and city ordinances by municipal police forces. Local government may be either of the mayor-council type; the commission form, in which there is joint government by a small number of commissioners, each assigned different functions (health, public safety, sanitation, and so forth); or the city manager form, in which a person trained as a city manager is hired to administer city affairs on the theory that a municipal corporation can be run like a business.

In big cities, the usual form of government is an elected mayor and city council. A municipal code or city charter sets forth the powers of the mayor and the mayor's relationship to the police and other departments. In Chicago, for example, the mayor is the "chief executive officer." The municipal code establishes "an executive department of the municipal government of the city which shall be known as the department of police."[3] With the exception of the superintendent of police, the mayor appoints all department heads with the advice and consent of the city council. The police superintendent is appointed by the mayor from three persons suggested by a police board, the members of which are appointed by the mayor with the consent of the city council. Once appointed, the mayor may remove the superintendent only by pressing a "formal charge." The superintendent "shall be responsible for the general management and control of the police department and shall have full and complete authority to administer the department in a manner consistent with the ordinance [sic] of the city, the laws of the state, and the rules and regulations of the police board."[4] The police board is to "adopt rules and regulations for the governance of the police department," but "the board's power" to adopt such rules and regulations "does not include authority to administer or direct the operations of the police department, or the superintendent of police. . . . "[5]

This statutory monstrosity might be expected to lead to jurisdictional squabbles if either the superintendent or the board were to seek more power. How this formal system works depends to a large extent on the mayor. A strong mayor ordinarily means that the executive departments are led with a firm hand. Even though the system is based on the principles of separation of powers and checks and balances, the removal power of the mayor, and the combined leadership of the government and the political party, are often enough to ensure command of the police department.

Decentralization factors

Several decentralizing factors, inherent in American federalism, however, substantially weaken a mayor's control. Power of local governments to create police departments and to administer them is provided by state legislation as are standards to be used in disciplining, discharging or permitting criminal justice personnel to form unions and bargain collectively. Laws governing the appointment of the police chief, the civil service and the police boards, as well as the laws to be enforced by the police, are also products of the state legislature. Ordinances promulgated by the city council must be in accord with these laws. It is the Civil Service Board that controls hiring and promotion through the rank of captain and it is the city council that prescribes, within statutory limitations, the duties of the police, and controls their salaries and departmental budgets. Moreover, police procedures are determined in part by the state legislature, in part by the state courts, and to a considerable degree by the United States Supreme Court. With the exceptions of violations of city ordinances and federal law, the state's attorney, an elected *county* official, politically responsible to that governmental unit (though legally considered a state official), will prosecute persons arrested by city police. On the periphery are the sheriff and coroner, elected county officers, who have uncertain and shadowy roles in city law enforcement.

Each elective office encourages personal advancement, best achieved by an appearance of individual activity rather than of cooperative effort. Further complicating the task was the 1960s entry of the federal government into local law enforcement through the Omnibus Crime Control and Safe Streets Act of 1968, and subsequent amendments. This Act sifted federal money through a series of regional, state, and local commissions to police and correctional agencies rather than to cities. Federal interest encouraged uniformity in standards and goals, in compiling national statistics, and since the 1972 amendments to Title VII of the Civil Rights Act of 1964, in requiring state and local governments to take affirmative action to raise minority and female representation in government employment, matters covered in chapter 2. Much of that "interventionist" role has been ended by the Reagan administration with the demise in April 1982 of the Law Enforcement Assistance Administration, and the withdrawal of substantially all federal assistance to local criminal justice agencies.

Political parties as unifying factors

As both a unifying and decentralizing factor, the political party is a ubiquitous and all-powerful force. The party links together loose ends. Many officials, members of different governmental units, have a common bond for cooperative action on behalf of the same political party. This factor unites a multitude of private interests because of the needs of the party for campaign funds and the financial ability of private interests to supply these funds in return for favors, direct or indirect. The party, through its governmental offices, can dispense contracts, influence the passage or nonpassage of laws affecting one interest or another, and can determine with what intensity and selectivity laws are enforced. One political party cannot usually capture all governmental units having law enforcement functions. For this reason, among others, city government does not, and in the nature of things, cannot agree on common goals, and on a common program for city law enforcement. Far from having common goals, it is not unusual for various units within city government or for city government and law enforcement authorities outside city government (county prosecutors and sheriffs, for example), to be in antagonistic confrontation on how to carry out the goals, or in argument over the inadequacies of the local criminal justice system.

Conservative and liberal attacks on the system

Moreover, the system is constantly used as the scapegoat for the "growth" of crime in the city by "conservative" and "liberal" politicians and citizen groups representing various social and economic interests. "Liberals" charge the police with brutality, urge police review boards to control police misconduct, file civil rights and damage actions against police, police departments, and prison officials; claim that the prisons brutalize the inmates and deprive them of constitutional rights, demand that more convicted persons be released on probation and parole, and that more probation and parole officers be provided. "Conservatives," on the other hand, ask for more police and prison guards, demand more arrests, more convictions, longer sentences, or capital punishment, and call for court decisions "untying" the hands of the police and correctional officials.

These conflicting demands are transmitted to politicians who sometimes apply one and sometimes another (or a combination of the two) of these perspectives. As a result, criminal justice policies have a tendency to fluctuate from what appears to be a too-tough to what appears to be a too-lenient policy, and after a time, back again. The reason for this vacillation is that both of these perspectives are based on appearances. Because neither "conservatives" nor "liberals" deal with the basic problems encouraging criminal behavior (poverty, inadequate schooling, unemployment, limited economic opportunity, racism, etc.), each group sees the others' solution as a cause of the failure and urge their own in its stead. Because neither deals with real causes, each is correct in arguing that the others' solutions are wrong, thereby providing a certain basis for believing that their own views are correct.

Liberals and conservatives therefore conform to a common belief system which places responsibility for burgeoning crime on the ineffectiveness of police, probation, parole, and prisons—that is, on criminal justice personnel. As a consequence, departmental control mechanisms, both external and internal, are aimed at making criminal justice personnel, particularly the police, "accountable to the democratic process."[6] These influences are illustrated by Tables III–V below.[7]

For the reasons cited in chapter 4, none of these remedies (external controls) are particularly useful to the claimant in changing conduct of criminal justice institutions. Despite all the hurrah about such things as police review boards, they have had little effect on the life of most police. Such is not the case with internal controls. These are listed below and clearly involve the rights of criminal justice personnel. Problems of disciplinary action against criminal justice personnel will be treated in chapter 6.

Police as workers

It will be recalled that one characteristic of criminal justice personnel is that they are essentially workers. Their primary relationship, therefore, is that of employer-employee. The classic case setting forth this relationship is McAuliffe v Mayor of the City of New Bedford[8] involving the dismissal of a policeman who violated a departmental regulation that forbade him to "solicit money . . . for any political purpose whatsoever."

Justice Holmes, speaking for the Massachusetts Supreme Court, in these famous words, wrote:

> The petitioner may have a constitutional right to talk politics, but he has no constitutional right to be a policeman. There are few employments for hire in which the servant[9] does not agree to suspend his constitutional rights of free

Table III
Legal and Political Environment Surrounding
the Criminal Justice System

FEDERAL AND STATE SYSTEMS
United States Constitution
(Supremacy clause, 14th amendment—due process, equal protection, 8th amendment—
cruel and unusual punishment; bill of rights)

FEDERAL JUDICIARY	LEGISLATURE	EXECUTIVE
United States Supreme Court	*Congress*	*President*
Appointed by President, confirmed by Senate; nationalization of the bill of rights; decisions affect both federal and state laws and procedures: provides constitutional limits for actions of criminal justice personnel.	Federal criminal laws; enforcement of Title VII (female, and minority employment).	Department of Justice, FBI; collects statistics, may train some local police; supervises federal prison system; provides funds for and encourages uniform adherence to set standards; interest in "subversive" political activities; enforces minority and female representation in employment.
STATE JUDICIARY	STATE LEGISLATURE	GOVERNOR
Trial and appellate courts; judges, usually elected; interprets laws.	Criminal laws and procedures; defines rights and duties of criminal justice personnel. Creates bureau of corrections and parole system.	Chief state law enforcement officer; administers bureau of corrections; issues regulations governing prison systems and parole. parole. Attorney general provides opinions of validity of state law and practice.
		District Attorney State officer, elected by county, prosecutes state offenses.

Table IV
Municipal Political System

Political Party Patronage	Mayor	Corporation counsel (lawyer
	Elected, appoints public safety director and/or chief of police (often on recommendation of Police Board).	for city, appointed by mayor).
City Council Elected, determines police funding and workload—how many police are hired.	*Director of Public Safety*	*Police Board* Appointed by mayor, may supervise department policy, but usually only buffer for mayoral responsibility.
	Police Department (police chief)	
	Police Officer (sometimes organized in unions)	
Civil Service Commission Appointed by mayor; in charge of recruitment standards and disciplinary hearings for major charges.	Political demands by politicians	*City Courts* City prosecutor, prosecutes city offenses—ordinances.
	Demands by middle class, business interests (vocal, organized)	
		Demands by lower class (inarticulate, unorganized, occasional violence.)

speech as well as of idleness by the implied terms of his contract. The servant cannot complain, as he takes the employment on the terms which are offered him. On the same principle the city may impose any reasonable condition upon holding offices within its control.

Although this rather stark approach to the relative rights of employer and employee was a sign of the times, its interest lies in the clear recognition that one basis for restricted rights of the policeman is because he is the *employee* in the employer-employee relationship, and that an employer, under the law, has a certain call and control on how employees spend their time. It is likewise of consequence that that employer is the state. That special relationship has been recognized in many cases. A typical statement is that appearing in a 1939 Illinois case, Coane v Geary:

Table V

External Influences on Police Departments	Internal Controls
1. Judicial System (bill of rights, civil and criminal sanctions; affirmative action lawsuits)	1. Organizational and management devices
	a. selective recruitment affirmative action
2. Citizen groups or "victims" (civil actions)	b. training at time of and after hiring
3. Civilian Review Board	c. decentralization of decision-making
4. The Press	d. planning and budgeting
5. Public Opinion	e. allocation of manpower and personnel policies
6. Organized Crime	
7. Police Unions	2. Internal investigation of citizen complaints
a. improve economic benefits	
b. threat of strikes, slow-downs	
c. political lobbying and other political activities	3. Disciplinary action
d. collective bargaining and grievance machinery	
e. court action	

A police force is peculiar . . . in its formation and in its relation to the city government. It is practically an organized force resembling in many respects a military force, organized under the laws of the United States and equally as important as to the functions it is required to perform.

It is not an ordinary branch of the executive government like the mayor's office, even, your water department, the comptroller's department, the health department. . . . It is a department which requires that the members of it shall surrender their individual opinion and power to act, and submit to that of his commanding officer. And there is the same necessity of discipline—of regulation existing in the police department that exists in regard to the military department. Strict discipline must be enforced, and it must be enforced in a manner that is effective, and without the supervision or regulation of any other department of the state, and particularly, without any attempt on the part of the judicial department . . . to regulate it in any way, and particularly, to regulate its discipline.[10]

The legal relationship set forth in these quotations recognizes the police as an instrument of the state. One definition of the state is as the sole organization in society that has the monopoly of force and the power to use it. It is the police which exercises that monopoly on behalf of the state to protect the state when domestic disharmony threatens, just as the army protects the state in time of foreign trouble. Court statements comparing the police to the "military department" should not therefore be unexpected. There seem to be two explanations for the continuity of this view of the police. Both demand a disciplined force.[11] It is essential that the police act as a unit when military-like they are used to counteract riot or rebellion. Such a function requires absolute discipline and unquestioned loyalty. Even where, however, this need is not made explicit, discipline is often seen as a good in itself. This view is apparent in the quotation from *Geary*. Where the courts take this perspective on the police, the result is the same as that doctrine which courts once employed in prison litigation—a "hands off" policy for police departments.

Challenges by unions of criminal justice personnel, in particular, police unions, have been important in forcing the state to formulate a legal and political posture toward its criminal justice employees. Therefore, it will be useful to recount the history of criminal justice employee unions and the reaction of the state of this challenge.

Trends in union organization

In general, unionization of workers has followed changes in the economic structure of the country. Until recently, however, unionization of workers in criminal justice has lagged behind unionization of other workers. From the end of the 19th century to the 1930s, unions consisted principally of skilled craftsmen; the emergence of mass manufacturing during the period from the mid-30s to the mid-50s transformed the typical union member from a skilled to a semi-skilled or unskilled worker; starting in the mid-50s the white collar and the service worker became predominant, and finally, beginning with the mid-60s, the public employee became an important component of the union workforce.[12] Both police and correctional employee unionism have followed a somewhat similar but separate history. Police unions were the first to develop.

The growth of police unionism

Until well into the 20th century the police were subjected both to intolerable working conditions and to manipulation by politicians. They were at the same time employed to further the political needs of others and legally prevented from pursuing their own.[13] Police were usually political appointees, without job tenure. They depended on the political party in power for their jobs, promotions, and assignments. No police unions developed until the civil service reforms at the end of the century provided some job tenure.[14] Poor working conditions, low pay, inadequate job security,[15] together with the growth of unions for other workers, naturally led police to become interested in organizing unions to improve their lot.

Police organizations began to be formed at the end of the nineteenth century primarily for the purpose of fulfilling fraternal-social needs (death benefits and health insurance).[16] The Patrolmen's Benevolent Association (PBA) was formed in New York City in 1894.[17] In 1897 a charter was sought from the American Federation of Labor by police in Cleveland, Ohio. The AFL rejected the request, giving the reason that it could no more organize the police than it could the military "as both police and militiamen were often controlled by forces inimical to the labor movement."[18]

This position on the part of the AFL was reversed in 1919 and was one of the precipitating causes of the important Boston Police Strike of that year, a strike that affected police organizational efforts for years thereafter. Other causes of the strike involved deterioration of the economic conditions of the police due to war-time inflation, bad working conditions, refusal on the part of the city government to recognize or negotiate with the union, no provision for grievance machinery, numerous strikes in other parts of the country among both private and public employees, and pledges of support from other unions, giving the police a feeling of solidarity with other workers. The immediate cause of the walkout, however, was the dismissal of police organizers for their union activity.[19] At almost the same time and for almost the same reasons the London police also went on strike.[20] Both strikes were lost and strikers in both police forces were dismissed. Nevertheless, the strike did bring to the attention of city officials the dangers of long-time avoidance of improving police working conditions. For the Boston police, the strike had two consequences: The amelioration of pay and working conditions, and the passage of ordinances in many cities banning police unions. Where unions survived or formed during this period, they usually issued a no strike pledge.[21]

Police employee organizations thereafter proceeded with extreme caution, avoiding affiliation with labor organizations, but nevertheless, following their developmental pattern. In the 1920s and 1930s, an anti-labor period, police employee organizations showed little growth. Police management continued to oppose unionization during the 1940s. Nevertheless, police social and fraternal organizations proliferated, and in a few cities, union locals affiliated with national organizations.[22] In the

1940s and 1950s, police employee groups found some official recognition by entering into a common pact with police management for the promotion of police professionalism.[23] The result of such alliances was domination by management. Where police officers demanded an independent union, they were stiffly opposed by police administrators and city officials on the ground that for officers to join a union would be to enter into a "dual allegiance," whereas their sole loyalty was to be to the government they served. The courts sustained this argument.[24] As late as 1957, the International Association of Chiefs of Police (IACP) issued a statement opposing police unions,[25] that is, the organization opposed those employee organizations that insisted on the right to collective bargaining over pay and working conditions.

By the 1960s, police unions, with other public employees, entered the "decade of the public employee."[26] Police unionization could already be said to be "widespread."[27] While unionization of private employees stagnated, that of public employees more than doubled, and in numbers and percentages of those unionized, surpassed private workers.[28] From 1958 to 1968 the number of government employee strikes per year rose from 15 to 254; the number of workers involved rose from 1700 to 202,000, and days of work lost as a result of strike activity increased from 7,500 to 2.5 million.[29] Such growth in unions merely reflected the rise in government sector employment as compared to the private sector. "The number of public sector workers has nearly tripled since 1947, while private manufacturing employment increased by only about 14 percent. The ratio of public sector workers to all such workers rose from 12.5 percent in 1947 to 18.8 percent in 1976."[30] Such a growth in public employee unionism is all the more astonishing when it is realized that, as a whole, union membership has been on a steady decline, from a peak of nearly 36% in 1956 to its 1986 low of 14%.[31] With reference to police, the percentage of municipal departments with employee organizations increased from 50 percent in 1978 to 69 percent in 1984, while the percentages covered by collective bargaining contracts during those same years, rose from 63 to 77 percent.[32] Therefore, the reverse trend of public union membership, in this case police unionism, and its relative militancy as compared to private sector unions, requires some explanation.

Factors contributing to police unionization

Two questions arise with reference to police unionization: What job factors pushed police toward unionization and why did it occur when it did, in the middle to late 1960s? Commentators have suggested that police job dissatisfaction was promoted by the following grievances:

(1) increased law and order demands, while at the same time the courts, particularly the Supreme Court, were seen as restricting police powers to act;

(2) increased job hazards, while at the same time police were subjected to hostility by black and middle-class youth;

(3) low pay, poor working conditions, a coercive command structure, and a lack of any internal means for asserting and resolving grievances.[33]

To a lesser degree, each of these factors had been present for years. But, it was not until the addition of several activating ingredients that the consciousness of the police was sufficiently raised to act collectively and militantly. Such factors included the change in the composition of the labor force from industrial blue collar to white collar. Police could identify with union "nurses, teachers, airplane pilots, engineers, and skilled technicians," as fitting into the developing police image of themselves as professionals.[34] Many of these groups, particularly the teachers, scored considerable gains both in pay and working conditions through collective bargaining. Further encouragement was provided by minorities that improved their position by collective and militant actions, and by police confrontations with blacks and young people protesting the Vietnam War. There was also the influx of young officers who no longer stood in awe of police command authority.[35]

Finally, the paramilitary structure, the communal experience of facing danger, and being treated by the public as a stereotypical body, promoted occupational solidarity, and permitted police to see that they had common goals that could be best attained by common action. In effect, the police found themselves "out of step" with the rest of the working class, and took the obvious steps to remedy that disjuncture.

Nevertheless, they did not lockstep with others in the working class because of the way management had been able to separate them from the rest of the union movement. The New York City PBA has similar characteristics to other large city police unions. One detailed study found that since the entry of the post-World War II generation of young police mavericks it has been democratically run, with its membership tending to reject settlements and leaders it did not approve. But at the same time, the PBA

lobbied against fairer treatment for women, homosexuals, blacks, and other minority groups. . . . fought to preserve entry criteria based on strength, height, and mental tests . . . , oppos[ed] the Public Review Board during the 1960s, and . . . consistently defend[ed] what appeared to be serious police abuse during the arrest and confinement of minority group suspects.[36]

Moreover, the PBA, "unlike in other city municipal unions, . . . have not attempted to advance their membership's understanding on issues of race or gender." In fact, the election of some leaders often depended on their advocacy of these prejudices. It has been suggested that one of the reasons for this intrangency is just because management required separation of the PBA from other city employees, many of whom were female and minorities, thereby preventing them from understanding the common ground of all their complaints.[37]

The character and legal status of police labor organizations

Functionally, there are three types of police employee organizations: (1) locally organized, oriented, and controlled, police-only; (2) national police-only; and (3) those affiliated with traditional labor organizations.

The first category is illustrated by the Fraternal Order of Police (FOP) and the Patrolmen's Benevolent Association (PBA). FOP began in 1915, and in 1988 became the National Fraternal Order of Police. It reputedly has the largest membership, estimated to be 203,500, stating its purpose to be to seek "economic benefits and professional advancement." Although earlier the organization was mostly concerned with social and fraternal benefits for its members, FOP is now turning more to a labor union orientation in the face of challenges from nationally affiliated non-police only unions.[38] The PBAs are state-wide associations, although they may be affiliated with one of the national police unions. Historically, they are the oldest of the groups, going back to the fraternal organizations of the late 19th and early 20th centuries. They are strongest in the northeast.[39]

In the second category are the International Brotherhood of Police Officers (IBPO) and the National Association of Police Associations (NAPA).[40] IBPO was formed in the early 1960s and is oriented toward complete organizational control from its national office in Boston. All labor services, except for its Washington, D.C. lobbying office, emanate from there. NAPA, as its name indicates, is an association of local organizations rather than a membership of individual officers. It is a splinter group from the International Conference of Police Associations (ICPA), created in 1954, but dissolved over the issue of membership in the AFL–CIO.[41] ICPA split into groups for and against affiliation with traditional labor unions, an important and divisive issue for police employee organizations. NAPA represents those local organizations that are against such affiliation, and provides them with seminars on collective bargaining, and a nucleus of national representation to lobby for federal legislation of interest to its members. Organizational members of NAPA are completely independent.[42]

In the third category are police locals affiliated with traditional national labor organizations: the International Union of Police Associations (IUPA); affiliated with the AFL–CIO; and established in 1978; the American Federation of State, County, and Municipal Employees (AFSCME), also affiliated with the AFL–CIO; the Service Employees International Union (SEIU), and the International Brotherhood of Teamsters, Chauffeurs, Warehousemen and Helpers Union (Teamsters).[43] By the very fact that these unions are nationally organized themselves, they are leaders in moving the police toward a national union. IUPA, the other splinter group from ICPA, claims 0,000 police officers throughout the country and has for its object to bring police within the mainstream of the union movement.[44] AFSCME, the oldest of the national unions in organizing police, founded its first police local in 1937. But intense management opposition during the 1940s slowed its growth, and it has generally lost to local representation since then. SEIU has had little success in its attempts at organization. The Teamsters has both an advantage and disadvantage over other unions in its organizing efforts. Militant officers at times have turned to this union because of its aggressive reputation in taking on management, but these same confrontation tactics have turned off some officers as contrary to their "professional" status.[45] One example of such a union confrontation can be cited. In a community with 50 officers, the PBA in 1974 won two to one over the Teamsters the right to represent the officers. But after three years of management intransigence and what the officers saw as "bad faith" on the part of city negotiators, in 1977, the Teamsters overwhelmingly were selected as the officers' bargaining agent.[46]

At the present time there exists no truly national police organization.[47] This concentration of police unions on the local level is understandable because departments with which the unions must negotiate are "local," that is, they are creatures of city and state governments.[48] One consequence of the growth of so many police organizations is that there is intense competition for membership.

Black police unions

Black officers in Detroit in 1963 organized the Guardians of Michigan. More militant officers formed the Concerned Officers for Equal Justice. In Atlanta, black officers in November 1969 formed the Afro-American Patrolmen's League. In New York City, the strongest of the black police unions, organized as the New York Guardians.[49] In 1972, the National Black Police Association was formed and at present claims 100 associations with 30,000 individual members.[50] A survey of black police organizations in the early 1970s found that such organizations existed in almost every city examined which had more than 25–30 black officers. Specifically mentioned were Baltimore, Chicago, Cincinnati, Cleveland, Dayton, New Haven, Detroit, New York, Oakland, Philadelphia, Pittsburgh, and San Francisco. Such organizations interested themselves primarily in (1) the relations between black and white police within the department and (2) relations between the department and the black community.[51]

Primary concerns of black unions, however, were found to center around departmental work practices and racist conduct of whites toward black officers, including restricted promotional opportunities or assignment, prejudicial treatment by white officers or discipline by command staff,[52] well illustrated by the actions of white officers in the Detroit department (chapter 2). Black and white unions are usually found on opposite sides of Title VII suits attacking police department hiring and promotion polices (chapter 2).[53] Where the white police command has been pushed to support affirmative action efforts, white-dominated unions have challenged their authority.[54] For the most part, however, the white command structure has been one with their men. In one instance of prejudicial assignment, only black officers were assigned to police black ghetto areas, thus reserving for black officers the areas with the highest crime and most dangerous work. Connecticut Guardians met this *de facto* segregation with a demand that they be distributed throughout the city. When the grievance went unresolved, mass sick calls by black officers resulted, one of the rare job actions taken by such organizations.[55]

Other specific actions taken by black officer associations include:

engaging in recruiting efforts to increase the number of black police; protesting police mistreatment of prisoners (primarily black prisoners); offering assistance to black citizens in filing complaints against policemen; forming alliances with black activist groups in the city; giving speeches to black community groups; sponsoring athletic, social, and recreational programs for black youth;

and in general, trying to reduce citizen distrust of police and to create a better police image in the black community.[56]

Most such groups place their major emphasis on attempts at internal change rather than on efforts to modify societal conditions. It appears easier to obtain a satisfactory resolution of specific intradepartmental greviances than to somehow improve the general state of relations between hundreds of policemen and thousands of citizens: in many cities an order from the top has opened assignments and promotional opportunities to blacks; similar orders have not been as effective in changing the relations between officers and the community.[57]

On the other hand, the Afro-American Patrolmen's League in Chicago considers itself primarily a community service organization. It has established a citizen complaint referral service, has conducted voter registration drives, and has filed a suit which succeeded in blocking millions of dollars in federal funds going to the Chicago police department, alleging that the department discriminated against black officers in violation of federal law.[58]

The most common means for black police organizations to assert their claims are by lobbying with the chief's office or with city officials, by litigation, or by publicizing issues of concern. They do not engage in collective bargaining although some function as *de facto* grievance representatives to press minority claims. Job actions do not seem useful because black associations do not control enough of the service to pose a threat. Actions which result in bringing their grievances to public attention have often been successful because militant actions by black organizations usually receive substantial publicity.[59]

Relations between black and white police have been worsening rather than improving. Prejudice may have increased in recent years as blacks assert themselves and have less tolerance for abuse. More black officers mean more black-white contacts. Whites are fearful and disgruntled over affirmative action agreements which often restrict their promotions and assignments. Blacks are angry that their long-sought gains are now threatened by the last hired, first fired policy during these years of restricted city budgets.[60]

In most cities black officers are content to allow the "white" majority union to fulfill its traditional collective bargaining role as to wages, seniority rights, and working conditions, and restrict themselves to racial aspects of the job. Blacks generally believe that the white-dominated union cannot represent black officer interests, and that blacks have no chance to capture or influence the white union. The National Black Police Association (NBPA) has bridged some of these difficulties and brought black locals together into a national organization dedicated to information sharing, education, and a common strategy.[61]

Detroit as a case study in police unionism[62]

Reacting to the loss of jobs resulting from mechanization of agriculture, and the pull of northern industrial work, large numbers of blacks emigrated to northern cities. By the 1930s, Detroit's population was 24% black. Because of job competition, tension grew between black and white workers, and between the black community and the white-dominated police department, until it erupted in the 1943 race riot. Battered by the almost unanimous press criticism for the way they had handled the riot, and the appointment of a "reform" commissioner to revise the department's racist policies, rank and file police morale was low.

A Fraternal Order of Police (FOP) chapter, established in 1943 before the riot, had been ineffective in convincing the commissioner to deal with it. Soon after the commissioner took office, a national union of government workers attempted to unionize the police. In response, the commissioner issued an order banning police from joining any organization that prevented officers from performing "full and complete police duty," or required "dual allegiance," thus implicitly allowing officers to join an organization independent of national or state affiliation, and consisting only of police officers. The Detroit Police Officers' Association (DPOA) was formed in 1944, and within six months had enlisted 2800 of the 3700 officers. Management had, in effect, accepted what amounted to a company union in an effort to stifle incipient rank and file militance.

Initially, the DPOA acted as a social and benevolent society, providing legal services, entertainment, and charitable events. But, in addition, it lobbied in the state capitol for the 40 hour, five day week and better wages. In 1965, with other public employee unions, it successfully urged passage of the Michigan Public Employee Relations Act (PERA) providing for public sector bargaining, which unlike many other such laws included the police in its provisions. Undoubtedly, one important factor in its passage was the success employers had had in the private sector, especially in the auto industry, in working with unions for uninterrupted production. By January 1960, under PERA, the DPOA had gained recognition as the exclusive bargaining agent for the police rank and file. Also recognized was the Lieutenants and Sergeants Association, and the Detectives Association.

In 1965, a Black Police Officers' Caucus was formed to protest the absence of blacks on the DPOA executive board. Reportedly, when black officers pressed their demands for black union representation at a DPOA meeting, they were laughed at. The Caucus, which largely consisted of younger members, thereafter engaged in direct, and militant opposition to both union and police management.[63]

PERA's success inspired a new, younger leadership to run for and be elected to union office. DPOA's first bargaining session in 1966 gained a hefty increase ($1,000), but by 1967 the first signs of a city budget crisis appeared, and the mayor took a firm stand against further increases, claiming there was no money for a wage hike. The union's response was an unofficial ticket writing slowdown, which potentially threatened millions of dollars in city revenue; the officers also stopped volunteering for overtime duty, required because of a severe manpower shortage. Threats of disciplinary action by the mayor and police chief were answered by calls by large numbers of officers reporting in sick with "blue flu." The city sought an injunction to halt the work stoppage, as well as $50,000 in compensatory and punitive damages against the union for each day of the sick-in. But even after the chief suspended 70 officers, about one-fourth of the force continued to call in sick.

The costs for both sides had escalated to such an extent that both management and labor were motivated to enter into a vague agreement to negotiate, and to submit unresolved issues to a mutually acceptable panel. Agreement was obtained on certain noneconomic issues: grievance procedures were to be established; seniority was recognized; arbitration was to be used for unresolved issues. In general, the action could be viewed as a challenge to and a victory over the quasi-military police authority structure. This struggle was interrupted in July 1967 by nine days of riot in the black Detroit ghetto. Although liberals lambasted police, and conservatives applauded their efforts in the riot, both groups agreed that there was a need for increased police protection. City officials were intent on maintaining the morale and stability of the force in the face of such protests. The police chief rescinded the suspensions, and two weeks following the riots, the City Council approved the DPOA contract. The independent panel, set up to consider wages and other issues, found that the city could pay the $10,000 salary demanded.

In effect, union-management collective bargaining did not prevent but did institutionalize conflict by making conflict more predictable and manageable just as it had in the private sector. At the same time, the pressures of public employees, coming at the same time as the fiscal crisis of the cities, has the effect of worsening the crisis, while placing some of the blame for that crisis on the workers. Finally, when layoffs came, the unions found themselves unable to prevent them, but, by reliance on the seniority clause in union contracts, were able to place much of the burden of unemployment on the backs of newly-hired black and female officers (see chapter 2).

Political environment surrounding correctional personnel[64]

Whereas the basic political focus of police organization is the municipality, for correctional personnel it is the state. The chief executive of the state, the governor, proposes and approves (or vetoes) all legislation, and initiates the budgetary process, which may include the selection of sites, and the building of prisons. The state legislature is responsible for appropriating funds, drafting and passing legislation, implementing its own or the governor's proposals, and approving or rejecting the governor's appointments to executive departments. The legislative function includes the creation of a department of corrections, whose powers are statutorily determined by the legislature, and whose head is appointed by the governor with legislative consent.

Prisons are divided into maximum, medium, and minimum security, the exact mix depending on the dominant correctional philosophy in vogue at the time, approximately along the same liberal and conservative lines as suggested in the section on the political environment of the police. Likewise, the flow in and out of prison, and the composition of the prison population, are determined by factors substantially beyond the control of prison administrators: acts made criminal by the legislature and the sentences affixed to the crime; crime and arrest rates, successful prosecutions, unemployment, law and order campaigns, numbers of convicted persons given prison sentences rather than non-prison alternatives; numbers released by the parole board, the building of new prisons, the deterioration of the old; and determination by courts as to what constitutes overcrowding.

The warden or superintendent is the executive officer of the prison and exercises his functions under the state director of corrections. Below the warden is a paramilitary structure similar to that found in the police department: captains, lieutenants, sergeants, and at the bottom, the correctional officer. Following the federal structure, there is both a federal and state system of prisons. I will discuss only the state system where about 90% of prisoners are found.

Prison workers can be divided into the three main tasks of the prison: (1) custodial—correctional officers; (2) treatment or program staff—academic and vocational teachers, caseworkers, chaplains, mental health workers, social workers, psychological, medical and dental personnel; (3) clerical, culinary, maintenance, and skilled trades.

Until the 1950s, substantially all of the prison staff was custodial. In the last 30 years, however, new theories of treatment and rehabilitation have brought numbers of program staff into the prison. To understand the resulting organizational, social, and political changes, it is worth recalling the more formal structure that it replaced:

> Throughout the history of the American prison, the most obvious characteristic of the guard force was its paramilitary organization. At the apex of the pyramid stood the warden whose "orders" flowed through his captains and lieutenants down to the rank-and-file line officers. While the prison guard was the lowest member of the formal organization, every guard ranked higher than even the most senior prisoner. The authoritarian control exercised by the staff over the prisoners paralleled the control that the warden and the custodial elite exercised over the rank and file. Traditional thinking in penology required a highly disciplined work force to meet the prison's special requirements for order, discipline, and control. The guard force took its model from the armed forces rather than from organizations of industrial production.[65]

One study of a maximum security prison in Illinois, Stateville, found that until 1970 the staff "was characterized by racial and ethnic homogenity, intense personal loyalty to the institution," to the warden, and to the captains, as well as a "pervasive belief" in the institution's mission to control the prison population.[66] But after 1970, the staff was transformed by an incoming reform administration that adopted new "professional" roles, by public employee unions, and by racial integration.

How was this unipolar, relatively stable, unchanging structure, where the administration had unchallenged power, transformed to a tripolar world in which power was shared with prisoners and guards in an unpredictable pattern? The post World War II period was full of expectations of change and reform. When state governments made no serious effort to improve prison conditions, such opposition to change may have contributed to the 1952–3 prison riots. The riots, in turn, brought forth more calls for reform.[67] Additional fundamental causative factors included the increased use of technology and statistical analysis as a means of problem solving in industry and the social sciences; the concomitant rise of the middle-class helping professions of social work, psychology, and counseling, utilizing this new found science to shape a treatment and therapeutic philosophy for the training and treatment of prisoners.

The convergence of technocratic knowledge and occupational expansion brought a new group of more educated, science-oriented, and idealistic professionals into prisons. This group, forming the program and treatment staff, gradually modified the job description and the correctional officer's relationship to the prisoner from that of a social helpmate and disciplinarian to that of custodian alone.[68] Consistant with this philosophy, but in conflict with the real world behind the walls, prison systems were renamed "departments of corrections," and guards were redesignated "corrections officers."[69] As such, they were expected to perform as "agents of change" and as "front-line treatment staff." These same influences were at work on administrators. Earlier, most correctional administrators had moved up through the ranks like police chiefs. But during the 1960s, contemporaneous with the rehabilitation philosophy, many administrators were replaced by those trained in social work, sociology and psychology, espousing a treatment as opposed to a security-first philosophy. These men often looked down on guards as being reactionary and behind the times. As a result, guards could no longer regard administrators as representing their interests. On the contrary, most administrators now seemed to be concerned only with prisoners' welfare, seeing the guards as obstacles to achieving the reforms they proposed.[70]

The prison population had also changed. As cities filled with minorities, principally blacks and hispanics seeking work, but seeing their dream of employment foundering, state prisons filled with these groups just as it did earlier in the century with white immigrants from the same socioeconomic layer. Aggravating the situation was the fact that most state prisons were located in rural areas. Thus, while a majority of prisoners were urban blacks, their guards were usually rural whites. External problems of racial conflict, gang warfare, gang control of prison population, loss of respect for authority, all led to violent confrontations between prisoners and guards, and became day to day problems of prison administration. As middle-class Vietnam protestors entered prisons in the late 60s and early 70s, conditions of violence, sexual abuse, and depraved living conditions were documented and brought to the attention of the reading public. Much of this literature was critical of guards and prison administrators.[71]

At the same time, courts were dropping their hands-off attitude and began recognizing prisoners rights: the right of access to courts and to legal materials; the right to challenge inadequate medical attention, food, and living conditions; rights to certain procedural guarantees during disciplinary proceedings; which in their totality represented the right to challenge the guard's authority.[72] Prisoners were organizing and actively asserting their rights. In the early 1970s there were hunger strikes, work stoppages, and riots. The formation of the National Prisoners Rights Association in 1971 argued that prisoners were employees of the state and had a right to bargain collectively. In Massachusetts they did succeed in negotiating improvements in living and working conditions.[73] Many guards attributed the prison violence occurring during the late 1960s and early 1970s to these changes, making their job more dangerous and anxiety provoking.[74]

For guards, this increasingly bad and unstable environment was aggravated by low pay and job prestige, lack of clarity in what was expected of them, and a feeling that they had been betrayed both by the college-trained staff and by the administration.[75] Under these conditions, it was natural for guards to feel a sense of solidarity in the face of common problems and to look for some force other than the warden to represent their interests and to solve their problems. That force was the union.

Rise of the correctional union

Correctional officers, in unionizing, followed an almost identical path to that of police officers. Beginning in the early 1900s, the New York City Department of Corrections Prison Keepers' Association provided welfare and death benefits, and did some lobbying for higher wages. In the 1930s, the American Federation of State, City and Municipal Employees (AFSCME), the union that continues to represent most correctional employees, lobbied before several state legislatures for higher wages. By the 1940s, Wisconsin state prisons, for example, were more than 95% unionized by AFSCME.[76] The New York Correction Officers' Benevolent Association in the late 1950s was the first correctional employee organization to collectively bargain with an employer. By the 1960s the social and fraternal type of organization was on the wane, to be replaced by a trade union interested in a one-to-one collective bargaining relationship with management.[77] The best account of the growth of unionism in one prison is that of Stateville, an Illinois maximum security institution.[78]

Stateville was built in 1925 as an attempt to alleviate overcrowding at nearby Joliet prison and to try what was thought to be a superior European prison design, a circular construction in which a guard, looking from the center, could see any part of the structure. Stateville's early history is dominated by Warden Joe Ragen, who reigned from 1936 to 1961, when he was moved up to state director of public safety. Ragen, a kind of prison replica of his contemporary J. Edgar Hoover of the FBI, demanded and obtained absolute personal loyalty from his staff. His rule epitomized the description of prison structure set forth in the prior section, a rule inconsistent with sharing power with a union. Attempts to organize guards in the mid-1950s met with little success. Ragen refused to meet with groups of employees. Another effort to organize in 1962 was snuffed out when Ragen had organizers transferred to different shifts, to tower duty, or to other posts where they would be out of contact with coworkers.

When, in 1965, because of illness, Ragen was replaced as state safety director, organizing efforts increased, this time aided by AFSCME. Ragen's replacement, Ross Randolph, a former school teacher and FBI man, had served an earlier tour as warden of Menard. His relaxed administration brought him to the attention of reformers. He became a favorite of academicians and introduced the first civilian into Stateville administration, a supervisor of parole with a master's degree in sociology. Soon after Randolph assumed the post, he was approached by Stateville guards for approval to form an employee union. Not only did he give approval but he pledged that he would allow no retaliation against union members for their activity. Union dues checkoffs were authorized in 1966.

As part of the general growth in unionization of professionals described earlier, AFSCME was in the process of expansion. By 1966, it was able to provide the young guard local with organizers who helped draft by-laws and a union charter. Negotiation with management began in 1967 over wages, seniority rights, and pay for a 15 minute daily period during which guards stood formation. The next few years involved jockeying between the two sides in which management often denied the AFSCME representatives entrance to the prison or otherwise harassed them, and the union looked for ways to attract more members. Successes of union attorneys in handling workmen's compensation claims and in contesting disciplinary proceedings were particularly fruitful. A breakthrough came in 1970 when lieutenants became members. Thereafter, the captains joined when one of their number was helped with a grievance. The issue of whether lieutenants and captains, "as management," could be part of an employees' union has been a crucial issue for all correctional unions. Such membership is frequently a key to successful growth for it is in these groups that unions find their most stable and competent leadership.[79]

About 1970, union concerns switched from concentration on salary to security issues. Guards perceived that as the authoritarian Ragen administration gave way to a more bureaucratized, impersonal, more even-handed management of prison affairs, and as prisoners obtained more rights, those of guards appeared to diminish, and their authority was under continuous challenge. Demands by the union included increased disciplinary powers for line officers and supervisors; separating out prisoner trouble-makers; reforming the abolished riot squad; enforcement of a grooming code for prisoners and correctional personnel (including counselors); hiring more guards; creation of a special segregation unit, and the like. The union's responsiveness to taking on management in disciplinary situations also boosted their membership: it challenged the discharge of guards for allowing inmates to escape; and defended a captain, not a member of the union, when he was suspended for throwing a teacher, who demanded that an inmate be assigned to his school, out of his office. Following the death of a guard in a 1973 riot, the union voted to lock up the prison if security demands were not met. The warden, John Twomey, threatened to fire the guards. AFSCME representatives made direct contact with the governor's office. The governor's representative ended the walkout by promising to negotiate all the demands, thus undercutting the warden's authority. By 1975, the union had a collective bargaining agreement.

The changes in the organizational and political structure of the prison were brought about by the convergence of the external and internal forces described. As guards became educated to union values they were drawn away from the earlier paramilitary perspective. Their former sense of an institutional mission was replaced with a new perspective of themselves as workers whose major concern was to earn enough to support their families. As workers, they began to see their work as "just a job," and that they weren't "being paid to be a hero."[80]

Factors contributing to correctional unionization[81]

Assertion of rights by other groups and the growth of public employee unions pushed guards as well toward unionization during the period. By

1978 it has been estimated that approximately half of the nation's correctional agencies were involved in collective bargaining with their employees. Recent moves toward unionization of guards have been in reaction against overcrowded prison conditions in deteriorating institutions. Overcrowding is an old problem in prisons. But the increase in state prison population from 174,000 to 225,000 or a rise of 30% between January 1, 1973 and January 1, 1976, has been due to a number of factors outside the control of prison administrators: (1) increase in crime related to high unemployment among minority males who now populate prisons; (2) limited job opportunities for those on probation and parole; (3) increased number of persons in the 18–30 age group which produces a disproportionate percentage of persons who are most likely to commit the violent crimes which result in long prison terms; (4) a rising number of arrests and convictions because of rising crime rates and increasing pressure of law and order groups for more and longer prison terms.

Such pressures, in turn, have resulted in the decreased use of parole and probation and the increased use of mandatory sentences for serious felonies. Complicating the problem was the fact that the increasing prison population came at a time when prisons were already overcrowded in outmoded, inadequate facilities, many of which have been condemned by court decisions, and when there was a fiscal crisis restricting the options available to state policy makers.

Character of correctional unions

Correctional union organization has deviated somewhat from police unionization in that correctional institutions are state-based, most correctional unions have both supervisory and rank and file members, and correctional employers are divided into security and program staff. Unionization had been of four types: (1) local, independent, (2) state or national law enforcement association, (3) state employee association, and (4) national labor unions. The type of organization has been affected by the legal authority of the organization to engage in collective bargaining, a matter to be discussed hereafter. Before such right is gained, the type of organization is usually (1) or (3); after the right is obtained (generally by statute), it is most likely (4).

In 1976, AFSCME, an all public employee AFL–CIO union, was reported to represent 20,000 of 75,000 correctional officers, and to have a total membership of 750,000. The Service Employees International Union (SEIU), also an AFL–CIO affiliate, draws its membership from both public and private sectors, and in corrections attracts mostly program staff. The National Association of Government Employees (NAGE), at first exclusively composed of federal employees, is now organizing police and correctional employees, its correctional branch being the International Brotherhood of Correctional Officers. Correctional unions support or oppose politicians according to their stand on issues of interest to correctional employees; increase member's economic benefits, and seek safety measures that will protect workers from potential dangers of their job. As one commentator put it, "the union's bargaining power in the public sector consists of its ability to manipulate the political costs of agreement and disagreement of the various managers rather than the economic cost manipulation that characterizes union power in the private sector."[82]

Development of organizational rights of criminal justice personnel

Rights of criminal justice personnel, like the rights of labor generally, waited until criminal justice personnel were able to form unions and force their public employers to bargain with them collectively. Those rights developed slowly after a long struggle. As has been earlier indicated, not only did most criminal justice personnel not participate in union activity, but in the case of police, they were often an instrument of management in denying unionization to other parts of the working class.

Two major constitutional and public policy issues are presented by the formation of criminal justice employee unions: (1) the right of criminal justice employees to join a union; and (2) the right of employee organizations to demand that their public employer bargains collectively with them.

Public employees now generally have the statutory right to bargain collectively but legislatures have been reluctant to grant the same right to criminal justice personnel. Nevertheless, criminal justice personnel now have an established constitutional right to join unions. Conversely, there is no constitutional right to require public employers to bargain collectively with the unions formed. In terms of state statutes, there is more resistance to, and more restrictions on, these rights in the case of criminal justice personnel than with other public employees. Both court decisions and statutes have treated differently the right to join a union and the right to bargain collectively. Even where the first right is granted by a state, the second does not automatically follow.

Right of workers to organize

There could be no union of workers until there were workers. Workers did not exist until the era of capitalism created the employer-employee relationship consisting of two antagonistic classes, one owning the means of production, and the other propertyless, and job dependent. The social organization of the new factory system, which grouped men and women with common interests and problems under the same roof, encouraged the formation of unions to contend with their more powerful employer.[83] But workers were not always free to organize for the purpose of demanding better pay and working conditions. Employers had an interest in maintaining wages as low as possible and any combination of employees which by their actions interfered with what employers argued were natural market forces were accused of entering into a criminal conspiracy. During the early years of the 19th century English courts followed this view. But American courts of the 1830s and 1840s rejected the notion that a combination of workers attempting to change pay and working conditions was a criminal conspiracy.[84] Between the 1860s and 1890s, a period of increasing labor-management strife, injunctions replaced criminal prosecutions as the management weapon against union activity.[85]

In 1921, the Supreme Court, in the following words, expressed the dominant American view—the union was an equalizing force in bringing together the contracting parties, the employer and employee:

> Labor unions were organized out of the necessities of the situation. A single employee was helpless in dealing with an employer. He was dependent ordinarily on his daily wage for the maintenance of himself and family. If the employer refused to pay him the wages that he thought fair, he was nevertheless unable to leave the employ and to resist arbitrary and unfair treatment. Union was essential to give laborers opportunity to deal on equality with their employers.[86]

Prior to the First World War the federal government's sole intervention in labor disputes involved the calling in of the national guard to break strikes or to control disorder. Federal courts also frequently enjoined strike activity (chapter 4). But with the inception of the First World War, uninterrupted production in major industries became essential for the conduct of the war. Thus, in 1918, the federal War Labor Conference Board (soon renamed the National War Labor Board), was created to establish "principles and policies which will enable the prosecution of production without stoppages of work."[87] The "good times" following the war and the return of the veterans provided a plentiful labor supply, weakening the position of unions. But the 1929 depression, leaving millions of workers unemployed, exposed the inability of individual workers to successfully negotiate with their economically much stronger employer. Workers thereupon joined unions in great numbers. Some workers even called for a different organization of society, a socialist state that would protect workers' jobs, and give workers more say in their future. In reaction against this call for a radical structural change, President Roosevelt, elected in the Democratic landslide of 1932, instituted a host of New Deal legislation, including the National Labor Relations Act of 1935 (NLRA, known as the Wagner Act, after its sponsor, Senator Robert Wagner).[88] This Act guaranteed the right to form a union, required employers to bargain in good faith, and guaranteed the right to strike. Public employers, however, were seen as falling in a separate category from private employers. This specific exclusion was embodied in the original Wagner Act: the term "employer . . . shall not include . . . any State or political subdivision thereof . . . "[89] This exclusion has been continued in later legislation.

Development of public employee organizational rights

In response to demands by public employees for equal rights to those gained by labor in the private sector, federal and state courts evolved theories of sovereign authority and unlawful delegation of power which enabled them to reject these claims. It was held that in the absence of express statutory authority a public employer had no power to bargain or to enter into a contract with a labor union.[90] Even where the state authorized collective bargaining with public employees, it has been held that the public employer is not required to bargain.[91]

One extreme example of this view is stated in a 1943 New York case:

> To tolerate or recognize any combination of Civil Service employees of the Government as a labor organization or union is not only incompatible with the spirit of democracy, but inconsistent with every principle upon which our Government is founded. Nothing is more dangerous to public welfare than to admit that hired servants of the state can dictate to the Government, the hours and conditions under which they will carry on essential services vital to the welfare, safety and security of the citizen. . . . Collective bargaining has no place in government service. The employer is the whole people. It is impossible for administrative officials to bind the Government of the United States or the State of New York by any agreement made between them and representatives of any union. Government officials and employees are governed and

guided by laws which must be obeyed and which cannot be abrogated or set aside by any agreement of employees and officials.[92]

Such a view of public employees' right to organize becomes even more restricted when it concerns criminal justice personnel. Although the cases cited below factually involve the dismissal of firefighters for joining labor unions, the same reasoning has been applied to the police. In a 1923 Pennsylvania case, the court said:

> It is generally conceded that association with an organization which, on any occasion or for any purpose, attempts to control the relations of members of either the police or fire departments toward the municipality they undertake to serve, is, in the very nature of things, inconsistent with the discipline which such employment imperatively requires, and therefore must prove subversive of the public welfare and detrimental to the general welfare. . . . If plaintiffs desired to retain their positions in the public service, they should have obeyed the director's order; having elected not to do so (which, of course, was the privilege of each of them, as individuals), they cannot successfully complain of the ensuing result.[93]

In a 1935 case, a Virginia court stated:

> Police and fire departments are in a class apart. Both are at times charged with the preservation of public order and for manifold reasons they owe to the public their undivided allegiance. The power in the City of complete control is imperatively necessary if discipline is to be maintained.[94]

Historically, private employees were the first conceded the right to join unions, then public employees, excluding criminal justice personnel and firefighters, and then only recently, were first amendment, freedom of association rights accorded police.[95]

The duty to bargain

To be able to bargain over wages is a prelude to the entry of parties into a contractual relationship. The idea that parties should be free to contract, to buy and to sell in accordance with market conditions, is accepted as the prime mover of a capitalist society based as it is on a market economy. The same notion applies to the sale of one's labor: employees dealing with employers arriving at a bargain—the wage for given work. But the imposition of a statutory duty to bargain, and the requirement to bargain with an organization representing the employees as a *group* rather than the individual employee, appears to go contrary to this belief system. It should not be surprising, therefore, that courts have taken the view that the right to collectively bargain may be granted by the state at its pleasure but is not a constitutional right. In Indianapolis Education Assn v Lewallen, a 1969 7th circuit decision, the court stated:

> [T]here is no constitutional duty to bargain collectively with an exclusive bargaining agent. Such duty, when imposed, is imposed by statute. The refusal of the [public employer] to bargain in good faith does not equal a constitutional violation of [the public employee's] positive rights of association, free speech, petition, equal protection, or due process. Nor does the fact that the agreement to collectively bargain may be enforceable against a state elevate a contractual right to a constitutional right.[96]

In Atkins v City of Charlotte,[97] a federal district court upheld a state statute barring the state from entering into a contract with a public employee union:

> We find nothing unconstitutional in [the law]. It simply voids contracts between units of government within North Carolina and labor unions and expresses the public policy of North Carolina to be against such collective bargaining contracts. There is nothing in the United States Constitution which entitles one to have a contract with another who does not want it. It is but a step further to hold that the State may lawfully forbid such contracts with its instrumentalities.

In the 1979 decision of Smith v Arkansas State Highway Employees,[98] the Supreme Court followed these cases, actually citing the Indianapolis Education Assn case in its support. *Smith* involved a practice of the Arkansas state highway department to refuse to consider grievances submitted by the public employee's union. Grievances would be considered by the agency only if submitted by the individual employee. In a per curiam decision, with only Justice Marshall dissenting, the Court replied to a claim that the practice violated first amendment rights:

> But the First Amendment is not a substitute for the national labor relations laws. The fact that procedures followed by a public employer in bypassing the union and dealing directly with its members might well be unfair labor practices were federal statutory law applicable hardly establishes that such procedures violate the Constitution. The First Amendment right to associate and to advocate "provides no guarantee that a speech will persuade or that advocacy will be effective." The public employee surely can associate and speak freely and petition openly, and he is protected by the First Amendment from retaliation in doing so. But the First Amendment does not impose any affirmative obligation on the government to listen, to respond or, in this context, to recognize the association and bargain with it. . . . [Because the Highway Commission has not] prohibited its employees from joining together in a union, or from persuading others to do so, or from advocating any particular ideas . . . [and because] there is . . . no claim of retaliation or discrimination, . . . far from taking steps to prohibit or discourage union membership or association,

all the Commission has done in its challenged conduct is simply to ignore the union. That it is free to do.[99] [Citations omitted].

The Court took this idea a step further in Babbitt v United Farm Workers Natl Union.[100] There the union complained about an Arkansas statute that provided them with statutory collective bargaining procedures the union claimed were "ineffective." The Court responded:

> Accepting that the Court guarantees workers the right individually or collectively to voice their views to their employees [citations omitted], the Constitution does not afford such employees the right to compel employers to engage in a dialogue or even to listen. Accordingly, Arizona was not constitutionally obliged to provide a procedure pursuant to which agricultural employees, through a chosen representative, might compel their employers to negotiate. That it has undertaken to do so in an assertedly niggardly fashion, then, presents as a general matter no First Amendment problems.[101]

While *Babbitt* deals with private employees, its principles seem to apply equally to public unions. Taking *Babbitt* and *Smith* together, it appears that public employees cannot rely on the federal constitution to force states to bargain collectively with them. Therefore public employees are limited to their ability to "associate and speak freely and petition openly" to convince the state legislatures to agree to collective bargaining. How successful have public employees been in their efforts to secure such legislation?

Development of the statutory right to bargain

Acceptance by the state and by municipalities that they must bargain with their public employees came slowly in a series of halting steps. One of the first breakthroughs for municipal employees was the creation in 1953 by New York City Mayor Robert F. Wagner, Jr. (the son of the sponsor of the NLRA), of a labor relations system for municipal employees, which, however, excluded uniformed personnel.[102] In 1958, Mayor Wagner, by executive order, authorized uniformed personnel to bargain collectively "through freely chosen representatives in the determination of the terms and conditions of their employment."[103] The first state giving public employees the right to bargain collectively was Wisconsin.[104] New York City, again under Mayor Wagner in 1961, provided a formal grievance procedure for the police, a gain which for the first time enabled the union to represent its members before management and thus impress them with its efforts in their behalf. A further Wagner executive order in 1963 codified a *de facto* series of agreements which had grown up between management and the police union: there was to be no non-police affiliation; the police commissioner was to have the last say in resolution of grievances rather than having employee complaints decided by the state department of labor as was the case with other public employees; a properly certified union was to have exclusive bargaining rights, and there was to be no right to strike.[105]

Mayor Wagner's executive orders no doubt encouraged, if they were not the cause, of Executive Order 10,988 of President Kennedy. That order provided that federal employees "shall have . . . the right . . . to form, join and assist any employee organization. . . . "[106] Employees were authorized to join any organization that included private employees, but were prohibited from joining an organization that asserted the right to strike against the federal government or that discriminated with regard to race, color, creed or national origin.[107] The parties, through their representatives, were to "meet at reasonable times and confer with respect to personnel policy and practices and matters affecting working conditions. . . . "[108] In 1969, by Executive Order 11,491, President Nixon added sex and age as bases for excluding discriminating organizations, and established a three person Federal Labor Relations Council to administer and interpret the order, to make policy, and issue necessary rules and procedures. A Federal Service Impasse Panel was created to help to settle negotiation impasses. The requirement to meet and negotiate was strengthened in that the parties "shall meet at reasonable times and confer in good faith with respect to personnel policies and practices and matters affecting working conditions. . . . "[109] A refusal to "consult, confer, or negotiate with a labor organization" could form the basis of an unfair labor practice.[110]

With the passage of the Civil Service Reform Act of 1978, federal employee relations underwent the first significant change since the Pendleton Act of 1883. The Civil Service Reform Act abolished the federal Civil Service Commission, and created in its place two new agencies: (1) the Office of Personnel Management and (2) the Merit System Protection Board. The former Civil Service Commission had had the conflicting responsibilities of overseeing management of federal hiring of civil service employees and at the same time protecting employee rights. These functions are now split between the two new agencies. The Act also creates the Federal Labor Relations Authority which oversees labor relations matters including the resolution of labor disputes. The Act does not apply to the FBI, the CIA, or other agency "which has as a primary function intelligence, investigation, or security work. . . . "[111]

An Ohio court sets forth the spirit behind the state public employees collective bargaining acts:

> With the enactment of the Public Employees Collective Bargaining Act, Ohio adopted a comprehensive law to govern labor relations between public employees and their employers. . . . By the time the new Act went into effect, Ohio was the fortieth state to have enacted some form of legislation to regulate their public-sector labor relations.
>
> Until the Act went into effect, Ohio had no legal framework governing public-sector labor relations, and dealt with these issues on an *ad hoc* basis. . . . The new Act is a positive step forward. It sets forth firmly defined legal guidelines that minimize the possibility of public-sector labor disputes and provides for the orderly resolution of any disputes that occur. This law brings stability and clarity to an area where there had been none and will facilitate the determination of the rights and obligations of government employees and employers, and give them more time to provide safety, education, sanitation, and other important services. In addition, the Act assures that both public employers and employees will be accorded many of the same rights and be governed by many of the same responsibilities as employees and employers in the non-public sector. In now being treated relatively equally with employees in the private-sector, public employees have been removed from second-class citizenship.[112]

Recent Supreme Court decisions affecting organizational rights

Labor generally found state legislatures unreceptive to attempts to secure collective bargaining for public employees. Such was particularly true in the southeast, a region historically hostile to labor unions. Labor, therefore, turned to the federal government for aid.[113] But the federal government's first regulation of wages in the Fair Labor Standards Act of 1938, excluded public employees from coverage. Continued lobbying resulted in the 1974 amendments establishing minimum wage standards for state and local government employees. This legislation was contested in the 1976 case of National League of Cities v Usery.[114] There, the Court, relying on the tenth amendment (stating that all rights not specifically delegated to the federal government are retained by the states), held that Congress lacked power under the Commerce Clause to pass such legislation. Ten years later, in Garcia v San Antonio Metro Transit Authority,[115] the Court overruled *National League of Cities.* Conceivably then, if Congress wished to pass such legislation, it would have power to do so.

Types of representation developed by criminal justice employees

Police unions have developed the following alternative ways of representing their members. With due regard to the different structure of corrections, the same alternatives may be employed by correctional personnel.

(1) Individual officers may communicate with their superiors through normal administrative channels. Police organizations restrict their activities to informal meetings with police officials;

(2) The police organization actively undertakes to present officer views on questions of salaries and/or working conditions through appearances at city council meetings, and lobbies for its views for or against legislation before state legislatures;

(3) The police organization meets with police chiefs or their representative for the purpose of developing mutually acceptable proposals on salaries and/or working conditions for submission to the city council;

(4) Representatives of the police organization, from the outset of negotiations, meet with a committee that represents the city council and/or the mayor's office. This alternative is closest to normal bargaining.[116]

Where there is a statute providing for a right to bargain, statutes may:

(1) require the employer to bargain;
(2) permit bargaining by local option;
(3) require no collective bargaining but require parties to "meet and confer";
(4) requires collective bargaining but restricts the areas over which bargaining may take place, usually those considered "inherent management policy";
(5) deny the right to bargain with public employees;
(6) remain silent on the issue.[117]

Where collective bargaining is authorized, the statutes usually take one of three forms: (1) meet and confer statutes—requiring employers to meet with union representatives to discuss working conditions and other matters affecting employees but where there is no procedure provided for resolving disputes; (2) nonwage collective bargaining, in which wages are specifically excluded from bargaining issues; and (3) bargaining open in all matters. Meet and confer laws, sometimes called collective begging statutes by unions because public employers under such laws cannot be forced to bargain in good faith, have been historically a step toward collective bargaining statutes. In practice, they often lead to the same negotiations and agreements as the more comprehensive statute.[118]

Between 1960 and 1970, over 20 states enacted statutes requiring public employers to negotiate over wages, hours, and other conditions of employment.[119] By the end of 1987, "40 states, the District of Columbia, the federal government, and the Virgin Islands have the right to bargain collectively under the protection of various federal, state and local statutes."[120] As of 1984, 27 states provided a right for local police to bargain, generally with compulsory arbitration or some other impasse resolution mechanism, as a substitute for the right to strike which is banned.[121]

Characteristics of police departments organized

One of the factors pushing toward such recognition is the number of departments already unionized. As early as 1968, a survey of police departments showed that:

> At least one police employee organization was reported by 84 percent of the respondents. Of cities over 50,000 in size, 89 percent had at least one police employee organization and of cities under 50,000 population, 72 percent.... Second, these organizations are police-only local units. While some have affiliated with organized labor, most have remained independent or are local affiliates of police-only organizations.
>
> Third, most of these organizations function as unions regardless of their affiliation. Practically one third of the cities over 50,000 in population engage in collective bargaining with their police employee organization, and another 20 percent permit the police employee organization to represent the membership with respect to wages, hours and conditions in a relationship other than bargaining.[122]

A more recent estimate is that 300,000 of the approximately 500,000 federal, state, and local law enforcement officers are members of some police employee organization, about one-half of which engage in some form of collective bargaining.[123] The highest degree of police employee organization is found in cities of the Northeast and North Central states while the South and West represent the lowest in organization. Such a dissemination is consistent with that found in the private sector.[124]

Right to strike

While the right to strike on the part of American workers in the private sector has been legally protected since the passage of the NLRA of 1935, except in a few jurisdictions, that right had been denied public employees. Particularly as concerns the police, that denial has a long history and is intimately tied to the importance of the police as one of the main pillars in sustaining a state structure that in part rules and maintains by force an unstable harmony among disputing and competing groups. Earlier in this chapter, the police strikes in Boston and London have been described. Here, it is the reaction of the governments to this threat of a police strike that is of significance. Lloyd George, English Prime Minister at the time of the London police strike, in a message to his police commissioner, expressed his understanding of the relationship of the police to the state:

> The police force is so essential to the stability of social order that at all hazards we must take steps to ensure that we have a body of men at the disposal of the state who can be relied upon. That we cannot command at the present moment as long as you have thousands of men who are under contract to disobey the authorities at the behest of an outside committee.[125]

Referring to the Boston strike, President Wilson stated:

> A strike of policemen of a great city, leaving that city at the mercy of an army of thugs, is a crime against civilization. In my judgment the obligation of a policeman is as sacred and direct as the obligation of a soldier. He is a public servant, not a private employee, and the whole honor of the community is in his hands. He has no right to prefer any private advantage to the public safety.[126]

Perhaps remembered best is the statement of then Governor Calvin Coolidge of Massachusetts, who rode to the presidency on the basis of his apparent unbending stand before striker demands. Answering a request by Samuel Gompers, the head of the AFL, for clemency for the discharged strikers, Coolidge righteously opined: "There is no right to strike against the public safety by anyone, anytime, anywhere."[127]

Even President Roosevelt, who was responsible for many rights accorded working people in the 1930s, pulled back from recognizing the right to strike for public employees:

> A strike of public employees manifests nothing less than an attempt on their part to prevent or obstruct the operations of government until their demands are satisfied. Such actions looking toward the paralysis of government by those who have sworn to support it is unthinkable and intolerable.[128]

The modern rejection of the right to strike on the part of public employees has been based on the supposed differences between public and private employees in relation to market forces:

> [T]he demand for government services is inelastic because there is very little substitutability of services, especially in fire and police protection and that government is not bound by the necessity to make a profit. Absent these market constraints which limit the amount which can be coerced from a private employer by a strike, there is no limit on the amount that could be coerced from the public employer by strikes other than the legislative appropriation.

Therefore, the strike prohibition is an economic necessity in order to keep labor from financially destroying the public employer.[129]

It is further argued that to grant the right to strike to public employees would "distort the political process" by giving "labor an unfair advantage over other interest groups competing for tax dollars in the budgeting process." The process may be further damaged when the frustrated public vents its anger at elected officials who refused to give in to what may have been unreasonable labor demands "while those who submit to such demands early may be returned to office as peacemakers and statesmen."[130] These arguments, based on the supposition of calamitous results from granting the right to strike to public employees, are giving way to the more moderate experience of recent years in which a few states have allowed public employees the right to strike, part of a trend toward finding that public and private collective bargaining are more similar than different.

> First, it means that judiciary and administrative tribunals are placing more stress on the word "bargaining" and less on the word "public." There is a dawning realization that public employees are primarily *employees* and only secondarily *government* employees. Therefore, they should be denied bargaining rights available to other employees only when there are compelling government or public policy reasons for such restrictions.[131]

Constitutional issues raised by denial of right to strike

Neither state nor federal courts have recognized a constitutional right to strike on the part of public employees. For the reasons cited earlier, this denial is particularly firm in the case of criminal justice employees. Three arguments have been advanced and rejected for the right to strike: (1) to deny public employees the right to strike while authorizing the strike for employees in the private sector is a violation of equal protection of the laws. This argument is turned aside because of the asserted differences in the two groups;[132] (2) the denial violates due process of law. This argument is rejected because "the State, in governing its internal affairs, had the power to prohibit *any* strike if the prohibition was reasonably calculated to achieve a valid state policy in an area which was open to state regulation;"[133] and (3) it is claimed that to be refused the right to strike is a violation of the thirteenth amendment prohibition against involuntary servitude, in that a strike is a voluntary withdrawal of labor, an argument rejected on the ground that the employees may withdraw their labor by quitting the employ without going on strike.[134]

Courts have been merciless in their rejection of the right of public employees to strike. Thus, even where the public employer failed to bargain in good faith, as it was required to do so by statute, or where there was unlawful racial discrimination, there was no right to respond by strike.[135] Although there is no right to strike, there are certain first amendment protections, for example, in which the right to strike is not in issue but what is involved is the mere assertion of the right to strike. A statute denying that right is unconstitutional.[136] The same is true if there is a prohibition against joining a union that claims the right to strike.[137] But the protection of the first amendment applies only to individual employees and not to the union, a holding most recently upheld in Smith v Arkansas State Highway Employees, discussed earlier in the chapter. Thus, a state law requiring as a condition of certification of a union as bargaining agent for public employees that it does not assert the right to strike is constitutional.[138]

As a result of this anti-strike pressure, all major police unions maintained a no-strike and often a no-picketing clause in their contracts until 1970 when AFSCME repealed the clause. ICPA followed the next year. One result was the immediate increase in strike activity among police.[139] Regardless of such no strike clauses in contracts or the lack of a legal right to strike, police, when faced by management opposition to their needs, have not refrained from engaging in "slowdowns, mass sick calls, blue flu epidemics, moratoriums over writing traffic tickets, stepped up issuance of summons, mass resignations, marathon professional meetings and mass demonstrations."[140]

Gains by criminal justice employees from unionization

It is impossible to demonstrate a clear cause and effect basis between unionization of criminal justice employees and the substantial gains accruing to employees in wages and working conditions. But it is a fact that during a period of increasing union activity and militance, ameliorations in these areas have been considerable.

Taking 1967 as the index year from 1924 to 1967, a period of 43 years, police quadrupled their salaries, while from 1967 to 1977 their salaries doubled. Bearing in mind that the original 1924 starting salary was exceedingly low compared to the 1967 salary, the salary growth from 1967 to 1977 has been considerable.[141]

Police in years past have kept slightly ahead of the Consumer Price Index (CPI), though lately, as with other working groups, they have been losing ground. Unions have been unable to resist this trend. From January 1 1975 to January 1 1976, the CPI increased 6.8% while the average maximum salaries for police increased 7.6%. For the following year the CPI increased 5.2% while police salaries went up 6.9%. In the year 1977–78, the differential was CPI 6.7%, and police salaries 7%. But in 1978–1979, as the fiscal crisis deepened, the CPI increase was 9.4% while police salaries rose only 7.1%. During 1979–80, this trend continued. The CPI increased 14% while police salaries went up 8.2%. Over the period 1975–80 the CPI increased 49.6% while police salaries rose 42.6%. Manpower levels also decreased during this period. Such growth slowed and then picked up again in more recent years. While during the period, January 1979 to January 1984, inflation amounted to 49.6%, salary increases for police officers amounted to only 40.9%. But from December 1983 to December 1988, inflation amounted only to 18.9%, while mean entrance salaries for officers increased 24.7% and mean maximum salaries rose 28.4%.[142]

Nonmonetary benefits of unionization

At least as important to criminal justice employees as pay increases has been the ability of the union to form a counterweight against the power of the public employer. Both police and correctional unions have been successful in obtaining contracts which have spelled out rights to grievance and disciplinary procedures, nondiscrimination clauses, and guarantees as to indemnification against civil suits arising out of their employment.[143] A typical 1982 correctional agreement between the New York State Security Unit, AFSCME and the state of New York[144] begins with a "Bill of Rights," giving employees the right to have a union representative at all stages of grievance and disciplinary proceedings, or at any interrogation, with a stipulation that any statement or admissions obtained when the employee was not given the opportunity to have a union representative may not be used against the employee in a disciplinary proceeding.

The agreement provides for exclusive bargaining rights for AFSCME, a detailed grievance procedure, with arbitration for disputes not earlier satisfactorily resolved, and that discipline may be imposed "only for just cause." During disciplinary proceedings the employer is required to provide certain procedural guarantees: notice in writing giving detailed description of the alleged acts, and restriction as to when the employee may be suspended pending determination of the discipline. Provision is also made for employee education and training, indemnification and defense of employees against any claims or judgments arising out of their jobs; an obligation on the part of the employer to provide safe working conditions, and a seniority clause to cover job assignments and shift selection. The contract also contains a no strike clause.

Summary and conclusions

The rights of criminal justice personnel are largely determined by two characteristics: They are members of the working class and they are employees of the state. Thus, just as for workers in private industry, unions have been important in asserting and protecting rights of criminal justice personnel. Their status as workers has meant that the unionization of criminal justice personnel has generally followed that of other workers. Early police and correctional unions arose during the last years of the 19th century as fraternal-social associations. They grew out of poor working conditions, low pay and prestige, and inadequate job security. Their growth was highly influenced during the 1960s, the "decade of the public employee," by the increase in government employment generally. Criminal justice personnel, who had trouble identifying with blue-collar workers, now felt closer to the many professional groups, such as teachers and nurses, which unionized during the same period.

Although police and correctional unions followed a somewhat similar history of development, they part company in their organization and affiliation. Police unions are locally oriented because most police are attached to local government units while correctional officers are state employees. Thus police negotiate on a local level while correctional personnel negotiate at a state level. Apart from the split in police ranks caused by multiple organizations seeking to represent them, there is also the breach between black and white officers caused by white domination of the union's political structure, prejudicial treatment by white officers of black citizens and their fellow black officers, and friction caused by affirmative action gains made by blacks and resented by whites. These dissatisfactions have given rise to black police unions primarily concerned with correcting white officer and departmental comportment toward black citizens and bettering their own status in the department.

The lot of correctional personnel was substantially modified during the 1960s when administrative philosophy underwent a transition from a security to a rehabilitative persuasion. These changes were caused by a number of influences outside the prison including prison riots, incoming groups of minority prisoners, and an advanced industrial society which encouraged problem solving through science and technology, exemplified in corrections by a treatment and therapeutic therapy. These new administrators challenged the authoritarian model that guards had been used to and often took the side of the prisoners against guards. Violence and questioning of guards' authority increased and guards turned to unions to help regain that authority. The appearance of the union in the prison completed a three-sided power structure involving administrators, guards and prisoners in a dynamic ever-shifting power base.

In asserting organizational rights, two issues have been primary: the right to join a union, and once formed, the right of unions to force public employers to bargain collectively. While the right to join a union is guaranteed by the first amendment, recent decisions of the United States Supreme Court have made it clear that unions have no constitutional right to require public employers to bargain collectively. Court decisions also seem to have foreclosed federal legislation to require state and local governments to collectively bargain. Criminal justice unions are therefore left to the political process to apply pressure on state legislatures to enact such legislation.

Public employee unions have traditionally been treated differently from unions in the private sector. This view is especially prevalent when the right to strike is involved. Public employees, especially criminal justice personnel, are compared with soldiers deserting their post. Arguments that to deny the right to strike to public employees is a violation of equal protection or due process of law have been turned aside by the courts on the basis of these asserted differences. Until recently, most public unions have accepted this restriction and have written no strike clauses into their constitutions. But, in the face of the current fiscal crisis resulting in layoffs, some unions have removed this restriction.

Overall, it would seem that unions have helped criminal justice personnel substantially upgrade their pay and working conditions. They have been less successful lately in opposing layoffs and pay-cuts as a result of economic problems cities and states now face.

ENDNOTES

1. Freeman, Richard B and Ichniowski, Casey (eds), When public sector workers organize, Chicago, U of Chicago Press, 1988, pp 12–13.
2. This section substantially follows Robinson, C: "The mayor and the police— The political role of the police in society," Mosse, G, ed, Police forces in history, London, Sage, 1975, pp 277, 279–81. See also Goldstein, H: Policing a free society, Cambridge, Ballinger, 1977, ch 12.
3. Municipal Code of Chicago § 11-1 (1984). For discussion of Chicago's governmental structure, see Auriemma v City of Chicago 747 FSupp 465 (ND Ill 1990); for Illinois Village Government structure relating to appointment of police chiefs, see Robinson v Scurto 1990 US Lexis 5462 (ND Ill).
4. Municipal Code of Chicago at § 11-5.
5. Id at § 11-3.
6. Bent, A: The Politics of law enforcement, New York, Heath, 1974, p 63.
7. Tables III–V are modified from those found in Bent pp 71, 75–76, *supra* n 6.
8. 155 Mass 216, 29 NE 517 (1892).
9. The legal relationship of employer-employee was at this time referred to as master-servant.
10. 298 Ill App 199, 206, 18 NE2d 719, 722–723 (1939).
11. Such a perspective must be compared with the view of many sociologists who see the police as largely having a social service function with wide discretion being exercised by the individual police officer.
12. Tyler, F: "Why they organize," Ayres, R and Wheelen, T, eds, Collective bargaining in the public sector, Gaithersburg, Md, Intern Assoc of Chiefs of Police, 1977, p. 108; Maddox, C: Collective bargaining in law enforcement, Springfield, C C Thomas, 1975, p 12.
13. Hilligan, T: "Police employee organizations: Past developments and present problems," 24 Labor Law Journal 288, 295 (1973); Robinson n 2.
14. Juris, H and Feuille, P: Police unionism, power and impact in public-sector bargaining, Lexington, Lexington books, 1973, p 15.
15. Salerno, C: Police at the bargaining table, Springfield, C C Thomas, 1981, pp 3–5.
16. Juris and Feuille p 16, *supra* n 14.
17. Maier, Mark H, City unions, managing discontent in New York City, New Brunswick, Rutgers University Press, 1987, pp 20–21. This union has continued in existence to the present time.
18. Bent p 78, *supra* n 6.
19. Russell, F: A city in terror, 1919, The Boston police strike, New York, Viking, 1975; Spero, S: Government as employer, Carbondale SIU Press, 1972, pp 252–84.
20. Reynolds, G and Judge, A: The night the police went on strike, London, Weidenfeld and Nicholson, 1968.
21. Spero p 281, *supra* n 19.
22. Gammage, A and Sachs, S: "Development of public employee/police unions,"

Ayres and Wheelen pp 83–6 n 12; Smith, J: "Police unions, an historical perspective of causes and organizations," Police Chief (Nov 1975); Spero, ch pp 288–91, *supra* n 19.

23. Smith, *supra* n 22. In New York City at least, the union was controlled by a president who ruled from 1914 to 1938, and maintained a cozy and trouble-free accommodation with police management. Younger officers entering the force after World War II changed the union and thereafter the union-management relationship, Maier p 21, *supra* n 17.

24. Spero pp 282, 293, *supra* n 19. In the 1950s, in New York City, the president of the PBA was able to win a 50% increase for his force in return for keeping the police "out of the activist labor movement." Maier, *supra* n 17 at 94.

25. Smith, *supra* n 22.

26. Shaw, L and Clark, Jr R: "The practical differences between public and private sector collective bargaining," Ayres and Wheelen p 47 n 12.

27. Juris and Feuille p 18, *supra* n 14. For a more detailed history of the New York City police union, see Maier, ch 7 *supra* n 17.

28. Shaw and Clark p 47, *supra* n 26; Edwards, H: "The emerging duty to bargain in the public sector," Ayres and Wheelen p 464, *supra* n 12.

29. Yates, M: "Public sector unions and the labor movement," Reader editorial collective, ed, Crisis in the public sector, New York, Monthly Review Press, 1981 p 229.

30. Imundo, Jr L: "Some comparisons between public sector and private sector collective bargaining," Ayres and Wheelen p 67, *supra* n 12.

31. Id at 221; Freeman, R: "Contraction and Expansion: The divergence of private sector and public sector unionism in The United States," 2 Journal of Economic Perspectives 63 (Sp 1988).

32. Freeman, Ichniowski, *supra* n 1 at 387. Although the statistics are not strictly comparable, the percentage of full-time police state and local government employees organized in 1987 is 64.9 percent. 1987 Census of Governments, Vol 3, No 3, Labor-Management Relations, US Dept of Commerce, Table B, US GPO 1987.

33. Juris and Feuille pp 19–23 *supra* n 14; Hilligan pp 290–1, *supra* n 13; Salerno p 15, *supra* n 15; Maddox, C: Collective bargaining in law enforcement, C C Thomas, 1975, p 8.

34. Maddox p 12, *supra* n 33; Kassalow, E: "White-collar unionism in the United States," White-collar trade unions, A Sturmthal, ed, Urbana, U of Ill Press, 1967, ch 7.

35. Salerno p 15, *supra* n 15; Juris and Feuille pp 22–3, *supra* n 14; Goldstein p 311, n 2; Maier, pp 105–107 *supra* n 17, suggests that increased militancy of NYC officers can be partly attributed to a combination of a highly active rank and file constantly pressuring its leadership, and a management thereby having to "cave in" for fear that a more radical union would replace the PBA if they didn't make concessions. Maier, pp 154–156, lists "protests by New York City Municipal Employees: 1950–1980," including those of police. See also Magenau, John M, Sociopolitical Networks for police

role-making, 42 Human Relations 547–60 (June 89) describing police union's use of their political influence to limit regulation of restrictive use of force policies.

36. Maier, p 164 *supra* n 17.

37. Id at 164–65.

38. Burpo, J: "The police labor movement, prospects for the 1980's," 50 FBI Law Enforcement 9, 10 (Jan 1981); Juris, H and Hutchison, K: "The legal status of municipal police employee organizations," 23 Indus and Lab Rel Rev 352, 353, 362 (1970); Stieber, J: Public employee unionism: Structure, growth, policy, Washington, DC, Brookings Institute, 1973, pp 55–8; National Trade and Professional Associations of the United States, 1990 Annual ed.

39. Juris and Hutchison p 355, 357, *supra* n 38, Gammage and Sachs pp 89–90, *supra* n 22.

40. The IBPO paid dues to the National Association of Government Employees (NAGE) "with whom IBPO was affiliated until 1982. After 1982, IBPO members were affiliated with Service Employees International Union (SEIU) since NAGE was absorbed by SEIU." Freeman, Ichniowski, p 367 *supra* n 1.

41. Id at 368.

42. Burpo p 11, *supra* n 38.

43. Gammage and Sachs pp 83–9, *supra* n 22, National Trade, supra n 38.

44. Burpo p 11, *supra* n 38.

45. Gammage and Sachs pp 83–7, *supra* n 22.

46. Sirene, W.: "Management, labor's most effective organizer," 50 FBI Law Enforcement Bulletin, 4–6 (Jan 1981).

47. Juris and Hutchison p 357, *supra* n 38.

48. Juris and Feuille p 27, *supra* n 14.

49. Levi, M: Bureaucratic insurgency, The case of police unions, Lexington, Heath, 1977, pp 99, 137–8, 147 fn 25.

50. National Trade *supra* n 38.

51. Juris and Feuille p 165, *supra* n 14.

52. Id at 166.

53. See Afro-America Patrolmen's League v Atlanta 817 F2d 719, 721 (11th Cir 1987) (black union filed Title VII suit claiming discrimination and the Fraternal Order of Police countered with a claim of reverse discrimination). In Calvin v Conlisk 520 F2d 1, 11 (7th Cir 1975) (black plaintiffs and black police union complained of police brutality).

54. National Minority Council on Criminal Justice, The inequality of Justice: A report on crime and the administration of justice in the minority community, Washington DC, Government Printing Office, Jan 1982, pp 232–3.

55. Juris and Feuille p 165, *supra* n 14.

56. Id at 167.

57. Juris and Feuille pp 167–8, *supra* n 14.

58. Id at 167; United States v City of Chicago 631 F2d 469 (7th Cir 1980).

59. Juris and Feuille p 168, *supra* n 14. See ch 2 for the many actions against their

own departments claiming discrimination in hiring, promotions and assignments.

60. Juris and Feuille pp 171–3, *supra* n 14. See ch 2.

61. Juris and Feuille *supra* pp 173–5, *supra* n 14. A good description of a black police union's experience in Chicago is told in McClory, R: The man who beat clout city, Chicago, Swallow Press, 1977.

62. This section substantially follows Levi chap 5 n 49.

63. Stieber p 62, *supra* n 38.

64. Wynne, J: Prison employee unionism: The impact on correctional administration and programs, Washington DC, Government Printing Office, Jan 1978.

65. Jacobs, J and Crotty, N: Guard unions and the future of the prisons, Ithaca, Institute of Public Employment, NY State School of Industrial and Labor Relations, IPE Monograph No 9, 1978, p 41.

66. Jacobs, J: Stateville, The peniteniary in mass society, p 175, Chicago, U of Chicago Press, 1977.

67. Jacobs and Crotty pp 6–7, *supra* n 65.

68. Wynne p 58, *supra* n 64; Jacobs pp 93–100, *supra* n 66.

69. Jacobs and Crotty p 7, *supra* n 65.

70. Jacobs ch 7, *supra* n 66; Wynne pp 38–9, *supra* n 64; Jacobs and Crotty p 7, *supra* n 65.

71. See, for example, Bach, J and Snyder, M: Danbury: Anatomy of a prison strike, 17 Liberation 32–42 (May 1972) and Davis, R: Conspiracy day in Cook County Jail, 15 Liberation 31–33 (March 1970).

72. Christianson, S: "Corrections law development: How unions affect prison administration," 15 Criminal Law Bulletin 238, 239 (May–June 1979); Cohen F: "The discovery of prison reform," 21 Buffalo L Rev 855 (1972).

73. Wynne pp 38–39, *supra* n 64; Christianson p 242, *supra* n 72.

74. Jacobs and Crotty pp 7–8, *supra* n 65.

75. Jacobs pp 21–2, 83–5, *supra* n 66; Jacobs and Crotty p 7, *supra* n 65.

76. Conversation with Joseph Coughlin, former Wisconsin correctional administrator.

77. The material on early history of correctional unions relies on Wynne pp 43–44, *supra* n 64.

78. Unless otherwise noted this summary on Stateville has been taken from Jacobs pp 15–16, 31, 55, 188–193, *supra* n 66.

79. Wynne pp 110–16, *supra* n 64.

80. Jacobs p 194, *supra* n 66.

81. The following two sections are based on Wynne, *supra* n 64.

82. Wynne pp 123–4, *supra* n 64.

83. Commons, J and Andrews, J: Principles of labor legislation, 4th rev ed, Augustus M Kelly, 1967, p 381.

84. Commonwealth v Hunt 45 Mass (4 Metcalf) 111, 129, 38 Am Dec 354, 355; Commons and Andrews p 382, *supra* n 83.

85. Forkosch, M: A treatise on labor law, 2d ed, Indianapolis, Bobbs-Merrill, 1965, pp 320–22, 368–70.

86. American Steel Foundaries v Tri-City Central Trades Council 257 US 184, 209.

87. Brody, D: "Steelworkers in America: The nonunion era," New York, Harper Torchbooks, 1960, p 208.

88. 49 Stat 499 (1935), 29 USCA § 151 (West Supp 1991).

89. 29 USCA § 152(2) (West Supp 1991).

90. Operating Engineers Local 321 v Water Works Board 276 Ala 462, 463, 163 S2d 619, 620 (1964); Edwards, H: "The emerging duty to bargain in the public sector," Ayres and Wheelen, p 467, *supra* n 12. This section relies heavily on this article. See also Westbrook, J: "The use of the nondelegation doctrine in public sector law: lessons from cases that have perpetuated an anachronism 30 St Louis L Rev 331, 384 (1986).

91. Edwards p 468, *supra* n 90. Bd of Education v Scottsdale Education Assn 17 Ariz App 504, 510, 511–512, 498 P2d 578, 582, 585 (1972), vacated 509 P2d 612 (1973) on procedural grounds; Spero pp 342–4, *supra* n 19.

92. Railway Mail Assn v Murphy 180 Misc 868, 875, 44 NYS2d 601, 607–8 (Sup Ct 1943), revd on other grounds sub nom; Railway Mail Assn v Corsi 267 App Div 470, 47 NYS2d 401, affd 293 NY 315, 56 NE2d 721 (1944), affd 326 US 88 (1945).

93. Hutchinson v Magee 278 Pa 119, 120, 122 A 234.

94. Carter v Thompson 164 Va 312, 317, 180 SE 410, 412.

95. Hilligan pp 295–6 n 13, citing People v Chicago 278 Ill 318, 116 NE 158 (1917); McAuliffe v City of New Bedford 155 Mass 216, 29 NE 517 (1892) against police right to join unions; Fraternal Order of Police v Harris 306 Mich 68, 10 NW 2d 310, cert den 321 US 784 (1944) (1943); Coane v Geary 298 Ill App 199, 18 NE2d 719 (1939). *McAuliffe* and *Coane* are discussed above. For first amendment rights, see ch 7.

96. 72 LRRM 2071, 2072 (7th Cir 1969).

97. 296 FSupp 1068, 1077 (WD NC 1969).

98. 441 US 463.

99. Id at 464–5.

100. 442 US 289 (1979).

101. Id at 313.

102. Levi p 31, *supra* n 49.

103. Wynne p 45, *supra* n 64. See Maier, ch 6 *supra* n 17.

104. Municipal Employment Relations Act, ch 509, Wis Laws 623, as amended Wis Stat Ann § 111.70 (Supp 1969).

105. Levi p 51–55, *supra* n 49.

106. 27 Fed Reg § 1(a) Jan 19 1962 p 551.

107. Id at § 2(c) p 552.

108. Id at § 6(b) p 553.

109. 3 CFR 262 (1973).

110. Id at § 19(6).

111. 5 USC §§ 1101, 7101 3(b)3; Reorganization Plan No 2 of 1978 §§ 101-2, 303, 403

(1988). For a description of the workings of the Act, see Wood, Stephen L, Federal employers, federal unions, and federal courts: The duty of fair representation in the federal sector, 64 Chicago-Kent L Rev 271–334 (Winter 1988). For a short history of collective bargaining in the federal sector, see McMillion, Michael R, Collective bargaining in the federal sector: Has congressional intent been fulfilled? 127 Military L Rev 169–217 (Win 90).

112. Dayton Frat Order of Police v State Employ 488 NE2d 181, 184–85 (Ohio 1986). One study shows that passing of state collective bargaining laws, particularly ones with a duty-to-bargain provision, is followed within a few years by the formation of police unions, suggesting "some form of pent-up demand for unionization." Ichniowski, Casey, "Public sector union growth and bargaining laws: A proportional hazards approach with time—varying treatments," in Freeman and Ichniowski, *supra* n 1 at 36, 40. A political history of the enactment of such laws will be found in Saltzman, Gregory M, Public sector bargaining laws really matter: Evidence from Ohio and Illinois, in Freeman and Ichniowski, p 41 *supra* n 1.

113. Beaird, R: "Public employee labor relations in the Southeast—An historical perspective," 59 No Carolina L Rev 71, 77 (1980).

114. 426 US 833.

115. 469 US 528, 557 (1985)

116. Juris and Hutchison p 358, *supra* n 38.

117. Id at 360–1.

118. Edwards p 472, 474, *supra* n 90.

119. Wynne p 16, *supra* n 64. The most important factor in police formation of union was a state enabling statute. Where no such statute existed, even strikes to gain recognition were rarely successful in gaining their objective. Ichniowski, C.: "Police Recognition Strikes; Illegal and ill-fated," 9 J of Labor Research 183, 194–5 (1988).

120. Freeman, Ichniowski, p 387 *supra* n 1. Statutes are classified according to type. Id at 390, 406–416.

121. Douglas, Joel M, Collective bargaining and public sector supervisors: A trend toward exclusion? 47 Public Admin Rev 485 (Nov–Dec 1987); and Kracji, Thomas J, Labor Relations in the public sector (county level law enforcement negotiations) 30 Personnel Administration 43 (May 85).

122. Juris and Hutchison p 358, *supra* n 38.

123. Salerno pp 37, 50, *supra* n 15.

124. Juris and Hutchison p 352, 357, *supra* n 38.

125. Reynolds and Judge p 119, *supra* n 20.

126. Russell p 170, *supra* n 19.

127. Salerno p 22, *supra* n 15.

128. Letter to Luther C Steward Aug 16 1937, Spero p 2, *supra* n 19.

129. Wohlers, E: "One strike and you may be out: The legal realities of the hardball game of firefighter and police strikes," 15 Idaho L Rev 39, 46 (1978).

130. Id at 46–7.

131. Edwards pp 507–8, *supra* n 90 (emphasis in original). The modern view is

stated in County Sanitation Dist no 2 v Los Angeles Cty Employee's Assn 38 Cal 3d 564, 586 (1985), which exhaustively reviews the doctrine, holding "that it is not unlawful for public employees to engage in a concerted work stoppage for the purpose of improving their wages or conditions of employment, unless it has been determined that the work stoppage poses an imminent threat to public health or safety," noting that this exception would apply to firefighters and law enforcement personnel.

132. School Committee v Westerly Teachers Assn 111 RI 96, 299 A2d 441, 444 (1973), revd in part on other grounds 363 A2d 1349 (1976); but see Exeter-West Regional School District v Exeter-West Green Teachers' Assoc 489 A2d 1010 (1985) (school board "bound by and must fund, the valid collective bargaining agreements entered into by its school committee"); Wohlers p 41, *supra* n 129.

133. City of New York v De Lury 243 NE2d 128, 131 (1968) (emphasis in original).

134. Wohlers p 41, *supra* n 129.

135. Id at 49–50.

136. Id at 42, citing United Fedn of Postal Clerks v Blount 325 FSupp 879 (DDC), affd 404 US 802 (1971).

137. Wohlers p 42, *supra* n 129, citing Police Officers' Guild Nat Union of Police Officers v Washington 369 FSupp 543 (DDC 1973).

138. Wohlers p 42, *supra* n 129.

139. Id at p 39; Steiber pp 179–82, *supra* n 38.

140. Steiber p 182, *supra* n 38.

141. US Dept of Labor, Handbook of Labor Statistics, 1978, Washington, Government Printing Office, June 1979, p 371.

142. International City Management Assoc, The Municipal Yearbook, Washington DC., 1980, pp 93–4; 1990 p 127. One study showed that collective bargaining and the availability of arbitration are strongly associated with higher police salaries. Other factors having influence on higher salaries: western, larger cities with high crime rates, for example, pay better than southern smaller cities with a lesser crime rate. Feuille, P and Delaney, J T: "Collective bargaining, interest arbitration, and police salaries," 39 Industrial and Labor Relations Journal 228, 238–39 (Jan 1986). For a view that unions are responsible for higher police salaries, nationally and internationally, see Skolnick, Jerome H, and Bayley, David, H, Community Policing, Issues and Practices around the world, p 57, National Institute of Justice, Washington, DC 1988; but see Kearney, Richard C and Morgan, David R, The effect of employee organizations on the compensation of police officers 9 J Collective Negotiations 17, 29 (1980), a study of police unionized cities of more than 10,000 population in the Southcentral United States showed differences of only one percent. Police have been shown to "have the largest effect on compensation through collective bargaining" of any group of public employees. Zax, Jeffrey and Ichnowski, Casey, the effects of public sector unionism on pay, employment, department budgets, and municipal expenditures, in Freeman and Ichniowski, pp 356, 394 *supra* n 1.

Correctional officers also obtained wage increases as a result of union activity. Zimmer, L E: Women guarding men, p 32, Chicago, University of Chicago Press, 1986.

143. It has been held that a collective bargaining agreement providing for a probationary period for police officers, supersedes city ordinances setting forth the time of the period. Biddle v City of Dayton 548 NE2d 329, 333 (Ohio App 1988). See chaps 2 and 4 for numerous cases in which black and white police associations filed anti-discrimination or reverse discrimination suits on behalf of their members. See, for example, Black Law Enforcement Officers Assoc v City of Akron 1990 US App Lexis 21742 (6th Cir); and Police Officers v City of Columbus 916 F2d 1092 (1990).

144. Tentative agreement between the state of New York and Security Unit Employees Council 82 AFSCME, Afl-CIO, effective April 1 1982 to March 31 1985.

Chapter 6

PROTECTION OF CRIMINAL JUSTICE PERSONNEL FROM ARBITRARY DISMISSAL AND RESTRICTIVE WORKING CONDITIONS

Introductory remarks

Dismissal is an area in which the rights of criminal justice personnel is particularly sensitive, in part because the threat of dismissal can also be the basis for other types of control. One author has properly designated dismissal as the capital punishment in the hierarchy of managerial disciplinary measures.[1] The right of criminal justice personnel to be free from arbitrary dismissal is, therefore, an essential guarantee not only of employment but of freedom from oppressive working conditions.

> At common law, the power to appoint a police officer included the unlimited power to remove, suspend, or demote the officer. A municipality could discipline a police officer without assigning reasons or holding a hearing.[2]

This chapter will analyze the social and economic aspects of the employment relationship as it impinges on the procedural and substantive rights of criminal justice personnel on their job; and will show how that relationship developed out of new social relations coming into force as the capitalist era evolved from feudal relations. From the permanent, life-long, status-dominated feudal society of slaves, serfs, soldiers, priests, nobles and king, in which the state played a crucial role in economic organization, society changed to one principally composed of owners and nonowners of the means of production for products for sale, where social relations were characterized by short-term economic rather than long-term social ties, and in which the state's role was substantially diminished. Whereas in the feudal period there had developed a series of clear-cut responsibilities of landlords for the health, welfare and security of their serfs, under capitalism, the sole responsibility of the owner of capital to his worker was to pay the agreed-upon wage, that is, the lowest wage the market would bear.

Thus social relations in the capitalist era were based on contractual rather than on status relations. The employer-employee relationship was conceived in law as a contract between the two parties for the employee's services, based on a fiction that the two parties stood in economic equality before the law. They were to be considered to be equal as contractees entering into the employment contract. It logically followed that the contract could be terminated by either party at any time. For the employer to dispense with the services of the employee was not a matter of personal malice on his part, but was a result dictated by the economic fluctuations of a boom and bust capitalist economy which relied on the unpredictable demands of the market. Under such a system, the employer's need for labor might be more at one time and less at another. Courts responded to that need in formulating a rule to encourage industrial growth—the termination of employment at will rule. This rule had the effect of placing the costs of slack periods of work on the employee rather than on the employer. Under the rule, employers could terminate employees for any reason or for no reason without notice, when in their view, business conditions required it.[3]

We will look at how this doctrine developed in England and the United States, how it affected the law of public employees, including criminal justice personnel, the right, if any, of criminal justice employees to a government post, the rights of probationary and nonprobationary employees to freedom from arbitrary dismissal, and how the Supreme court has applied the due process clause of the fourteenth amendment to substantive and procedural rights of criminal justice personnel. The chapter will further examine specific restrictions on working conditions of criminal justice personnel, questions involving age discrimination, charges of conduct unbecoming an officer, on and off duty, including sexual and criminal activity; the procedural rights of criminal justice personnel under civil service statutes, and problems raised by insubordination on the part of lower-level employees.

Historical development of the employment at will rule

The rule that the employer has the absolute power to discharge an employee at will followed from the logic of capitalist social relations. Capitalist social organization was sustained by its ideology, denoted laissez faire (letting people do as they will), that entrepreneurs should be free to go about their business without government interference. Rather than trying to control business, as was the case in feudal times, the purpose of government in a capitalist society was to foster conditions whereby each individual could take advantage of opportunities to make a profit. As individuals sought their own advantage, the social effect would be to increase the wealth for all. This was the basic message of Adam Smith's *Wealth of Nations* published in 1776—that persons left to pursue their own economic interests would be lead by an "invisible hand" to the betterment of all society. The employment at will rule was developed by the courts to accommodate this policy in giving employers maximum freedom to react to economic conditions of competition and changing economic circumstances by having absolute control of their labor force so as to be able to react instantly to these fluctuations.[4] Its present importance is apparent: 67% of all U.S. employees work under the rule.[5]

The early English rule was based on an analysis of the response to two questions: the duration of the employment relation when there was no specific contract as to term, and the notice that would have to be given before such an employment relationship could be terminated.[6] Blackstone, an eighteenth century legal writer, set forth the rule as follows:

> If the hiring be general, without any particular time limited, the law construes it to be a hiring for a year; upon a principle of natural equity, that the servant shall serve, and the master maintain him, throughout all the revolutions of the respective seasons, as well when there is work to be done as when there is not.[7]

The rule reflected Blackstone's time—a period of transition from an agricultural to an industrial employer-dominated society. As in feudal society, there was a principle of "natural equity," that is, a continuing obligation running from the lord to the serf, here referred to as master and servant, after the still current employment relationship of the eighteenth century domestic servant. The servant should work for the master all the year, including the growing season, during all of which time, the master had the continuing obligation to pay the worker even though there was no work to do.

Perhaps because the United States never experienced a feudal period as part of its history, and thus began its existence just as capitalism was developing in Europe, the law took a turn more favorable to employer interests than it did in England. Toward the end of the nineteenth century the character of employment in the US changed from a personal, small business system, to one where more and more workers were employed by large organizations in which their employer no longer was the owner but was rather a supervisory foreman.[8] At the time, the law was confused, reflecting the transitional nature of the period. Nevertheless, capitalist laissez-faire ideology suffused the law of contracts which proclaimed that employers took on only those obligations they had voluntarily and expressly assumed. The law looked on the employer and employee as equals. Because the employee could terminate the employment contract at any time, it followed that the employer could do so with or without reason.[9] Taking this rule of contracts and combining it with the laissez-faire ideology, in 1874, a writer on the subject of master and servant, relying on some very questionable authority, stated the rule to be:

> With us the rule is inflexible, that a general or indefinite hiring is *prima facie* a hiring at will, and if the servant seeks to make it out a yearly hiring, the burden is upon him to establish it by proof. . . . [It] is an indefinite hiring and is determinable at the will of either party, and in this respect there is no distinction between domestic and other servants.[10]

In the next 25 years, this rule took hold throughout the United States. As one oft-quoted 1884 Tennessee case stated, where there was an employment contract for no specified period, the employee may be discharged "for good cause, for no cause, or even for cause morally wrong, without being thereby guilty of a legal wrong."[11] Such a court-constructed rule was only one of a number of rules intended to encourage industrial growth and to shift the cost of that growth to workers. Other court decisions during the last years of the nineteenth century, a period of enormous industrial expansion, struck down social legislation designed to protect employees; created defenses to defeat employee claims for damages for on-the-job injuries, and blocked worker attempts to unionize so as to press claims for higher wages and better working conditions.[12]

The United States Supreme Court raised the employment at will rule to the level of a constitutional right in decisions such as Adair v United States[13] in 1908 and in 1915, Coppage v Kansas.[14] Any legislation, the Court said, that interfered with the employer's right to discharge his employees violated his freedom to contract, and thus invaded the employer's liberty and property interests under the due process clause of the fourteenth amendment. In effect, these decisions allowed the employer to treat the offer of employment as his own property.[15] This narrow view of employment relations was maintained until the 1930 depression years when millions of workers were thrown out of work through no fault of their own. Together with the pressure from the unions (see chapter 5) and the new ideology of social responsibility of employers proposed by the New Deal, the Supreme Court modified the Adair-Coppage doctrine. In NLRB v Jones & Laughlin Steel Corp[16] and in Phelps Dodge Corp v

NLRB,[17] the Court turned back constitutional attacks on the National Labor Relations Act and upheld the right of employees to unionize, while rejecting the right of employers to discharge employees for union activity. In effect, the Court reduced the employer's claim to something less than a constitutional property right, thus making it possible for courts to balance the claims of employer and employee.

Following the passage of the NLRA,[18] state and local governments passed statutes and ordinances prohibiting discrimination in employment on the basis of race, creed, nationality, sex or age;[19] such legislation was extended to the national scene in 1964 with the passage of Title VII of the Civil Rights Act.[20] (See chapter 2.) Thereafter, there were a number of Acts, which in one way or another restricted the employer's right to discharge: the consumer Credit Protection Act[21] prohibited discharge because of garnishment of wages for any one indebtedness; a law entitling veterans, upon release from military service, to return to the jobs they held before entering the military;[22] the Fair Labor Standards Act[23] and the Occupational Health & Safety Act[24] forbid retaliatory discharge against those exercising rights under those Acts; and of course, statutes against race, sex and age discrimination. There are also state statutes that restrict discharge for the exercise of jury duty, the refusal to take lie detector tests, or because of participation in political activity.[25] Many of these statutes, however, are unenforced and unenforceable, and therefore ineffective in curbing employer discharges.[26] Even with some protection in specific areas, the general right of discharge at will remains intact.[27] Although public employees are usually protected by statutes that limit discharge at will, these statutes normally apply only to "permanent" employees. Temporary, probationary, and non-tenured employees, unless covered by a specific agreement, may usually be discharged at the will of the employer. In some states, in recent years a tort cause of action developed for unjust dismissal.[28] From a constitutional standpoint the question becomes when, if at all, employees acquire a property or liberty interest in their employment under the due process clause of the fourteenth amendment so that, as a matter of procedural due process, they are entitled to a hearing before they can be discharged; or whether, having a property or liberty interest in the job, the cause for the discharge is so arbitrary and capricious that it is a denial of substantive due process.

Supreme Court development of rules for protection against arbitrary dismissal

The Burger Court was torn between two views of rights derived from the due process clause of the fourteenth amendment. That debate roughly follows the lines that rights either derive from the nature of man or that persons have only those rights bestowed by the state.[29] The more conservative members of the Court at the time of these decisions (Justices Burger, Rehnquist, Powell, O'Connor) take the first view while the more liberal members (Justices Marshall, Blackmun, and Brennan) take the second. Justices Stevens and White sometimes swing between the two. Most government employees, both federal and state, are covered by some kind of civil service law which requires that a permanent employee be fired only for "just cause." In most of the cases that follow, therefore, the question has been whether the status of the plaintiff employee is such that the employee is entitled to a hearing (that is, to procedural due process); and, assuming the employee has such a right, to determine whether there is "just cause" for the employee's discharge. Generally, if employees do not have permanent status, they do not have a constitutionally-protected interest in their position under the liberty and property provisions of the fifth and fourteenth amendments.

In Board of Regents v Roth,[30] a 1972 case, a nontenured teacher alleged that his post had not been renewed because of his exercise of constitutionally protected free speech. He argued that he could not be terminated without a hearing. The Court decided that procedural due process was due only when an individual's interest in "property" or in "liberty" is infringed by government action. Within the meaning of the due process clause of the fourteenth amendment, a person has a property "interest in a benefit" if he or she has

> more than an abstract need or desire for it. He must have more than a unilateral expectation of it. He must, instead, have a legitimate claim of entitlement to it. It is a purpose of the ancient institution to protect those claims upon which people rely in their daily lives, reliance that must not be arbitrarily undermined. It is a purpose of the constitutional right to a hearing to provide an opportunity for a person to vindicate those claims.[31]

Because Roth had no tenure, he had "absolutely no claim of entitlement to re-employment," and therefore, no protected *property* interest.[32] Nevertheless, there might be some situations in which a *liberty* interest would be engaged: (1) where the state, for example, based its contract nonrenewal on a charge that the employee had been guilty of dishonesty or immorality, or any other instance in which the person's "good name, reputation, honor or integrity"[33] was at stake, or (2) where the discharge involved some stigma or other disability that foreclosed the employee's freedom to take advantage of other employment opportunities, for example, in barring Roth from public employment at other state universities. In such situations he must have an opportunity to refute the charges. Roth would not be protected, however, where "he is simply not rehired in one job but remains free as before to seek another."[34] To have a legitimate claim of entitlement, he must show that the alleged "property interest" was created by "existing rules or understandings that stem from an independent source such as state law—rules or understandings that secure certain benefits and support claims of entitlement to those benefits."[35] Thus, the Court has not found the loss of a government job, in itself, to be a significant loss. It is only when the loss extends beyond the particular job to the occupation, as where the discharge places on the employee a "badge of infamy" that carries beyond the particular discharge that a liberty interest is engaged.

In a companion case to *Roth,* Perry v Sindermann,[36] also involving a teacher without a formal tenure agreement, Sindermann alleged that there was a de facto tenure system. Returning the case to the trial court to determine the nature of these alleged agreements, the Court held that the basis for a property interest was not limited to formalized rules but that agreements could be implied from the contracting parties' words and conduct in the light of the surrounding circumstances. "Just as this Court has found there to be a 'common law of a particular industry or of a particular plant' that may supplement a collective bargaining agreement. . . . so here may be an unwritten 'common law' in a particular university that certain employees shall have the equivalent of tenure."[37] One writer, summing up *Roth* and *Sindermann,* suggests that "every government employee, whether or not a civil servant, is protected against infringement of liberty interests, while only those with government-created rights have protected property interests."[38]

Two years later, the Court was called on to decide whether once having granted a property right, Congress could at the same time establish procedures limiting that right. But because of the divisions in the Court on the issue no clear opinion was produced. That case, Arnett v Kennedy,[39] involved a federal civil service employee, who was discharged, in part, for falsely charging a superior with attempted bribery. As a career civil servant, Kennedy could be removed under a statute covering all federal civil service employees, only for "such cause as will promote the efficiency of the service."[40]

Relying on *Roth,* Kennedy asserted a constitutionally-protected property interest in his job. He further asserted that the procedures provided by the Civil Service statute and executive order—notice and right of reply prior to dismissal, and a full trial-type hearing only on appeal after dismissal—were constitutionally insufficient. He claimed that he had a right to a trial-type (a pretermination) hearing in front of an impartial hearing officer before being discharged. Justice Rehnquist, writing for a plurality of three, concluded that the public employee, granted a property right by the statute, "must take the bitter with the sweet"[41] when the grant of a substantive liberty or property interest is inextricably intertwined with limitations on procedure. The entire statute, including what it confers on the employee (the sweet), and what it denies (the bitter), must be accepted. The Act provided that nonprobationary employees could be removed only for "cause," but it also provided limited procedural means to determine how that cause was to be determined.

Six of the judges, however, agreed that the Lloyd-La Follette Act had given Kennedy a property interest in his job, and that that property interest could not be taken away without constitutionally-approved procedures. In dissent, Justice White chastised the contrary view of Justice Rehnquist:

> While the State may define what is and what is not property, once having defined those rights the Constitution defines due process, and as I understand it, six members of the Court, are in agreement on this fundamental proposition.[42]

In the 1978 case of Carey v Piphus,[43] the Court decided that "procedural due process rules are meant to protect persons not from the deprivation [of property], but from the mistaken or unjustified deprivation . . . of property."[44] The purpose of the due process clause is not to give an employee a windfall. If it can be shown that the plaintiff "would have been [fired] even if a proper hearing had been held, then [the plaintiff] will not be entitled to recover damages to compensate . . . for injuries caused by the [firing]."[45]

Justice Rehnquist's "bitter with the sweet" theory was specifically rejected by the Court in Cleveland Board of Education v Loudermill,[46] which found that permanent employees were entitled to a pretermination hearing as a matter of constitutional due process. Loudermill, the complainant, was hired in 1979 as a security guard. At the time of his application, he stated that he had never been convicted of a felony. In a routine check of employment records, it was discovered that Loudermill had been convicted of grand larceny in 1968. He was thereupon sent a letter dismissing him for dishonesty in filling out his employment application. No opportunity was provided him to respond to the charge. Under Ohio law, however, he was entitled to a post-termination hearing as a "classified civil servant" and could be discharged only for "just cause." Loudermill defended in the hearing that he believed that the conviction was for a misdemeanor rather than a felony. The referee hearing the case recommended that he be reinstated but the Commission upheld his discharge, at which point he filed this 1983 suit.

Loudermill was consolidated with another suit in which a bus mechanic for a state board of education was fired for failing an eye examination. Like Loudermill he was denied a pretermination hearing. After a post-termination hearing he was reinstated but without back pay.

In lower courts both employers relied on the Rehnquist theory in Arnett that substantive rights (property right in the job) and procedural rights (procedure to be used in determining whether the employer could discharge the employee) were "inextricably intertwined."[47] After pointing out that this view had been "specifically rejected by the other six justices," the Court further emphasized its point by stating that "the 'bitter with the sweet' approach misconceives the constitutional guarantee."[48]

> the Due Process Clause provides that certain substantive rights—life, liberty, and property—cannot be deprived except pursuant to constitutionally adequate procedures. The categories of substance and procedure are distinct.[49]

Relying on its prior cases the Court quickly determined that before a person could be deprived of any significant property interest a pretermination hearing was necessary, a principle "evident from a balancing of the competing interests at stake. These are the private interest in retaining employment, the governmental interest in the expeditious removal of unsatisfactory employees and the avoidance of administrative burdens, and the risk of an erroneous termination."[50]

After setting forth the advantages to both the employee and the employer of providing a pretermination hearing the Court set out the "essential requirements of due process":

> [T]he pretermination hearing need not definitively resolve the propriety of the discharge. It should be an initial check against mistaken decisions—

essentially, a determination of whether there are reasonable grounds to believe that the charges against the employee are true and support the proposed action. The essential requirements of due process . . . are notice and an opportunity to respond. The opportunity to present reasons, either in person or in writing, why proposed action should not be taken is a fundamental due process requirement. . . . We conclude that all the process that is due is provided by a pretermination opportunity to respond, coupled with post-termination administrative procedures as provided by the Ohio statute.[51]

Application of these principles to criminal justice personnel

In a series of cases following *Kennedy* a new majority of five formed around the theory that the sources of property and liberty interests, as protected by the fourteenth amendment, were limited (1) to those defined and recognized by state law; or (2) those defined independently by Supreme Court decisions in interpreting constitutional provisions—such as a right to privacy, to travel, or to freedom of expression. Bishop v Wood,[52] involving a police officer who was terminated without a hearing, clearly expressed this view. Wood contended in a § 1983 action that "since a city ordinance classified him as a 'permanent employee,' he had a constitutional right to a pretermination hearing."[53] The Court first set forth the appropriate queries to determine the existence of constitutionally protected property and liberty interests: "(1) whether petitioner's employment status was a property interest protected by the Due Process clause of the Fourteenth Amendment, and (2) assuming that the explanation for his discharge was false, whether that false explanation deprived him of an interest in liberty protected by that clause."[54] While admitting that a property interest in employment can be created either by ordinance or by implied contract, citing *Sindermann,* the Court concluded that "the sufficiency of the claim of entitlement must be decided by reference to state law."[55] Then relying on a construction of the ordinance by the United States District Court judge below, the Court concluded, as did the district judge, that petitioner "held his position at the will and pleasure of the city,"[56] and thus, "petitioner's discharge did not deprive him of a property interest protected by the Fourteenth Amendment."[57] The Court, by this simple maneuver, returned to constitutional status the state employment at will doctrine that had seemingly been rejected in the 1930s. Having disposed of Wood's property interest, the Court then looked to the liberty interest. Wood claimed both "that the reasons given for his discharge are so serious as to constitute a stigma that may severely damage his reputation in the community; in addition, he claims that those reasons were false."[58] Because the case came up on summary judgment (that is, opposing affidavits as to the facts), the Court assumed that Wood's discharge, as he contended, "was a mistake and based on incorrect information."[59] Referring to the language in *Roth* that a nonretained employee is not thereby deprived of liberty as long as he remains free to seek another job, the Court concluded that the same reasoning "applies to the discharge of a public employee whose position is terminable at the will of the employer when there is no public disclosure of the reasons for the discharge."[60] As to the point that the reasons given for his discharge were false, because they were stated to him in private, the Court concluded they "had no different impact on his reputation than if they had been true."[61]

In closing, the Court referred to a motivating factor in this and other decisions—its concern with the use of the federal courts to supervise state (that is, executive) agencies (discussed in chapter 4):

> The federal court is not the appropriate forum in which to review the multitude of personnel decisions that are made daily by public agencies. We must accept the harsh fact that numerous individual mistakes are inevitable in the day-to-day administration of our affairs.[62]

Finally, in a footnote, the Court added that "the ultimate control of state personnel relationships is, and will remain, with the States; they may grant or withhold tenure at their unfettered discretion."[63]

The next year, in Codd v Velger,[64] a probationary policeman complained that he had been wrongly discharged. Being still on probation, it was clear that Velger did not have a property interest in his job. He asserted, however, that he had been stigmatized by derogatory material placed in his personnel file which in turn had caused his subsequent dismissal from a position with the Penn-Central Railroad Police Department.[65] Information in his file showed that he had been dismissed as a trainee because he had placed "a revolver to his head in an apparent suicide attempt."[66] The Court, however, never reached the issue of whether these facts established stigmatization because "[n]owhere in his pleadings or elsewhere has respondent affirmatively asserted that the report of the apparent suicide attempt was substantially false" and therefore a hearing, the purpose of which would be to "provide the person an opportunity to clear his name," would be pointless.[67] A pretermination hearing would be required "[o]nly if the employer creates and disseminates a false and defamatory impression about the employee in connection with his termination. . . . "[68] The Court had earlier held that a person whose name and photograph are circulated to merchants as being a shoplifter, but who had not been convicted of that crime, does not have a 1983 claim because such claim for defamation does not deprive him of liberty or property within the meaning of the due process clause of the fourteenth amendment.[69]

These cases tend to show trends which have been continued and refined in further cases brought under the due process clause of the fifth and fourteenth amendments: (1) There is no fundamental right to government employment;[70] (2) to be recognized by the courts, the property interest in a government job must be shown to be a government-created entitlement (right); (3) the liberty interest must be either a government-created entitlement or be an independent right arising from the Court's interpretation of the due process clause; and (4) the procedural due process provided by the Court to protect these substantive interests is either that set forth (a) by the governmental statute that created the substantive right or (b) a kind of procedural due process that does not interfere with governmental organizational or security interests.[71] Support for these propositions can be found in the cases discussed above and cases to be briefly discussed below. An overlaying principle from which the above propositions naturally flow is the Court's deference to the institutional hierarchy (police and corrections departments) represented by supervising employees—chiefs of police and prison officials. A number of recent cases have made this trend clear, the Court majority making a conscious retreat behind the hands-off doctrine abandoned by the Warren Court in the 60s.

In Kelly v Johnson[72] (a case considered in chapter 7), the Court upheld a police department regulation establishing hair grooming standards for police employees because the officer could not "demonstrate that there is no rational connection between the regulation, based as it is on the county's method of organizing its police force, and the promotion of safety of persons and property."[73] Not only did now Chief Justice Rehnquist (who appears to be the ideologue for the conservative majority) defer to the organizational structure as against the interest of the employee, but, in addition, he requires the public employee to show that the regulation in question has no rational connection to the broadly construed interests of the employer organization. Moreover, as we will see, the personal interests of the supervisor are assimilated to the interests of the government.

Statutory protection for public employees

Except for the short period from the mid-30s to the late 1960s, courts have been generally hostile to workers' rights. Workers have therefore organized unions (see chapter 5) to assert their rights. A principal demand has been to replace the employment at will contract as a result of which the worker could be discharged for any or for no reason with a "just cause" provision which would permit firing only if workers failed to properly perform their job. Almost every union contract has such a clause.[74] But less than one-third of the US work force has that protection, leaving 67% of the nations' workers who can be fired at will.[75] About 16.4% of U.S. workers in 1989 were unionized, and of these 80% have collective bargaining agreements with a "just cause" clause included. About 16% of the work force are federal, state or local government employees. Over 90% of federal employees are tenured under the federal civil service statute, which permits discharge "only for such cause as will promote the efficiency of the service."[76] Each federal agency may have its own detailed procedure for suspensions or dismissals.[77] More than half of state employees have similar protection, one survey showing that 34 states and almost all cities over 100,000 population have comprehensive civil service laws.[78] On the other hand, many other local government employees have little or no protection.[79]

Where civil service protection is provided, discharged employees "are entitled to notice and hearing, review by an administrative agency, and an ultimate appeal to the courts on both procedural and substantive grounds."[80] Illinois, for example, provides both the procedural protection of notice of charges and a hearing, and requires a showing of a cause which is detrimental to the service.[81] In Pennsylvania, the exact procedure described depends on the class into which the city falls. In Philadelphia, no police officer may be disciplined without "just cause." That term is undefined by the statute and the civil service commission is given wide latitude in its definition. Charges must be filed and a hearing held before final action may be taken. A superior may suspend an officer without pay for a period not to exceed 30 days. Once an action for dismissal or demotion is taken, written reasons must be given ten days prior to the effective date of the disciplinary action. The officer may reply in writing, and may appeal the decision to the civil service commission, whereupon the commission must hold a public hearing to affirm or reject the reasons assigned for any action taken against the officer. At the hearing, the burden is on the municipality (1) to present clear, convincing, and substantial evidence to support the charges filed against the officer, and (2) to prove that the charges are sufficient to warrant the discipline imposed.[82]

The statutory and regulatory framework within which allegations of misconduct resulting in discharge or disciplinary sanctions are heard is well set forth in the Arizona case of Civil Service Comn of City of Tucson v Livingston:[83]

> [T]he relationship between the City of Tucson and appellee is that of employer and employee. The laws relative to that relationship have been modified by the civil service laws, the object of which is to protect the employees and public from the spoils system [see chapter 7]. The purpose of civil service is to secure more efficient employees and thereby promote better government. One of the objectives of civil service laws is to take from the appointing officer the right of arbitrary removal of an appointee. Absent such laws a public employee has no protection against suspension and removal with or without cause.
>
> Chapter XII of the Charter of the City of Tucson creates a civil service commission and a classified service for certain city employees, officers, deputies and clerk. § 3(c) of the said chapter provides in part:
>
> > "Persons who have served through their probationary period and who have received permanent appointment in the classified service shall not be . . . discharged . . . except for *just cause,* which shall not be religious or political."
>
> Section 10-10 of the Tucson City Code in furtherance of the Charter makes further provisions relative to the discharge of persons in the classified service. It directs the Commission to adopt rules and regulations governing the classified service. Among the rules and regulations to be promulgated § 10-10(12) directs the Commission to provide a procedure for the discharge or suspension of employees for cause. This rule further states:
>
> > "The following shall constitute just cause, although enumeration thereof shall not exclude other causes, namely: Incompetence; subordination; inattention to duties; discourteous treatment of the public or fellow employees; violation of the ordinances of the mayor and council, the rules and regulations of the department in which an employee is employed; absence from duty without leave; physical or mental unfitness to perform prescribed duties; excessive use of intoxicating liquors; addiction to the use of narcotics; immoral conduct; conviction of a crime involving moral turpitude; failure to pay or failure to make reasonable provision for payment of just debts due and owing; and conduct, while either on or off duty, tending to cause scandal to the service. In no case shall any political or religious belief or affiliation or any indefinite or vague charges, such as for the good of the service be considered just cause."
>
> The Chief of Police of the City of Tucson has promulgated certain rules for

internal management of his department. § 6-8.401(7) of the rules prohibit "conduct unbecoming an officer while on or off duty, detrimental to the service." The manual which contains this rule also contains the following explanation of conduct unbecoming an officer:

"A police officer is the most conspicuous representative of government, and to the majority of the people he is a symbol of stability and authority upon whom they can rely. An officer's conduct is closely scrutinized; and when his actions are found to be excessive, unwarranted, or unjustified, they are criticized far more severely than comparable conduct of persons in other walks of life. Since the conduct of an officer, on or off duty, may reflect upon the Department, an officer must at all times conduct himself in a manner which does not bring discredit to himself, the Department, or the City.' "[84]

Procedural issues relevant to disciplinary proceedings

A number of legal and constitutional issues are raised when criminal justice personnel are subjected to disciplinary proceedings growing out of charges of misconduct. These include the power of supervisory personnel to require answers to questions concerning their work, the corresponding right of refusal to respond, and what sanctions, if any, may be attached to that refusal. Whether the regulation under which the employee is charged is unconstitutionally vague and overbroad is considered in chapter 7. Other procedural issues include: the degree of proof required at the hearing and that used by the reviewing court in deciding whether to sustain the findings and sanction of the hearing board; adequacy of notice of the charge; whether during the probationary period a hearing is required for termination; the right to refuse to take a polygraph test, the nature of the hearing due, and the relation of the penalty to the misconduct alleged.

Rights of criminal justice personnel
under background or criminal investigation

All officers, before they are hired, ordinarily must pass a background investigation, which are likely to make inquiries into their personal life.[85] In addition, because of the nature of their daily activity, police officers, in particular, are often subject to charges of various types of corruption, brutality, racism and the like. Investigations into corruption in police departments was particularly active in the 1960s and 1970s resulting in a series of cases defining the rights of police officers, and hence other criminal justice personnel. Questions arose about the rights of police under interrogation. The Supreme Court in 1967 dealt with this question in Garrity v New Jersey.[86] Borough police officers were questioned about fixing traffic tickets as part of an investigation into corruption in the municipal courts. During questioning by a state deputy attorney general, Garrity was warned that anything he said could be used against him in a state criminal proceeding. He was then given a Hobson's choice. He could refuse to answer if the response would tend to incriminate him; but if he refused to answer, he was told he could be removed from office because a state statute provided that any public official who refused to answer a material question about his official duties by a proper official would thereby forfeit his office.[87] Thereafter, the state prosecuted some officers for obstructing the administration of traffic laws on the basis of the answers given. The Supreme Court reversed the convictions, concluding that the statements provided by the officers were coerced and therefore involuntary admissions or confessions in violation of the due process clause of the fourteenth amendment. The state cannot "use the threat of discharge to secure incriminatory evidence against the employee."[88] In the following year, the Court considered Gardner v Broderick[89] in which the police officer was presented with a somewhat similar choice, this time concerning a "waiver of immunity." Gardner was subpoenaed before a grand jury investigating bribery of certain police officers by persons involved in an unlawful gambling operation. The officer was constitutionally entitled to take the fifth amendment and not testify. He was so advised but he was then requested to sign a "waiver of immunity" that would waive his fifth amendment rights. For refusing to sign the waiver he was dismissed. The Supreme Court ordered Gardner reinstated because the job forfeiture provision of the statute violated Gardner's fifth amendment guarantee against self-incrimination.

Although criminal justice personnel cannot be penalized directly for asserting constitutional rights, the Court in *Gardner* did indicate by dictum that officers could be dismissed for refusal to answer specific direct questions narrowly related to the performance of their official duties.[90] The case of Sanitation Men's Assoc v Sanitation Comr[91] and the case that flowed from it after remand, illustrate the bounds of permitted questioning. As in *Gardner,* the public employee was ordered reinstated. He was then called before a high ranking official of his department and informed that he had a right to remain silent. He would be subject to departmental discipline, however, for failure to answer relevant questions relating to the performance of his official duties. He was further informed that the answers given could not be used in criminal proceedings against him except for false answers for which he might be subject to a perjury prosecution. The employee failed to answer several questions material to the performance of his duties. He was discharged for the continued refusal to answer these questions. The New York Court of Appeals decided that because he was not faced with criminal prosecution, the public employee was not placed in the unconstitutional choice disapproved by the Supreme Court in *Gardner* —a choice between job forfeiture and self-incrimination. Here, the state was merely asserting its interest as an employer. Such an assertion of the employer's interest in discharging an employee who refuses to respond to relevant inquiries concerning his work performance does not preclude criminal prosecution as long as the prosecution does not rely on the information disclosed by the employee in the interview.[92] Thus, it followed from these decisions that police officers could be suspended for failure to fill out a questionnaire seeking financial information "specifically, directly, and narrowly relating to the performance of their official duties."[93]

An allied question involves the giving of adequate *Miranda* warnings within the context of a disciplinary interview.[94] A detailed discussion of the *Miranda* rule is not within the scope of this book but where the public employee is placed in a similar situation to *Gardner,* any disciplinary action taken against an employee will be reversed. In Peden v US,[95] a 1975 Court of Claims case, an Internal Revenue Service agent was interviewed concerning the bribery of other IRS employees. Upon being given *Miranda* warnings Peden refused to answer questions. He was then warned that the refusal to answer questions on matters of official business could result in his discharge. He was thereafter arrested, charged with bribery, and was fired for refusal to answer the questions. The court found the instructions "a masterpiece of confusion," stating that for the instructions to be constitutionally adequate the officer must be assured that his responses will not be used against him in a criminal proceeding.[96] Where, however, there is a proper warning of the consequences of not answering pertinent questions, discharge is proper for refusal to answer.[97] On the other hand, where the questions pertain to a police officer's personal life, not involving departmental performance, such questions may be prohibited.[98] The applicable rules may be summarized as follows:

1) As a matter of constitutional law, any statement given by public employees based upon a threat of dismissal from their job if they fail to respond will be inadmissible against the employee in a subsequent criminal proceeding;
2) Employees being questioned in any proceeding about a matter that could

result in a criminal prosecution against them may not be discharged solely for invoking their fifth amendment privilege and refusing to answer or for refusing to sign a waiver of immunity;

3) Public employees do have an obligation to answer employer's work-related inquiries. Therefore, if employees are assured that their answers or information obtained as a result of those answers cannot be used against them in a criminal proceeding, and that they may be disciplined or discharged for failure to respond, then they may properly be disciplined or discharged for any refusal to answer such questions;[99]

4) Conversely, questions *directed* at an officer's personal activities, not affecting on-duty performance, need not be answered.

Use of polygraph results

The polygraph or "lie detector" has been used as a pre-employment screening device[100] and as a means of investigation both by the police in investigating crimes and by criminal justice agencies in investigating charges against their own employees.[101] State courts are split on the admissibility in evidence of the test results. Two legal questions arise from its use in such proceedings: (1) Are the results of a polygraph examination admissible in a disciplinary hearing, and (2) if a public employee refuses to take the test on a direct order from a superior, can that employee be dismissed for that refusal? As a well reasoned Illinois Supreme Court opinion held, the answer to the second question depends on the answer to the first. Kaske v The City of Rockford[102] was a consolidation of two cases, each of which raised one of the above questions. In one case, an officer, Collura, was accused of sexually touching a female detainee. He was ordered to and did submit to a polygraph examination. Over his counsel's objection, the test results, tending to show he had lied in answering questions about the contact, were admitted in evidence. He was found guilty of the charge and ordered discharged.

In the other case, Kaske and another officer were accused by Kaske's estranged wife of having smoked marihuana.[103] Although the woman later withdrew the charge as false, the department ordered the officers to take polygraph tests, warning them that the result could be used against them in a disciplinary hearing, or alternatively, that a refusal to take the test could result in charges being brought for refusal to follow an official order. Appellate courts were split on the issue of admissibility of polygraph tests in administrative proceedings. The Illinois Supreme Court resolved the issue against admissibility because "polygraph evidence is not reliable enough to be used as substantive evidence in an administrative proceeding before the board in which the findings must be based upon facts proved by competent evidence."[104]

Logically, the court also found that the refusal of an officer to take a polygraph test could not be made the basis of a disciplinary hearing:

> We are mindful of the need for public employees to maintain personal integrity in the eyes of those they serve; we also understand that a police chief has to have the authority to require officers to answer questions specifically related to the performance of the officer's official duties in cooperation with the investigation into an officer's official conduct. And while we recognize that a polygraph examination is an instrument of some investigatory utility and value, we nevertheless conclude in view of our disposition as to the admissibility of polygraph results at the officer's administrative hearing that a municipal police officer can refuse to submit to a polygraph examination and such a refusal cannot be used as a basis for filing of charges seeking disciplinary action against the officer.[105]

Some other states, however, do not follow this reasoning, but view the police as a quasi-military organization, depending on internal discipline to survive. They require the officer to take the polygraph test. Therefore, a refusal to follow an official order to take the test is a basis for discharge.[106] Conversely, there are statutes that protect criminal justice personnel from being forced to take such tests on pain of discharge.[107]

For example, subsequent to the decision in *Kaske,* Illinois enacted the Uniform Peace Officers' Disciplinary Act which, among other provisions, states:

> In the course of any interrogation no officer shall be required to submit to a polygraph test . . . except with the officer's express written consent. Refusal to submit to such tests shall not result in any disciplinary action nor shall such refusal be made part of his or her record.[108]

Power of employer to search

In the 1987 Supreme Court case of O'Connor v Ortega (a decision by a plurality of four in which Justice Scalia made his view a majority by concurring in the result), the court asked:[109] whether public employees have a reasonable expectation of privacy in their offices, desks, and file cabinets at their place of work, and if so, the appropriate fourth amendment standard for a search. Ortega was a doctor employed by a state hospital who came under suspicion in connection with possible improper acquisition of a computer and for sexual harassment of two female employees. While Ortega was on administrative leave, his employer entered his office several times removing numerous documents from his desk and file cabinets, some of which were later used in an administrative proceeding against him.

Within such a "workplace context," a public employee has "a reasonable expectation of privacy at least in his desk and file cabinets."[110] But in "searches conducted by a public employer, we must balance the invasion of the employees' legitimate expectations of privacy against the government's need for supervision, control and the efficient operation of the work place." No warrant need be obtained by the employer because such a requirement "would seriously disrupt the routine conduct of business and would be unduly burdensome."[111]

Looking toward the proper standard to be employed in approving such a search, the Court examined the "government interest justifying intrusion by public employers" and found it to be "the efficient and proper operation of the workplace."[112] Finding the probable cause standard "impractical" in view of the need for efficient operation, the Court held that "public employer intrusions on the constitutionally protected privacy interests of government employees for noninvestigatory, work-related purposes, as well as for investigations of work-related misconduct, should be judged by the standard of reasonableness under all the circumstances," that is, "when there are reasonable grounds for suspecting that the search will turn up evidence that the employee is guilty of work-related misconduct, or that the search is necessary for a work-related purpose such as to return a needed file."[113] Because the lower courts made no determination as to the reasonableness of the search, the Court returned the case to the trial court for this determination to be made.

Justice Blackmun, writing for three other dissenters in this five to four decision, complained that the majority acted on "'assumed' facts . . . weighted in favor of the public employer, and as a result, the standard that emerges makes reasonable almost any workplace search by a public employer."[114]

It seems virtually certain that if this same issue arose in a criminal justice agency where the "workplace context" is subject to military-like discipline, that the expectation of privacy of the employee would be proportionally diminished and the power of search of the employer enlarged.

The probationary period

Does a probationary public employee have sufficient property interest in the desired job to be entitled to a disciplinary hearing? As discussed above, probationary employees, not having a property interest within the meaning of the due process clause of the fourteenth amendment, are not entitled to a hearing before their dismissal for any or no cause.[115] Of course, a state could give probationary employees a property interest in their jobs, but the very purpose of the probationary period is to provide the state a period when employees may be discharged at the will of the employer. Nevertheless, there are some restrictions. Probationary employees cannot be discharged for the exercise of their constitutional rights. In practice, this usually means the use of first amendment rights (see chapter 7), although the same issue might arise for refusal to obey an unconstitutional order (discussed below), or where the whole purpose of the period, the training of the employee, is frustrated by the state itself.[116] Moreover, if the dismissal is based on alleged misconduct on the part of the probationer, a hearing may be required.[117] Such a stigmatization represents a denial of a liberty interest and the officer has a right to refute the charge.[118]

Adequacy of notice

In order for an employee to defend against a charge, the employee must have a clear idea of what must be defended against. For example, it would be completely unfair to charge the individual with sleeping on the job and then find her guilty upon evidence produced at the trial for misuse of a firearm; or to notify the employee he will receive one punishment, and then later dole out another.[119] There must be concurrence between the charge and the finding against the employee. Reviewing courts, however, do not look to see "whether a technical distinction exists, but whether the Appellant has been denied substantial justice."[120] In that case, the officer was found guilty of making false statements to his commanding officer about damage to his squad car. No specific charge alleged these facts but two charges, when combined, did so allege and the court held that under its standard of review he was sufficiently notified that he might be punished for lying to his commanding officer about the damage. The basic criterion is that "the charges be sufficiently clear and specific to enable the respondent to intelligently prepare for defense."[121]

Nature of the hearing

The minimum procedural guarantees necessary for a hearing have been set forth above and most civil service statutes provide these essentials. At a minimum there is a right to respond to formal charges before unbiased individuals;[122] a right to call sworn witnesses, a right to confront and to see evidence used against the officer,[123] and a right to confront opposing witnesses by cross-examination,[124] but probably no right to presence of counsel.[125] Such rights, however, are set forth in detail in the Law Enforcement Officers' Bill of Rights, adopted by several states.[126]

Degree of proof required by reviewing court

In a hearing to dismiss a public employee, the burden of proof is on the agency to prove the charge made. The accused officer need respond with a defense only after the state makes out a prima facie case.[127] Even where a criminal charge against an officer is dismissed he may still be proceeded against for violations of departmental rules.[128]

Standards usually used by reviewing appellate courts allow decisions of civil service boards to be reversed only if the decision is supported by no substantial evidence,[129] or is arbitrary and contrary to the manifest weight of the evidence.[130] A court may not make an independent finding as to facts but must base its decision entirely on the record of the administrative hearing.[131] Another means of examining the sufficiency of the evidence to support the agency's findings is to determine whether the decision is without any evidence to support it, or that the decision is absolutely contrary to uncontradicted and unconflicting evidence upon which it purports to rest.[132] Relying on the doctrine of separation of powers, this standard of review by appellate courts is consistent with the presumption of validity courts accord administrative decisions. An Illinois court has expressed this appellate approach as follows:

> [T]he findings of the Board on questions of fact are to be held prima facie true. Such finding may not be reversed unless it is against the weight of the evidence. An administrative finding may not be adjudged to be against the manifest weight of the evidence unless, from the record, it appears that an opposite conclusion is clearly evident.[133]

For federal civil service employees, the Civil Service Reform Act of 1978[134] provides a Merit Systems Protection Board (MSPB) to hear disciplinary charges. By the same Act, the reviewing court is required to:

review the record and hold unlawful and set aside any agency action, findings, or conclusions found to be—(1) arbitrary, capricious, an abuse of discretion, or otherwise not in accordance with law; (2) obtained without procedures required by law, rule, or regulation having been followed; or (3) unsupported by substantial evidence. . . . 5 USC § 7703(c) (Supp IV 1980). . . . The term "substantial evidence" has been interpreted to mean "such relevant evidence as a reasonable mind might accept as adequate to support a conclusion."[135]

In Department of Navy v Egan,[136] a 1988 case, the Court decided that when an employee is discharged because his navy employer denied him a security clearance, the Merit Systems Protection Board had no statutory authority to review such action. The rationale of the decision was that "the protection of classified information must be committed to the broad discretion of the agency responsible, and this must include broad discretion to determine who may have access to it."[137] As to the right of review of the agency decision to deny security clearance, the Court said:

> Placing the burden on the Government to support the denial by a preponderance of the evidence would inevitably shift this emphasis and involve the Board in second-guessing the agency's national security determinations.[138]

Substantive issues

Even where criminal justice personnel are protected by civil service statutes having just cause clauses, a number of substantive issues are raised including the meaning of "just cause." Few statutes define the term. Occasionally rules issued by the civil service board, as set forth in the Arizona case quoted above, provide instances of just cause dismissal. Some bases of just cause dismissal such as homosexuality, mandatory retirement at a certain age, the requirement of residency within the jurisdiction, or an officer's illicit sexual activity, raise constitutional questions about the power of criminal justice institutions to control the officer's personal life (a right to privacy) while not on duty. Particularly in the case of police officers, courts have not often distinguished on and off duty behavior, relying on the public image of police officers as a representative of law and order in the community.

Just cause defined

An Illinois appellate court has defined just cause for discharge as follows:

> The word "cause" is not defined by statute but our courts have construed it to be some substantial shortcoming which renders the employee's continuance

in office in some way detrimental to the discipline and efficiency of the service and which the law and sound public opinion recognizes as good cause for his no longer holding the position. Further our courts have held that cause is to be defined and applied in the discretion of the Board and a court should not reverse unless the Board's findings are so unrelated to requirements of the service or are so trivial as to be unreasonable and arbitrary.[139]

The almost total discretion courts allow boards and commissions is affected by their conception of the employer-employee relationship. Thus, an Arizona case states that while "just cause" may not be based on "arbitrary or capricious reasons,"

a finding of misconduct which justifies suspension or discharge need not be predicated upon the violation of any particular rule or regulation. A finding of misconduct may be based upon the violation of the implicit standards of good behavior imposed upon one who stands in the public eye as an upholder of that which is morally and legally correct, provided certain standards are met. . . . Since appellee is in the classified service and cannot be discharged except for "just cause," his discharge for cause may be upheld only if it meets two criteria of reasonableness: One, that it is reasonable to discharge him because of certain conduct, and the other, that he had fair notice, express or fairly implied, that such conduct would be ground for discharge. These standards comport with substantive due process when dealing with the employer-employee relationship. The very nature of this relationship makes it infeasible to spell out in detail all that conduct which will result in discharge. . . . This standard is an objective one. Would the reasonable police officer under the circumstances know that his conduct was prohibited?[140]

The constitutional "requirement that the government afford reasonable notice of the kind of conduct that will result in deprivation of liberty and property" is rarely required by reviewing courts.[141]

Taken together, the loose construction and narrow appellate review, gives to civil service boards substantial power to control both the public and private lives of public employees. Older cases tended to apply this broad definition both to on-duty and off-duty misconduct, and therefore to make no separation between conduct related to official duties and the personal lives of officers. More recent cases, however, attempt to restrict just cause discharges to instances in which the department can show that the conduct adversely affected the officers' ability to perform their official duties. In addition to discharge there are of course other kinds of discipline such as loss of pay, suspension, and reprimands, oral and written. Transfers to less attractive areas or kinds of work may also be used as a disciplinary measure by criminal justice management. Such transfers may not always be seen as punishment entitling the officer to a hearing.[142] But where the transfer is politically motivated (see Chapter 7), it is a violation of the employee's first amendment rights and he is entitled to reinstatement.[143] One writer has divided grounds for discharge into three categories: (1) physical or mental disability; (2) conduct unbecoming an officer, and (3) neglect or violation of official duty or law.[144] Categories two and three often overlap but they will serve as a loose means of organizing the cases that follow.

Physical or mental disability

This issue arises when the state asserts an interest in protecting itself against physical disability assumed to accompany the aging process by prescribing a mandatory retirement age, by requiring a physical standard the officer must maintain on the force, or by discharging officers who, because of some off-duty or on-duty injury or illness, are believed to be physically or mentally incapable of continuing to perform their job.

Age as a disability

The Age Discrimination in Employment Act of 1967 (ADEA),[145] as amended, substantially patterned after Title VII of the Civil Rights Act of 1964, requires employers to consider aging persons (that is, those 40–69) in their individual capacity rather than as a group. Under the ADEA, it is unlawful for an employer to discriminate against any employee or potential employee on the basis of age except "where age is a bona fide occupational qualification reasonably necessary to the normal operation of the particular business, or where the differentiation is based on reasonable factors other than age."[146] In 1974, the ADEA was extended to include state and local governments. Age-related legislation was first proposed in the 1950s and then as part of the floor debate on Title VII of the Civil Rights Act banning employment discrimination on the basis of race, color, religion, sex, or national origin (see chapter 2). Amendments to this effect were rejected because it was argued that Congress did not then have enough information to make a considered decision about age discrimination. When such a study was shortly thereafter available it confirmed that age limitations were important both in public and private employment, that age lines were often drawn in an arbitrary manner unfounded in fact, and that such discrimination was costly to government due to claims for early retirement benefits, as well as because of the

economic and psychological injury to the workers themselves. Originally limited to ages 40 through 65, the Act was extended in 1978 to age
70.[147] Because ADEA is specifically limited to the protection of the rights
of people in that group, there can be no development akin to that of
reverse discrimination found in Title VII cases "because a worker achieves
no kind of protection under the Act until 40, and loses it promptly . . . on
his 70th birthday.[148]

That part of the statute that extended coverage to the states and local
governments was challenged in Equal Employment Opportunity Commission v Wyoming.[149] The case arose when a supervisor for Wyoming's
Game and Fish Department was involuntarily retired at age 55 under a
statute that permitted employment after age 55 only with the employer's
approval. After a finding for the employee before the Equal Employment Opportunity Commission, the Commission sued the state in federal court. The state responded that the federal statute was unconstitutional
because it restricted the state's sovereign powers as forbidden by National
League of Cities v Usery.[150] That case held legislation which attempted
to extend wage and hour provisions of the Fair Labor Standards Act to
state and local governments, unconstitutional because it interfered with
"the essentials of state sovereignty." It was argued that the ADEA equally
interfered with state sovereignty to control its employment policies.
National League of Cities has now been overruled (see chapter 5)[151] and
therefore that objection is no longer valid.

(i) State regulation

The matter of a state regulation requiring retirement at a certain age
first came before the Supreme Court in a 1976 case, Massachusetts Board
of Retirement v Murgia.[152] That case involved a 50-year-old officer who
was forced into retirement by a state law requiring state police officers to
retire at that age, even though admittedly Murgia was in "excellent
physical and mental health," still capable of performing the duties of a
uniformed officer. Murgia claimed that to treat him thus denied him
equal protection of the law in violation of his fourteenth amendment
rights. Murgia could not take advantage of the ADEA because his case
arose before the statute had been extended to the states. In a per curiam
opinion, Justice Marshall dissenting, the Court first determined that
"the class of uniformed state police officers" constitutes no suspect class,[153]
thus eliminating the need for the Court to subject the Massachusetts
statute to a strict scrutiny analysis. Rather, the court sought a rational

connection between the state's interest in seeking "to protect the public by assuring physical preparedness of its uniformed police" and the mandatory retirement at age 50.[154] "Since physical ability generally declines with age, mandatory retirement at 50 serves to remove from police service those whose fitness for uniformed work presumptively has diminished with age."[155] Even though the state may not have chosen the best and most humane means to carry out its purpose, that question was for the state and not for the Court to resolve.

In response to the *Murgia* situation involving state regulation of the age of retirement of law enforcement officers, in 1986, Congress ratified that decision by providing that "it shall not be unlawful" for a state employer of firefighters or law enforcement officers "to fail or refuse to hire or to discharge any individual because of such individual's age if such . . . individual has attained the age of hiring or retirement in effect under applicable State or local law on March 3, 1983, and (2) [is an action taken] pursuant to a bona fide hiring or retirement plan that is not a subterfuge to evade the purposes of this chapter."[156]

In the 1989 case of Public Employees Retirement System of Ohio v Betts,[157] the Court interpreted the language, "pursuant to a bona fide . . . retirement plan that is not a subterfuge," so as to allow a state to pay lesser benefits to an older disabled person than to a younger person retiring with disability benefits. The statute construed[158] was similar enough in language and purpose to the above section so that this case should apply to the statute applicable to law enforcement personnel. Betts, age 61, a speech pathologist employed by the County Board of Mental Retardation and Developmental Disabilities, became so physically incapacitated that her employer concluded she could no longer perform her job. She was given the choice of retiring or being medically tested, which could result in her being placed on unpaid medical leave. Her choice to retire made her eligible for retirement benefits from PERS.

Because Betts was over 60 the statutory scheme denied her disability retirement benefits. Betts would have received substantially more in benefits if she had been permitted by statute to take disability retirement. It was evident that the statute, on its face, denied disability retirement benefits. The question was whether the statutory language of 29 USC § 623(f)(2) allowed such discrimination. There was no question that the plan was "bona fide," in that it "exists and pays benefits."[159]

After a review of the legislative history of the section, the majority concluded that "Congress intended to exempt employee benefit plans from the coverage of the Act except to the extent plans were used as subterfuge for age discrimination in other aspects of the employment relation."[160] In arguing that such a plan is a subterfuge a plaintiff must show "actual intent to discriminate . . . in some non-fringe-benefit aspect of the employment relation."[161] Applying that reasoning to the Betts' situation, the Court found "that PERS' disability retirement plan is the type of plan subject to the § 4(f)(2) exemption, and PERS' refusal to grant [Bett's] request for disability benefits was required by the terms of the plan."[162]

Justice Marshall, in dissent, summarized the effect of the decision:

> The majority today immunized virtually all employee benefit programs from liability under [ADEA]. Henceforth, liability will not attach under the ADEA even if an employer is unable to put forth any justification for denying older workers the benefits younger ones receive, and indeed, even if his only reason for discriminating against older workers in benefits is his abject hostility to, or his unfounded stereotypes of them.[163]

(ii) Federal regulation

An analogous provision to the section authorizing states, as an exception to ADEA, to set certain age limits to the employment of state law enforcement officers, is a federal law which authorizes "the head of any agency [to] fix the minimum or maximum limits of age whenever the original appointment can be made to a position as a law enforcement officer. . . . [164] Such law has been held to be an exception to ADEA.[165]

ADEA proof requirements—the 1978 amendments

Lower courts have generally agreed that because the ADEA was modeled on Title VII, proof requirements would also follow that title, namely, a plaintiff must show:

"(1) she is a member of a protected group;
(2) adverse employment action was taken against her;
(3) she was replaced by a person outside the protected group; and
(4) she was qualified for the position she held."[166]

The 1978 amendments, although eliminating almost all age limits on federal employment, in response to *Murgia,* left those on certain occupations including firefighters, law enforcement officers and air controllers. Federal law provides that these groups retire at age 55.[167] What effect, if any, does this federal provision have on state employees in these categories?

Baltimore firefighters challenged an ordinance which required fire-fighters below the rank of lieutenant to retire at age 55. They claimed that the ordinance violated the ADEA and the city defended with a BFOQ defense. When the case reached the court of appeals, that court applied the federal statute as a standard, concluding that "the City was not required to make any factual showing at trial as to its need for the mandatory retirement age."[168]

After reviewing the statutory history of ADEA and of the civil service statute dealing with federal employees' retirement age, the Supreme Court concluded that the civil service provision establishing the federal retirement age for firefighters "does not articulate a BFOQ for firefighters, that its presence in the United States Code is not relevant to the question of a BFOQ for firefighters, and that it would be error for a court, faced with a challenge under the ADEA to an age limit for firefighters, to give weight, much less conclusive weight, to the federal retirement provision."[169] Although this case dealt with firefighters, there seems to be no reason why the same logic would not apply to police and other law enforcement officers.

In Western Air Lines v Criswell,[170] the Court affirmed requirements (set forth in an earlier court of appeals decision) necessary for an employer to assert a BFOQ exception.

> [T]he court recognized that the ADEA requires that age qualifications be something more than "convenient" or "reasonable"; they must be "reasonably necessary . . . to the particular business" [the statutory requirement] . . . This showing could be made in two ways. The employer could establish that it " 'had reasonable cause to believe, that is, a factual basis for believing, that all or substantially all [persons over the age qualification] would be unable to perform safely and efficiently the duties of the job involved.' " . . .
>
> Alternatively, the employer could establish that age was a legitimate proxy for the safety-related job qualifications by proving that it is "impossible or highly impractical" to deal with the older employees on an individual basis.[171]

The Court summed up these criteria as follows:

> It might well be "rational" to require mandatory retirement at *any* age less than 70, but that result would not comply with Congress' direction that employers must justify the rationale for the age chosen. Unless an employer can establish a substantial basis for believing that all or nearly all employees above an age lack the qualifications required for the position, the age selected for mandatory retirement less than 70 must be an age at which it is highly impractical for the employer to insure by individual testing that its employees will have the necessary qualifications for the job.[172]

Fitness for duty

Where the discharge is based on physical disability, injuries resulting in the disability that are incurred on the job are treated differently from those that occur off duty.[173] Disabilities arising out of and in the course of the employee's duties, are often covered by state retirement pension statutes. An Illinois statute provides:

> If a police officer as the result of sickness, accident or injury incurred in or resulting from the performance of an act of duty, is found to be physically or mentally disabled for service in the police department, so as to render necessary his or her suspension or retirement from the police service, the police officer shall be entitled to a disability retirement pension of 65% of the salary attached to the rank on the police force held by the officer at the date of suspension of duty or retirement. A police officer shall be considered "on duty", while on any assignment approved by the chief of the police department of the municipality he or she serves, whether the assignment is within or outside the municipality.[174]

A public employee is properly discharged when he is no longer able to perform the duties of his office;[175] but an officer already on leave because of psychiatric problems arising out of his police work, cannot be discharged for conduct directly arising out of those psychiatric problems.[176] It has also been held that a municipal ordinance could validly require physical examinations as a condition precedent to employment or continued employment as a police officer.[177] But such removal for failure to pass a physical examination is removal for incompetence and the board must comply with state statutory procedural requirements for discharge for incompetence.[178]

There are, however, certain constitutional and statutory protections for employees with physical disabilities. In one case, a village, while supplying injury and sick leave, sought to place restrictions on the movement of employees who were receiving these benefits. The village fire and police commission issued regulations providing that employees on injury and sick leave must remain in their residences at all times except for matters relating to their injury or illness. The employee argued that such restrictions infringed his fundamental rights to vote, to practice his religion and to travel. The district court found that village interests "(1) to provide an efficient method of administering the sick and injury leave policies while providing for the personnel needs of the [police department], or (2) preventing abuse of those policies" were not compelling enough to override the fundamental rights violated, nor were the regulations sufficiently narrowly drawn to avoid trampling on fundamental rights.[179] But in Crain v Board of Police Comrs of St. Louis, the court concluded:

> We have no doubt that requiring officers to remain in their homes while on sick leave is rationally related to the St. Louis Police Department's legitimate interests in speeding the recuperation of its officers, maintaining discipline and morale, and preventing abuses of the department's liberal sick leave policy. Appellants' claim that the sick leave regulations violate their constitutional rights fails because they have not shown the absence of a rational relationship between the regulations and the important interests they are designed to serve.[180]

Statutory rights of handicapped persons

There are two major sources of rights for handicapped persons, the Rehabilitation Act of 1973, as amended,[181] and the various state Human Relations Acts.[182]

(1) Rehabilitation Act of 1973

The purpose of the Rehabilitation Act of 1973, among others, is "the guaranty of equal opportunity . . . for individuals with handicaps in order to maximize their employability, independence, and integration into the workplace and the community."[183]

The Act forbids, "solely by reason of her or his handicaps," the exclusion of a "qualified individual with handicaps" from participation in or denial of benefits in, or subjection "to discrimination under any activity receiving Federal financial assistance or under any program conducted by any Executive agency or by the United States Postal Services." While Title VII requires only that discrimination be one factor, the Rehabilitation Act requires the handicap be the *sole* reason for the decision.[184]

Even though the Act applies only to recipients of federal assistance, it has been estimated that at least one-half of all businesses, employing at least one-third of the workforce, fit that category.[185]

An "individual with handicaps" is defined by the Act as "any person" who

(1) has a physical or mental impairment that substantially limits one or more of such person's major life activities.
(2) has a record of such an impairment, or
(3) is regarded as having an impairment.[186]

Handicaps have not been restricted by cases decided under the Act to "traditional" disabilities such as deafness or blindness, but have included epilepsy, back conditions, disfiguring scars, alcoholism, drug addiction, compulsive gambling, allergies, amputations, cancer, cerebral palsy, diabetes, dyslexia, heart problems, high blood pressure, tuberculosis, mastectomy, mental and nervous conditions, multiple sclerosis, paraplegia, repeated shoulder dislocations, crossed eyes, transexuality, but not homosexuality or transvestism, or mere sensitivity to tobacco smoke, left-handedness, varicose veins, or other trivial or temporary conditions.[187]

The key enforcement provision states:

> No otherwise qualified individual with handicaps in the United States . . . shall, solely by reason of her or his handicap, be excluded from the participation in, be denied the benefits of, or be subjected to discrimination under any program or activity receiving Federal financial assistance or under any program or activity conducted by any Executive agency or by the United States Postal Services.
>
> Each department, agency, and instrumentality . . . in the executive branch shall . . . submit . . . an affirmative action program plan for the hiring, placement, and advancement of individuals with handicaps. . . . [188]

Under regulations developed by the EEOC pursuant to the statute, a

> "Qualified handicapped person" means with respect to employment, a handicapped person who with or without reasonable accommodation can perform the essential functions of the position in question.[189]

A further section makes remedies available under either Titles VI or VII of the Civil Rights Act of 1964, including the award of attorney fees to the attorney of the prevailing party.[190]

For the "public safety officer," the Act provides for "special consideration" to be

> "given to the rehabilitation . . . of an individual with handicaps whose handicapping condition arises from a disability sustained in the line of duty while such individual was performing as a public safety officer if the proximate cause of such disability was a criminal act, apparent criminal act, or a hazardous condition resulting directly from the officer's performance of duties in direct connection with the enforcement, execution and administration of law . . . or related public safety activities.[191]

Interpretation under the Act

Numerous questions are raised concerning interpretation of the statutory language: What is meant by handicap? What is a "qualified individual?" To what extent do the words "financial assistance" impose a limit on the statutory coverage? What is meant by "substantial limits" and "major life activities"? Only a few of these questions can be discussed here.

In School Bd of Nassau Cty v Arline,[192] the Court interpreted § 504 of the Rehabilitation Act of 1973 to cover a teacher afflicted with tuberculosis as a "handicapped individual" within the meaning of that statute. An elementary school teacher had been discharged when her tuberculosis, inactive for many years, again became active. Reviewing the legislative history of the statute, the Court concluded that "the Act is carefully structured to replace [prejudiced] reactions to actual or perceived handicaps with actions based on reasoned medically sound judgments: the definition of 'handicapped individual' is broad, but only those individuals who are both handicapped *and* otherwise qualified are eligible for relief."[193] That the teacher had tuberculosis, a contagious disease, does not alone bar coverage by the section.

The Court then looked into whether the teacher was still qualified for the job, which would require an individualized inquiry, in which courts would "normally" defer to the reasonable medical judgments of public health officials."[194] Because the lower courts had not determined "the duration and severity of [the teacher's] condition, nor . . . the probability that she would transmit the disease," the case was remanded to the lower court to make this finding of fact.[195]

The question of who is "otherwise qualified" was raised in Copeland v Philadelphia Police Department.[196] There, a police officer was discharged as a result of a positive urine test for marihuana. In part, he relied on the Rehabilitation Act, arguing that the city had discriminated against him because they had a rehabilitation program for alcohol problems, while there was none for drug addiction. The court responded that "accommodating a drug user within the ranks of the police department would constitute a 'substantial modification' of the essential functions of the police department and would cast doubt on the integrity of the police force."

> Because a police department is justified in concluding that it cannot properly accommodate a user of illegal drugs within its ranks, we conclude that Copeland is not otherwise qualified for the position and thus does not qualify for the protections afforded by the Act.[197]

Copeland may be contrasted with Nisperos v Bush,[198] in which the opposite result was obtained in another drug use case, but in which the discharged employee was an attorney for the Immigration and Naturalization Service. Nisperos, on his own, entered a drug rehabilitation facility where he was cured. The court determined from the Act's legislative history that there was no intention to exclude from coverage rehabilitated drug users. *Copeland* was distinguished on the basis that "Nisperos has no responsibilities for the investigation, apprehension, or detention, of individuals suspected of criminal offenses". Section 791 of the Act requires the employer to make "reasonable accommodation" to the handicap to the extent possible, and here this requirement can be satisfied merely by shifting the case load so that Nisperos is not assigned cases involving violation of drug laws.[199]

(i) State Human Rights Statutes

According to one survey, as of 1990, all states, except for Delaware and the District of Columbia, have laws prohibiting discrimination against the handicapped. These laws vary greatly in their coverage and effectiveness,[200] but in general follow both the language and the cases interpreting the Rehabilitation Act. It will not be necessary therefore to extensively set forth case law under these statutes.

The change in attitude toward the handicapped from the 1960s to the 1980s is well-illustrated by Melvin v The City of West Franklin,[201] a 1981 case in which the Illinois court held unconstitutional a section of the Illinois Municipal Code of 1961 that prohibited a municipal fire or police department from hiring an amputee. Seven years later, the court, in Police and Fire Comrs v Human Rights Comn, stated

> In reaching that conclusion, we reiterated the express policy of this state that eligibility for employment be based on individual capacity and that blanket restrictions in hiring handicapped individuals which are not related to the ability of the particular applicant to perform the particular work are prohibited.[202]

Police and Fire Comrs involved a police applicant who qualified to be a probationary police officer except for the requirement that he have 20-20 uncorrected vision. The applicant argued that such a denial discriminated against him because of his visual handicap even though he was otherwise qualified to do the job. The court agreed and ordered him readmitted as probationary officer. Where, however, a probationary officer has an off-duty automobile accident that would not allow him to fully perform his duties as a police officer, his condition does not fall within the definition of "disabled," and therefore he has no claim to the continued probationary status.[203]

(ii) AIDS sufferers as handicapped persons

AIDS, the acquired immune deficiency syndrome, is at the same time so well-known and the object of so much suspicion, fear and speculation that it is not surprising that it has spawned cases involving all parts of the criminal justice system. One early question was whether those infected with the disease were to be considered "handicapped" within the meaning of the Rehabilitation Act of 1973 and the more recent Disabilities Act of 1990.

In order to clarify this question, the US Justice Department, October 6, 1988, issued a legal opinion that found that § 504 of the Rehabilitation Act protects HIV [Human Immunodeficiency Virus] infected individuals "against discrimination in any covered program and activity on the basis of any actual, past or perceived effect of HIV infection that substantially limits any major life activity . . . ", provided that "he or she is able to perform the duties of the job and does not constitute a direct threat to the health or safety of others."[204] A majority of state fair employment practice agencies have interpreted their state handicap discrimination laws as protecting AIDS victims and as prohibiting involuntary testing of employees for the AIDS virus.[205]

AIDS cases can be divided into four categories: 1. demands for more controls over persons with AIDS; 2. complaints by persons with AIDS concerning restrictions on them; 3. problems of confidentiality; and 4. mandatory testing of AIDS-infected persons.

1. Demands for more controls over persons with AIDS

In Davis v Stanley,[206] a prisoner asserted that the sheriff negligently placed plaintiff in a cell with a person who later tested positive for AIDS. The prisoner asked that all persons entering the prison be tested for the HIV virus. Rejecting this demand, the court concluded that the sheriff was in the best position to be able to determine if testing is necessary for the security of the jail and its prisoners. In another case, Welch v Sheriff, Lubbock County, Texas,[207] a jail inmate filed a § 1983 action alleging that he was placed in the same cell with another inmate, who the jailer knew had tested positive or reacted to a blood test for HIV. Because the court found that the plaintiff had not alleged sexual contact nor engaged in any other activities with the inmate that are known to transmit AIDS, and there was even a question whether the inmate had tested for AIDS, the plaintiff's claim was denied.

2. Complaints concerning restrictions on persons with AIDS

This category of cases involve complaints by persons, usually those who have not yet developed AIDS, are asymtomatic, but have tested positive for the HIV antibody, about restrictions imposed on them because others are said to fear contraction of the disease. In Leckelt v Board of Comrs of Hosp Dist No 1,[208] plaintiff, a practical nurse in a hospital, was discharged for failure to submit a blood test for AIDS when it came to the hospital's attention that plaintiff was a homosexual and lived with someone who was infected with AIDS, and when asked to take a blood test, plaintiff replied that he had recently taken one but never supplied the hospital with results of that test.

After being discharged, plaintiff filed this suit relying on the Rehabilitation Act of 1973. The court responded: "By refusing to submit the results of his HIV antibody test Leckelt prevented [the hospital] from knowing whether he had a handicap for which federal law arguably required reasonable accommodations." Not having provided the test, under the Act he was not "otherwise qualified." His discharge was based on his failure to submit the test, not on the results themselves.

As with homosexuality, it is the military services that deal most harshly with AIDS sufferers. A sailor, who tests positive for AIDS, may be released from the Navy even though he had developed no symptoms,[209] or although allowed to reenlist in the Army may not be permitted to take training that would lead to an occupational specialty.[210]

Prison administrators faced with problems of balancing the rights of HIV positive prisoners and the general prison population have generally been upheld by the courts in deciding to segregate HIV-positive inmates. In Harris v Thigpen,[211] inmates testing HIV positive, were administratively segregated from other prisoners, had little use of recreation areas or libraries, and were unable to do work that might prepare them for an occupation on release. Incoming inmates were tested on admittance and all those found with HIV antibodies or active AIDS virus were separated. To fourth amendment, eighth amendment, and right to privacy objections, the court answered:

> The Eighth Amendment provides inmates with the right to a safe and secure environment. Allowing inmates with AIDS to be introduced into the general population may be violative of the general population inmates' Eighth Amendment rights. . . . The Court is of the opinion that the policies currently in effect are appropriate measures to prevent the situation about which the Court has expressed grave concern.[212]

3. Confidentiality of AIDS information

Regardless of the assurances that the scientific community has given that AIDS can be acquired only through exchange of blood or genital fluids, the certainty of death if the disease is acquired, makes AIDS the modern equivalent of leprosy. Therefore, spreading information that anyone has AIDS or has tested HIV-positive represents such sensitive communication that duties of confidentiality have arisen concerning AIDS. In Doe v Borough of Barrington,[213] a truck in which plaintiffs were riding was stopped by defendant police. As the police were about to search the husband, the husband informed the police that he had tested HIV-positive, and because he had "weeping lesions," they should be careful in searching him. Later that same day, in an unrelated traffic accident opposite plaintiff's house, the police defendants, during a conversation, informed the neighbors of the plaintiff's AIDS infection. Neighbors panicked, contacted other people, many of whom pulled their children out of school where plaintiffs' children attended; these facts were reported in the local newspapers, and on TV, causing plaintiffs embarrassment and humiliation, and resulted in discriminatory behavior towards them.

In finding for the plaintiffs, the court remarked:

> The sensitive nature of medical information about AIDS makes a compelling argument for keeping the information confidential. Society's moral judgments about the high-risk activities associated with the disease, including sexual relations and drug use, make the information of the most personal kind. . . . The potential for harm in the event of a nonconsensual disclosure is substantial. . . . [214]

The court also noted that it was clearly in the public interest to encourage persons with AIDS in the situation such as was this plaintiff, to disclose to police officers their AIDS infection without penalty of later disclosure of that information by the police.

4. Mandatory drug testing

In Johnetta J v Municipal Court,[215] plaintiff challenged California Proposition 96 which provided for mandatory AIDS blood testing for persons charged with interfering with official duties of public safety employees when there was probable cause to believe the person's bodily fluids have mingled with those of the employee. In this case, plaintiff was removed from a court room when she became disruptive, in the course of which she bit a deputy's arm, penetrating the skin and drawing blood.

Although there had been no documented cases of transmission of AIDS through biting, the court upheld the constitutionality of the law and ordered the testing:

> Here the electorate has enacted a statute that finds public safety officers at risk from anxiety and fatal infection in the course of their duties. In the unique circumstances of the AIDS epidemic, medical opinion cannot rule out the possibility of HIV transfer to an officer suffering a bite. The assailant's blood is tested under the statute in a medically approved manner, test results are subject to limited disclosure, and a blood test of the assailant is highly useful to the treatment of the assaulted officer. Under these circumstances, the state's interest is sufficiently compelling to overcome petitioner's right of privacy against what we have already concluded is a minimal intrusion.[216]

But in Glover v Eastern Nebraska Community Office of Retardation,[217] mandatory testing of employees of the Community Office of Retardation was rejected as being an unreasonable search and seizure because the chance of their passing the disease on to their clients is "negligible," and the constitutional incursion does not "justify requiring employees to submit to a test for the purpose of protecting the clients from an infected employee.[218]

(2) Conduct unbecoming a police officer

This extremely vague term is found in almost all statutes or regulations covering police and correctional personnel. The claim that the wording is constitutionally vague and overbroad so as to be in violation of the first amendment is treated in chapter 7. The Supreme Court has not yet construed the term in the police context although the term has been held constitutional with reference to the military.[219] One court defining the term has stated: "Unbecoming conduct on the part of . . . a policeman . . . [is] any conduct which adversely affects the morale or efficiency of the bureau to which he is assigned . . . [or] any conduct which has a tendency to destroy public respect for municipal employees and confidence in the operation of municipal services."[220] The following are some matters that have been found to be conduct unbecoming a police officer: homosexuality, illicit sexual relations, misuse of firearms, refusal to cooperate with an investigation, association with persons of ill repute, failure to pay debts, neglecting to consider that his wife was supporting their expenditures by embezzlement, and filing a law suit against a superior, among others. Until recently, courts did not distinguish between acts committed on and off duty. As one Illinois appellate court stated:

> It has long been settled in our state that there is no distinction between "off duty" or "on duty" misconduct by a police officer. Should a police officer engage in misconduct which is detrimental to the service it would be absurd to say that he is clothed with a cloak of immunity if such misconduct occurred during off duty hours. By the very nature of his employment a police officer is in the eyes of the public and for the good of the department must exercise sound judgment and realize his responsibilities to the department and the public at all times.[221]

As noted earlier, more recent cases appear to be requiring a direct relationship between the misconduct charged and the job performed by the officer. If the board cannot convincingly show that misconduct interfered with the officer's job performance, the discharge may be overturned by a reviewing court. This trend becomes more apparent in the following sections.

(a) Homosexuality

Homosexuality has long been considered a reason for discharge of public employees. This approach has been especially true for criminal justice employers because of the strong male (macho) image that these agencies often seek to portray. Reasons given for the impropriety of homosexuals in public employ have been (1) they are subject to blackmail and they may thereby be forced into making compromises inconsistent with their job performance; (2) such conduct is criminal in most states and thus the state would be employing criminals; (3) their conduct is immoral, unprofessional and involves moral turpitude; (4) their employment will result in the public's losing respect and confidence in the agency; (5) their employment tends to show tacit approval by the agency of their conduct; (6) their employment will foster similar behavior on the part of fellow employees and will create disharmony and disrupt working relations.[222] Like other groups in our society, homosexuals in recent years have asserted rights that have increasingly been recognized by the courts. In addition, as one writer has observed, "the effect of disqualifying from public employment all individuals who have engaged in homosexual conduct would be to eliminate virtually 37% of the caucasian male population. Simply excluding those individuals who are exclusively homosexual in orientation would eliminate upwards of three to four million Americans."[223]

Discrimination in public employment because of homosexuality may be found in three areas: (1) the military; (2) those requiring security clearance; and (3) civil service. Restrictions on homosexuals are most rigid in the military. From 1982 to June, 1990, 13,307 military personnel were discharged because of allegations of homosexuality. Department of Defense guidelines require the military to discharge those who engage in homosexual acts,[224] but as the cases will show, the regulation is interpreted to result in discharge of any admitted or discovered homosexual.

For civilians, on the other hand, the developing majority rule is that, for a government civilian employee, homosexuality, in itself, is not "just cause" for discharge; such discharge would violate the due process clause of the fifth and fourteenth amendments.[225] Neither Title VII nor the ADEA cover homosexuality as an employment classification or a disability.[226] The general rule is that civilian employees may not be discharged solely for sex preference unless the trait affects job performance. Because of the different way courts look at homosexuality in civilian and military contexts, it becomes crucial for criminal justice personnel to be seen by courts as having more civilian than military characteristics.

The ruling case, decided in 1988, from which all others take their cue, is the lone Supreme Court case involving employment of homosexuals, Webster v Doe.[227] Doe, a clerk-typist, employed by the CIA, voluntarily informed his security officer that he was a homosexual. He was thereafter terminated because his homosexuality was said to be a security risk. The initial question for the Court was whether, under the National Security Act, the Director's decision was reviewable. That Act authorized termination whenever the Director deemed it "necessary or advisable in the interests of the United States," a standard that the Court said foreclosed any meaningful review.[228] Nevertheless, the Court left open a door through which review can proceed—where the person terminated can assert a constitutional right violation.

Another Supreme Court case, Bowers v Hardwick[229] upheld a Georgia law making sodomy a felony even when performed by consenting adults in the privacy of their home. Even though *Bowers,* as a criminal case, should be irrelevant to cases involving employment of homosexuals, it has been persuasive for many courts in deciding that homosexuals are not a "suspect class," and therefore that any law, regulation, or decision affecting them need only pass the test of rationality—that is, that the rule need have no more than a rational relationship to the legitimate end sought to be attained by the decisionmaker. In Woodward v US,[230] a 1989 case, Woodward, at the time he enlisted in the Naval Reserves, answered a question that he would like to engage in sexual activity with members of his own sex but had never done so. Woodward was released from the Reserves under a statute authorizing the Secretary of the Navy to at any time "release a Reserve . . . from active duty."[231] Woodward argued that homosexuals were a suspect class, but on the authority of *Bowers,* the court rejected that theory, answering that the Navy policy was rationally related to a permissible end—the maintenance of "discipline, good order and morale."[232]

Webster, as noted earlier, did leave an opening for agency dismissal of homosexuals (and others) when they could assert a "colorable" constitutional claim, that is, one that has a fair chance of being upheld. It is too early to see how courts will ultimately apply this important doctrine but in Dubbs v CIA,[233] an openly gay woman working as senior technical illustrator for a defense contractor, was refused security clearance because of her homosexuality. On authority of *Webster,* she was barred from the right to press her appeal of the CIA's decision to denial her clearance, but because she had asserted an equal protection constitutional claim, the case was remanded to the district court to hear that claim.

In US Information Agency v Krc,[234] while on duty in Yugoslavia, Krc voluntarily disclosed that he had sex with other males. He was removed from the job he was doing as foreign service officer and given another job in which no security clearance was required. On the authority of *Webster,* his equal protection claim was remanded for consideration by the district court, with the comment: "as this case illustrates, those constitutional claims may well be the *only* check on agency actions that determine a person's career fortunes. Courts have an obligation to listen to those claims clearly and to consider them carefully."[235]

Most recent cases involving civilian public employment have adhered to the newer rule requiring a showing that the homosexuality affected on-duty performance before disciplinary action would be allowed. In a well-reasoned 1980 District of Columbia court of appeals opinion,[236] a non-investigative FBI employee was called into his superior's office where he was accused of being a homosexual. Upon admitting to the fact, he was forced to resign. The question was whether the fact of plaintiff's homosexuality without any inquiry as to its job-relatedness, justified his dismissal. There was nothing in the FBI's rules which denominated homosexuality as an automatic cause for dismissal. Following Norton v Macy[237] followed by Society for Individual Rights v Hampton,[238] the Civil Service Commission instructed supervisors[239] that they could dismiss employees for homosexuality only if it affected their fitness for the job.[240] Therefore, the court concluded: "We are convinced that the FBI has fostered rules and understandings which, by entitling appellant to believe that he would lose his job only for a job-related reason, gave him a property interest in his position such that he could be fired only with the procedural protections of the Due Process Clause."[241] But where the employee's on-duty conduct was found to be related to his homosexuality in that as a houseparent for mentally retarded boys he made advances or remarks to other employees about dressing up boys in girl's clothing, he could be discharged.[242]

One author has distilled a series of standards applicable to criminal justice agencies from his analysis of cases of termination due to homosexuality:

> (1) the termination may not be based upon factors unconnected with the responsibility of the employment; (2) the reasons upon which termination is based bear a rational relationship to the performance; (3) the individual's conduct/lifestyle might bring the public service into contempt; (4) there is an established nexus between the conduct and its effect on job fitness; (5) removal of the individual would promote efficiency of the particular service; and (6) the decision to terminate may not be arbitrary or capricious.[243]

The above cases dealt with an agency's decision to discharge. Where the decision is to hire, an agency has considerably more latitude. In a case arising in the District of Columbia circuit, the issue was whether the refusal of the FBI to employ a woman applicant as a special agent because of her active homosexuality was in violation of either bureau policy or the equal protection guarantee of the Constitution.[244] As to the first of these grounds, the court of appeals noted that Congress has exempted the FBI's hiring decisions from traditional schemes of reviewability, and that therefore "there is no meaningful statutory standard against which to judge the FBI's exercise of discretion."[245] Further, the FBI, in its policy statements, has never made sexual preference irrelevant to its hiring decisions, but on the contrary "does indeed look to an applicant's sexual orientation," for it might "involve conduct that is relevant to employment."[246]

Rejecting the argument that government policy should be strictly scrutinized where homosexuality is a basis of decision, the court said such decision need only justify itself "in terms of some government purpose." That purpose the court found to be that the FBI was a national law enforcement agency, that homosexual conduct was criminal in about one-half of the states, and that the secret work that the FBI does might expose homosexual agents to the danger of blackmail. Thus, the FBI's action in rejecting the homosexual applicant, did not violate the applicant's constitutional rights.

(b) Illicit sexual activity

Because of the values asserted by criminal justice institutions, particularly police departments, they have been sensitive to employees' violations of traditional sexual mores. Such violations have included instances of adulterous relationships in which either the officer or the sexual partner is married, where the woman is particularly young, is a prostitute, or is a resident of a house of ill repute. Changing sexual mores or the entrance of women into these agencies, have not clearly made a difference in the way courts have decided these cases. More important seems to be the notoriety occasioned by the incident, whether it is accompanied by other objectionable conduct, and whether the employee had been warned by a superior to end the conduct, but despite the warning, the conduct has continued. Nevertheless, if the few cases available suggest a trend, it is in accentuating the constitutional right of privacy over the "higher standard" required of criminal justice personnel to preserve the institutional image.

One such case is Thorne v City of El Segundo[247] in which the female police applicant, Thorne, passed all parts of the police screening except that under questioning she revealed she had had sex with a married man. She was denied eligibility to become an officer and thereupon filed this § 1983 action claiming damages for invasion of her privacy interests. The court stated:

> In the absence of any showing that private, off-duty, personal activities of the type protected by the constitutional guarantee of privacy and free association have an impact upon an applicant's on-the-job performance, and of specific policies with narrow implementing regulations, we hold that reliance on these private non-job-related considerations by the state in rejecting an applicant for employment violates the applicant's protected constitutional interests and cannot be upheld under any level of scrutiny.[248]

The court pointed out that no deviant conduct was shown, that the sexual affair was not a matter of public knowledge, and thus could not diminish the department's image, and that there was no reason to believe Thorne would engage in such conduct while on duty. Another case, in which the officer was accused of having sex with an unmarried woman, required that the act be "publicly visible." "Such private activities do not establish the requirement of a nexus between the activities and either poor job performance or reputation and integrity of the department."[249]

Where however those cohabiting were both officers of the same force of different rank, "a rational connection [exists] between the exigencies of Department discipline and forbidding members of a quasi-military unit, especially those different in rank, to share an apartment."[250]

Those cases in which the offensive sexual conduct takes place on-duty, of course, raise no right to privacy, and uniformly result in discipline.[251] Where conduct is especially offensive, courts also hold officers accountable because "the state has such as overriding and compelling interest in protecting the public and preserving the integrity of the Police Department that such interests overrides" the officer's right to privacy.[252]

Another view, now in the minority, but still important, is presented by a 1975 Pennsylvania case that strongly relied on the public image of the police officer in the community.[253] There, Officer Faust had a liaison with a married woman. The affair came to the attention of his superior who told him it was in his and the department's best interests if the relationship ended. Faust nevertheless continued the relationship, whereupon it was discovered by the woman's husband and her father. The father called the chief of police. Faust was then fired. Faust claimed that because adultery was no longer a crime in Pennsylvania and because he was neither in uniform nor on duty at the time of the incidents they were constitutionally protected rights of privacy and that such activity was "in keeping with the modern 'changed community standards of the last ten years'."[254] The court remained unconvinced.

> Faust's reasoning overlooks the fact that police officers are held to a higher standard of conduct than other citizens, including other public employees. This high standard, grounded in common sense, is statutorily mandated by the Borough Code. There is undoubtedly a compelling state interest in the maintenance of a high degree of public respect for police officers.[255]

Police officers have also been discharged for having sexual intercourse in "an establishment of ill repute";[256] and for the officer inducing his wife to consent to an affair with another officer and his having an affair with the wife's 18-year-old sister.[257] This same sort of reasoning has been turned on its head in more recent cases. In *Shuman v City of Philadelphia*,[258] a 1979 Pennsylvania district court opinion, a police officer being investigated by his department about his relationship with an 18-year-old girl, on advice of counsel, refused to answer questions. The charge under investigation was that of involvement in "crimes of moral turpitude."[259] Relying on this charge to make its point, the court took a position exactly the opposite to that of *Faust,* decided just four years before.

> Adultery has not been a crime in Pennsylvania since the enactment of the Crimes Code [1973]. Therefore, adulterous behavior is not a "*crime* of moral turpitude" and does not violate any express regulations of the Police Department.... In the absence of a showing that a policeman's private off-duty activities have an impact upon his on-the-job performance, we believe that inquiry into those activities violates the constitutionally protected right of privacy.[260]

A similar position was taken by an Arkansas district court[261] where a police chief forbade an officer separated from his wife to have more than a "casual" relationship with a female police civilian employee, and then disciplined the officer when he announced plans to marry the employee. Such action was held to be an unconstitutional interference with the officer's right to privacy.

> The court would agree that the police department has an interest and may investigate some areas of the personal sexual activities of its employees if the activities have an impact upon job performance. In the absence of a nexus between the personal, off-duty activities and poor job performance, inquiry into these activities violates the Constitutionally protected right of privacy.... [262]

Likewise, a police officer who dated a married woman did not violate a standard that requires " 'associations with women while off-duty [that] shall be of the quality acceptable by good social standards' " because the court found such norms "clearly are the standards of the general public, not some higher standard."[263] And a police officer who had been discharged for the "immoral act" of having a second unwed pregnancy, was reinstated because such action cannot be taken merely on "the appearance of 'immorality' as defined by the chief of police and the mayor.... "[264]

(c) Sexual harassment

With the rise of the women's movement in the 1970s and the inclusion of "sex" as one basis for claims under Title VII of the Civil Rights Act of 1964 (see chapter 2), women began to file claims based on sexual harassment at their workplace.[265] The infusion of women into criminal justice agencies in greater numbers, together with their increased consciousness as to their rights, provided support for women to object to the various means by which males in superior positions used those positions to demand sexual favors, to deny promotion where advances were repelled, or to make the working environment so hostile that the employee was forced to resign (constructive discharge). Under Title VII claims, two legal questions have arisen from such sexual advances by fellow workers or by superiors:

(1) Must there be "employment consequences" associated with the harassment?
(2) What knowledge, acquiescence or approval of the wrongful conduct of the employee on the part of the employer is necessary?[266]

These and other questions were answered by Meritor Savings Bank v Vinson.[267] All justices joined in finding that employers who maintain a hostile or offensive working environment as a result of sexual harassment are subject to a Title VII claim; that no economic consequences need be shown to prove such a claim; and that traditional agency principles should be used to determine the employer's liability for the employee's misconduct. Four justices in a separate concurring opinion stated that where sexual discrimination by a supervisor leads to a discriminatory work environment for the employee, Title VII liability "should be imputed to the employer for Title VII purposes regardless of whether the employee gave 'notice' of the offense."[268]

Vinson had been a bank teller-trainee. During her training and probationary period, her supervisor, a bank vice-president, suggested sexual relations. She initially refused, but upon his continued insistence, she had sexual intercourse with him between 40 and 50 times over the next few years. During this time he also raped her several times and fondled her in front of other employees. In proving a Title VII hostile working environment action, the Court found a plaintiff must show conditions are "sufficiently severe *or* pervasive 'to alter the conditions of [the victim's] employment and create an abusive working environment'."[269]

Even when the sex-related conduct was "voluntary," as it often was in this case, recovery is not precluded as long as the advances were "unwelcome." As to the liability of employers for employee sexual misconduct, the Court rejected strict liability, that is, "that employers are automatically liable for sexual harassment by their supervisors." On the other hand, mere "absence of notice to an employer does not necessarily insulate that employer from liability."[270] These vague principles of employer liability were to be worked out in later lower court decisions.

Plaintiffs can file sexual harassment claims under Title VII, section

1983 or under state Human Rights Acts. For § 1983 claims, claimants normally assert that their due process or equal protection rights have been violated. Each section must stand on its own. Claimants cannot encompass a Title VII claim within a § 1983 claim, in an attempt to expand the reach of both.[271]

From 1980, when the EEOC adopted guidelines recognizing sexual harassment was a form of sexual discrimination, and that it might arise from two types of activity—quid pro quo (in consideration of) and hostile working environment—courts have used these criteria to measure unlawful sexual discrimination. The portion of the guidelines defining sexual harassment states:

> Harassment on the basis of sex is a violation of Sec. 703 of Title VII. Unwelcome sexual advances, requests for sexual favors, and other verbal or physical conduct of a sexual nature constitute sexual harassment when (1) submission to such conduct is made either explicitly or implicitly a term or condition of an individual's employment, (2) submission to or rejection of such conduct by an individual is used as the basis for employment decisions affecting such individual, or (3) such conduct has the purpose or effect of unreasonably interfering with an individual's work performance or creating an intimidating, hostile, or offensive working environment.[272]

Courts have accepted this dichotomy, delineating the two as either (1) a *quid pro quo* arrangement, or (2) a working environment, where sexual harassment was so pervasive that it had the effect of creating an intimidating, hostile, or offensive work environment.[273]

(i) *Quid pro quo*

Although the *quid pro quo* theory appears easy to prove, in practice, few cases have been found where women employees have been successful.

In Chamberlin v 101 Reality, Inc[274] the plaintiff was hired for the eventual purpose of supervising a real estate project. During a nine month period of employment she was subjected to five sexual advances by her employer, and claims she was fired in retaliation for her rejection of his advances. In finding for her on a theory of *quid pro quo* harassment, the court set forth a five-part test for employer liability:

> (1) the plaintiff-employee is a member of a protected group; (2) the sexual advances were unwelcome; (3) the harassment was sexually motivated; (4) the employee's reaction to the supervisor's advances affected a tangible aspect of her employment; and (5) *respondeat superior* liability has been established.[275]

After reviewing the evidence of the five sexual overtures the court concluded

> Chamberlin was discharged because she did not submit to sexual discrimination in the workplace, clearly a retaliatory termination from employment. Sexual discrimination in employment contravenes New Hampshire public policy [citing the state civil rights statute].[276]

There is an important distinction between a hostile sexual working environment claim and a *quid pro quo* claim in that in the latter it is not necessary to show knowledge by the employer of the sexual harassment for the employer to become liable. This point is well expressed in Carrero v New York City Housing Authority[277]

> The gravamen of a *quid pro quo* claim is that a tangible job benefit or privilege is conditioned on an employee's submission to sexual blackmail and that adverse consequences follow from the employee's refusal. Unlike in hostile environment cases, in *quid pro quo* cases the harassing employee acts as and for the company, holding out the employer's benefits as an inducement to the employee for sexual favors. Accordingly, in a *quid pro quo* sexual harassment case the employer is held strictly liable for its employee's unlawful acts [citing *Vinson* 477 US at 70–71].[278]

(ii) Hostile working environment

In order to prevail under this theory, a plaintiff must prove: "(1) she is a member of a protected group; (2) she was subjected to unwelcome sexual harassment; (3) the harassment was based upon sex; (4) the harassment affected a term, condition, or privilege of employment; and (5) the employer knew or should have known of the harassment and failed to take appropriate remedial action."[279]

Women working in criminal justice often have difficulty in showing that the harassment is "unwelcome" because banter in police stations and prisons is male-dominated and sexual remarks are often pervasive. But as one court responded:

> Although defendants' counsel vigorously argues that a police station need not be run like a day care center, it should not, however, have the ambience of a nineteenth century military barracks.[280]

Likewise, it is difficult for women criminal justice workers not to be caught up in the banter themselves, just so they can be one of the "guys." Such natural desire for acceptance leaves them open to charges that the "harassment" was welcome. One court, has recognized this problem:

> We agree that [plaintiff's] conduct is relevant to the determination of whether the alleged sexual harassment by [the offending officers] was unwelcome. The record shows that [the plaintiff] sometimes gave as much as she got. Nevertheless, it also shows that she repeatedly indicated to [the harassing officers] and her superiors that this state of affairs was offensive and unacceptable. She acted reasonably under the circumstances.[281]

In proving a sexually hostile working requirement, courts have found a multitude of offensive activities of fellow employees and superiors that victimizes plaintiffs "by offensive conduct 'sufficiently severe or pervasive' to render her working environment hostile. . . . Physical assaults of a sexual nature obviously constitute incidents that tend to satisfy this criterion of severity."[282] Cases disclose an incredible number of offensive activities by males targeting women. In Sanchez v City of Miami Beach,[283] the plaintiff filed a Title VII action claiming a sexually offensive work environment. At trial the court found she had been subjected to

> kissing, moaning, sighing and other disruptive noises transmitted over the police radio, and was the subject of a plethora of sexually offensive posters, pictures, graffiti, and pinups placed on the walls throughout the Police Department. She received a soiled condom, a sanitary napkin, two vibrators, and a urinal device in the mailbox . . . and generally withstood innumerable childish, yet offensive sexual and obscene innuendoes and incidents aimed at her on the basis of sex (fn 9. The posters and graffiti appearing throughout the police department accused Plaintiff, among other things, of being a lesbian [a common accusation in these cases], having male genitalia, and challenging male co-workers to various physical competitions. . . .).[284]

In Ross v Double Diamond,[285] repeated sexual overtures during an employee's first two days of work as a salesperson by the manager who hired her was enough to create a sexually harassing work environment. Because the company had notice of similar claims by another female employee against the same manager, and neither took action against him nor provided an effective policy against sexual harassment, the court found that "the employer knew or should have known of the harassment in question, and failed to take prompt remedial actions."[286]

Plaintiff also must show that the harassment was severe and persistent enough to change her conditions of employment. On a motion for summary judgment to dismiss plaintiff's claim of harassment, one court found nine incidents during a five month period could "show a pattern of something beyond the occasional crude joke, trivial remark, or accidental slip of the tongue. . . . Thus, in order to satisfy the requirement of *Vinson,* [plaintiff] need only show that the discriminatory hostility was sufficiently pervasive to change the work atmosphere, rather than being merely episodic, and thereby to change also a condition of employment."[287]

(iii) Supervisor liability

Compensation for such harassment is only likely if plaintiffs are able to hold supervisors and thus employers liable. *Vinson* tied such liability to agency principles but gave no further aid. Lower courts therefore have been searching for guidelines between strict liability, which *Vinson* forbade, and a necessary finding of fault on the part of the superiors themselves. Where superiors engage in or clearly condone the offensive conduct,[288] there is no problem in holding employers liable. One court put the criterion for employer liability tersely: "if a plaintiff proves that management-level employees had actual or constructive knowledge about the existence of a sexually hostile environment and failed to take prompt and adequate remedial action, the employer will be liable."[289]

A case in which the employer successfully avoided liability will show the necessity for the criminal justice employer to make a proper and prompt response to evidence of sexual harassment. In Hirshfeld v New Mexico Correction Dept,[290] plaintiff was a typist at a correctional facility who had been subject to a number of unsolicited advances by a captain. Although the captain was liable the court found that the facility was not. At the first opportunity after the warden was informed of plaintiff's complaint, he interviewed the offending captain, and immediately placed him on administrative leave. After a thorough investigation, the captain was demoted to lieutenant. Thereafter, the plaintiff had no further problems with the captain. Moreover, after remedial action was taken, the action was monitored to see that it had the desired effect. The generally accepted standard seems to be that employer liability results when "an employer who is aware of sexual harassment in the workplace acts negligently or recklessly by failing to take 'reasonable steps to eliminate such offensive conduct.' "[291]

Conditions of work may be so unbearable that the plaintiff may quit. The question then arises whether that resignation is the result of the sex harassment, that is, was the sexual harassment severe enough so, in effect, she was "constructively discharged?"

> [C]onstructive discharge occurs when the employer 'deliberately makes an employee's working conditions so intolerable that the employee is forced into an involuntary resignation . . . [that is,] a reasonable person in the employee's shoes would have felt compelled to resign.' "[292]

(3) Section 1983-based harassment claims

Asserting a § 1983 claim for sexual harassment requires the same proof as for any other § 1983 claim, as set forth in chapter 1. For example, explaining the nature of an equal protection basis for sexual harassment, one court said: "Forcing women and not men to work in an environment of sexual harassment is no different than forcing women to work in a dirtier or more hazardous environment than men simply because they are women," and is a violation of her rights under the equal protection of the law clause.[293]

A female Chicago police officer, relying on § 1983, asserted a violation of her rights of equal protection of the law in that she was treated differently because of her sex.[294] Charges of sexual harassment by a lieutenant, which went uninvestigated by his superiors, was sufficient to state a cause of action against those superiors, including the chief of police, for their failure to act.

(4) Disciplinary action against criminal justice personnel

Earlier cases dealing with sexual harassment by male criminal justice personnel seemed to have treated the offense lightly.[295] More recent cases, however, have often resulted in dismissals instead of fines or short suspensions where the charges are upheld. Such cases either arise as disciplinary appeals by the accused officer from the determination of the state disciplinary board or from § 1983 actions by the officer complaining of deprivation of his constitutional rights. Grievance of Gorruso[296] was an appeal by the state from a decision of the Vermont Labor Relations Board reinstating the grievant who had been dismissed as a correctional officer for sexual harassment of female employees at the Correctional Center. One of the legal questions raised was whether sexual harassment constituted "just cause" for dismissal. The court responded:

> Grievant's repeated sexual harassment clearly constituted a substantial short-coming detrimental to the State's interest. See 21 V.S.A. § 495 (sexual harassment prohibited under state law). Workers in a correctional center environment must be able to depend upon their co-workers. Sexual harassment clearly undermines this necessary dependence.[297]

Drug testing of criminal justice employees

As drugs have become an everyday feature of American life, and the effects of drug-abuse on the workplace have become better understood, both federal and state governments have taken measures to detect and eliminate drugs from that environment. In July, 1986, President Reagan provided a legal base to procedures for drug testing by issuing an executive order mandating a drug-free federal workplace. Each federal agency was required to establish drug-testing for all employees who were engaged in sensitive work.[298] Later, in the Drug-Free Workplace Act of 1988, Congress extended this requirement to every "person" receiving a grant from any federal agency.[299] Agencies under the jurisdiction of these measures were required to and did issue regulations setting forth procedures by which the testing was to take place, for its accuracy, protections for the employee's privacy; and the resulting sanctions if the employee refused to take the test, or if it was positive.

Two 1989 United States Supreme Court cases, National Treasury Employees Union v Von Raab[300] and Skinner v Railway Labor Executives Assn,[301] have naturally dominated the debate on the issue. Their holdings, together with the lower-case law that was developed since then can be briefly summarized as follows: (1) mandatory drug tests of government employees fall under the search and seizure clause of the fourth amendment and therefore can be valid only as long as they are "reasonable"; (2) the analytic approach adopted by the Supreme Court requires a balancing of the government's interest to be served by the test and the individual employee's expectation of privacy; (3) it is usually reasonable to require tests of employees whose jobs invoke security or safety interests; (4) because criminal justice employees normally fall within these security and safety concerns, testing is likely to be required for those employees engaged in that type of work; (5) given these governmental interests, the type of testing can be random, warrantless and without individualized suspicion as long as procedures used reduce as much as possible intrusions into the individual's privacy; (6) where special circumstances of the job cannot be called upon to show government interests, that is, where the government cannot show that the job falls into a particular category of safety or security so as to give the government a compelling interest in the testing, then the privacy and fourth amendment interests of the individual employees outweigh the interest of the government, and the attempt to test without individualized suspicion will fail.

Of the two Supreme Court cases, *Skinner,* because it deals with railway workers who were tested only after a train accident triggered the necessity for such tests, was easier to decide than *Von Raab* which required tests of workers in the Customs Service who sought transfer or promotion into positions where they were involved in the interdiction of drugs.

In *Skinner,* the Federal Railroad Administration (FRA) promulgated regulations that mandated blood and urine tests of employees who were involved in train accidents, or who have violated safety rules. Such regulations presented the issue, whether mandatory testing under these conditions violated the search and seizure provisions of the fourth amendment. The Court noted that between 1972 and 1983, at least 21 serious train accidents, involving 25 fatalities, and 61 non-fatal injuries, resulted from alcohol and drug abuse. According to the regulations, test samples were to be provided by involved employees on the occurrence of a "major train accident," as defined in the regulations. Those who refused to take the test were to be disciplined. The Court decided that mandated urine tests were searches under the fourth amendment's search and seizure clause and therefore, to be constitutional had to be reasonable. Nevertheless, no warrant or individualized suspicion was required before the test was given. In finding that such testing procedure was reasonable the Court reasoned:

> [T]he government interest in testing without a showing of individualized suspicion is compelling. Employees subject to the tests discharge duties fraught with such risks of injury to others that even a momentary lapse of attention can have disastrous consequences.[302] . . . In light of the limited discretion exercised by the railroad employers under the regulations, the surpassing safety served by toxicological tests in this context, and the diminished expectation of privacy that attaches to information pertaining to the fitness of covered employees, we believe it is reasonable to conduct such tests in the absence of a warrant or reasonable suspicion that any particular employee may be impaired. We hold that the drug tests contemplated by subparts C and D of the FRA's regulations are reasonable within the meaning of the Fourth Amendment.[303]

In *Von Raab,* the United States Customs Service required a urinalysis test of employees who sought transfer or promotion into any positions having responsibility for the interdiction and seizure of contraband, including illegal drugs. Customs employees who test positive and can offer no satisfactory explanation for the positive test are subject to dismissal. The employee's union sued claiming a fourth amendment violation.

> We hold that the suspicionless testing of employees who apply for promotions to positions directly involving the interdiction of illegal drugs, or to positions which require the incumbent to carry a firearm, is reasonable. The Government's compelling interests in preventing the promotion of drug users to positions where they might endanger the integrity of our Nation's borders

or the life of the ordinary citizenry outweigh the privacy interests of those who seek promotion to these positions, who enjoy a diminished expectation of privacy by virtue of the special, and obvious, physical or ethical demands of those positions. We do not decide whether testing those who apply for promotion to positions where they would handle "classified" information is reasonable because we find the record inadequate for this purpose.[304]

Thus, the Court left the determination of the reasonableness of testing employees who had jobs outside the sensitive areas of drug interdiction and guncarrying for later cases. Because employee testing in *Skinner* and *Von Raab* did not occur until triggered either by an accident or some entry into jobs where potential drug use posed some special hazard, several questions were left to later cases: Was random testing, that is, where there was no individualized suspicion, "reasonable"? Where was the line to be drawn in the balancing process between the security and safety needs of the agency and the privacy needs of the employee? How would the court treat the expectation of privacy rights of criminal justice employees in a profession often compared to the military? Would courts distinguish between off and on-duty activity? Answers to these questions were not long in coming.

In National Federation of Federal Employees v Cheney,[305] the circuit court for the District of Columbia had to determine if compulsory, random urine testing of the Department of the Army's civilian employees, including guards and police, was in violation of the employee's fourth amendment rights. The program affected some 9,000 of the department's 450,000 civilian employees. Four categories of employees were to be tested. The first were approximately 2800 civilians who flew and serviced airplanes and helicopters. The court first rejected the argument that the test was invalid because it did not test on-duty impairment and therefore was unable to distinguish between on or off-duty use or impairment. Without directly answering this argument, the court pointed out that the Supreme Court decisions made no such distinction.

The court had no trouble finding that tests for this first group were reasonable because "employees in each of the covered positions . . . perform tasks that are frought with extraordinary peril: A single drug-related lapse by a covered employee could have irreversible and calamitous consequences."[306]

The second group involved both chemical and nuclear surety positions as well as secretaries and animal caretakers. Unable to determine what risk, if any, drug use would imply for this mixed group, the court remanded this issue to the district court for further hearings.

The next category, civilian police and guards, because they carried firearms, fit into the safety concerns of the court:

> Because the civilian guard's expectations of privacy are severely reduced as a condition of employment in a high-security-military context, mandatory, random urinalysis testing constitutes a modest additional privacy intrusion, and cannot, on this basis, be deemed unreasonable.[307]

The fourth group included the civilian treatment staff of the Alcohol and Drug Abuse Prevention and Control Program who work with the civilian employees of the Army's Drug testing Laboratories as well as all employees involved in the chain of custody of the testing process. The government argued that testing for this group was necessary to protect the "credibility" and "integrity" of the testing process. The court rejected these general assertions. "*Von Raab* rested not so much on the Service's undifferentiated interest in ensuring its reputation and credibility as on the myriad dangers posed by drug-using interdiction agents."[307] Following this rationale, the court found that for drug counselors, "successful performance of their assigned duties may reasonably be viewed as depending on their abstinence from illicit drug use."[308] Likewise, employees in the department's drug rehabilitation program may be tested to determine the success of the program. But other employees whose only connection to drugs was their job in the chain of custody, threatened no important government interest such as was evident with other groups of workers considered.

> Because we have not been shown that the government interests in testing either laboratory workers or those in the specimen chain of custody outweigh the privacy expectations of those employees, we hold that the testing of these employees is not reasonable within the meaning of the Fourth Amendment.[310]

Almost all of the cases dealing with line criminal justice personnel have decided, following *Von Raab,* that testing, as long as it was accompanied by procedures to protect the confidentiality of the results and to reduce the invasion of privacy to a practical minimum, were reasonable searches within the fourth amendment. In McCloskey v Honolulu Police Department,[311] the plaintiff, a female police officer, refused to submit a drug sample as demanded under the department's random drug-testing program. In an apparent effort to avoid the United States Supreme Court's *Skinner* and *Von Raab* cases, plaintiff relied on similar search and seizure provisions and the privacy provisions of the Hawaiian constitution. While the right of privacy under the US Constitution emanates from case law, such a right is written into the Hawaiian constitution. Nevertheless, the Hawaiian Supreme court found the urine testing procedure non-intrusive, and serving "three compelling interests: (1) insuring that individual police officers are able to perform their duties safely; (2) protecting the safety of the public; and (3) preserving HPD's integrity and ability to perform its job effectively."[312]

> Police officers, since they are authorized to make arrests, conduct searches, and carry and use firearms, even when not on duty, must be mentally alert and exercise sound judgment at all times. They may be placed in a life threatening situation in which they must exercise split second judgment in the use of their firearms. In addition, police officers must control and exercise proper judgment in the use of their motor vehicles. Thus, drug use by a police officer, which can substantially impair the user's judgment and ability to react quickly, threatens police and public safety. Drug use within HPD seriously affects the integrity of the department and undermines the public's trust and confidence in the police.[313]

In rejecting the privacy claim, the court noted that "a police officer, by reason of the employment as a police officer, has a diminished expectation of privacy. HPD's rules prohibit the illegal use of drugs even when off-duty, and all police officers know they are subject to regulations which affect their private non-professional lives."[314]

Neglect or violation of official duty

This category represents the criminal code of disciplinary offenses and therefore is more precise than accusations such as conduct unbecoming an officer. Charges of neglect or violation of duty can include the participation in or commission of a crime, for example, writing checks on an account with insufficient funds;[315] failing to arrest and then disposing of a substance believed to be controlled[316] or driving while intoxicated.[317] Likewise, personal use of a police vehicle to transport or to meet female companions is grounds for discharge.[318]

Disclosing confidential information,[319] and abuse of citizens, fellow officers or prisoners can also result in disciplinary action.[320] Unreasonable or negligent use of force against an unarmed suspect can result in discharge.[321] Lying to a superior where it relates directly to the duty performed by the officer can be grounds for discharge. In an Illinois case, an officer had an accident on private property while on patrol but lied to his superior about it. The court reasoned that "[t]he key factor is the subject matter of the falsehood, more specifically, how it directly relates to a policeman's duties to the public. . . . The instant case does not involve a lie about attending to personal business while on duty but a lie directly connected to an officer's duty to the public. . . ."[322]

Officers may also be discharged for incompetence, inefficiency, failure to follow proper orders or improper use of authority. Dismissal has been upheld where a commander failed to properly supervise personnel under his command or failed to respond to calls;[323] or doing his job in a grossly negligent manner.[324]

Restrictions on off-duty activities

Criminal justice personnel have often been restricted by their employing agencies in two areas—their right to additional employment and their right to live where they wish. Generally, where reasonable, these regulations have been upheld.[325]

In McCarthy v Philadelphia Civil Service Comn,[326] the Supreme Court found constitutional a municipal regulation requiring city employees to be residents of the city. The plaintiff's employment of 16 years with the city's fire department was terminated because he moved his permanent residence from Philadelphia to New Jersey in violation of the regulation. The Court rejected plaintiff's claim that such a regulation was in violation of his right to travel. The Court referred to and found constitutional two types of residency requirements: one that required city residency at the time of the employment application, and the other continued residency during employment.[327]

Discharge for failing to follow an unconstitutional order

Criminal justice agencies are hierarchal systems. In such pyramidal organizations those on top make policy and those on the bottom are employed to obey. Failure to follow orders is ordinarily grounds for discharge.[328] But what if the order given is illegal or unconstitutional? That question was posed in the case of Harley v Schuykill County.[329] There, a prison guard, ordered by an acting warden to have a prisoner "stand check" in front of his cell, "even if he had to be dragged from his cell," refused to carry out the order and was discharged.[330] Harley refused to act because he discovered that the prisoner had previously been maltreated for his refusal to stand check and that the refusal was motivated by the prisoner's religious beliefs. If he was to carry out the

order, Harley concluded he would have to use force, which would aggra-
vate injuries the prisoner received in a previous attempt. He therefore
refused to obey the command, arguing that it was immoral and unconstitutional. He was discharged, the reasons given thereafter being insubordination and causing dissension between the warden and the other
guards. Harley sued under § 1983 claiming that to comply with the
order would violate the prisoner's fourth, eighth and fourteenth amendment rights, and would subject Harley to civil liability. In response, the
district court ruled that such refusal to obey an order to perform an
unconstitutional act is a constitutionally protected right which could be
asserted under § 1983 and that therefore Harley could not be fired for his
action. Judge Huyett's research showed that there were "surprisingly few
authorities on this issue . . . and no case which discusses the matter in any
great depth."[331] Failing to find any authoritative cases on the precise
issue before the court, Judge Huyett looked to the more general doctrine
that for every right there exists a reciprocal duty to observe that right.

> [P]laintiff had a clear duty under the constitution to refrain from acting in a
> manner that would deprive [the prisoner] of his constitutional rights. If
> plaintiff is under a *duty* to refrain from performing an act, then we believe that
> he has the concurrent *right* to so act. To hold otherwise would create an
> unconscionable burden upon one charged with the duty to uphold another's
> constitutional rights.[332]

Because Harley relied on § 1983, it must be shown that such a right was
"secured by the Constitution." Rather weakly, the judge reasoned that "it
is logical to believe that the current *right* is also one which is created and
secured by the Constitution." More forthrightly, the court rested its
ruling on "strong policy considerations."

> Parties such as [the] plaintiff, who are acting in the capacities of prison
> administrators, policemen and the like, may daily be faced with situations
> where they are required to act in a manner which is consonant with the
> constitutional rights of others who are subject to their authority. The potential
> for abuse in these situations scarcely needs to be mentioned. If such persons
> are to be *encouraged* to respect the constitutional rights of others, they must at
> least have the minimal assurance that their actions are also protected by the
> constitution in those cases where they are confronted with the difficult choice
> of obeying an official order or violating another's constitutional rights.[333]

The most often cited precedent to Harley is Parrish v Civil Service
Commission[334] in which a county social worker refused to participate in
early-morning mass raids on welfare recipients for the purpose of locat-

ing any "unauthorized males," because he believed the raids to be illegal under the fourth amendment. Upon his dismissal for insubordination he sued and was reinstated with an order for backpay. The California Supreme Court set forth three criteria for determining when a public employee could disobey a superior's order: (1) when the order creates a *reasonable belief* that it is unconstitutional; (2) when the employee in fact holds a *good faith belief* that the order is unconstitutional; and (3) when the order is *in fact unconstitutional.*[335]

Summary and Conclusions

Dismissal from a job has been rightly called the capital punishment of disciplinary measures available to an hierarchal organization. As such, it is of overriding importance to criminal justice personnel. The linchpin that holds together and determines all successive rules is the employment at will principle. Underlying that principle is the capitalist system of organization in which private employers control the means of production — factories, machines and work tools. Such a system, based as it is on a market economy, has ups and downs of economic activity. During slack periods it would be extremely costly for employers to continue to pay wages when workers were unneeded to produce products for sale. After the Civil War, during a period of high industrial growth in the United States, courts recognized this need and accepted the employment at will rule which provided that employers could discharge employees at any time without giving any reason whatsoever.

The holdings of recent Supreme Court cases on the procedural and substantive rights of public employees under the fifth and fourteenth amendments due process clause can be summarized as follows: (1) There is no fundamental right to government employment; (2) the property interest in a government job, to be recognized by the courts, must be shown to be a government-created right; (3) the liberty interest must be either a government-created right or be an independent right arising from the Court's interpretation of the due process clause; and (4) the procedural due process provided by the Court to protect these substantive interests is either that set forth (a) by the governmental statute that created the substantive right or (b) a kind of procedural due process that threatens to interfere with government organizational or security interests. Overall, the Court has shown a continued deference to the institutional hierarchy (police and correctional departments) represented by decisions of supervisory employees.

In the 1930s, following the depression in which millions of workers organized, and thereafter in the 1960s, when blacks and other groups asserted their rights, the states and the national government passed legislation providing for exceptions to the employment at will rule. The most important protection against the rule for public employees, including criminal justice personnel, is civil service laws which contain "just cause" clauses. These permit firing classified, that is, permanent workers, only after a "just cause" for dismissal has been shown in a procedurally proper hearing.

Such legislation usually provides for a framework in which there is a requirement for a formal charge, followed by a hearing at which the state must prove a prima facie case by convincing and substantial evidence. Officers charged with misconduct have a right to confront and cross-examine witnesses against them, to present their own witnesses and evidence and to have retained counsel present. There is a right to appeal from the administrative board's decision to a trial court, and thereafter to have both the board's and the trial court's decisions reviewed by an appellate court. The usual appellate court standard of review is that the appellate court will affirm the board's decision unless it is found to be arbitrary and supported by no substantial evidence. This standard is consistent with the presumption of validity accorded administrative (executive) agencies by the judiciary.

In preliminary inquiries into alleged employee misconduct public employees have an obligation to answer specific, narrowly-drawn questions, directly related to their official duties. If the employees are told that answers given cannot be used against them in criminal proceedings and that they may be disciplined or discharged for refusal to answer, subsequent refusal to answer such questions can be made a ground for discipline or discharge. Employees may not be sanctioned, however, merely for invoking their fifth amendment privilege not to answer.

Lie detection is one means sometimes used as an aid to interrogation in a disciplinary proceeding against criminal justice personnel. Evidence obtained from use of lie detectors has almost uniformly been rejected by courts when attempts have been made to introduce it into disciplinary proceedings. Officers, therefore, may refuse to submit to such tests where they are used as investigative devices. Criminal justice employers are empowered to search an employee's desk and other workplace areas when there are reasonable grounds for suspecting that the search will turn up evidence that the employee is guilty of work-related conduct, or that the search is necessary for a work-related purpose.

"Just cause" for discharge has been defined as "some substantial short-coming that renders the employee's continuance in office in some way detrimental to the discipline and the efficiency of the service and which the law and sound public opinion recognizes as good cause for his no longer holding the position." Older cases tend to apply this broad definition both to on-duty and off-duty misconduct, and therefore to make no distinction between conduct related to official duties and officers' personal lives. More recent cases, however, restrict just cause discharges to instances in which the department can show that the conduct adversely affected the officers' ability to perform their official duties. Grounds for discharge may be separated into three categories: (1) physical or mental disability; (2) conduct unbecoming an officer, and (3) neglect or violation of official duty or law.

Physical or mental disability as a legal issue arises when agencies have rules prescribing a mandatory retirement age, or require employees to maintain a physical standard to remain on the force, or to discharge officers who, because of off-duty injury or illness, are believed to be physically or mentally incapable of doing their job.

The Age Discrimination Act of 1976, patterned after Title VII, prohibits discrimination in employment for persons 40–69. State legislation, however, that retired criminal justice personnel at earlier ages has been upheld by the Supreme Court on the theory that a criminal justice agency could rationally decide that ability to perform such a job declines with age. Power to set mandatory retirement ages has now been embodied in both federal and state laws. Nevertheless, in order for a state to set an age for retirement less than 70, it must establish a substantial basis for believing that all or nearly all employees above that age lack the qualifications required for the position.

The Rehabilitation Act of 1973 prohibits, among other things, employment discrimination "solely by reason of her or his handicaps." The Act calls for "special consideration" to be given to "public safety officers" who suffer a disability in the line of duty. In addition to the federal act almost all states have analogous acts protecting handicapped persons.

AIDS, the acquired immune deficiency syndrome, is generally considered a handicap under both federal and state employment discrimination laws. Because of the fear engendered by the illness, there have been a number of attempts to control exposure to disease by both criminal justice personnel and by prisoners. These may be divided into four categories: (1) demands for more control over prisoners with AIDS; (2) complaints by persons with AIDS concerning restrictions on them; (3) problems of confidentiality; and (4) mandatory testing of AIDS-infected persons. In general, courts have rejected claims by prisoners for segregation of AIDS-infected prisoners or for specially testing procedures to identify HIV-positive new prisoners, and at the same time have supported efforts of administrators to segregate or otherwise specially deal with HIV-positive inmates.

Distinction is made between physical or mental disability that results from on or off-duty injuries. Disability resulting from on-duty injury or illness cannot be a basis for discharge. Agencies can, however, require employees to maintain a reasonable level of physical fitness commensurate with the requirements of the job.

Conduct unbecoming an officer has been defined by the courts as "any conduct which adversely affects the morale or efficiency of the bureau to which he is assigned." In the past, courts, for example, have found the following conduct by officers to be embraced by this definition: homosexuality, illicit sexual relations, misuse of firearms, association with persons of ill repute, failure to pay debts, and filing a law suit against a superior, among others.

Because of the values asserted by criminal justice institutions, particularly police departments, they have been sensitive to employees' violations of traditional sexual mores. These have included instances of adulterous relationships where either the officer or the sexual partner is married, where the woman is particularly young or is a prostitute or a resident of a house of ill repute. Changing sexual mores and the entrance of women in the up to now male work environment seems to have changed the focus of courts in cases of sexual violation from merely considering *supposed* damage to the department to its *actual* effect, if any, on the ability of the officer to properly perform his job. Homosexuality seems to be developing along the same line. For the most part, cases reject discharge on this basis unless the department can demonstrate an adverse effect on the employee's ability to carry out official duties. More latitude may be given in some sensitive services such as the FBI where homosexuality may be an accepted factor on the hiring decision.

Sexual harassment claims may be filed either under Title VII, Section 1983, or under various state Human Rights Acts. Harrassment claims usually fall into two categories: (1) *quid pro quo,* in which the plaintiff employee must show that she suffered some direct loss in employment because she refused her employer's sexual advances, or (2) her working environment was made hostile, intimidating and offensive by sexual harassment. For an employer to be liable in a case of hostile workplace harassment, the plaintiff must prove that management-level employees had actual or constructive knowledge about the existence of a sexually hostile environment but failed to take prompt and adequate remedial action. Constructive discharge occurs when the employer deliberately makes an employee's working conditions so intolerable that she is forced into involuntary resignation.

Concern about the effect of the use of narcotics on government employees engaged in sensitive operations has resulted in government regulations requiring mandatory drug-testing. In the *Von Raab* and *Skinner* cases, the Supreme Court set forth certain guidelines, in general, approving mandatory blood or urine tests, random, and without individualized suspicion. Such testing was found to be reasonable within the search and seizure provisions of the fourth amendment. If proper precautions are taken to protect the employee's privacy, under the US Constitution such testing is not a violation of the employee's privacy because of the government's interest in those employees engaging in security and safety functions. Where, however, special circumstances of the job cannot be called upon to show such government interests, then the privacy and fourth amendment interests of the individual employees outweigh the interest of the government, and the attempt to test without individualized suspicion will fail.

Charges involving neglect or violation of official duty have involved participation in corrupt activities such as fixing traffic tickets or participation in gambling operations; the use of some controlled substance; abusing citizens, fellow officers or prisoners in their custody; intoxication or sleeping on the job; lying to an officer where it relates to official duty, or discharge for incompetence or inefficiency. Rules have been upheld where they regulate outside employment, whether those rules restrict the time the officer can spend otherwise employed or the type of employment permitted. Regulations have also been upheld that require municipal employees to be residents of the city where they are employed both at the time of application and on a continuing basis.

A difficult question is posed when a public employee is discharged for refusing to follow an order of a superior that the employee contends is unconstitutional. One such situation arose in the *Harley* case. There, a prison guard was given an order that he rightly believed would violate a prisoner's constitutional rights. His refusal to obey resulted in his discharge. His § 1983 suit for reinstatement was upheld by a federal district court on the principle that every right rests on the reciprocal duty to observe that right and that to permit punishment of a person who had upheld the constitutional rights of another under his tutelage would be contrary to public policy.

ENDNOTES

1. Moore, W: The conduct of the corporation 28 (1962), as cited in Blades, Employment at will vs individual freedom: On limiting the abusive exercise of employer power, 67 Col L Rev 1404, 1406 fn 11.
2. Mancke, J: Removal, suspension or demotion of a municipal police officer: A review and analysis, 79 Dickenson L Rev 380 (1975).
3. Peck, C: Unjust discharges from employment: A necessary change in the law, 40 Ohio St L J 1, 11 (1979); Comment, Protecting at will employees against wrongful discharge: The duty to terminate only in good faith, 93 Harv L Rev 1816, 1824–5 (1980); Note, Non-statutory causes of action for an employer's termination of an "at will" employment relationship: A possible solution to the economic imbalance in the employer-employee relationship, 24 NYU L Rev 743, 747 (1979).
4. Comment, Recognizing the employee's interests in continued employment— The California cause of action for unjust dismissal, 12 Pacific L J 69, 73 (1980).
5. Douglas, J A: "Is it and look out: Employment discrimination against homosexuals and the new law of unjust dismissal," 33 Wash U J Urb & Contemp L 73, 77 (1988).
6. Feinman, J: The development of the employment at will rule, 20 Am J Legal Hist 118, 119 (1976).
7. Id at 120, citing 1 Blackstone, Commentaries 425.
8. 20 Am J Legal Hist at 120.
9. Note, NYU L Rev pp 745–6, *supra* n 3.
10. Am J Legal Hist 126, *supra* n 6, citing Horace Gray Wood, Master and Servant § 134.
11. Payne v Western & Atl RR Co 81 Tenn 507, 519–20 (ovrld by Hutton v Matters 132 Tenn 527 (1915)), cited in Summers, C: Individual protection against unjust dismissal: Time for a statute, 62 Va L Rev 481, 485 (1976).
12. Pacific L J p 73, *supra* n 4.
13. 208 US 161.
14. 236 US 1.
15. NYU L Rev p 747, *supra* n 3.
16. 301 US 1, 45–6 (1937)

17. 313 US 177, 187 (1941).
18. Act of July 5 1935, Pub L No 74-198, ch 372, Stat 449, codified at 29 USC § 151-68, as amended (Supp IV 1980).
19. Va L Rev pp 492–3 n 11.
20. 42 USC §§ 2000e-2000e-15 (1988).
21. 15 USC § 1674(a) (1988).
22. 38 USC § 2021(a) (1988).
23. 29 USC § 215(a)(3) (1988).
24. 29 USC § 660(c) (1988).
25. See generally Harv L Rev p 1827 fn 65, *supra* n 3; Ohio St L J p 15, *supra* n 3; Va L Rev pp 492–99, *supra* n 11 and Pacific L J p 83, *supra* n 4.
26. Va L Rev pp 495–6, *supra* n 11.
27. Harv L Rev p 1828, *supra* n 3.
28. Wash U J Urb & Contemp L p 82, n 5.
29. These views are detailed in ch 1 of the first edition of this book.
30. 408 US 564. This analysis relies, in part, on Rosenblum, V: Schoolchildren: Yes, Policemen: no—some thoughts about the Supreme Court's priorities concerning the right to a hearing in suspension and removal cases, 72 NW L Rev 146 (1977).
31. 408 US at 577.
32. Id at 578.
33. Wisconsin v Constaniteau 400 US 433, 437 (1971).
34. 408 US at 575.
35. Id at 577.
36. 408 US 593, 602 (1972).
37. Id at 602.
38. Frug, G: Does the Constitution prevent the discharge of civil service employees? 124 U of Pa L Rev 942, 948 (1976).
39. 416 US 134 (1974).
40. Id at 140. The Lloyd-La Follette Act, 5 USC § 7501 (1988).
41. 416 US at 154.
42. Id at 185, White dissenting.
43. 435 US 247.
44. Id at 259.
45. Id at 260 (citations omitted). See Brewer v Parkman 938 F2d 860 (8th Cir 1991) (before back pay award may be made for violation of procedural due process, district court must determine if deputy sheriff would have been discharged anyway).
46. 470 US 532 (1985).
47. Id at 540.
48. Id at 541.
49. Id.
50. Id at 542–43.
51. Id at 545–48 (citations omitted). *Loudermill* seems to raise questions about the holding in an earlier case, Davis v Scherer 468 US 183, 192 (1984), a five to

four decision. There, procedural due process was said to be satisfied by the discharge of a state trooper without any formal pretermination or post-termination hearing. The trooper was discharged for taking outside employment in violation of orders from his superior not to do so. The Court majority found that a simple exchange of letters concerning the employee's outside employment "provided the fundamentals of due process" even though there was no notice to the employee that his conduct might subject him to the discharge and even though the failure to provide a hearing violated a state regulation.

52. 426 US 341 (1976).
53. Id at 343.
54. Id.
55. Id at 344.
56. Id at 345.
57. Id at 347.
58. Id.
59. Id at 348.
60. Id.
61. Id at 349.
62. Id at 349–50.
63. Id at 350 fn 14.
64. 429 US 624 (1977)
65. Id at 625.
66. Id at 626.
67. Id at 627.
68. Id at 628.
69. Paul v Davis 424 US 693, 712 (1976).
70. Massachusetts Board of Retirement v Murgia 427 US 307, 313 (1976).
71. Id.
72. 425 US 238 (1976).
73. Id at 247.
74. Harv L Rev p 1832, *supra* n 3.
75. Wash U J Urb & Contemp L p 77, *supra* n 5.
76. Civil Service Reform Act of 1978 § 204(a), 5 USC § 7501(a); 7503 (1988); Wash U J Urb & Contemp L p 77 fn 14, *supra* n 5.
77. 5 USC § 7501(a) (1988).
78. See Arnett v Kennedy 416 US 134 (1974).
79. Ohio St L J p 9 fn 49, *supra* n 3; Harv L Rev p 1832, *supra* n 3; Va L Rev p 481, *supra* n 11.
80. Va L Rev p 498, *supra* n 11.
81. Ill Rev Stat ch 24 § 10-1-18(b) (1989). Illinois also has promulgated the Uniform Peace Officers' Disciplinary Act, Ill Rev Stat Ch 85 § 2551 et seq (1989) which guarantees certain procedural rights to peace officers subject to administrative charges.
82. Purdon's 53 Pa Stat Annot § 12638 (1990); Mancke pp 382–85 n 2.

83. 22 Ariz App 183, 525 P2d 949 (1974).

84. 525 P2d at 952-3 (citations omitted. Emphasis added).

85. It is unclear whether in a polygraph pre-employment examination, questions about the applicant's personal activities are in violation of the individual's right to privacy. See Hedge v County of Tippecanoe 890 F2d 4, 7 (7th Cir 1989), questions whether female applicant had had sexual relations with another female not within police applicant's right to privacy, Walls v City of Peterburg 895 F2d 188, 195 (4th Cir 1990).

86. 385 US 493.

87. Id at 495 fn 3.

88. Id at 499.

89. 392 US 273 (1968).

90. 392 US at 278, and Sanitation Men's Assn v Sanitation Comr 392 US 280, 284-5 (1968).

91. 392 US 280, 284-5 (1968).

92. Uniform Sanitation Men's Association v Commn 426 F2d 619, 626 (2nd Cir 1970) cert den 406 US 961 (1972); in Gniotek v City of Philadelphia 808 F2d 241, 245 (3rd 1986) cert den 481 US 1050 (1987) police officers, identified by witnesses as taking bribes, who were thereafter called to respond to the charges, and not responding, were dismissed, could not rely on the self-incrimination privilege because "they were compelled to choose between asserting the privilege and responding."

93. O'Brien v Digrazia 544 F2d 543, 546 (1st Cir 1976) cert den O'Brien v Jordan 431 US 914 (1977).

94. Miranda v Arizona 384 US 436 (1966). The Uniform Peace Officer's Disciplinary Act, Ill Rev Stat ch 85 § 2561 et seq provides for *Miranda*-type warnings. US v Frederick 842 F2d 382, 401 (DC Cir 1988), where lack of clear warnings to FBI agent under investigation for lying about his own prior investigation required dismissal of charges against him.

95. 512 F2d 1099.

96. Id at 1101-2. For a horror story of interrogation of police officers suspected of a disciplinary breach, see Oddsen v Board of Fire and Police Comrs 321 NW2d 161, 172 (1982) (police officers interrogated without sleep for long hours without adequate warnings).

97. Williams v Pima County 791 P2d 1053, 1056 (1989), cert den 111 SCt 441 (1990).

98. Shuman v City of Philadelphia 470 FSupp 449 (ED Pa 1979) (refusal of officer to answer questions about adulterous relationship with 18-year-old girl while separated from wife upheld where no showing officer's conduct affected job performance).

99. Davis, J: Interview of public employees regarding criminal misconduct allegations: Constitutional considerations, Part I, 49 FBI Law Enforcement Bulletin 30-31 (1980). This section has partially relied on the analysis of this article. See Williams v Pima County 791 P2d 1053, 1056 (1989), cert den 111 SCt 441; Braje v Bd of Fire & Police Comrs 487 NE2d 91, 94 (1985); Ross

v Public Employment Relations Board 417 NW2d 475, 477 (1987); Brown v City of North Kansas City 779 SW2d 596 (Mo App 1989).

100. In Anderson v City of Philadelphia, 845 F2d 1216, 1225 (3rd Cir 1988), the court rejected constitutional objections from police and correctional officers to the use of pre-employment testing by the use of lie detectors, concluding "that in the absence of a scientific consensus, reasonable law enforcement administrators may choose to include a polygraph requirement in their hiring process without offending the equal protection clause." See also Rust v City of Vallejo 263 Cal Rptr 839, 849 (Cal App 1st Dist 1989), rev den, op withdrawn from publication by order of ct 1990 Cal Lexis 847 (officer seeking reinstatement could be required to take polygraph test).

101. After charges that large numbers of employers were using lie detector tests for employee testing, as a result of which "each year about 400,000 honest workers are misidentified as deceptive and suffer adverse employment consequences," Congress passed the Employee Polygraph Protection Act of 1988, 29 USCA 2001 et seq (West Supp 1991). See Employee Polygraph Protection Act of 1988, Law and explanation, Chicago, CCH, p. 6 (1988). § 2006 exempts "any state or local government, or any political subdivision of a state or local government."

102. 96 Ill2d 298 (1983), cert den Rockford v Kaske 464 US 960 (1983).

103. 96 Ill2d 298.

104. 96 Ill2d at 309.

105. Id at 310. *Kaske* is confirmed in Collura v Board of Police Comrs 498 NE2d 1148 (1986).

106. See Annotation, Refusal to submit to polygraph examination as ground for discharge or suspension of public employees or officers, 15 ALR4th 1207 (1982), and US v Piccinonna 885 F2d 1529, 1533, 1535, 1536 (11th Cir 1989) where the court evaluates "new empirical evidence" supporting the polygraph's "widespread acceptance as a useful and reliable scientific tool. The evidence is admissible where (1) both parties stipulate to its admission, or (2) when it is used to impeach or collaborate the testimony of a trial witness. See also US v Miller 874 F2d 1255, 1261 (9th Cir 1989) where the court holds itself out as "inhospitable" to the test but would admit it "for a limited purpose that is unrelated to the substantive correctness of the results of the polygraph examination."

107. Public Safety Officers Procedural Bill of Rights Act, Gov Code § 3300 et seq. Section 3307 allows police officers to refuse to submit to polygraph examination and prohibits discriminatory action for such refusal. See Long Beach City Emp Assoc v City of Long Beach 719 P2d 660, 667–68 (Cal 1986). See Note, Lie detectors in the workplace: the need for civil actions against employers, 101 Harv L Rev 806–825 (Feb 1988).

108. Ill Rev Stat ch 85 § 2564 (1989).

109. 480 US 709.

110. Id at 719.

111. Id at 719–20, 722.

112. Id at 723, 725.

113. Id at 726; see generally, LaFave, W R: Search and Seizure 2d ed Vol I § 2.4(b) (1987).

114. 480 US at 734.

115. In re application of John Ferone v Koehler 554 NYS2d 526 (AD I Dept 1990). In Cain v Larson 879 F2d 1424, 1427 (7th Cir 1989) cert den 110 SCt 540, the court rejected the view that the Uniform Peace Officers' Disciplinary Act provides a probationary officer with a property interest. Normally, a permanent police officer has a property right as a "permanent civil service employee," City of Philadelphia v Fraternal Order Lodge No 5 572 A2d 1298, 1302 (Pa Cmwlth 1990), app den 592 A2d 466 (1991); but see *contra,* City of Clinton v Loeffelholz 448 NW2d 308, 311 (Iowa 1989) ("a municipal police officer does not have an entitlement to that employment under state law").

116. Schuster v Thraen 532 FSupp 673, 677 (1982).

117. Major v DeFrench 286 SE2d 688, 698 (WVa 1982).

118. Paul v Davis 424 US 693, 712 (1976) and Codd v Velger 429 US 624 (1977).

119. Zavala v Arizona State Personnel Bd 766 P2d 608, 615 (Ariz App 1987).

120. Kupkowski v Board of Fire and Police Comrs 389 NE2d 219 (Ill 1979); Panozzo v Rhoads 905 F2d 135, 139 (7th Cir 1990) (even a written notice less than one day before hearing sufficient).

121. 389 NE 2d at 222. Ealey v Board of Fire & Police Comrs 544 NE2d 12, 16 (1989) app den 548 NE2d 1068 (1990) allegations of "acts of moral turpitude, neglect of duty, conduct unbecoming an officer, acts tending to discredit the police department, allowing unauthorized persons to ride in a squad car, acts of oppression and sexual harassment" held sufficient).

122. City of Philadelphia v Fraternal Order of Police, Lodge No 5 572 A2d 1298, 1302 (Pa Cmwlth 1990); app den 590 A2d 466 (1991) McDonald v McCarthy 1990 US Dist Lexis 11957 (1990 ED Pa) affd without op 932 F2d 960 (3rd Cir 1991), ("A hearing before biased individuals [The chief of police and the mayor] who have a personal interest in the outcome does not satisfy due process."

123. Swank v Smart 898 F2d 1247, 1255 (7th Cir 1990) cert den 111 SCt 147 (1990) (public officer was entitled to see and rebut witness' statement that was described by police chief at hearing).

124. City of Anderson v State of Indiana 397 NE2d 615 (Ind 1979).

125. Williams v Pima County 164 Ariz 170, 791 P2d 1053, 1055 (1989), cert den 111 SCt 441 (1990).

126. Law Enforcement Officers' Bill of Rights and Md Code Annot Art 27 § 727, and Public Safety Officers Procedural Bill of Rights Cal Code Annot Gov § § 3300 et seq; and § 2562 of the Uniform Peace Officer's Disciplinary Act, Ill Rev Stat § 2551 et seq (1989) where right to counsel is guaranteed. A violation of the LEOBR does not provide a basis for violation of constitu-

tional rights. Lolling v Patterson 1990 US Dist Lexis 18717 (CD Ill), p 15 n 2.

127. Ealey v Board of Fire & Police Comrs 544 NE2d 12, 17 (1989) app den 548 NE2d 1068 (1990), stating "the first step [in reviewing an administrative agency's decision] considers whether the findings were against the manifest weight of the evidence. In the second step, the court is to determine if the findings of fact provide a sufficient basis for the agency's conclusions that cause for discharge does exist."

128. In re Phillips 569 A2d 807 (1990) (criminal charge against police chief for DWI violation dismissed but chief demoted to patrolman after departmental hearing); Metropolitan Police Dept v Baker 564 A2d 1155, 1161 (DC App 1989) (charge as accomplice to wife's embezzlement dismissed but officer still subject to discharge).

129. Norton v City of Santa Ana 93 Cal Rptr 37, 40 (1971).

130. Braje v Bd of Fire & Police Comrs 487 NE2d 91, 95 (1985).

131. Williams v Pima County 791 P2d 1053, 1056 (1989), cert den 111 SCt 441 (1990).

132. Arizona Department of Public Safety v Dowd 573 P2d 497 (1978); Bishop v Law Enforcement Merit System Council 581 P2d 262, 266 (1978).

133. Kupkowski v Board of Fire and Police Commrs 389 NE2d 219, 224 (1979) (citations omitted); Metropolitan Police Dept v Baker 564 A2d 1155, 1159 (DC App 1989). But see In re Phillips 569 A2d 807, 813 (1990) where statute provides for new trial so that the hearing board's findings are "not controlling."

134. 5 USCA §§ 1101, 1201 (West Supp 1991).

135. Hoska v US Department of the Army 677 F2d 131, 135 (DC Cir 1982) (citations omitted).

136. 484 US 518.

137. Id at 529.

138. Id at 531.

139. Davenport v Board of Fire & Police Comrs 278 NE2d 212, 215 (1972); confirmed in Walsh v Bd of Fire & Police Comrs 449 NE2d 115, 117 (1983); court definitions of "just cause" are usually not very helpful; Philadelphia v Fraternal Order of Police, Lodge No 5 572 A2d 1298, 1302 (PaCmwlth 1990) (off-duty discharge of gun during altercation—"cause should be personal to the employee which renders him unfit for the position he occupies . . . "); Johnson v Welch 388 SE2d 284, 287 (WVa 1989) (just cause "restricted to something of a substantial nature affecting the rights and interest of the public"); See Swanson v Board of Police Comrs 555 NE2d 35 (Ill App 2 Dist 1990), app den 561 NE2d 708 (1990) (" 'cause' is defined as some substantial shortcoming, recognized by law, and sound public opinion as a good cause of termination, which renders the employee's continued employment detrimental to the discipline and efficiency of the service").

140. Civil Service Comn of City of Tucson v Livingston 525 P2d 949, 953–54 (1974), cert den Livingston v Civil Service Comn 421 US 951 (1975) (citations omitted).

141. Whisenhunt v Spradlin 464 US 965, 407 (1983), Justice Brennan dissenting (police officers in sexual relationship disciplined for violating regulation calling for "diligent and competent" performance of their duties).

142. White v County of Sacramento 183 Cal Rptr 520, 646 P2d 191, 195 (1982) (deputy sheriff reassigned from detective to patrol division because of alleged deficient performance not a demotion but merely "an intra-class assignment in a different position"); but see Batten v NC Dept of Correction 389 SE2d 35, 41 (NC 1990) (correctional lieutenant, who was "reallocated" to a lower grade when his facility was converted to another use, was entitled to contest the matter even though he suffered no loss in pay or benefits).

143. Derringer v Civil Service Comn 383 NE2d 771 (1978) (assistant warden transferred to another prison for political purposes entitled to reinstatement).

144. Mancke p 391, *supra* n 2.

145. 29 USCA § 621 et seq (1985); see generally, Cook, JG and Sobieski, jr, JL: Civil Rights Actions Vol 5, ch 22 Age discrimination in employment, New York, Matthew Bender 1990, and Larson, A and Larson, L: Employment Discrimination, Vol 3A, New York, Matthew Bender, 1990.

146. Equal Employment Opportunities Commission v Wyoming 460 US 239 (1983).

147. Employment Act Amendments of 1978 § 3, 92 Stat 189 (Supp IV 1980).

148. Larson and Larson, *supra* n 145 § 985.2.

149. 460 US 239 (1983). Notice provisions of the ADEA were discussed by the Court in Stevens v Dept of Treasury 111 SCt 1562 (1991).

150. 426 US 833 (1976).

151. See Garcia v San Antonio Metro Transit Authority 469 US 528(1985).

152. 427 US 307.

153. Id at 313.

154. Id at 314.

155. Id at 315.

156. 29 USCA § 623(i)(1990); § 622 provides for a joint study by the Secretary of Labor and EEOC to result within five years of "guidelines for the administration and use of physical and mental fitness tests to measure the ability and competency of police officers and firefighters to perform the requirements of their jobs."

157. 492 US 158

158. 29 USC § 623(f)(2) (1988).

159. Id at 166.

160. Id at 180.

161. Id at 182.

162. Id.

163. Id.

164. 5 USCA § 3307(d) (West Supp 1991).

165. Stewart v Smith 673 F2d 485, 495 (DDC 1982) (statute authorized exception to ADEA "to promote the 'youth and vigor' of the law enforcement profession"); see also Patterson v US Postal Service 901 F2d 927, 930 (11th Cir 1990) distinguishing *Johnson, infra* n 168. In Gilmer v Interstate/Johnson Lane

Corp 111 SCt 1647, 1657 (1991), the Court decided that companies could avoid employee claims under the ADEA by requiring employees, as a condition of employment, to enter into arbitration agreements as exclusive remedies.

166. Baker v Sears, Roebuck & Co 903 F2d 1515, 1519 (11th Cir 1990), but "unlike race or sex," age is a continuum along which the distinctions between employees are often subtle and relative ones. Thus, "a plaintiff's inability to show that she was replaced by someone under 40 is not an absolute bar to the establishment of a prima facie case" [citations omitted]. See Lorillard v Pons 434 US 575, 584 (1978), where the Court, in dicta, says "the prohibitions of the ADEA were derived [in the very words] from Title VII", approved in Trans World Airlines, Inc v Thurston 469 US 111, 121 (1985).

167. "A law enforcement officer or a firefighter who is otherwise eligible for immediate retirement under section 8336(c) of this title shall be separated from the service on the last day of the month in which he becomes 55 years of age or completes 20 years of service if then over that age. . . . " Title 5 USC § 8335(b) (1988).

168. Johnson v Mayor and City Council of Baltimore et al 472 US 353, 360 (1985).

169. Id at 370.

170. 472 US 414 (1985). Western Air Lines had a rule that flight engineers must retire at age 60. The company defended the rule on the basis of a BFOQ exception.

171. 472 US 414.

172. Id at 422–423 (emphasis in original). In EEOC v State of Tenn Wildlife Resources Agency 859 F2d 24, 26 (6th Cir 1988), cert den Tennessee Wildlife Resources Agency v EEOC 489 US 1066 (1989), state was unable to show that "physical and coronary fitness are reasonably necessary to the job" of wild life officer). BFOQ applies only to the job at issue, for example, police chief, and not to other jobs in the occupation, for example, street cops. As stated in EEOC v City of St Paul 671 F2d 1162, 1166 (8th Cir 1982) a state employer cannot "retire a police dispatcher because that person is too old to serve on a SWAT team." See also EEOC v Mississippi State Tax Comn 873 F2d 97, 99 (5th Cir 1989). For a good discussion, see Larson and Larson, *supra* n 145 at ch 21 § 100 16(c).

173. This distinction should be largely removed by the American with Disabilities Act of 1990, PL No 101-336 signed into law July 26, 1990, and scheduled to go into effect two years from that date. The law's purpose is "to provide a clear and comprehensive national mandate for the elimination of discrimination against individuals with disabilities." It covers both private and public (city, county and state, but not federal employees) and specifically waives the immunity defense.

174. Ill Rev Stat ch 108½ § 3-114.1 (1989); see also, Mich Compiled Laws 419.101 (1985), and Tenn Code Annot 7-51-201 (1990).

175. Swanson v Board of Police Comrs 555 NE2d 35, 46 app den 561 NE2d 708 (1990) (psychological problems prevented officer from returning to police work);

Williams v Policeman's & Fireman's Ret S 543 NYS2d 211 (AD 3 Dept 1989) (back injury result of prior conditions); Wall v Police Pension Board 533 NE2d 458, 463 (1988) (complaint of stress not unique to police officers); Anastasi v Civil Service Comn of Philadelphia 488 A2d 384, 387 (PaCmwlth 1988) (officer dismissed on the basis of medical finding of her mental instability); but where police officer is severely injured on duty and after treatment can fully return to duty, she cannot be discharged. Childress v Dept of Police 487 So2d 590 (La App), 592 cert den 489 So2d 918 (1986).

176. Walsh v Bd of Fire & Police Comrs 449 NE2d 115, 118 (1983). See Maffeo, Patricia A, Making non-discriminatory fitness-for-duty decisions about persons with disabilities under the Rehabilitation Act and the Americans with disabilities Act, 16 Amer J of Law & Medicine 279–326 (Fall 1990).

177. City of Pittsburg, Civ Serv Comn v SP Weger 505 A2d 398 (Pa Cmwlth 1986) (nodes on spine disqualifying applicant from police work); Brletic v Municipality of Monroeville 440 A2d 686 (Pa Cmwlth 1982) (weight tables upheld as valid bar to employ as police officer).

178. Tafoya v New Mexico State Police Board 472 P2d 973 (NM 1970); Myers v City of Oakdale 409 NW2d 848, 853 (Minn 1987) (citing *Tafoya*—similar fact situation but here veteran's preference statute entitled officer to hearing).

179. Pienta v Village of Schaumberg 536 FSupp 609, 612 (ED Ill 1982) affd 710 F2d 1258 (1983); an officer could not be discharged where his failure to take a urine test was preceded by a six year tour of duty as an undercover agent that left him disoriented and confused. Puig v McGuire 501 NYS2d 49, 51 (AD1 Dept 1986); Daley v Koch 892 F2d 212, 216 (2nd Cir 1989) (police applicant who is found to have "poor judgment, irresponsible behavior and poor impulse control" does not qualify as a handicapped person).

180. 920 F2d 1402 (8th Cir 1990), reh den en banc 1991 US App Lexis 2044 (1991).

181. 29 USCA § 701 et seq (West Supp 1991), and see comment on the Disabilities Act of 1990, supra n 173. For an exhaustive discussion, see Larson and Larson, supra n 145 at ch 22 § 106 et seq (1990).

182. See, for example, Illinois Human Rights Act Ill Rev Stat ch 68, § 1-101 et seq (1989).

183. 29 USCA § 701 (West Supp 1991).

184. Leckelt v Board of Comrs of Hosp Dist No 1 909 F2d 820, 825–26 (5th Cir 1990).

185. Note, Facial discrimination: Extended handicap law and employment discrimination on the basis of physical appearance," 100 Harv L Rev 2035, 2043 (1987).

186. 29 USCA § 706(8)(B)(1990); the accompanying regulations are found at 29 CFR 1613.701 et seq (1990). See School Board of Nassau Cty v Arline 480 US 273 (1987), and Note, "The Rehabilitation Act of 1973: Focusing the definition of a handicapped individual," 30 Wm and Mary L Rev 149–179 (1988).

187. Larson and Larson, *supra* n 145 at § 106.14(a), and Harv L Rev *supra* n 185 at 2044.

188. 29 USCA § § 794, 791(b) (West Supp 1991).

189. 29 CFR 1613.702(f) (1990).

190. 29 USC § 794a(1)(2) (1988).

191. Id § 721(a)(13)(B).

192. 480 US 273 (1987).

193. Id at 284–85 (emphasis in original).

194. Id at 288.

195. Id.

196. 840 F2d 1139 (3rd Cir 1988), cert den 490 US 1004 (1989).

197. Id at 1149. See also Desper v Montgomery County 727 FSupp 959, 963 (ED Pa 1990) (police narcotics undercover officer who used drugs "violates the laws he or she is sworn to uphold" and therefore is not entitled to his job back after resigning).

198. 720 FSupp 1424 (ND Cal 1989), affd without op Nisperos v McNary 936 F2d 579 (9th Cir 1991).

199. But see Salmon Pineiro v Lehman 653 FSupp 483, 493 (D Puerto Rico 1987) (Navy criminal investigator who has epilepsy "cannot meet all of the position's requirements. . . . "); and Duran v City of Tampa, 451 FSupp 954 (MD FLA 1978) denial of employment to a police applicant who has a childhood history of epilepsy but who is otherwise fit would be a violation of his equal protection rights under the Rehabilitation Act of 1973, 29 USC § 701 et seq.

200. Larson and Larson, *supra* n 145 at ch 22 § 107.30 et seq where several examples are given.

201. 417 NE2d 260.

202. Belleville, Bd of Police and Fire Comrs v Human Rights Comr 522 NE2d 268, 272; app den 530 NE 2d 241 (1988).

203. O'Hare v New York City Police Dept 555 NYS2d 753 (AD 1 Dept 1990).

204. FEP § 405:1-2 Labor Relations Rptr BNA (1990). The 1988 memorandum was a reversal one in 1986 that came to the opposite conclusion on the basis of the *Arline* decision. See Connolly, Walter B, Jr and Marshall, Alison B, An employer's legal guide to AIDS in the workplace, 9 St. Louis University L Rev 561, 565 (1990).

205. Id at § 421:675. See Raytheon v Fair Emp Housing Comr 261 Cal Rptr 197, 203 (Cal App 2 Dist 1989) ("there can be no doubt that AIDS is a physical handicap").

206. 740 FSupp 815, 818 (ND Ala 1987). See also Feigley v Fulcomer 720 FSupp 475 (MD Pa 1989) (inmate's demand that all incoming prisoners be tested for AIDS rejected because AIDS not transmitted on casual contact and prison has policy against sex between inmates). The National Institute of Justice provides intermittent updates on AIDS as it affects criminal justice. See Hammett, TM, and Moini, S, "Update on AIDS in Prisons and Jails," AIDS Bulletin Sept 1990. As of October 1989, there were 3,661 AIDS cases among inmates in the 45 state/federal correctional systems reporting. Id at p 2.

207. 734 FSupp 765, 768 (ND Tex 1990).

208. 909 F2d 820 (5th Cir 1990).

209. Doe v Ball 725 FSupp 1210, 1216–17 (MD Fla 1989) affd Doe v Garrett 903 F2d 1455 (11 Cir), cert den 111 SCt 1102 (1990) (Navy regulation that denies extended active duty to personnel testing HIV positive precludes expectation of property interest, and Rehabilitation Act not applicable to Navy personnel).

210. SP4 John Doe v Marsh 1990 US Dist Lexis 1442.

211. 727 FSupp 1564 (MD Ala 1990). Present trends, however, are away from segregation toward "mainstreaming" AIDS-infected inmates, that is, maintaining them in the general inmate population. Hammett and Moini, *supra* n 206 at 8.

212. 727 FSupp at 1572. See also Roe v Fauver 1988 US Dist Lexis 4272 (DC NJ) (female inmate with AIDS in remission could be assigned to hospital room, and although she is in effect in solitary confinement, and male inmates in a similar situation have a special facility, taking into consideration that a prison is in process of being built for women, such deprivation does not violate her eighth amendment rights); and Farmer v Moritsugu 742 FSupp 525 (WD Wis 1990) (inmate testing HIV positive was properly restricted from working in prison food service because "security and order are threatened by the inmates' fear of the transmittal of the disease and their actions based on this fear"); but see Wilson v Franceschi 735 FSupp 395 (MD Fla 1990) (unexplained six month delay in responding to AIDS sufferer's demand for a drug, AZT to help remit his illness enough to sustain claim of deliberate indifference).

213. 729 FSupp 376 (D NJ 1990). The mere fact that most AIDS plaintiffs sue anonymously dramatically testifies to the problem. See also Doe v Hirsch 731 FSupp 627 (SD NY 1990) (police officers who came in contact with blood of HIV-infected victim filed § 1983 action to declare law unconstitutional which made information about AIDS blood tests confidential).

214. 729 FSupp at 384.

215. 267 Cal Rptr 666 (Cal App Dist 1990).

216. Id at 683.

217. 867 F2d 461 (8th Cir 1989), cert den 110 SCt 321 (1989).

218. 867 F2d at 464. Some of the legal and public policy questions involved tests for AIDS and other tests to which employees are increasingly being subjected are discussed in Bible, Jon D, When employers look for things other than drugs: the legality of AIDS, genetic, intelligence, and honesty testing in the workplace, 41 Labor L J 195–213 (April 1990).

219. Parker v Levy 417 US 733 (1974). But see City of North Muskegan et al v Briggs 473 US 909 (1985) where Justice White dissented from a denial of certiorari. Although the officer was charged with "conduct unbecoming" because he lived with a woman not his wife, the issue was right to privacy and not vagueness. See Briggs v North Muskegon Police Dept 563 FSupp 585 (WD Mich 1983) affd without op 746 F2d 1475 (6th Cir 1984).

220. In Zeber's Appeal 156 A2d 821, 825 (1959); Kramer v City of Bethlehem 289 A2d 767 (Pa Cmwlth 1972); Fugate v Phoenix Civil Service Bd 791 F2d 736,

742 (9th Cir 1986) ("conduct unbecoming an officer and contrary to the general orders of the police department," while admittedly vague, is clearly intended to protect the legitimate interests of the department from potentially damaging behavior of the department's officers); Flanagan v Munger 890 F2d 1557, 1569 (10th Cir 1989) (such vague phases are "unavoidable").

221. Davenport v Board of Fire and Police Comrs 278 NE2d 212, 216 (1972) (citations omitted); slightly modified in Kloss v Bd of Fire & Police Comrs, etc 438 NE2d 685, 689 (1982) (citing *Davenport*, "The infraction can be a factor in determining whether . . . it constitutes statutory cause for dismissal").

222. Clark, P: Homosexual public employees: Utilizing section 1983 to remedy discrimination, 8 Hastings Const Law Q 255, 284–5 (1981); Jones, Marsha, Comment, When private morality becomes public concern: homosexuality and public employment, 24 Houston L Rev 519–547 (May 1987); Sexual orientation and the Law, 102 Harv L Rev 1508, 1560 (1989).

223. Hastings Const L Q, p 284, *supra* n 218. See generally, Larson and Larson, supra ch 23 § 109, *supra* n 145.

224. Duke, Lynne, The military's final labor lingers in the closet, Washington Post National Weekly ed Aug 26–Sept 1, 1991, p 31, 32, According to interviews with high defense department officials, no change in their policy toward homosexuals is contemplated. Id. Harvard L Rev p. 1554, *supra* n 222.

225. Douglas, J A: "I sit and look out: Employment discrimination against homosexuals and the new law of unjust dismissal," 33 Wash U J Urb & Contemp L J 73, 103 (1988).

226. Generally state Human Rights statutes do not protect sexual preference, but see California Civil Code § 51.7 wherein "sexual orientation" is defined as "heterosexuality, homosexuality or bisexuality."

227. 486 US 592.

228. Id at 594. The same reasoning with reference to nonreviewability of terminations for lesbianism was used for an FBI termination in Padula v Webster 822 F2d 97 (DC Cir 1987).

229. 478 US 186.

230. 871 F2d 1068 (Fed Cir), cert den 110 SCt 1295 (1990).

231. 871 F2d at 1070.

232. Id at 1076. To same affect, see High Tech Gays v Defense Ind Secur Clearance Off 895 F2d 563, 571 (9th Cir), reh den, en banc 909 F2d 375 (1990) (Department of Defense employee discharged for homosexuality—suspect category rejected. Constitution confers no fundamental right to engage in homosexual sodomy). But where a homosexual soldier was allowed to reenlist over a period of 14 years, even though the Army had a rule precluding homosexuals from enlisting, equity requires the Army be estopped from refusing to accept the reenlistment. Watkins v US Army 875 F2d 699, 711 (9th Cir 1989), concurring judge, on an equal protection theory, finds homosexuals to be a suspect class (at 728), cert den 111 SCt 384 (1990). See also Doe v Sparks 733 FSupp 227, 234 (WD Pa 1990) (prison policy of barring a female lover of a homosexual female prisoner is a

violation of her equal protection rights: "the asserted goal of maintaining internal security and safety of inmates is so remote as to be arbitrary"); but see Endsly v Naes 673 FSupp 1032, 1038 (D Kan 1987) where sheriff's road deputy, a lesbian, was involved in a fight with the husband of her lover to which police were called; she often rode in lover's police car when plaintiff was off-duty; in discharging her, the department "acted to protect the public image of the Department and to maintain close working relationships internally and externally with the community."

233. 866 F2d 1114 (9th Cir 1989).

234. 905 F2d 389, 400 (DC Cir 1990).

235. 905 Fed at 400 (emphasis in original). Dissenting in Reed v Collyen 487 US 1225, 1226 (1988) cert den Justice Scalia argued for granting certiorari in order to "begin the necessary process of limiting *Webster* to its facts," that is, to eliminate the chance of constitutional challenge to national security employment disciplinary decisions.

236. Ashton v Civiletti 613 F2d 923.

237. 417 F2d 1161 (DC Cir 1969) (civil servant cannot be discharged for homosexual activity unless related to job performance).

238. 63 FRD 399 (ND Cal 1973).

239. Civil Service Bulletin Dec 21 1973.

240. 613 F2d at 927.

241. Id at 928.

242. Safransky v State Personnel Board 215 NW2d 379 (1974). And see Childers v Dallas Police Department 513 FSupp 134, 140 (ND Tex 1981) (department could rationally conclude that homosexuality of officer would interfere with its function), Etscheid v Police Board of Chicago 47 Ill App2d 124, 197 NE2d 484 (1964) (discharge of police officer appearing in public attired in women's undergarments upheld); and Sommers v Iowa Civil Rights Comn 337 NW2d 470, 471, 476 (Ia 1983) (transsexual, anatomically male, but emotionally female, hired to do clerical work, can be discharged without violating state civil rights statute); Ealey v Bd of Fire & Police Comrs 544 NE2d 12, 17 (Ill App 5 Dist 1989), app den 548 NE2d 1068 (1990) (female police officer who allowed female lover, also police officer to operate squad car while intoxicated, used police phone for personal calls; both rode in squad car while only one was on duty, could be discharged).

243. Franscell, G J: "Legal protection for those with alternative lifestyles," The Police Chief 33 (Sept 1989).

244. Padula v Webster 822 F2d 97, 98 (DC Cir 1987). See also Childress v Dallas Police Department 513 FSupp 134, 142 (ND Tex 1981) (applicant patrol officer, admitted homosexual, "will undoubtedly foment controversy and conflict within the department . . . [and] the concern of the police department to protect its public image and to avoid ridicule and embarrassment [justify] refusal . . . to hire. . . . ").

245. 822 F2d at 100. This point, of course, is the same one raised later in Webster v Doe, *supra* n 228.

246. 822 F2d at 101.
247. 726 F2d 459 (9th Cir 1983); likewise Briggs v North Muskegon Police Dept 563 FSupp 585, 591 (WD Mich 1983), affd 746 F2d 1475 (1984) (no evidence that police officer who lived with married woman "flaunted" the relationship). For earlier cases, see Annotation, "Sexual misconduct or irregularity as amounting to 'conduct unbecoming an officer,' justifying officer's demotion or removal or suspension from duty, 9 ALR4th 614 (1981).
248. 726 F2d at 471.
249. Duckworth v Sayad 670 SW2d 88, 92 (MoApp 1984).
250. Shawgo v Spradlin 701 F2d 470, 483 (5th Cir 1983) cert den Whisenhunt v Spradlin 464 US 965, 971 (1983) in which Justice Brennan, in his dissent argues that such "lawful, off-duty sexual conduct clearly implicates 'the fundamental . . . right to be free . . . from unwanted governmental intrusions into one's privacy."
251. Fugate v Phoenix Civil Service Bd 791 F2d 736, 742 (9th Cir 1986) (on-duty sex with prostitutes carried on "openly and publicly"); Kazmarek v New Bethlehem Borough Council 478 A2d 514, 517 (Pa Cmwlth 1984) (police chief made "improper remarks and request to three female members of the community").
252. Matter of Raynes 698 P2d 856, 861 (Mont 1985) (officer sexually molested patients he had hypnotized); Matula v City of Omaha 390 NW2d 500, 503 (Neb 1986) (officer attempted to rape police civilian employee at private party).
253. Faust v Police Civil Service Comn 317 A2d 765 (Pa 1975).
254. Id at 768.
255. Id.
256. Civil Service Comn of Tucson v Livingston 525 P2d 949 (1974); cert den Livingston v Civil Service Com 421 US 951 (1975). see also Warren v State Personnel Board 156 Cal Rptr 351 (Cal App 1979) (police officer dismissed for participating in transvestite party and lying about it to superior officers. In upholding the dismissal, the court found the "critical question" to be not whether the officer's "conduct violated the morals of the public or of the Highway Patrol, but whether such conduct indicates an unfitness for employment with the Highway Patrol."
257. Fabio v Civil Service Comn of City of Philadelphia 414 A2d 82 (Pa 1980).
258. 470 FSupp 449, 461 (ED Pa 1979) And see Major v Hampton 413 FSupp 66 (ED La 1976) (off-duty extra-marital sexual acts of Internal Revenue Service agent no basis for discharge where acts brought no discredit on service).
259. 470 FSupp at 454.
260. Id at 459.
261. Swope v Bratton 541 FSupp 99, 108 (WD Ark 1982).
262. Id at 108.
263. Risner v State Personnel Board of Review 381 NE2d 346, 350 (1978).
264. Willis v Willis 454 So2d 429, 431 (La App 3 Cir 1984).
265. About 4,000 sex harassment complaints are annually filed with the EEOC; 90%

of large corporations receive such complaints. Surveys show that up to 50% of American working women experience employment-related sexual harassment at some time in their careers. Larson and Larson *supra* n 145, Vol I Supp June 1991 p 8–159. The first case to recognize sexual harassment as a form of gender discrimination was Williams v Saxbe 413 FSupp 654 (DDC 1976), rev sub nom 587 F2d 1240 (DC Cir 1978). See Sperry, M: "Hostile environment sexual harassment and the imposition of liability without notice: a progressive approach to traditional gender roles and power based relationships," 24 New England L Rev 917 (1990).

266. Larson and Larson *supra* 145 at § 41.60.

267. 447 US 57 (1986).

268. Id at 78.

269. Id at 67 (emphasis added).

270. Id at 72.

271. Huebschen v Dept of Health & Social Services 716 F2d 1167, 1172 (7th Cir 1983).

272. 2CFR Ch XIV § 1604.11(a) Sexual harassment (7-1-90 ed).

273. Andrews v City of Philadelphia 895 F2d 1469, 1482 (3rd Cir 1990).

274. 915 F2d 777 (1st Cir 1990).

275. Id at 783.

276. Id at 786.

277. 890 F2d 569 (2nd Cir 1989).

278. Id at 579; see also Steele v Offshore Shipbuilding, Inc 867 F2d 1311, 1316 (11th Cir), reh den en banc 874 F2d 821 (1989).

279. Staton v Maries Cty 868 F2d 996, 998 (8th Cir 1989). See also *Andrews* 895 F2d at 1482.

280. Andrews v City of Philadelphia 895 F2d 1469, 1486 (3rd Cir 1990).

281. Lynch v City of DesMoines 454 NW2d 827, 834 (IA 1990). But where she "was a willing and welcome participant" in such sexual on-duty innuendo, such conduct was fatal to her claim. Reed v Shepard 939 F2d 484 (7th Cir 1991).

282. Watts v New York City Police Dept 724 FSupp 99, 104 (SD NY 1989). See Annotation, When is work environment intimidating, hostile or offensive, so as to constitute sexual harassment in violation of Title VII of CRA of 1964, as amended (42 USCS §§ 2000e et seq), 78 ALRFed 252 (1986); and Annotation, Sex discrimination in law enforcement and corrections employment, 53 ALRFed 31 (1981).

283. 720 FSupp 974, 977–78 (SD Fla 1989). See also Andrews v City of Philadelphia 895 F2d 1469, 1486 (3rd Cir 1990); Bennett v New York City Dept of Corrections 705 FSupp 979, 981 (SD NY 1989); Lynch v City of Des Moines 454 NW2d 827 (Ia 1990); and Bohen v City of East Chicago, Ind 799 F2d 1180, 1188 (7th Cir 1986).

284. 720 FSupp at 977.

285. 672 FSupp 261 (ND Tex 1987).

286. Id at 273.

287. Bennett v New York City Dept of Corrections 705 FSupp 979, 986–87 (SD NY 1989).

288. Bohen v City of East Chicago, Ind 799 F2d 1180, 1188 (7th Cir 1986).

289. Andrews v City of Philadelphia 895 F2d 1469, 1486 (3rd Cir 1990). See Annotation, sexual advances by employee's superior as sex discrimination within Title VII of Civil Rights Act of 1964, as amended 46 ALR Fed 224 (1980); Blake v City of Chicago 1991 US Dist Lexis 2918, p 8 (ND Ill) (termination of sexually harassed plaintiff by superintendent of police is ratification of such conduct and results in superintendent's liability; and Brooms v Regal Tube Co 881 F2d 412 (7th Cir 1989) (employer liable for sexual harassment engaged in by their supervising employee where employer knew of his actions but failed to take remedial measures); Gilardi v Schroeder 833 F2d 1226 (7th Cir 1987) (Title VII claim against employer who sexually harassed, raped and discharged employee); Board of Directors, Green Hills Country Club v Illinois Human Rights Comm 514 NE2d 1227 (Ill 1987) (employers are strictly liable under state law for actions of their supervisory personnel).

290. 916 F2d 572, 576–79 (10th Cir 1990).

291. Watts v New York City Police Dept 724 FSupp 99, 106, (SDNY 1989); but Sanchez v City of Miami Beach 720 FSupp 974, 979 (SD Fla 1989) found that although the city and department issued policy statements, no "meaningful steps" were taken to disseminate them, to train officers, or to discipline anyone pursuant to the policy.

292. Id at 108–9.

293. Bohen v City of East Chicago, Ind 799 F2d 1180, 1188–89 (7th Cir 1986). [T]he legal elements of a section 1983 claim and a Title VII disparate treatment claim are identical; for both the plaintiff must prove intentional discrimination." Jordan v Wilson 649 FSupp 1038, 1045 (MD Ala 1986).

294. Woerner v Brzeczek 519 FSupp 517, 26 FEP 897 (ND Ill 1981).

295. Washington v Civil Service Comn of Evanston 423 NE2d 1136, 1142 (1981) (penalty of 29-day suspension for proposing sex to female prisoner in exchange for release found "unduly harsh" and reduced to 5 days); but after a second such incident, this time involving a female motorist, Washington was discharged, Washington v Civil Service Comr of Evanston 496 NE2d 1109 (Ill App 1986). Altman v Board of Fire and Police Comrs 442 NE2d 305, 307 (1982) (officer suspended one day for passing finger over female civilian police employee's back after earlier objections to similar incidents); but see Robinson v Cook County Police & Corrections Merit Board 436 NE2d 617, 622 (1982) (deputy sheriff, who had been earlier found guilty of driving while intoxicated, discharged for attempting to solicit "sexual favors" in exchange for a "pass" on traffic tickets).

296. 549 A2d 631 (Vt 1988).

297. Id at 636. See also Roberts v Greiner 386 SE2d 504 (WVa 1989) (sheriff's deputy terminated because of attempts over five year period to use official position to obtain sexual favors); Howard v Dept of Air Force 877 F2d 952, 956 (Fed Cir 1989) (removed from position for harassing female co-workers. Govern-

ment must establish same proof in disciplinary actions for sexual harassment as necessary in establishing sexual harassment); Buckner v City of
Highland Park 901 F2d 491, 497 (6th Cir 1990), cert den 111 SCt 137 (officer
grabbed and attempted to fondle complainant at her apartment properly
discharged), but see Zavala v Arizona State Personnel Bd 766 P2d 608 (Ariz
1987), where dismissal for sexual harassment was overturned because of
procedural irregularities, including failure to provide proper notice.

298. Order 12,564 Fed Reg 32, 889, 28 CFR 550 (1986).
299. 41 USCA § 702 (1990).
300. 489 US 656 (1989).
301. 489 US 602 (1989).
302. Id at 628.
303. Id at 634.
304. 489 US at 679.
305. 884 F2d 603 (DC Cir 1989), cert den 110 SCt 864 (1990).
306. Id at 610.
307. Id at 613.
308. Id.
309. Id at 614.
310. Id at 615. See also Hartness v Bush 919 F2d 170 (App DC 1990), cert den 111
     SCt 2890 (1991) (employees of Executive Office of the President with
     "secret" national security clearances could be randomly tested for drugs
     based on earlier approval of testing "Top Secret" employees, Harmon v
     Thornburg 878 F2d 484 (DC Cir 1989) cert den Bell v Thornburgh 488 US
     934 (1990). National Treasury Employees Union v Yeutter 918 F2d 968
     (App DC 1990) (US Department of Agriculture motor vehicle operators
     subject to random testing for drugs reasonable because of "obvious safety
     interests," but as to other employees, "the government may search its
     employees only when a clear, direct nexus exists between the nature of the
     employee's duty and the nature of the feared violation" and no such nexus
     was here made); Thomson v Marsh 884 F2d 113 (4th Cir 1989) (civilian
     Army employees working with highly lethal chemical warfare agents rea-
     sonably required to take random drug tests because of diminished expecta-
     tions of privacy and government's compelling interest in the safety of the
     workplace); and Willner v Thornburgh 928 F2d 485, 1193 (DC Cir 1991)
     (attorney applying for Justice Department's Anti-Trust Division has a
     "significantly diminished" right to privacy, and could be required to take
     urine test to qualify for employment even in the absence of individualized
     suspicion). For some earlier cases that found drug testing as applied to
     criminal justice personnel unconstitutional, see Annotation, Validity, under
     federal constitution, of regulations rules, or statutes requiring random or
     mass drug testing of public employees or persons whose employment is
     regulated by state, local, or federal government 86 ALR Fed 420 (1988).
311. 799 P2d 953 (Hawaii 1990).
312. Id at 958.

313. Id.

314. Id at 959. See also O'Connor v Police Comr of Boston 557 NE2d 1146 (Mass 1990) (compelling interest in police department to test to determine by random urine test if police cadet taking academy training was using drugs); Seelig v Koehler 556 NE2d 125 (NY), cert den 111 SCt 134 (1990) (random drug testing for correctional officers reasonable in that "by choosing to work in the paramilitary milieu of the City Correction Department, guards voluntarily sacrifice certain cherished freedoms"); McKenzie v Jackson 557 NYS2d 265 (Ct App 1990) (probationary corrections officer could be randomly tested on the basis of "a serious drug abuse problem among a significant number of its members"); but see Taylor v O'Grady 888 F2d 1189, 1201 (7th Cir 1989) (sheriff's correctional employees subjected to random annual mandatory urine testing program not applicable to employees who have (1) no regular access to inmate populations; (2) no reasonable opportunity to smuggle-in drugs; and (3) no access to firearms); Matter of Carberry 556 A2d 314 (NJ 1989) (Well-Trooper program to detect cardiac deficiencies, including narcotic testing without trooper's knowledge, reasonable; Annapolis v United Food & Commercial Workers 565 A2d 672, 682 (Md 1989) (urinalysis test as part of regularly scheduled physical upheld against argument that no on-duty impairment was shown); and Policeman's Benev Assn of NJ v Washington 850 F2d 133, 141 (3rd Cir 1988), cert den 490 US 1004 (1989) (strong statement that "police officers are members of quasi-military organizations" and "intensely regulated" and subject to random drug testing). But see Jeanette A v Condon 728 FSupp 204, 206 (SD NY 1990) where a police officer whose urine tested positive for cocaine during her participation in the department's alcohol counseling program could not thereby be discharged because 42 USC § 290dd-3 prohibits disclosure of patient's records in a federally-assisted program.

315. Rogers v Director of Labor 767 SW2d 319 (Ark App 1989); Metropolitan Police Dept v Baker 564 A2d 1155 (DC App 1989) (as police officer he should have known that his wife was embezzling the money used to purchase new car and other expensive items).

316. Kinter v Board of Fire and Police Comrs 550 NE2d 1126 (Ill App 1990); McDowell v Koehler 553 NYS2d 116 (NY App 1990) (convicted of petty larceny and failed to notify department).

317. Laborde v Alexandria Municipal Fire & Civil Service Bd 566 So2d 426 (La App) cert den 568 So2d 1055 (1990). Minneapolis v Moe 450 NW2d 367 (Minn App 1990) (possession of cocaine enough to merit discharge even though Moe had "exemplary record"); Wayering v County of St Lawrence 546 NYS2d 258 (NY App Div 1989) (purchased alcohol for person under drinking age).

318. Ealey v Board of Fire & Police Comrs 544 NE2d 12 (Ill App 1989), app den 548 NE2d 1068 (1990).

319. Kvidera v Board of Fire & Police Comrs 549 NE2d 747 (Ill App 1 Dist 1989) (assisted in the composition of a letter that alleged marital infidelity of the

husband of a candidate for the school board, and thereafter attempted to impede police investigation of the incident); Odell v Village of Hoffman Estates 443 NE2d 247, 251 (1982) (civilian police radio dispatcher who disclosed information about arrested juveniles to outsiders properly discharged); Tuzzio v Ward 554 NYS2d 227 (App Div 1990) (officer made personal use of department's computer system and failed to safeguard printout of confidential information); Doe v Borough of Barrington 729 FSupp 376 (D NJ 1990) (officer who disclosed to others that person he arrested had AIDS was liable to injured party).

320. Boyce v Ward 551 NYS2d 7 (AD 1 Dept 1990) (officers solicited oral sex at massage parlor; when rebuffed went on drunken rampage with other officers); Bultas v Board of Fire & Police Comrs 524 NE2d 1172, app den 530 NE2d 239 (1988) (kicked female prisoner); Bolster v Carboy 451 NYS2d 909 (1st Dist Ill 1988) (deputy sheriff who, after a prison disturbance, opened up all windows in cell block in 0° weather, and then returned to warm office, could be discharged); Savoie v State Dept of Corrections 394 So2d 1285 (La App 1981) (juvenile officer discharged on disciplinary charge of beating juvenile escapees, even though acquitted on criminal charges).

321. Putz v Civil Service Comm 557 A2d 458 (Pa Cmwlth 1989) app den 577 A2d 546 (1990); City of Philadelphia Fraternal Order of Police 572 A2d 1298 (Pa Commw 1990), app den 592 A2d 46 (1991) (officer entered bar with gun exposed, confronted bar owner and gun discharged); City of Jackson, Miss v Froshour 530 So2d 1348 (Miss 1988) (officer who struck handcuffed prisoner repeatedly apparently because of way prisoner treated his own wife); In re application of Sean O'Brien 555 NYS 2d 764 (App Div 1990) (punched, choked and placed gun to head of person detained for investigatory stop); Vacchio v Ward 554 NYS2d 523 (App NY 1990) app den 555 NYS 2d 983 (in response to complaint that person was threatened with gun, officer exited police car with gun in hand, and in apparent accident shot and killed unarmed civilian).

322. Kupkowski v Board of Fire & Police Comrs 389 NE2d 219 (IllApp 1979); see also Foran v Murphy 342 NYS2d 4 (1973), and Freyre v Ward 555 NYS2d 102 (App Div 1990) (lied while under oath at suppression of evidence proceeding).

323. O'Malley v Bd of Fire & Police Comrs 538 NE2d 888 (Ill App 1 Dist 1989); Holcomb v City of Los Angeles 259 Cal Rptr 1 (2d App Dist 1989) (failed to respond promptly to lieutenant's radio call to return to station—because of other infractions, 30 day suspension); Rouse v City of Birmingham 535 So2d 167 (Ala Cir App 1988) (police captain, involved in on-duty auto accident improperly placed himself on injury with pay status although able to work); O'Connor v Oakland County Sheriff's Dept 426 NW2d 816 (Mich App 1988) (when bartender ordered officer out of bar because officer was found having oral sex in men's room, officer threatened to arrest bartender for traffic violation).

324. Swanson v The Board of Police Comrs 555 NE2d 35 (Ill App) app den 561

NE2d 708 (1990). Civil Service Comm of West Miflin v Vargo 553 A2d 102 (Pa Commw 1989) (officer suspended for five days for leaving keys in police car which was eventually stolen and wrecked); Emmons v City of Miamisburg 1989 Ohio App Lexis 1224 (demoted from lieutenant to sergeant for unfairly criticizing employees; making sarcastic and profane remarks over radio and the like); Eberhart v Ward 555 NYS2d 329 (App Div 1990) (failed to conduct proper investigation). In a justly famous incident, Milwaukee officers were dismissed for failing to investigate an instance in which a bleeding, naked 14-year-old Laotian immigrant boy, complained to them of a beating by Jeffrey Dahmer who later confessed to multiple killings, including the boy, who was killed shortly after the officers ignored his plea. New York Times, Sept 8, 1991, p 12.

325. Fraternal Order of Police v City of Evansville 559 NE2d 607 (Ind 1990) (regulation restricting off-duty employment where alcoholic beverages sold or consumed valid); Allison v City of Southfield 432 NW2d 369, 374 (Mich App 1988) (denial of right of officer to engage in business of private investigation upheld against attack of vagueness); but see Dale v City of Phillipsburg 1989 US Dist Lexis 11622, p 24 (suspension of police officer for consuming two beers while attending a ball game cannot be sustained "simply because of general community disapproval of the protected conduct").

326. 424 US 645 (1976).

327. Id at 646. See Albrechta v Borough of Shickshinny 565 A2d 198 app den 577 A2d 891 (1990) (police chief of three-person force could be terminated due to his refusal to relocate in Borough). *McCarthy* was favorably referred to in Martinez v Bynum 461 US 321, 326 N 5 (1983) and noted in United & Contr Trades v Mayor 465 US 208, 219 (1984). See Ferguson v Board of Police Comrs 782 SW2d 814 (1990) (police officer terminated for violation of residence regulation).

328. Wadman v City of Omaha 438 NW2d 749 (Neb 1989) (even if disagreement with punishment meted out to subordinates is opposed in good faith, chief of police who willfully refused to sign the dismissal notices as directed by safety director is insubordinate and is properly discharged); Guarino v Dept of Social Welfare 410 A2d 425, 428 (1980) (youth home supervisor left home after being ordered to remain); Watts v Civil Service Board 606 SW2d 274 (1980), cert den 450 US 983 (1981) (police officer who pursued prosecution after dismissal by prosecutor and appeared before grand jury instead of presenting evidence to detective bureau after order to proceed through department, could be fired); and Department of Corrections v Cage 418 So2d 3 (La App) cert den 422 So2d 164 (1982) (tower guard discharged for defying order to report for work on election day).

329. See Note, Harley v Schuykill County—Section 1983 protects a "new" constitutional right to privacy from an "old" duty, 1980 Utah L Rev 617, 476 FSupp 191 (ED Pa 1979).

330. 476 FSupp at 193.

331. Id at 194.

332. Id (emphasis in original).

333. Id (emphasis in original).

334. 425 P2d 223 (Cal 1967).

335. 425 P2d at 234, Emphasis in Utah L Rev 620–21, *supra* n 329. See also Belmont v California State Personnel Board 111 Cal Rptr 607 (1974) (upholding five day suspension for state-employed psychiatric social workers for willful disobedience of a lawful order to furnish patient information for computer files), and Petermann v Teamsters Local, 174 Cal App2d 184, 344 P2d 25 (1959) (employer had instructed employee to give false testimony at legislative hearing; firing when he refused found to be against public policy) and, Vaughn, Public employees and the right to disobey, 29 Hastings LJ 261, 285 (1977).

Chapter 7

FIRST AMENDMENT RIGHTS OF
CRIMINAL JUSTICE PERSONNEL

Introductory remarks

This chapter will discuss the place of freedom of expression in the spectrum of rights of US citizens, the specific applications of that right to criminal justice personnel, and their right to express themselves, both inside and outside their organizations, including their right to engage in political activity. This chapter also illustrates the use to which criminal justice personnel may put civil rights § 1983 (see chapter 1) in assertion of these rights. Almost all first amendment cases filed by criminal justice personnel employ this section. First amendment issues, as applied to criminal justice personnel, raise the following kinds of questions: Do criminal justice employees lose any first amendment rights they would otherwise have as citizens because of their public employment? Should criminal justice personnel be treated like other public employees in terms of first amendment rights, or should special rules apply to them related to the nature of their employment? Which principle should dominate public employment: that of private employment—that employers may discipline or discharge their employees at will, or first amendment principles that citizens should be free to say what they will, subject to certain post-speech penalties for defamation or criminal behavior? Discipline and discharges resulting from the use of free speech by criminal justice employees may be seen as a special case of arbitrary dismissal discussed in chapter 6.

The Supreme Court, after a period of non-attention to first amendment rights of public employees, stretching from the feudal-like concept exemplified by *McAuliffe* (see chapter 5), through the stifling McCarthyite 1950s, finally, in 1968, arrived at a rather unsatisfactory balancing test—balancing interests of the state ("society") against those of the individual. That case, Pickering v Board of Education,[1] involving the first amendment rights of a high school teacher, has spawned numbers of cases, some of which have supported first amendment rights and others that have denied them. Because by the nature of the Pickering rule, the "balancing" of interests is done after the fact, such an approach is bound to have a chilling effect on the free speech rights of government employees, who in 1980 numbered almost 17% of the civilian labor force.[2] Restriction of first amendment rights of such a large portion of the population, and a part so intimately and actively involved in the political life of the country, cannot fail to have serious consequences on the ability of citizens to learn of and to take corrective action against arbitrary and wrongful governmental acts, a major reason for the ratification of the amendment in the first place.

The first amendment and its place in democratic society

Thomas I. Emerson, a Yale law professor, and a leading interpreter of the first amendment, opens his discussion of freedom of expression with the following statement:

> A system of freedom of expression, operating in a modern democratic society, is a complex mechanism. At its core is a group of rights assured to individual members of the society. This set of rights, which makes up our present-day concept of free expression, includes the right to form and hold beliefs and opinions, and information through any medium—in speech, writing, music, art, or in other ways. To some extent it involves the right to remain silent. From the obverse side it includes the right to hear the views of others and to listen to their version of the facts. It encompasses the right to inquire, and to a degree, the right of access to information. As a necessary corollary, it embraces the right to assemble and to form associations, that is, to combine with others in joint expression.[3]

Emerson suggests that freedom of expression rests on four premises:

1. It is essential as a means of assuring individual fulfillment.
2. It is an essential process for advancing knowledge and discovering truth.
3. It is essential to provide for participation in decision-making by all members of society.
4. It is a method of achieving a more adaptable and hence a more stable community, or maintaining the precarious balance between healthy cleavage and necessary consensus.[4]

In the United States, a dominant concern has been that the federal government, that is, centralized power, is the main danger to the maintenance of a system of full expression. The addition of the first amendment to the Constitution results from and is directed at that fear:

> Congress shall make no law respecting an establishment of religion, or prohibiting the free exercise thereof; or abridging the freedom of speech or of

the press; or the right of the people peaceably to assemble, and to petition the Government for a redress of grievances.

But the inclusion of such a guarantee in the Constitution creates a contradiction. While the first amendment places restrictions on the government so as to limit government power over the individual, it also relies on that same government to protect the individual from government power. As part of the doctrine of checks and balances, it is to the judiciary to which the task of oversight is assigned. Yet, we know that the judiciary and the decisions it renders are a part and product of the structure of that society. Therefore, to understand the free speech rights of criminal justice personnel, it will be necessary to examine the development of free speech rights in US society.

Significant events affecting the development of free speech rights

Until well into the 20th century almost all activity engaged in by citizens involved private transactions among private citizens. Employer-employee relations fell into that category. In capitalist society, private and public relations are seen as being separate domains, governed by distinctly different legal relations. Thus, while the first amendment applies to governmental (public-state) action, it does not apply to private action. The first amendment prohibits Congress from making laws abridging freedom of speech. There is no restriction on private parties doing so.[5]

Heavily influenced by this privatization of American life, courts did not conceive of legal issues in terms of free speech challenges. Before World War I, the Supreme Court virtually ignored the issue, and where the issue was presented, both state and federal courts showed a "pervasive hostility to the value of free speech."[6] Thus scholars have concluded that on the federal level, no right of free speech was recognized by courts before 1919.[7] That the United States has a long-standing and continuous tradition of free speech is more myth than fact.[8]

Presently-constituted free speech rights begin their evolution in the period just preceding World War I. Following the Civil War, the country experienced rapid growth of cities, large combines and trusts, labor unions, the importation of increasing numbers of European immigrants to work northern factories, huge pockets of urban poverty, management-labor conflict, and resulting protest against these conditions. In the years before World War I, writers such as Lincoln Steffens and Upton Sinclair described the worst excesses of capitalist enterprise. Ideas on the rights of women, sexual freedom, the new Freudian psychology, the popularization of the arts, socialism, and the class struggle were current. New publications such as the socialist magazine, *The Masses,* appeared to expound these ideas. With the coming of the Russian Revolution of 1917, propertied groups perceived these views as threats to established order. Government, at their urging, moved to suppress such unwelcome expression. Attempts to eliminate these ideas, in turn, activated others to organize in their support: the Free Speech League, and in 1917, the National Civil Liberties Bureau, the forerunner of the American Civil Liberties Union, formed in 1920.[9]

The War forced the Supreme Court to confront first amendment issues. It produced a wave of patriotic fervor and anti-German feeling which was answered by antiwar sentiment. Antiwar critics charged that the war was for the benefit of a small group of capitalists. Some of those opposing the war conscientiously objected to being drafted to fight such a war. To counter this opposition, Congress passed the Espionage Act of 1917 which made it a crime to "willfully make or convey false reports or false statements with intent to interfere with the operation or success of the [US armed forces] or to promote the success of its enemies," to "willfully cause or attempt to cause insubordination, disloyalty, mutiny, or refusal to duty," or to "willfully obstruct . . . recruitment and enlistment."[10] In 1918, the Sedition Act also made criminal the "uttering, printing, writing, or publishing any disloyal, profane, scurrilous, or abusive language, or language intended to cause contempt, scorn, contumely or disrepute as regards the form of government of the U.S., the Constitution, the flag, the uniform of the Army or Navy, or any language intended to incite resistance to the U.S. or promote the cause of its enemies."[11]

These laws resulted in the indiscriminate indictment, trial and jailing of hundreds of members of the International Workers of the World (IWW), conscientious objectors, Non-Partisan Leaguers, socialists, German-Americans, and the silencing of radical publications such as *The Masses.*[12] Those most interested in such laws and the repression which followed were "propertied men with a stake in society and in the preservation of its hierarchy of economic authority and social control."[13] Such concerns were continued in the post-war period because these groups saw the need for rapid economic reconversion, reducing, with a minimum of public criticism, excessively high wartime wages; undermining union strength through a vigorous nation-wide open-shop campaign and the revival of the labor injunction; and a return to a minimum of government interference in the management and use of property.[14]

Suppression could be rationalized because under this system any man could travel as fast and as far as his abilities would carry him to the ownership of property. Complaining malcontents, according to this view, were merely people who refused to play by the rules and wanted something for nothing. Such criticism, which fomented labor violence, strikes, mob action, and other clashes with authority, merely prevented others from attaining the proper ends for which the system provided, and thus must be silenced. The cases growing out of this legislation forced the Court to deal with the free speech issues it had heretofore ignored. The question then became, what legal test would it apply?

Setting the limits to free speech rights

Two tests have dominated the Court's treatment of free speech—the supposed "bad tendency" of speech to provoke unlawful action; and the clear and present danger test. Justice Holmes, the author of the clear and present danger test, used the bad tendency test in his earlier decisions. In Patterson v Colorado,[15] Holmes upheld the conviction of an editor for contempt for criticizing a judge. He rejected the editor's defense of truth of his allegations holding that the first amendment prohibits only "previous restraints upon publications," permitting "the subsequent punishment of such as may be deemed contrary to the public welfare.... Publications criticizing judicial behavior in pending cases *tend to* obstruct the administration of justice, whether or not the allegations are true."[16]

Holmes began his rejection of the bad tendency test in Schenck v United States.[17] Schenck, a Socialist Party leader, was charged, in violation of the Sedition Act, with having distributed a pamphlet to draftees criticizing the war, alleging that the draft was unconstitutional, and urging draftees to legally challenge their conscription. Although Holmes formulated a clear and present danger test, he found that Schenck's actions satisfied that test and upheld his conviction. Thus, the test, though an improvement on earlier tests, was vague enough to allow convictions for speech far removed from actual danger to the state.[18] When the Court thereafter resumed its use of the bad tendency test,

Holmes, with Brandeis, in a number of dissents, formulated a theory of free expression consistent with and derived from the principles of market capitalism.[19]

Dissenting in Abrams v United States,[20] a conviction based on a leaflet condemning US intervention in the Soviet Union in 1918, and advocating a general strike, Holmes set forth a theoretical and practical foundation for free expression. To Holmes, the "theory of our Constitution" is that

> the ultimate good desired is better reached by free trade in ideas—that the best test of truth is power of the thought to get itself accepted in the competition of the market, and that the truth is the only ground upon which their wishes safely can be carried out. . . . It is an experiment, as all life is an experiment. Every year if not every day we have to wager our salvation upon some prophecy based upon imperfect knowledge. While that experiment is part of our system, I think that we should be eternally vigilant against attempts to check the expression of opinions that we loathe and believe to be fraught with death, unless they so imminently threaten immediate interference with the lawful and pressing purposes of the law that an immediate check is required to save the country. . . . Only the emergency that makes it immediately dangerous to leave the correction of evil counsels to time warrants making any exception to the sweeping command, "Congress shall make no law . . . abridging the freedom of speech."[21]

Brandeis, somewhat later, took the logic a step further, stating "that the greatest menace to freedom is an inert people; that public discussion is a political duty; and that this should be a fundamental principle of the American government."[22] The clear and present danger test, as stated by Holmes, and the test still viable today, is that speech may be limited by government only when there is a "present danger of immediate evil, or intent to bring it about."[23] Brandeis refined that statement in declaring that no danger flowing from speech can be deemed to be clear and present "unless the incidence of the evil apprehended is so imminent that it may befall before there is an opportunity for full discussion. If there be time to expose through discussion the falsehood and falacies, to avert the evil by the process of education, the remedy to be applied is more speech, not enforced silence."[24]

It was not until 1925 that a majority of the Court by dictum agreed that the first amendment applied to the states,[25] and not until 1931, that the Court reversed a state conviction in reliance on the first amendment—a conviction for displaying a red flag at a Young Communist League summer camp.[26]

It is not possible in this brief review to continue a detailed analysis of the amendment to the present day. Suffice it to say that the breadth of free speech rights in the US has been dependent on the relative strength of those asserting these rights as compared to the perceived threat to the established order, and the state's power to suppress that threat. Thus, in the 1930s during a depression, as labor's strength increased, and propertied forces were in disarray, free speech grew apace; while in the 1950s when the exact opposite was true, when labor was weakened by internal divisions, and the country was seized by a paranoia of communist threats to its security, free speech suffered. In the 1960s, a time of relative prosperity, when criticism posed little threat to established order, free speech rights again were given protection.[27] We turn now to the analytic approach used by the Court in its more recent decisions and the application of first amendment rights to public employees.

Analytic approach to first amendment issues

Consistent with the central political role that the Supreme Court has lately seen the first amendment playing in US society, the Court has carved out a special constitutional doctrine for that amendment, denoting it as having a "preferred position" as compared to other constitutional provisions. The primary efect of such a court-created doctrine is to overcome the usual presumption of constitutionality that government action, particularly statutes and administrative rules, carry into court. Analysis follows the "compelling interest" theory as in other substantive due process cases. Where a statute or rule interferes with first amendment rights, the presumption of constitutionality is reversed. The government must initially show a "compelling interest" to interfere with that right, and secondly that it has restricted that right as little as necessary to carry out the state interest.

Justice Rutledge, in Thomas v Collins,[28] overturning a Texas law requiring a license before one could solicit members for a labor union, wrote:

> This case confronts us again with the duty our system places on this Court to say where the individual's freedom ends and the State's power begins. Choice on that order, now as always delicate, is perhaps more so where the usual presumption supporting legislation is balanced by the preferred place given in our scheme to the great, the indispensible democratic freedoms secured by the First Amendment. . . .[29]

For these reasons any attempt to restrict those liberties must be justified by clear public interest, threatened not doubtfully or remotely, but by clear and present danger. The rational connection between the remedy provided and the evil to be curbed, which in other contexts might support legislation against attack on due process grounds, will not suffice. These rights rest on firmer foundation. Accordingly, whatever occasion would restrain orderly discussion and persuasion, at appropriate time or place, must have clear support in public danger, actual or impending.

Over a period of time the courts have utilized a "variety of devices" that guarantee the first amendment its "preferred position."[30]

> Among these are the clear and present danger test; narrowing of the presumption of constitutionality; strict construction of statutes to avoid limitation of first amendment freedoms; the prohibitions against prior restraint and subsequent punishment; relaxation of the requirement of standing to sue where first amendment issues are involved; and generally higher standards of procedural due process where these freedoms are in jeopardy. Not one, but the sum total of these—and more—make up the preferred position concept.[31]

The application of first amendment rights to public employees

For the reasons set forth in chapters 5 and 6, the application of the law to public employees is largely determined by their employer-employee relationship, and particularly by their employment by the state, and the same is true in first amendment cases. In chapter 5, the 1892 case of McAuliffe v Mayor of New Bedford[32] was cited, in which Justice Holmes, then a judge of the Massachusetts supreme court, analogized a policeman's first amendment rights in public employment to a person's rights in private employment, stating with his characteristic brevity: "The petitioner may have a constitutional right to talk politics, but he has no constitutional right to be a policeman."[33]

Over the years, as recounted below, that restrictive view of the rights of public employees has been weakened until in 1968, the Court decided Pickering v Board of Education.[34]

Development of public employees' first amendment rights

The development of first amendment rights for public employees can be divided into pre and post-*Pickering* cases.[35] The period before *Pickering* in turn can be separated into (1) a time from the *McAuliffe* case (1892) through the *Adler* case (1952),[36] during which public employees were regarded as "slaves" of the state in that the effect of taking government employment was said to be an abandonment of all first amendment rights; and (2) the 16-year period between *Adler* and *Pickering* when the

Court was searching for a more flexible stance. *Pickering* was the watershed that established the balancing test: that the rights of the public employee to free speech must be balanced against the interest of the public employer in an efficiently run government. The post-*Pickering* years saw a working out of this test using factors relevant to each professional grouping.

It is apparent that these changes in Court posture toward public employees were influenced by the huge increase in the numbers of employees affected by such treatment, and the rights revolution that saw many other groups acquire rights forbidden to public employees. These changes eventually placed public employees "out of step" with other employees and encouraged their viewing their own employment relationship as being inconsistent with the newly-accepted concept of the employer-employee relationship. One consequence of this developing rights consciousness on the part of public employees has been the growth of public employee unions, and their assertion of public employee rights (see chapter 5). That *Pickering* was decided in 1968, in the midst of these developments, is hardly surprising. Neither is it by chance, that most of the keynote cases involve school teachers, who had the first and strongest union among professionals. Thus, in *Pickering*, Justice Marshall no longer analyzes the state-employee relationship from the perspective of an employee subject to the whims of the sovereign. Instead, he applies the same criterion as he would to a private employee, namely "the interest of the State, as an employer, in promoting the efficiency of the public services it performs through its employees."[37] In doing so, however, he effectively jettisons the preferred position of the first amendment and lays the groundwork for the court's embrace of the private employment model for public employee first amendment rights.[38]

The pre-*Pickering* period

McAuliffe represents a period when courts, reflecting real relations of the period, viewed the employer-employee relationship as that of master-servant. Under such dominant-subordinate relations the master sets the terms and the servant obeys them. From this perspective, the statement in *McAuliffe* that "The petitioner may have a constitutional right to talk politics, but he has no constitutional right to be a policeman,"[39] is understandable. Otherwise put, such a statement represents government employment as a privilege, a reflection of a feudal period when the seigneur gave employment at his pleasure and took it back in the same fashion. This position continued in force through the 1950s when it began to run counter to the forces described in Chapter 5. Thereafter, the court gradually came around to a position more consistent with other employer-employee relationships. The battle revolved not around privilege, but what "rights" in a public setting accrued to that relationship.

Adler v Bd of Education[40] represents the tail end of the *McAuliffe* period. That period was undoubtedly prolonged by authoritarian values of the McCarthy era out of which this case arose. *Adler* attacked the New York Feinberg Law which authorized the dismissal of any public school teacher who was a member of an organization classified by the New York Board of Regents as "subversive." In upholding the statute, the Supreme Court echoed *McAuliffe* in stating:

> It is clear that [teachers] have the right under our law to assemble, speak, think and believe as they will. It is equally clear that they have no right to work for the State in the school system on their own terms. They may work for the school system upon reasonable terms laid down by the proper authorities of New York. If they do not choose to work on such terms, they are at liberty to retain their beliefs and associations and go elsewhere.[41] [citations omitted.]

Teachers were given the choice of abandoning their first amendment rights or their careers. As one writer has observed, "This reasoning overlooks the job market realities for many professionals, such as school teachers and police officers, who essentially must rely on the government as an employer or face unemployment."[42] There was a glimmer of light, however, in the dissent by Douglas, with Black concurring. They expressed the relationship in a way more consistent with capitalist social organization in which private and public behavior is conceived of as separate:

> So long as she is a law-abiding citizen, so long as her performance within the public school system meets professional standards, her private life, her political philosophy, her social creed should not be the cause of reprisals against her.[43]

Later that same year, in Wieman v Updegraff,[44] the Court was already on its way to rejecting *Adler*, to replace it with Douglas' professional standard. *Wieman* involved a public employee who, like Adler, was discharged when he refused to take a loyalty oath. But here the Court invalidated the discharge, stating in passing:

> We are referred to our statement in *Adler* that persons seeking employment in the New York public schools have "no right to work for the State in the school system on their own terms." . . . To draw from this language the facile generali-

zation that there is no constitutionally protected right to public employment is to obscure the issue. . . . We need not pause to consider whether an abstract right to public employment exists. It is sufficient to say that constitutional protection does extend to the public servant whose exclusion pursuant to a statute is patently arbitrary or discriminatory.[45]

The Court thereafter would examine two factors in loyalty cases: the relationship of the oath to the employee's fitness for the position, and the effect of the oath requirement upon the employee's first amendment rights, tests almost indistinguishable from the Douglas-Black standard.[46]

The 1956 case of Slochower v Bd of Higher Education,[47] though not a first amendment case, allowed the Court to place even more distance between itself and *Adler Slochower* was an attack on a section of the New York City charter which provided that city employees who used the privilege against self incrimination to avoid answering a question relating to their official conduct would thereby forfeit their office. Slochower, a long-time tenured professor of a city university, was terminated under these conditions.[48] Reworking the authoritarian *McAuliffe* and *Adler* cases to fit contemporary society, the Court said:

> To state that a person does not have a constitutional right to government employment is only to say that he must comply with reasonable, lawful and nondiscriminatory terms laid down by the proper authorities. . . . This is not to say that Slochower has a constitutional right to be an associate professor. . . . The State has broad power in the selection and discharge of its employees, and it may be that proper inquiry would show Slochower's continued employment to be inconsistent with a real interest in the State. But there has been no such inquiry here. We hold that the summary dismissal of appellant violates due process of law.[49]

Eleven years later in Keyishian v Bd of Regents[50] *Adler* was finally swept out of the Court's closet, held up to view, and overruled.

> [T]he Feinberg Law was . . . before the Court in *Adler* and its constitutionality was sustained. But constitutional doctrine which has emerged since that decision has rejected its major premise. That premise was that public employment, including academic employment, may be conditioned upon the surrender of constitutional rights which would not be abridged by direct government action. [The Court then quoted the *Adler* language referred to above.] . . . However, the Court of Appeals . . . correctly said . . . "[T]he theory that public employment which may be denied altogether may be subjected to any conditions, regardless of how unreasonable, has been uniformly rejected."[51]

Pickering

The abandonment of *Adler* signaled more than the reversal of a single case. It symbolized a movement from conceiving claims by government employees as privileges to be graciously granted at the discretion of the sovereign to rights to which public employees are constitutionally entitled. *Pickering*[52] represented the Court's groping for a way to deal with this new approach. The case involved an Illinois high school teacher who was dismissed by the board of education for writing a letter to a local newspaper that was sharply critical of the school administration. Some of Pickering's statements were allegedly incorrect and the Board dismissed him on the ground that publication of the letter was "detrimental to the efficient operation and administration of the schools of the district."[53] Justice Marshall, in holding that Pickering's first amendment rights were violated, rejected any hard and fast rule. Instead, he chose a balancing test to "indicate some of the general lines"[54] in evaluating the competing rights of Pickering and the state:

> [I]t cannot be gainsaid that the State has interests as an employer in regulating the speech of its employees that differ significantly from those it possesses in connection with regulation of the speech of the citizenry in general. The problem in any case is to arrive at a balance between the interests of the teacher, as a citizen, in commenting upon matters of public concern and the interest of the State, as an employer, in promoting the efficiency of the public services it performs through its employees.[55]

The Court seemed to be saying that first amendment protection would depend on the extent the speech was distanced from the employer-employee relationship. In the course of his opinion, Marshall suggested that (1) it would be necessary to evaluate "the conflicting claims of First Amendment protection and the need for orderly school administration," and (2) the effect on this evaluation of the falsity of the speech claiming protection.[56] Marshall pointed to certain factors concerning Pickering's relation to the board of education that would later return to haunt criminal justice personnel. Pickering's expression was not directed at any person with whom he would normally be in contact during his workday, so that questions of "discipline by immediate superiors or harmony among coworkers" was not involved.[57] Neither did his "employment relationships" with the board or the superintendent depend on "the kind of close working relationships for which it can persuasively be claimed that personal loyalty and confidence are necessary to their proper functioning;"[58] or whether the statements "have in any way impeded [the employee's] proper performance of his daily duties ... or ... interfered with the regular operations of the [office]."[59] The Court therefore concluded that on matters of public concern that are substantially correct, criticism of the kind here involved was not a ground for dismissal.

As for the statements found to be false, there was no evidence that they were damaging to the board or its members, and therefore no question was raised about Pickering's fitness to perform in a classroom. Pickering could not be dismissed for such remarks unless the degree of falsity reached the kind of actual malice the Court required in its decision in New York Times v Sullivan.[60] That case involved the asserted liability of the *Times* for an alleged libelous advertisement published in the newspaper by a civil rights organization. Some of the statements printed were incorrect. The Court held that a public officer could not recover against a newspaper for such false statements unless, quoting the *New York Times* case, they were shown to be printed with "knowledge of their falsity or with reckless disregard for their truth or falsity."[61]

Justice Marshall concluded that in this case:

> [T]he interest of the school administration in limiting debate is not significantly greater than its interest in limiting a similar contribution by any member of the general public.[62]

The Court left to future cases the relative weight to be accorded the various cited factors. It is, however, noteworthy that the Court measured Pickering's rights by his rights as a citizen and not by his rights as a public employee. To the extent that the public employee's use of first amendment rights impinges on the employment relationship, to that extent the Court seemed to accept the fact that they would diminish, a point the court made more explicit in Connick v Myers,[63] discussed below. Moreover, the Court substituted a balancing test (the public employee's first amendment rights against the state employer's interests) for the preferred status of first amendment rights in which the state has the burden of justifying any incursion on first amendment freedoms. Of equal consequence is the trivialization of public employee first amendment rights by balancing the state's ("society's") rights against the public employee's individual rights—thereby ignoring Brandeis' reasoning that free speech "is a duty as well as a right for its exercise is more important to the Nation than it is to" the party exercising it.[64]

Post-*Pickering* developments

For almost ten years lower federal courts struggled with the ambiguities of *Pickering*, particularly "how large a factor the speech had to be in the decision to implement the disciplinary action."[65] Did free speech have to be the sole, the partial, the substantial, or the predominant reason for the dismissal? Was the issue to be seen from the perspective of the employee: that any threat of dismissal for the exercise of first amendment rights would act as a chilling effect on those rights, or was it to be seen from the perspective of the employer, that to invalidate a dismissal whenever free speech played a part in it would allow government employees to insure their retention by invoking constitutionally-protected speech?[66]

These issues were presented to the Court in Mt. Healthy City School District Bd of Education v Doyle.[67] The case facts must have made first amendment advocates wince, and certainly had an effect on the Court's decision, a unanimous opinion authored by Justice Rehnquist. Doyle was an untenured teacher whose apparently abrasive style resulted in a series of incidents during the year before the refusal to rehire decision: a physical dispute with another teacher, an argument with school cafeteria employees over the amount of food being served him, his reference to certain students as "sons of bitches," and obscene gestures made to girls who refused to obey his commands as a cafeteria supervisor. The first amendment incident, however, arose out of Doyle's conveying a disputed school memorandum on teacher dress and appearance to a local radio station.

Shortly thereafter, the school superintendent, in his annual tenure report, recommended that Doyle not be rehired. Doyle was informed that the reasons for the nonhiring decision were that he had shown "a notable lack of tact in handling professional matters which leaves much doubt as to your sincerity in establishing good school relationships," specifically citing the radio station and obscene gesture incidents.[68] In analyzing these facts, the Court constructed a three-tiered test. First, government employees have the burden of showing that their conduct was constitutionally protected; and secondly that the conduct was a "substantial" or "motivating" factor in the government's decision not to rehire.[69] Finally, the government is entitled to show "by a preponderance of the evidence that it would have reached the same decision as to [the employee's] reemployment even in the absence of the protected conduct."[70]

The Court had no trouble finding that Doyle's communication to the radio station was protected by the first amendment. "There is no suggestion by the Board that Doyle violated any established policy, or that its reaction to his communication to the radio station was anything more than an ad hoc response to Doyle's action in making the memorandum public."[71] The Court then faced the issue whether a government employer who would otherwise have had the power to dismiss an employee is prevented from doing so where "the protected conduct played a 'substantial part' in the actual decision not to renew. . . . "[72] The Court was concerned that "a rule of causation which focuses solely on whether protected conduct played a part, 'substantial' or otherwise, in a decision not to hire, could place an employee in a better position as a result of the exercise of constitutionally protected conduct than he would have occupied had he done nothing."[73] "The constitutional principle at stake," the Court concluded, "is sufficiently vindicated if such an employee is placed in no worse a position than if he had not engaged in the conduct."[74] The case was remanded to the lower court to make this factual determination. A later case applied this same reasoning to private as well as public communication with the employer, and reformulated the inquiry in terms of causation: whether the public employee "would have been hired *but for*" the first amendment activity.[75] The Court also added another balancing factor to those it had enumerated in *Pickering:* when the communication is made privately to an employee's immediate supervisor, "The employing agency's institutional efficiency may be threatened not only by the content of the . . . message but also by the manner, time, and place in which it is delivered."[76] How have these principles been applied to criminal justice personnel?

First amendment rights of criminal justice personnel

It is apparent that in considering the use of first amendment rights in the context of public employment, it is the fact of employer-employee relations that the Court has found to be the dominant factor, and not first amendment preferred rights as in other free speech contexts. Therefore, in construing the extent of first amendment rights in public employment, it will be crucial to consider how the nature of that relationship may define the contours of that right.

In wrestling with first amendment cases involving criminal justice personnel, courts have had to decide whether the nature of their work is closer to that of teachers as in *Pickering,* and therefore that they should have substantial first amendment rights, or whether they are closer to the military, and therefore they should have a truncated version of such rights. Further considerations include whether the free speech involved takes place on or off the job; whether it is aimed at supervisors, and whether the state must show that the first amendment activity resulted in any disruption or disharmony in work relationships; and from a procedural standpoint, whether the departmental rule under which they were disciplined is in violation of the first amendment because it is vague, overbroad, or both.

Nature of the job—the military analogy

Because *Pickering* concerned school teachers, the question naturally arose as to what extent the nature of the job might determine the scope of first amendment rights—whether criminal justice personnel are closer to teachers, at one end of the spectrum, or the military at the other.[77] In *Pickering,* the Court found that

> Teachers are, as a class, the members of a community most likely to have informed and definite opinions as to how funds allotted to the operation of the schools should be spent. Accordingly, it is essential that they be able to speak out freely on such questions without fear of retaliatory dismissal.[78]

Pickering also suggested the other side of the equation, a minimum of free speech rights where "the need for confidentiality is so great that even completely correct public statements might furnish a permissible ground for dismissal."[79] The Court found such a fit in the work of the CIA. That agency could restrain past and present employees from publishing information derived from classified sources on the theory that such employment involved an "extremely high degree of trust."[80]

Criminal justice personnel have not been compared with the CIA, but the police have been contrasted with the military. Although there are no recent Supreme Court cases involving first amendment rights of criminal justice personnel, such cases do exist for the military. The Court tackled the issue at the worst of times for the amendment, during wartime, in this case, the Vietnam War. In Parker v Levy,[81] the Court compared the use of free speech rights in military and civilian societies. Levy was an army physician who made statements to enlisted personnel at his post criticizing the Vietnam War and urging blacks to refuse to go there if ordered to do so. Levy was charged with violations of the military code.

In the course of its analysis the Court distinguished military from civilian society and military law from civilian law:

> This Court has long recognized that the military is, by necessity, a specialized society separate from civilian society. We have also recognized that the military has, again by necessity, developed laws and traditions of its own during its long history.... "An army is not a deliberative body. It is the executive arm. Its law is that of obedience. No question can be left open as to the right to command in the officer, or the duty of obedience in the soldier."[82]

A military code, the Court said, cannot be compared with a criminal code, because the military law regulates "a much larger segment of the activities of the more tightly knit military community."[83]

In Kelly v Johnson,[84] a 1976 case, Johnson, a police officer on the Suffolk County (NY) force and president of the Patrolmen's Benevolent Association, brought a 1983 action challenging a hair-grooming standard regulating hair-length applicable to male officers. Although the Court decided the case on the basis of Johnson's "liberty" interest under the due process clause of the fourteenth amendment rather than the first amendment, the importance of the case lies in its recognition of the primacy of the employer-employee relationship in the Court's balancing act. In his opinion, Justice Rehnquist accentuated *Pickering's* language:

> it cannot be gainsaid that the State has interests as an employer in regulating the speech of its employees that differ significantly from those it possesses in connection with regulation of the speech of the citizenry in general.[85]

While the Court accepted the court of appeals conclusion that "there was no historical or functional justification for the characterization of the police as 'para-military,'" that determination in

> no way detracts from the deference due Suffolk County's choice of an organizational structure for its police force. Here the county has chosen a mode of organization which it undoubtedly deems the most efficient in enabling its police to carry out the duties assigned to them under state and local law. Such a choice necessarily gives weight to the overall need for discipline, esprit de corps, and uniformity.... We believe ... that the hair-length regulation cannot be viewed in isolation, but must be rather considered in the context of the county's chosen mode of organization for its police force.
>
> The promotion of safety of persons and property is unquestionably at the core of the State's police power, and virtually all state and local governments employ a uniformed police force to aid in the accomplishment of that purpose. Choice of organization, dress, and equipment for law enforcement personnel is a decision entitled to the same sort of presumption of legislative validity as are

state choices designed to promote other aims within the cognizance of the State's police power.[86]

The case places a heavy burden of proof on the officer who wishes to assert the invalidity of a departmental regulation. Rather than demanding that the department establish the need for such regulation, the Court requires the officer to "demonstrate that there is no rational connection between the regulation, based as it is on the county's method of organizing its police force, and the promotion of safety of persons and property."[87] While *Kelly* was decided on the due process clause of the fourteenth amendment rather than on the first amendment (and therefore did not have to cope with first amendment preferred status analysis), it has been frequently cited to support denial of first amendment rights for police.[88]

To date, most federal courts have rejected the argument that because of their "quasi-military" organization police have only limited first amendment rights. In Muller v Conlisk, a 7th circuit court of appeals case, the defendant police chief attempted to distinguish *Pickering* in that "policemen are different than teachers and that police departments are quasi-military forces dependent upon rigid internal discipline for their effectiveness."[89] The court countered this argument by citing earlier Supreme Court dicta that "policemen, like teachers and lawyers, are not relegated to a watered-down version of constitutional rights."[90] Such military characteristics, to the extent they exist, do

> no more than to influence the balance which *Pickering* says must be struck in each case. To the extent that being a policeman is public employment with unique characteristics, the right of the employee to speak on matters concerning his employment with the full freedom of any citizen may be more or less limited. It is not, however, destroyed. . . . Thus, it is clear that the First Amendment would reach and protect some speech by policemen which could be considered "derogatory to the department."[91]

First amendment rights of criminal justice personnel are likely to be highly restricted if courts accept the military analogy. That such an analogy is inapplicable to the police is well articulated in the following commentary:

> The argument that the First Amendment freedoms of police officers are more limited than those of other public employees stems from the premise that the police force usually depends on strict and rigid discipline. . . . This is reflected in the police force's centralized administrative structure, hierarchy of command and uniform dress and appearance, all designed to promote competent public service and harmony within the department.

Even though many police departments are organized along paramilitary lines, they remain significantly different in character from the military. Police departments are locally managed and organized, and are more directly controlled by the electorate. Police officials are given broad discretion in running a department and dismissals are subject to review by civil rather than provincial military tribunals. Most importantly, the discipline necessary for the efficient functioning of the military and of police forces is not of the same variety. Instant unquestioning obedience, while essential for a soldier in action, is not necessary for an effective police force. It has even been suggested that the military model of organization and discipline be discouraged somewhat in police departments because a police officer, unlike a soldier, must frequently act on his or her own initiative without immediate direction or supervision.[92]

Effect of Speech on "Efficiency of the Workplace"

Pickering suggested that first amendment rights might be restricted where "the relationship between superior and subordinate is of such a personal and intimate nature that certain forms of public criticism of the superior by the subordinate would seriously undermine the effectiveness of the working relationship between them...."[93] Most cases involving public employees' first amendment rights fall into this category. It is easy to see why. In this industrial society, nearly all employment, including government employment, is based on a hierarchal structure in which the assumption is that the "superior" makes policy which the subordinate carries out. Equally strong are the assumptions that superiors know more about what they are doing than do subordinates, and that therefore the efficiency of the organization depends on subordinates carrying out superiors' orders. Accepting these assumptions, it is understandable why courts are tempted to equate first amendment activity, particularly criticism of superiors by subordinates, with disruption of organizational efficiency and harmonious working relations.

Because these assumptions are unarticulated by courts, the case reasoning in this area is often murky and unconvincing, and frequently is determined by the peculiar facts of the case rather than by any clearly-defined legal principles. Nevertheless, cases may be roughly divided into those relying on a test (a) requiring "material and substantial disruption" of the working relationship before free speech may be suppressed; or (b) in which mere criticism of superiors by their immediate subordinates will be *presumed* to result in disruption of the working relationship, and therefore of the agency's operating efficiency. Each test uses the factors cited in *Pickering* but balances them differently, the first test requiring objective evidence of damage to the operation of the workplace, or the ability of employees to perform the duties of their office and the second showing more concern for the *presumed* disruption of the work relationship.

"Material and substantial" disruption as a test

The Supreme Court first suggested a test requiring actual or probable agency disruption as a result of free speech activity in the 1962 case of Wood v Georgia.[94] Wood, an elected sheriff, was held in contempt of court for issuing press releases questioning the advisability of conducting a grand jury investigation of alleged payments by politicians to purchase the "Negro vote." The Court noted that although the state court found that the sheriff's statements "created a serious evil to the fair administration of justice," it "did not indicate in any manner *how* the publications interfered with the grand jury's investigations, or with the administration of justice."[95] No one was on trial whose rights might be affected by such statements and there were no allegations that the fact that Wood was a sheriff would lead such statements to cause more harm than would those of a private citizen. Finally, there was no evidence that the publications interfered with the performance of his duties in connection with the investigation. Thus, the sheriff, as a public officer, had the right to enter the field of controversy. *Wood* required the state to show that the employee's first amendment activity in some way interfered with the normal operations of the public employer.

It was not, however, until the 1969 case of Tinker v Des Moines Independent Community School District[96] that the Court first enunciated the test in its present form. In that case, high school students were suspended for wearing black arm bands to protest the Vietnam War. School authorities demanded the arm bands be removed, and when the students refused, they were suspended. In upholding the students' right to engage in such first amendment activity the Court observed that the students had engaged in no "disruptive action"; nor did they interfere with school work or with the rights of other students. The district court had based its decision on what it considered the reasonable fear that the wearing of armbands might cause a disturbance. Such reasoning must be rejected, said the Court, because "in our system, undifferentiated fear or apprehension of disturbance is not enough to overcome the right of freedom of expression. . . ."[97]

In order for the State in the person of the school officials to justify prohibition of a particular expression of opinion, it must be able to show that its action was caused by something more than a mere desire to avoid the discomfort and unpleasantness that always accompany an unpopular viewpoint. Certainly where there is no finding or no showing that engaging in the forbidden conduct would "materially and substantially interfere with the requirements of appropriate discipline in the operation of the school," the prohibition cannot be sustained.[98]

Deference to the employer's judgment

The 1983 case of Connick v Myers[99] reversed this trend, changing emphasis from requiring a showing of actual disruption to a mere showing of a perception by the employer of disruption. Myers was a competent New Orleans assistant district attorney who had been assigned to a criminal branch in which part of her assignment was counselling convicted defendants. She was informed that she was to be transferred to another criminal court section. Concerned that her transfer might cause a conflict of interest with her former clients, she objected to the transfer. In discussing the transfer with the first assistant district attorney, Myers indicated that her own concerns were shared by others in the office. When the first assistant expressed doubt that this was true, Myers said that she would "research" the matter. She distributed a questionnaire concerning transfers, office morale, confidence in superiors, and whether employees felt pressure to work in political campaigns. Charging that she was starting a "mini-insurrection" in the office, the district attorney discharged Myers.

Justice White, writing for a five to four majority, first posed the *Pickering* problem of balancing the interests of the employee and the state: "the interests of the [employee] as a citizen, in commenting upon matters of public concern and the interest of the State, as an employer, in promoting the efficiency of the public services it performs through its employees."[100] The Court thus set out to determine if Myers' speech was "of public concern." "Private" expression is entitled to a lesser protection when it "cannot be fairly considered as relating to any matter of political, social, or other concern to the community.... "[101] In such a case, "government officials should enjoy wide latitude in managing their offices, without intrusive oversight by the judiciary in the name of the First Amendment."[102] Summing up, the Court held that

when a public employee speaks not as a citizen upon matters of public concern, but instead as an employee upon matters only of personal interest, absent the most unusual circumstances, a federal court is not the appropriate forum in which to review the wisdom of a personnel decision taken by a public agency allegedly in reaction to the employee's behavior.[103]

Applying those principles to Myers, the Court concluded that, except for one question, Myers' queries were "mere extensions of Myers' dispute over her transfer. . . . "[104] Myers neither sought to bring the dispute to public attention, nor did she expose some "actual or potential wrongdoing or breach of public trust" on the part of her superiors.[105] The Court then turned to the one question that did raise first amendment concerns: whether assistant district attorneys "ever feel pressured to work in political campaigns on behalf of office supported candidates."[106] The district and circuit courts had required a two-tier test. First, the plaintiff must show that her expression was one of "public concern," after which the burden shifted to the state to "clearly demonstrate" that the speech "substantially interfered" with official responsibilities.[107]

This approach is wrong, said the Court, because *Pickering* "requires full consideration of the government's interest in the effective and efficient fulfillment of its responsibilities to the public."[108] While the distribution of the questionnaire did not interfere with Myers' ability to perform her job, her superiors concluded that the questionnaire did represent "an act of insubordination which interfered with working relationships."[109] Where as here such relationships were essential to fulfilling her responsibilities, "a wide degree of deference to the employer's judgment is appropriate."[110] There was no need for the employer to wait until these events occurred before taking action. A "stronger showing," however, may be required if the "speech more substantially involved matters of public concern."[111] The "manner, time and place" was also of consequence where as here Myers distributed the questionnaire at the office, thus supporting the district attorney's "fears" that office functions may be "endangered."[112] Added weight is to be given to the fact that the speech involved defies the authority of the superior in carrying out policy. Therefore, because Myers' expression is best "characterized as an employee grievance concerning internal office policy, [t]he limited First Amendment interest involved does not require that Connick tolerate action which he reasonably believed would disrupt the office, undermine his authority, and destroy close working relationships."[113] Finally, the Court suggests that under appropriate circumstances there may be an exception to this general rule when "[e]mployee speech which transpires entirely on the employee's own time, and in non-work areas of the office, bring different factors into the *Pickering* calculus, and might lead to a different conclusion."[114] Such conflicts must be dealt with on the same terms as any other employment dispute:

> Perhaps the government employer's dismissal of the worker may not be fair, but ordinary dismissals from government service which violate no fixed tenure or applicable statute or regulation are not subject to judicial review even if the reasons for the dismissal are alleged to be mistaken or unreasonable.[115]

A few years after *Connick,* the court decided Rankin v McPherson,[116] in which a probationary clerical employee working in a county constable's office was discharged for remarking, shortly after she heard of the attempt on President Reagan's life, "If they go for him again, I hope they get him." The remark was reported to her employer, Constable Rankin, who questioned her about it, and then when she admitted making the remark, fired her.

In deciding the case, the Court reasserted the basic premise of constitutional employment law: even though as a probationary employee, she could have been fired for any or no reason, she could not be fired in violation of her constitutional rights. In this regard, the Court cautioned:

> Vigilance is necessary to insure that public employers do not use authority over employees to silence discourse, not because it hampers public functions but simply because superiors disagree with the content of employer's speech.[117]

After quickly concluding that the comment touched on a matter of "heightened public attention," and therefore was a matter of public concern, the Court next turned to the time, manner and place of the employee's expression in balancing state and individual interests.

> ... the state interest element of the test focuses on the effective functioning of the public employer's enterprise. Interference with work, personnel relationships, or the speaker's job performance can detract from the public employer's function; avoiding such interference can be a strong state interest. From this perspective, however, [the public employer fails] to demonstrate a state interest that outweighs McPherson's First Amendment rights. While McPherson's statement was made at the workplace, there is no evidence that it interfered with the efficient functioning of the office. The Constable was evidently not afraid that McPherson had disturbed or interrupted other employees.... nor was there any danger that McPherson had discredited the office by making her statement in public.... not only was McPherson's discharge unrelated to the functioning of the office, it was not based on any assessment by the Constable that the remark demonstrated a character trait that made [McPherson] unfit to perform her work.[118]

McPherson's discharge was found therefore to be improper in violation of her first amendment rights.

The effect of *Rankin,* therefore, was to shift the emphasis from *Connick's* apparent concern with an employer's "fear" of potential disruption as a result of an employee's speech to *Rankin's* search for actual "evidence" of interference with "efficient functioning" of the workplace.

Post-Connick-Rankin cases

According to the teaching of *Connick,* before public employees can claim that their first amendment rights have been violated, they must show that the speech involved a matter of "public concern" rather than a matter that merely concerned that employee alone. As Brawner v City of Richardson, TX simply put it,

> An employee contending that his termination from employment violates the First Amendment must initially establish that his speech addressed a matter of public concern. If the speech did not address a matter of public concern, then the employee is not entitled to constitutional protection against discharge, even if he was fired for what he said.[119]

What then is a "matter of public concern" as defined by the courts? *Connick* defined matters of public concern as "any matters of political, social, or other concerns to the community. . . . "[120] *Connick* also defined the term in a negative sense: "when a public employee speaks not as a citizen upon matters of public concern, but instead as an employee upon matters of only personal interest."[121] In Barkoo v Melby,[122] plaintiff Barkoo was an emergency dispatcher with the Village of Skokie who claimed that she was constructively discharged for exercising her right to free speech. The claim arose out of a radio report she received of a stolen car. She delayed action on the report and did not follow proper procedure to record its receipt. Following a reprimand she wrote an interoffice memo to various supervisors complaining about a Village plan calling for dispatchers and other employees occasionally to work two consecutive shifts.

The *Barkoo* court asks: "Was it the employee's point to bring wrongdoing to light? Or to raise issues of public concern, because they are of public concern? Or was the point to further some purely private interest?"[123] The court concluded that the subject of the interoffice memo did not reach the level of public concern:

> The context in which the memo was written was one of increasing hostility between Barkoo and her superiors; discipline for the . . . incident already had been handed down, grievances had been filed, and Barkoo was in the process of flooding her superiors with complaints, appeals and other memoranda. This was just one of those memoranda and its subject matter related to the "internal operations within a government agency" that . . . were not matters of public concern.[124]

Conversely, Zamboni v Stamler[125] seems to be a typical situation in which a court is most likely to find "public concern." Zamboni, a detective in the county prosecutor's office, was disciplined in retaliation for expressing opposition to changes in personnel policies and procedures. The incident arose out of the prosecutor's intention to reorganize his office. One of the proposed changes affected the way promotions would thereafter be made. Stamler, who was adversely affected by the plan, wrote a letter to the Civil Service Commission charging the prosecutor with an attempt to "subvert the Civil Service System and to carry out his own plans, without regard to the law."

> The thrust of Zamboni's speech related to his opposition to Stamler's reorganization plan and, in particular, to how promotions were made under the plan. That opposition raised significant issues concerning, *inter alia,* whether the county prosecutor had impermissibly circumvented the civil service laws, the role of civil service employees in the county prosecutor's office, and the manner in which the county prosecutor, the county's highest law enforcement official, performed his administrative functions. . . . This court has repeatedly found that public employees' criticism of the internal operations of their places of public employment is a matter of public concern.[126]

The fact that the speech represents a "mixture of public and personal concerns" does not remove it from the ambit of speech of "public concern."[127]

Balancing the interests

Connick, in particular, emphasized the primacy of the employer-employee relationship, and tended to push the balance of interests in favor of the "efficiency of the workplace," with the employer being in the catbird seat of determining when that "efficiency" was "disrupted." Although the Supreme Court implicitly invited courts to jettison the substantial disruption test, this has not generally been the way courts of appeals have interpreted that decision. In reviewing these cases, I start with those involving obvious "disruption," that is, those involving insubordination. These are followed by cases in which the issue is first criticism of the employee's superior, and then those involving disruption of the workplace.

(a) insubordination

In Wheaton v Webb-Petett,[128] Wheaton, manager of a branch office of Oregon's Adult and Family Services Division (AFSD), criticized and decided to implement the NEW JOBS program in a different way from that ordered by the central office. While the court recognized that Wheaton had "a strong interest in the unfettered exercise of his first amendment franchise,"

> Wheaton spoke as a dissenting manager. . . . In contrast to *Rankin,* here the risk that Wheaton's persistence might endanger the AFSD's successful implementation of the NEW JOBS pilot was far greater than "minimal." . . . Almost simultaneously with Wheaton's suspension, the participation of the [branch] in the NEW JOBS pilot was halted because Wheaton . . . agreed that [the administration] would not be ready to implement NEW JOBS . . . as scheduled. . . . [AFSD's] interest outweighed any personal interest that Wheaton had in expressing his dissent. . . . [129]

(b) criticism of superior

Criticism of one's superior goes to the heart of the threat to the working relationship, named by the Court as one of the factors that could reduce the employee's freedom of expression. But where the employee is sufficiently "distant" from the target of the criticism or is "independent" of that target, employees may more safely express that criticism.

In Biggs v Village of Dupo,[130] Biggs, a part-time police officer, with the other officers of the village force (five full-time and four part-time) were the subject of interviews by a local newspaper, running a feature, "Meet Your Police." Such interviews were approved by the chief of police. Biggs' interview contained statements such as: "it's hard to distinguish the politicians from the criminals," together with complaints about "politicians" interfering with the police force. Shortly thereafter, upon the recommendation of the mayor, to the Village Board of Trustees, Biggs' commission was revoked, and this suit followed. The court concluded that the interview posed no threat to working relationships.

> Mr. Biggs did not criticize his fellow officers, his supervisors . . . , nor the current Police Commissioner; he was "on the bottom rung" while the "politicians" he was criticizing were at the top. . . . While Mr. Biggs personally knew each member of the Board of Trustees (not surprising in a small town), there was no

evidence of any working relationship, let alone one calling for loyalty and confidence, between the Board and him.[131]

In Scott v Flowers,[132] Scott, a justice of the peace, had noted that large percentages of traffic cases that were appealed were thereafter dismissed or the fines substantially reduced. This practice meant that those "in the know" obtained a different result from those unlearned in this practice. Scott wrote an "open letter" to county officials, attacking the district attorney's office and the county court. Several newspaper articles resulted. The Texas Commission on Judicial Conduct sent Scott a letter of reprimand stating that his letter had the effect of casting "public discredit upon the judiciary."

As an elected official, the court noted, "the state cannot justify the reprimand of Scott, as it could the discipline of an ordinary government employee, on the ground that it is necessary to preserve coworker harmony or office discipline."[133]

(c) "Disruption" of the workplace

Key to the employee's right to free expression in the workplace is whether courts interpret the *Connick-Rankin* disruption in the workplace test to require *actual* or merely *potential* disruption; in other words, to require material and substantial evidence of disruption, or some variant of the bad tendency test. A further issue involves who has the burden of proving disruption. Taking this last question first, the majority of courts appear to require the employer to show disruption.[134] The burden of proof requirement is clearly set forth in Jackson v Blair:

> The burden to establish that the speech in issue was upon a matter of legitimate public concern is upon the employee but if this burden is carried, the burden to establish that public employer interest outweighs the employee's first amendment interest is upon the public employer.[135]

The case of Zamboni v Stamler,[136] considered above in the subsection on public concern, provides a good statement of the application of the *Connick-Rankin* admonition that public employees lose first amendment protection to the extent that they interfere with "the effective functioning of the public employer's enterprise."[137] Because the case was disposed of on a motion for summary judgment, the court of appeals instructed the district court how to procede on remand. The question, the court stated, was

> whether Zamboni's speech caused any disruption in [the prosecutor's] office and, if so, whether that disruption was so severe as to override both Zamboni's

and society's First Amendment interests.... At the outset, we reject [the prosecutor's] suggestion ... that a finding of *potential* disruption could be sufficient to outweigh Zamboni's interests. To the contrary, in cases such as this involving speech on matters of significant public concern, a showing of actual disruption is required.... A finding of actual disruption, while necessary, is not sufficient to a determination that the employee's speech is not protected.... In considering whether any disruption was, in fact, material and substantial, consideration of Zamboni's role in the office will be important.... whether Zamboni's functional role in the prosecutor's office was of such proximity to [the prosecutor] that his speech destroyed "a needed close working relationship."... Furthermore, in evaluating the disruption, if any, that resulted from Zamboni's criticism of [the prosecutor's] reorganization plan, the district court must consider whether any unrest was caused directly by Zamboni's speech or whether it was exacerbated by defendant's actions.[138]

A court may also recognize that the speech being defended by the public employee was founded in constitutional core values, and therefore the burden of proof on employers to show a balance in their favor would require a "higher showing." In Eiland v City of Montgomery,[139] Eiland, a police officer, posted a poem in the police station, satirizing the mayor just before a mayoral election was to take place.

Although an employer need not allow events to deteriorate to the point of actual disruption before taking action, the Court in *Connick* cautioned "a stronger showing may be necessary if the employee's speech more substantially involved matters of public concern." Clearly matters directly affecting an electoral campaign go directly to the heart of the democratic electoral process ... which requires that we give utmost deference to the speech that is possible.... Once this factor is recognized, we conclude that a higher showing of potential disruption was required than was shown here in order to conclude that the [employer's] interest outweighed the [public employer's] interest in his constitutionally protected speech.[140]

The whistleblower

The *Connick* and *Rankin* cases have raised but hardly settled the phenomenon of the government whistleblower: to what extent does the first amendment protect government employees who blow the whistle on the fraud, corruption, mismanagement, waste, incompetency, dishonesty, or public danger creation of their fellow workers or superiors? This issue, dressed in first amendment terms, often pits entrenched government bureaucracies and their corporate allies against both their own subordinate employees and outside accusers who are able to advance their cause by use of the inside information gained from whistleblowers. Such leaks bring cries of "insubordination" and "disloyalty" from the ranks of the wounded upper hierarchy. This section will examine how the Supreme Court, Congress and state legislatures have begun to reach into this area.

One well-known case, that of A. Ernest Fitzgerald, illustrates the problem. In 1965, Fitzgerald worked for the Air Force as deputy for management systems. A practice had developed in which large corporations engaging in airplane production, here Lockheed, made exceedingly low bids for contracts, and then later, when there was a cost overrun, requested more money for completion, requests heretofore routinely granted. Production of the C-5A cargo transport by Lockheed ran into all kinds of breakdowns because of shortcuts taken to reduce costs. Fitzgerald had leaked some of this information to the press. In Fall, 1969, he was called before Senator Proxmire's committee investigating cost overruns on government contracts. Fitzgerald testified that cost overruns on the contract could be expected to equal two billion dollars. This news received wide news coverage. Shortly thereafter, Fitzgerald was notified that his job had been eliminated, ironically for reasons of "economy."[141] After congressional hearings on the dismissal and considerable press attention, President Nixon asked that his staff arrange for Fitzgerald to be assigned to another job. In an internal memorandum of January 1970, Fitzgerald was described by a Nixon aide as "a top-notch cost expert, but he must be given low marks on loyalty; and after all, loyalty is the name of the game."[142] The recommendation, therefore, was that Fitzgerald be allowed to "bleed, for a while at least."[143] Although a civil service hearing and extensive litigation finally restored Fitzgerald to his former position, in June 1982 certain of his claims for damages were still in litigation. Because of Fitzgerald's courage and persistence, the extensive publicity given his case, and the support by Senator Proxmire and the American Civil Liberties Union, Fitzgerald was able to cut his losses. But most whistleblowers, who do not have such support systems, are casualties to the "low marks on loyalty" given by their superiors. Their sense of duty to a larger public or to their integrity does not usually count for much to higher ups threatened by such "disloyalty."[144] The result is to chill potential whistleblowers from exposing managerial excesses, which is exactly what such tactics are intended to do.

Statutory remedies for whistleblowers

Cases such as that of Fitzgerald have motivated successful efforts to pass whistleblower statutes. About two-thirds of the states have such laws.[145] The Pennsylvania Whistleblower statute, in pertinent part, reads as follows:

§ 1423. protection of employees

(a) Persons not to be discharged. — No employer may discharge, threaten or otherwise discriminate or retaliate against an employee regarding the employee's compensation, terms, conditions, location or privileges of employment because the employee or a person acting on behalf of the employee makes a good faith report or is about to report, verbally or in writing, to the employer or appropriate authority an instance of wrongdoing or waste.

(b) Discrimination prohibited. — No employer may discharge, threaten or otherwise discriminate or retaliate against an employee regarding the employee's compensation, terms, conditions, location or privileges of employment because the employee is requested by an appropriate authority to participate in an investigation, hearing or inquiry held by an appropriate authority or in court action.[146]

Federal employees are protected by the Whistleblower Protection Act of 1989.[147] In signing the bill on April 10, 1989, President Bush stated:

The bill will strengthen the protections and procedural rights available to those Federal employees, often called "Whistleblowers," who report waste, fraud, or abuse in Federal programs. It will ensure that those employees will not suffer adverse personnel actions because of their whistleblowing activities."[148]

The Act creates an Office of Special Counsel that is to "receive and investigate allegations of prohibited personnel practices, and where appropriate" is to "bring petitions for stays, and petitions for corrective action . . . and, file a complaint or make recommendations for disciplinary action."[149] The statute applies to "any disclosure of information by an employee, former employee, or applicant for employment which the employee . . . reasonably believes evidences

(A) a violation of any law, rule or regulation; or
(B) gross mismanagement, a gross waste of funds, an abuse of authority, or a substantial and specific danger to public health or safety."[150]

An individual right of action is provided by seeking "corrective action" from the Merit Systems Protection Board. If the decision of the Board is considered unsatisfactory, the employee may seek judicial review, and if the employee prevails in the action, the employee may be awarded attorney fees.[151]

Whistleblowing has been defined as "a good faith public or intra-organizational disclosure or documentation of real or perceived employer misconduct by a past or present employee of the organization."[152] Whistleblowers are a rare and much endangered species. According to government studies, in 1983, about 70% of federal government employees with knowledge of fraud, waste and abuse failed to disclose it.[153] In 1985, the Office of Special Counsel reported that there were about 130 complaints received, and in 1990 the number was about 250.[154] One of the reasons that the 1989 Whistleblower Protection Act was enacted was that the earlier review procedures for government reprisals against whistleblowers had proved either inadequate, or the Office of Special Counsel (OSC), that agency under both the old and new act that was designated to protect whistleblowers, often proved hostile to them.[155]

According to one commentary, the new act has certain advantages over its predecessor: (1) the Office of Special Counsel is now separated and is independent of the Merit Systems Protection Board, and "shall act in the interests of employees who seek assistance from the office . . . ;"[156] (2) the employee has a reduced burden of proof: instead of having to show that the whistleblowing was a significant or motivating factor in the reprisal, now the employer needed to show it was merely a factor leading to the adverse action;[157] (3) although the OSC still submits its initial investigative results to the target agency for its investigation and response, the whistleblower now has a right to comment on the agency's response.[158]

In addition, an amendment to Merit System Principles, a chapter setting forth the rules to the applied in hiring and working conditions of federal employees, specifies:

> (9) Employees should be protected against reprisal for the lawful disclosure of information which the employees reasonably believe evidences—
>
>> (A) a violation of any law, rule, or regulation, or
>> (B) mismanagement, a gross waste of funds, an abuse of authority, or a substantial and specific danger to public health or safety.[159]

This language may have the effect of separating whistleblower cases involving federal employees from other free speech cases. In principal, whistleblowers should not be subject to the *Pickering-Connick* balancing test but should only have to show, in accordance with the above language, that (1) the employee reasonably believed that (2) (a) agency action was in violation of a law, rule, or regulation or (b) there was mismanagement or some other abuse set forth in the section.[160]

Nevertheless, one author is pessimistic about the likelihood of the new act curing the defects of the old:

> Tension in the jurisprudence of whistleblowers which is reflected in the 1989 Act derives from two competing desires. The first desire is to make the management of the federal government possible by insuring that agency control resides in the hands of those responsible for the agency and able to build a unified team to carry on government's work. Competing with the first is the desire to prevent waste, fraud, and corruption in the administration of federal agencies on the other hand.... [I]n the name of promoting efficiency and preventing illegality, Congress authorizes whistleblowers and thereby undermines the authority of those it makes legally responsible for the agency's operation. Congress' response to this efficiency/management dilemma implicit in the 1989 Act is to opt for management by allowing the agency head to respond to the whistleblower's complaints in a written report.... Although the 1989 Act's amendments to [the Civil Service Reform Act's] whistleblower protections provide some added help to the whistleblower, the balance now, as in the past, remains tilted in favor of agency management.[161]

Whistleblower cases relevant to criminal justice personnel

McDonald v McCarthy[162] illustrates a case that combines a § 1983 action with Pennsylvania's Whistleblower law, quoted above. McDonald was discharged as a part-time policeman after he reported that the chief's brother was dumping trash at the town's waterworks. McDonald was discharged in part because he violated a chain of command directive in going over the chief's head to the attorney general with the complaint. The court responded as follows:

> Enforcement of the chain of command directive, requiring subordinates to report problems to immediate superiors, is a legitimate means of promoting efficiency. But the Borough's interest is outweighed by the public's interest in encouraging investigation of alleged wrong-doing, particularly in circumstances where the speech concerned an investigation of the superior's relative, an elected public official.[163]

Relying on the Pennsylvania Whistleblower statute, the court stated that "reports of official efforts to impede investigation of unlawful activity is precisely the type of disclosure encouraged by the Whistleblower Law,"[164] To the objection that "whistleblowing is limited to unobligatory reports and that McDonald, as a police officer, was required to report illegal activity," the court replied that the law "does not require the absence of an obligation to report wrongdoing, because the purpose of the Whistleblower Law is to protect individuals who report wrongdoing in the course of their employment from having their employment terminated."[165]

Likewise in Solomon v Royal Oak Tp,[166] plaintiff police officer informed a newspaper reporter that the second in command was using police equipment for his own security business and was hiring unqualified personnel. To the suit brought by Solomon seeking relief for the reprisals taken against him for his exposures, the township argued that he had a duty to go through the chain of command rather than to the newspaper with his charges. To this argument the court replied:

> If Solomon had followed the perceived chain of command, his efforts probably would have proved futile because Dawson, his direct supervisor, was the protagonist in the corruption. Moreover, it was reasonable for Solomon to assume that no investigations of Dawson would result by informing Gatewood or any Board members since they had twice demoted him within the past six months, and since many of them were the subjects of corruption investigations initiated by Solomon. Even assuming that a break in the chain of command amounted to some disruption of the department's routine operation, this claim is not consistent with the Pickering analysis, which focuses on disruption resulting from the speech, not from events prior to the speech.
>
> Although Solomon's statements directly questioned his superior's work performance, no evidence was presented that this form of disloyalty adversely affected the proper functioning of the department. On the contrary, Solomon's statements were made because the office was not functioning properly due to Dawson's malfeasance.[167]

But as one case said, there is, for many courts, "a thin line between disruptive rumor-spreading and protected 'whistle-blowing' "[168] In that case, Price v Brittain, Price, a social worker leading drug and alcohol discussion groups in a mental health hospital, was discharged for making numerous charges against staff members including sale and distribution of drugs, beatings of patients, stealing of money, and accusing the head of the institution of complicity in the alleged murder of one of the patients. When Price received no satisfaction within the institution, he contacted the FBI. Although the matters about which Price spoke were clearly of public concern, because of the context in which the speech took place—involving disturbed and dangerous individuals, in an old, dilapidated, understaffed facility, the court concluded "that here the employer's need to prevent disruption and violence was paramount. Price's communications to the staff and patients of the facility therefore were not protected expression."[169]

A like case is Guercio v Brody,[170] in which a confidential secretary's documentation of corrupt bankruptcy assignments resulted in the reorganization of the district's bankruptcy courts. When a new judge, Woods, was appointed, the plaintiff sent to the newspapers, press reports she had found on him, disclosing that he had reputedly represented some organized crime figures when running for office in 1969. Woods warned the Chief Judge that he would not take the post if Guercio remained, at which point the Chief Judge ordered her terminated. According to the court Guercio's campaign against the current judge had overstepped the line:

> Guercio's expression and activities had become a force counterproductive and disruptive to the ongoing effort to rehabilitate and revitalize the operation of the Detroit Bankruptcy Court; [she] was no longer speaking out on matters of public interest, but rather had begun to speak as an employee on matters primarily of personal concern.[171]

Federal employee assertion of first amendment claims

The Supreme Court, in Bush v Lucas,[172] decided that a federal civil service employee whose first amendment rights were violated by a superior was restricted to asserting his first amendment claim through the established civil service administrative procedures and could not seek relief under a *Bivens*-type remedy (see Chapter 1) in federal court. In a unanimous opinion the Court stated:

> Because such claims arise out of an employment relationship that is governed by comprehensive procedural and substantive provisions giving meaningful remedies against the United States, we conclude that it would be inappropriate for us to supplement that regulatory scheme with a new judicial remedy.[173]

Bush was an aerospace engineer who in 1974 was reassigned to a job to which he objected. He appealed to the Civil Service Commission. While his administrative review was pending, he gave TV interviews complaining that his reassigned post provided him with no meaningful work and that it was a waste of taxpayer's money. Shortly after these statements, in August 1975, Bush was charged by his superior, Lucas, with making false, misleading and intemperate public remarks demeaning to the agency for which he worked, impeding its efficiency, and reducing public confidence, thereby undermining morale and causing disharmony among fellow workers. Following a hearing, Bush was demoted in grade and salary. After proceeding through the appeal procedure to the Civil Service Commission's Review Board, Bush in November 1975 was retroactively restored to his former post and was awarded approximately $30,000 in back pay. In the meantime, Bush filed an action in state court for damages. This action was removed by the government to federal court. When the case eventually reached the Supreme Court, the Court assumed for the purpose of the case that Bush's first amendment rights had been violated by his superior's actions, and that the civil service remedies would not provide as effective compensation as an individual action for the harm Bush had suffered. Because Congress had not specifically authorized a remedy outside the civil service structure, the question became whether the Court should authorize the same kind of common law-like remedy as it had in *Bivens*. After reviewing the history of the development of the procedural rights of federal employees, the Court posed the question in a way that could have only one answer: "whether an elaborate remedial system that had been constructed step by step, with careful attention to conflicting policy considerations, should be augmented by the creation of a new judicial remedy for the constitutional violation at issue."[174] The Court declined to provide a separate and independent remedy for first amendment violations for federal civil service workers where Congress had refused to do so.

Claims that regulations are vague and overbroad

A penal statute or regulation which is so vague that persons of common intelligence must guess at its meaning and differ as to its application is void for vagueness because it fails to give "fair warning" as to what conduct must be avoided to remain within the confines of the law, and therefore lends itself to arbitrary and erratic application by enforcement authorities. In first amendment matters, vagueness is an even more serious defect because it tends to have a "chilling effect" on the use of free speech rights. A law overbroad in its coverage is equally objectionable. Such a law covers constitutionally protected as well as prohibited activity and thus makes both types of conduct equally subject to criminal or other penalty.

Meehan v Macy,[175] a 1968 court of appeals case, has been much cited, more because of its florid dicta than because of its reasoning. *Meehan* was originally decided before *Pickering* and then reheard and remanded in light of *Pickering*. The case grew out of the 1964 Panama Canal Zone riots by Panamanians against US policies. In order to ameliorate relations, the US government planned to hire Panamanians to serve as police officers. Meehan, president of the local police union, attended an official meeting during which the governor informed him and others of this proposal, and "cautioned" those attending to avoid disclosing the information to the press, and to confine any protests to regular channels.[176] Meehan, sought out by the Associated Press, gave an interview, the results of which appeared in both the local and continental press. He thereafter circulated a letter and poem highly critical of the governor. Meehan was discharged for, among other things, "conduct unbecoming" a police officer, the charge being based on the distribution of the above-described critical material.[177] He argued that such a charge was unconstitutionally vague. The court replied with a modified version of the *McAuliffe* philosophy:

> We think it is inherent in the employment relationship as a matter of common sense if not common law that an employee in appellant's circumstances cannot reasonably assert a right to keep a job while at the same time he inveighs against his superiors in public with intemperate and defamatory lampoons. We believe that Meehan cannot fairly claim that discharge following an attack like that presented by this record comes as an unfair surprise or is so unexpected and uncertain as to chill his freedom to engage in appropriate speech.[178]

The court conjectured that in the circumstances of the tense Canal Zone, the information released by Meehan "could have had an incendiary effect upon the public,"[179] a test quite similar to the "bad tendency" test.

Meehan took on added significance when it was cited by the Supreme Court a few years later in Arnett v Kennedy.[180] There, a nonprobationary federal civil service employee was discharged for publicly stating that his superior had attempted to bribe a representative of a community action organization. The allegation was without proof and in disregard of facts reasonably discoverable by him. Kennedy was discharged under a federal law that provided that a federal employee "may be removed or suspended without pay only for such cause as will promote the efficiency of the service."[181] Such language, the employee asserted, was vague and overbroad and therefore interfered with his first amendment rights.

Pointing to "long-standing principles of employer-employee relationships, like those developed in the private sector,"[182] Justice Rehnquist concluded for the Court that the statutory language should be interpreted with that relationship in view. After quoting with approval the *Meehan* language cited above, he stated:

> The Act proscribes only that public speech which improperly damages and impairs the reputation and efficiency of the employing agency, and it thus imposes no greater controls on the behavior of federal employees than are necessary for the protection of the Government as an employer. Indeed the Act

is not directed at speech as such, but at employee behavior, including speech, which is detrimental to the efficiency of the employing agency. We hold that the language "such cause as will promote the efficiency of the service" in the Act excludes constitutionally protected speech, and that the statute is therefore not overbroad.[183]

The decision, in analogizing government employment to employment in the private sector, where no first amendment right exists, gravely attenuates the substance of that right.

A few months later, the court decided Parker v Levy,[184] a case discussed above. Levy, an army physician, criticized the Vietnam War, urging blacks to refuse to go if ordered to do so. He was charged with the violation of a section of the military code providing for punishment for "conduct unbecoming an officer and a gentleman."[185] After reciting the differences between military and civilian society, quoted above, the Court reasoned that any problem of vagueness or overbreadth was diminished by prior interpretation of the language by the US Court of Military Appeals and by examples of violation in the Manual for Courts-Martial, giving the words an established "custom and usage."[186] Moreover, said the Court,

> Since appellee could have had no reasonable doubt that his public statements urging Negro enlisted men not to go to Vietnam if ordered to do so were both "unbecoming an officer and gentlemen," and "to the prejudice of good order and discipline in the armed forces," in violation of the [military code], his challenge to them as unconstitutionally vague under the Due Process Clause of the Fifth Amendment must fail.[187]

Would the rigors of *Arnett* and *Parker* be applied to cases involving criminal justice personnel? As indicated earlier in the chapter, the military analogy has usually been rejected. In Muller v Conlisk,[188] a Chicago detective, during an interview with TV news reporters, criticized the department's Internal Inspection Division, stating that "The IID is like a great big washing machine. Everything they put into it comes out clean."[189] When Conlisk was reprimanded for thereby violating a rule prohibiting officers from "engaging in any activity, conversation, deliberation, or discussion which is derogatory to the Department or any member or policy of the Department," he sued, arguing that the rule was vague and overbroad in violation of the first and fourteenth amendments. The court had to confront the claim that police were really more like the military ("quasi-military forces") than teachers and were therefore "dependent upon rigid internal discipline for their effectiveness."[190] Acknowledging the relevance of the claim, the court nevertheless replied that the right of the officer "to speak on matters concerning his employment with the full freedom of any citizen may be limited, but is not destroyed."[191]

> Thus, it is clear that the First Amendment would reach and protect some speech by policemen which could be considered "derogatory to the department." Rule 31 on its face prohibits all such speech, even private conversations, and is for that reason unavoidably overbroad in violation of the First Amendment as it applies to the states through the Fourteenth Amendment.[192]

Another 7th circuit case with similar facts, Bence v Breier,[193] involved a police union president who was reprimanded for sending a letter to Milwaukee's chief negotiator, and for placing copies of the letter on the police bulletin board. The information in the letter, which related to unpaid overtime compensation, was incorrect. Bence was charged with violation of a departmental rule which included the language "conduct unbecoming a member and detrimental to the service. . . ."[194] Such language is too vague to conform to "the constitutionally-mandated 'rough idea of fairness' " because "any apparent limitation on the prohibited conduct through the use of these qualifying terms is illusory, for 'unbecoming' and 'detrimental to the service' have no inherent, objective standards defining the proscribed conduct. . . . "[195]

> The subjectivity implicit in the language of the rule permits police officials to enforce the rule with unfettered discretion, and it is precisely this potential for arbitrary enforcement which is abhorrent to the Due Process Clause. Further, where, as here, a rule contains no ascertainable standards for enforcement, administrative and judicial review can be only a meaningless gesture. There is simply no benchmark against which the validity of the application of the rule in any particular disciplinary action can be tested. The language of the rule additionally offers no guidance to those conscientious members of the Department who seek to avoid the rule's proscription.[196]

In Gasparinetti v Kerr,[197] Gasparinetti, president of the police union, after being transferred from a Tactical Patrol to a less prestigious unit following the end of a racial dispute in Newark, charged that the transfer was motivated as a result of political pressure and threats. He also criticized the chief of the tactical force and other superior officers. He was charged with violating several departmental rules, one of which read:

> Department members shall not publicly disparage or comment unfavorably or disrespectfully on the official action of a superior officer, nor on the Rules, Regulations, Procedures or Orders of the Police Department.[198]

While the court recognized that there was "a significant government interest in regulating some speech of police officers in order to promote efficiency, foster loyalty and obedience to superior officers, maintain morale, and instill public confidence in the law enforcement institution,"[199] this end must be achieved by regulations that "extend only as far as is necessary to accomplish a legitimate governmental interest,"[200] This regulation, however, "indiscriminately casts its net so as to catch, along with that speech which the Department may properly regulate, much speech in which the Department's legitimate interest is minimal."[201]

There is another type of police department regulation that has found more favor with courts. In Kannisto v City and County of San Francisco,[202] a police lieutenant who made disparaging remarks before his officers was suspended under a regulation providing that

> Any . . . conduct . . . which tends to subvert the good order, efficiency, or discipline of the Department . . . shall be considered unofficerlike conduct. . . . [203]

To a suggestion that the regulation was vague and overbroad the court, citing *Kelly,*[204] stated that such regulations were entitled to substantial deference, and concluded that one "could scarcely doubt such talk would tend to subvert the good order, efficiency or discipline of the department,"[205] clearly a bad tendency test.

Restrictions on political activities of public employees

As we have seen, government cannot generally demand that persons give up constitutional rights as the price for public employment. Nevertheless, statutes that have required that public employees refrain from partisan political activity have been upheld. The following sections will describe the historical background that led Congress to pass such restrictive legislation, summarize the most significant legislative restrictions, set forth the important cases determining the constitutionality of that legislation, interpreting its provisions, and show its applicability to criminal justice personnel.

Historical background to political restrictions

Post-Revolutionary War ideas about job tenure[206] were reactions partly to English feudal property concepts that had been transferred to the colonies. Under this doctrine, the king could grant to his favorites property rights to government office. Because many offices involved collection of fees from which the owner of the office was entitled to retain a hefty percentage, these offices were much sought after. The owner could retain the office for life, pass it on to his heirs, or sell it. To deprive the "owner" of the office would be a violation of his right of private property.[207]

Under colonial administration, this practice continued to be a way to maintain the dominance of the "upper social classes."[208] Although provisions in the Articles of Confederation and the Constitution aimed directly or indirectly at eliminating such a proprietary view of public employment, considerations of class and kinship remained the main basis for government appointment through the late eighteenth and the early nineteenth centuries. Washington, for example, looked to "fitness of character" exemplified by "standing in the community and personal integrity," a standard which limited appointments to the social and economic elite of the day.[209] Adams continued this practice but restricted political appointments almost exclusively to members of his own party, thus giving appointments a political bent not present in Washington's administration. Both agreed, however, that government was to be limited to a select few. In Adams' words,

> The proposition that [the people] are the best keepers of their liberties, is not true. They are the worst conceivable; they are no keepers at all. They can neither act, judge, think, or will.[210]

Jefferson was the first to succeed a president of the opposing political party. As a Republican, surrounded by Federalists, he appointed as many as he could from his own and removed as many as he could from the opposing party. Nevertheless, he was the first to develop the concept of political neutrality for political appointees. In a circular, Jefferson stated that employees "will not attempt to influence the votes of others, nor take any part in the business of electioneering, that being deemed inconsistent with the spirit of the Constitution and his duties to it."[211] But like others before him, Jefferson made his appointments from the "natural aristocracy," rather than from an "artificial aristocracy," which he believed could result in a "mischievous ingredient in government."[212] The same policy continued through the administrations of Presidents Madison, Monroe and John Quincy Adams.

The spoils system and the age of egalitarianism

The beginnings of the Industrial Revolution in the early nineteenth century brought forth a new ruling class, an "artificial aristocracy" to replace the older "natural" landed and merchant aristocracy that had ruled America since colonial times. New capital—manufacturing—was replacing old capital.[213] Forces contributing to these changes included the immigration of Irish, Scotch and German peasants, a higher birth rate, the emigration west, the growth of cities, and the extension of canals and railroads to link east and west. These events were associated with the growth of capitalist enterprise, particularly manufacturing in the northeast. In turn, the ideas generated by these changes—free public education, male white sufferage, the "universal ambition to get forward"—led to demands for political as well as social and economic equality.[214] Government offices, as the property of an aristocratic class, could not persist in the face of these changes.

In 1828, Andrew Jackson was able to ride to the presidency on the crest of such a wave of egalitarianism. Politically, these ideas were expressed during Jackson's administration by the "spoils system," and the birth of the political party in its modern form.[215]

> The political party became a permanent institution . . . , a source for government jobs and offices. The prospective elective officeholder petitioned the party for support in the general election; in return for that support he in effect pledged to fill those government offices and jobs which he would control with party faithful.[216]

Although earlier presidents had used a form of patronage, Jackson was the first president to systematize it as a means of maintaining political power. He was also the first to use a system not based on class and to give it an ideological justification. His views can be contrasted with those of John Adams, quoted earlier. In his First Annual Message, Jackson attacked the idea of government office as a "species of property," limited to a privileged few, stating that "the duties of all public officers are, or at least admit of being made, so plain and simple that men of intelligence may readily qualify themselves for their performance. . . . "[217]

The spoils system brought in new leaders who were intent on maintaining their dominance through the insertion in government of political workers whose interest it would be to perpetuate themselves and their administration in office. In furtherance of that plan, government workers, on penalty of job loss, were required to work for their party before and during elections, contribute to party coffers, and vote for the party ticket.[218]

As the economy expanded after the Civil War, more western states entered the Union, industrialization intensified, and a professional and technically-educated middle class evolved to service industrial needs. Federal government employment multiplied to respond to these developments. While in 1851 the federal government employed 26,274 employees, by 1871 this number had jumped to 51,020, by 1881 to 100,020, and by 1891, to 157,442.[219] In the post-Civil War period, groups of professionals (lawyers, editors, clergyman, professors) and business groups (merchants and financiers), previously excluded from government or from its benefits, began a reform movement to apply the same standard to government as they did to their own businesses: a politically neutral employee. "They wanted to disassociate the civil servant from politics and politics from the civil service."[220] For them, civil service reform was to correct the "chief evil" of " 'the alliance between industrialists and a political class which thinks like industrialists.' " Civil service reform [part of the Progressive Movement], would unseat such vandals and put in their place " 'gentlemen . . . who need nothing and want nothing from government except the satisfaction of using their talents,' or at least 'sober, . . . middle class persons who have taken over . . . the proper standards of conduct.' "[221] They looked down on the immigrant groups that occupied many state and federal positions, seeking a means to eliminate these "unqualified" political appointees and replace them with a technically-educated civil service that had permanent tenure, thereby substituting employment security for control by a political boss. Their means to this end was to substitute political appointments with merit-based open competitive examinations for nonpolicymaking government posts.[222]

Statutory reform[223]

Reform was stalled until the July 1881 assassination of President James A. Garfield by a disgruntled Chicago lawyer who had been refused a political appointment.[224] Public reaction was strong against the spoils system. Even more important to the passing of reform legislation was the desire of the Republican party to protect itself against what appeared to be an imminent Democratic victory in the next election, with its likely cleanout of Republican officeholders.[225]

The congressional debate that preceded the final passage of the Civil Service Act of 1883 (the Pendleton Act) focused on the fairness of competitive examination for government employment. At the time, only a small percentage of the population had a high school education. Such education was almost exclusively reserved to the wealthy. Some feared that the exams would be an " 'opening wedge to aristocracy in this country' by excluding the common people from the civil service." The issue was fought out on the question of whether the exams were to have "a practical or a literary character," with the former winning out.[226]

The act finally passed created a Civil Service Commission of three persons, no more than two of whom could be members of the same political party; the members were to be appointed by the president with the advice and consent of the Senate, and could be removed by the president.[227] The Commission was authorized to draw up rules providing for open competitive practical examinations, selection to be from the highest scorers, with a probationary period for appointees.[228] The act did not restrict the president's power to remove an employee. It merely provided that a public employee was "under no obligation to contribute to any political fund, or to render any political service, and that he will not be removed or otherwise prejudiced for refusing to do so," and that "no person" may "use his official authority or influence to coerce the political action of any person or body."[229] The act covered about 10% of employees as compared with about 80% today.[230]

While attempting to remove coercive political influences from forcing partisan political activity on federal employees, the act did not restrict employees from asserting their own beliefs. Although President Hayes in 1877, and President Cleveland in 1886 issued orders requiring neutrality, it was not until President Theodore Roosevelt issued an order in 1907 that employees' assertion of their own beliefs was restricted.[231] That order amended Civil Service Rule 1 as follows:

> Persons who by the provisions of these rules are in the classified service while retaining the right to vote as they please and to express privately their opinions on all political subjects, shall take no active part in political management or in political campaigns.[232]

Until the coming of the Great Depression of 1929 and the ensuing 1932 election victory of Franklin Delano Roosevelt and the New Deal, the use of patronage had been a means to accumulate and maintain power and wealth through politics, particularly for immigrant groups closed out of the business world. The New Deal used the federal government to pump-prime a paralyzed private economy. By the end of 1934, 60 government agencies had been created, only five of which were under the Civil Service Commission rules. Roosevelt's purpose was to place people in these agencies highly motivated with his ideas to solve the economic crisis. Among these were many college-educated middle-class intellectuals attracted to federal employment for the first time. By Roosevelt's second term, one-third of federal employees were outside the civil service system.[233]

Roosevelt's political enemies and those opposed to his economic policies used the issue of political neutrality to restrict his control of the federal bureaucracy. Senator Hatch declared his bill would "prohibit Federal officeholders from misuse of positions of public trust for private partisan ends."[234] The unspoken aim, which would repeatedly surface as a first amendment issue, was to silence potential criticism of Congress or the administration by government officials who had access to facts that would give their criticism credibility and create a "potent force in the public debate."[235]

What became known as the First Hatch Act passed in 1939, the most important provision of which, section 9(a), as amended, read as follows:

> An employee in an Executive agency or an individual employed by the government of the District of Columbia may not—
>> (1) use his official authority or influence for the purpose of interfering with or affecting the result of an election; or
>> (2) take an active part in political management or in political campaigns.
> For the purpose of this subsection, the phrase 'an active part in political management or in political campaigns' means those acts of political management or political campaigning which were prohibited on the part of employees in the competitive service before July 19, 1940, by determinations of the Civil Service Commission under the rules prescribed by the President."[236]

As the Supreme Court later said of the application of § 9,

> It applied to all persons employed by the Federal Government, with limited exceptions [the president, vice-president, and specified officials in policy-making positions]; it made dismissal from office mandatory upon an adjudication of a violation; and whereas Civil Service Rule I had stated that persons retained the right to express their private opinions on all political subjects, the statute omitted the word, "private" and simply privileged all employees "to express their opinion on all political subjects."[237]

The Second Hatch Act of 1940 extended its provisions to state employees paid in whole or in part through federal funds.[238] Later amendments allowed the Commission to impose a lesser penalty than removal.[239] The importance of statutory enactment over earlier executive rulemaking was that statutes make adherence mandatory for all federal employees rather than depending on the uneven enforcement at the discretion of each executive officer.[240]

Constitutionality of the Hatch Acts

The constitutionality of the Hatch Act was challenged in the 1947 case of United Public Workers v Mitchell.[241] Several federal employees of the competitive civil service sought an injunction against the enforcement of § 9(a) claiming that it was unconstitutional under the first, fifth, nineth and tenth amendments, in particular, the portion of § 9(a) that provided that "No officer or employee . . . shall take any active part in political management or in political campaigns."[242] Poole, a roller in the mint and a ward committeeman who worked at the polls during elections, had been charged by the Commission with political activity in violation of the statute.

The Court agreed that the section interfered with Poole's first amendment rights "to act as a party official or worker to further his own political views."[243] But, said the Court, this right must be balanced "against a congressional enactment to protect a democratic society against the supposed evil of political partisanship by classified employees of government."[244] The Court reasoned that Congress and the President, being responsible for efficient public service, decided that such efficiency could best be obtained by prohibiting active participation in politics by classified employees. "To declare that the present supposed evils of political activity are beyond the power of Congress to redress would leave the nation impotent to deal with what many sincere men believe is a material threat to the democratic system."[245]

Pointing out that "it is only partisan activity" that is prohibited, thereby leaving other first amendment activity by public employees untouched, the Court concluded:

> For regulation of the employees it is not necessary that the act regulated be anything more than an act reasonably deemed by Congress to interfere with the efficiency of the public service. . . . Congress may regulate the political conduct of government employees "within reasonable limits," even though the regulation trenches to some extent upon unfettered political action. The determination of the extent to which political activities of governmental employees shall be regulated lies primarily with Congress. Courts will interfere only when such regulation passes beyond the generally existing conception of governmental power.[246]

Justice Douglas, in dissent, protested against the use of the reasonable relationship test in first amendment cases. He called attention to "the interests of the employees in the exercise of cherished constitutional rights."

> If those rights are to be qualified by the larger requirements of modern democratic government, the restrictions should be narrowly and selectively drawn to define and punish the specific conduct which constitutes a clear and present danger to the operations of government. It seems plain to me that that evil has its roots in the coercive activity of those in the hierarchy who have the power to regiment the industrial group or who undertake to do so. To sacrifice the political rights of the industrial workers goes far beyond any demonstrated or demonstrable need.[247]

Douglas' critique of the majority for refusing to use the clear and present danger test and for their lack of understanding that coercion emanates from the hierarchal arrangement in government, foreshadows the vital or paramount (compelling) interest test later used by the Court to measure first amendment violations. Likewise, Douglas's distinction between "industrial" and "administrative" workers[248] later is taken up by the Court in terms of policy and non-policy decisionmakers.

In the 1973 case of Civil Service Commission v Letter Carriers,[249] the Hatch Act language prohibiting a public employee from taking "an active part in political management or in political campaigns" was attacked as unconstitutionally vague and overbroad.[250] By time this case was decided, the Court had jettisoned the *McAuliffe* doctrine designating government employment as a privilege, substituting instead the balancing test of *Pickering*.[251] Using that test, the Court found that the balance struck by Congress was sustained "by the obviously important interests sought to be served by the limitations on partisan political activities now contained in the Hatch Act."[252] In answer to the argument that the statutory language was vague and overbroad, the Court pointed with approval to the case-by-case body of law developed by the Commission since 1907, which the Commission has restated from time to time in detailed regulations setting forth what activities are permitted and what prohibited. In 1939, the Commission had issued a pamphlet to all employees that had reduced its 3000 decisions to a series of detailed do's and don'ts.[253] In a companion case, the Court considered the same objections and similarly rejected them with reference to the little Hatch Acts, enacted by all states to apply to their employees' political activity.[254]

If governments can restrain political activities of their employees, can they also make their employment conditional on their membership or support of the governing political party?

Patronage dismissals as first amendment violations

In the 1976 case, Elrod v Burns,[255] Justice Brennan, speaking for a plurality of three, found the practice of patronage dismissals in violation of the first amendment's right to freedom of political belief and association. A separate opinion by Justice Stewart, with Justice Blackmun joining him, concurred but on narrower grounds. In 1970, a Democratic sheriff, Richard Elrod, was elected to replace a Republican. Plaintiffs, a chief deputy of the process division, a bailiff, and a process server, were all nonmerit employees, appointed by the prior administration. Of 3,000 Cook County Illinois sheriff office employees, about half, at the time challenged, were in "nonmerit" positions awarded by incoming politicians on patronage grounds.[256] These employees replaced incumbent employees of the losing political party. As the Court put it,

> It has been the practice of the Sheriff of Cook County, when he assumes office from a Sheriff of a different political party, to replace non-civil-service employees of the Sheriff's Office with members of his own party when the existing employees lack or fail to obtain requisite support from, or fail to affiliate with, that party. Consequently, subsequent to Sheriff Elrod's assumption of office, [plaintiffs]...were discharged for their employment solely because they did not support and were not members of the Democratic Party and had failed to obtain the sponsorship of one of its leaders.[257]

Patronage was a pervasive means of control of Chicago political and economic life by Democratic party Chief Mayor Richard Daley who thereby had maintained party and city control since 1955.[258] The case therefore held substantial importance for state and local party structures. But the Court stated the issue simply as "the constitutionality of dismissing public employees for partisan reasons."[259]

In its analysis, the Court returned to the use of strict scrutiny analysis. Such analysis required a determination as to how the dismissals impacted on political belief and association, "the core of those activities protected by the First Amendment."[260]

> Under that practice, public employees hold their jobs on the condition that they provide, in some acceptable manner, support for the favored political party. The threat of dismissal for failure to provide that support unquestionably inhibits protected belief and association, and dismissal for failure to provide support only penalizes its exercise.[261]

Having decided that the practice contravenes the first amendment, the Court looked to see if the state had a paramount interest that would outweigh the employee's first amendment rights. Before considering this balance, the Court brushed aside any remaining doubt that it still adhered to the right-privilege distinction with reference to government employment. In order for the practice to surmount first amendment objections it

> must further some vital government end by a means that is least restrictive of freedom of belief and association in achieving that end, and the benefit gained must outweigh the loss of constitutionally protected rights.[262]

The Court recognized that the state had a vital "need for political loyalty of employees . . . to the end that representative government not be undercut by tactics obstructing the implementation of policies of the new administration. . . ."[263] But such an interest would not "validate patronage wholesale. Limiting patronage dismissals to policymaking positions is sufficient to achieve this governmental end." The rationale for this policy-nonpolicymaking distinction is that "nonpolicymaking individuals usually have only limited responsibility and are therefore not in a position to thwart the goals of the in-party." The Court recognized that "no clear line can be drawn between" these two positions.[264] In any particular instance, "it is the government's burden to demonstrate an overriding interest in order to validate an encroachment on protected interests, . . . cases of doubt being resolved in favor of the" employee.[265] The Court distinguished the cases of *Mitchell* and *Letter Carriers* by subordinating "the category of political campaigning and management" in the first amendment spectrum to individual belief and association on the theory that the proper functioning of a democratic system depends "on the unfettered judgment of each citizen on matters of political concern."[266]

Justice Stewart, in his concise concurring opinion, one which provided the standard for future cases, narrowed the question before the Court to:

> whether a nonpolicymaking, nonconfidential government employee can be discharged or threatened with discharge from a job that he is satisfactorily performing upon the sole ground of his political beliefs.[267]

Here, the plaintiffs were nonpolicymaking, nonconfidential employees. Hence they could not be discharged for their political beliefs.

These two opinions were formed into a cohesive whole by Justice Stevens in the 1980 decision of Branti v Finkel.[268] There, county public defenders, appointed by a Republican, were discharged by the incoming Democratic Public Defender "solely because they were Republicans and thus did not have the necessary Democratic sponsors."[269] The Court again found the test to be whether the state had the "overriding interest" to interfere with first amendment rights. Using Justice Stewart's framework, the Court stated:

> the ultimate inquiry is not whether the label "policymaker" or "confidential" fits a particular position; rather, the question is whether the hiring authority can demonstrate that party affiliation is an appropriate requirement for the effective performance of the public office involved.[270]

Those issues were resolved by the Court in determining that "the primary, if not the only, responsibility of an assistant public defender is to represent individual citizens in controversy with the State." With reference to the question of confidentiality, the Court concluded that "although an assistant is bound to obtain access to confidential information arising out of various attorney-client relationships, that information has no bearing whatsoever on partisan political concerns."[271]

Thus, the *Elrod-Branti* rule can be said to be that public employees are not "policymakers" for the purpose of a permissible politically-motivated discharge even where decisionmaking is an important part of their responsibility if the decisions themselves play no part in "partisan political concerns." The cases further establish that discharge based on political affiliation can be sustained only if the government can show that "party membership was essential to the discharge of the employee's governmental responsibilities."[272] An executive exercising the discharge power for political reasons, when challenged, must show "either (1) proof that political affiliation is a proper criterion for the position, or (2) a statement of legitimate reasons for discharge other than political affiliation."[273] The cases protect the rights of public employees to be free from discharge from a government job because of their political beliefs, and the right to belong to a political party of their choice.[274]

Elrod-Branti Rule Expanded

Ten years after *Branti*, Mr. Justice Brennan, speaking for a five to four majority in Rutan v Republican Party of Illinois,[275] faced the issue whether the *Elrod-Branti* rule should be extended to cover "promotion, transfer, recall, and hiring decisions involving low-level public employees" as well as those *discharged* for failure to adhere to or support the political party of the government employer. The majority decided that such political patronage practices did come within the rule and that therefore government action to so penalize government employees was a violation of their first amendment rights.

The action arose out of a 1980 executive order of the Illinois governor that froze all 60,000 jobs subject to his control. Exceptions to the order were permitted only upon requests submitted to the Governor's Office of Personnel that operated a system of political patronage, approving hiring, promotions, transfers and recalls only for those who supported the Republican Party.

Plaintiffs included Rutan, a rehabilitation counselor, who allegedly had been denied promotion to a supervisory position; an employee of the Illinois Department of Transportation, who claimed he had been denied a transfer to an office nearer his home; another who claimed he had been denied employment as a prison guard; and others who charged they were not recalled after layoffs, all because they did not work for, and therefore did not have the support of, Republican Party officials for their applications.

Mr. Justice Brennan first set forth the first amendment rationale behind *Elrod:*

> The plurality explained that conditioning public employment on the provision of support for the favored political party "unquestionably inhibits protected belief and association." It reasoned that conditioning employment on political activity pressures employees to pledge political allegiance to a party with which they prefer not to associate, to work for the election of political candidates they do not support, and to contribute money to be used to further policies with which they do not agree. The latter, the plurality noted, had been recognized by this Court as "tantamount to coerced belief"[276]

Placing this case within the rules of both *Elrod* and *Branti*, Brennan wrote:

> In *Elrod*, we suggested that policymaking and confidential employees probably could be dismissed on the basis of their political views. In *Branti*, we said that a State demonstrates a compelling interest in infringing First Amendment rights only when it can show that "party affiliation is an appropriate requirement for the effective performance of the public office involved." The scope of this exception does not concern us here as respondents concede that the five employees who brought this suit are not within it.[277]

To the argument that because the plaintiffs had no "right" to promotions, transfers or recall from layoffs, they had no legal claim, the Court replied: "For at least a quarter-century, this Court has made clear that even though a person has no 'right' to a valuable government benefit and even though the government may deny him the benefit for any number of reasons, *there are some reasons upon which the government may not rely. It may not deny a benefit to a person on a basis that infringes his constitutionality protected interest—especially, his interest in freedom of speech.*"[278]

The Court concluded therefore that the *Elrod-Branti* rule applied

> to the patronage practices at issue here. A government's interest in securing effective employees can be met by discharging, demoting or transferring staff members whose work is deficient. A government's interest in securing employees who will loyally implement its policies can be adequately served by choosing or dismissing certain high-level employees on the basis of their political views. Likewise, the "preservation of the democratic process" is no more furthered by the patronage promotions, transfers, and rehires at issue here than it is by patronage dismissals. First, "political parties are nurtured by other, less intrusive and equally effective methods." ... Second, patronage decidedly impairs the elective process by discouraging free political expression by public employees. ... Respondents who include the Governor of Illinois and other state officials, do not suggest any other overriding government interest in favoring Republican Party supporters for promotion, transfer, and rehire.
>
> We therefore determine that promotions, transfers, and recalls after payoffs based on political affiliation or support are an impermissible infringement on the First Amendment rights of public employees.[279]

Application of the Elrod-Branti-Rutan rule

Elrod and *Branti*, and now *Rutan* have been criticized in that they "created a hopelessly inconsistent and unpredictable jurisprudence in this area that fails to protect the very interests *Elrod* and *Branti* seek to uphold. ... The test chosen by the majority in *Rutan* has proven impossible to apply in a consistent and logical manner, because determining whether a particular government job is appropriately a 'political' appointment is an inheritantly political question—one poorly suited for judicial determination."[280]

Another commentator has stated the problem of forging such a test as follows:

> [L]ower court treatment of workers at opposite ends of the employment spectrum has been straightforward and predictable. For example, a cleaning woman in the governor's executive mansion clearly receives *Elrod/Branti* protection. At the other end of the spectrum, lawyers—other than assistant public defenders— generally have not received protection from patronage dismissals. Difficulties arise, however, because most jobs fall somewhere in the middle of

this continuum. As a result, lower courts have attempted to create objective criteria by which to determine where the continuum dividing line occurs and on which side a specific job lies.[281]

The First Circuit Court of Appeals, for example, arrived at a "two-step inquiry":

> The first step in this inquiry requires a determination of whether the position from which the plaintiff/employee was removed involves decisionmaking on issues where there is room for political disagreement on goals or their implementation." The second step of the inquiry examines the particular responsibilities of the position in order to determine whether the position is one of a policymaker, one where the appointee is a communicator, or some other type of position whose function is such that party affiliation is an equally appropriate requirement. The court emphasized that the focus of the inquiry should be on the inherent powers of the position itself, rather than on the function performed by the individual holding the particular position.[282]

More recent cases, some of which are Post-*Rutan,* can be divided into those in which dismissal or other sanction is based (1) solely on political affiliation; (2) or those in which there is some other motive for the sanction in addition to political affiliation—mix motive dismissal; and (3) in which political affiliation is not a factor in the sanction.

Sanction solely because of political affiliation

This classification can be further divided into those cases (a) in which states have statutorily declared certain government jobs to be "exempt" or "policymaking" that is, to be positions for which political affiliation is a proper qualification; (b) those cases in which the sanction was purely for political reasons; and (c) cases in which a confidential relationship or loyalty between employer and employee was the basis of dismissal.

(a) "Exempt" or "policymaking" classifications

In Savage v Gorski,[283] three employees, Confidential Secretary to the Director of the County Correctional Facility; Co-ordinator for Pre-Trial Release Services for the county; and First Deputy Service Officer for the county Veterans Agency claimed their first amendment rights had been violated because they were terminated for political reasons soon after the County Executive assumed office. Each of these positions was classified as "exempt" under New York State Civil Service law.

Although the statute was not the deciding factor in the decision, the court in part relied on the statute, setting forth the statute's rationale:

[D]etermining whether it makes sense to exempt appellees' positions from First Amendment protection involves many of the same factors that New York State already has considered in exempting these public employment positions from its constitutionally-mandated civil service system. "The criteria . . . are the confidential nature of the position, the performance of duties which require the exercise of authority or discretion at a high level, or the need . . . to have some expertise or personal qualities which cannot be measured by a competitive exam." Here, [the secretary's] duties were confidential; [the co-ordinator] was exempt from taking a competitive exam; and [the First Deputy] duties required the exercise of discretion at an important level. Both the interests of federalism and the conservation of judicial resources would ordinarily be better served by the federal courts' giving substantial deference to the state's judgment where government positions are so defined. Otherwise, federal courts will be embroiled in determining at each change of state or local administration which positions are appropriately within the political patronage system. Such a determination not only creates the possibility of a super-civil service overseen by the courts, but allows the federal judiciary to intrude undesirably into the very structure of state and local governments.[284]

Courts have been varied in their acceptance of the legislature's designation of certain positions as "exempt." One circuit has decided that such a statute creates "a presumption at law that discharge or demotion was proper."[285] The seventh circuit rejects such a presumption. In Lohorn v Michal,[286] a newly elected mayor reduced the rank of an assistant chief of police to detective sergeant based on an Indiana Statute that authorized an executive to reduce in grade any member of the police department "who holds an upper level policy making position." To a demand by the defending mayor that the statute was determinative, the court replied:

The court cannot give conclusive weight to the government assertion that it has a compelling interest in infringing on the protected interests at issue here. Rather, the court must scrutinize the government's professed justification for impairing these first amendment interests.[287]

(b) sanction solely for political association or activity

The case of Zold v Township of Mantua[288] sets forth the test and burden of proof in these cases:

"the ultimate inquiry is not whether the label 'policymaker' or 'confidential' fits a particular position; rather the question is whether the hiring authority can demonstrate that party affiliation is an appropriate requirement for the effective performance of the public office involved." This court has stated, "should a difference in party affiliation be highly likely to cause an official to be ineffective in carrying out the duties and responsibilities of the office, dismissals for that reason would not offend the First Amendment." The burden of proof is on the defendant to demonstrate "an overriding interest" in order to validate an encroachment on an employee's First Amendment rights.[289]

Zold involved a claim by a township clerk who was not reappointed by an incoming mayor. The clerk handled the day-to-day duties of the clerk and filled in when the clerk was unavailable. "[D]efendants have failed to carry their substantial burden of demonstrating that political affiliation is an appropriate requirement for the effective performance of the deputy municipal clerk. . . ."[290]

On the other hand, where in Terry v Cook,[291] a newly elected sheriff refused to rehire his deputies, the court, on the basis of a state statute making a deputy sheriff the general agent who was empowered to act for the sheriff, decided that "the closeness and cooperation required between sheriffs and their deputies necessitates the sheriff's absolute authority over their appointment and/or retention."[292]

(c) sanction because position involves confidential relationship or loyalty

Soderstrum v Town of Grand Isle[293] illustrates a number of factors that bring it within the *Elrod-Branti* exception. Soderstrum was appointed to her post of secretary to the chief of police by newly elected officials. To her claim for reappointment, the court responded:

> [The new chief] should not be prevented by the First Amendment from replacing his defeated opponent's secretary and relative, at least when that person . . . has unambiguously expressed her lack of confidence in the incoming official and her unwillingness to work in the new administration.[294]

(d) Sanction because of mixed motives

In Duffy v Sarault,[295] plaintiffs, who had been city clerk and director of the department of parks and recreation, were eliminated by a reorganization plan soon after the entry of a new mayor in office. Plaintiffs had supported the present mayor's opponent and there was acrimony between them. The court concluded that even though

> the political affiliations of [the plaintiffs] were impermissibly considered in the decision to reorganize the City of Pawtucket which eliminated their jobs. . . . the two would have lost their jobs anyway regardless of their political ties, and thus that no First Amendment violation occurred.[296]

(e) Sanction where political affiliation not a factor

In Wright v Phipps, former sheriff's deputies and employees from other county departments were terminated when a new administration was elected. In each case the court rejected claims that the terminations were politically based. In one case there was a reduction in force because the new administration found that three persons were doing a job when only one was needed and no one was hired to take his place; in others, a secretary was clearly incompetent; a deputy sheriff had a serious drinking problem; a chief jailer had been involved in a traffic accident while intoxicated; and in the case of another deputy, there were many citizen complaints that he was not doing his job.[297]

Mr. Justice Scalia and the future of *Elrod-Branti*

Mr. Justice Scalia filed a long dissent in *Rutan* arguing that when "a practice [political patronage] not expressly prohibited by the text of the Bill of Rights bears the endorsement of a long tradition of open, widespread, and unchallenged use that dates back to the beginning of the Republic, we have not proper basis for striking it down."[298] In Justice Scalia's view, "the desirability of patronage is a policy question to be decided by the people's representatives . . ."[299]

> The choice in question, I emphasize, is not just between patronage and a merit-based civil service, but rather among various combinations of the two that may suit different political units and different eras: permitting patronage hiring, for example, but prohibiting patronage dismissal; permitting patronage in municipal agencies but prohibiting it in the police department; or permitting it in the mayor's office but prohibiting it everywhere else. I find it impossible to say that, always and everywhere, all of these choices fail our "balancing" test. The last point explains why Elrod and Branti should be overruled, rather than merely not extended. Even in the field of constitutional adjudication, where the pull of stare decisis is at its weakest, one is reluctant to depart from precedent. But when that precedent is not only wrong, not only recent, not only contradicted by a long prior tradition, but also has proved unworkable in practice, then all reluctance ought to disappear. In my view that is the situation here.[300]

Given the fact that two of the five man majority, Brennan (who wrote the opinion) and Marshall have retired, and been replaced by justices more likely to agree with Justice Scalia's view of things, the *Elrod-Branti* doctrine may not long endure.

Summary and conclusions

Government employees, state and federal, now represent 18% of the civilian workforce. Restriction of first amendment rights of such a large part of the working population is therefore bound to have an adverse effect on democratic government, especially when it is further recognized that it is just such employees to whom we must look for the most informative criticism of government operations.

In a democratic society, free speech includes the right to form and hold beliefs, to communicate ideas, to associate with and hear the views of others, to have access to information, and to engage in joint expression. The first amendment was added to the Constitution by the newly-independent states for fear that the creation of a centralized power, the federal government, would lead to the curbing of the people's rights. But because government in early America had relatively little to do with people's lives (most activity was private and the first amendment only applies to government action), the amendment, during the first 150 years of its existence, was little noticed by the courts, and played a minor role in American politics. It was only during World War I that protests against our participation, together with legislation to repress those protests, thrust upon the Supreme Court first amendment issues.

In confronting such issues the Court developed two tests: the supposed "bad tendency" of some speech to provoke unlawful action; and the clear and present danger test—that speech may be limited by government only when "the incidence of the evil apprehended is so imminent that it may befall before there is an opportunity for full discussion." Not until 1925 did the Court agree that the first amendment applied to the states through the fourteenth amendment. In general, at any particular time, the strength of first amendment rights has depended on the strength of those asserting rights as compared to the perceived threat to the established order and the state's power to suppress that threat.

In more normal times, constitutional doctrine has given the amendment a "preferred position" among constitutional guarantees so that where a statute or regulation interferes with first amendment rights, the government must show that it has both a compelling or overriding interest in such legislation and that the particular law has restricted first amendment rights as little as possible to carry out that state interest.

The development of first amendment rights can be divided into a pre and post-*Pickering* period. The pre-Pickering period (extending from the 1892 *McAuliffe* decision to the 1968 *Pickering* case), saw multiple societal changes affecting the employer-employee relationship, including the huge increase in government services and employees, the growth of public unions, and their assertion of public employee rights. This period represented a transition for public employees from master-servant to employer-employee relations. In the 1950s the Court began to reject the *McAuliffe* doctrine. It concluded that constitutional protection did extend to public employment, arriving at the unconditional conditions theory—that while government employment is not a right, neither can a government employee be required to maintain that employment at the price of being subjected to unconstitutional conditions.

Pickering, still the major guideline in this area, found that a teacher who had criticized a schoolboard would not be dismissed even though some of his statements were incorrect. The Court, using a balancing test that compared the competing rights of the teacher and those of the state employer, concluded that in this case the "interest of the school administration in limiting debate is not significantly greater than its interest in limiting a similar contribution by any member of the general public." In arriving at the decision, the Court noted that Pickering's expressions were not directed at anyone with whom he had daily contact so that questions of discipline by his immediate superior, or work harmony, were not involved; neither was his employment one of close working relations or one that required personal loyalty or confidence.

Pickering left up in the air the degree to which the employee's expression had to motivate the dismissal before it would serve as a basis for constitutional complaint. *Mt Healthy* determined the point by setting forth a three-tiered test: (1) employees have the burden of showing that their conduct was protected by the first amendment; (2) the expression must have been a "substantial" or "motivating" factor in the government's decision to dismiss; and (3) the government can show by a preponderance of the evidence that it would have reached the same decision even in the absence of the first amendment expression. The purpose of the test was to prevent employees from being able to place themselves in a better position as a result of their assertion of first amendment rights. Such a view is obviously contrary to that taken by Justice Brandeis in urging that public expression is a political duty. Exercise of first amendment rights by government employees is always a risky affair and the decision to "take that risk" is a weighty one. The shift in that balance provided by *Mt Healthy* is likely to result in more employees deciding that they are better off if they do "nothing."

Courts have looked at whether criminal justice personnel appear to be closer to teachers as in *Pickering* or to the military. For example, the Court has found the CIA to be an organization requiring such a "high degree of trust" of its employees that there is little room for the exercise of first amendment rights. Several cases have recognized that the military is "a specialized society" which has developed its own laws and traditions and requires obedience and discipline. Though the Court has refused the invitation to categorize the police as "para-military," it has required deference to a police department's hair-grooming regulation "in the context of the county's chosen mode of organization for its police force." While the Court at this point seems unlikely to accept the paramilitary analogy, in a balancing of interests, the Court can be expected to come down on the side of departmental needs rather than "individual" criticism of departmental policies.

Of the several rationales used to suppress public employee speech, the most important is that the effect of the employee's speech has been to interfere with agency morale or efficiency. Such a rationale for suppression of speech ultimately derives from the acceptance of the belief that the views of persons higher in the hierarchy have more worth than the views of those lower down. Courts have two tests: (a) whether the speech has "materially and substantially" disputed the working relationship, or (b) the mere criticism of the superior is presumed to result in the disruption of that relationship, and therefore of the agency's efficiency.

Courts which use the first of the above tests usually find for the employee while courts using the second usually find that the likelihood of the free speech disrupting the employment relationship supersedes the employee's free speech rights. There are also a number of decisions emphasizing the basic values of free speech as expressed by Brandeis. Often such courts are more realistic in looking at the context in which the speech took place. They note that far from provoking disharmony, the speech is more likely to be a symptom of it, or that even where there is disruption, that is the price this society pays for an informed citizenry. Conversely, some speech, such as insulting remarks to other employees, is unprotected.

In the 1983 case, Connick v Myers, a slim Court majority opts for a hierarchal model of employer-employee relations akin to that of private industry in which agency "efficiency" and workplace "harmony" are defined from the supervisor's point of view. In terms of first amendment law, the Court seems to be favoring a sort of bad tendency test over a substantial injury or clear and present danger test.

The Court places considerable obstacles before the public employee seeking protection from his public employer for the use of his free speech rights. A public employee is protected only when his speech can be said to be a matter of "public concern," that is, it relates to "any matter of political, social, or other concern to the community." The Court set forth a number of factors considered by lower courts in subsequent cases: acts of insubordination interfering with the working relationship; deference to the employer's judgment; no need for the employer to wait until disruption occurs before taking action. On the other hand, where the speech transpires on the employee's own time, and in non-work areas of the office, the result may be different.

In a later case, Rankin v McPherson, the Court upheld the free speech rights of an employee who made an off-hand remark upon the attempt on President Reagan's life largely because her discharge was "unrelated to the functioning of the office."

Post-Connick-Rankin cases flushed out the meaning of "public concern." In general, the employee's use of free expression had to raise some question about public administration that went beyond the employee's personal grievance. Once courts have dealt with the issue of public concern, they must balance interests between employer and employee. Cases fall into three categories: those concerning insubordination; criticism of the employee's superior, and those involving disruption of the workplace.

Insubordination, or refusal to carry out orders of a superior, accompanied by criticism of those orders, has been disposed of by courts on a disruption of the workplace rationale. Criticism of superior is least likely to result in a disruption of the workplace where the person criticized is sufficiently "distant" either because the person is not the employee's immediate superior, or is in some "independent" status such as judge where no working relationship is involved. With reference to criticism that is alleged to lead to disruption in the workplace, such condition must be proved by the employer-defendant. Actual disruption must be shown and the employer's actions in contributing to the disruption may also be considered. Where certain "core values" are present, such as those represented by an election campaign, a higher showing may be required.

Government employees who have the courage to report fraud, abuse, or mismanagement on the part of their superiors, would seem to be a prime example of the fundamental value of free expression. Until recently, however, such expression by whistleblowers has received little protection from either courts or legislatures. Today, however, two-thirds of all states and the federal Whistleblower Protection Act of 1989 provide some protection to whistleblowers. Nevertheless, the clash between those who see government as needing a strong management team acting without fear of challenge and those who believe that the very likelihood of challenge if they do wrong, some fear, has been tipped in favor of management. Courts have not been able to work out a distinctive whistleblower doctrine based on the superior free expression value to society of the whistleblower, and therefore have largely followed the *Connick-Rankin* reasoning.

Federal employees are restricted in their claims by the civil service administrative procedures and have no Bivens-type remedy available.

Provisions restricting public employee free speech are frequently attacked as vague and overbroad. Phrases such as "conduct unbecoming an officer and a gentleman," or "such cause as will promote the efficiency of the service," have been upheld for federal employment and the military. But the rationale of these cases has not generally been transferred to criminal justice personnel. Broadly stated provisions, which deny criminal justice personnel all right to criticize their departments and superiors, are generally struck down while a more narrowly drawn regulation is more likely to be upheld.

Another area of regulation of public employee speech lies in the state's restriction on their political activities. Political office in colonial times was looked on as the property of the ruling classes, as one means of maintaining power. As political parties developed in the nineteenth century, and new groups of immigrants challenged this monopoly of power, President Jackson and those who followed him, used the "spoils system" (to the victor belongs the spoils), to replace public employees of the losing party with those employees who would be loyal to the incoming victors. To preserve their own jobs such workers had an interest in perpetuating the incumbent in power. In most cities they represented new immigrant groups that had pushed out, through the use of political machines, the older aristocracy. By the end of the 19th century, however, as the country industrialized, a new middle class of bureaucrats and professional-technocrats combined with business groups to form a reform movement asserting new values. These newer groups sought a politically neutral, technically-educated civil service with permanent tenure, substituting employment security for control by a political boss. Their goal was to replace political appointments with merit based open competitive examinations for nonpolicymaking government posts.

The legislative result of this reform movement was the Civil Service Act of 1883, the Pendleton Act, which created a Civil Service Commission authorizing competitive examinations and providing that public employees had no obligation to render political service. Employees were further prohibited from using their official authority to coerce political action in others. During the Great Depression, to deal with the economic crisis, the Roosevelt administration created a government bureaucracy and government programs heretofore unknown. Many college-educated middle class intellectuals, imbued with an ideological fervor to make the New Deal work, entered federal service for the first time. Roosevelt's political enemies, opposed to his programs and fearing that the wave of new employees would be politically dedicated to them, in 1939, proposed and passed the Hatch Act which prohibited federal employees from taking an active part in political campaigns. The legislation applied to all federal employees except to appointive policymaking positions. The Second Hatch Act of 1940 extended coverage to state employees paid in whole or in part with federal funds and state little Hatch Acts completed the process for state employees.

The constitutionality of the First Hatch Act was challenged and sustained in the 1947 case of United Public Workers v Mitchell on the ground that the act restricted only "partisan activity," leaving other first amendment activity untouched. The act was also upheld against a vagueness attack in the *Letter Carriers* case on the basis of the case-by-case body of rules the Civil Service Commission had developed over the years. Likewise, in *Broadrick,* the state Little Hatch Acts were found constitutional.

The modern equivalent of the spoils system, party patronage, came under attack in Elrod v Burns. That system was struck a death blow when *Elrod* made dismissals based on party affiliation, a violation of the employees' first amendment rights to freedom of political belief and association. The government's interest in employee loyalty could be preserved by limiting patronage dismissals to policymaking positions. Nonpolicymakers have only limited opportunities to thwart the aims of the in-party. It is the government's burden to show an overriding interest in such dismissal. Justice Stewart's concurring opinion supplied the criteria for establishing the burden of proof: whether the discharged employee was a nonpolicymaking, nonconfidential employee.

In the 1980 decision of Branti v Finkel public defenders complained that they were fired when another political party gained the election. Because the employer could not demonstrate that party affiliation was an appropriate qualification for effective job performance, such firing was in violation of plaintiffs' first amendment rights.

Ten years after *Branti*, the Court, in Rutan v Republican Party of Illinois, expanded the rule against political patronage discharges to include, as well promotions, transfers, recalls and hiring decisions. In the years since *Elrod-Branti*, there has been considerable criticism that the decisions have "created a hopelessly inconsistent and unpredictable jurisprudence . . . impossible to apply in a consistent and logical manner." Nevertheless, recent cases can be divided into those in which the sanction was (1) solely based on political affiliation; (2) those which have mixed motives; and (3) those in which political affiliation is not a factor.

Some states have attempted to designate certain positions as "exempt" from their civil service and thus subject to replacement by incoming officials. Courts have varied in the deference they have given to such statutes, frequently looking behind them to see if party affiliation is really a proper qualification for the job. A requisite for a confidential relationship would be such a qualification.

Justice Scalia, in a long dissent in *Rutan*, joined by three other justices, urged that the rule was unworkable and should be overruled. Because two of the majority have now left the Court, the *Elrod-Branti-Rutan* rule has an insecure future.

ENDNOTES

1. 391 US 563 (1968).
2. In recent years, the percentage of government workers as compared to total employed has been steadily growing. In 1965, 1978, and 1980, 1987 the percentages were respectively 14.8, 15.9, 16.75, and 17.8. While the number of federal employees have remained substantially unchanged (about 3 million) during these years, state and local employees have increased over 100% from 8,000,000 in 1965 to 17,281,000 in 1987. The total of both federal and state/local employees in 1987 is 17,281,000. Statistical Abstract of the United States, Washington, DC, US Government Printing Office, 1966, 1979, 1990, Tables 488, 494, 519. The federal government is the country's largest single employer.
3. Emerson, T: The system of freedom of expression, New York, Vintage, 1970, p 3.
4. Id at 6–7.
5. Dwoskin, R: Rights of the public employee, Chicago, American Library Assoc, 1978, p 15; Davis v Williams 617 F2d 1100, 1103 (5th Cir), cert denied 449 US 937 (1980); Kairys, D: "Freedom of Speech," in The politics of law, a progressive critique, Kairys, D, ed, New York, Pantheon, 1982, pp 163–4. I have heavily relied on this article in writing this section.

6. Rabban, D: "The first amendment and its forgotten years," 90 Yale Law J 514, 542, 557 (1981); Murphy, P: World War I and the origin of civil liberties in the United States, New York, Norton, 1979; Murphy, P: The meaning of freedom of speech: First amendment freedoms from Wilson to FDR, Westport, Greenwood, 1972, p 248. For a somewhat different view that analyzes state first amendment decisions, see Blanchard, M: "Filling in the void: Speech and press in state courts prior to *Gitlow,*" The first amendment reconsidered: New perspectives on the meaning of freedom of speech and press, Chamberlin, B, and Brown, C, eds, New York, Longman, 1982, pp 14–59. But the thesis that state courts' conception of the first amendment as inapplicable to "disgruntled minorities" and to unions is supported. See pp 28–30.

7. Kairys p 141, *supra* n 5; Murphy, The meaning of freedom of speech, p 248, *supra* n 6.

8. Kairys p 145, *supra* n 5.

9. Id at 157; Fishbein, L: Rebels in Bohemia: The radicals of *The Masses,* 1911–1917, Chapel Hill, U of No Carolina, 1982, Ch 1 and 2.

10. Act of June 15, 1917, c 30, I § 3, 50 USC 33 (repealed 1948).

11. Act of May 16, 1918, c 75, § 1, 40 Stat 533, 1359–60; Murphy, The meaning of freedom of speech, p 22, *supra* n 6.

12. Murphy, the meaning of freedom of speech, p 22, 249, *supra* n 6; Fishbein pp 24–29, *supra* n 9.

13. Murphy, The meaning of freedom of speech, p 25, *supra* n 6.

14. Id.

15. 205 US 454 (1907).

16. Id at 462 (emphasis added).

17. 249 US 47 (1919).

18. Kairys p 154, *supra* n 5.

19. Id at pp 155–6; Rabban pp 591–3, *supra* n 6; Murphy, Freedom of speech pp 254–5, *supra* n 6.

20. 250 US 616 (1919).

21. Id at 630–31.

22. Whitney v California 274 US 357, 375 (1927).

23. Abrams v United States 250 US 616, 628 (1919).

24. Whitney v California 274 US 357, 377 (1927).

25. Gitlow v New York 268 US 652 (1925).

26. Stromberg v California 283 US 359 (1931); Near v Minnesota 283 US 697, 7707, 713–22 (1931).

27. Kairys pp 141, 156, *supra* n 5; Murphy, Freedom of speech pp 270–71, *supra* n 6.

28. 323 US 516 (1945).

29. Id at 529.

30. McKay, R: "The preference for freedom," 34 NYU L Rev 1182, 1183–4 (1959).

31. Id at 1184.

32. 155 Mass 216, 29 NE 517.

33. 155 Mass at 220, 29 NE at 517.

34. 391 US 563.
35. Much of the following case analysis is indebted to Finck, K: "Nonpartisan speech in the police department: The aftermath of *Pickering,*" 7 Hastings Const L Q 1001–1029 (1980).
36. Adler v Bd of Education 342 US 485 (1952).
37. Pickering v Bd of Education 391 US 563, 568 (1968).
38. See Connick v Myers 461 US 138 (1983), discussed below.
39. 155 Mass at 220, 29 NE at 517 (1892), and see Van Alstyne, "The demise of the right-privilege distinction in constitutional law," 81 Harv L Rev 1439 (1968).
40. 342 US 485 (1952).
41. Id at 492.
42. Finck p 1006, *supra* n 35.
43. 342 US at 511.
44. 344 US 183 (1952).
45. Id at 191–192.
46. Finck p 1006, *supra* n 35.
47. 350 US 551
48. Id at 554.
49. Id at 555, 559.
50. 385 US 589 (1967).
51. Id at 606. This proposition has now been placed in doubt by Rust v Sullivan 111 SCt 1759, 1765 (1991) in which the Court upheld an interpretation of Title X of the Public Health Service Act by the Secretary of the Department of Health and Human Services prohibiting family planning "from referring a pregnant woman to an abortion provider, even upon specific request." To the argument that the regulation prohibited all discussion about abortion, the Court responded that "this is not a case of the government "suppressing a dangerous idea, but of a prohibition on a project grantee or its employers from engaging in activities outside its scope." Id at 1772. The implication of this decision is enormous, namely, allowing the state to eliminate first amendment activities associated with any activity it funds.
52. 391 US 563 (1968).
53. Id at 564.
54. Id at 569.
55. Id at 568.
56. Id at 569–570.
57. Id at 570.
58. Id.
59. Id at 572–3.
60. 376 US 251 (1964).
61. 391 US at 573.
62. Id.
63. 461 US 138 (1983).

64. Gilbert v Minnesota 254 US 325, 338 (1920).

65. Finck p 1014, *supra* n 35.

66. Id at 1015.

67. 429 US 274 (1977).

68. Id at 282–3.

69. Id at 287.

70. Id.

71. Id at 284.

72. Id at 285.

73. Id.

74. Id at 285–6.

75. Givhan v Western Line Consolidated School District 439 US 410, 417 (1979) (emphasis in original).

76. Id at 415 fn 4.

77. Dwoskin pp 86–9, *supra* n 5.

78. 391 US 563, 572 (1968).

79. Id at 570 fn 3.

80. Snepp v United States 444 US 507, 510 (1980).

81. 417 US 733 (1974).

82. Id at 743–4. A more recent case, Chappell v Wallace 462 US 296, 305 (1983), denied the right of military personnel to sue their superior officers under § 1983 because of "[T]he special nature of military life. . . . "

83. 417 US 749. In Brown v Glines 444 US 348, 354 (1980), a captain who circulated a petition complaining of Air Force grooming standards could be charged with violation of an Air Force regulation that required him to get his commander's authorization before circulating the petition because "the different character of the military community and of the military mission require a different application of first amendment freedoms."

84. 425 US 511.

85. Id at 245, citing Pickering v Board of Education 391 US 563, 568 (1968).

86. Id at 246–247.

87. Id. See also Goldman v Weinberger 475 US 503, 510 (1986) in which the Court held that the wearing of a skull cap, traditionally worn by orthodox Jews, in this case, a rabbi in an army study program, could be regulated "in the interest of the military's perceived need for uniformity."

88. In Rathert v Village of Peotone 903 F2d 510, 516 (7th Cir) cert den 111 SCt 297 (1990), two police officers who wore ear studs could not claim first amendment protection because in a small community such behavior "caused an adverse impact on police discipline, *esprit de corps* and uniformity;" see also Kannisto v City and County of San Francisco 541 F2d 841, 844–5 (9th Cir 1976) cert den 430 US 931 (1977); Gasparinetti v Kerr 568 F2d 311, 321 (3d Cir 1977), Rosenn dissenting; Davis v Williams 617 F2d 1100, 1104 fn8 (5th Cir 1980), cert den 449 US 937 (1980), and Barrett v Thomas 649 F2d 1193, 1198 (5th Cir 1981), cert den 456 US 925 (1982). Jurgensen v Fairfax County, Va 745 F2d 868, 880 (4th Cir 1984) ("In analyzing the weight to be

given a particular job . . . 'nonpolicy making' employees can be arrayed on a spectrum from university professors at one end to policemen at the other. State inhibition of academic freedom is strongly disfavored. In polar contrast is the discipline demanded of and freedom correspondingly denied to policemen"). See also Busby v City of Orlando 931 F2d 764, 774 (11th Cir 1991) and Eiland v City of Montgomery 797 F2d 953, 960 (11th Cir 1986); cert den Montgomery v Eiland 483 US 1020 (1987).

89. 429 F2d 901, 904. See also Bence v Breier 501 F2d 1185, 1192 (7th Cir 1974), cert den Breier v Bence 419 US 421 (1975), where the court responded to an argument that the police should be legally treated like the military, reasoning that such treatment was inapplicable because " '[t]he fundamental necessity of obedience,' and the consequent necessity for imposition of discipline . . . is less exigent in a civilian police context."

90. Garrity v New Jersey 385 US 493, 500 (1967).

91. Muller v Conlisk 429 F2d at 904.

92. Finck pp 1012–13, *supra* n 35.

93. 391 US at 570 fn 3.

94. 370 US 375.

95. Id at 386, 387. Emphasis in original.

96. 393 US 503.

97. Id at 508.

98. 393 US at 509. See also Battle v Mulholland 439 F2d 321 (5th Cir 1971) in which a white police officer was discharged for allowing two female anti-poverty workers to board at his home. Overturning the discharge on first amendment grounds of freedom of association, the court required the police chief to show that the officer's "conduct would materially and substantially impair his usefulness as a police officer;" and Williams v Board of Regents 629 F2d 993, 1003 (5th Cir 1980), cert den Saye v Williams 452 US 926 (1981); in which Williams, a lieutenant of the University of Georgia's police security force, filed a report that the town's police chief was driving while intoxicated. When that report was modified by his chief, Williams protested; the court found that even though William's first amendment activity would damage the relationship between himself and the chief, the matter was so important to the public that "the employee's right to speak must be vigorously protected if the public is to be informed."

99. 468 US 138 (1983).

100. 461 US at 142, citing Pickering v Board of Education 391 US 563, 568 (1968).

101. 461 US at 146.

102. Id.

103. Id at 147.

104. Id at 148.

105. Id.

106. Id at 149.

107. Id at 150.

108. Id.

109. Id at 151.
110. Id at 151–52.
111. Id at 152.
112. Id at 153.
113. Id at 154.
114. Id at 153 fn 13.
115. Id at 146–147. See ch 6 for an explanation of this variant of the employment at will rule.
116. 483 US 378 (1987).
117. Id at 384.
118. Id at 388–89.
119. 855 F2d 187, 191 (5th Cir 1988). As full "public concern" analysis requires the court to examine "the content, form, and context of a given statement, as revealed by the whole record." *Connick* 461 US at 147–148.
120. 461 US at 416.
121. Id at 147.
122. 901 F2d 613 (7th Cir 1990).
123. Id at 618.
124. Id at 620.
125. 847 F2d 73 (3rd Cir 1988), cert den 488 US 899.
126. Id at 77. See also Thompson v City of Starkville 901 F2d 456, 462–63 (5th Cir 1990) (police officer who filed grievance and aided others to do the same, complaining about promotion procedures, acts of dishonesty, mistreatment of black persons, and theft of confiscated property "addressed far more than one employee's dissatisfaction with the status quo or his own lot"); Harris v Evans 920 F2d 864, 867 (11th Cir 1991) (prisoner complaining of Department of Corrections' policy prohibiting guards from making parole recommendations directly to the state board of paroles is voicing a matter of public concern); but see Hoffman v Mayor Councilmen and Citizens of Liberty 905 F2d 229, 234 (8th Cir 1990) (police officer's filing of a grievance is not of itself a matter of public concern); Thomas v Carpenter 881 F2d 828, 830 (9th Cir 1989), cert den Carpenter v Thomas 110 SCt 3236 (1990) (lieutenant in sheriff's department who criticized sheriff in running against him for sheriff is clearly a matter of public concern); Fiorillo v US Dept of Justice, Bureau of Prisons 795 F2d 1544 (F2d Cir 1986), affd 824 F2d 978 (1987) (correctional officer voicing personal complaints, even when published in newspaper, does not raise speech to matter of public concern); and Flanagan v Munger 890 F2d 1557, 1564 (10th Cir 1989), where department forbid its police employees, who had opened a video rental store, from renting sexually explicit films, the court found "that the public concern test does not apply when public employee expression does not occur at work or is not about work"; and McEvoy v Shoemaker 882 F2d 463, 466 (10th Cir 1989) (where police officer's principal purpose was "to air his frustration at having failed to receive a promotion," not a matter of public concern).

127. Thompson v City of Starkville 901 F2d 456, 463 (5th Cir 1990) and Zamboni v Stamler 847 F2d 73, 78 (3rd Cir 1988), cert den Stamler v Zamboni 488 US 899.

128. 931 F2d 613 (9th Cir 1991); one of the best reasoned cases involving subordination is Moore v City of Kilgore 877 F2d 364, 373–375 (5th Cir 1989) cert den Kilgore v Moore 110 SCt 562 (1989), in which a firefighter criticized fire department policy that he charged resulted in the death and injury of firefighters).

129. 931 F2d at 618. In Domiano v Village of River Grove 904 F2d 1142, 1147 (7th Cir 1990) a fire chief was terminated because he termed two newly-passed ordinances changing procedures "ridiculous" and refused to follow them. The court, in response to a first amendment claim, countered that "an employer is not obliged to allow events to unfold to the extent that the disruption of working relationships is manifest before taking action."

130. 892 F2d 1298 (7th Cir 1989).

131. Id at 1304.

132. 910 F2d 201 (5th Cir 1990).

133. Id at 212. See Thomas v Carpenter 881 F2d 828, 831 (9th Cir 1989), cert den 110 SCt 3236 (1990) (sheriff cannot use an unsupported claim of disruption to sustain his retaliation against lieutenant who ran against and criticized him in an election). For cases involving more direct criticism of superiors, see hereafter, section on whistleblowing.

134. Burden on the public employer: Zamboni v Stamler 847 F2d 73 (3rd Cir 1988); Scott v Flowers 910 F2d 201 (5th Cir 1990); Powell v Basham 921 F2d 165 (8th Cir 1990); and Eiland v The City of Montgomery 797 F2d 953 (11th Cir 1986).

135. 851 F2d 714, 718 (4th Cir 1988).

136. 847 F2d 73 (3rd Cir 1988).

137. *Rankin* 483 US at 388.

138. 847 F2d at 78–79 (emphasis in original, citations omitted). See also Flanagan v Munger 890 F2d 1557, 1566 (10th Cir 1989) ("The record is devoid of actual, or potential disruption of the department's internal operations. . . . "; Melton v City of Oklahoma City 879 F2d 706, 715–16 (10th Cir 1989) reh en banc, revd on other grounds 928 F2d 920 (1991). ("Although we recognize the *potential* impact that a breach of confidentiality may have on the department, we must point out that the government must introduce evidence of an actual disruption of its services resulting from the speech at issue"). Cases may also rely on the question of interference with the "effectiveness" or "efficiency" of the workplace: Powell v Basham 921 F2d 165, 168 (8th Cir 1990) (no evidence that deputy sheriff's criticism of promotion procedure "affected the efficiency of the department"). Scott v Flowers 910 F2d 201 (5th Cir 1990) (Judicial Commission which reprimanded judge for criticizing judicial procedures failed to show "goals of promoting an efficient and impartial judiciary" were impeded); Biggs v Village of

Dupo 892 F2d 1298, 1303 (newspaper interview "caused no significant disruption in the efficient operation of the village police department").

139. 797 F2d 953 (11th Cir 1986).

140. Id at 958 (citations omitted).

141. Ewing, D: "Do it my way or you're fired": Employee rights and the changing role of management prerogatives, New York, John Wiley, 1983, pp 193–6. This book also covers whistle blowing in private employment. See also Glazer, Myron and Migdal, Penina, The Whistleblowers, New York, Basic Books, 1989.

142. Nixon v Fitzgerald 457 US 731, 736 (1982).

143. 457 US at 736.

144. See the many instances cited in Ewing n 168; Ewing, D: Freedom inside the organization: Bringing civil liberties to the workplace, New York, E P Dutton, 1977, and The Whistleblowers, Committee on Governmental Affairs, US Senate, Washington, US Government Printing Office, 1978.

145. Whistleblowing IERM 505.21 Labor Relations Rep BNA (1987), and see Boyle, Robert D, A review of whistleblower protections and suggestions for change, 41 Labor L J 821, 825 (Dec 1990).

146. 43 PS §§ 1423(a) and (b).

147. PL 101-12, 103 Stat 16, 5 USCA 1201 et seq (West Supp 1991).

148. 2 USSCAN 101-12, Legis Hist P11 (1989).

149. 5 USCA § 1212 (West Supp 1991).

150. Id at § 1213; the 1989 act, which defines protected disclosures of "gross mismanagement," actually narrows the coverage compared to the act it replaced which covered "mismanagement." The purpose of this change is to eliminate "bad faith" whistleblowers who might "expose" some minor management examples of inefficiency to protect themselves from impending agency action. See Vitaris, Richard W, The Whistleblowers: Exposing Corruption in Government and Industry 127 Military Law Rev 219–221 (1990).

151. 5 USCA §§ 1212, 1221(a)(e)(g) and h(1) (West Supp 1991). A more detailed description of procedures in the Office of Special Counsel will be found at 133 FRD 392–412 (1991). For the Act's legislative background, see Id at 380–81.

152. Boyle, *supra* n 145 at 822.

153. Fisher, Bruce D, The Whistleblower Protection Act of 1989: A false hope for whistleblowers 43 Rutgers Law Rev 355, 372, fn 92.

154. Id at fn 80; 133 FDR at 399.

155. Fisher, *supra* n 153 at 386.

156. 5 USCA § 1201(b)(2)(B) (West Supp 1991).

157. Id at 1214(b)(4)(B)(i).

158. Id at 1213(e)(1). Fisher, *supra* n 153 at 394–95.

159. 5 USCA 2301(b)(9) (West Supp 1991).

160. 133 FRD at 402.

161. Fisher, *supra* n 153 at 415–16.

162. 1990 US Dist Lexis 11957 (ED Pa), affd without op 932 F2d 960 (3rd Cir 1991).

163. Id at 19–20.

164. Id at 23.

165. Id. See also Clemens v Hastings 1989 US Dist Lexis 4875 (MD Pa) (sheriff deputies who reported wrongdoing by sheriff's wife could sue under Pa Whistleblower law).

166. 842 F2d 862 (6th Cir 1988).

167. Id at 866. See also Wulf v City of Wichita 883 F2d 842, 862 (10th Cir 1989) ("the evidence supports the conclusion that Wulf's letter was seeking to rectify malfunctions already present in the department"); and in Brockwell v Norton 732 F2d 664, 667 (8th Cir 1984), where there is inefficiency, disharmony and unwritten rules of chain of command, officer could ignore the rules in reporting misconduct, but see Busby v City of Orlando 931 F2d 764, 774 (11th Cir 1991) (heavily relying on military analogy, court applied chain of command rule suggesting "they merely sought to delay access to a public forum until the OPD's internal affairs division could investigate his complaints").

168. Price v Brittain 874 F2d 252 (5th Cir 1989); and see Bryson v City of Waycross 888 F2d 1562, 1567 (11th Cir 1989), reh den en banc 894 F2d 414 (1990) (police captain, who charged police chief with theft from supply room by sending letter to city manager, and spent police department time broadcasting his rancor, was engaged in a personal dispute, and could be discharged); and Warner v Town of Ocean City 567 A2d 160 (1990) (police officer who wrote anonymous letter to mayor and city council charging recently promoted captain with misconduct was part of a quasi-military force "founded on principles of discipline and rank, and the type of criticism at issue would per se undermine the relationship between Lieutenant Warner and his superiors").

169. 874 F2d at 259.

170. 911 F2d 1179 (6th Cir 1990), reh den en banc 1990 US App Lexis 22082.

171. Id at 1188 (1990), cert den 111 SCt 1681 (1991). See also Breuer v Hart 909 F2d 1035, 1042 (7th Cir 1990) (deputy sheriff properly discharged after making charges that sheriff was favoring female employee, and was engaged in gathering evidence and urging other deputies to join him. Although such speech was on a matter of public concern, in such "a small tightly knit" department (16 members), where "his method . . . was to immerse himself in an intra-departmental contest with the sheriff," the employer's interest becomes the more substantial one.

172. 462 US 367 (1983).

173. Id at 368.

174. Id at 388.

175. 392 F2d 822 (DCC 1968).

176. Id at 826.

177. Id at 828.

178. Id at 835.

179. Id at 834.
180. 416 US 134, 161 (1974).
181. Id at 140.
182. Id at 160.
183. Id at 162.
184. 417 US 733 (1974).
185. Id at 738.
186. Id at 753–4.
187. Id at 757.
188. 429 F2d 901 (7th Cir 1970).
189. Id at 902.
190. Id at 904.
191. Id.
192. Id.
193. 501 F2d 1185 (7th 1974).
194. Id at 1187.
195. Id at 1190.
196. Id.
197. 568 F2d 311 (3rd Cir 1977), cert den 436 US 903 (1978).
198. Id at 314.
199. Id at 315–16.
200. Id at 316.
201. Id at 317.
202. 541 F2d 841 (9th Cir 1976), cert den 430 US 931 (1976).
203. 541 F2d at 842.
204. Kelly v Johnson 425 US 238, 246 (1976), discussed above.
205. 541 F2d at 844–5; see also Paulos v Breier 507 F2d 1383 (7th Cir 1974), and Davis v Williams 617 F2d 1100 (5th Cir 1980) (regulation facially valid against fireman's constitutional attack); and Barrett v Thomas 649 F2d 1193 (5th Cir 1981) cert den 456 US 925 (1982) (upholding the words "conduct subversive of the good order or discipline of the department," and "abusive, insulting or indecent language to a superior officer" as not vague or overbroad); more recent cases include: Jurgensen v Fairfax County, Va 745 F2d 868 (4th Cir 1984) (police officer releasing information violating regulations against such release was "presumed" to have "knowledge of these plain and understandable regulations" and should have known "that his action in releasing the report was in violation thereof"); Zook v Brown 865 F2d 887, 892 (7th Cir 1989) (regulation requiring prior approval by sheriff before communicating with the public upheld); Brown v City of Trenton 867 F2d 318 (6th Cir 1989) (police department regulations prohibiting officers from "publically criticizing orders given by a superior . . . provide adequate notice of what is proscribed"); and State ex rel Trautman v Farmington 799 SW2d 638, 643 (Mo App 1990) (municipal ordinance prohibiting police officers from taking "an active part in a political campaign" forbids only "active participation"); but see Pierson v Gondles 693 FSupp

408, 414–15 (ED VA 1988) (regulation prohibiting sheriff's deputies from "publicly criticiz[ing] other officers or office operations" were "overly broad and vague" because "the regulation fails to take into account that employers at different levels within the sheriff's office are guaranteed different free speech protections" and also undermines the rights of the deputies to support whomever they wish during elections). See Note, "Limiting public expression by public employees: The validity of catch-all regulations," 18 Houston L Rev 1097–1108 (1981).

206. Problems of job tenure are discussed in considerably more detail in ch 6.
207. Rosenbloom, D: Federal Service and the Constitution: The development of the public employment relationship, Ithaca, Cornell U Press, 1971, pp 4–5; Dwoskin pp 10–11 n 5.
208. Rosenbloom, Federal service p 20 n 207.
209. Id at 35.
210. Id at 37.
211. Id at 40.
212. Id.
213. Miller, W: A new history of the United States, new rev ed, New York, Dell, 1968, pp 155–72; Hofstadter, R: The United States, a history of a republic, 2d ed, Englewood Cliffs, Prentice-Hall, 1967, p 548, Rosenbloom pp 56–7 n 207.
214. Benson, L: The concept of Jacksonian democracy: New York as a test case, New York, Atheneum, 1967, p 12.
215. Id at 7–15; Miller pp 154–72 n 213.
216. Dwoskin p 144 n 5.
217. Rosenbloom pp 48–9 n 207.
218. Id at 56–66.
219. Id at 2.
220. Id at 95, 227.
221. Hofstadter p 549 n 213.
222. Rosenbloom pp 72–73, 75–77 n 207.
223. Statutory history is recounted in more detail in Civil Service Commission v Letter Carriers 413 US 548, 550 (1973).
224. Hofstadter p 549, *supra* n 213.
225. Rosenbloom pp 80–1, *supra* n 207.
226. Id at 78.
227. Civil Service Act of 1883 22 Stat 403 (1883).
228. Rosenbloom p 82, *supra* n 207.
229. Civil Service Act of 1833 22 Stat at 404.
230. Rosenbloom p 83, *supra* n 207.
231. Id at 96–8.
232. Exec Order no 642 (June 3 1907), codified as 5 USC § 1101 et seq and Civil Service Rule 5 CFR § 151.101 et seq.
233. Rosenbloom pp 103–4, *supra* n 207, Dwoskin pp 147–8, *supra* n 5.
234. Rosenbloom p 105, *supra* n 207.

235. Dwoskin p 153, *supra* n 5.
236. The Hatch Political Activities Act Pub L No 76-252, 53 Stat 1147 (1949), codified as 5 USC 7324(a) (1976).
237. Civil Service Commission v Letter Carriers 413 US 548, 561 (1973).
238. 5 USC § 1501(4).
239. Hatch Political Activities Act, amendment Pub L No 87-756, 76 Stat 750 (1962).
240. Dwoskin p 148, *supra* n 5.
241. 330 US 75.
242. Id at 78.
243. Id at 94–5.
244. Id at 95.
245. Id at 99.
246. Id at 102–3.
247. Id at 126.
248. Id at 122.
249. 413 US 548.
250. Id at 550, 554.
251. Pickering v Board of Education 391 US 563, 568 (1968), 413 US at 564.
252. 413 US at 564.
253. USCSC, Political activity and political assessment of federal officeholders and employees, Washington, US Government Printing Office, 1939, and periodically thereafter.
254. Broadrick v Oklahoma 413 US 601, 604 fn 2 (1973). See also State ex rel Trautman v Farmington 799 SW2d 638 641 (Mo App 1990) (police chief discharged for violating municipal ordinance prohibiting officers from taking "an active part in a political campaign. . . . ")
255. 427 US 347.
256. For the extended litigation that "cracked" the Chicago patronage machine, see Shakman v The Democratic Organization of Cook County 481 FSupp 1315 (ND Ill 1979), and cases cited hereafter.
257. 427 US at 351.
258. Robinson, C: The mayor and the police—The political role of the police in society, Police forces in history, Mosse, G, ed, London, Sage, 1975, pp 298–305.
259. 427 US at 353.
260. Id at 356.
261. Id at 359.
262. Id at 363.
263. Id at 367.
264. Id.
265. Id at 368.
266. Id at 371–2.
267. Id at 375.
268. 445 US 507.
269. Id at 510.

270. Id at 518.
271. Id at 519.
272. Id at 518.
273. Note, Patronage, arbitrary discharge, and public policy: redefining the balance of interest in employment, 14 John Marshall L Rev 785, 815 (1981); and Martin, Susan L, A decade of *Branti* decisions: A government official's guide to patronage dismissals, 39 Amer L Rev 11, 22 (Fall 1989).
274. Note, Patronage dismissals not permitted unless party affiliation relevant to job performance—Branti v Finkel, 29 Kan L Rev 286, 293 (1981). A number of states have specific statutes forbidding public officials to coerce employees to pay, lend, contribute, or render political services. BNA Labor Relations Rep IERM §§ 544.9-585.17 (1991).
275. 110 SCt 2729.
276. Id at 2734 (citations omitted).
277. Id at 2735 fn 5 (citations omitted).
278. Id at 2736 (emphasis in original).
279. Id at 2737 (citations omitted).
280. Heinen, Steven, Note, Political patronage and the first amendment, Rutan v Republican Party of Illinois, 14 Harvard J of Law & Public Policy 292, 303 (Winter 1991); see also Brinley, Martin, Note, Despoiling the spoils 65 North Carolina L Rev 719–740 (March 1991).
281. *Supra* n 273, Martin at 23–24.
282. Id at 25.
283. 850 F2d 64 (2nd Cir 1988).
284. Id at 69. The court also relied on the failure of the plaintiffs to reapply for their jobs as they had been advised to do by their new employer; there was no evidence that their new employer has any knowledge of their political affiliation; and all three positions were located "at the policymaking end" of the county government spectrum. Id at 68.
285. Stott v Haworth 916 F2d 134, 142 (4th Cir 1990). See also Monks v Marlinga 923 F2d, 423, 426 (6th Cir 1991) "Because Michigan law statutorily imposes the inherent policymaking responsibilities of the prosecutor on the assistant prosecutor, we hold that the job of assistant prosecutor is a policymaking position."
286. 913 F2d 327 (7th Cir 1990).
287. Id at 334.
288. 935 F2d 633 (3rd Cir 1991).
289. Id at 635 (citations omitted).
290. Id at 640.
291. 866 F2d 373 (11th Cir 1989).
292. Id at 377. Others fired such as a clerk, investigator, dispatcher, jailer and process server are not positions requiring "political loyalty" to the sheriff and therefore cannot be fired. Id at 378. But see Sweeney v Bausman 1989 US Dist Lexis 16491, 12 (ND Ill) (no "overriding interest" for sheriff deputies" to conform their political beliefs and associations to the political

belief of a sheriff"), and Robinson v Scurto 1990 US Dist Lexis 5462, pp 19–20 (ND Ill 1990) (statutes show that both village police chief and treasurer are policymaking posts and thus employees may be discharged by incoming mayor, but chief, who has property right in his job as sergeant, not a policymaking job, may have a claim of politically-motivated firing).

293. 925 F2d 135 (5th Cir 1991).

294. Id at 141. See also Williams v City of River Rouge 909 F2d 151, 156 (6th Cir 1990) ("The record shows that [the City Attorney] was clearly allied politically and personally to the former mayor and his policies . . . "); Savage v Gorski 850 F2d 64, 69 (2nd Cir 1988) ("Savage's secretarial position involves confidentiality, discretion in disseminating information to the public, and independent judgment regarding department policies and procedures"); and Balogh v Charron 855 F2d 356, 357 (6th Cir 1988) (judges must be able to rely on the confidentiality of their bailiffs who could be replaced by newly elected judge); but see Pierson v Gondles 693 FSupp 408, 413 (ED Va 1988) ("the sheriff has failed to present sufficient evidence that [his deputies] are highly placed or that their positions are so visible that mutual trust and confidence is important).

295. 892 F2d 139 (1st Cir 1989).

296. Id at 142. See also Wright v Phipps 1990 US Dist Lexis 18934, p 14 (WD Va) (the sheriff "has met his burden of showing that the unrelated motive was an independently effective motive. . . . In a rural county . . . where people know their deputies on a personal basis, sobriety is a necessity for a person to be an effective police officer, no matter what his political affiliation"); and Laidley v McClain 914 F2d 1386, 1393 (10th Cir 1990) ("Although there may have been legitimate budgetary reasons for the district attorney to terminate an assistant, there is also evidence that the assistant's support of the DA's opponent was a factor").

297. See also McMillan v Svetanoff 878 F2d 186, 191 (7th Cir 1989) (newly appointed judge replaced black female court reporter with white female with whose work he was familiar; and fact judge may have been of different party was insufficient to show political motivation where there was no proof judge knew of employee's political party); Byron v Clay 867 F2d 1049, 1053 (7th Cir 1989) (political appointee who did no work cannot rely on political patronage principle); Neely v Mangum 396 SE2d 160 (WVA 1990) (employee who worked in tax department was discharged for her own official misconduct and not for political reasons).

298. Rutan v Republican Party of Illinois 110 SCt 2729, 2748 (1990).

299. Id at 2752.

300. Id at 2756.

TABLE OF CASES*

---

*Numbers refer to page numbers on which the case appears or to cases in the footnotes appearing on that page.

INDEX